T0202994

Lecture Notes in Computer Science 11566

Commenced Publication in 1973
Founding and Former Series Editors:
Gerhard Goos, Juris Hartmanis, and Jan van Leeuwen

More information about this series at http://www.springer.com/series/7409

Masaaki Kurosu (Ed.)

Human-Computer Interaction

Perspectives on Design

Thematic Area, HCI 2019
Held as Part of the 21st HCI International Conference, HCII 2019
Orlando, FL, USA, July 26–31, 2019
Proceedings, Part I

 Springer

Editor
Masaaki Kurosu
The Open University of Japan
Chiba, Japan

ISSN 0302-9743   ISSN 1611-3349 (electronic)
Lecture Notes in Computer Science
ISBN 978-3-030-22645-9   ISBN 978-3-030-22646-6 (eBook)
https://doi.org/10.1007/978-3-030-22646-6

LNCS Sublibrary: SL3 – Information Systems and Applications, incl. Internet/Web, and HCI

This Springer imprint is published by the registered company Springer Nature Switzerland AG
The registered company address is: Gewerbestrasse 11, 6330 Cham, Switzerland

Foreword

The 21st International Conference on Human-Computer Interaction, HCI International 2019, was held in Orlando, FL, USA, during July 26–31, 2019. The event incorporated the 18 thematic areas and affiliated conferences listed on the following page.

A total of 5,029 individuals from academia, research institutes, industry, and governmental agencies from 73 countries submitted contributions, and 1,274 papers and 209 posters were included in the pre-conference proceedings. These contributions address the latest research and development efforts and highlight the human aspects of design and use of computing systems. The contributions thoroughly cover the entire field of human-computer interaction, addressing major advances in knowledge and effective use of computers in a variety of application areas. The volumes constituting the full set of the pre-conference proceedings are listed in the following pages.

This year the HCI International (HCII) conference introduced the new option of "late-breaking work." This applies both for papers and posters and the corresponding volume(s) of the proceedings will be published just after the conference. Full papers will be included in the *HCII 2019 Late-Breaking Work Papers Proceedings* volume of the proceedings to be published in the Springer LNCS series, while poster extended abstracts will be included as short papers in the HCII 2019 *Late-Breaking Work Poster Extended Abstracts* volume to be published in the Springer CCIS series.

I would like to thank the program board chairs and the members of the program boards of all thematic areas and affiliated conferences for their contribution to the highest scientific quality and the overall success of the HCI International 2019 conference.

This conference would not have been possible without the continuous and unwavering support and advice of the founder, Conference General Chair Emeritus and Conference Scientific Advisor Prof. Gavriel Salvendy. For his outstanding efforts, I would like to express my appreciation to the communications chair and editor of *HCI International News,* Dr. Abbas Moallem.

July 2019   Constantine Stephanidis

HCI International 2019 Thematic Areas and Affiliated Conferences

Thematic areas:

- HCI 2019: Human-Computer Interaction
- HIMI 2019: Human Interface and the Management of Information

Affiliated conferences:

- EPCE 2019: 16th International Conference on Engineering Psychology and Cognitive Ergonomics
- UAHCI 2019: 13th International Conference on Universal Access in Human-Computer Interaction
- VAMR 2019: 11th International Conference on Virtual, Augmented and Mixed Reality
- CCD 2019: 11th International Conference on Cross-Cultural Design
- SCSM 2019: 11th International Conference on Social Computing and Social Media
- AC 2019: 13th International Conference on Augmented Cognition
- DHM 2019: 10th International Conference on Digital Human Modeling and Applications in Health, Safety, Ergonomics and Risk Management
- DUXU 2019: 8th International Conference on Design, User Experience, and Usability
- DAPI 2019: 7th International Conference on Distributed, Ambient and Pervasive Interactions
- HCIBGO 2019: 6th International Conference on HCI in Business, Government and Organizations
- LCT 2019: 6th International Conference on Learning and Collaboration Technologies
- ITAP 2019: 5th International Conference on Human Aspects of IT for the Aged Population
- HCI-CPT 2019: First International Conference on HCI for Cybersecurity, Privacy and Trust
- HCI-Games 2019: First International Conference on HCI in Games
- MobiTAS 2019: First International Conference on HCI in Mobility, Transport, and Automotive Systems
- AIS 2019: First International Conference on Adaptive Instructional Systems

Pre-conference Proceedings Volumes Full List

1. LNCS 11566, Human-Computer Interaction: Perspectives on Design (Part I), edited by Masaaki Kurosu
2. LNCS 11567, Human-Computer Interaction: Recognition and Interaction Technologies (Part II), edited by Masaaki Kurosu
3. LNCS 11568, Human-Computer Interaction: Design Practice in Contemporary Societies (Part III), edited by Masaaki Kurosu
4. LNCS 11569, Human Interface and the Management of Information: Visual Information and Knowledge Management (Part I), edited by Sakae Yamamoto and Hirohiko Mori
5. LNCS 11570, Human Interface and the Management of Information: Information in Intelligent Systems (Part II), edited by Sakae Yamamoto and Hirohiko Mori
6. LNAI 11571, Engineering Psychology and Cognitive Ergonomics, edited by Don Harris
7. LNCS 11572, Universal Access in Human-Computer Interaction: Theory, Methods and Tools (Part I), edited by Margherita Antona and Constantine Stephanidis
8. LNCS 11573, Universal Access in Human-Computer Interaction: Multimodality and Assistive Environments (Part II), edited by Margherita Antona and Constantine Stephanidis
9. LNCS 11574, Virtual, Augmented and Mixed Reality: Multimodal Interaction (Part I), edited by Jessie Y. C. Chen and Gino Fragomeni
10. LNCS 11575, Virtual, Augmented and Mixed Reality: Applications and Case Studies (Part II), edited by Jessie Y. C. Chen and Gino Fragomeni
11. LNCS 11576, Cross-Cultural Design: Methods, Tools and User Experience (Part I), edited by P. L. Patrick Rau
12. LNCS 11577, Cross-Cultural Design: Culture and Society (Part II), edited by P. L. Patrick Rau
13. LNCS 11578, Social Computing and Social Media: Design, Human Behavior and Analytics (Part I), edited by Gabriele Meiselwitz
14. LNCS 11579, Social Computing and Social Media: Communication and Social Communities (Part II), edited by Gabriele Meiselwitz
15. LNAI 11580, Augmented Cognition, edited by Dylan D. Schmorrow and Cali M. Fidopiastis
16. LNCS 11581, Digital Human Modeling and Applications in Health, Safety, Ergonomics and Risk Management: Human Body and Motion (Part I), edited by Vincent G. Duffy

34. CCIS 1033, HCI International 2019 - Posters (Part II), edited by Constantine Stephanidis
35. CCIS 1034, HCI International 2019 - Posters (Part III), edited by Constantine Stephanidis

http://2019.hci.international/proceedings

Human-Computer Interaction Thematic Area (HCI 2019)

Program Board Chair(s): **Masaaki Kurosu,** *Japan*

- Jose Abdelnour-Nocera, UK
- Mark Apperley, New Zealand
- Kaveh Bazargan, France
- Simone Borsci, The Netherlands
- Kuohsiang Chen, P.R. China
- Stefano Federici, Italy
- Isabela Gasparini, Brazil
- Ayako Hashizume, Japan
- Wonil Hwang, Korea
- Mitsuhiko Karashima, Japan
- Shinichi Koyama, Japan
- Naoko Okuizumi, Japan
- Takanobu Omata, Japan
- Katsuhiko Onishi, Japan
- Philippe Palanque, France
- Alberto Raposo, Brazil
- Guangfeng Song, USA
- Hiroshi Ujita, Japan

The full list with the Program Board Chairs and the members of the Program Boards of all thematic areas and affiliated conferences is available online at:

http://www.hci.international/board-members-2019.php

HCI International 2020

The 22nd International Conference on Human-Computer Interaction, HCI International 2020, will be held jointly with the affiliated conferences in Copenhagen, Denmark, at the Bella Center Copenhagen, July 19–24, 2020. It will cover a broad spectrum of themes related to HCI, including theoretical issues, methods, tools, processes, and case studies in HCI design, as well as novel interaction techniques, interfaces, and applications. The proceedings will be published by Springer. More information will be available on the conference website: http://2020.hci.international/.

General Chair
Prof. Constantine Stephanidis
University of Crete and ICS-FORTH
Heraklion, Crete, Greece
E-mail: general_chair@hcii2020.org

http://2020.hci.international/

Contents – Part I

Redefining the Human in HCI

Emotional Design, Kansei and Aesthetics in HCI

Narrative, Storytelling, Discourse and Dialogue

Contents – Part II

Eye-Gaze, Gesture and Motion-Based Interaction

Interaction in Virtual and Augmented Reality

Contents – Part III

Design for Culture and Entertainement

Design for Intelligent Urban Environments

Design and Evaluation Case Studies

Design and Evaluation Methods and Tools

End-User Requirements Elicitation Using Narratives

Fernanda Amâncio[1(✉)], Camilo C. Almendra[1], and Gustavo Coutinho[2]

[1] Federal University of Ceara, Quixadá, Brazil
famancio0@gmail.com, camilo.almendra@ufc.br
[2] Instituto Federal do Ceará, Jaguaribe, Brazil
gustavo.coutinho@ifce.edu.br

Abstract. End-User Development comprises the study of tools and techniques to foster the development by end-user of their applications. However, some problems arise when end-user build their applications, such as the quality of those solutions. End-User Software Engineering research aims to support end-user in their applications development. A main challenge of EUSE is to find ways to blend typical software engineering activities into daily work of end-users. End-User Requirements Engineering refers to the incorporation of Requirements Engineering in end-user development. Requirements techniques need to be adapted so that they can bring value to end-user, without changing too much of their work nature and priorities. This work presents an empirical study on the use of narratives by end-user in applications development. We observed school teachers using SideTalk tool and applying the narrative technique to analyze the influence of the latter in the end-user development. The study concluded that narratives helped end-users in planning their development activities before build conversations in SideTalk tool, getting the same benefits the technique brings in professional development.

Keywords: End-user development ·
End-user requirements engineering · Empirical study

1 Introduction

Computer users are rapidly increasing in numbers and diversity [1]. These users include managers, accountants, engineers, teachers, researchers, health workers, salespeople, and administrative assistants. Such users perform a variety of tasks that evolve and deals with lots of data and business rules. Traditional development of professional software may not adequately meet such needs because when establishing a contracting relationship between users and solution providers, one of the first challenges is the transfer of domain knowledge [2]. Passing domain knowledge and experience to professional developers is something that requires effort and time, and needs to keep pace with changing user tasks. As end-users have an internalized understanding of the business rules and objectives, they may be able to construct applications without gaps of knowledge. However, they lack abilities to organize these developments efforts.

EUP (End-User Programming) refers to software development activities carried out by non-professional developers [3]. When a user engages in development activities, she seeks to create a program for herself, that is a different perspective from professional development [2]. Typically, end-user programming emerges in a context in which domain experts are seeking more automation in day-to-day tasks and for any reasons can not contract professionals to develop solutions. EUP efforts benefit from end-users knowledge of business context and need better than anyone else, and their awareness of changes in the corresponding domain. However, some issues arise when end-users produce their applications, system quality is one of these problems.

It is expected for end-users to struggle in understanding the general view of the problem and reason about all the functionalities they wish to have [3]. End-User Software Engineering (EUSE) refers to the adoption by end-users of software engineering practices and techniques. A challenge of EUSE research is to find ways to incorporate software activities into the end-users' workflow without the need for them to substantially change the nature of their work or priorities [3]. In the context of Requirements Engineering, end-users are generally not motivated to build a program to be used by others, so the focus on system quality is expected to be low [3]. People involved in end-user programming rarely have an interest in being explicitly linked to requirements, so there will be a need to make explicit to end-users the benefit of using EUSE.

The objective of this work is to motivate end-users to apply requirements engineering in their activities, leading to the development of user applications with more quality and completeness. We focus on end-users developers of web applications in the educational field and proposes the use of narrative writing technique for them to understand their needs better and plan requirements accordingly. Narrative writing promotes better end-user reflect upon its needs and facilitates registering their ideas. We expect that use of a requirements engineering technique contributes to better end-user development.

This article is organized as follows: in the next section, we present the related works and then the theoretical basis. Subsequently, there is the methodology section, where we describe the profile of the participants, and the steps required to conduct the research. After the methodology section, we present the study planning and execution section and then the results section. Subsequently, there are the final considerations also encompassing future work.

2 Background

According to Sommerville [4], Software Engineering is a discipline focused on aspects of software production, from the early stages of system specification to maintenance, when the system is already in use. In general software engineers adopt a systematic and organized approach to their work, as this is often the most efficient way to produce high-quality software [4]. Requirements Engineering (ER) "involves the surveying, modeling, specification, verification and maintenance of the properties that a software product or service must manifest before, during and after its realization" [5]. Key stakeholders are identified, and the constraints and needs that customers impose on the system are discovered while the RE process is taking place. After discovery, there is a need for documentation, analysis, and validation later, so that software can be built that presents customer satisfaction. RE activities are crucial to design and create quality software application and require practitioners to have some level of training and experience to work throughout the entire requirements lifecycle.

End-users act as non-professional software developers, who at some point may create, modify or extend software artifacts [6]. Professional software developers cannot directly address all of these needs, because of their limited domain knowledge and because their development processes are prolonged. On the other side, end-users know their context and needs better than anyone else, and often they have a real-time perception of changes in their respective domains [3].

End-user motivations are not related to software quality, so there is no explicit interest in explicitly documenting requirements [3]. They are less likely to learn formal or structured languages to express requirements or follow prescribed development methodologies. This work investigates the usefulness of requirements techniques that require little or no training by users.

3   Narrative Writing

For many years, analysts have employed usage scenarios to trigger customer needs. A scenario is a description of how a system will be used, and it is well employed to describe requirements for interactive applications and system-to-system interfaces [5]. Barbosa and Silva [7] still define scenarios as a narrative textual or pictorial, concrete and rich in contextual details of a situation of use of the application. Scenarios can then put real, potential users, processes, and data in a joint perspective.

According to Cockburn [8], a narrative is a use case in action, a highly specific example of an actor using the system. This narrative is not a use case, and in most projects, it does not remain in the official document of requirements, but it is a handy technique.

Narratives can be used to assist in the construction of a web application for example, in the case of this research the end-users used to plan how the structure of conversations in the SideTalk tool would be. Sheets of paper were used to describe the whole process of what was planned for construction, and later the end-users themselves continued the process by programming the narrative into the tool, thus creating a conversation in SideTalk. Therefore, we had as input the preparation of a script and how to exit the whole plan transformed into a conversation in SideTalk, both thought and created by themselves.

4   Methodology

This study was carried out following the next steps:

1. Analyze end-users profile: First there was an analysis of the people to be invited, who did not need to be experts in programming knowledge, but they had to have the desire to develop something that involved other people. It was decided to use teachers with needs to instruct students about the use of some service on the internet.
2. Invite end-users to join the survey: After defining the end-user profile, a formal invitation was made to participate in the survey. Six people agreed to participate in the survey.
3. Define search development location: On account of the public involved, and the municipality of the application, the place of the application was defined to be the home of each end-users, causing the study to be carried out one by one.
4. Conduct technical application sessions with end-users: The conduction of the application is described in Sect. 5.

End-users were identified from their professional profiles of education with the desire to develop something differentiated to help in the interaction of students in the classroom. We have the participation of six volunteers, aged between 20 and 25 who teach elementary and high school classes. End-users were recruited according to their profiles of education professional with the desire to develop something differentiated to help in the interaction of students in the classroom.

The elaboration of the technique of narratives was performed at this stage. The narrative method was applied to serve the end-users better and could contribute better to the development of their web applications, enabling a job with more quality and satisfaction.

The application of the technique was structured in this way: a use narrative training was created explaining step by step from what it is, what it is for and how it can be used. Then an example was presented, and soon we created three scenarios for the end-users to execute them, telling us that the first two were just to make the end-user more involved and that he could learn about narratives, and the last one would later be put into practice in a tool.

Before the application of the technique, we trained each participant in the narrative technique. Subsequently, the end-users themselves wrote their usage narratives, and then the end-users were trained on the SideTalk tool, and finally the construction of SideTalk conversations by each end-user. Throughout these steps, we observed participants regarding their engagement in the creation and later use of narrative during end-user programming.

SideTalk (formerly called WNH - Web Navigation Helper) is a Firefox browser extension, built from the CoScripter macro recorder [9]. SideTalk "inherited" from CoScripter the ability to write different interactions on Web pages, generating navigation scripts. It is in tune with the actions recorded in the script that the mediation dialogs appear [10]. Figure 1 illustrates the SideTalk splash screen, which provides a brief explanation of the tool and where the conversations are already created, the conversation import icon, and the link for editing.

Fig. 1. SideTalk Home screen

SideTalk also has the function of creating dialogs for the commands, with this functionality users can better explain the steps to be followed and can create dialogs of opening and closing their activities, Fig. 2 shows the example of this functionality.

Fig. 2. SideTalk dialog creation screen

5   Technical Application Sessions

The end-users were labeled P1, P2, P3, P4, P5, and P6, so that the anonymity was preserved, as presented in the end-users consent form. Table 1 below shows the end-user data, and the time each took to complete the proposed tasks.

Table 1. End-users data

Users	Age	Level of education	Time spent
P1	24	High School	47 min
P2	24	High School	52 min
P3	21	Elementary School	60 min
P4	25	High School	40 min
P5	22	Elementary School	58 min
P6	23	Elementary School	44 min

The study was done sequentially with one end-user at a time. The research was carried out in a place with Internet access so that it was possible to build conversations by end-users. Following the training, end-users were instructed to elaborate narratives, taking into account three proposed goals.

The goal is a high-level requirement that represents what a user could achieve using a system. From a high-level requirement there are several ways to build a system, and in the elaboration of the narratives, the end-user will produce a specific scenario to meet the requirement. The first two goals are focused on the training of end-users so that they can become familiar with the technique of writing narratives. The third objective is what will be used for the elaboration of the narrative for the creation of the SideTalk conversation.

The first goal reads as follows: "Imagine that you need to send pdf texts to your students over the weekend so they can do a particular job, how would you do to pass these texts on to them?" As an example of narrative, the end-user P1 wrote the narrative of Table 2.

Table 2. Narrative written by P1

> It would select the texts for work, convert to pdf format, go to the browser, open the email, attach the desired file and send it to the students.

The second goal reads: "You need to teach your students how to get a book from a particular subject on the internet because this book is not sold in the city bookstore. How would you go about teaching them to get this particular product?" As an example of narrative, the end-user P5 wrote the narrative in Table 3.

Table 3. Narrative written by P5

> I asked everyone to open the browser on the Google page, then enter the following address 'www.blogliverson-line.com', thus selecting the book that was indicated.

The third goal reads as follows: "You will give a computer class to your class, and you need to teach your students how to do a social networking account (Facebook)." As an example, the end-user P6 wrote the narrative of Table 4.

Table 4. Narrative written by P6

First step, open the browser, type in the
url www.facebook.com, then open
the Facebook registration screen,
then the following data need
to be entered: name, surname, email,
email confirmation, password, date,
month, year of birth, then click open account.

The narratives of the six end-users related to the last objective are presented as follows:

- P1 - Open the browser, search for 'facebook.com', in the search box when opening the page will fill the requested data, (name, surname, email address, password, date of birth), after filling the data, click on the button to open an account. Dialog to enter at the beginning: Welcome! Today's challenge is to make a Facebook account! Dialog to type at the end: You just created an account on the social network Facebook! Fill in the data!
- P2 - It would open the browser and search for the word 'Facebook', access the link and access the page that would be targeted. Fill in the data that is requested, and if everything is right and available, click open an account, and then you can use your account on the social network. Dialogue to Open: Hello, we will start the process of creating a Facebook account now! Dialogue to Finish: We have finished creating the account on Facebook. Enjoy the experience! Data needed for account creation on Facebook!
- P3 With the browser open, we enter the site 'www.facebook.com', in the search box of the browser click enter, and enter the home page of the site. We look for the 'open an account' box, highlighted in blue and click. From there we fill in the spaces with our data, answering each space with what is requested, for example, name, surname and so on. The part of the email will have to be filled with valid and active email. For those who already have is just typing, for those who do not have to be created (just go to the gmail.com website, for example, click on create an account, and do the same process). The password will be created according to your imagination (I advise it to be a date or word that has some meaning and difficult oblivion). After all the information is filled, we will have your profile on Facebook. Text to open: Well, today we will do a different lesson, the proposal is to create a Facebook account, you should just follow the guidelines below. Good class! Text to close: As you have followed the guidelines and it worked very well, you now have a Facebook account! User data!

- P4 - First go to 'www.facebook.com', and then enter your data, first name, phone or email, male or female, birthday, day/month/year, and password. After that, click open an account. Ready your Facebook social network has been finalized. Text to start: Hello, today we will create a Facebook account. Text to finalize: The account was created successfully. Fill in the data!
- P5 - With all the students in the computer lab I asked them to turn on the computer and open the internet browser, then type in the URL 'www.facebook.com'. Opening the site will fill the following register to create the account in the social network where you will be asked for name, surname, email, etc. Then click the button to open an account. When done this everyone will be able to enjoy. Opening dialogue: Hello, today we will create a new Facebook account! The task is simple; you just need to follow the steps as shown below. Good performance! Final dialogue: Congratulations, you just created a new Facebook account! Enter the data!
- P6 - First step is to open the browser, type in the URL "www.facebook.com", then open the Facebook registration screen, then the following data need to be entered. First name, last name, email, confirmation email, password, date, month and year of birth and then click open account. Initial text: Well, today we will do something different, we will learn how to create an account on the social network Facebook, so that it is done correctly, please keep an eye on the step by step information that will be displayed. Good performance!

Subsequently, the SideTalk tool training was started so that end-users could check how it should be used. After the training, the end-users began to create the conversation, asking them to create it according to the third objective, just to see if the end-users relied on the narratives to reach the goal of creating the conversation in the SideTalk. In the creation of the conversations, the end-users started from the opening the browser until the creation of the account in Facebook including the dialogues requested in the tool, and they had the support of the researcher with the syntax of the tool and the technical problems. In Figs. 3, 4, 5 and 6 an example of the creation of SideTalk conversation performed by end-user 4 is displayed.

Figure 3 illustrates the steps that the End-user P4 performed to reach the Facebook page and then begin the data fill step and then, with all the data filled, concluded with the click of the "open one account".

Table 5 shows a representation of the scripts that were generated in the creation of a new Facebook account by the end user 4.

6   Results

In this section, we report the results of the research, based on the users' answers collected through the interview at the end of the application, the observations made by the researcher and the comparison between the written narratives and the conversations built on the SideTalk tool. The analysis seeks to answer whether the use of the narrative writing technique by end-users helps in the development of conversations in the SideTalk tool.

Fig. 3. Screenshot of creating a Facebook account by end-user 4

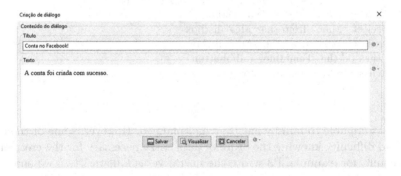

Fig. 4. Creation of opening dialog created by end-user 4

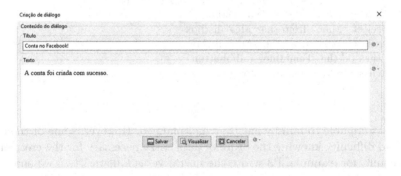

Fig. 5. Closing dialog creation screen performed by end-user 4

6.1   Interview Analysis

After the end-users created their conversations, an interview was conducted with six questions related to the development and training contained in the research. The first question was "Could you build what you had planned?", The six end-users responded positively to this question. Analyzing the writing of the narrative and the construction of the conversations in SideTalk it was noticeable that all

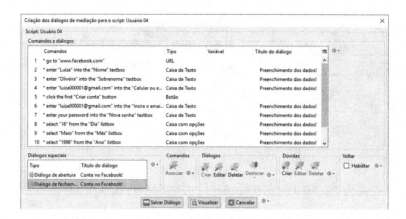

Fig. 6. Screen of all dialogs made by end-user 4

Table 5. Representation of account creation scripts on Facebook

(usuário 4)
go to "www.facebook.com"
enter "Luiza" into the "Nome" textbox
enter "Oliveira" into the "Sobrenome" textbox
enter "luiza000001@gmail.com" into the "Celular ou email" textbox
click the first "Criar conta" button
enter "luiza000001@gmail.com" into the
"Insira o email novamente" textbox
enter your password into the "Nova senha" textbox
select "16" from the "Dia" listbox
select "Maio" from the "Mês" listbox
select "1996" from the "Ano" listbox
turn on the "Feminino" radiobutton
click the first "Criar conta" button

the users were able to build what they had planned. However, some of the end-users had difficulty knowing the order of data entry necessary for the creation of the account, for example, P3 wrote the narrative as follows: "(...) we enter the home page of the site, we search for the link 'Open an account', highlighted in blue and click, from there fill the spaces with our personal data (...)". In fact, the completion of personal data happens before the option to open the account. This difference between the planned narrative and what it was actually possible to do on the social network did not affect the construction of the conversations.

The second question was "Have you developed something you had not planned?". Three end-users, P3, P4, and P6, responded that they had not developed anything beyond what was planned. The end-users P1 and P2 replied that they had to create a new email account to test the conversation built on SideTalk. The end-user P5 replied that he did not develop anything in SideTalk beyond

what he had planned, but his narrative begins with step-by-step, from the operation of turning on the computer, opening the browser until the creation of the
account in the social network. Some end-users have answered this question also
considering the data that should be prepared for the test created in the SideTalk
tool. However, this is not configured as an additional functionality implemented.
Taking into account the conversations created and the planned narratives, it was
noticeable that some of the end-users forgot the detail of having to create a new
email that was not associated with any Facebook account. P1 and P2 created a
fictitious email at the time of the research, P3 prepared the creation of e-mail
during narrative writing, while P4, P5 and P6 already had an email not yet used
in the social network Facebook. For the end-users who did not remember putting
the creation of an e-mail in the preparation of the narratives, they were given an
already created e-mail. It was noticeable that the preparation of the narratives
reminded some of the end-users of the need to create valid test data for account
creation on the social network.

The third question read as follows: "Beyond the narrative, did you prepare an
outline, plan or artifact before development?". P1, P2 responded positively. P1
and P2 used a sheet beyond the narrative to write the data needed to create the
account on Facebook. And P1 still illustrated how the button creates account.
P4 also responded positively ("Yes, before I made a plan to run it then.") but in
actually the end-user referenced the narrative itself as a kind of plan. The other
end-users, P3, P5 and P6, responded negatively to this question. Expectations
would be that the end-users did not need any other plan beyond the narrative,
but P1 and P2 thought it best to make a separate sketch of the narrative to put
the account creation data.

The fourth question reads as follows: "What were your difficulties during
development?". Four end-users, P1, P2, P3, and P6, had difficulties, P1 and P6
reported that "In a few moments the program locked, in the time of putting
the month and the year of birth, in the data register of the Facebook account".
P2 said that "had difficulty understanding the context of the narrative", the
difficulty found by P3 was "Not knowing exactly the sequence of steps to create
the account on Facebook," P4 and P5 answered the question negatively. Even
though some of the end-users reported some problems, it was noticeable that
it did not affect them in relation to not being able to complete what they had
planned.

In the fifth question was asked with the end-user if "Before developing something similar, would you again use the preparation of narratives?". P1, P2, P3,
P5 and P6 responded positively to this question. P1 reported that "I would use
it, it's a simple and quick way to help and even if I'm a person who has never
seen it, I can easily understand it." P2 commented that "it was great to have
written everything I needed, so I did not forget any details". P3 reported "Yes,
because it helped me to create the conversation on Facebook". P5 commented
that "to understand the narrative it is essential to know it before" and also
said that "I found the preparation very useful, because what I planned it went
as I wanted". The end-user P4 was the only one with an undecided response,

reporting that "I thought so." It was noticeable that the end-users P1, P2, P3, P5 and P6 quite liked the narratives and even if P4 responded indecisively, it was noticed that he used a lot of narrative preparation to build his SideTalk conversation. Therefore, it is concluded that the preparation of narratives was very important for the accomplishment of this study.

The sixth question was related to the training "Did the brief explanation of use narrative help you when you do it yourself?" P1, P3, P5 and P6 responded positively, P2 reported that "yes, but at first I had difficulty understanding, but when I started doing the narratives myself I felt that I had really learned." P4 was brief, only responding that "helped". The training of narrative was very satisfactory, it was noticeable that in explaining it to some, it was clear to others not, but when they themselves began to make the narratives, they managed to do them well. In this way, the narrative proved to be a technique for easy understanding and a tangible benefit.

6.2   Direct Observation Analysis

The end-user P1 was very attentive throughout the process and quickly understood the narratives, the only question was whether it was doing it right or not since it was the first contact with a certain subject. Interesting that in addition to the narratives, P1 put some data in a separate draft that would need to create the account on Facebook and still illustrated by sketching a button "Open an account". It was noticeable that the end-user liked the interaction and commented that he would use in his work as a teacher as a way to improve the communication with the students.

P2 had difficulty beginning to understand the concept of use narrative, but then managed to understand thoroughly and write the narratives with ease. This user also used the draft to put the data needed to create the account on Facebook and at the time of the creation of the conversation resorted to the two roles, both the draft and the written narratives.

P3 was one of the most enthusiastic, had no difficulty understanding the concept of narratives, and also proved to be participatory throughout the research. P3 pointed out that would be interesting to perform lectures with more interactivity. P3 added, "It was important to have written the narrative before creating the conversation because it helped me when it was time to create it".

P4 did not prove to be involved with the research as the other end-users, understood the concept of the narratives well, wrote them well, but at the time of the interview when the question was asked "before developing something similar would you again use the preparation of narratives of use?", he replied that "he thought so", it was noticeable that there was not much interest, but there is a contradiction because in the construction of the conversation it was realized that he drew much attention to the narrative.

P5 was participative, his understanding and writing were satisfactory, he was a bit worried if he was writing the narratives correctly, and added "can I look on the internet and find more examples?", But even with the doubt managed to do well, and made a comment that called attention, that he had found legal the construction of the narratives and the conversations, and that actually preparing before had been better, because he did not forget anything. It was the only end-users who wanted to create the conversations first and then write the narratives, but then realized that the form used was the best way.

P6 was participatory throughout the research, it was noticeable that he understood the concept of narratives well and was able to do them well, became interested in writing narratives and added that they helped when he needed to create the conversation in the tool.

After analyzing the participation of the end-users, it was concluded that the narrative explanation was presented in a simple and easy-to-understand way for the end-users, as well as the narrative writing training, which provided the end-users with a greater knowledge and facility to elaborate the narrative that would be used as intended to create the conversations in SideTalk. Also, it was noticed that the narrative served as a guide to end-users in the creation of scripts and the development of dialogues within SideTalk, although this tool is a novelty for those involved.

Rosson et al. [11] observed that the scenario technique, similar to narratives, is a low-cost technique and that it gave end-users a better view of what needed to be done in the application development. This research has achieved similar results in a context of entirely different user profiles and programming tools.

7   Related Work

Requirements engineering in the context of EUSE is a topic of interest that needs to be explored [3]. Notably, we are interested in requirements specification and planning activities. The work of Rosson et al. [11] reports an exploratory research project that investigates the impact of different forms of project planning performed by end-users. End-users were asked to make a simple application using a web development tool for end-users. The study aimed to investigate the influence of planning techniques in end-user development. Conceptual maps elaboration, interaction scenarios writing, and non-guided free planning were compared among groups of end-users. Conceptual map stood out from the three approaches. Conceptual maps were highlighted because end-users were able to work harder in less time, while the end-users who worked with the scenarios also managed to develop their planned activities but with a longer time compared to the conceptual maps. On the other hand, users who did not use any technique had difficulty getting the construction of an application. Users who did not create a pre-development plan were found to have more problem in development.

The study of Rode et al. [11] aims to understand what end-user developers need, how they think, and what can be done to help them when it comes to developing their applications. A simple web application was created for the study, ten participants were chosen who had some familiarity with websites, but had little programming experience, five were female, and five were male. Participants have given a general introduction to the objectives of the study, so they were asked to view and label all elements of the application's three functionalities: login, member list, and add members. This first phase of the study was designed to report on languages that the public uses to refer to visible screen elements, then end-users were allowed to explore the application until they were comfortable using it.

After the familiarization phase, participants were given seven user tasks (login, pagination, user-specific profile, add a member, sort, search, delete) and were asked to be taught these behaviors to a magic machine. A paragraph of text within the written instructions explained this scenario to the participants. The seven tasks were presented by concise instructions that were designed to guide the user without polarization to their response. Participants wrote responses using screenshots and blank paper, emphasizing that they were free to choose how to communicate with the magic machine (using written words or drawing), but also that they should fully specify the behavior of the application.

The work of Rode et al. [12] and the research in question are identified by the fact that end-users will work with their ideas for an application. In Rode et al. [12], the end-users will explore an application that is already built, and in this research, end-users will build an application from planning done by them.

8   Final Considerations

This work presents an evaluation of the outcomes and perceptions of end-users using a requirements engineering technique for planning purposes. The narrative writing helped end-users in the prior planning of what would be built on the SideTalk tool, achieving similar benefits that such a technique would bring in a professional development context.

The elaboration of narratives helped end-user reflecting and registering their ideas so that throughout the development work important characteristics were not lost. Also, the upfront planning facilitates that the objectives of their application could be discussed with other potential users. It is worth mentioning that the profile of the end-users (elementary and middle school teachers) is of people who already have the culture of preparing themselves before executing their professional actions (lecture, for example). This suggests that requirements engineering and other software engineering activities may better be adopted by end-users depending on the culture of their professions.

As future work, we propose that the evaluation of the use of the narratives be performed with experienced end-users in the tool used so that we can verify how narrative writing related to this audience happens. We also propose that the narratives be used in context with more extensive user requirements that require the planning of more narratives, and that are used to prepare activities in other systems.

References

1. Scaffidi, C., Shaw, M., Myers, B.: Estimating the numbers of end-users and end-user programmers. In: 2005 IEEE Symposium on Visual Languages and Human-Centric Computing, pp. 207–214. IEEE (2005)

2. Burnett, M.M. Scaffidi, C.: End-user development in "the encyclopedia of human-computer interaction, 2nd edn.". In: DAM, R.F., Soegaard, M. (Eds.) [s.n.] (2014). https://www.interaction-design.org/encyclopedia/end-user_development.html
3. Ko, A.J., et al.: The state of the art in end-user software engineering. ACM Comput. Surv. (CSUR) **43**(3), 21 (2011)
4. Sommerville, I.: Engenharia de Software, 9th edn., 529 p. Pearson Prentice Hall, São Paulo (2011)
5. Wiegers, K., Beatty, J.: Software Requirements, 3 edn., 637 p. Microsoft Press, Redmond (2013)
6. Lieberman, H., Paterno, F., Wulf, V. (eds.): End-User Development. Kluwer/Springer, Dordrecht (2006)
7. Barbosa, S.D.J., Silva, B.S.: Interação Humano-Computador, 379 p. Elsevier, Rio de Janeiro (2010)
8. Cockburn, A.: Escrevendo Casos de Usos Eficazes: Um guia prático para desenvolvedores de software, 245 p. Bookman (2005)
9. Leshed, G., Haber, E.M., Matthews, T., Lau, T.: CoScripter: automating & sharing how-to knowledge in the enterprise. In: Proceeding of the 26th Annual SIGCHI Conference on Human Factors in Computing Systems, CHI 2008, pp. 1719–1728. ACM, New York (2008)
10. Monteiro, I.T.: Autoexpressão e engenharia semiótica do usuário-designer, 312 f. Tese (Doutorado em Informática) – Centro Técnico Científico, PUC-Rio, Rio de Janeiro (2015)
11. Rosson, M., et al.: Design planning by end-user web developers. J. Vis. Lang. Comput. **19**(4), 468–484 (2008)
12. Rode, J., Rosson, M.B., Quiñones, M.A.P.: End-user development of web applications. In: Lieberman, H., Paternò, F., Wulf, V. (eds.) End User Development. Human-Computer Interaction Series, vol. 9, pp. 161–182. Springer, Dordrecht (2006). https://doi.org/10.1007/1-4020-5386-X_8

Interactive Search Profiles
as a Design Tool

Maram Barifah$^{(\boxtimes)}$ and Monica Landoni

Università della Svizzera Italiana (USI), Faculty of Informatics,
Lugano, Switzerland
{maram.barifah,monica.landoni}@usi.ch

Abstract. *Interactive Information Retrieval* (IIR) research studies how users interact with IR systems and evaluates the users' satisfaction with the retrieval process. Thus, it focuses on how users behave when they interact with IR systems. The involvement of potential users, and access to dynamic and individual information needs are essential elements in IIR studies. User-oriented evaluations investigate the ability of users to engage with a system, thus requiring real users to be involved in the evaluation process. Despite its importance in driving the design of better and more usable IR systems, the user-oriented evaluation approach has been criticised for: (i) being expensive and time consuming in its application, (ii) failing to capture a holistic understanding of the context, as it focuses on users, (iii) delivering not reusable data, often of qualitative nature, and (iv) generating experiments and results that are not reproducible. In this paper, we propose an alternative approach, based on data extracted from *Log File*s (LF) and automatically extracted *Usage Pattern* (UP)s. *Interactive Search Profiles* (ISP)s are then created as tools to guide the design of more usable IIR systems, specifically considering *Digital Libraries* (DL).

Keywords: Evaluation · Digital library · User interaction · Interface

1 Introduction

IIR systems are designed to target users regardless of their numerous and complicated attributes [4]. DLs, as an example of IIR systems, define as "distributed systems with the capability to store various electronic resources and provide convenient access for end users via networks" [33]. Users tend to use DLs to fulfil their information needs. Their interactions are embodied in the information seeking behaviour which are affected by different attributes including expertise in using the system, familiarity, frequency of using the system and knowledge. Lacking expertise and knowledge result in poor usage of the system's functionalities and content identification. Therefore, it is important to enlarge the scope of the evaluation of IIR systems by considering more user attributes [3]. Evaluation of DL assessed the decision makers to determine the usefulness, usability, and economics of a DL [7].

M. Kurosu (Ed.): HCII 2019, LNCS 11566, pp. 18–30, 2019.
https://doi.org/10.1007/978-3-030-22646-6_2

Trischler and Scott emphasised the needs for developing new techniques and tools to redesigning service systems in such a way that users become value co-creators of their own experiences [28]. Such new methods need to be driven by deep understanding of human experience to support the users in co-creating their desired experiences [27]. Collaboration and co-production can lead to open innovation and continuous improvements to increase efficiency, and to develop better interaction experiences [28].

Different approaches can be followed to understand the user interactions and their experiences with the systems. For example, conducting naturalistic studies with real users, and running laboratory-controlled experiments where surrogate users are recruited. Conducting such experiments with test subjects is time consuming, expensive, laborious in terms of organising and running them. Besides, experiences are subjective, and the experiments are difficult to reproduce [1].

Alternatively, researchers may investigate users' digital footprints or UPs recorded in the LF. UPs are a means to represent the search strategies found in the LF [17]. The analysis of the UP enables the researchers to understand the recorded searching experiences [13]. LF analysis can reveal a wealth of information about the user interactions and their preferences. Such analysis does not only results in providing information about the system performance, but also provides a more in-depth analysis of the user interactions with the systems [10].

This work introduces ISP, as a design tool, which can be constructed on top of real data gathered while the users interact with the system. Different ISPs depict the types of interaction a segment of users performs with the system. Such profiles can complement existing user-oriented techniques e.g. personas. The paper starts with reviewing related works, it then describes the research platform, presents the methodology, discusses examples of ISPs, and concludes by suggestion of some practical benefits.

2   Background

Due to the interdisciplinary research domain of the DL covering information retrieval systems, human-computer interaction, and information science, the literature is rich with various evaluation frameworks and techniques [29]. Generally, the existing DL evaluation research can be classified into: general DL evaluation, evaluation of specific components of DLs, and user-oriented evaluation [15,31].

- General DL evaluation studies encompassed the comprehensive evaluation frameworks and models which encourage the researchers and librarians to consider wide range components when evaluating a DL. Scholars e.g. [19,23] suggested to evaluate a DL as a unit by assessing: (i) *content* including digitised resources selection and structure, collection building, repository managing, and preservation. (ii) *policy* counting service, process, quality, access, development, and sustainability. (iii) *technology* considering architecture, algorithms, functionality, interface, and design. (iv) *user* covering perceptions, activities, needs, and tasks.

- Evaluation of specific components of DLs: due to the complexity nature of the DL and its components [7], some researchers contributed to the DL evaluation field by deeply investigating individual aspects. Some evaluation studies [3] targeted the system components and information retrieval performance. Others, considering the metadata [32], and the system interfaces [16].
- User-oriented evaluation: the system performance can be assessed by the established system-oriented approach to measure the effectiveness and efficiency of the underlying search algorithms [26]. The system-oriented approach has been criticised for lacking insights into the user-system interaction and disregarding iterative and exploratory user interactions [20]. Thus, user-oriented evaluation gives the priority to the users by considering their characteristics, information needs and information seeking behaviour [7].

  Consequently, a group of researchers assessed the DLs in relation to the user needs and satisfactions. Such evaluation studies conducted by involving and considering the users and their needs [20]. Three frequent user dimensions considered in the evaluation: usability [30], accessibility [31], and interactions [16].

Accordingly, there is no universal accepted evaluation frameworks or tools, the choice between the available frameworks mainly depends on the evaluators and their aim of the evaluation [7]. Saracevic [22] claims that the impact of such studies are non visible which can be due to the complexity of the DLs, the limited evaluation interest and funds, the lack of the evaluation as a core activity in the operating DL culture [22]. This suggested for more handy and inexpensive evaluation tools.

Evaluation can be conducted at different phases of the DL projects with various purposes [7]. At the initial and during stage of the project, a *formative* evaluation can be conducted to establish goals and to minimise imperfections before release. In contrast, *summative* evaluation is conducted in the final stages to assess the goals are met. *Comparative* evaluation where different systems or components are compared. And *iterative* evaluation aiming to improve the system incrementally [7]. Iterative evaluation is recommended for the DLs as new material are added, metadata are updated and users characteristics changed or new users joined [20, 30]. Thus, there is a need for more user-oriented, practical, and inexpensive iterative evaluation tools.

Because DLs are designed to provide support for seeking activities, Sumner [25] emphasised the impact of understanding user, innovative user interfaces and interaction mechanisms on providing better experiences of digital library.

A number of user-oriented design techniques and tools were developed to help designers to make user-informed decisions. Mapping techniques and personas are examples. Such techniques capture the dynamism of processes, and the ongoing interactions during the user experience. Personas, in particular, are a medium for communication which is created or used as an interaction design technique introduced by Cooper [8]. The usefulness and value of personas is increasingly recognised because they offers insight regarding users' attitudes, preferences, and interests [28]. Personas are created fictionally based on extracted attributes from real users. Courage and Baxter provide idealised attributes list including: identity (demographic data), status of the users to the system e.g. (primary, secondary), goals of using the system, skill set, tasks, relationship, and requirements, expectations, and photograph [9]. Personas assist developers and designers to keep the user present in the design process, and move away from a developer's perspective to a perspective of user [12].

There are different applications of personas: enhancing user testing and evaluation, scenario generation, design exploration, and solution brainstorming. They are usually produced in the initial phases of the design process. Where the real users are complex and non consistent, personas are instead well defined and clear and therefore better suited as a starting point for design work [9]. Personas can be obtained by simple observational methods or in-depth interviews, surveys or studies. Personas are rich but static descriptions of fictive users. Once they are built, the contents of their description are not changeable [12]. The challenge of creating personas is embodied on focusing on a specific segment of the targeted users, or design vaguely for everyone [28]. Persona also has been criticised by being too flat to engage designers, and there is a need for developing characters with richer personalities and better descriptions [12]. Designing for user-experiences is difficult since the experiences do not yet exist. The design situation is therefore only partly known, thus personas need to be invented [28]. Therefore, in this research we make the most of using the existing experiences of the users recorded on the LFs, and presenting ISPs. Such profiles can complement existing techniques for user modelling while offering unique features as described in Table 1, where they are compared with personas.

Table 1. Comparison between persona and ISP

	Persona	ISP
Purpose	representing potential users	representing existing users
Nature	static	dynamic
Data source	qualitative tools e.g. survey	log files
Effort	manually made	automatically made
Cost	costly, time consuming, intensive	cheap, quick, repeatable
Construction	user data collection and analysis	machine learning techniques
Time of use	initial phases of design	after launching systems
Design Effect	reminding about user needs	involving users to improve design

This paper describes how to build and use ISPs, which require a profound understanding of the users searching experiences, the so-called customer journey. The focus is on analysing diverse UPs that occur during the interactions with a system of heterogenous users. We propose to use these ISPs to inform the design and improvement of interactive systems. The profiles also can be used timely while the users interact with the system where the interactions are captured from the LFs. The proposed methodology will enable to run iterative evaluations, by limiting and possibly avoiding the problem of recruiting participants, and running laborious user studies.

3   RERO Doc

This study is conducted in collaboration with RERO Doc[1]. RERO Doc is a digital library connecting libraries of Western Switzerland as a public service. Figure 1 shows the homepage of the library. The library offers free access to its contents and services. The users can discover the content by simple (1) and advance (2) search functions. Or by navigating the content by the collection (3), institutions (4), content (5), or digitised press (6). The users also may check the latest news of the library (7). The geographical locations of the users are world-wide. Thus, RERO Doc serves a diverse population. LF analysis was conducted aiming to investigate users' interactions and habits recorded in the LFs. Ultimately, the found UPs used to build different ISPs by generating various interaction scenarios.

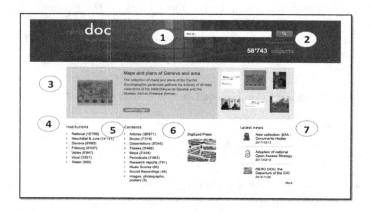

Fig. 1. RERO Doc interface

4   UPs Exploration

For a better understanding of the users journeys on RERO, we draw a hierarchical taxonomy of RERO as shown in Fig. 3. Users may start (B) their sessions by accessing through landing pages including search engines, their emails, or directly through the different functions available on the home page. They can discover (C) the content by searching (G) or navigating (H), After reviewing the search result page, they do have different options of displaying (D) the items. There are different other (E) services the users might implement.

---

[1] https://doc.rero.ch.

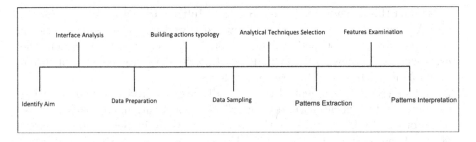

Fig. 2. The framework of exploring UPs in LFs

A dataset of 28 Million records obtained from RERO Doc DL was adopted for our study. Two different unsupervised techniques, namely: K- means, and Birch (Agglomerative) clustering, were applied to data samples of different sizes. The data processing and analysing is described in [2]. Figure 2 shows the framework of exploring UPs.

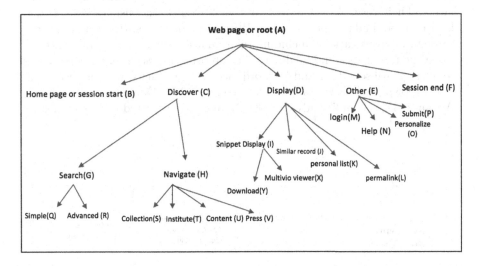

Fig. 3. Hierarchical taxonomy of RERO

This research concluded that UPs can be characterised by: session duration, session starting points, discovering content actions, functions used, and determination session points. Three main UPs were found in the LF, those are: item seekers, navigators, and searchers. Each one of those patterns has sub-patterns. Those patterns and their descriptions are as the following:

1. *Item seeker* (IS): the first category of the UPs is the ISs where they redirected from search engines or emails seeking authorised items. Their sessions characterised by conducting one action download or view items. There are four sub

UPs under this category: Satisfied IS (SIS), Multivio IS (MIS), Average (AIS), and Advance (DIS) item seekers. They are varied in the session durations: short (60), average (60–300), advance (900–1800) seconds. MIS represent the users who prefer viewing items by using Multivio viewer (a viewer application available in RERO Doc) instead of pdf format.

2. *Navigator* (N): this segment of the users discovers RERO Doc by navigating its content which is categorised into: collection, institution, content, or press. Some of the Ns filter and sort the search results by implementing different facets. Their session durations vary between short (60), average (60–300), and long (900–1800) seconds. Their termination actions are: view results list, display item, download item, and add to personal list. Accordingly, we classified them into: Light (LN), Average (AN), Advance (DN), and Press (PN) navigators.

3. *Searcher* (S): the S interacts with RERO Doc by submitting queries through simple or advance search functions. They vary in terms of: session durations, filtering or sorting results, and termination actions. Their session durations vary between short (60), average (60–300), and long (900–2700) seconds. Some of the S filter and sort the search results by implementing different facets. Their termination actions are: view results list, display item, download item, and add to personal list. With some of the Ss, the searching went through many iterations, including reformulation queries. The differences of using the functions could be due to their information needs e.g. KS searchers frequently utilise author and keyword facets. Accordingly, we classified them into: Known item (KS), Simple (SS), Average (AS), Familiar average (FAS), Advance (DS), Familiar advance (FDS), and Sophisticated (PS) searchers.

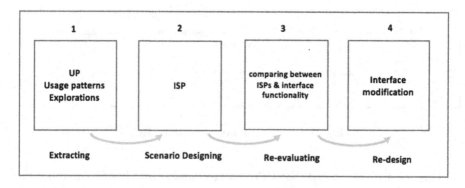

Fig. 4. The implementation of ISPs

5   From UPs to ISPs

Motivated by [5] who emphasised the usefulness of the scenarios for better understanding of the new user situations, we created different scenarios extracted from
UPs to be presented in the ISPs. ISPs are specific instances of the UPs, they can
represent any of the possible variations inside the same pattern. Figure 4 shows
the roadmap of the implementation of the ISP. The process starts with exploring UPs from LF, these can be used to construct different ISPs, and different
experience scenarios can be designed accordingly. Finally, such information can
assist the designers to re-evaluate their systems.

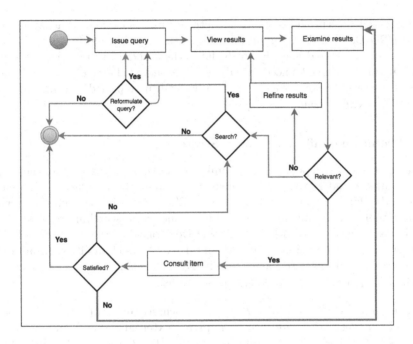

Fig. 5. Searcher model

We developed different interaction models, Fig. 5 is an example of the searcher
model. The flowchart illustrates the key actions of the model represented in
the rectangles, along with decisions to be taken by the user in diamonds. The
visualisation of the interaction models helps us to generate various scenarios.

For example, we identified the UP of Light Navigator, LN, whose session
duration last for 60 s and navigate the DL without going beyond the result page.
Out of this pattern, we can extract sub LN pattern by simulating all LN features
with modification of the search path. For example, instead of finishing up the
session with view results page (VRP), a LN may also select a result and apply
some functions. Accordingly, slight changes of the termination points also may
apply where a LN may download or display the documents. Another example

of deriving different ISPs out of the same UP is that of the KS Searcher. This pattern represents users who usually spend 60 s as a maximum duration and search by author and keyword filters. Their search usually ends with the viewing of the page with the result list. Out of this pattern, a further ISPs can be extracted with different scenarios, what if the KS searchers could not find their information needs? Different paths/tactics might be applied e.g. a KI searcher might return to home page and reformulate the query without filtering the facets i.e. author or keyword.

6   Design Implications

The large-scale logs provided a holistic picture of user behaviour while interacting with RERO Doc DL. Developing different scenarios may help in improving the existent DL interface design. Figure 6 shows the standard result page interface. Consequently, the specific needs of DL users are served effectively and efficiency.

Here we propose some suggestions on how DL may provide mechanism that support user engagement.

6.1   Promoting Different Search Strategies

The usage of the DL depends on the familiarity and experience levels of the users. Stelmaszewska and Blandford [24] investigated how the interface can support users to develop different search strategies. Thus, providing DL interfaces with assistive tools may result in faster, and more successful searching results.

The existing interface design of RERO Doc considers the needs of different searchers by providing simple and advanced search functionalities. In addition to the traditional keyword-based search, DL administrators can enhance the searchers? experiences by the following solutions:

- *Visualising the search results*: Hajra and Tochtermann proposed an approach for visualising search interface by applying external thesauri and suggested terms through machine learning techniques [11]. Consequently, the mental workload of the user is reduces and this results in better search experiences. This suggestion is in line with Cao et al who emphasised the importance of using visual representation rather than textual interfaces to search document collections [6].
- *Providing auto completion function*: although RERO Doc enhances the searching experiences by utilising Auto Correct function, it also could add the Auto Complete or "Popular Terms" function. This might accelerate the searching time [14]. The previous suggested solutions are applicable in the case of the FDS and PS searchers where they reformulated their queries many times during their searching process.
- *Better utilisation of the filter and sort functions*: Niu and Hemminger [18] emphasised the importance of the facets as a supplementary feature for better interaction. They concluded that facets improve the search accuracy for

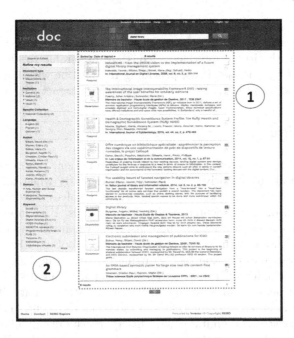

Fig. 6. Result page interface

complex and open-ended tasks by filtering the search results. We found that the KI searchers utilised author and keyword facets more frequently and rarely used the other facets. This indicates that their information needs are more precise than open-ended tasks where different facets where used. Besides, it is worth noticing how not all of the users are aware of the functionality of the facets. As a suggestion, the DL designers might provide a drop-list of the facets instead of having a long static facets bar. The drop-down list might draw the attention of the different available facets.

In terms of sorting the results, RERO Doc offered result sorting function where users can sort their results by: Ascending (SA), Descending (SD) Date (Default), Title (ST), Author(SU), or by including only full-text results. Presenting all the results including abstract, non-full text and full-text documents might causes frustrations for some users and can adversely affect the discovery experience [14]. Although RERO Doc located "search in fulltext" in the upper right corner of the search result page, the sorting functions are rarely used during the interaction processing. Instead, the designers could provide a pop-up window suggesting to limit the search results to include only the full-text results.

6.2   Improving Navigation Experiences

Considering the heterogenous users of RERO Doc, offering navigational icons might improve the navigation interactions. Rahrrovani emphasised the importance of the icons as a significant feature for better navigation experiences [21]. They concluded that the users with higher mental modules are more compatible with the iconic interfaces. Icons are preferable to abstract text as they are easier to memorise. Thus, providing RERO Doc with navigation icons may assist this segment of users to more effectively interact with the interface.

7   Conclusion

In contrast to the formative and summative evaluation, this paper emphases the importance of the iterative evaluation, particularly when targeting interface design. Iterative evaluation of user interfaces involves steady refinement of the design based on user-oriented evaluation methods. User interactions, as a significant influence factor, need to be considered when refining the interfaces. Based on a wealth and rich user-centred evaluation tool. i.e LFs, this research proposes an iterative evaluation tool. Starting by extracting UPs, we construct ISPs and generate different scenarios to be used for studying design implications and recommend possible improvements. It may be stated that ISP as a data-driven profile, and iterative evaluation tool can be used to continually refine and improve DL interface. The limitations of this approach are embodied in the validation of the found UPs from the LF analysis. Thus, we are planning to conduct a user study to investigate to what extent LFs are informative. We also plan to investigate the usefulness of such profiles for system designers with a future expert study involving experts in DL design and development.

Acknowledgments. The authors thank RERO Doc administrators for their collaboration. Our special thanks to Mr. Johnny Mariéthoz for his effort. And to Mr. Alessio Tutino from BUL (https://www.bul.sbu.usi.ch) for the enlightening conversations on DLs, users and librarians.

References

1. Azzopardi, L., Ìarvelin, K.J., Kamps, J., Smucker, M.D.: Report on the SIGIR 2010 workshop on the simulation of interaction. ACM SIGIR Forum **44**(2), 35–47 (2011)
2. Barifah, M., Landoni, M.: Interactive search profiles as a means of personalisation. In: CHIIR (2019)
3. Behnert, C., Lewandowski, D.: A framework for designing retrieval effectiveness studies of library information systems using human relevance assessments. J. Doc. **73**(3), 509–527 (2017)
4. Belkin, N.: On the evaluation of interactive information retrieval systems. Rutgers University Community Repository document (2010)
5. Blandford, A.: Understanding user's experiences: evaluation of digital libraries. In: DELOS Workshop on Evaluation of Digital Libraries, Padova, Italy (2004)
6. Cao, N., Sun, J., Lin, Y.R., Gotz, D., Liu, S., Qu, H.: FacetAtlas: multifaceted visualization for rich text corpora. IEEE Trans. Vis. Comput. Graph. **16**, 1172–1181 (2010)

7. Chowdhury, S., Landoni, M., Gibb, F.: Usability and impact of digital libraries: a review. Online Inf. Rev. **30**, 656–680 (2006)
8. Cooper, A.: The Inmates Are Running the Asylum. Sams Publishing, Indianapolis (1999)
9. Courage, C., Baxter, K.: Understanding Your Users: A Practical Guide to User Requirements. Methods, Tools, and Techniques. Elsevier, San Francisco (2005)
10. Gooding, P.: Exploring the information behaviour of users of welsh newspapers online through web log analysis. J. Doc. **72**(2), 232–246 (2016)
11. Hajra, A., Tochtermann, K.: Visual search in digital libraries and the usage of external terms. In: 2018 22nd International Conference Information Visualisation (IV) (2018)
12. Johansson, M., Messeter, J.: Present-ing the user: constructing the persona. Digit. Creat. **16**(04), 231–243 (2005)
13. Joo, S.: Investigating user search tactic patterns and system support in using digital libraries (2013)
14. Kay, J.: Improving access to e-resources for users at the university of derby: enhancing discovery systems with library plus 2.0. Insights (2019)
15. Li, Y., Liu, C.: Information resource, interface, and tasks as user interaction components for digital library evaluation. Inf. Process. Manag. **56**, 704–720 (2019)
16. Matusiak, K.K.: User navigation in large-scale distributed digital libraries: the case of the digital public library of America. J. Web Librariansh. **11**, 157–171 (2017)
17. Ndumbaro, F.: Understanding user-system interactions: an analysis of opac users' digital footprints. Inf. Dev. **34**(3), 297–308 (2018)
18. Niu, X., Hemminger, B.: Analyzing the interaction patterns in a faceted search interface. J. Assoc. Inf. Sci. Technol. **66**, 1030–1047 (2015)
19. Noonan, D.: Digital preservation policy framework: a case study. EDUCAUSE Review Online (2014)
20. Petrelli, D.: On the role of user-centred evaluation in the advancement of interactive information retrieval. Inf. Process. Manag. **44**(1), 22–38 (2008)
21. Rahrovani, S., Mirzabeigi, M., Abbaspour, J.: The trained and untrained users' mental models compatibility with the icons of search modules in Iranian digital library applications. Library Hi Tech (2017)
22. Saracevic, T.: Evaluation of digital libraries: an overview. In: Notes of the DELOS WP7 Workshop on the Evaluation of Digital Libraries, Padua, Italy (2004)
23. Shen, R., Goncalves, M.A., Fox, E.A.: Key issues regarding digital libraries: evaluation and integration. Synth. Lect. Inf. Concepts Retr. Serv. **5**, 1–10 (2013)
24. Stelmaszewska, H., Blandford, A.: Patterns of interactions: user behaviour in response to search results. In: Proceedings of the JCDL Workshop on Usability of Digital Libraries Usability of Digital Libraries 2002 (2002)
25. Sumner, T.: Report on the Fifth ACM/IEEE Joint Conference on Digital Libraries – Cyber Infrastructure for Research and Education, 7–11 June 2005, Denver, Colorado. D-Lib Magazine (2005)
26. Tamine-Lechani, L., Boughanem, M., Daoud, M.: Evaluation of contextual information retrieval effectiveness: overview of issues and research. Knowl. Inf. Syst. **24**(1), 1–34 (2010)
27. Teixeira, J., Patrício, L., Nunes, N.J., Nóbrega, L., Fisk, R.P., Constantine, L.: Customer experience modeling: from customer experience to service design. J. Serv. Manag. **23**(3), 362–376 (2012)

28. Trischler, J., Scott, D.R.: Designing public services: the usefulness of three service design methods for identifying user experiences. Public Manag. Rev. **18**(5), 718–739 (2016)

29. Tsakonas, G., Kapidakis, S., Papatheodorou, C.: Evaluation of user interaction in digital libraries. In: Notes of the DELOS WP7 workshop on the evaluation of Digital Libraries, Padua, Italy (2004)

30. Xie, I., Cool, C.: Understanding help seeking within the context of searching digital libraries. J. Am. Soc. Inf. Sci. Technol. **60**(3), 477–494 (2009)

31. Xie, I., Joo, S., Matusiak, K.K.: Multifaceted evaluation criteria of digital libraries in academic settings: similarities and differences from different stakeholders. J. Acad. Librariansh. **44**, 854–863 (2018)

32. Zavalina, O., Vassilieva, E.V.: Understanding the information needs of large-scale digital library users. Libr. Resour. Tech. Serv. **58**(2), 84–99 (2014)

33. Zha, X., Wang, W., Yan, Y., Zhang, J., Zha, D.: Understanding information seeking in digital libraries: antecedents and consequences. Aslib J. Inf. Manag. **67**(6), 715–734 (2015)

Trends and Changes in the Field of HCI the Last Decade from the Perspective of HCII Conference

André Calero Valdez$^{(\boxtimes)}$ and Martina Ziefle

Human-Computer Interaction Center, RWTH Aachen University,
Campus-Boulevard 57, Aachen, Germany
{calero-valdez,ziefle}@comm.rwth-aachen.de

Abstract. In order to identify trends and changes in the field of HCI, we used the full-texts of the papers of the HCII conferences from 2007 to 2017 in a text-mining approach. From a set of approx. 7500 documents we looked at word frequencies and topic modelling using latent dirichlet allocation (LDA) in order to detect changes and trends. We identified 50 topics using the LDA model. We found that the topics around social aspects, gamification and datafication play an increasing role. We find evidence for this in both LDA and word frequencies. We qualitatively asses the topic models using our own publications and find a high match of detected topics and our ground truth.

Keywords: Latent dirichlet allocation · Text mining · tfidf ·
Bag-of-words model · Bibliometrics

1 Introduction

The field of HCI was established in the early 1980s by Card, Newell, and Moran (The psychology of human-computer interaction [12]). It was the realization that computers are more than simple tools, with singular application uses, but rather a "partner" in continuous interaction that drove the emergence of a novel field of research. The interaction component was new and HCI was more than pure "ergonomics" or "human factors" research. It included the computer sciences and in particular interface design that enables a continuous interaction with the device. According to the ACM the field encompasses research on design, evaluation, and implementation of techniques and methods for interactive computer use, as well as phenomena that are derived from it.

In recent times the computer has become an integral part of everyday life. Computing devices are carried around by most human beings on the planet, as smartphones, tablets, smart watches, or laptops. Further, computing devices surround us in pervasive computing environments and even voice-activated access to data stored in the cloud has become a commodity. HCI has become the key research activity to design everyday life for future societies. This also becomes apparent in the changes of topics in HCI research.

© Springer Nature Switzerland AG 2019
M. Kurosu (Ed.): HCII 2019, LNCS 11566, pp. 31–45, 2019.
https://doi.org/10.1007/978-3-030-22646-6_3

In this paper we look at all publications from the HCI conference between 2007 and 2018 and conduct several text-mining approaches to understand trends and changes in the focus of the conference.

2 Text-Mining Approaches

In order to automatically understand larger bodies of text several methods can be used to understand the content of a corpus of documents. In order to understand the results, however, it is necessary to understand the underlying methods and why they are employed.

2.1 Data Cleaning

Textual data, as in our case, is often available in the form of PDF files. PDF files contain layout information, text, figures, and tables. Not all of the information contained in PDF files can sensibly used to understand the topic of the document.

We first must separate the text into meta-data and textual data. For this purpose it is helpful to first unify encoding and rely on UTF-8 encoding for all documents. Often, depending on the settings of the word processor, characters that look identical to the human reader can be encoded in several ways digitally. Unifying these is called *UTF-8 normalization*. This helps algorithms further down the processing pipeline.

Next, it is helpful to separate the main body of text from meta data such as authors, keywords, and references. Luckily, scientific publications have relatively standardized textual structures. The use of regular expressions is very helpful in separating text from meta-data.

A last step in improving general applicability of text mining, especially in the English language, is putting all text in lower case. This allows to ignore capitalization in text, which in English serves no other purpose than sentence separation. Lastly, numerals, commas, and full stops are removed, as they carry little meaning in *bag-of-words* models [24]. The *bag-of-words* model is a simplified model of text, removing all information regarding word order or semantics that rely on deixis or grammatical parsing.

2.2 Tokenization and Lemmatization

The process of *tokenization* is used to separate a document into individual words. Word delineation can be quite non-intuitive as hyphenation might separate a word into its syllables. The result of *tokenization* is a set of tokens per document. However, different inflections of the same word (e.g., "user" and "users") are not recognized as the same word by computers.

The process of *lemmatization* is used to map all inflections of a word to its basic form. Often, especially in the English language, stemming is used for *lemmatization*. Stemming removes the inflection postfix of the word leaving only the stem of the word. A typical approach is the porter-stemming algorithm [19].

The downside of this approach is that many stems are hard to read for the human user (e.g., analysis to analy). In our approach we use the lemmatization of the `textstem` package [20].

A third approach can be applied by tokenizing not only single words, but by creating n-gram tokens. A bi-gram token is a set of two consecutive words in the text (e.g. "user experience"). This improves interpretability as terms like "user" can appear in very different bigrams.

2.3   Term Frequencies

One approach of identifying topics in documents is to compare the frequency of tokens (i.e., words) relative to other documents. Typical metrics here are term-frequency and inverse-document frequency.

The *term-frequency (tf)* measures the proportion each word takes in a given document. The assumption is, the higher the *tf* the more important the word is for the document. The *inverse-document-frequency (idf)* measures how often a word occurs in all documents. The less often it appears, the higher the *idf*. Thus, *idf* is often used to identify words that occur in only few documents. By combining *tf* and *idf* we can identify words that are specifically relevant to their respective document [21].

By using *tf-idf* as a means to measure the importance of words for a document, we automatically remove *stopwords* from the equation. *Stopwords* are words that carry little meaning for a document in a bag-of-words text model (e.g., "the", "and", etc.).

2.4   Topic Modelling

The process of topic modelling refers to algorithms that identify topics in documents from token frequencies. A variety of approaches exist in determining topic models from a corpus of documents. Most renowned are *latent semantic analysis (LSA)* [13] and latent dirichlet allocation (LDA) [4].

The *LSA* method applies a singular value decomposition method to the occurrence of tokens in paragraphs or documents. This will identify topics from the empirical covariance in the documents. Using this method, topics are relatively easy to understand when token frequencies follow gaussian distributions. However, most real text documents contain token distributions that follow Zipf's Law distributions. Therefore, a different approach is more typically used when identifying topics.

Latent Dirichlet Allocation (LDA) [4] is a generative method that tries to estimate multivariate distributions between terms and topics, as well as topics and documents. This means every topic contains several terms, and every document may contain multiple topics. The challenge in LDA is that a required parameter for the algorithm is the count of topics called k, which must be given in advance. In order to find the parameter k, one must generate multiple models using different k values and evaluate them against each other. In addition, LDA runs in $O(Vnk)$, meaning that it increases linearly in the size of the corpus (n), linearly in the size of the vocabulary (V), and linearly in the size of topics (k). This means it pays of to limit the size of the vocabulary, either by filtering by term-frequency (tf) or by *tf-idf.*

3   Method

In order to understand what has shaped HCI research in the last decade, we have analyzed all papers published between 2007 and 2017 at the HCI International Conference. All papers and their PDF files were generously made available by Springer after the 2018 HCI International Conference in Las Vegas, USA. From this data-set of over 7700 papers we extracted all written text and utilized this text for a text-mining procedure written in the R language. The following steps were conducted to gather and clean the data:

1. First, all text was extracted from all PDF files using the `pdftools` package [18].
2. Meta data was extracted from the text of the document using regular-expression matching, identifying title, authors, keywords, year of publication, and references. Documents that contained no references (e.g., case-studies) were removed from the corpus.
3. All words were then tokenized using the `tidytext` package [23]. We generated both word-tokens as well as bigram and trigram tokens.
4. Then all stopwords were removed using the `stopwords` package [3]. All bi- and trigrams containing at least one stopword were removed as well.
5. After stopword removal, similar terms were unified using stemming from the `SnowballC` package [5] and also lemmatized using the `textstem` package [20].
6. Then *tf-idf* [22] was applied to the frequencies of words normalized across documents.
7. Lastly, relative frequencies are plotted over time to visualize changes in frequency using the `ggplot2` package [25] and the `viridis` palette [15].

As a means of further investigation, we then generate topic models using the `topicmodels` package [17] and try to verify whether topics change similarly as derived from word frequencies alone. Here, we use latent dirichlet allocation (LDA) [4] to create topic models. The amount of topics was estimated using the `ldatuning` package and the four contained metrics [2,11,14,16].

As a third means of understanding changes in trends, we look at the individual frequencies of terms and how we can predict their frequencies a few years into the future. For this purpose we use the `imputeTS` package as well as the `forecast` package to determine were individual word frequencies would be predicted assuming continuous drift.

4   Results

In this section we look at the different results using both the token frequency approaches as well as the latent dirichlet allocation approach. In order to ensure, that these methods are sensible, we further verify that our data follows typical frequency distributions. Overall, 7554 papers were analyzed.

4.1 Data Regularity

As a first sanity check, we verify Zipf's Law in our corpus, to see how well the distribution fits Zipf's prediction.

The linear regression that predicts frequency from rank (both on a logarithmic scale) yields an intercept of $y_0 = -0.9647$ ($SE < 0.001$, $p < 2e^{-16}$) and a slope of $b = -0.8669$ ($SE < 0.0005$, $p < 2e^{-16}$), matching the prediction of -1 for both intercept and slope (adj. $r^2 = .91$, see also Fig. 1). This means, the words in this corpus occur very much in a power-law-distribution with very few outliers.

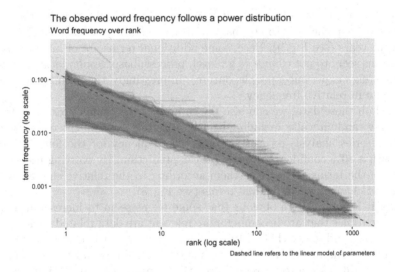

Fig. 1. Evidence for the power law distribution of terms in the dataset

4.2 Trends in the Data

After showing that the data is usable for bag-of-words style text mining, we next look into the absolute and relative word frequencies for all individual years (see Fig. 2). For this purpose we draw the top-10 words of every year, and then look-up their frequencies in all other years.

First, we see the typical trend in scientific publishing, that the overall amount of publications increases, hence the increase on absolute word counts. Furthermore, we see that these top terms do not show strong differences across the years. The only term that seems to indicate slight changes over time is the term *datum*, which is the stem for data as in data analysis, data mining, etc.

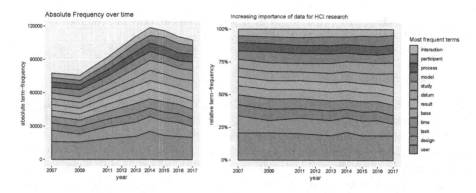

Fig. 2. Absolute and relative frequency of top terms in the last 10 years

In order to understand changes, it seems, we need to look not only at absolute and relative frequencies of top terms, but also at the different ratios of changes in the recent years (see Fig. 9). Here, some additional terms are of interest. While many terms seem to not change (e.g., level, process, base, result), others increase over time (e.g., experience, people, datum). Interestingly, the term *human* seems to decrease in relative frequency.

Based on these data, we can also try to predict the changes for these terms, by running random walks including drift on the time series of these data points. The time series analysis returns an expected frequency for the following year, along with a 80% confidence interval on the prediction. By plotting the relative changes of the terms and sorting them according to the relative change, we see the biggest changes for individual terms (see Fig. 3).

Here, it becomes more obvious that some terms seem to increase in importance. The topics that are becoming more relevant are data related topics, gamification topics and topics that address learning and cognitive aspects (see Fig. 4). On the other hand terms that have a strong traditional root in HCI (e.g., human, display, usability) seem to decrease in relative importance and continue to do so in the future.

4.3   Topic Modelling

In order to understand how the changes in the field of HCI play a role in the topics published at HCII we further look at topic models to represent content of publications. The general idea of a topic model is to generate matching word-frequencies given a set of topics per document. The word-topic frequencies and the document-topic frequencies are generated using Bayes theorem and an iterative process.

The challenge is to identify the number of topics k. For this purpose we have used the `ldatuning` package. This package allows to generate a multitude of topic models using multiple k-values and allows to calculate metrics to evaluate these topics. Additionally, this process needs hyperparameter setup.

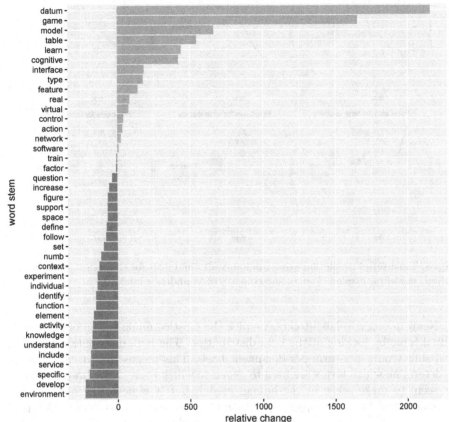

Fig. 3. Predicted changes of term frequencies using random walk and drift.

For our purpose we used *Gibbs* sampling, a burn-in time of 2500 iterations, a total 7500 iterations and 5 randomized local starts. We used automatic alpha-parameter optimization and ram the topic models on a 2.2 GHz Intel Core i7 with 12 cores and 32 gigabytes of ram. The models took several hours to converge onto a solution and using the combined metrics [2,11,14,16]. We identified 50 topics to be an ideal solution (see Fig. 5).

In order to see whether this topic model actually yields topics that are distributed among the different documents we look at the so-called gamma distribution. The gamma-distribution of the LDA returns a per-topic-per-document-probability table. If for each document several topics become relevant, the topic model is able to differentiate multiple topics. In our case the model returns such a distribution (see Fig. 6).

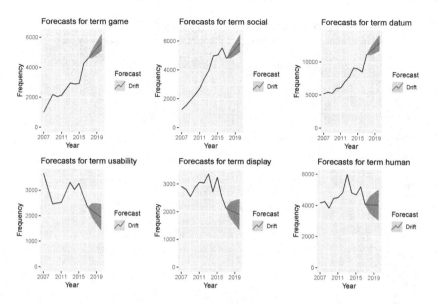

Fig. 4. Time-series prediction using random-walks and drift for the terms *game, social, datum, usability, display, human* showing a 80% confidence interval.

Next, in order to label topics, we pick the most common token for each individual topic by looking at the beta-distribution. The beta-distribution contains probability on a per-term-per-document basis. This means that it can be used to determine which terms are used to generate which topic. Not always will topics seem to make sense to the human reader, but it is nevertheless necessary to understand how the topics are constructed. In our case we found 50 topics regarding the 4 metrics mentioned earlier. Very clear topics are the topics 3, 16, 21 for the respective fields: gestures, visualization, or robotics (see Fig. 10).

In the next step, we try to track these topics over the years of the conference. For this purpose we measure the overall probability on a per year basis for the topic to occur. This is achieved using the sum of all gamma values per year (see Fig. 7).

As investigating all 50 topics would not fit the scope of this document, we look at the 16 most frequent topics across all years. Some of the topics, here indicated by their most probable term, show a large increase over time, while others seem to go in and out of trends. For example, the topics *children, games,* and *social* seem to increase in importance from the LDA topic modelling. This is particularly interesting, as these were also terms that we identified using the word frequencies from a regular bag-of-words model. The topic of *data* was not found as one of the top terms in the topics. So there are some differences in the modelling processes, although the similarities are striking.

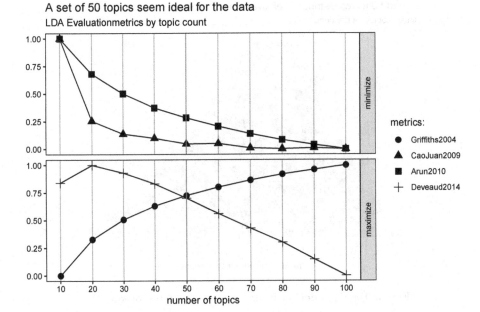

Fig. 5. Evaluation metrics for all investigated k-parameters.

4.4   Qualitative Validation of the Topic Model

In order to qualitatively evaluate how well our topic model works we look at five papers by the authors to test how well the topics match the content (see Fig. 8).

The first paper [26] is a paper about the acceptance of robots in health care for the elderly. The top three topics identified were the topics *robot*, *elderly*, and *eye*. Two topics matching exactly the content of the article. The eye topic is also related to accessibility, which matches the paper well.

The second paper [9] is a paper about a visualization that should help researchers to improve interdisciplinary collaboration. It was a user study on the usability of the visualization. The best recognized topics were *visualization*, *hci*, and *learn* which match the main idea in the paper, however the aspect of interdisciplinary research is not discovered.

The third paper [8] is a study on insights on visualization in multi-dimensional data. This paper is assigned the topics *visualization*, *behavior*, and *brand*. The first topic is a very good match, while the other topics do not seem to match the content very well. The *behavior* topic has a second almost equally important term (i.e., evaluation), which does play a large role in the paper. Thus, only the *brand* topic seems to be a mismatch. Still, the second most important term here is *management*, which was a good match for the paper.

The fourth paper [10] is a paper on the rejection of mobile assistance systems by older users in the field of diabetes management. The matched topics are *patient*, *mobile*, and *elderly*. All three topics match the content of the paper.

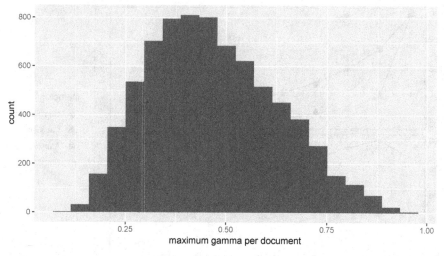

Fig. 6. Topic per document distribution (gamma) for $k = 50$.

The last paper [7] is a paper on a visualization prototype that should help researchers identify knowledge in their organization. The matched topics are *visualization*, *prototype*, and *behavior*. Here, the first two topics are a perfect match, while for the topic *behavior* we again have to look at the second most important term—evaluation. Overall, the topic model was able to detect the main topics of the authors' papers and yielded meaningful terms for categorizing these documents.

5 Discussion

We have utilized the archive of all HCII papers from 2007 to 2017 to determine changes and trends in topics of the HCI community. This method can be continuously applied in future HCII international conferences identifying future hot topics and areas for which interest might be decreasing. The trends witnessed in our data reflect the changes in public discourse about the societal impact of computing. Questions of social implications and data-driven approaches to address the large societal challenges are the cornerstones of many funding calls.

The predictions generated in this paper can be verified using the data of the upcoming years. Independently of the large body of documents, only the few years are considered as data points for the longitudinal prediction of term frequencies. This explains why there are relatively large confidence intervals around the predictions. Only very clear increases (e.g., as for *game*) have narrow CIs.

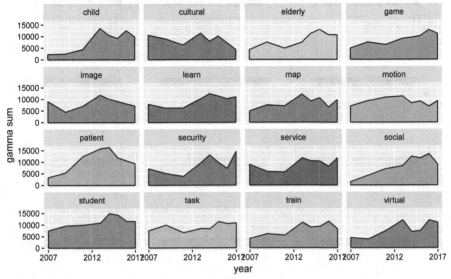

Fig. 7. Summed gamma values of the top sixteen topics over the years.

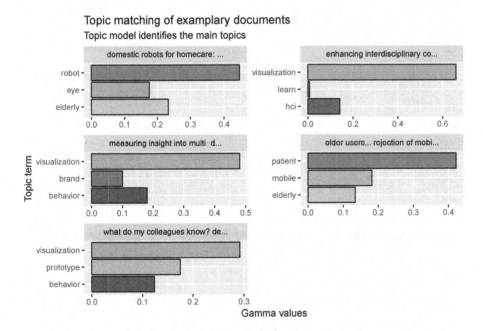

Fig. 8. Summed gamma values for the five example papers of the authors.

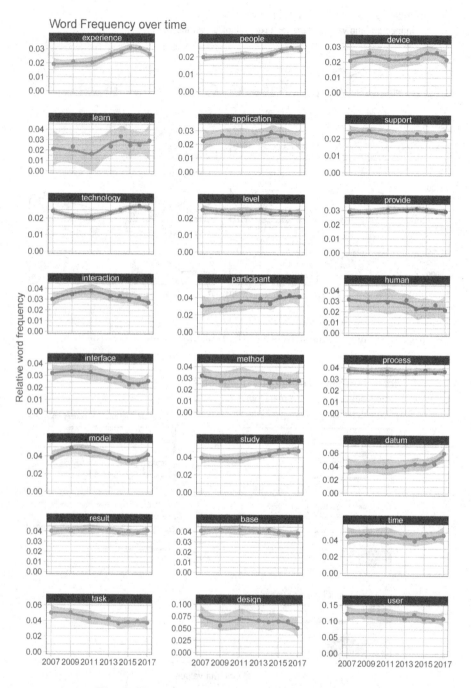

Fig. 9. Time-series analysis of the top 24 key terms.

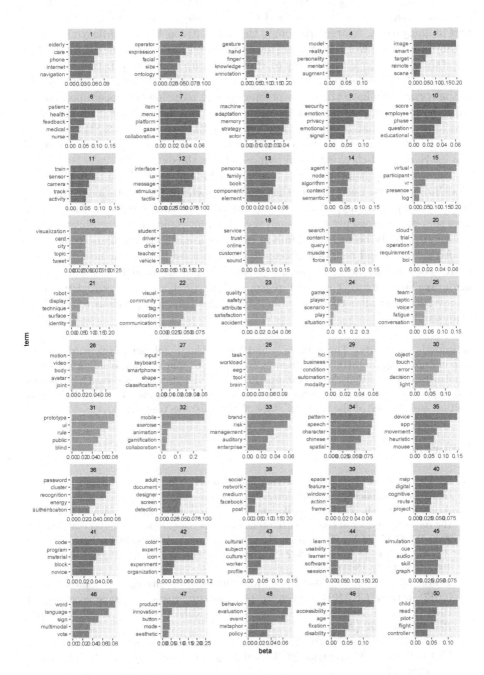

Fig. 10. Top five terms of all discovered topics.

The topic modelling showed similar results as the bag-of-words model. However, the topics generated from the LDA modelling are relatively hard to interpret in many cases. A large problem in the LDA approach is that idiosyncracies of authors and their favorite topics are hard to differentiate. The name of an expert of a certain technology is more likely to appear high up in the beta-distribution than the name of the technology, simply because the name of the author occurs rarely in the corpus. We have tried to overcome this be reducing the vocabulary size of the LDA by both *tf-idf* thresholds and *absolute* thresholds. This prevents terms that appear less than 5 times to show up in the LDA results at all. Still, common spelling errors occurred multiple times and were thus recognized as meaningful tokens. Here, spell-checking could reduce noise in the data.

Another really helpful approach was to include bi- and tri-grams in the topic modelling process. Even though they do not appear in the top-terms for models, they seemed to have helped the process immensely. Using only token data, topics were sometimes crosscutting through very different topics (e.g., visualization and security) possibly because of common evaluation methods and thus terms.

All methods and results will be published in a osf project including analysis source-code using the `rmarkdown` package [1]. The original PDFs will not be made available out of copyright reasons.[1] The analysis was pre-registered on Friday 26th 2018 after the collection of PDF-files data, but previous to the data-analysis.

Acknowledgements. The authors would like to thank Johannes Nakayama for his help in improving this article. Further, we would like to thank Annie Waldherr and Tim Schatto-Eckrodt for their help on improving the LDA hyperparameters. This research was supported by the Digital Society research program funded by the Ministry of Culture and Science of the German State of North Rhine-Westphalia.

References

1. Allaire, J., et al.: rmarkdown: Dynamic Documents for R (2018). https://CRAN. R-project.org/package=rmarkdown, r package version 1.10
2. Arun, R., Suresh, V., Veni Madhavan, C.E., Narasimha Murthy, M.N.: On finding the natural number of topics with latent dirichlet allocation: some observations. In: Zaki, M.J., Yu, J.X., Ravindran, B., Pudi, V. (eds.) PAKDD 2010, Part I. LNCS (LNAI), vol. 6118, pp. 391–402. Springer, Heidelberg (2010). https://doi.org/10. 1007/978-3-642-13657-3_43
3. Benoit, K., Muhr, D., Watanabe, K.: stopwords: Multilingual Stopword Lists (2017). https://CRAN.R-project.org/package=stopwords, r package version 0.9.0
4. Blei, D.M., Ng, A.Y., Jordan, M.I.: Latent dirichlet allocation. J. Mach. Learn. Res. **3**, 993–1022 (2003)
5. Bouchet-Valat, M.: SnowballC: Snowball stemmers based on the C libstemmer UTF-8 library (2014). https://CRAN.R-project.org/package=SnowballC, r package version 0.5.1
6. Calero Valdez, A.: HCII Text-Mining, October 2018, osf.io/cfaez

---

[1] All related materials are available at http://osf.io/cfaez [6].

7. Calero Valdez, A., Bruns, S., Greven, C., Schroeder, U., Ziefle, M.: What do my colleagues know? Dealing with cognitive complexity in organizations through visualizations. In: Zaphiris, P., Ioannou, A. (eds.) LCT 2015. LNCS, vol. 9192, pp. 449–459. Springer, Cham (2015). https://doi.org/10.1007/978-3-319-20609-7_42

8. Calero Valdez, A., Gebhardt, S., Kuhlen, T.W., Ziefle, M.: Measuring insight into multi-dimensional data from a combination of a scatterplot matrix and a hyperslice visualization. In: Duffy, V.G. (ed.) DHM 2017, Part II. LNCS, vol. 10287, pp. 225–236. Springer, Cham (2017). https://doi.org/10.1007/978-3-319-58466-9_21

9. Calero Valdez, A., Schaar, A.K., Ziefle, M., Holzinger, A.: Enhancing interdisciplinary cooperation by social platforms. In: Yamamoto, S. (ed.) HIMI 2014, Part I. LNCS, vol. 8521, pp. 298–309. Springer, Cham (2014). https://doi.org/10.1007/978-3-319-07731-4_31

10. Calero Valdez, A., Ziefle, M.: Older users' rejection of mobile health apps a case for a stand-alone device? In: Zhou, J., Salvendy, G. (eds.) ITAP 2015, Part II. LNCS, vol. 9194, pp. 38–49. Springer, Cham (2015). https://doi.org/10.1007/978-3-319-20913-5_4

11. Cao, J., Xia, T., Li, J., Zhang, Y., Tang, S.: A density-based method for adaptive LDA model selection. Neurocomputing 72(7–9), 1775–1781 (2009)

12. Card, S.K.: The Psychology of Human-computer Interaction. CRC Press, Boca Raton (2017)

13. Deerwester, S., Dumais, S.T., Furnas, G.W., Landauer, T.K., Harshman, R.: Indexing by latent semantic analysis. J. Am. Soc. Inf. Sci. 41(6), 391–407 (1990)

14. Deveaud, R., SanJuan, E., Bellot, P.: Accurate and effective latent concept modeling for ad hoc information retrieval. Doc. Numér. 17(1), 61–84 (2014)

15. Garnier, S.: viridis: Default Color Maps from 'matplotlib' (2018). https://CRAN.R-project.org/package=viridis, r package version 0.5.1

16. Griffiths, T.L., Steyvers, M.: Finding scientific topics. Proc. Natl. Acad. Sci. 101(Suppl. 1), 5228–5235 (2004)

17. Grün, B., Hornik, K.: Topicmodels: an R package for fitting topic models. J. Stat. Softw. 40(13), 1–30 (2011). https://doi.org/10.18637/jss.v040.i13

18. Ooms, J.: pdftools: Text Extraction, Rendering and Converting of PDF Documents (2018). https://CRAN.R-project.org/package=pdftools, r package version 1.8

19. Porter, M.F.: An algorithm for suffix stripping. Program 14(3), 130–137 (1980)

20. Rinker, T.W.: textstem: Tools for stemming and lemmatizing text, Buffalo, New York (2018). http://github.com/trinker/textstem, version 0.1.4

21. Salton, G., Buckley, C.: Term-weighting approaches in automatic text retrieval. Inf. Process. Manag. 24(5), 513–523 (1988)

22. Salton, G., McGill, M.J.: Introduction to modern information retrieval (1986)

23. Silge, J., Robinson, D.: tidytext: Text mining and analysis using tidy data principles in R. JOSS 1(3) (2016). https://doi.org/10.21105/joss.00037

24. Sivic, J., Zisserman, A.: Efficient visual search of videos cast as text retrieval. IEEE Trans. Pattern Anal. Mach. Intell. 31(4), 591–606 (2009)

25. Wickham, H.: ggplot2: Elegant Graphics for Data Analysis. UR. Springer, Cham (2016). https://doi.org/10.1007/978-3-319-24277-4. http://ggplot2.org

26. Ziefle, M., Calero Valdez, A.: Domestic robots for homecare: a technology acceptance perspective. In: Zhou, J., Salvendy, G. (eds.) ITAP 2017, Part I. LNCS, vol. 10297, pp. 57–74. Springer, Cham (2017). https://doi.org/10.1007/978-3-319-58530-7_5

Design Patterns to Support Personal Data Transparency Visualization in Mobile Applications

Thiago Adriano Coleti[1,2,3,4(✉)], Marcelo Morandini[1,2,3,4(✉)],
Lucia Vilela Leite Filgueiras[1,2,3,4(✉)], Pedro Luiz Pizzigatti Correa[1,2,3,4(✉)],
Igor Goulart de Oliveira[1,2,3,4(✉)],
and Cinthyan Renata Sachs Camerlengo de Barbosa[1,2,3,4(✉)]

[1] Politechniq School of University of Sao Paulo, Brazil, Sao Paulo, Brazil
{thiagocoleti,m.morandini,lfilguei,pedro.correa}@usp.br,
igorgoulartoliveira96@gmail.com, cinthyan@uel.br
[2] School of Arts, Science and Humanities of University of Sao Paulo,
Sao Paulo, Brazil
[3] Northern Parana State University, Brandeirantes, Brazil
[4] Londrina State University, Londrina, Brazil

Abstract. This paper presents a study to select and evaluate Mobile Design Patterns to support Personal Data Transparency. This research was considered as important for the Human-Computer Interaction analysis since Mobile Devices are the main resource used by subjects to interact and thus, produce personal data. Providing Transparency can require a lot of information and the Personal Transparency is being requiring by regulations of the GDPR (General Data Protection Regulation). Thus, we assumed that it could be complex to provide a mobile interface to support these issues. We selected some mobile patterns which were assumed that can support Personal Transparency Visualization and developed prototypes using the Android technology. These prototypes were evaluated providing data to conclude that the studied patterns were quite appropriated, but they required improvements related to navigation capacity.

Keywords: Personal data · Transparency · Human-data interaction · Mobile Design Patterns

1 Introduction

Transparency is the ability to provide information about the tasks involved in the collecting, processing, disclosing and use of personal data by any kind of organization or people that aim to obtain some advantage [1]. Among several concerns related to the use of personal data, provide information that allow subjects[1] to understand which events are conducted in their data and who is working with it is the more meaningful [1].

---

[1] In this paper, the word subject refers to people who produce personal data.

© Springer Nature Switzerland AG 2019
M. Kurosu (Ed.): HCII 2019, LNCS 11566, pp. 46–62, 2019.
https://doi.org/10.1007/978-3-030-22646-6_4

In this sense, Transparency can be considered as a new requirement for all software that intend to use personal data in order to ensure knowledge [2], privacy [3], security [4], anonymity [5] and that subjects rights are met [6].

Several tools usually request access permissions to personal data at the beginning of the installation that may be poorly written and/or follow a *black box* strategy which application just presents texts such as: *To use software, you need to allow us to access your contacts.* However, details about which specific data are collected or which process are performed are not showed avoiding subjects to understand, monitoring and/or acting in the use of data [7].

Government agencies, researchers and software development teams that work with personal data are increasing their concerns on providing Personal Data Transparency using specifics software known as Transparency Enhancing Tools (TETs) [6], users' interfaces [3] and regulations as General Data Protection Regulation (GDPR) [8].

Although necessary, providing Transparency is not a simple tasks, mainly in mobile devices [2] since it can be influenced by:

1. The amount of information can be large making it difficult to visualize;
2. A Transparency's requirement is related to show the processes conducted with the personal data and, according to Mortier [1] and Haddad [2], convert the processing in a visual strategy can be really complex; and
3. Most of the personal data production is done using mobile devices and it has small screen with considerable restrictions on the adequacy of information in the screen [9].

Thus, we had as research question: is it possible to provide Transparency for subjects in mobile devices even though it's a small screen? To answer this question, the following tasks were conducted: (1) We analyzed the GDPR regulation to understand how Transparency should be presented; (2) Based on the GDPR and using Android development tool, interfaces prototypes were created to simulate the Personal Data Transparency information; and (3) To validate the design, heuristic evaluation were conducted by HCI and Computing experts that inspected the prototypes according mobile heuristic criteria.

Next section presents succinct background areas that support this research.

2 Background

This section presents background about Transparency, GDPR and Mobile Design Patterns.

2.1 Transparency

Personal Data Transparency, according to GDPR in Recital 58 requires that software must provide information for subjects about activities realized in personal data such as collecting, processing, disseminating and sharing. Since 2010 the concerns about Transparency became more meaningful due to the expansion of personal data usage for several commercial and non-commercial reasons. However, tasks performed in personal data are opaque for subjects and have a strong relationship with people's privacy, security and agency [1].

Transparency can support personal data privacy and understanding through two properties:

- **Visibility** is a property discussed by Turilli [10] and Mortier [1]. Turilli presents that it refers as the form to provide information and the possibility of accessing intentions, behaviors and processes performed by controllers. Mortier [1] discuss that personal data can guide several and critical decisions took by companies and organization that can interfere in subjects' life, for example, government can use data about foreign in social networks and e-commerce for ranking people and allow (or not) he/she visit some country; and
- The **Trust** property is discussed by Murmann and Fischer-Hubner [6], by Cuppens-Boulahia [5], by Patrick [11] and by Froehlich [12] as a mean to provide real information about the use of personal data avoiding the predominance of black box strategy which subject has enough knowledge about events related to their data. Authors present that the user can have more confidence in using a software whether he/she know how his/her data are used and also known how to act case the controller/processor conduct any illegal tasks.

Haddad [2] presents that Transparency is strongly related to HCI because the visibility property requires information design in order to provide the understanding by subjects that can be traditional users (without advance knowledge about computing) and due to this reason the designer must concern about appropriate User Experience (UX). However, definitions about Transparency can be subjective and all actions involved in the use of data can lead to a complex environment to be designed [13]. In this sense, the GDPR can be used as a guideline to design Transparency information because it presents a list of items required for Transparency and considered as a right for subject.

Transparency also provides challenges related to human behavior once the interaction with data and the data-driven life is uncommon and unknown. Oliver [14] presents the passive posture and lack of custom to deal with data. Passive posture is related to the fact that systems can provide good Transparency, but to access it, subjects must choose, have time, means and/or skills to do it. Also, people use smart phones, Internet and other services and automatically interact with personal data, but they usually do not know how to use, act, analyze or lead with personal data.

Next section we present information about the GDPR and Transparency Requirements.

2.2 GDPR

GDPR is a regulation that provides criteria and rules for the use of personal data created by the Europe Union to ensure the subject's privacy and freedom rights. GDPR started in 2016 and are definitively in force since April 2018 when several companies in Europe Union and all the world should suit it processes to be conform to GDPR [8]

This regulation provides a list of requirements that must be considered to ensure Transparency for subjects [15]. This list is composed by three main articles focused on guiding controllers in the aspect as visibility, control and understanding of the personal data use by subjects [16]. In short, the GDPR requires that information about the follow items must be presented as Transparency:

- Controllers, Processors and Protection Office contact details;
- Information about purpose of use, legal basis and subjects' rights;
- Information about collecting process, period of use and the processes performed; and
- Information about disclose and sharing procedures.

Somehow, we can conclude that GDPR is a regulation that should be followed to provide Transparency even for countries that do not belong to the European Union. The guidelines well-defined and few subjective that can support the development of clear components for Transparency's interface.

Next section presents information about the Mobile Design Patterns.

2.3 Mobile Design Patterns

Design patterns have become a widely used concept in the Human-Computer Interaction field, as well as in Software Engineering. Design patterns in Computing stem from the works of Alexander [17], who develops the concept of the recurrency of solutions in architecture and the nature of order. Tidwell [18] says that "patterns are structural and behavioral features that improve the 'habitability' of something - a user interface, a website, an object-oriented program or a building." Patterns are thus valid representations of commonsense in a given field and a useful tool for designing applications for that field. Libraries of patterns have been built in several areas to help designers in finding reusable solutions to common situations in design and implementation of user interfaces (UI), in different abstraction levels [19].

Mobile devices is one of the most used computational resource. Since smartphones is working many models and types of this devices aroused and all of them has a similar features: it work as a small computer and some devices have more processing powerful than a traditional computer [20].

In fact, smartphones change several ways of software development and users can work with mobile devices for several activities and due to this reason some people does not have computers anymore [9,21].

In HCI field some challenges aroused because the design of interfaces had to be improved. Mobile screens are smaller than traditional computers, the icons and visual components are also small and the interaction is usually based on touch-screen. Other different features from traditional computer is that users are not working totally focused on the task, but it may be using the cell phone in parallel with another task creating a sharing of attention and interaction [22].

All these features require new approaches to develop mobile interfaces in a way that all components, UX and information organization must be created specially for small interfaces and mobile interaction [23]. The amount of information in screen should be carefully designed because a prioritization of resources and components must be considered in order to avoid a high density information and an unusable interface [24].

To support the mobile interface development several Mobile Design Patterns were created and/or selected based on scientific researches or practical software development experience. The patterns aim to provide means to create interface to be suitable for mobile devices in size, working and interaction [24]. Without the patterns it was not difficult to identify the process of miniaturization which desktop components had it sized reduced on canvas creating a terrible interface and UX [23]. Some examples for Mobile Design Patterns are:

- Springboards: provide a group of buttons in a main interface that allow users to access any kind of information from this interface;
- Headerless Table: is a concept of table special design for mobile interface and is considered appropriate for quick visualization and actions. In this pattern, column's title are hidden to improve the data visualization through the organization of a items collection per row. The rows can display several different components as images, charts, colors and text;
- User Guide: require an information organization by topics that allow the user to conduct a systematic search (also supported by search fields);
- Maps and markers: present information using maps services as Google Maps and use markers to point to a specific information or present more content;
- Time-lines and charts: is an interface component that provides a line with interactive resources to manipulate and visualize information; and
- Thresholds: present information based on a range with markers to indicate how many items of the context were done

Patterns presented by Neil [24] were created for Android and IoS operational systems and are being improved according to new mobile interfaces needs to provide increasingly UX.

The next section presents the selection of Mobile Design Patterns for Personal Data Transparency.

3   Patterns for Transparency in Mobile Devices

This section presents the process conducted to select Mobile Design Patterns to support Personal Data Transparency visualization in mobile devices. Highlighting that the main challenge was to look for interfaces' components to provide a good experience in the visualization of Transparency. Also, GDPR Transparency guideline was used to establish which information must be presented. Thus, the follow tasks were performed:

- analyzing GDPR to identify which information must be presented to provide Transparency;
- search and analyze Mobile Design Patterns that could support the development of interfaces for Transparency visualization. Important to highlight that in this stage we did not create new patterns, but selected existed patterns, mainly those proposed by Neil [24] and Nuldemann [23];
- prototyping interfaces using the selected patterns in Android Platform; and
- evaluating the prototypes using Mobile Heuristic evaluation.

3.1 Transparency Requirements

In this stage we analyzed the GDPR's articles number thirteen, fourteen and fifteen in order to identify which elements should be presented to provide Transparency. The Transparency items were classified according to type of information required by each one as followed:

1. **Contact Data Information**: Several companies/people can be involved in the use of some personal data and due to this reason GDPR requires that information to allow subject to contact any organization or people that are working with the data must be presented. Also, GDPR classified companies and people in: controllers, processors, protection office and recipients;
2. **Purposes and Legal basis, Rights of subjects**: One of the main objectives of GDPR is provide information to avoid the "black box" strategy. In this sense, Transparency can be achieved presenting information about the purpose of use, whether the purpose is legal and how subjects can exercise his/her rights;
3. **Location**: Besides data for contact, GDPR requires that the location must be clearly presented in order to allow subjects to know where his/her data is being used in the world since Internet and Cloud Computing allow that computational tasks can be performed using a distributed strategy and different places. Location is also required to support to identify companies which data are sharing or disclosed;
4. **Processing information**: Using interface's components to explaining the execution of an algorithm is complex, but according to GDPR, show minimum information about the data processing which allow subject to understand how data is used must be done;
5. **Data Source**: The data can be collected by the users' device or obtained from third parties and in this case, the subject must to know the datasource; and
6. **Period of use**: Subjects must know about the period of use (processing/storage) the data.

Based on these Transparency's needs, we started to analyzed which patterns could be used to present these information in mobile devices.

3.2 Mobile Design Patterns

The interface for Transparency was developed considering the limitations of small mobile screens which does not have area for large amount of components and because of this it requires an better analysis to ensure that all the resources presented are really necessary to avoid the waste of resources. An approach named Mobile First [21] that was developed for Web-Mobile was considered to support this project because it purpose is to input in the interface just components that are really important for context beside to consider the development for mobile before development for desktop.

Two interaction properties were concerned for Transparency delivery: (1) Navigation: Subjects can have different needs of Transparency and intentions of use and due to this reason the interface must allow he/she to navigate among different information; and (2) Information Display: provide an appropriate design that allow user to visualize and understand the information presented.

We started developing and prototyping the Navigation strategy that were classified, according to Neil [24] in Primary and Secondary.

For primary navigation we chose the Springboard pattern. As we classified Transparency's information in six main topics presented in previous subsection, we assumed that a springboard could be a simple and clear way to guide the subjects to navigate among the topics. Also, due to the reduced amount of information classes, springboard provide a clear interface and the buttons can have a size and position that did not overlap and also it were well defined areas avoiding uncorrected selections.

For secondary navigation that could be used to support a direct navigation (without use the springboard) among topics we decided to use the a pattern named Toggle Menu that is an interaction component that is showed as an overlay always the user select another component as a button or a label. This navigation should not interfere in the data visualization and due to this reason a Transient pattern were select, i.e, the navigation is hidden until the user active the option thought an interface component.

In Fig. 1 is presented a prototype for primary navigation with Springboard and the secondary navigation with Toggle Menu with few options once more options could be defined later.

After, we chose a design pattern to present the items for Transparency required by GDPR. First item designed was to display **Contact Data Information**. To select the patterns for this requirement, the follow aspects were considered: (1) GDPR requires that the identification and contact details of entities must be presented, but it does not point out specific data, so the follow data were considered for identification: the name and a picture with the company's logo (or people's face image) and contact details (e-mail address, website address and full phone number); (2) these data were select considered as minimum information needed to identify a organization/person; and (3) the data select should occupy little space in the screen;

Thus, the design pattern selected for this information was the Headerless Table because it can presents several controllers, processors or protection offices

Fig. 1. Springboard and Toggle Menu prototype for transparency main menu

in a kind of list. For each contact a row should be provided with a image, identification with highlight letters and contact details in normal format letters. In Fig. 2 an example of list of contacts is displayed.

Provide information about **Purposes and Legal basis, Rights of subjects** is a concern of GDPR since most of users produce personal data without know about the controller's purpose of use and whether is legal or not.

This Transparency item can be one of more complex to be designed for mobile interfaces because it usually present a large amount of texts which can be uncomfortable and visually inefficient once size of fonts could be small and the user must read all the text in mobile.

To support it, we considered the use of a pattern named User Guide/Help System. The topics (Purpose, Legal basis and Rights) are organized in a main interface (similiar to Springboard) and according to user needs, he/she can navigate using a drill-down strategy. Also, each topic can guide to textual interface where user can read the text or search a specific word.

Thus, we proposed the use of User Guide/Help System pattern using at least three levels: (1) First level were organized as a Springboard with the options: (a) Purpose; (b) Legal Basis; and (c) Rights of Subjects; (2) Secondary level could present the subgroups of information, for example, for Legal Basis information, this level can present items such as: Number of Law, Date of Beginning, Responsible. Also for Right of Subjects some suggestion can be: How to cancel the use or How to obtain a copy; (3) This level presents textual information with a search field to make easy to find a word.

In Fig. 3 is presented an example of proposed pattern with explained level exemplified by Rights for Subject information.

For **Location** Transparency information the decision was relatively simple since people are accustomed to using maps because of the popularity of

Fig. 2. Prototype for contact details interface

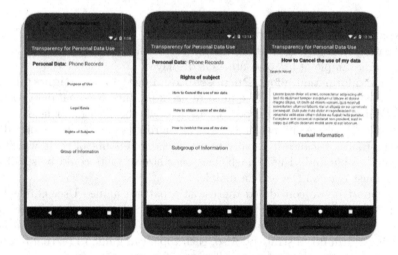

Fig. 3. Prototype for purpose, legal basis and rights of subjects

applications as Google Maps and Waze. Thus, to provide information about location of organizations, people or any entity that require the identification we propose the use of Maps that is a usual resource in mobile tools. To support the details visualization we suggest the use of markers to provide, at least, the name, phone, e-mail, address or any information that can help user to understand the location.

In Fig. 4 an example is presented, which a marker displays information about a hypothetical Data Processor located in Sao Paulo Brazil. Data as phone, e-mail address helps to identify the actor.

Fig. 4. Prototype for location information using maps and markers

Providing details of data **Processing** is considered one of biggest challenge for Transparency information as discussed by Mortier [1] and Haddad [2] . It is not simple create a visual demonstration about how data and algorithms works. However, GDPR requires that subjects have access to minimum information that allow him/her understand the processing tasks mainly whether a computer-based decision is performed using personal data.

What the word "minimum" means is not detailed presented leading us to assume that the user should understand at least: which stages (name), the sequence when it happens and a brief and lay description. Details about the operation of algorithm can be hidden since the vast majority of people could not desire (and need) to know execution low level details.

Thus, we propose the use of a timelime concept based on the pattern named Interactive Timelime. The time-lime could be presented in vertical orientation with markers in a reasonable distance that can present the number of sequence, the name of task and a single description. In certain way, it can be similar to road map or to a subway map that can be find in the stations. In Fig. 5 an example of timelime pattern is presented containing three stages and the third marker is selected and presenting the information.

The next Transparency item is the **Data Sources**. It is common for people receive e-mail, phone calls or be surprised by information of your interest without information about the source of data. In this sense, GDPR proposes that data source information must be presented mainly if data is obtained from 3rd sources and not directly by subjects' device.

We assumed that information must be classified in two types as presented in Fig. 6: Data collected directly from subject; and Data obtained from 3rd. For first type, we suggest an approach where data is presented using an image to represent the data source and a panel with three other data:

Fig. 5. Prototype for processing minimum details

- Source: description of the data source, for example, smart phone, subway service or credit card machine;
- Resource: component that performs the data collecting such as camera, surveillance camera, payments in the credit card machine; and
- Collection period: the interval for data collecting.

For data obtained from three controllers, we assume that it can be complex to detail which resources or devices were used to collect the data because the controller that is providing Transparency could not have this information. Therefore, display information about who is the responsible for data collecting is possible. Also, details about the moment which data were transferred from the source to the actual controller and data explaining whether the source is public or private is also needed since it is required by GDPR.

Thus, we propose to use the same Pattern used for **Location** presented in Fig. 4. A map with markers to set the data-source location and for each marker, data about the controller or processor could be presented. Besides the data already discussed in location requirement, the date of acquisition must be presented.

Period of use is the last Transparency item identified and is considered important since users must know about the time the data will be used. This is a subjects' right because it can interfere in privacy, freedom and security. Also, the use of data can be expired according to the context of use, so the subjects need to know if his/her data is not being used incorrectly.

For this requirement we propose the use of a calendar adapted by a pattern named Thresholds. For example, a personal data is collected to be used by one year and the rate is composed from the collect date until the end date. The marker must be positioned to indicate how much of a period has elapsed since the beginning of use of the data. Thus, we propose a pattern adaptation to be

Fig. 6. Prototype for data source information

used to indicate the period of use of the data. As presented in Fig. 7 this pattern must have at least two information: Start date of data usage; and End data of data usage.

This section presented the proposition of Mobile Design Patterns for Personal Data Transparency's visualization based on GDPR. The concern in create this kind of interaction is justified because Transparency can required a large amount of information conflicting with mobile screen features such as size and interaction ways.

With the proposed patterns we assumed that Transparency information could be visualized in mobile devices in a way that would allow subject to identify some events related to their personal data.

Next section presents the validation of the proposed patterns.

4   Validation

The validation was performed using Heuristic Evaluation strategy that is a systematic inspection of the user interface's design to identify ergonomic problems [25]. The prototypes (developed using Android technology) were organized in cards and presented for 7 evaluators with advanced knowledge in HCI or Computer Science. The number of evaluators is according to Nilsen [25] proposition that required at least 5 evaluators-specialists.

The evaluators received the cards with: (1) the instructions to understand the heuristics and the criteria to be evaluated; and (2) the prototype images with the description. We suggested that evaluators focused on verify whether the patterns selected, and levels organization (if applicable) were appropriate in order to provide Transparency information visualization in Mobile Device.

Fig. 7. Prototype for period of use

The heuristics selected are based on the research of Rocha [26] that used eleven criteria for mobile interface evaluation. However, the evaluation were conduct in cards using the prototypes based on Android user interface, but without computational interactions and due to this reason we selected six heuristics (Table 1) that could better answer questions about data visualization, design, organization and user experience in prototype/static images.

Table 1. Mobile Heuristics select for evaluation

Heuristic	Name
HM1	Good use of screen space
HM2	Visibility and easy access to all information existing
HM3	Suitability between the component and its functionality
HM4	Message matching to functionality and user
HM5	Ease access to features
HM6	User memory load minimization

Each heuristic were evaluated based on the criteria presented in Table 2. Next section presents the results and discussions.

5 Results and Discussions

The results were described in a way similar to [26], in three tables that classified the results as followed:

Table 2. Criteria to evaluate the heuristics

Severity	Problem description
0 - No relevant	Does not severely affect the interface and does not cover all users which excludes the need for adjustments
1 - Design	No relevant, but can be improved as possible
2 - Simple	Can be repaired but has low priority
3 - Serious	Must be repaired as soon as possible
4 - Catastrophic	Must be repaired immediately because it affects/prevents the use of the interface

1. Total of problems and severity average (Table 3);
2. Amount of problems and severity average per Interface (Table 4);
3. Amount of problems and severity average per Heuristics (Table 5).

To be considered as a problem, a heuristic must be evaluated among the rates 1 (one) and 4 (four). Each evaluator could answer about 54 problems, thus, as 7 (seven) evaluators worked in the evaluation 378 problems were possible. The severity average were calculated using traditional average mathematics technique.

Table 3. Total of problems and severity average

Total of problems	General severity average
74	1,37

Results in Table 3 present that the evaluated interfaces had few amount of problems since 15% of all possible problems were found and that the problem severity average was between 1 and 2 leading to assume that the interfaces had aesthetic and simple problems.

Also, results in Table 4 present that from the nine functions evaluated, just two functions were classified with greater severity than 2. Two interface were very well evaluated because it severity average was between zero and one. Other interfaces presented severity between 1 and 2 similar to the general evaluation severity.

Coincidentally, worst severities were found in navigation interfaces in which one were the pattern named Toggle Menu and other one was about Purposes and Legal basis, Rights of subjects that used a Guide/Help design pattern. We assume that this problems happened because provide navigation for many interfaces and information in a small screen can required that information be divided, classified or using strategies as filters and/or drill-down. In this sense, the interface can required that user conduct several clicks, tips or other commands to find/access an information making the task for finding something difficult.

Table 4. Problems by interface/functions

Interface/function	Total of problems	Severity average
Springboard	10	1,6
Navigation	19	3,1
Contact data details	1	0,16
Purpose, legal basis and rights	15	2,5
Location	6	1
Processing information	4	0,67
Data source (by subject)	0	0
Data source (by other sources)	8	1,33
Period of use	11	1,83

On the other hand, the best evaluated interfaces used simple, direct and easy visualization patterns that allowed a good components organization in a little screen space and thus, the information was in a unique interface, in a visible way and well and easy interactive allowing user to find information with few tasks.

With results presented in Table 5 we concluded that the navigation pattern was the main problem of the proposed interfaces. The heuristic HM2 related to navigation was the worsted evaluated being the unique with severity Two and eighteen errors. All the other were severity between 1 and 1.5 and the amount of errors was about 15% similar to general severity values.

Table 5. Problems identified by Heuristic

Heuristic	Total of problems	Severity average
HM1	14	1,5
HM2	18	2
HM3	11	1,2
HM4	10	1,1
HM5	9	1
HM6	12	1,2

Considering the results, we concluded that the interfaces are quite appropriate to provide Personal Data Transparency. Except navigation heuristics, all others were considered irrelevant or simple and that do not interfere or impede the views of information.

For Navigation issues, we proposed to study how to find, improve and/or create new patters that can support navigation among several Transparency information with more quality and reducing the number of tasks among the screens. For information that was visualized using navigation pattern we intend to look for new patterns that can present the information in few (or just one) interfaces and avoid changes between multiple screens.

Next section presents the Final Considerations and Futures Works.

6   Final Considerations and Future Works

Personal Data Transparency became an important requirement to be provide for users in order to allow him/her to understand how their personal data are used and by who. The more usually resource used for subjects to do their tasks is the smartphone that has small screens leading to challenges in design interfaces for visualization of many contents such as Transparency.

The Mobile Design Patterns could support the development of interface for Transparency and due to this reason we selected, developed and evaluated a group of mobile interfaces that were based on mobile patterns and Transparency requirements from GDPR.

The evaluations were conducted using Heuristic evaluation techniques and presented that the patterns can support most of Transparency Requirements, but Navigation issues were not considered appropriated and must be improved mainly to support the navigation among all the resource and also to support navigation in a drill-down concept which is a kind of interaction that could be common in Transparency for personal data.

As future work we intend to improve the navigation capability to facilitate the interaction with big amount of information in different interfaces. The development of an usable release in order to realize usability testing and understand how the subjects interact with Transparency information and whether the patterns really support the interaction between user and interface. Also we intend to expand the patterns for other digital platforms as IoS and Web-Responsive.

References

1. Mortier, R., Haddadi, H., Henderson, T., Mcauley, D., Crowcroft, J., Crabtree, A.: Human-data interaction: the encyclopedia of human-computer interaction. In: The Encyclopedia of Human-Computer Interaction, pp. 1–48 (2016)
2. Mortier, R., Haddadi, H., Henderson, T., McAuley, D., Crowcroft, J.: Human-data interaction, no. 837, pp. 1–9. University of Cambridge (2013)
3. Iachello, G., Hong, J.: End-user_privacy_in_human_computer_interaction - 2007.PDF
4. Ackerman, M.S., Mainwaring, S.D.: Privacy Issues and Human-Computer Interaction, pp. 1–19. O'Reilly & Associates, Sebastopol (2005)
5. Munier, M., Lalanne, V., Ardoy, P.-Y., Ricarde, M.: Legal issues about metadata data privacy vs information security. In: Garcia-Alfaro, J., Lioudakis, G., Cuppens-Boulahia, N., Foley, S., Fitzgerald, W.M. (eds.) DPM/SETOP -2013. LNCS, vol. 8247, pp. 162–177. Springer, Heidelberg (2014). https://doi.org/10.1007/978-3-642-54568-9_11
6. Murmann, P., Fischer-Hübner, S.: Tools for achieving usable Ex post transparency: a survey. IEEE Access 5, 22965–22991 (2017)

7. Schneier, B.: Data and Goliath: The Hidden Battles to Collect Your Data and Control Your World. Norton, New York (2015)
8. Voigt, P., von dem Bussche, A.: The EU General Data Protection Regulation (GDPR): A Practical Guide, 1st edn. Springer, Heidelberg (2017). https://doi.org/10.1007/978-3-319-57959-7
9. Lee, V.R., Dumont, M.: An exploration into how physical activity data-recording devices could be used in computer-supported data investigations. Int. J. Comput. Math. Learn. **15**(3), 167–189 (2010)
10. Turilli, M., Floridi, L.: The ethics of information transparency. Ethics Inf. Technol. **11**(2), 105–112 (2009)
11. Patrick, A.S.: From privacy legislation to interface design: implementing information privacy in human- computer interactions. In: Lecture Notes in Computer Science, March 2003. NRC Publications Archive (NPArC), January 2015
12. Froehlich, J., Findlater, L., Landay, J.: The design of eco-feedback technology. In: Proceedings of the SIGCHI Conference on Human Factors in Computing Systems (CHI 2010), pp. 1999–2008 (2010)
13. Mortier, R., et al.: Personal data management with the databox: what's inside the box? (2016)
14. Oliver, R.W.: What is Transparency?. McGraw-Hill, New York (2004)
15. Bellamy, B., Alonso, C.: Reframing data transparency. Centre for Information Policy Leadership and Telefónica Senior Roundtable, vol. 1, pp. 1–20, June 2016
16. Bonatti, P., Kirrane, S., Polleres, A., Wenning, R.: Transparent personal data processing: the road ahead. In: Tonetta, S., Schoitsch, E., Bitsch, F. (eds.) SAFE-COMP 2017. LNCS, vol. 10489, pp. 337–349. Springer, Cham (2017). https://doi.org/10.1007/978-3-319-66284-8_28
17. Alexander, C.: The origins of pattern theory: the future of the theory, and the generation of a living world. IEEE Softw. **16**(5), 71–82 (1999)
18. Tidwell, J.: Designing Interface: Patterns for Effective Interaction Design. O'REILLY, Sebastopol (2011)
19. Miyamaru, F., Leite, L., Bertuzzi, A., Filgueiras, L.: Task patterns for e-government services. In: Proceedings of the VIII Brazilian Symposium on Human Factors in Computing Systems, IHC 2008, Porto Alegre, Brazil, pp. 276–279. Sociedade Brasileira de Computação (2008)
20. Fling, B.: Mobile Design and Development. OReilly, Sebastopol (2009)
21. Wroblewski, L.: Mobile First (2011)
22. de Abreu Cybis, W., Holts, A.B., Faust, R.: Ergonomia e Usabilidade: Conhecimentos, Métodos e Aplicações. Novatec Editora, São Paulo (2015)
23. Nudelman, G.: Padrões de Projeto para o Android - Soluções de projetos de Interação para desenvolvedores. 1 edn. Novatec Editora (2013)
24. Neil, T.: Mobile Design Pattern Gallery, 2nd edn. OReilly, Sebastopol (2014)
25. Nielsen, J.: Usability Engineering, 1st edn. Morgan Kaufmann, San Diego (1993)
26. Rocha, L.C., Andreade, R.M.C., Sampaio, A.L.: Heurísticas para avaliar a usabilidade de aplicações móveis: estudo de caso para aulas de campo em Geologia. In: Nuevas Ideas en Informática Educativa TISE, pp. 367–378 (2014)

The IoT Design Deck 2.0: Improving the Tool for the Co-design of Connected Products

Massimiliano Dibitonto[(✉)], Federica Tazzi, Katarzyna Leszczynska,
and Carlo M. Medaglia

DASIC, Link Campus University, via del Casale di S. Pio V, 44,
00165 Rome, Italy
{M.Dibitonto, F.Tazzi, K.Leszczynska,
C.Medaglia}@unilink.it

Abstract. Designing the User Experience of an Internet of Things (IoT) product is a complex activity that requires multidisciplinary and specific competencies and that raises new challenges for designers. In this context the IoT Design Deck [1] is a method to help design teams to collaborate in order to design a connected product and an omnichannel service. The main strengths of the method are: to create a common language and a common knowledge base to help multidisciplinary teams working together; to focus on UX factors rather than on technological ones; to discover and use the potential of the IoT and take into account its threats; to have a service oriented approach rather than a device centrical one; to accelerate the design process. In this work we present the evolution of the method, obtained through a test campaign, made with experts and non-experts, and a redesign phase based on tests results.

Keywords: User experience design · Internet of Things ·
Human computer interaction · Co-design · User centered design ·
Service Design

1 Introduction

The Internet of Things is a new technological paradigm that is changing the way we interact and relate with digital contents and services, reshaping our world. As an evolution of the concept of Ubiquitous and Pervasive Computing [2] physical elements like objects and spaces are becoming connected and able to share information. From the perspective of the user it means that digital contents and services may be accessed by a multiplicity of new channels (i.e. a smart fridge could suggest a recipe and then share it with a smart food processor) but the most important point is that the fusion of digital and physical worlds, together with AI and machine learning, enables a huge number of new services and possibilities (i.e. a smart fridge could learn the habits of the user, suggest a diet that takes into account the user's activity level and her health conditions and so on).

Designing this new type of services and products means to face a wide set of new challenges [1] like trust, privacy, human-human and human-machine relationship and many others. It requires also multidisciplinary and specialized competencies and

© Springer Nature Switzerland AG 2019
M. Kurosu (Ed.): HCII 2019, LNCS 11566, pp. 63–74, 2019.
https://doi.org/10.1007/978-3-030-22646-6_5

presents an high level of complexity due to the multiplicity of variables to be considered. For this reason new methods and tools are needed to support designers and professionals involved in the design of connected products and omnichannel services. The IoT Design Deck, as described in our previous work [1], is a method to help multidisciplinary teams to co-design the User Experience of connected products and omnichannel services. In this work we present the evolution of the method based on a series of tests and a redesign phase.

2 IoT Design Deck

As described in our previous work [1] The IoT Design Deck is a method for the co-design of the User Experience of connected projects and services. Its main objectives are to help design teams to:

- to create a common language and a common knowledge base to help multidisciplinary teams to work together, also with the involvement of users and stakeholders;
- to focus on UX aspects rather than on technological ones;
- to discover and use the potential of the IoT and to take into account its threats;
- to have a service oriented approach rather than a device centrical one;
- to accelerate the design process.

The method could be used for the design of "real" projects but also for exploring and teach how to design the UX for a connected product.

It is physically composed by several decks of cards and "boards". The method follows a design process that mixes the use of cards and boards with common techniques and methods for user research, idea generation and sorting, testing and prototyping, to guide the team from the first idea to the prototype.

2.1 Testing the IoT Design Deck

After the development of the first version of the method, we decided to test its effectiveness in order to improve it. At the best of our knowledge there is no agreement on a standard method to evaluate a co-design method, so we decided to use a qualitative approach to measure if the proposed method was able to help a design team in the expected way.

Moreover we were invited to take part to the IoT Ideation Expert Workshop organized by the Chemnitz University of Technology. During this workshop several co-design method for the IoT were tested and compared.

In the following paragraphs we will describe the tests and subsequent redesign phase based on the tests results.

First Tests. The first tests were intended to be merely qualitative as, according to the objective of the method, the outcomes are more related to the experience of the participants rather than to a measurable parameter. Moreover, according to the intrinsic characteristics of the method and to the need of a facilitator, it was possible to manage just few small groups that, however, could be representative of a real-world condition.

As the main objective was to test the usability and the effectiveness of the tools we adapted the well-known Nielsen heuristics [3] and used those evaluation criteria:

- Self-explanation and understandability (system visibility, consistency and standards, help and documentation): ability of the tools to be understood without explanation. Awareness of the user about why she is doing something and which are the next steps. This is also related with the understandability of the labelling and the textual contents by an heterogeneous audience but also at the logical order of the elements in the cards.
- Efficiency and ease of use (flexibility and efficiency): it refers to the ability of the cards to support the action they are designed for with the right amount of user effort i.e. if there is enough space to write the characteristics, but also if the card dimensions allows to be sorted, managed and red by several people at once. Regarding the flexibility, we were also interested to see if experts could "bend" the tools to use them with the methods they are familiar with.

Moreover, as a way to measure efficiency, we added another indicator:

- Group interaction: the ability of the method and the tools to encourage the interaction within the group, the discussion and the exchange of ideas.

We organized a series of workshops to test the method both with non-experts (students) and experts of UX and Service Design. During the workshops people were asked to develop a possible solution (concept) starting from a brief (randomly extracted), defining personas, context of use, functionalities and touchpoints, and creating a user journey. The workshop had a duration of 3 h.

To collect the data we used the following techniques:

- Observation: made by the facilitators and by the researchers to detect the behaviour of the participants and the interactions within the group.
- Thinking aloud: the participants were asked to comment while they were using the cards.
- Focus group: made at the end of the workshop to collect information about the three points reported above and to let emerge participants' opinion.

Four tests were made with design students with basic knowledge of UX Design. We recruited 12 students (different for each test), aged between 23 and 25 years. They were divided in 3 groups.

The second test was made with the involvement of the members of the UX Book Club of Rome. Participants were experts and professionals working in the field of UX, Visual and Service design and software development. They were 18, aged between 25 and 47. They were divided into 4 groups.

There were two facilitators to help the groups. The facilitator had the role to help the group to use the method and to focus on the project, suggesting tools and techniques and keep the group discussion moving smoothly.

Results. Regarding the three main criteria selected we obtained the following qualitative results:

- Self-explanation: The tools are quite self explaining. Even non-experts were able to identify the scope and the use of the cards. The preferred one was the "Personas" card. Even experts and non-expert were able to use it intuitively. Although the "Functionality" cards was not easily understood by non-experts. Moreover the process was perceived as not clear, the participants couldn't easily guess the next steps of the design process and they needed to be guided by the facilitator. Also the usefulness of "Action" cards was understood only when explained by the facilitator.
- Efficiency and ease of use: The participants found the dimension of the cards useful to write and draw concepts. The limited space was identified by someone as an invitation to be concise. The majority of the participants preferred to write instead of sketching inside the "Context" and "Functionality" cards.
- Group-Interaction: Participants used the cards to discuss ideas within the group. As an example they intuitively used the "Personas" and the "Context" cards to describe some scenarios or possible use cases to other participants. The "Touchpoints" and the "Threats" cards were used as a library to find inspiration.

During the focus group with the experts we asked them if they would use the method or some tools in their work. Especially the "Personas", the "Context" and the "Threats" cards were addressed to be useful and that could be used even outside the method.

The IoT Ideation Expert Workshop. On October 2018 our team was invited to the two days IoT Ideation Expert Workshop organized by the Chemnitz University of Technology, during which several co-design methods for the IoT were tested and compared to find the benefits and different approaches of the different ideation tools. For each method there was a brief workshop follow by a post-hoc questionnaire and a q&a session.

We condensed the main phases of the method in one hour and a half and we focused on the main steps of the design process. We started from predefined briefs, randomly chosen by the participants. The successive steps were defining personas, context of use, functionalities and touchpoints and creating at the end of the process a short user journey. The participants were divided into three groups of six persons each, composed by IoT experts (designers and engineers) and students from the Chemnitz University of Technology. In each group there was a facilitator who guided the participants during the different phases.

This test was very helpful to analyze and improve the method and also to compare it with the six other IoT design techniques. It allowed us to focus on specific topics as: the target (experts or not), the focus (teaching, exploring, designing), the type of support used (cards, objects, etc.) and the necessity or not of a facilitator during the workshop.

It was useful to see how the different methods involved were different from each other, despite all of them was IoT ideation tools. After all the workshops we identified some main differentiation between the different ideation methods and we so have been able to position our method more clearly in relation to the identified variables:

- The ideal target for which the method is created (students, experts, etc.). Looking at the ideal target for which the tools have been designed we notice that some methods seems to be more appropriate for teaching context while others are more business oriented. The IoT Design Deck can start from an idea generation process, useful for consultancy purposes in business contexts, or can start from a predefined brief for shorter teaching context.
- The focus (on technology, user experience, product design, etc.). From this point of view, the IoT Design Deck has clearly its roots in the UX Design, while other methods seems to have more influences coming from product design or from computer science. The biggest difference with the other methods is that in the "Actions" cards there are some user research methods that can be used in the first part of analysis.
- The type of supports used (cards, objects, etc.). About the type of supports used, all the methods have cards, most of the methods have boards and, in some cases, they use also 3D printed elements (i.e. U4IoT [4] and Cards'n'Dice [5]). The IoT Design Deck doesn't include other elements in addition to the cards and to the canvas.
- The necessity of the facilitator's presence during the workshop. Each method has a different flow that has to be known or explained at the beginning of the workshop. The IoT Design Deck needs a facilitator, expert of UX, that masters the method and that can perform actions like giving the "Actions" and the "Threats" cards to the participants. This could be a weakness if compared to more self explaining methods like Tile Cards [6] or Know Cards [7].

Results. The feedback from the post-hoc questionnaire and the q&a session with the other experts have highlighted different aspects of the IoT Design Deck, already partially emerged after the first qualitative results. The received feedbacks were very useful for the redesign of the second version of the method and we grouped them according to the criteria previously identified:

- Self-explanation and understandability: The method was perceived generally as not self-explaining for non experts. Indeed it was perceived especially suitable for design experts, like product designers, interaction designers and service designers. Half of the workshop participants has also perceived it useful for technology experts (i.e. engineers and computer scientist) and professionals working in the smart city, smart home, health and cultural heritage fields. It was interesting to note that only few experts involved in the workshop session perceived the tool useful for non-experts, aspect closely related to the necessity of the presence of a facilitator during the design phases. The facilitator has been indicated as fundamental for the understanding of the process and the correct execution of the workshop. The aspects considered less clear were principally the order of when introduce the different cards, the lack of a overview of all the design steps and the relation and interaction between the cards, the brief and the concept. Another pain point emerged during the workshop was the lack of a support to document the scenario, the ideation process and the solution. Some participant suggested to create a user manual and/or boards that could explain better the design sequence also to non-experts and making the presence of a facilitator less essential.

- Efficiency and ease of use: The aspects considered most positive were the good color scheme used, that allows a clear distinction between the card groups, and the appealing design. The "schemas" cards, with fields to be filled up with text or sketches, were considered useful to enlarge and customize the project, allowing to go beyond a simple assemblage of reference cards.
- Group Interaction: The tool was considered a useful tool for generating, detailing, presenting and discussing ideas with others.

As regards the application context of the IoT Design Deck it was perceived as not focused on a specific context and useful to design different connected products or services. From the methodology point of view "Action", "Input", "Output" and especially "Threats" cards were considered the most interesting to provide inspiration during the design phases.

3   Redesign of the IoT Design Deck

According to the tests results we began a redesign process to fix the problems emerged but also to integrate new research outcomes and new technological trends. The redesign process was focused on the following key point:

- Self-explanation and self-use of the method: the method should be used without the presence of the facilitator and the design process should be smooth composed by clearly separated steps. In order to achieve this results other two sub-steps where needed:
  - Process redesign: to make it simpler and clearer;
  - Design of a Quick-Start Guide: an handbook to guide an individual or a group to the use of the method even without a facilitator;
  - Cards and boards redesign: fixing the labelling problems (to allow self explanation) and design/re-design of the boards to support the new process.
- Cards update: adding new cards according to new research outcomes and new technological trends.

3.1   Process Redesign

The objective of the redesign of the process was to make it faster, agile and self explanatory, with the possibility to avoid a facilitator using a handbook. The first step was to consider the starting point of the method. As it could be used on real projects or for teaching we must take into account if the users will start from a brief or should generate ideas. For this reason we kept and updated the "Brief" cards, a deck with a set of precompiled briefs useful for teaching purposes. Moreover we designed some techniques to use the cards, to find inspiration and generate new ideas.

Moreover we defined precise steps, defining the inputs, the outputs and the tools and methods to be used (or suggestion well-known methods for experts). To do this we took as a reference the Double Diamond process [8] that maps the design process through two cycles of divergent and convergent thinking, one for the problem definition and one for the design of the solution. As one of the goal of a design team is to produce project documentation, we identified some key moments in the design process in which the team could save useful information like the research results, the value proposition the user journey map, just arranging the cards and taking pictures or writing information on the canvases.

A Quick-Start Guide, further described, was created to guide the user through the new process.

The steps are the following:

- WarmUp: It is a preparation of the design stage and it shows some exercises for ice-breaking before starting to design; moreover, the warm up section also illustrates the Design Double Diamond.
- Discover: This is the first step of the design process and it helps users to seek for a specific problem to solve. Designs do not have all the same starting point: some designs arise from a specific request from a customer or a company, while others start from a given brief or an intuition or a problem to be solved. Whatever it is the starting point of a design, it is important for the designers to discover the context they are moving around, to find out as much as possible about the problem to be solved, its characteristics and current solutions. Exploring a problem's space at this stage will help later to clearly define what is the problem to be solved. This stage of the design process is mainly based on research, that could be made in several ways, starting from sources like online or academic sources, personal experience or observation and interviews with customers. The problem discovery stage can be accomplished by filling the "Problem Discovery Canvas".
- Define: The definition step is an important moment of the design process that can compromise or support the future design choices. As the design process is iterative, designers should carefully refer to the "Problem Discovery Canvas" filled before and check whether if they are following the emerged insights or if they are going off the road. The definition stage consists in the filling of the final section of the "Problem Discovery Canvas": the "How Might We" section.
- Concept: The concept stage drives the design team into the definition of the value proposition of the concept they are willing to develop. The concept stage consists in diverging and then converging on ideas: a first part of the exercise asks designers to generate as many ideas as possible, by using the "how might we" section on the "Brainstorming Canvas". Each participant of the design session tries to address five creative answers, keywords, inspirations related to the "how might we" challenges. All ideas collected should be selected, organized in clusters, voted in order to define a ranking of emerged ideas; then each participant tries to ideate, sketch and present to the others a personal concept idea related to the selected themes, by using the Brainstorming Canvas. A further discussion is necessary to select the concepts presented. Participants should be aware that this process of divergence and then convergence on a concept could lead to divert from the initial challenge. The concept stage is iterative and could be repeated as many times as needed. If designers notice that they are going off-topic or if ideas are not satisfying, the concept stage could be started again.

- Design: The design stage has the objective to help designers in defining all the core elements of the project and to let them use these elements to visualize all the project in a glance. Using a physical support for each element of the project helps designers, especially in co-design sessions, to quickly prototype a user journey and easily understand whether if it works or not, or to have an overview of the touch points in the project ecosystem. During the design process, designers define personas, contexts and micro moments by using the specific fillable cards. Subsequently the guide drives designers in the definition of the core functionalities, the touch points through which functionalities are enabled and the related inputs and outputs.
- Prototype and Test: this phase is to be seen as complementary of the Design one. Indeed prototyping is a way to answer to a question. For this reason there are different types of prototypes like functional prototypes, to check is the idea is feasible, or experiential prototypes, to test if our design choices will give a good experience to the user. During the prototype phase designers will be invited to create and test experiential prototypes even of a single feature of the project especially if they need to decide among design alternatives.

3.2 Cards Redesign and Update

During the redesign process we undertake different actions:

- redesign of the structure and labelling of existing cards ("Functionality" had become "Function" cards);
- reorganizing the content and the category of existing cards ("Action" cards had become "Tool" Cards);
- creation of new set of cards, "Micromoment" cards, useful in certain part of the process;
- updating of the content of the existing cards: revising the text of the cards adding some new research outcomes and popular technological trends.

Function Cards. Since the first test we noticed that the "Functionality" cards where hard to be understood in their scope and use so we redesigned them. As nobody used the sketch field we canceled it and we provided 4 fields: function's name, what the system does, user's action/intent supported, notes. In that way we want the designer to focus on the objective/task that the function helps to accomplish and what the system should do (i.e. the user wants to eat and the systems automatically orders the preferred food). We also changed the name in "Functions".

Tool Cards. This was a rearrangement and an update of the "Action" cards. A problem in the comprehension and the autonomous use of the "Action" cards was that it contained techniques that are useful in different moments of the design process. We decided to change the name of the deck to make it more understandable and to divide it into 4 sub-categories that are useful in certain steps of the new design process designed:

- Inspiration: Techniques or design principles to find inspiration. Useful in the idea generation phase and, in general, in every moment when the creative process needs a boost. As an example the "Empathy tools" card suggests to use objects or simulate a situation context to experience how your user would feel like.

- Research: Techniques to collect qualitative and quantitative data useful to develop the project. As an example the "Quick Ethnography" card suggests to spend some time with people that represent the target, trying to understand how they behave.
- Sorting: Techniques to sort ideas, useful after a process of idea generation or when you have to choose among different alternatives. As an example there is the "dot voting" technique that helps a group to quickly vote and rank different ideas.
- Test: Techniques to test the solution designed, even in an early stage, as an usability test.

Micromoment Cards. This new type of fillable card is used to have a more detailed description of the context and the intention of the user that is about to do something. This is based on a research made promoted by Google [9] which define a micro-moment as an "Intent-rich moment when a person turns to a device to act on a need- to know, go, do or buy". As Google made this research to understand how people use smartphones to have support in the accomplishment of a certain tasks we adapted the concept to the IoT scenario, focusing on how a user could use smart and connected objects/environments to answer to a certain need. In the "Micromoment" cards the user should indicate the intention of the user in that moment, the contextual needs and constraints and the objects and environments that could be used. Especially the last two fields could be used to have inspiration to create innovative touch-points for the service that will support the user.

The "Micromoment" card could be considered a child of the "Context" card. Indeed in the definition of the user journey the micro-moment is a detail of something that happens inside a context. As an example if the context is a smart-kitchen the micro-moment could be "I want to prepare the dinner", the contextual need could be finding a recipe based on the food available and the objects that could be "enchanted" with IoT features are the fridge and a frying pan.

Updating of Existing Cards. We updated the "Input" and "Output" cards stressing more on the interaction with conversational interfaces like vocal assistants. In the "Threats" we added cards about the design for failure (i.e. considering false-positives and false negatives in an Artificial Intelligence system) and the "Inspiration" deck we suggest to design for trust (i.e. trust that a self driving car will turn when we expect it to do it). (Fig. 1)

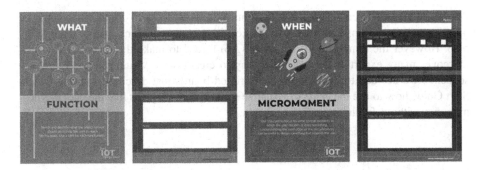

Fig. 1. "Function" and "Micromoment" cards front and back.

3.3 Design of New Tools

In order to guide the designer during the design process we created some tools that are helpful in certain phases to synthesize ideas and to create project documentation.

Problem Discovery Canvas. The Problem Discovery Canvas is divided into different sections that examine the characteristics of the problem, the people involved and contexts where the problem takes place. The impact of the problem can be analysed under the social, economic, environmental perspective, so does the context, that can be analysed on physical or social perspectives. The strength of the canvas is that it helps designers to look at the problem from different points of view and to split it in sub-sections in order to analyse every single element of the problem.

The Problem Discovery Canvas also invites designers to think about the competitors already working on the problem identified, in order to identify who is already solving that problem and how. Analysing the state of the art is also an useful tool to find out best practices in a specific field.

The last section of the Problem Discovery Canvas makes designer think about possible solutions to the problem identified. The "How might we" method is largely used in service and user experience design and its output is not the perfect, final solution, but a set of opportunities for design. A good "how might we" session is a powerful tool to frame the problem identified and to generate insights for the brain-storming stage.

Brainstorming Canvas. During the idea generation phase the participants needs to share ideas. It is useful to make it in a written form because it helps to share, compare, select but also to save all the alternatives that have been considered. The canvas is really simple, it has a space for a title, a sketch, for a description (that have to be short because the space is small).

Concept Definition Canvas. Its objective is to help the team to focus on the value proposition of the product/service. A fill-the-blank form helps the user to create a concise and effective value proposition that the team will use in all the design process. The fill the blank is: "Our project (project name) allows (target users) to (users'goal) so (outcome)".

However, as the process is iterative, this definition could change over time so there is the field notes that will help to keep track of the changes with the corresponding motivations.

Boards. In the first version we designed some boards or decks to organize the cards in order to visualize specific aspects of the project like the user journey map or the system map. However the dimension of the cards (A6) forced to make the boards really big, moreover many experts have their own way to create those visualization. As a consequence we decided to avoid the use of printed boards just describing on the Quick Start Guide how to use the cards to visualize some specific aspects like the user journey map, but without forcing to a fixed schema.

4   The Quick Start Guide

The Quick Start Guide for the IoT Design Deck was created as an answer to the need for a guidance revealed during the test session in Chemnitz. We decided to design a guide to be included in the IoT Design Deck box, useful to those who want to use the tool by themselves.

The Quick Start Guide is an introduction to the IoT Design Deck methodology and objectives; it is divided into seven sections, each of them corresponds to a different stage of the design process. In order to introduce readers to their first usage of the deck, there is also a "welcome" introduction, describing materials and information that will be valid for all the future design sessions.

A relevant element introduced in the Quick Start Guide is the chance to skip some steps of the design process, according to the needs and time constraints. Many of the design stages have optional tasks to be performed only in longer design sessions.

Furthermore, the welcome section introduces the icons that occur during the reading, suggesting the use of a certain card in a specific moment. Some of the icons refer to the tool decks and represent a call to action. For example, the "sorting deck" icon appears when it is necessary to pick up a specific sorting technique from the deck.

Another symbol often present during the reading is the camera symbol, that suggests readers to take pictures of what they are doing in order to get documentation of the design process. Taking pictures can also be useful to save all the possible cards configurations: designers can realize a touchpoint matrix or a customer journey without the need of replicating certain cards. Moreover, pictures can be useful tools for further presentations of the project.

The structure of each section in the Quick Start Guide is organized as follows, except for the welcome section.

Every stage is presented with a short description page and step by step indications, that also indicates if a step is mandatory or optional. This allows the team to choose between a full or fast design session.

The short description is a page that quickly illustrates:

- What designers will do;
- Which materials of the IoT Design Deck are needed to complete the task;
- The average duration of the task;
- How many participants can be involved in this activity, expressed in a range;
- The energy effort required;
- Whether the facilitator is necessary, optional or unnecessary;
- The expected output.

The step by step description, instead, offers a deeper understanding of the actions that will be performed in that stage, including useful tips about the usage of certain cards (i.e. how and when it could be helpful to have insights from the tool decks). (Fig. 2)

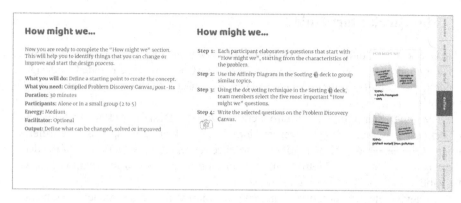

Fig. 2. Contents from the Quick Start Guide.

5 Future Works

In relation to its topic the method is in a constant evolution. In the next steps we are planning another test campaign, to evaluate the redesign implemented. Moreover as the method at the moment is general purpose, we are planning to develop domain specific cards (i.e. smart home, smart city, e-health, etc.) in collaboration with domain experts, to make it more specific and helpful for a professional use.

References

1. Augusto, J.C.: Ambient intelligence: the confluence of ubiquitous/pervasive computing and artificial intelligence. In: Schuster, A.J. (ed.) Intelligent Computing Everywhere, pp. 213–234. Springer, London (2007). https://doi.org/10.1007/978-1-84628-943-9_11
2. Dibitonto, M., Tazzi, F., Leszczynska, K., Medaglia, C.M.: The IoT design deck: a tool for the co-design of connected products. In: Ahram, T., Falcão, C. (eds.) AHFE 2017. AISC, vol. 607, pp. 217–227. Springer, Cham (2018). https://doi.org/10.1007/978-3-319-60492-3_21
3. Nielsen, J.: Finding usability problems through heuristic evaluation. In: Proceedings of the SIGCHI Conference on Human Factors in Computing Systems, pp. 373–380. ACM (1992)
4. U4IoT Project. https://u4iot.eu/. Accessed 11 Jan 2019
5. Lefeuvre, K., et al.: Loaded dice: exploring the design space of connected devices with blind and visually impaired people. In: Proceedings of the 9th Nordic Conference on Human-Computer Interaction, p. 31. ACM (2016)
6. Asheim, J., Divitini, M., Kjøllesdal, A., Mora, S.: Tiles Cards: a Card-based Design Game for Smart Objects Ecosystems. SERVE@AVI (2016)
7. Know-Cards. https://know-cards.myshopify.com/. Accessed 11 Jan 2019
8. Design Counsil. https://www.designcouncil.org.uk/news-opinion/design-process-what-double-diamond. Accessed 10 Jan 2019
9. Ramaswamy, S.: How micro-moments are changing the rules. Think with Google (2015)

Heuristic Evaluation of eGLU-Box:
A Semi-automatic Usability Evaluation Tool
for Public Administrations

Stefano Federici[1]([⊠]) [iD], Maria Laura Mele[1] [iD], Rosa Lanzilotti[2] [iD],
Giuseppe Desolda[2] [iD], Marco Bracalenti[1] [iD], Arianna Buttafuoco[1] [iD],
Giancarlo Gaudino[3], Antonello Cocco[3], Massimo Amendola[3],
and Emilio Simonetti[4]

[1] Department of Philosophy, Social and Human Sciences and Education,
University of Perugia, Perugia, Italy
stefano.federici@unipg.it, marialaura.mele@gmail.com,
marco.bracalenti90@gmail.com,
arianna.buttafuoco@gmail.com
[2] Department of Computer Science, University of Bari Aldo Moro, Bari, Italy
{rosa.lanzilotti,giuseppe.desolda}@uniba.it
[3] ISCOM – Superior Institute of Communication and Information Technologies,
Ministry of Economic Development, Rome, Italy
{giancarlo.gaudino,antonello.cocco,
massimo.amendola}@mise.gov.it
[4] Department of Public Service, Prime Minister's Office, Rome, Italy
e.simonetti@funzionepubblica.it

Abstract. This paper illustrates the heuristic evaluation of a web-based tool for usability testing for Public Administrations called eGLU-box. eGLU-box is an online platform aiming at supporting practitioners in the process of designing usability tests, analyzing data, and helping step-by-step participants to complete assessment tasks. Web users of Public Administrations can report their perceived quality of experience by completing a library of questionnaires shown to them by eGLU-box at the end of the test. This work is part of a multi-step user experience (UX) evaluation methodology to assess the platform. The UX evaluation methodology of eGLU-box uses standard and bio-behavioural evaluation methods. This work shows the results of the heuristic evaluation of eGLU-box involving five human factors experts and 20 practitioners working in Italian Public Administrations. Findings show that most of the problems are rated as minor problems and related to Nielsen's heuristic, "visibility of the system." Only 9% of problems are rated as major problems. These major problems are related to the "problematic match between system and the real world" heuristic. Evaluators provided indications for improvements that will be applied for the next version of the platform.

Keywords: User experience · Heuristic evaluation ·
Remote semi-automatic usability assessment · Usability assessment tools

M. Kurosu (Ed.): HCII 2019, LNCS 11566, pp. 75–86, 2019.
https://doi.org/10.1007/978-3-030-22646-6_6

1   Introduction

Remote usability evaluation tools are becoming more and more relevant in the field because they allow practitioners to reach wide and differentiated pools of test users at the same time, with lower costs and efforts than traditional laboratory usability approaches. Remote and automatic usability evaluation methodologies ask users to test web interfaces in their usual work or living environments while evaluators collect and analyze data by remotely controlled systems [1]. During the remote automatic assessment, evaluators do not directly monitor users during the interaction, but they remotely analyze their behavior collected by log files (e.g., [2, 3]). The limits of these tools are that (i) they often capture users' logs without analyzing them, (ii) they are not able to detect detailed information about users' actions such as facial expression recognition, (iii) they need to be pre-installed in the client's device (e.g., Morae, https://www.techsmith.com/morae.html), and (iv) they are often not platform-independent [4].

This work describes the heuristic evaluation of eGLU-box, a new remote semi-automatic usability assessment tool that overcomes each of the aforementioned limits. eGLU-box is a re-engineered version of a previous platform called UTAssistant [5–8], a web-based usability assessment tool developed to provide the Italian Public Administration with an online tool to conduct remote user studies. Both UTAssistant and its renewed version eGLU-box are designed according to usability guidelines provided by GLU, a group working on usability founded by the Department of Public Function, Ministry for Simplification and Public Administration in 2010. The latest version of the eGLU protocol (eGLU 2.1) was released in 2015 [9, 10].

The re-engineering process of UTAssistant was made possible by previous studies by Federici and colleagues, who evaluated user experience (UX) expert users of public administration (PA) websites [6]. In laboratory conditions, they used psychophysiological techniques [5] to measure the underlying reactions of participants through the recognition of facial expressions and electroencephalography (EEG). This work describes the usability evaluation of the renewed platform by a heuristic evaluation with both UX experts and PA practitioners. A heuristic evaluation is a usability assessment method in which an expert user performs a simulation of a typical user-system interaction with the aim of identifying critical points and weaknesses by means of heuristics. Heuristics in the UX context are simple and efficient rules that have been proposed since 1990 [11] to explain how people perceive, judge, and make decisions when facing interaction problems with a given system.

The rest of the paper is organized as follows. Section 2 describes the proposed usability assessment platform. Section 3 introduces the experimental methodology for the assessment of eGLU-box. Section 4 describes the results. Section 5 is for discussions, conclusions, and future directions.

2 From UTAssistant to eGLU-BOX: A Remote Usability Testing Tool for Public Administrations

Italian public administrations are the main public services that can benefit from simple and easy-to-use remote usability tools for assessing their websites. This is why in 2017 a web platform called UTAssistant was developed in line with the last Italian PA usability protocol, eGLU 2.1 [9]. Thanks to a UX evaluation of UTAssistant with expert users [6] and in laboratory conditions with two biobehavioral implicit measures [5], a re-engineering process of UTAssistant led to the development of the current version of the platform, eGLU-box. It is divided into two modules, one (the "tester module") for the practitioner who has to create, administer, and analyze the test, and another (the "end-user module") for end-users for whom the test is intended.

eGLU-box aims to facilitate evaluators in performing evaluation design activities such as creating a script, defining a set of tasks, or deciding which questionnaire to administer by means of three wizard procedures. Firstly, it guides the evaluators in specifying general information (e.g., a title, the script), data to gather during user task execution (e.g., mouse/keyboard data logs, webcam/microphone/desktop recordings), and post-test questionnaires to administer. The second procedure assists evaluators in creating the task lists and, for each task, specifying the starting/ending URLs, the goal, and the duration. The third procedure allows evaluators to decide which users to evaluate by selecting them from a list of users already registered to the platform or by typing their email addresses.

The second aim of eGLU-box is to help practitioners to manage all the tasks necessary for usability test execution such as emailing users with information, carrying out the evaluation test, capturing the session, and privacy policies regarding data from mouse/keyboard logs or webcam/microphone/desktop recordings. Each task is strongly guided by the platform, which shows the task description in a pop-up window and opens the web page from which users begin the test. To keep the platform as non-invasive as possible during the evaluation test, all the functions and indications (such as the current task goal and instructions, duration time, task number, and buttons to proceed to the next task or stop the evaluation) are grouped in a toolbar placed on top of the web page. Moreover, the button to proceed to the next task becomes "Complete Questionnaire" when the users finish the last task and must complete a questionnaire. During the task execution, the platform collects all data set by the evaluator in the study design in a transparent and non-invasive way.

eGLU-box automatizes all activities (such as collecting, storing, merging, and analyzing) related to data analysis, removing barriers in gathering usability test data. The evaluators access the data analysis results in their control panel by exploiting different tools that provide useful support in finding usability issues. The next subsection provides an overview of the tools. Moreover, the platform calculates the task success rate (the percentage of tasks that users correctly complete during the test, which can also be calculated for each task estimating the percentage of users who complete that task) and visualizes them in a table in which the columns represent the tasks while the rows represent the users. The last row reports the success rate for each task, and the last column depicts the success rate for each user. The global success rate is reported under the table.

When the test is concluded, summarizing the questionnaire results would improve the efficiency of evaluations. With eGLU-box, the evaluators can administer one or more questionnaires at the end of the usability evaluation. The platform automatically stores the user's answers and produces results by means of statistics and graphs.

The platform analyses audio-video information by collecting and storing the participants' voices with a microphone, their facial expressions with a webcam, and desktop activity with a browser plugin. The implemented player also provides an annotation tool so that when evaluators detect difficulties externalized with verbal comments or facial expressions, they can annotate the recorded audio/video tracks. If the evaluators decide to record both camera and desktop videos, their tracks are merged in a picture-in-picture fashion.

Finally, starting from the collected data, the platform shows performance statistics for each task as well as mouse and keyboard user logs.

Section 3 illustrates the heuristic evaluation for each of the above-described features of eGLU-box.

3   The Heuristic Evaluation of eGLU-Box

The study is a heuristic evaluation of the proposed web platform for remote and semi-automatic usability assessment of a PA website. The evaluation focuses on both the "tester module" and the "user module" of eGLU-box. Two groups of experts performed the evaluation, UX experts and PA practitioners involved in the design, development, and/or management of PA websites. As typically three to five UX experts are required to find 80% of usability issues [12], the group of experts is composed of four participants. A second group composed of 20 PA practitioners also performed the heuristic evaluation. The two groups followed the heuristic evaluation procedure as described in the following subsections.

3.1   Methods and Techniques

Heuristic evaluation is a usability evaluation method by which an expert evaluator performs a simulation of using a system to identify its critical points and weaknesses. The evaluation method uses heuristics, which are "simple and efficient rules that have been proposed to explain how people solve, make judgments, or make decisions about complex problems or incomplete information" (https://it.wikipedia.org/wiki/Euristica).

In a heuristic evaluation, the expert evaluator interacts with the system interface by simulating the actions and thoughts of a typical user following representative tasks. Tasks should guarantee that the system applies the main usability rules. For this study, we adopted the 10 Nielsen's heuristics (Table 1) [11], which consist of 10 principles derived from the factorial analysis of a list of 249 problems detected by numerous usability assessments. Nielsen's heuristics are used for the evaluation of the two modules of eGLU-box, the evaluator module and the end-user module.

Table 1. Nielsen's heuristics as described in the seminal work [12].

1.	**Visibility of system status.** The system should always keep users informed about what is going on through appropriate feedback within a reasonable timeframe
2.	**Match between system and the real world.** The system should speak the user's language with words, phrases, and concepts familiar to the user rather than system-oriented terms. It should follow real-world conventions, making information appear in a natural and logical order
3.	**User control and freedom.** Users often choose system functions by mistake and will need a clearly marked "emergency exit" to leave the unwanted state without having to go through an extended dialogue. It should support undo and redo functions
4.	**Consistency and standards.** Users should not have to wonder whether different words, situations, or actions mean the same thing. Follow platform conventions
5.	**Error prevention.** Even better than helpful error messages would be a careful design that prevents a problem from occurring in the first place
6.	**Recognition rather than recall.** Make objects, actions, and options visible. The user should not have to remember information from one part of the dialogue to another. Instructions for the use of the system should be visible or easily retrievable whenever appropriate
7.	**Flexibility and efficiency of use.** Accelerators – unseen by the novice user – can often speed up the interaction for the expert user such that the system can cater to both inexperienced and experienced users. Allow users to tailor frequent actions
8.	**Aesthetic and minimalist design.** Dialogues should not contain information that is irrelevant or rarely needed. Every extra unit of information in a dialogue competes with the relevant units of information and diminishes their relative visibility
9.	**Help users recognize, diagnose, and recover from errors.** Error messages should be expressed in plain language (no codes), precisely indicate the problem, and constructively suggest a solution
10.	**Help and documentation.** Although it is better if the system can be used without documentation, it might be necessary to provide help and documentation. Any such information should be easy to find, focused on the user's task, list concrete steps to be carried out, and not be too large

An impact rating is assigned to each problem. The problems are rated considering the frequency of the problem and the severity ratings assigned by the UX experts to each problem based on the scale shown in Table 2 [13].

Table 2. Nielsen's severity rating scale [13].

0	**Not a usability problem at all**
1	**Cosmetic problem only.** Need not be fixed unless extra time is available
2	**Minor usability problem.** Fixing this should be given low priority
3	**Major usability problem.** Important to fix. Should be given high priority
4	**Usability catastrophe.** Imperative to fix this before product can be released

The impact is calculated as the weighted average of the frequency of a problem and the related severity rating and defines how much a problem would affect the interaction with a system. Impacting problems with high frequencies and severity are then rated with high impact ratings.

3.2 Materials and Apparatus

During the assessment, both UX experts and PA practitioners are asked to report any violated heuristics in two grids, one for the assessment of the "tester module" and another for the assessment of the "end-user module." For each heuristic, the practitioner is asked to report any violated heuristics, the specific problem, the frequency of the problem, and suggestions on how to solve the issue. The grids were distributed in the spreadsheet file format. Participants are allowed to use their own laptop devices in indoor conditions. All tests were done in the Google Chrome web browser and the latest Windows operating system.

Instructions and tasks were created for the evaluation of the "tester module" and the "end-user module" and described as follows. The eGLU-box platform was tested on the PA website Ministry of Economic Development (MISE) (URL: https://www.sviluppoeconomico.gov.it).

3.3 Procedure

Both UX experts and PA practitioners are asked to evaluate the two main modules composing eGLU-BOX, the tester module and the end-user module. During each evaluation, participants are asked to compile the provided spreadsheet file format.

The expert is asked to evaluate the tester's experience for each of the following tasks.

Task 1 – Tester Module. Create a new test – Basic information.

- Login
- Create a new study, name it "Usability evaluation of the MISE website"
- Set website URL: to http://www.sviluppoeconomico.gov.it
- Set description, name it "Evaluation of UTAssistant"
- Ensure anonymity for the participants
- Set the following input peripheral devices to capture: microphone, webcam, and desktop
- Set duration to 5 min
- Select questionnaires to be administered to users at the end of the test: NPS, UMUX, and SUS

Task 2 – Tester Module. Define tasks for end-users.

- Create four tasks by setting a title, description, maximum duration, and start and end URLs (tasks for end-users are reported below in this section)

Task 3 – Tester Module. Invite participants to the test.

- The tester should invite participants to their test

Task 4 – Tester Module. Open the test to users.

- Save the test and make it public to participants
- Logout
- Once the test is created, the expert is asked to evaluate the end-users' experience for each of the following tasks. Before starting, end-users should log in to the eGLU-box platform and agree to participate in the test. The heuristic evaluation begins at the login phase.

Task 1 – End-User Module. *Scenario 1.* You inherited a farmhouse in Italy from your elderly grandmother. You go to the MISE website to search for information about the energy redevelopment of your type of building, and you come to know that the Ministry of Economic Development allows you to benefit from a bonus of tax deductions in the case of interventions on individual units. To find out more, you need to:

1. Identify the website area related to the incentives for the citizen;
2. Identify the deadline for requesting incentives in case of interventions on the single real estate units;
3. Look for the designated office to call for more information about it.

    - Start URL: https://www.sviluppoeconomico.gov.it/
    - End URL: https://www.sviluppoeconomico.gov.it/index.php/it/component/organigram/?view=structure&id=563.

Task 2 – End-User Module. *Scenario 2.* You are a non-EU citizen. In your country of residence abroad, you have obtained a professional hairdresser qualification. You would like to do your profession in Italy. You go the MISE website to search for information about it. To find out more, you need to:

1. Identify the list of recognized professional qualifications;
2. View the most up-to-date document regarding the recognition of your profession.

    - Start URL: https://www.sviluppoeconomico.gov.it/
    - End URL: https://www.sviluppoeconomico.gov.it/images/stories/impresa/mercato/MethnaniMounir.pdf.

Task 3 – End-User Module. *Scenario 3.* You are a journalist for a national information magazine for agricultural companies. For the article you are working on, you are looking for the 2018 statistics on rice export authorizations. Starting from the MISE homepage, you need to:

1. Identify the existence of a page containing the import/export statistics of agri-food products;

2. Look for statistics relevant to the export of rice issued in 2018.

- Start URL: https://www.sviluppoeconomico.gov.it/
- End URL: https://www.sviluppoeconomico.gov.it/images/stories/commercio_internazionale/agroalimentare/statistiche_2018/export_2018.pdf.

Task 4 – End-User Module. *Scenario 4.* A friend of yours recently told you that the Italian citizens are provided with an online information tool that monitors fuel prices in both Italy and Europe. You want to know more about it. Starting from the MISE homepage, you try to:

1. Identify the actual existence of an observatory for fuel prices;
2. Identify the existence of an observatory for fuel prices in Italy.

- Start URL: https://www.sviluppoeconomico.gov.it/
- End URL: https://carburanti.mise.gov.it/OssPrezziSearch/.

3.4   Subjects

Four UX experts (50% female, mean age 33 years old) and 20 practitioners working for the Public Administration in the field of website development and management (70% female, mean age 52 years old) participated in the study. The experimental sessions were conducted separately for UX experts, who accessed the eGLU-box platform through the servers of the University of Perugia and in a single session in a laboratory with multiple workstations through the PA servers.

4   Results

Severity ratings were computed for the usability problems identified for the tester module and the end-user module, respectively, as explained in Sect. 3.1.

The numbers of heuristic violations for the two modules assessed by the two groups of experts according to Nielsen's heuristics were calculated (Fig. 1). In the tester module of eGLU-box, heuristics were violated 19 times. The violated heuristics were "1. Visibility of system status" (68.4%), "5. Error prevention" (26.3%), and "3. User control and freedom" (5.3%). No other heuristics were violated in the tester module. In the end-user module, heuristics were violated 31 times. The most frequently violated heuristics were "1. Visibility of system status" (35.5%), "3. User control and freedom" (22.6%), and "4. Consistency and standards" (19.4%), followed by "2. Match between system and the real world" (9.7%), "5. Error prevention" (9.7%), and "7. Flexibility and efficiency of use" (33.2%). Across both modules, the heuristic "1. Visibility of system status" comprised 48% of all violations.

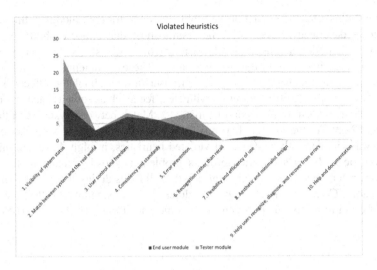

Fig. 1. Violated heuristics for both end-user and tester modules.

Comparisons of the two modules show no significant difference in the frequency of usability problems between the two modules (t(8) = 1.315, p > .05), meaning that the two modules have an equal chance of generating errors.

Figure 2 shows the level of severity of the usability problems found in both the tester and end-user modules. The severity ratings calculated for the tester module revealed 20% major severity problems, 60% minor severity problems, and 20% cosmetic usability problems. In the end-user module, 100% of problems were rated as minor usability problems. Overall, the problems belonging to the most violated heuristics in both modules (i.e., "1. Visibility of system status," 48% of all the violations) were rated as minor usability problems.

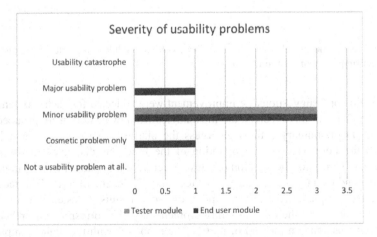

Fig. 2. Severity of the usability problems found for both modules as defined by the UX experts.

Figure 3 illustrates the impact of the problems found for both modules. Impact was calculated as described in Sect. 3.1. The results show that minor usability problems related to the first Nielsen's heuristic "1. Visibility of system status" have an impact of 24.5% on the interaction during the test. These problems are related to misleading/missing feedback that notifies end-users/testers about the effects of their actions – for example, "notify end-users with clear feedback as soon as each test ends." Major problems related to the second heuristic "2. Match between system and the real world" had 22.3% of the impact. This result shows that although the second Nielsen's heuristic was violated only 9.7% of all violated heuristics, it might have a significant impact on the end-user's experience. This problem is mostly related to the tester module and refers to a missing mark warning that all fields during the creation of a test are mandatory. Comparisons of the two modules show no significant difference in the impact of usability problems between the two modules ($t(9) = 0.922$, $p > 0.05$).

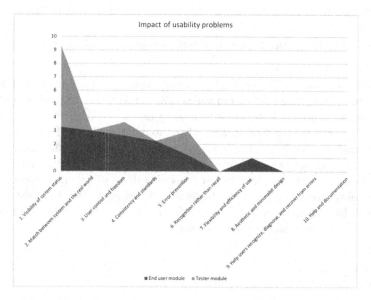

Fig. 3. Impact of the usability problems found for both modules calculated by considering severity and frequency of each problem.

The evaluators' suggestions for improvement were collected for each problem. The areas of the platform that received the most advice from evaluators were grouped into five parts: (1) preliminary actions to access the platform (e.g., access via link and login), (2) the homepage (i.e., exploration of the functions displayed in the user's dashboard), (3) areas for the creation of a test or agreement to participate, (4) invitation of users to conduct a test or participate in a test, and (5) the end of a test (i.e., feedback to users after completing the test or reports of users' results to testers). In the tester module, the areas with the most usability problems and the corresponding indications of improvements concern the end of part 3. The problems with the highest impact on usability were related to the heuristic "5. Error prevention" and are related to missing/unclear feedback during the invitation of users to take part in the test. In the end-user module, the areas with the highest number of suggestions for improvement concern the end of part 5. These problems are linked to the heuristic "1. Visibility of system status" and are mostly linked to missing feedback to users after completing each task or the whole test.

5 Conclusions

This paper proposed the heuristic evaluation of eGLU-box, a web-based platform for the remote and semi-automatic evaluation of websites. The platform is specifically designed for Italian Public Administrations, and it follows the latest usability guidelines for PAs as recommended by the eGLU 2.1 protocol. eGLU-box is divided into two modules specifically designed to be used by two main categories of users: the tester who creates and administers usability tests and the end-user who performs the required tasks. eGLU-box overcomes the main issues related to remote automatic tools for usability assessment because it (i) is able to capture users' logs and provide pre-processed analysis reports; (ii) detects information about users' interactions through the main peripheral devices such as microphones, webcams, and desktops; (iii) does not need to be pre-installed; and (iv) is platform-independent. eGLU-box is the result of a re-engineering process on a previous version of the platform called UTAssistant subsequent to its UX evaluation with PA practitioners and in laboratory conditions with bio-behavioral measures. The heuristic assessment of eGLU-box involved two groups of evaluators, UX experts and PA practitioners. The evaluators highlighted the critical points and weaknesses of the system by using the 10 heuristics provided for the first time by Nielsen and Molich [11]. Results show that the modules of the system have an equal chance of generating usability errors. No differences in the extent to which errors impacted the interaction were found. Most of the problems found in both modules were minor usability problems (60%) related to visibility of the system status. Major problems (20%) were due to functions that are more system-oriented than user-oriented in the way they are presented to users. Updates and error fixes of the system will be performed by following the evaluators' suggestions for improvement provided in this study. Future work will focus on the assessment of the updated platform with end-users recruited via an online platform.

Acknowledgements. This study was supported by ISCOM under grant Project "eGLU-box PA".

References

1. Andreasen, M.S., Nielsen, H.V., Schrøder, S.O., Stage, J.: What happened to remote usability testing? An empirical study of three methods. In: SIGCHI Conference on Human Factors in Computing Systems: CHI 2007, pp. 1405–1414 (2007). https://doi.org/10.1145/1240624.1240838

2. Obendorf, H., Weinreich, H., Hass, T.: Automatic support for web user studies with scone and tea. In: Extended Abstracts on Human Factors in Computing Systems, CHI 2004, pp. 1135–1138. ACM, Vienna, AT (2004). https://doi.org/10.1145/985921.986007

3. Atterer, R.: Logging usage of Ajax applications with the "Usaproxy" Http Proxy. In: Workshop on Logging Traces of Web Activity: The Mechanics of Data Collection, pp. 1–4 (2006)

4. Sauer, J., Sonderegger, A., Heyden, K., Biller, J., Klotz, J., Uebelbacher, A.: Extra-laboratorial usability tests: an empirical comparison of remote and classical field testing with lab testing. Appl. Ergon. **74**, 85–96 (2019). https://doi.org/10.1016/j.apergo.2018.08.011

5. Federici, S., Mele, M.L., Bracalenti, M., Buttafuoco, A., Lanzilotti, R., Desolda, G.: Bio-behavioral and self-report user experience evaluation of a usability assessment platform (UTAssistant). In: International Conference on Human Computer Interaction Theory and Applications, HUCAPP 2019, pp. 73518 (2019)

6. Federici, S., et al.: UX evaluation design of utassistant: a new usability testing support tool for italian public administrations. In: 20th International Conference on Human-Computer Interaction, pp. 55–67 (2018). https://doi.org/10.1007/978-3-319-91238-7_5

7. Catarci, T., et al.: Digital interaction: where are we going? In: Proceedings of the 2018 International Conference on Advanced Visual Interfaces, AVI 2018, pp. 1–5 (2018). https://doi.org/10.1145/3206505.3206606

8. Desolda, G., Gaudino, G., Lanzilotti, R., Federici, S., Cocco, A.: UTAssistant: a web platform supporting usability testing in italian public administrations. In: CHItaly, CHItaly 2017, 12th edn., pp. 138–142 (2017)

9. Dipartimento della Funzione Pubblica: Il Protocollo Eglu 2.1: Come Realizzare Test Di Usabilità Semplificati Per I Siti Web E I Servizi Online Delle Pa. Formez PA, Rome, IT (2015)

10. Borsci, S., Federici, S., Mele, M.L.: Eglu 1.0: un Protocollo Per Valutare La Comunicazione Web Delle Pa. Diritto e Pratica Amministrativa, vol. 1, pp. 9–10. Il Sole 24 Ore, Milan, IT (2014)

11. Nielsen, J., Molich, R.: Heuristic evaluation of user interfaces. In: SIGCHI Conference on Human Factors in Computing Systems: CHI 1990, pp. 249–256 (1990). https://doi.org/10.1145/97243.97281

12. Nielsen, J.: Heuristic evaluation. In: Nielsen, J., Mack, R.L. (eds.) Usability Inspection Methods. Wiley, New York (1994)

13. Nielsen, J., Mack, R.L. (eds.): Usability Inspection Methods. Wiley, New York (1994)

Designing Design Resources: From Contents to Tools

Carles Garcia-Lopez[(⊠)] [iD], Susanna Tesconi[(⊠)] [iD],
and Enric Mor[(⊠)] [iD]

Universitat Oberta de Catalunya (UOC), 08018 Barcelona, Spain
{carlesgl,stesconi,emor}@uoc.edu

Abstract. This paper presents the design process and implementation of a design knowledge repository. In recent years, design evolved into a broad discipline with a large application field. From an educational point of view, this design expansion brings the need to rebuild design contents and resources for both practitioners and learners. We designed and developed a repository of design resources. The design process followed a user-centered design approach, taking into account different types of users with learning needs. Design contents were analyzed taking into account the new challenges and disciplines of design and the educational needs of practitioners and learners. Three main types of design contents were identified and also the need to provide tools instead of simply contents, that is, up-to-date and actionable resources that, at the same time, lead to reflection and critical thinking. These tools were arranged into a toolbox, a knowledge repository that became a toolkit. The toolkit provides an adaptable navigation system that allows either direct access or exploration of the available tools.

Keywords: Design · Education · Learning contents · Learning resources · User-centered design

1 Introduction

Design is a ubiquitous human activity used in every problem-solving situation. Over the years, especially in the second half of the 19th century, the design has been closely linked to industrial development and associated with artifact production in a variety of fields [1]. This association between design and product development has led to usually focus on the application rather than addressing to design itself. Indeed, this is one of the reasons why generally design has not been deeply studied like a research field. In recent years design has suffered a significant evolution that led to redefine the discipline and the designer role. This evolution has displaced the focus from products to ideas, people and experiences. Consequently, new design disciplines have appeared such as design thinking, service design, co-design or open design [2]. Despite this expansion and diversification, there is a shared set of common elements in the design practice, especially on asking questions, solving problems and the transversality of their methods and techniques. This evolution brings the need to update the design knowledge field and the related contents for learners and practitioners to use.

© Springer Nature Switzerland AG 2019
M. Kurosu (Ed.): HCII 2019, LNCS 11566, pp. 87–100, 2019.
https://doi.org/10.1007/978-3-030-22646-6_7

Currently, the availability of design content and resources is very scattered. Most design content and resources are created and shared within the context of a design discipline such as product design, graphic design, interaction design or learning design. This makes difficult to extend the use of these contents to other practitioners or learners who often come from other design disciplines or even from other fields. Consequently, these very focused design contents often become isolated and obsolete in a short time.

In addition to that, most of the design contents are published either in a traditional manner through books or by short specific publications, mostly online, oriented to the different design communities. This way of distributing and accessing contents makes difficult for the design practitioners to keep updated on the knowledge of the field and to learn new competencies and skills in order to explore new possibilities of problem-solving as well as making and to be able to apply it to projects from diverse fields [1]. As a response, the design community started developing design resources under the tool perspective, promoting the aggregation of contents through toolboxes. Also, most of design toolkits are addressed to practitioners. Therefore, there is an opportunity for providing an open-ended organization of design resources for both practitioners and design students. Both user profiles are learners, since practitioners are lifelong learners that face the new challenges of the design disciplines and, in a more autonomous way, they try to be up-to-date on their discipline. From an educational point of view, students and practitioners need to learn and be updated with actionable contents and resources. Therefore, instead of one dimensional and static contents there is a need for dynamic tools, fostering among other things reflection and critical thinking as key professional competencies for the 21th century. This proposal aims to provide users access to educational design resources in several ways from direct access to exploration, using a navigational system to empower teachers and learners [3]. In addition to that, we want to provide different levels of depth for each content, depending on the educational needs of each user.

This paper is organized as follows; the state of the art of learning content repositories is presented in Sect. 2. Section 3 presents our approach to design and develop design learning contents. The implementation and evaluation of our proposal are presented in Sect. 4. Finally, in Sect. 5, the conclusions, limitations and future work are discussed.

2   The State of the Art

The design of digital knowledge repositories requires a deeper understanding of the expected users: teachers and learners. Consequently, it is necessary to get a first-hand look to students learning and to know how these repositories can support them in their learning processes. Focusing on the students learning, during the industrial age, the students were expected to learn specific contents through explicit directions from the teachers, emphasizing the compliant understanding in concordance with the external and professional expectations [4].

Over the last decades, design education has changed, becoming more flexible and student-centered. These changes not only imply a different point of view of how to involve students during the education design, but it has also changed the learning goals: from understanding learning contents to acquiring professional competencies and skills. In this regard, Samavedham [5] particularly emphasizes the relevance of the creative and critical skills within the professional competencies for the 21st century. Therefore, any learning implementation should aim to improve these students' skills. One way to improve them is through Problem-Based Learning (PBL) learning environments [6]. In this scenario, students are expected to resolve unknown problems in a dynamic, critic and collaborative way by informed decisions making [7]. This process is self-directed by the learner, who, by implication, get more autonomy in his/her own learning process. Furthermore, during this process, they are expected to show what they have learned along the process of problem-solving [8]. In this context, sometimes also known as Student-Centered Learning (SCL), students become the very center of their learning process in an open-ended learning environment [9]. Glasgow emphasizes in [10] the importance of the learner autonomy in SCL, where "students learn to decide what they need to know to find success within the class and educational format". Thus, learners decide the key components of their own learning process in order to acquire their individual or collective goals. [9]. It could be understood as a creative work where learners have to navigate the problem space and iterate solutions to achieve the result, which is not necessarily known at the outset of the process. Even though, the role of the lecturer should not be underestimated because they have an important purpose: acting as a learning facilitator by encouraging learners to explore their learning process [11] and providing students with the adequate scaffolding in order to build it.

Focusing on the resources used during the learning processes, Wiley [12] defines the learning objects as "any digital asset which can be used to enable teaching and learning". It is commonly accepted that the digital education resources created by teachers and learners are key components of the knowledge assets in the education communities [13–15], especially in e-learning settings. In this way, there are a variety of initiatives that reinforce the importance of providing educational resources to the educational community in order to reuse and share them through Learning Objects Repositories (LORs) [16, 17]. It should be noted that these educational resources are produced in diverse contexts. Rodes-Paragarino et al. [18] analyzing the use of repositories in digital education highlight the Kooper identification of the three levels of reuse of educational resources: (a) first level, where the creator of the resource reuses it, (b) second level, where a member of the same community reuses it and (c) third level, when it is reused by an outside community member [19]. Thus, this use of educational resources emphasizes the need to develop a digital educational repository [18] in order to provide access to the community and allow them to reuse these educational resources. In this way, some research outcomes show an evolution of the discussion on labeling these educational resources in order to be found and used by others, as well as the debate on how to label the "whole learning experience" facilitated by these resources in order to be transferred to other learning environments [20]. With the aim to create and share open educational resources, some learning initiatives have been presented in the last years. These initiatives enable users to use and explore these educational resources [21] through digital repositories.

Although this work focuses on digital repositories, it is important to keep in mind that the knowledge dissemination has not always needed the use of the technology. In this way, books had been a way to disseminate knowledge to the community who had access to them since the 17th century. Although, it has to be emphasized that due to the increment of Internet use during the late 20th century some other typologies of educational content had emerged. Hence, it is amply studied how this had changed the nature of resources and information [22]. Wikis are an example of these supports where the community can find, create and share knowledge. In the same way, specific databases and publications are also an example of content dissemination. Focusing on technology-based repositories, there are several specific software that allow users to create and adapt the repository to their needs. Examples of these educational repositories are MERLOT, CAREO, Paloma, Edua and Ariadne LOR. One of the most used software is Dspace, especially in academic communities [23]. This software allows users to recollect and tag digital content to be shared with their community. Note that it is not enough to just publish the contents in the repositories to facilitate their reuse. Accordingly, adding metadata to describe the content is very valuable. In this way, most repository software allows to tag content with the use of metadata. Nevertheless, the metadata must be well defined and completed and existing related work shows that the use of metadata in learning repositories is diverse and heterogeneous [24]. Some studies underline that the current metadata model for learning resources in repositories difficulties for general and universal re-use of contents by users or software pieces [24–26].

Providing tools to learners instead of contents stored in repositories has the potential of fostering exploration-oriented learning. In this sense, Resnick et al. outlined in [27] learning tools requirements: (a) Easy to try things out, and backtrack if it is needed; (b) Make clear to the user what can be done and (c) Pleasurable and fun to use. In this line, Clemente and Tschimmel [28] demonstrated the effectivity of implementing a toolkit in order to improve the students' performance enhancement. The design community has begun to channel the solution providing its members with design tools through the use of toolkits. In the case presented in this work, and taking these design toolkits as an example, it is necessary to adopt this solution to an educational purpose.

2.1 Design Knowledge Repositories

Currently, there are some design-themed repositories aimed to provide contents in a tool-oriented approach. These repositories are usually called toolkits. It is worth to mention that most of the analyzed design toolkits aim to provide contents and tools to design practitioners (Table 1).

Most of the design toolkits provide a predefined classification of the content according to the creators' criteria. This predefined classification can be seen as parallelism with the direct instruction learning where the instructors provide the content classified by their own criteria (sometimes based on external requirements) [29]. At the same time, only a few of them allow users to filter the results through a filter system. It should also be noted that most of these design toolkits are designed as action-oriented. It means that the content is provided by guides or booklets that facilitate the users to take action.

Table 1. Analysis of design toolkit's main features and contents

Toolkit	Content	Classification system	Filters
AC4D Design Library	Design methods and tools	Process phases and type of content	–
Data visualisation Catalogue	Data visualizations methods	Alphabetical or by function	–
Design-led research toolkit	Design tools and methods	Process phases and alphabetical order	–
DIY	Design tools and Methods	Purpose	–
D.P.D	Design principles		–
Dubberly Design Office	Design models	Projects	–
Ideos' DesignKit	Mindsets, methods and case studies	Process phases	–
Hi Toolbox	Methods and activities	Energizers, Innovation, Self-leadership, action and team	Time available and group members
High Resolution	Product design and design thinking	Chronological classification	–
Medialab Amsterdam	Design and research methods	Alphabetical	Purpose and time available
Project of how	Creative methods	Exercises, generate ideas, group dynamics, select ideas and structure projects	Time available and group members
Service Design Toolkit	Methodology of service design	Templates types	–
Usability.gov	Methods, templates and guides	Methods, resources, guides	–

This overview underlines the importance to provide a toolkit, to the design community, with design tools that allow explorative navigation and also with direct access to resources like the use of filters. In addition, there is a need to facilitate the share and re-use of educational resources. Furthermore, in this work, providing tools in the local language, Catalan and Spanish, was also an incentive, since most design tools are only available in English.

3   The UOC Design Toolkit

This work takes place at the Universitat Oberta de Catalunya (UOC, Open University of Catalonia). It is a fully online higher education institution with a community of more than 58,000 students and more than 3,100 teachers. Teaching and learning mainly take place in a virtual learning environment that integrates learning contents, asynchronous communication, academic services and interaction with teachers and peers. Blaschke [30] underlines that the main audience of distance learning is mature adult leaders. This is the case of UOC students, 68,87% of whom are older than 25 years old and 28,61% older than 35 years old. Moreover, this learner profile is not a full-time student, thus, it is important to offer them a good learning experience by providing all the components of the virtual learning environment. Lifelong learners have autonomy in their own learning process [30]. Furthermore, their personal life takes place in their educational field, due to the learning process occurs as a result of the learner personal experiences [31], and the process is adjusted to these experiences [32]. This self-control of the process facilitates learners to identify their needs and learning goals. Consequently, it affects the way they plan their learning process and the interactions with the virtual learning environment.

3.1   Design Process and Methodology

This work followed a user-centered design approach based on the principles of ISO 9241-210 human-centered design process [33]: understand and specify the context of use; specify the user requirements in sufficient detail to drive the design; produce design solutions which meet these requirements and conduct user-centred evaluations of these design solutions and modify the design taking account of the results. From a research point of view, an Action Research Methodology (ARM) [34] was followed, which emphasizes consecutive iterations, being modified accordingly on the experience of the previous iterations. Furthermore, this cyclical nature of the ARM has strong resemblances with the user-centered design process [35]. Thus, this work presents the results of the first process iteration and evaluation.

The first phase of the work focused on understanding the context, gathering information and defining the users. Since we focused on an educational context we needed to collect information about learners and teachers and the educational requirements.

With this purpose, the first project iteration was focused on understanding the UOC teachers' needs related to design contents. We conducted 8 face-to-face interviews with lecturers involved in learning courses where the Design Toolkit could be applied. In these interviews, they pointed out the need to improve the existing learning materials and transform them to more actionable content but including reflection and critical thinking. In addition to that, the need to easily access and navigate resources was identified. Learners should be able to explore the models, principles, and methods of design and create their own point of view about how they relate to one another and how they fit within a design process. Also, the need to find easy ways to update the contents was underlined. Finally, the need for an easy to access platform or repository was identified, that is, that students from different courses were able to explore the same learning resources in different ways and that alumni and design practitioners were able to access it as an open resource. The information obtained through the interviews was complemented with the outcome of the literature review, considering both design and learning science fields. During the research, the need for providing an interoperable and modular platform that allows easily to update the contents has been reinforced. As a result, the following findings were identified: unify scattered resources; easy updates of the contents; provide both direct an exploratory navigation system; provide different levels of contents depending on the students' needs and easily share the resources. Also, in order to foster exploratory learning, the need to provide design tools instead of design contents was identified.

3.2 Conceptualization and Design

The definition of the toolkit included several functionalities which were really important for improving the students' and teachers' experience in terms of developing and accessing design learning resources. Digital resources to be used within educational communities need to be organized, managed, shared and reused effectively [36]. Following the dimensions proposed by Mor et al. [37], conceptualization and design of each one of these dimensions had been done: users, content, and environment.

Regarding the first dimension, we noticed how challenging it is to define and implement a platform to be used both by individuals and a group of students [38]. In this case, the toolkit was designed to be used by different profiles: learners and lecturers. But it is mandatory to have a deeper view of each profile. On the one hand, learner profiles were subdivided, taking also into consideration the life-long learners (practitioners). On the other hand, the lecturers (teachers) who, in the UOC case, are both academics and practitioners.

The second dimension is the content and, therefore, design contents were analyzed according to the new challenges and disciplines of design and the educational needs of students and practitioners as life-long learners. This analysis, together with the analysis of the main design toolkits presented in Sect. 2.1 and the findings identified in Sect. 3.1, lead to the identification of three main types of design contents: models, methods, and principles [39]. In addition to that, we identified also the convenience of offering a toolkit that is action-oriented, providing practical step-by-step instructions through guides and, at the same time, cards (Fig. 1) for reflection and critical thinking, instead of providing just contents (Table 2). Even though this distinction was done in the type of content, it was decided to bring them together in one layout. Therefore, the step-by-step guides are accessible through links in the cards addressing the same content. Thus, the toolkit allows us to create decision-making systems that can provide a theoretical overview of the contents or can be a point of reference for decision making [40]. Furthermore, it was decided to provide external resources for each content that allow users to go in depth in the knowledge. These external resources offer real examples of each content, providing an overview of the practical appliance, and references to research publications, bringing the user closer to the academic world. This approach enabled a step forward towards a toolkit for educational purposes. In addition to that, the organization of the content through cards and guides allows two levels of navigation, that is, two levels of depth per content depending on the educational requirements for each user. Laurillard et al. pointed in [41] that the technology must be appropriated for its context of use and must have to add value to the learning process and enable the learners to achieve the learning outcomes. In this sense, a modular organization was designed to allow learner and practitioners to use these resources in their own context of learning and practice, integrating these resources in their own learning environment.

Fig. 1. User Journey card with access to the step-by-step guide

Table 2. Type of contents provided in UOCs Design Toolkit

Learning depth	Objective	Learning
Cards	Reflection and critical thinking	Design
Guides	Action oriented	Tasks

As already mentioned, one of the big challenges identified during the interviews was the need to provide a platform that allows the easy updating of the contents. That was the reason for choosing Wordpress as the CMS to build the platform since it provides simple mechanisms and interfaces to upload and update contents.

The third dimension was the environment. In this way, based on the previously identified requirements, we designed a toolkit that allows users to access resources in several ways: direct access, filtered access, and exploration. For example, users can either directly access a tool if they know which one they need, or they can access by filtering tools (Fig. 2) or they can explore the available tools in order to identify the one that best matches their needs. We designed a navigational system to empower teachers and learners [3], giving them autonomy of use [42]. The designed navigational system allows: (a) to use the educational resources in different teaching programs with similar learning goals but with different levels of depth; (b) to access learning resources to solve learning tasks; (c) to explore learning resources as a way to enhance learner's responsibility and autonomy. In this way, it should be noted that, from a constructivism perspective, students construct knowledge and skills and organize their understanding through interactions with the environment [43].

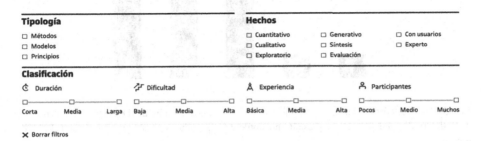

Fig. 2. Design toolkit filter options

4 Implementation and Evaluation

The Design Toolkit was developed as a research project at Universitat Oberta de Catalunya (UOC). It was used and evaluated in several courses and learning programs: Interaction Design course from the Digital Design and Creation Degree, Human-Computer Interaction course from the Computer Engineering Degree and User-Centered Design course from the User Experience Design Postgraduate. Also, the UOC Design Toolkit is available as an open source learning resource for anyone to access, explore and learn.

In order to have evidence about the usage and satisfaction of the Design Toolkit collected data with different approaches: interviews with users, a questionnaire sent to students and usage data collected by a web analytics application.

A questionnaire was sent to the students enrolled in two editions of the previously mentioned courses and a set 170 answers were obtained. The questionnaire addressed questions about the main design decisions of the toolkit. Catalan and Spanish versions of the same questionnaire where developed since UOC has both Catalan and Spanish speaking students. In order to process and analyze the answers, the collected data were merged into one database. According to the answers provided by the students, the implementation of the Design Toolkit seems to be successfully. As shown below, most of the students pointed out that Design Toolkit was useful for their academic and extra-academic activities. In this way, the students had to answer if they agreed that the design toolkit contents were useful to do the subject activities. From the 170 total responses, 82% of them answered they agree or strongly agree with that. Learners were also asked if the Design Toolkit contents were directly related to the contents they need to learn in order to follow the subject were the toolkit was proposed. From the totality of the answers, 78% of them agree or strongly agree that the content was aligned. Regarding the content, we asked learners if they thought this format was more suitable than the traditional one (see Fig. 3), 62% of them agree or strongly agree that the improvement provided by the Design Toolkit was beneficial to their goals.

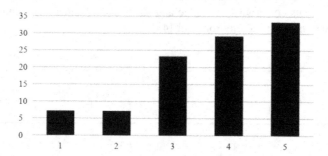

Fig. 3. Answers for the question "I think that the format provided by the Design Toolkit is better than the traditional format to present the contents" (5 indicates *strongly agree* and 1 *fully disagree*)

As pointed above in this work, exploratory navigation is a key factor for successful learnings. Thus, learners were asked if they used the Design Toolkit in an exploratory way. Of the totality of responses, 61% of them agree or very agree that the content had been useful for their extra studies activities (see Fig. 4).

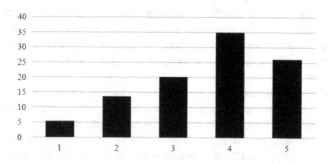

Fig. 4. Answers for the question "I explored the contents provided by the Design Toolkit further than the strictly asked by the subject" (5 indicates *strongly agree* and 1 *fully disagree*)

In this way, the data provided by Google Analytics shows that the guides have a 45% exit rate. This means 55% of the users that visit the guides continue exploring other pages of the Design Toolkit.

Apart from the questions related to learners' satisfaction with the implementation of the toolkit, we added some questions regarding the perception of the whole system and the navigation system. Regarding this last aspect, more than 63% of students say they see clearly the difference between guides and cards. Moreover, more than 66% of the students underline the usefulness of the separation between cards and the guidelines. Asking students about the navigation system and the filters, from the total of the answers, the 64% affirm they agree or strongly agree about the utility of the navigation system and the filers (Fig. 5).

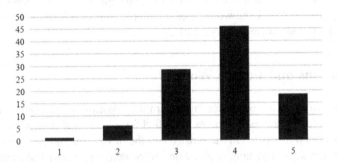

Fig. 5. Answers for the question "The navigation system and the filters provided by the Design Toolkit are clear and intuitive" (5 indicates *strongly agree* and 1 *fully disagree*)

Beside quantitative results gathered in the survey, qualitative results have been collected through questions with an open answer. We asked for proposals to improve the Design Toolkit, the implementation, and the contents. The most relevant outcome is the proposal to enable the PDF download of the guidelines provided by the Design Toolkit. Currently, this information is only available through the online platform and it is not presented in a printable way.

In this part of the first iteration phase, we also conducted three semi-structured interviews with UOC lecturers who had used the Design Toolkit in their class. In this way, the interview started with a set of questions related to the main goal of the interview: to know their satisfaction with the use of the Design Toolkit. All the responders were very satisfied with the UOC Design Toolkit and they expressed they will keep using the toolkit as a learning resource as well as a professional tool. Regarding the use of the toolkit they made, all the interviewed participants used the toolkit beyond the academic activity, making use of it in their non-academic professional tasks: "I have used the toolkit in professional projects to define the phases of the process we had to follow". This use beyond academic activity is also referred by students who, as shown in Fig. 4, said they used the toolkit in non-academic activities.

Asked about what they liked the most of the Design Toolkit, there were different answers. P1 said she liked to find a lot of design tools in the same place. P2 answered she liked the facility to integrate the tool content: "due to the modular classification of the content it is very easy to use it in different activities like a puzzle of knowledge".

P3 emphasized the filter system: "it allows me to find what I need very quickly". About the students' use of the toolkit, the responders said that "In addition to the use of the toolkit they (students) had to make to carry out the proposed activities, they explored the toolkit". This is actually what the students responded at the questionnaire (shown in Fig. 4). P2 referred that "some of those questions whose content were provided by the toolkit had better results than whose contents were provided by traditional resources". This is in line with the position sustained by Clemente and Tschimmel [28] and the responses of the students questionnaire shown in Fig. 4.

The last part of the semi-structured interview focused on obtaining suggestions for improvement to be taken into consideration in the next iteration phase. In one hand, P1 said "the usability of the toolkit needs to be improved, we must lead by example" and highlighted the need to "allow teachers to update content or add some case of study". On the other hand, P2 said she would like to "merge this toolkit resources with other UOC's toolkits (about interaction and art)".

5   Conclusions and Future Work

This paper provides a successful design and implementation of a Design Toolkit. On the one hand, it fulfills the requirements identified for educational design resources and content available on the web. On the other hand, the developed and deployed platform enables the compilation and update of the design content on an easy and intuitive way. Moreover, the implemented format to show the content, based on cards and guidelines, and the navigation structure, allows the adaptation of the platform to the specific needs of the students depending on the activity they are performing: an exploratory search or an action-based use. The results enable to conclude that the platform has provided students the opportunity to have an active behavior through the use of an educational design toolkit [40], acquiring greater autonomy in their learning process [3].

As shown by the results obtained through the research, most of the students were satisfied with the contents and format provided by the Design Toolkit. However, due to the qualitative questions, we had some feedback that shows us several opportunities for improvement, such as the possibility provided by the platform to download the guidelines as a PDF file, as well as the convenience to increase the amount of content.

As a future work, the navigation system has to be analyzed and, if needed, re-designed in order to improve the user experience with the toolkit. As part of the iterative process proposed in the methodology section, future works and improvements of the platform will be considered in future iterations. All the research provided in this manuscript can be considered as the first iteration that will be followed by incoming ones, improving the usefulness and intuitiveness of the Design Toolkit.

References

1. Buchanan, R.: Wicked problems in design thinking. Des. Issues **8**(2), 5–21 (1992)
2. Sanders, E.B.N., Stappers, P.J.: Co-creation and the new landscapes of design. Co-design **4** (1), 5–18 (2008)

3. Kalantzis, M., Cope, B.: The teacher as designer: pedagogy in the new media age. E-Learn. Digit. Media **7**(3), 200–222 (2010)
4. McCaslin, M., Good, T.: Compliant cognition: the misalliance of management and instructional goals in current school reform. Educ. Res. **21**, 4–17 (1992)
5. Samavedham, L.: Teaching students to think: a matter of engaging minds. Cent. Dev. Teach. Learn. **9**(2), 1–3 (2006)
6. Barrows, H.S., Tamblyn, R.M.: Problem-Based Learning: An Approach to Medical Education. Springer, Heidelberg (1980)
7. International Society for Technology in Education (ISTE). ISTE Standards for Students (2015). http://www.iste.org/standards/standards-for-students
8. Hmelo-Silver, C.E.: Problem-based learning: what and how do students learn? Educ. Psychol. Rev. **16**(3), 235–266 (2004)
9. Hannafin, M.J., Hill, J.R., Land, S.M., Lee, E.: Student-centered, open learning environments: research, theory, and practice. In: Spector, J., Merrill, M., Elen, J., Bishop, M. (eds.) Handbook of Research on Educational Communications and Technology, pp. 641–651. Springer, New York (2014). https://doi.org/10.1007/978-1-4614-3185-5_51
10. Glasgow, N.A.: New Curriculum for New Times: A Guide to Student-Centered, Problem-Based Learning. Corwin, Thousand Oaks (1997)
11. Fischer, G., Nakakoji, K.: Amplifying designers' creativity with domain-oriented design environments. In: Dartnall, T. (ed.) Artificial Intelligence and Creativity, vol. 17, pp. 343–364. Springer, Dordrecht (1994). https://doi.org/10.1007/978-94-017-0793-0_25
12. Wiley, D.A.: The Instructional Use of Learning Objects, vol. 1. Agency for Instructional Technology, Bloomington (2002)
13. Chen, I.Y., Chen, N.S.: Examining the factors influencing participants' knowledge sharing behavior in virtual learning communities. J. Educ. Technol. Soc. **12**(1), 134–148 (2009)
14. Carroll, J.M., Rosson, M.B., Dunlap, D., Isenhour, P.: Frameworks for sharing teaching practices. J. Educ. Technol. Soc. **8**(3), 162–175 (2005)
15. Hsu, K.C., Yang, F.C.O.: Toward an open and interoperable e-learning portal: OEPortal. J. Educ. Technol. Soc. **11**(2), 131 (2008)
16. Sampson, D.G., Zervas, P.: Learning object repositories as knowledge management systems. Knowl. Manag. E-Learn. **5**(2), 117 (2013)
17. McGreal, R. (ed.): Online Education Using Learning Objects. Psychology Press (2004)
18. Rodés-Paragarino, V., Gewerc-Barujel, A., Llamas-Nistal, M.: Use of repositories of digital educational resources: state-of-the-art review. IEEE Revista Iberoamericana de Tecnologias del Aprendizaje **11**(2), 73–78 (2016)
19. Koper, R.: Combining reusable learning resources and services with pedagogical purposeful units of learning. In: Littlejohn, A. (ed.) Reusing Online Resources: A Sustainable Approach to E-Learning. Kogan Page, Limited, pp. 12–19 (2003)
20. Kraan, W.: Learning Design and reusability. CETIS (2003). http://zope.cetis.ac.uk/content/20030902133812/index.html. Accessed 28 Jan 2019
21. Caswell, T., Henson, S., Jensen, M., Wiley, D.: Open content and open educational resources: enabling universal education. Int. Rev. Res. Open Distrib. Learn. **9**(1), 2 (2008)
22. Galbreath, J.: The Internet: past, present, and future. Educ. Technol. **37**(6), 39–45 (1997)
23. Kurtz, M.: Dublin Core, DSpace, and a brief analysis of three university repositories. Inf. Technol. Libr. **29**(1), 40–46 (2010)
24. Soto, J., García, E., Sánchez, S.: Repositorios semánticos para objetos de aprendizaje. Barcelona, Exolearning (2006)
25. Churchill, D.: Towards a useful classification of learning objects. Educ. Technol. Res. Dev. **55**(5), 479–497 (2007)

26. Sicilia, M.A., Garcia, E., Pagés, C., Martinez, J.J., Gutierrez, J.M.: Complete metadata records in learning object repositories: some evidence and requirements. Int. J. Learn. Technol. **1**(4), 411–424 (2005)
27. Resnick, M., et al.: Design principles for tools to support creative thinking. In: NSF Workshop Report on Creativity Support Tools, pp. 25–36, October 2005
28. Clemente, V., Vieira, R., Tschimmel, K.: A learning toolkit to promote creative and critical thinking in product design and development through design thinking. In: 2016 2nd International Conference of the Portuguese Society for Engineering Education (CISPEE), pp. 1–6. IEEE, October 2016
29. Lee, E., Hannafin, M.J.: A design framework for enhancing engagement in student-centered learning: own it, learn it, and share it. Educ. Technol. Res. Dev. **64**(4), 707–734 (2016)
30. Blaschke, L.M.: Heutagogy and lifelong learning: a review of heutagogical practice and self-determined learning. Int. Rev. Res. Open Distrib. Learn. **13**(1), 56–71 (2012)
31. Hase, S., Kenyon, C.: Heutagogy: a child of complexity theory. Complicity: Int. J. Complex. Educ. **4**(1), 112 (2007)
32. Mezirow, J.: Transformative learning: theory to practice. New Dir. Adult Contin. Educ. **1997**(74), 5–12 (1997)
33. ISO 9241-210: Ergonomics of human-system interaction. Part 210: Human-centred design process for interactive systems. ISO, Geneva (2008)
34. Oates, B.J.: Researching Information Systems and Computing. Sage (2005)
35. Swann, C.: Action research and the practice of design. Des. Issues **18**(1), 49–61 (2002)
36. Hsu, K.C., Yang, F.-C.O.: Toward an open and interoperable e-learning portal: OEPortal. Educ. Technol. Soc. **11**(2), 131–148 (2008)
37. Garreta Domingo, M., Mor Pera, E.: User centered design in e-learning environments: from usability to learner experience. In: Proceedings of the EDEN 2007 Annual Conference (2007)
38. Jacqueline Yannacci, M.P.P., Kristin Roberts, B.B.A., Vijay Ganju, P.D.: Principles from Adult Learning Theory, Evidence-Based Teaching, and Visual Marketing: What are the Implications for Toolkit Development? Center for Mental Health Quality and Accountability NRI, Inc. (2006)
39. Boeijen, A.V., Daalhuizen, J., Schoor, R., Zijlstra, J.: Delft design guide: design strategies and methods (2014)
40. Conole, G., Fill, K.: A learning design toolkit to create pedagogically effective learning activities (2005)
41. Laurillard, D., et al.: A constructionist learning environment for teachers to model learning designs. J. Comput. Assist. Learn. **29**(1), 15–30 (2013)
42. Shrader, S.R.: Learner empowerment—a perspective. Internet TESL J. **9**(11), 1–5 (2003)
43. Jonassen, D.H.: Objectivism versus constructivism: do we need a new philosophical paradigm? Educ. Technol. Res. Dev. **39**(3), 5–14 (1991)

Service-Oriented Control-Command Components for Designing Complex Systems

Olga Goubali[1(✉)], Abdenour Idir[1], Line Poinel[2], Laurianne Boulhic[1], Djamal Kesraoui[1], and Alain Bignon[1]

[1] SEGULA Technologies, BP 50256, 56602 Lanester Cedex, France
{olga.goubali,laurianne.boulhic,
djamal.kesraoui}@segula.fr,
idir.abdenour@hotmail.com, bignon.alain@neuf.fr
[2] SEGULA Technologies, 71 rue Henri Gautier,
44550 Montoir-de-Bretagne, France
Line.poinel@segula.fr

Abstract. An important task in designing control-command systems is defining components for two essential parts of the system: command and monitoring. Instead of developing a monolithic executable, designers use reusable blocs, named components, which are saved in a library. Services Oriented Architecture (SOA) was introduced in the design of control-command systems to improve flexibility and reusability [1]. However, this approach does not consider the composition of the services [2], disregarding this important characteristic in the design of control-command systems. In some industrial areas such as ship-building, the component-based approach is typically used since it enables better legibility for the applications; it uses a modular approach based on the system architecture recorded on the Piping and Instrumentation Diagram (P&ID) [3]. Each software component is associated with a unique type of equipment. This approach enables to produce components highly optimized to their functions. The counterpart is that services integrated in each component cannot be reused in designing another component. In fact, part of the component services can also be present in another component (Fig. 1). Including services in component does not optimize functions reusability. In this paper, we propose an approach that facilitate and improve the design of quality components whilst complying with specifications and timelines in a more efficient way; it also reduces efforts required to redesign services provided by these components.

Keywords: Control-command component · SOA · MDE · EUD

1 Introduction

Designing control-command systems includes an important step of components definition. These components are usually stored in a library. A component is an independent unit that is combined with other components to make an application. Therefore, designing a control-command system is made of the components with different views for the command and the supervision/monitoring parts.

© Springer Nature Switzerland AG 2019
M. Kurosu (Ed.): HCII 2019, LNCS 11566, pp. 101–113, 2019.
https://doi.org/10.1007/978-3-030-22646-6_8

Usually components are stored in a library which contains the required elements for creating command programs and control interfaces for the system being designed. The library often contains two types of components: standardized components which are highly specialized and white components. The white component is an empty component which initial function is not identified but that can be configured to be adapted to a specific case, this gives bespoke components.

Each software component is associated to a unique type of equipment. This approach enables to create components highly optimized for their functions. The counterpart is that services integrated in each component cannot be reused in the design of another component. Indeed, a part of the services (functions) of a component can also be present in another component (Fig. 1). Integration of services in each component does not enable to optimize functions reuse during the component design. To solve this issue, a service-oriented components model was proposed by [2]. Nevertheless, this model is not adapted to the design of control-command components.

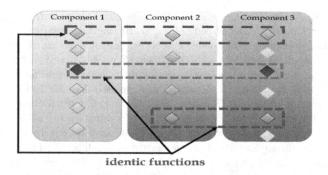

Fig. 1. Duplication functions in component design

Our aim is to improve the approach for components design, to reduce the effort required for re-designing services and to explore solutions to improve reusability during components design. For this, we take advantage of the SOA (Service Oriented Architecture) approach. This approach should enable to encourage quality components design while efficiently complying with the requirements specification and time constraints. We apply our solution to components of an EdS system (Eau douce Sanitaire in French, sanitary freshwater in English). In this system, several components have common functions which are redesigned for each new component.

2 State of the Art

Heterogeneity and fast evolution of applications confront designers with an ever growing complexity [4] and with major challenges of system engineering: scale-up, administration and autonomy. To propose potential solutions to this problem, industrial and academic communities looked towards component-based approaches, which are inescapable since 1990s. These are based on the construction of reusable, modular and spreadable software components. In the literature, there are several définitions of a "software component", amongst which we select the following:

"A software component is a unit of composition with contractually specified interfaces and explicit context dependencies only. A software component can be deployed independently and is subject to composition by third parties" [5].

A software component is therefore a code unit that can be characterised as a black box. Some component models have been proposed to facilitate design and composition of components, including models of software components.

Defined by OMG (Object Management Group), CORBA (Common Object Request Broker Architecture) component Model (CCM) [6] is a model of allocated software components that specifies distributed and heterogeneous components which are in turn independent of any platform and programming languages. A CORBA component model is defined in IDL3 (Interface Definition Language) language and has different types of ports and attributes that represent configurable properties. CCM enables to model the complete life cycle of a component by proposing a structure to define its behaviour, its integration in an application and its deployment in the CORBA distributed environment. Moreover, CCM provides a global framework for applications design based on distributed components: specification, installation, processing, assembly, deployment and execution of components. However, this model is not easy to implement and does not enable to model adaptive parallel components [7], which execute parallel activities.

To solve this issue of parallelism, CCA model (Common Component Architecture) [8] was defined. Indeed, parallelism does not act on CCA components because they are defined in the same way whether they are arranged in parallel or sequencially. CCA is a software component model written in SIDL (Scientific Interface Definition Language), software interface specification language. A CCA component has two types of ports: ProvidePort and UsesPort that enable, through interfaces, to provide and use functionality of other components. This way, CCA components can be connected to other components through their ports. Each application made of CCA components will be a CCA component itself. However, the use of CCA component requires to know its internal working, which is hardly understandable [4].

A Fractal component model [9] is a consortium project ObjectWeb defined by France Télécom R&D and INRIA. This model is presented as a specification for the design of complex software systems (middleware and operating systems), in different languages such as Java, C, C++, SmallTalk, .Net. Designing such systems requires definition of Fractal components. These are entities with two types of interfaces: server interfaces and client interfaces. Server interfaces correspond to services provided by a component and clients interfaces correspond to services required by the component. A Fractal component contains either its implementation code (primitive component), or other components (composite components). Indeed, Fractal enables to build shared components which can be included in several composites. One advantage of Fractal is that the developer can customize control capacities of each component, while taking into account functional and non-functional aspects. However, developers can quickly be confronted to an increase in programming complexity [4].

Whilst simplifying applications design, existing component models are not adapted to the designing of control-command applications because they do not allow for easy designing that type of applications. More and more supervision software propose predefined components to assist the designing of control-command systems. However, getting used to handling these components can take a considerable amount of time. It is sometimes easier for designers to develop their components themselves.

3 Problem Description

Designing components enables experts to focus on their expert knowledge where they have most added value [10]. With Component Oriented Programming (COP), designers use reusable blocs that are the components, instead of building a monolithic executable. However, reusability remains at high level (component level). A component used in a given context (subject area, application in the same area, etc.) is unlikely to be reusable in other contexts [11]. As an example, components defined for a sanitary freshwater system are not all reusable for a gasoil processing installation. In fact, some components are standards and other are bespoke, to respond to a requirement that is only relevant for the system to be designed. However, bespoke components are rarely maintainable, because such an approach favors spreading of hacked and incompatible versions of components that are vaguely similar, of which none is really reusable in the end [12]. Moreover, in some industrial areas where additional requirements modifying initial specifications can be added if necessary, inaccessibility to the component code inhibits adaptation of the code to specific needs by developers [13]. Even if models such as SMARTTOOLS [14] do focus on extensibility making it possible to add functionalities to the component as long as they are compatible, it is not possible to use internal services of one component to create another one. This limits the concept of reusability at the component level. Easily creating bespoke components and make them reusable is the first challenge we have identified.

A component designed are often integrated in a library. This library is therefore made of components that can be combined in different ways to respond to different needs. Usually, designing a component starts with the choice of programming language. Once this and the development environment chosen, how the components should be developed still needs to be defined. In the components definition, the COP approach focuses on the individual application rather than looking at a much larger software process. However, components engineering does not only focus on the development of software components but can concern all aspects of software development, from collecting and specifying requirements up to designing and implementing. Most advantageous to reuse artefacts are often not the software components themselves but the knowledge of the field and of the generic designs. Software reuse is more successful if prepared in advance. Until requirements are specified and systems designed, numerous reuse opportunities may have been wasted. It is then interesting to rethink, in applications life cycle, the way components should be designed as well as how to introduce new activities linked to services provided by components.

Search for new ideas led us to look at the definition of a component. A component should provide services that are specific, accurate, defined and implemented during its design. However, some of the services can be present in another component. Encapsulation of services inside a component makes it difficult to reuse them. Issues of interoperability and reuse at the structural level of the component, and not only during designing of the system, should be addressed. Identifying and modeling reusable services, and implementing them for component designing, is the second challenge we have identified.

4 Methodology

Our solution (Fig. 2) is based on the combination of Service Oriented Computing (SOC), Model Driven Engineering (MDE) and End User Development (EUD) approaches. It allows to capture expert knowledge for designing services oriented components and to facilitate fast integration of evolutions. Applying each of these approaches enables to build a solution to automatically generate a complete chain of control-command components from the requirements specification by the expert user (non-programmer).

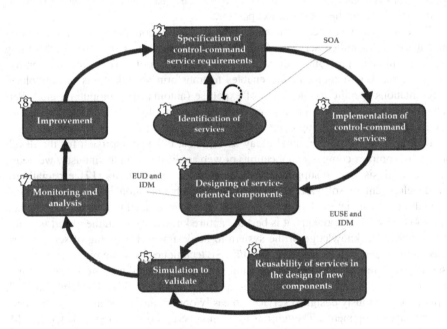

Fig. 2. Our approach

SOC [15] enables to address the limitations identified in the component approach. The aim is not to completely replace the existing component approach, but to reuse some of its principles while adding new ones from SOA. Based on SOA approach, we have identified and modelled control-command services. Identification of services is the same as identifying the most used functionalities of control-command systems, using a user centered approach [16]. HMI centered methods are used to collect business requirements from different actors in the designing process. The aim is to promote a loose coupling between the different technical functionalities of a component. This first step in our methodology is broken down in several analysis steps. First, we identify the main business actors of the designing of control-command systems, by analyzing different parts of the system. Then, we analyze the operators tasks on the components of control-command systems. This analysis enabled to break down a system in several sub-systems to identify and list the operator actions on the supervision components, as well as the system feedback. We also review existing control-command systems to identify functionalities that are reused inside their different components. With this, we can identify the main services reusable in the components. Eventually, these business services are categorized using SOA approach. The step of services identification is iterated until the designers are satisfied with the output.

After identifying the services, it is required to specify how they are to be built. The step of requirements specification for the control-command services enables to define the process by which we establish the physical designing of services and how to compose them to implement business components. During this step, services designers specify, for each identified service, its functionalities, exchanged variables and information sent back to the supervision operator.

Once these services requirements validated, control-command systems designers implement the identified services. Each designer focuses on its expertise field, using interfaces models previously described, and adapted tools. This step of control-command services implementation enables to transform specifications into graphical representations specific to each field of expertise (automatism, computing, etc.). Services implementation and promotion of reusability at this level enables to reduce designers effort for designing components.

Despite SOA being presented today as the most efficient approach for the development of complex company applications or web applications, in the industry we notice a lack of analysis tools to support development based on reusability [17], especially for the development of software components for which operation is known and documented, but not its internal structure. Indeed, in order to quickly and correctly obtain control-command components, it is best to capture knowledge from the expert who has all the functional knowledge of the system to be designed. Designing of services oriented components will be based on EUD/EUSE techniques, which have already proven useful in the area of industrial supervision [18]. Those techniques are integrated in a proof of concept enabling to validate our approach. A tool will be developed and will exploit the previously designed services to easily obtain reusable standard components and bespoke components. Though our tool, an expert who has no knowledge in HMI programming (computing) nor in command coding (automatism), easily composes services to design both command and supervision parts of components.

To quickly take into account component evolutions, the use of MDE is a well-adapted solution to issues of control-command system migrations from one platform to another [19]. Implementation of MDE therefore enables to get a complete control-command chain for the bespoke components and standard components the expert needs to design its system. The tool enables to design new components from existing components, promoting reusability at the level of components functionalities and ensuring a good coupling between services.

All designed components could then be simulated, analyzed and reintegrated in the tool to be improved. The specified services could also be improved and expanded depending on the identified shortcomings.

5 Case Study and Results

5.1 SOA Implementation: Services Identification and Implementation

SOA recommends to break down functionalities in a set of basic elements called «services». SOA implementation enables to finely describe the services interaction scheme as part of a business process. Services were then identified and deployed as independent software components. SOA use enabled to skip the step of heavy components construction (considered as black boxes) for which internal functionalities are not reusable. Analysis of components present in control-command systems led us to identify a set of services such as measurer, indicator light, command buttons, etc. Each service has inputs/outputs (Fig. 3) and service interfaces depending on the interface meta-model defined in Fig. 4.

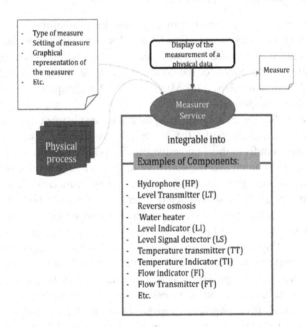

Fig. 3. Illustration of the measuring service

Figure 3 presents the measuring service that we defined, as well as examples of components in which we can find this service. Some components can be present in a same control-command system. Services definition reduce the designing effort on the system and increase the reusability on other systems, which can have different components using the same services. We therefore exploited service properties in the SOA meaning: reusability, composability, independence and variable granularity. In good respect of these properties, we described services interfaces based on the meta-model of Fig. 4a. Parameters contained in this meta-model have been entered in a spreadsheet by the business expert, then automatically translated in XML format (Fig. 4b).

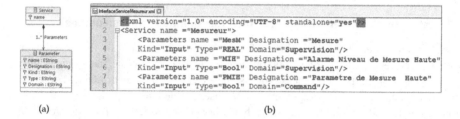

(a)   (b)

Fig. 4. Service interface meta-model

5.2 SOCD (Service Oriented Component Design) Tool for the Composition of Services in Components

Ideally, encapsulation of each service must ensure its reusability and its interoperability. The SOCD tool developed (Fig. 5) enables the designer without any HMI programming knowledge nor of command code to create, modify, visualize and delete command and supervision codes for the components of the system being designed. To do this, we used approaches based on MDE and EUD techniques to enable fast integration and reuse of components services.

By integrating these approaches, the proposed interface is made of three areas. The main area (1 on Fig. 5) displays the list of components already designed. The expert can modify a component from this interactive list. To modify a component, the user can click on the component name and the corresponding services are displayed in the area 2. He can modify service parameters by clicking on its name and save the changes («Enregistrer» in area 2). He can also delete a service from a component («Supprimer service» in area 2) or delete a component («Supprimer composant» in area 2). The third area regroups widgets enabling the user to create a new component from scratch or from an already existing component, to integrate the designed components in specific software («Test composant» in area 3) and to actualize the synoptic. Synoptic refers to a top-down approach for design [20] - it is an extract design of a control-command system which contains composition of necessary components for this system. Synoptic actualization is useful for designing bespoke components, to integrate them into automatic or manual design process and to take into account the changes made to components.

To add a new component from scratch, the user must enter the component name and choose the services he requires. The user has a choice between three pre-defined functions as services: measurer, indicator and command. He should be able to define the parameters characterizing each service through the interface.

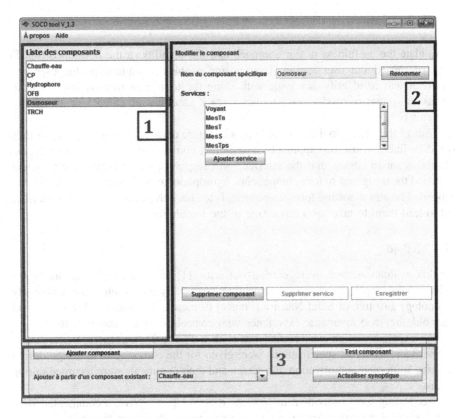

Fig. 5. SOCD tool for designing services oriented components

Adding a new component based on an existing component relies on the reusability mentioned in the EUSE approach [18]. The tool proposes a list of existing service oriented components for the expert to choose an existing component in the field «Ajouter à partir d'un composant existant» (Fig. 5) (in English "Add a component using existing one". Once the component chosen, the user can modify, delete or add new services to the component being created. This way, he chooses to reuse services of an existing component and to add new services; this leads to a time gain in the first designing steps.

Information related to user inputs during component designing is recorded in an XML file. This file enables MDE implementation for the automatic generation of command and supervision codes after the component creation. Once generated, the component can be tested by the expert using the «Test composant» button on Fig. 5. This button enables the expert to integrate component command codes in Straton tool [18] and its supervision codes in Panorama E2 tool [18], to visualize command views and components supervision respectively.

6 Evaluation

To validate the usefulness of our approach and the usability of the developed SOCD tool, we carried out user testing. User testing enables to understand the user real objectives and to identify any issue with using the tool. This method is efficient to increase a system or product ergonomics since it identifies up to 95% of ergonomic problems [21].

Tests of the SOCD tool are carried out with future designers, to check whether they would be likely to use our approach in designing component by services association. We also want to ensure that the interface will respond to their needs. We therefore evaluated the designing of four components: hydrophore, chlorination, water heater and osmosis. The aim of testing four components is to check the ease of use of the interface and to lead them to take most advantage of the reusability.

6.1 Method

For this evaluation, tests were carried out with 11 participants (6 students and 5 professionals) expert in process engineering from Polytech Nantes and University Technology Institute of Saint Nazaire (France) (9 men and 2 women). From 20 to 63 years old, they had a variable experience with control-command components.

The experimentation was carried out with a PC, a 23′ screen, a mouse and a keyboard and technical specifications were given for the components to design during the tests. With their authorization, the screen and their comments were recorded during the tests.

User testing were individual in separate rooms. Upon arrival, a commented slide show presented the context of the study to participants. They were then placed in front of the SOCD tool with an experimenter beside them.

Participants were asked to design the four components for which they had the technical specifications. They were asked to test at least one of the created component and to observe the result in the supervision view in Panorama E2. They were invited to think out loud for us to better understand their actions on the tool.

At the end of the test, they were asked to fill a questionnaire AttrakDiff [22] and another with more open questions to give their views on the tool.

6.2 Results and Interpretation

User testing results were encouraging even if some efforts remain to be made to improve the interface design. Some missing functionalities were highlighted, such as the possibility to all new services to components previously created or the arrangement of the elements on the interface. Despite these minor issues, we observed a good first use of the tool. Participants noticed it in their comments and the time required to build a component decreased from the 2nd component. Participants have been reported to appreciate the reusability of existing component services to create a new one. Furthermore, the approach of designing components by association of services was well received. They qualified the tool as controllable, foreseeable, practical, simple, clear, new, motivating, and easy to use; all being very positive.

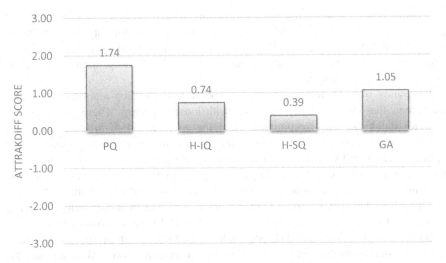

Fig. 6. Average score by items category (AttrakDiff questionnaire)

Figure 6 presents the AttrakDiff questionnaire results which evaluate the perceived quality of an interactive system. It includes 28 items in 4 sub-scales (pragmatic quality PQ, hedonic-stimulation quality H-SQ, hedonic-identity quality H-IQ and global attractivity GA). These different items are detailed in [22]. To analyze the results, average values are presented in the −3 to 3 range. Values between 0 and 1 are considered in a neutral zone, and values outside this zone are considered either as positive (1 to 3) or negative (−3 to −1).

Scores collected with the AttrakDiff questionnaire are very encouraging. The average PQ score of 1.75/3 describes the usefulness, utilisability and the success in carrying out the tasks when using the system. The analysis by sub-scale show that H-SQ and H-IQ have the lower average scores with 0.74/3 and 0.39/3 respectively. These sub-scales correspond to hedonic characteristics which are linked to emotions, affects, etc. These low scores are explained by the fact that the proposed tool is described as not fun, which some participants found normal since they qualified the tool as professional. These user tests have confirmed the usefulness of our approach, the usability of our tool and have evaluated the tool based on measuring scales linked to user experience. However, the tool must now be improved to better facilitate user tasks, since user centered design is an iterative process where evaluation is fully integrated in the designing process.

7 Conclusion

A component is a system element providing a predefined service and capable of communicating with other components. In the designing of control-command systems, component design is a very important step. Existing technologies, such as CORBA or

CCA components, do not fulfill our expectations. Moreover, limits of the component approach lead us to rethink the way we design components. Our approach combining SOA, EUD/EUSE and MDE enables us to bring solutions to identified challenges on reusability and interoperability of functionalities (services) encapsulated in the components during their designing.

Integration of SOA techniques made it possible to develop a solution to obtain components that are simple, modular and with loose couplings. These characteristics allow for quick and easy recombination of the arrangement of functionalities they provide. By its approach of designing and construction of services as independent applicative blocs, SOA facilitates process instrumentation. Our work demonstrates that this approach can be used for developing services more frequently found in control-command systems. It led us to the definition and implementation of the SOCD tool enabling a user that is expert in his field, but not an automatism or computing specialist, to create and modify or reuse standard components and bespoke components.

Integration of EUD and EUSE approach enabled the reusability of functionalities (services) internal to components, as well as errors correction. MDE through the DOM API for the XML files processing allowed for the joint and automatic generation of command and supervision codes for the components.

Our approach therefore facilitates the designing of components whilst respecting the information contained in the requirements specification and while promoting reusability of internal services of a component in different contexts. Thanks to this approach, the component is not seen as a black box but rather a flexible element for the designing, which can be handled by non-programmers. Usability (ISO 9241-11 and ISO-13407) of our tool was demonstrated during the users testing.

In the future work, we will improve the tool to better facilitate user tasks.

Acknowledgements. We would like to thank students and teachers of the Polytech Nantes and University Technology Institute of Saint Nazaire for their participation to the user tests.

References

1. Dai, W., Peltola, J., Vyatkin, V., Pang, C.: Service-oriented distributed control software design for process automation systems. In: 2014 IEEE International Conference on Systems, Man and Cybernetics, pp. 3637–3642 (2014)
2. Cervantes, H.: Vers un modèle à composants orienté services pour supporter la disponibilité dynamique. Ph.D. thesis. Informatique (2004)
3. Kesraoui-Mesli, S.: Intégration des techniques de vérification formelle dans une approche de conception des systèmes de contrôle-commande. Ph.D. thesis, no. Umr 6285 (2017)
4. Pichon, V.: Contribution à la conception à base de composants logiciels d'applications scientifiques parallèles. Ph.D. thesis, Ecole Nationale Supérieur de Lyon - Université de Lyon (2012)
5. Szyperski, C.: Component Software – Beyond Object-Oriented Programming, 2nd edn. Addison-Wesley Longman Publishing Co., Boston (2002)
6. OMG. CORBA component model, v4.0 (2006). http://www.omg.org/spec/CCM/4.0/
7. Courtrai, L., Guidec, F., Mahéo, Y.: Gestion de ressources pour composants parallèles adaptables. In: JC (2002)

8. Bernholdt, D.E., Elwasif, W.R., Kohl, J.A., Epperly, T.G.: A component architecture for high-performance computing: an overview of the common component architecture, pp. 1–10. SANDIA National LABS LIVERMORE CA (2005)

9. Bruneton, E., Coupaye, T., Leclercq, M., Quéma, V., Stefani, J.-B.: The FRACTAL component model and its support in Java. Softw. Pract. Exp. **39**(7), 701–736 (2006)

10. Bignon, A.: Génération conjointe de commandes et d'interfaces de supervision pour systèmes sociotechniques reconfigurables. UBS (2012)

11. Zachman, J.A.: Enterprise Architecture Artifacts Versus Application Development Artifacts, vol. 28 (2000)

12. Dami, L., Konstantas, D., Pintado, X.: Object-Oriented Software Composition, vol. 1. Prentice Hall, Englewood Cliffs (1995)

13. Ait Abdelouhab, K., Idoughi, D.: Conception centrée utilisateur de services dans le cadre des architectures orientées services. Thèse de doctorat, Université de bejana (2016)

14. Courbis, C., Degenne, P., Fau, A., Parigot, D., Variamparambil, J.: Un modèle de composants pour l'atelier de développement SmartTools. Journée systèmes à Compos. Adapt. extensibles (2002)

15. Papazoglou, M.P., Van Den Heuvel, W.: Service-oriented computing: state-of-the-art and open research issues. IEEE Comput. **40**(11), 38–45 (2007)

16. 9241-210:2010 ISO: Ergonomics of human-system interaction – Part 210: Human-centred design for interactive systems (2010)

17. Stojanović, Z., Dahanayake, A.: Service-Oriented Software System Engineering: Challenges and Practices. IGI Global, Hershey (2005)

18. Goubali, O.: Apport des techniques de programmation par démonstration dans une démarche de génération automatique d'applicatifs de Contrôle-Commande. ENSMA (2017)

19. Vernes, P.J.: Algorithmes de Contrôles Avancés pour les Installations à Gaz du LHC au CERN suivant le Framework et l'approche dirigée par les modèles du projet GCS. Ph.D. thesis, Université de Picardie Jules Vernes (2008)

20. Bignon, A., Berruet, P., Rossi, A.: Joint generation of controls and interfaces for sociotechnical and reconfigurable systems. In: 2010 IEEE International Conference on Systems, Man and Cybernetics (2010)

21. Boucher, A.: Ergonomie web: pour des sites web efficaces, 2nd edn. Eyrolles (2009)

22. Diefenbach, S., Hassenzahl, M., Eckoldt, K., Hartung, L., Lenz, E., Laschke, M.: Designing for well-being: a case study of keeping small secrets. J. Posit. Psychol. **12**(2), 151–158 (2017)

End User Designing of Complex Task Models for Complex Control-Command Systems

Olga Goubali[1(✉)], Patrick Girard[2], Laurent Guittet[2], Alain Bignon[1],
Djamal Kesraoui[1], Soraya Kesraoui-Mesli[1], Pascal Berruet[3],
Benjamin Morio[1], and Laurianne Boulhic[1]

[1] SEGULA Technologies, BP 50256, 56602 Lanester Cedex, France
{olga.goubali,djamal.kesraoui,soraya.kesraoui,
laurianne.boulhic}@segula.fr,
bignon.alain@neuf.fr, morio.benjamin56@gmail.com
[2] LIAS/ENSMA, 1 avenue Clément Ader, 86961 Chasseneuil, France
{girard,laurent.guittet}@ensma.fr
[3] Lab-STICC, BP 92116, 56321 Lorient Cedex, France
pascal.berruet@univ-ubs.fr

Abstract. In the design of control-command systems, task models are useful for collecting requirements about the use of the systems. Indeed, task models describe actions the supervisor performs to start, to control and to monitor the system events (alerts, performance messages), to evaluate, to stop a function (if needed), etc. Depending on the state of the supervised system (for example, presence of defects), these tasks can be numerous, repetitive and complicated. This complexity makes it difficult to describe task models, which are therefore complex, but essential for design. Task models are usually described by HMI designers using dedicated modeling tools and can be validated with business experts.

In this paper, we propose a specification process that enables to best capture system expert knowledge and to facilitate obtaining complex task models based on their operational expert knowledge. Our approach aims at formalizing and designing industrial system tasks models in our tool named Prototask Editor User. With our tool, system experts who are not tasks specialists can read and adapt the tasks pattern while simulating, verifying and validating it.

Keywords: Tasks pattern · Complex tasks model · Industrial system · EUD

1 Introduction

In the design of interactive systems, taking into account users through tasks models is inevitable because, for designers, it avoids a lot of errors related to the use of the system. Indeed, tasks models help to understand the human activity and the use of the system to be designed. With this model, HMI designers can express human tasks based on activity analysis to meet design needs. The basic principles of task models do not differ much from one tasks model to another [1]. The use of task models in a multi-disciplinary design has become increasingly popular [2].

© Springer Nature Switzerland AG 2019
M. Kurosu (Ed.): HCII 2019, LNCS 11566, pp. 114–130, 2019.
https://doi.org/10.1007/978-3-030-22646-6_9

Tasks are usually described according to structuring mechanisms. These mechanisms provide temporal operators that allow a hierarchical decomposition of tasks into sub-tasks, with categorization according to the type of tasks. For a more precise description of the activity, it is possible to add attributes to the tasks. These attributes can be optional, iterative, pre-condition and post-condition.

In designing sociotechnical and complex systems, a task leads to a goal (state of the desired system) that the user wishes to achieve by using a procedure that describes the means to achieve that goal [3]. Tasks analysis provides a set of data that can be used in design approaches. It is now accepted that task models are fully integrated into the design process of control-command systems. Faced with the complexity of these systems, where the user tasks must be precise and context-sensitive, the design of task models becomes more time-consuming. In fact, with the actions to be defined, the states of the system to be monitored (alarms, elements, faults, etc.), the possible actions depending on the context, the decision-making etc., the design of tasks models is laborious. In addition to that, the detection and correction of errors during the simulation of these models can delay the design of the control-command system. Indeed, tasks models are usually designed by the HMI designers and then simulated with the business expert until they are validated.

To solve these problems, existing approaches offer pattern-based solutions. Patterns provide a reusable structure for task models allowing designers to focus on the user needs.

Although tasks patterns facilitate tasks models designing, their definition is often not easy [4]. In order to facilitate the design of complex tasks models, we propose in this paper: an approach that allows to formalize and design industrial system tasks pattern; and a tool named Prototask Editor User. Based on the principle of End User Development, our tool contains modules enabling the designer to change the name of tasks, add a basic task, or delete a basic or complex task, in addition of the tasks simulation principles of the tasks simulator named Prototask [5]. In our tool, the adaptation process is performed jointly with the tasks pattern simulation.

To validate our approach, we evaluate the usefulness of on a real case study. We also evaluate our approach with tasks specialists to take into account their needs and the usability of our tool with practitioners' designer. Results are analyzed and detailed in this paper.

2 State of the Art

2.1 Analysis of Operators Activities

The description of user activities on a control-command system in tasks models, is based on the formalization of specifications. This formalization is firstly based on an analysis and a review of the literature [6–8] and secondly on feedback acquired through the analysis of specifications established in real projects and through interviews with expert designers. With this formalization, it is possible to identify necessary information contained in specifications, which must be modeled as tasks. The modeling of these information in tasks, brings out global recursive actions, necessary to control a control-command system.

The supervision of control-command systems consists in carrying out a certain number of commands which are described as "complex" and classified in four categories [7]. The first category is about monitoring of the system functions. This task is the main one for the system operators and takes an important part of their working time. The second category concerns the manipulation of orders. This task can be performed at any time (for example: when the system is in permanent regime, when faults are detected on the system, etc.). In a functional context, for most control systems, supervisory operations occur when a function starts, when the function stops normally, or when faults are returned [7]. The third category is the diagnosis of defects. This category of tasks occurs when a defect is identified by the supervisory operator. The fourth category relates to administrative tasks (e.g. surveillance tests, verification of technical specifications, journal maintenance and event reports). These four categories of tasks detailed in [9] are closely related in a control room.

Bovell, Carter and Beck presented a flow that shows the connection between the four categories described [7]. However, this flow does not allow to accurately take into account hierarchical organization of operator activities.

Kluge presented a table containing the sequences of actions which are performed by supervisory operators [8]. However, with this table, it is not possible to structure these actions with the necessary precision, to carry out the complex and various operators tasks in exceptional situations [10].

2.2 Designing of Complex Task Models

Typically, supervisory task templates take into account the specificities of each high-level function of control systems. One can imagine the complexity in the design of such models. Several works have attempted to provide a solution to this complexity. Therefore, during the SIGCHI'97 pattern workshop [11], participants considered patterns as a way to solve complexity and diversity problems increasing in the design of HMI. The main purpose of patterns is to create an inventory of solutions to help HMI designers to solve common and difficult design problems. A pattern is defined as a solution description format for recurring design problems [12].

The study of [4] is among the first work that integrated patterns in task modeling. They were motivated by the possibility of reusing good design solutions to solve recurring problems related to dialogue specification, in order to reduce design time. Their work has highlighted the use of task structures to speed up the process of building tasks models and integrating them into the design of large-scale industrial applications.

The PSA Framework [12] uses patterns throughout the software development cycle to extend reusability across all design models. This framework offers a reusability solution and allows designers to capture and propagate information between the proposed patterns (tasks, domain, structure and navigation patterns, etc.). However, the concept of linking patterns in a design is not addressed in this approach [13]. In addition, the approach does not address the transition from task patterns to task models.

Gaffar and his colleagues approach emphasizes another important aspect of the notion of pattern: the combination of patterns [14]. By combining different patterns, developers can use pattern relationships and combine them to produce an effective design solution. This approach offers a solution and a tool to facilitate the integration and adaptation of patterns into tasks models, then the transition from tasks models to concrete interfaces. In their work, several patterns have been proposed to represent generic tasks models and techniques to transform them into a concrete interface. However, this tool uses dialog patterns in addition to tasks patterns and when the user wants to achieve a single goal, he has to take several actions and make several decisions consecutively. The manipulation of patterns is therefore fastidious [13]. In addition, to be interpreted by the tool, tasks patterns must be expressed in XIML exclusively. To use the tasks models described in CTT, the authors use Dialog graph editor [15] to convert CTT files into XIML files.

The PD-MBUI Framework [16] offers a very interesting approach for instantiating and adapting all models involved in the design process, not just task models. However, this approach is based on a library of formalized and predefined patterns which are not usable in all areas of design. The authors plan to extend the modeling concept into an integrated pattern environment which will support their tool and others based on generalized patterns which will be independent of any platform and programming language.

In [13], a pattern language was constructed for the Smart meeting room domain. This language can assist the designer when he is building models and thus improve the design process. Tasks patterns belonging to this language allow integration of task fragments as a design block within the user's tasks model. The whole methodology is adaptable to the design of similar patterns in other domains. In addition, the consideration of pre-conditions and post-conditions in the definition of visualization constraints related to tasks patterns provides a precision in the description of the latter. However, the lack of tools does not facilitate use of this language.

3   Problem Description

The description that is made of user activities on a control system, in task models is a good illustration of the complexity of these models. Previous work has shown that using task patterns is a good solution.

The simple graphical representation of the supervisory tasks pattern as proposed in [7], presents only the tasks tree, but no information on the decomposition of tasks, operators, implementers, etc. The TPML language and its variants make it possible to represent the patterns graphically and textually, but the instantiation of the patterns is done with specific tools that exploit these languages. A task model that integrates these patterns must be described either in CTT [17], or in XIML. Other tasks modeling languages are not currently taken into account. However, the use of notation such as CTT to structure the complex activity of operators in supervision is difficult [10]. It is preferable to be able to describe patterns in any tasks modeling language. Therefore, the first challenge identified is the definition of complex task patterns. This requires an approach to build the patterns that describe the tasks of an operator in front of a control system. This also requires identification and formalization of the so-called tasks.

On the other hand, current approaches that exploit tasks patterns can reduce the complexity of designing tasks models. These approaches offer tools based on the use of task patterns which are stored in a database, for the description of task models. The limits of these tools are at two levels. First, it's very difficult to imagine all the possible patterns for storing them into a Framework. In fact, patterns designed in a warehouse are not suitable for all areas. This problem was encountered when one was trying to build task models for a "smart environment" for example [13] and a new pattern language adapted to this domain had to be built.

Some of the work presented provides tools for moving from tasks patterns to tasks models. These tools are generally used by HMI designers because they contain concepts that are still complex for end users (expert users). Once the tasks models are achieved, they are simulated with the end users who have operational knowledge, to verify and validate them. During the simulation, detected errors can lead to important modifications in the models. These changes may affect design time of the control system. The second identified challenge is enabling end users to build complex tasks models by using tasks patterns.

4   Proposition

Our approach aims at facilitating the design of complex tasks models. The transition from generic tasks patterns to tasks models is a way to promote reusability and to facilitate the definition of tasks models. Figure 1 describes the process used to define the tasks pattern and to transform it into tasks models. This process is detailed into three phases. During the first phase, we formalize and design the supervision tasks pattern, by analyzing state of the art and functional specifications information. At this stage, we analyze the typical situations which may exist in different applications, and the information that could be used to determine the instances of the patterns. Then, we choose TPML [14] as the representation formalism. This choice allows HMI designers to understand the pattern. This formalism contains a modular section which enables to represent the pattern tree structure. For the graphical representation, we use this formalism through the K-MADe task modeling tool [18], to describe the supervision tasks pattern. The advantage of this representation is to be able to take into account information about tasks decomposition, tasks operators, tasks performers, preconditions, event, etc. at the pattern level.

It would be better to use the pattern directly without going through transforming processes from a pattern language to a task model representation language. However, these processes are unavoidable if we want to go from one task notation to another. In order to facilitate these processes, we formalize and define a generic meta-model so call ATS (Anaxagore Task Structure), which standardizes the information contained in the different tasks notations.

For implementing the model transformations, it is necessary to identify the notation in which the pattern is described. This identification enables to execute the appropriate transformation and to obtain a uniform tasks pattern.

The standardization of tasks patterns facilitates the transition to tasks models, through our developed tool. Our tool is based on the techniques of End User Development since it allows business expert to design tasks models without training.

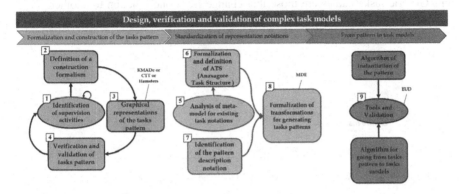

Fig. 1. Our approach

5   Implementation and Results

5.1   Pattern Construction Formalism

The description of the TPML formalism fields (Table 1) to adapt it to our context facilitates the design of the supervisory task pattern. In this formalism, classic fields such as Name, Problem, Context, Solution, and Relationship are described to help the designer understand the pattern. The graphic representation shows the tree structure of the pattern.

Table 1. Representation formalism of tasks patterns based on [19]

Field	Description
Name	Pattern name
Problem	Description of the problem solved by the pattern e.g. it allows designing task models for high-level function of control-command system
Context	Description of precondition that will be verified before applying the pattern
Solution	Description of the problem solution by presenting the procedure to follow
Relation	List of the pattern(s) to which this pattern is linked
Representation	Graphical representation of the solution

5.2   Graphical Representation of Tasks Pattern

We describe tasks pattern with K-MADe tool. The tasks patterns are generic tasks models. Unlike tasks models, task patterns must contain variables that can be adapted to different contexts of use, allowing it to be specialized in specific tasks models. For the pattern to be as generic and as flexible as possible, the description of the hierarchical structure of the tasks must include, at least, one variable (for example, instruction (n1) on Fig. 2). Variables contained in the pattern are tasks name and tasks descriptions. Generic tasks names are those that change from one function to another.

The complete tasks pattern for describing operators activities on a complex industrial system is presented in Annex 4 of [9].

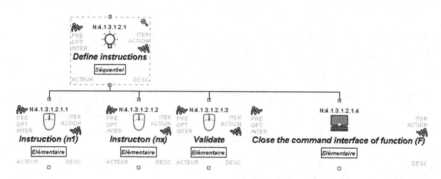

Fig. 2. Extract of tasks pattern

To make our approach generic, we used the PIM (Platform Independent Model) principle: the patterns whose descriptions contain variables can be specified with modeling tools other than K-MAD. HMI designers can represent these patterns with any task modeling notation (KMAD, CTT, Hamsters, etc.). However, to facilitate the exploitation of the patterns in our approach, we defined a phase to uniform the tasks representation notation.

5.3   Standardization of Tasks Modeling Language

To be independent from task modeling notations, an important step before getting tasks models is to transform the tasks pattern written in any task modeling notation into a platform-independent generic notation. For this, we have described a task meta-model (Fig. 3a) named ATS (Anaxagore Task Structure) that gathers all the information contained in all existing task notations.

The current created models transformations enable to convert the pattern described with K-MADe into a generic tasks pattern (Fig. 3b). These transformations will be further completed to take into account other task modeling notations, such as CTT and Hamsters. A new model transformation will only be created for using a new task notation, for the first time.

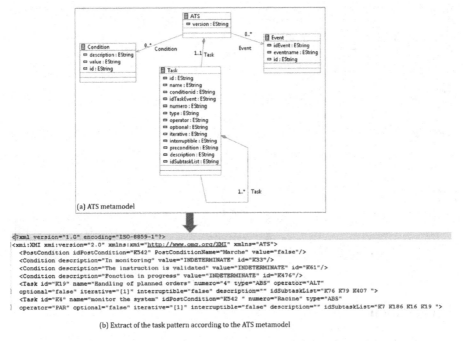

(a) ATS metamodel

```
<?xml version="1.0" encoding="ISO-8859-1"?>
<xmi:XMI xmi:version="2.0" xmlns:xmi="http://www.omg.org/XMI" xmlns="ATS">
    <PostCondition idPostCondition="K542" PostConditionName="Marche" value="false"/>
    <Condition description="In monitoring" value="INDETERMINATE" id="K33"/>
    <Condition description="The instruction is validated" value="INDETERMINATE" id="K61"/>
    <Condition description="Fonction in progress" value="INDETERMINATE" id="K476"/>
    <Task id="K19" name="Handling of planned orders" numero="4" type="ABS" operator="ALT"
    optional="false" iterative="[1]" interruptible="false" description="" idSubtaskList="K76 K79 K407 ">
    <Task id="K4" name="monitor the system" idPostCondition="K542 " numero="Racine" type="ABS"
    operator="PAR" optional="false" iterative="[1]" interruptible="false" description="" idSubtaskList="K7 K186 K16 K19 ">
```

(b) Extract of the task pattern according to the ATS metamodel

Fig. 3. Extract of the task pattern according to the ATS metamodel

5.4   From Task Pattern to Task Models

Once the generic tasks pattern is obtained, it can be reused for designing tasks models of most of control-command systems. Indeed, this pattern can be instantiated to be adapted to the specificities of the function of which one wants to describe the tasks model. The instantiation and adaptation are carried out with the Prototask Editor User tool (Prototask EU). The adaptation process is performed jointly with the simulation of tasks pattern. Different algorithms have been implemented to take into account all task model characteristics [9].

The developed interface gradually displays the tasks pattern loaded in the Prototask EU tool (Fig. 4), to enable the user to adapt it. In fact, the gradual display of tasks is carried out like task simulators. Simulation and adaptation are therefore closely linked.

The proposed interface is in four zones. The main one (frame 1 in Fig. 4) displays the tasks pattern gradually according to tasks hierarchical organization. It contains widgets for changing the name of an active task, changing the description of an active task, deleting an active task, or adding a basic subtask. Frame 2 displays the historic, as the user progresses into the task tree. Frame 3 groups all preconditions and post-conditions defined during the creation of tasks pattern. Finally, Frame 4 appears when the user clicks on the button "Ajouter une nouvelle tâche" (in English "Add a new task"). All required information needed to add a task must then be entered by the user.

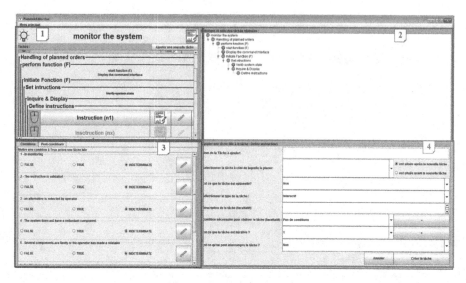

Fig. 4. Prototask Editor User

6   Validation

Our approach and the associated tool were evaluated in three different ways:

- By experimentation, to validate if our approach and tool are helpful to obtain complex tasks model of any control-command system. This validation is carried out by developer teams of our tool who have relied on specifications of seven high-level functions of a control-command system.
- By tasks specialists, who were consulted in unstructured interviews to validate if our approach and tool (Prototask EU) are relevant in designing of complex tasks models. We also validate if the usage of Prototask EU tool facilitates the description of complex tasks models in real project.
- By practitioners, first to validate if end user can use Prototask EU tool to describe tasks models; then to evaluate the actual usability of the interface.

6.1   Experimental Validation: Case Study

To validate our approach, we applied it for designing the tasks models of seven high-level functions of an industrial case study. The latter, is a system for the production, storage and distribution of fresh water, onboard a ship, called EdS (Eau douce Sanitaire in French, sanitary freshwater in English). Here we describe some steps of the adaptation process to present the different Prototask EU widgets and their usefulness. In Fig. 4, we simulated the tasks pattern up to the task "Fill instructions" to illustrate the adaptation to the tasks model design for the transfer function of EdS system.

The "pencil" icon (to edit) and "trash" icon (to delete) are active on achievable tasks. The pencil icon enables the user to modify the task name if needed. The "trash" icon enables the user to delete a task not required in the current tasks model. It is important to note that deleting a complex task removes all subtasks related to it.

The "paper pencil" icon enables the user to modify or enter a description for the active task. Adapting the pattern to obtain the tasks model of the transfer function exploits all widgets to modify preconditions, task names, and delete unnecessary tasks for this function. At the end of this operation, we obtain the tasks model (an extract of this model is shown in Fig. 5) which is verified and validated for the transfer function.

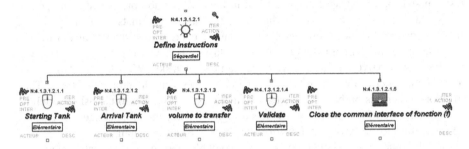

Fig. 5. Extract of the tasks model adapted for the transfer function

The same process of adaptation was followed to obtain all seven high-level tasks models of the EdS system in one hour and ten minutes instead of fifteen hours when using classical task modelling tool. The tasks models obtained this way contain required information for the specification of the EdS functions.

Our tool makes the task tree completely transparent to the expert user (system expert) who has no knowledge of task notations. It therefore gives the user the ability to customize the task pattern while simulating it, and to obtain checked and validated task models.

6.2   Tasks Specialist Validation

To evaluate the usefulness of our tool, we have asked two computer scientists (tasks specialists) for specifying two complex tasks models (composed of 64 tasks and 8 decomposition levels) with our tool and with an existing tool (K-MADe). Each tasks specialist had to specify the model with both tools. Time required for specification of the models with each tool was recorded, and the tasks specialists were asked to answer three questions about their overall impressions.

The results showed that the tasks specialists spent more time to specify the tasks models with the conventional tool (K-MADe) than with our tool (Table 2), five times more on average.

Table 2. Specification times with both tools

	K-MADe	Prototask Editor
Tasks model n°1	Tasks specialist 1: 00:46:24	Tasks specialist 1: 00:08:48
	Tasks specialist 2: 00:52:11	Tasks specialist 2: 00:15:01
Tasks model n°2	Tasks specialist 1: 01:12:17	Tasks specialist 1: 00:08:26
	Tasks specialist 2: 00:56:14	Tasks specialist 2: 00:16:31

They explained that the use of the pattern in our tool saved them a lot of time because they didn't need to start from the beginning for each model. With K-MADe, they had to rebuild the tree for each model and found it tedious. The integration of the simulation with the conception was also an advantage in terms of specification time. For them, the major advantage of K-MADe is the possibility to see and interact with the tree diagram. In fact, the absence of the diagram in our tool was disturbing for complex tasks models and tasks specialists felt lost in the specification process at some points.

Regarding tasks simulation in the tools, the tasks specialists explained that the frame showing the tasks during the simulation decreases systematically with the increase of the model complexity (number of tasks). Indeed, the number of displayed windows in K-MADe increases with the number of tasks. With Prototask EU (our tool), the number of lines (one for each task) increases with the number of tasks. They mentioned that this problem seems to be a major issue common to all tasks modelling tools in the case of complex tasks models designing. They therefore suggested it would be interesting to improve our tool for trying to solve this problem.

On the other hand, simulation is an unavoidable step in the verification and validation of task models. The tasks specialists appreciated the possibility of simulating the whole model in Prototask EU and not just a single scenario like with conventional task simulators such as K-MADe. For them, the complete simulation of the model offered by Prototask EU allows a considerable gain in terms of quality and completeness of the model. Indeed, they explained that our tool forces them to realize all the scenarios and thus to validate all the model and not only some parts. The tasks specialists mentioned that the Prototask EU does not allow them to deeply modify the tasks tree contrary to K-MADe. Indeed, Prototask EU tool allows the modification and addition of new single task. It does not enable to add a complex task with the choice of tasks operators, tasks types, etc. They suggested to add more functionalities (edition, insertion, deletion of operators) to Prototask EU tool for tasks specialists.

In summary, tasks specialists preferred to use Prototask EU for its ease of use, the completeness of its simulation and also the gain in quality (reduction of errors) and the time saving.

6.3   Practitioner Validation

To identify potential usability problems of our tool, we have solicited five plan designers for individual user tests sessions with our tool. They were men between 25 and 57 years old (32.8 years old on average). They didn't have previous experience in tasks models design and specification.

The user tests consisted of four steps. First, the context of the study was presented to the participants (objective of the study and of the tool, some technical notions about task models that were important for the understanding of the tool, and organization of the test session). Then, they were asked to use the tool to specify two simple tasks models (the first one was composed of four tasks, the second of six tasks, both models with two decomposition levels). The screen and the voice of the participants were recorded with their agreement during this step. After that, we asked them some questions to know their first impressions with the tool. Finally, they completed the Post

Study System Usability Questionnaire (PSSUQ) and a form with personal information such as age or profession.

These user tests identified some usability problems. We identify three minor problems. First, the function of creating a new task is misplaced in the tool. This creates confusion for some elements (for example, placing the new task against existing tasks) and mixes mandatory and optional fields in the same place, which unnecessarily complicates the creation process. We also observed problems of title and placement for some functionalities that were not clear for the participants (e.g. confusion between the description button and the modification button). Furthermore, they pointed out that the historic frame was not interactive. Indeed, they can only view their progression and they wished they could go back to previous tasks through it. We also identifies two major usability problems that we are going to present with further details.

The first one concerns the preconditions frame. During the test sessions, the participants had to activate a precondition for some of the tasks in the models before any modifications. We have reported the number of clicks participants have done for activating the precondition associated with the task they intend to specify, and compared it to the minimal number of clicks needed to activate a precondition with our tool (here, this number is two clicks). The Fig. 6 shows the results. The first time, the participants clicked 8.2 times on average (min = 5; max = 10), that represents 720% of additional clicks. Observation of the participants when they were using the tool showed that they haven't spontaneously thought to activate the precondition of the task the first time. In fact, they were clicking randomly on the interface and reported that they felt lost. Moreover, they had difficulties to identify which precondition is associated with which task. Indeed, four of the participants have first activated the wrong condition. However, for the other occurrences of this type of action, we observed a significant reduction of the number of clicks by the participants, which shows that they learnt how to do this type of action.

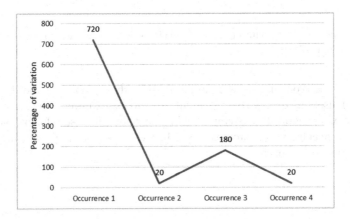

Fig. 6. Percentage of clicks number variations to activate the good precondition compared to minimal number of clicks needed

The second major problem concerns the mode of simulation, which consists in clicking on the task button to go to the next one. We observed that, the first time, participants made 3 clicks in average (min = 1; max = 7) while this action only requires one click the shortest way; that represents 200% of additional clicks (Fig. 7). Indeed, during the tests sessions, the participants didn't understand that they had to click on the task to simulate it and go to the next one. They found it by clicking at different places on the interface. The number of clicks decreased significantly the second time the action was required and reached the minimum number necessary for this action. We can conclude that, even if not very intuitive at the beginning, the minimum sequence of clicks quickly becomes automatic.

Nevertheless, the participants explained that, with this functioning, it is very easy to make an error. Some of them have expressed exasperation reactions after clicking involuntarily on the task button, and others were surprised by the appearance of the task when it is simulated (i.e. the task name is strikethrough). It seems that they thought they made a mistake while this was entirely correct.

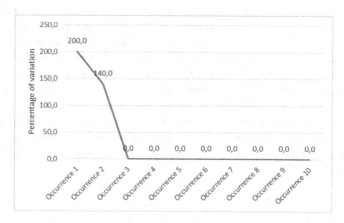

Fig. 7. Percentage of clicks number variations made to simulate the task compared to minimal number of clicks needed

Despite these problems, answers to the PSSUQ showed that our tool has a satisfying overall usability quality (Fig. 8). In this questionnaire, lower is the score, better is the quality of the tool. The overall usability and the other sub-dimensions of the questionnaire average scores are comprised between two and three, which is significantly superior to the mean.

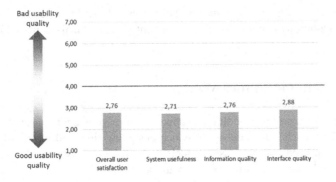

Fig. 8. PSSUQ dimensions average scores

6.4   Discussion

The validation of our tool showed that the presence of the pattern is an important advantage for specifying complex tasks models. We have demonstrated through experimental validation the applicability and the utility of our tool for the specification of complex task models. This validation, carried out on an industrial study, made it possible to specify complex task models in less time than other conventional tools. However, the correction of complex errors detected during tasks patterns simulation or the addition of complex tasks to the tasks pattern or model leads to starting again at the design phase of the pattern and repeating some steps our approaches. This may delay the design of the control system. This problem was also pointed by tasks specialists during their validation. Indeed, they mentioned the limits of our tool since it does not allow them to add complex tasks tree with appropriate tasks operators.

Tasks specialists validation has also shown that our tool is a great help in ensuring quality when specifying complex task models. The simulation of the entire task tree ensures the completeness of the tests and thus guarantees the quality of the validation of the tasks models. Using pattern also reduces design errors and avoids repetitive creation steps for redundant tasks. Tasks specialists also appreciated the integration of simulation into the adaptation phase (design). For them, this avoids interface changes for designing and simulation of tasks models compared to conventional tools. Nevertheless, they explained that they need a tool which takes into account more tasks modeling features such as operators, types for designing complex tasks. The information collected from analysis of tasks specialists validation will be used to propose them another tool which takes into account these features since different end users do not have the same needs.

To take into account end users needs, we have carried out practitioner validation. This validation made it possible to check if users who are not tasks specialists can use the tool for designing their tasks models. The practitioners' validation showed that the usability quality of our tool is satisfying. This is because the participants learned quickly when using the interface for the first time (designing the first task template). The design of the second task model was therefore quick since they understood the operation of the interface. The participants declared that the interface remains a tool of work which they must understand but after the first use it becomes easy. The usability problems detected were identified during the first use of the interface. The information from this validation will be used to improve the interface and make it more intuitive for the user.

7 Conclusion and Future Works

The presented work provides additional support over existing approaches for designing complex tasks models. Our goal is to reduce designing time and effort while getting verified and validated complex tasks models through an interface which can easily be used by our end users, i.e. non-tasks specialists.

The formalization, construction and use of tasks patterns have enabled us to solve the complexity and diversity problems that are increasing in the description of industrial system tasks models. Indeed, the identification of the structure of the supervisory tasks, based on state of the art and real design projects, led to the construction of a pattern which regroups the operator activities in a control room in a generic way.

The use of proven software for tasks modeling (K-MADe) to design tasks pattern by leaning on the TPML, enabled a better description of these patterns. The implementation of model transformations enables to overcome the constraints related to the choice of task notation. With our approach, the pattern can be designed with any task notation. This step may require large model transformations, but these transformations are only implemented when using a new task notation for the first time.

The implementation of Prototask Editor User tool to support our approach enables system experts (an expert user who are not task specialists) to read and adapt the tasks pattern for getting different tasks models.

The three types of validation carried out demonstrated the usefulness of our approach and the usability of the developed tool. Experimental validation enabled us to get seven complex tasks models of EdS system functions, in one hour and ten minutes instead of fifteen hours when using classical task modeling tool. In addition, our approach can be used in the design of new control-command systems.

Tasks specialist validation has highlighted the benefits of our approach for specifying complex task models. The time required for adaptation is five times less on our tool than on traditional tools. The accuracy and quality of the specified models are also improved by our tool which allows the simulation of the whole model and not only some scenarios. However, tasks specialists have brought out the need for more complex modifications in tasks patterns. Today, to widely modify tasks pattern, tasks specialists need to go back to their task notation tool (e.g. K-MADe), validate a new tasks pattern, and repeat the model transformation phase before using our tool.

Practitioners' validation showed that the usability quality of our tool is satisfying but can be improved to be more intuitive for the users.

In future work, we will solve the various usability problems of our tool and we will propose a tool for tasks specialists to enable them to widely modify task pattern and task models.

Acknowledgements. We are grateful to Line Poinel for her help.

References

1. Lachaume, T., Guittet, L., Girard, P., Fousse, A.: Task model simulators: a review. J. d'Ineraction Pers. **3** (2014)
2. Lewandowski, A., Bourguin, G., Tarby, J.-C.: De l'Orienté Objet à l'Orienté Tâches – Des modèles embarqués pour l' intégration et le traçage d'un nouveau type de composants. Rev. d'Interaction Homme-Machine **8**, 1–33 (2007)
3. Normand, V.: Le modèle SIROCO: de la spécification conceptuelle des interfaces utilisateur à leur réalisation. Joseph-Fourier - Grenoble I (1992)
4. Breedvelt-schouten, I.M., Paternò, F., Severijns, C.: Reusable structures in task models. Des. Specif. Verif. Interact. Syst. **97**, 225–239 (1997)
5. Thomas, L., Patrick, G., Laurent, G., Allan, F.: ProtoTask, new task model simulator. In: Winckler, M., Forbrig, P., Bernhaupt, R. (eds.) HCSE 2012. LNCS, vol. 7623, pp. 323–330. Springer, Heidelberg (2012). https://doi.org/10.1007/978-3-642-34347-6_24
6. AFNOR X50-151: Management par la valeur et ses outils, analyse fonctionnelle, analyse de la valeur, conception a objectif designe. French National Standards, Ed.
7. Bovell, C.R., Carter, R.J., Beck, M.G.: Nuclear power plant control room operator control and monitoring tasks. Oak Ridge, TN, July 1998
8. Kluge, A.: Controlling complex technical systems: the control room operator's tasks in process industries. In: The Acquisition of Knowledge and Skills for Taskwork and Teamwork to Control Complex Technical Systems, pp. 11–47. Springer, Dordrecht (2014). https://doi.org/10.1007/978-94-007-5049-4_2
9. Goubali, O.: Apport des techniques de programmation par démonstration dans une démarche de génération automatique d'applicatifs de Contrôle-Commande. ENSMA (2017)
10. Martinie, C.: Une approche à base de modèles synergiques pour la prise en compte simultanée de l'utilisabilité, la fiabilité et l'opérabilité des systèmes interactifs critiques. université de Toulouse (2011)
11. Bayle, E., et al.: Putting it all together: pattern languages for interaction design. A CHI 97 workshop. In: CHI 1997 Workshop, vol. 30, no. 1, pp. 17–23 (1998)
12. Granlund, Å., Lafrenière, D., Carr, D.A.: A pattern-supported approach to the user interface design process. In: HCI International 2001 9th International Conference on Human-Computer Interaction, vol. 1, pp. 282–286 (2001)
13. Seffah, A.: Patterns of HCI Design and HCI Design of Patterns: Bridging HCI Design and Model-Driven Software Engineering. HIS. Springer, Cham (2015). https://doi.org/10.1007/978-3-319-15687-3
14. Gaffar, A., Sinnig, D., Seffah, A., Forbrig, P.: Modeling patterns for task models. In: Proceedings of the 3rd Annual Conference on Task Models and Diagrams, vol. 2, no. 1, pp. 99–104 (2004)
15. Wolff, A., Forbrig, P., Dittmar, A., Reichart, D.: Linking GUI elements to tasks - supporting an evolutionary design process. In: 4th International Workshop on Task Models and Diagrams, pp. 27–34 (2005)
16. Radeke, F., Forbrig, P., Seffah, A., Sinnig, D.: PIM tool: support for pattern-driven and model-based UI development. In: Coninx, K., Luyten, K., Schneider, K.A. (eds.) TAMODIA 2006. LNCS, vol. 4385, pp. 82–96. Springer, Heidelberg (2007). https://doi.org/10.1007/978-3-540-70816-2_7

17. Paterno, F., Mancini, C., Meniconi, S.: ConcurTaskTrees: a diagrammatic notation for specifying task models. In: Howard, S., Hammond, J., Lindgaard, G. (eds.) Human-Computer Interaction INTERACT 1997. ITIFIP, pp. 362–369. Springer, Boston, MA (1997). https://doi.org/10.1007/978-0-387-35175-9_58
18. Baron, M., Lucquiaud, V., Autard, D., Scapin, D.L.: K-MADe: un environnement pour le noyau du modèle de description de l'activité. In: IHM 2006, vol. 133, pp. 287–288 (2006)
19. Sinnig, D.: The complicity of patterns and model-based UI development. Concordia, Montreal, Quebec, Canada (2004)

Redefinition of Benefits of Inconvenience

Toshihiro Hiraoka[1,2(✉)] and Hiroshi Kawakami[1,2]

[1] Institutes of Innovation for Future Society, Nagoya University,
Furo-cho, Chikusa-ku, Nagoya 4648601, Japan
`toshihiro.hiraoka@mirai.nagoya-u.ac.jp`
[2] Unit of Design, Kyoto University,
Yoshida-honmachi, Sakyo-ku, Kyoto 6068501, Japan
`kawakami@design.kyoto-u.ac.jp`
`https://sites.google.com/site/toshihirohiraoka/`
`http://www.design.kyoto-u.ac.jp/members/kawakami/`

Abstract. A new design methodology for a human-machine system, which is called *Benefits of Inconvenience (BI)*, has attracted lots of attention, especially from the people who worry about the harmful effects of too convenient products and systems. Nevertheless, the definitions of *"inconvenience"* and *"benefits"* of inconvenience differ not only among the researchers and the general public but also among the researchers. Therefore, the present manuscript clarifies the reasons why the misunderstandings of the above-mentioned definitions occur, and it redefines the BI by separation of effort and benefits into two types; objective ones and subjective ones. Moreover, the present manuscript analyzes some BI examples from the viewpoint of the new BI definition.

Keywords: Benefits of inconvenience ·
Design guidelines for human-machine systems · Redefinition ·
Objective and subjective effort · Objective and subjective benefits ·
Cognitive disuse atrophy

1 Introduction

The previous study [1] named the utilities obtained from inconvenience as "Benefits of Inconvenience (BI[1])", and also defined a system that provides BI to users as a BI system. We proposed design guidelines for the BI and support tools for designing of the BI system [2,3]. By using the guidelines and the tools, some BI researchers perform a field-based learning (FBL) or/and a problem-based learning (PBL) under the theme of designing the BI system. At the beginning of FBL/PBL, they explain the definition of the BI with plain expressions in order to promote easy understandings by the participants gathered not only from university students but also the general public. However, the participants' understandings of the BI are sometimes different from the original definition proposed by the BI researchers. This seems to be due to the fact that the definition of "inconvenience" in the BI is just a little part of conventional meanings commonly used in the Japanese general public.

---

[1] Please note that the BI is not "Basic Income" in this manuscript.

© Springer Nature Switzerland AG 2019
M. Kurosu (Ed.): HCII 2019, LNCS 11566, pp. 131–144, 2019.
https://doi.org/10.1007/978-3-030-22646-6_10

Furthermore, the differences in the understandings of the BI definition exist not only among the BI researchers and the general public but also among the BI researchers. Hence, this study provides a redefinition of the BI in order to clear up the misunderstandings, especially among the BI researchers.

The present section described the background and purposes of this study. Section 2 explains conventional definitions of inconvenience and the BI in the general public and the past BI researches. Section 3 discusses misunderstandings of the BI, and therefore Sect. 4 proposes the redefinition of the BI. Section 5 shows six different types of the BI definition based on the combinations of the BI elements, and also analyzes the BI examples from the viewpoint of the combinations of the BI elements. Finally, Sect. 6 mentions some concluding remarks and future works.

2   Conventional Definition

2.1   Conventional Meaning of Convenience and Inconvenience

A Cambridge Dictionary [4] explains meanings of "*convenient*" as follows:

- suitable for your purposes and needs and causing the least difficulty. Ex.: *a bike's a very convenient way of getting around.*
- near or easy to get to or use. Ex.: *a very convenient bus service.*

The meanings of convenient in Japanese dictionary are almost the same as the above definitions. And a meaning of "*convenience*" is described as

- the state of being convenient.

On the other hand, a meaning of "*inconvenient*" is described as

- causing problems or difficulties. Ex.: *It will be very inconvenient for me to have no car.*

And a meaning of "*inconvenience*" is described as

- a state or an example of problems or trouble, often causing a delay or loss of comfort.

Consequently, the word "*inconvenience*" has negative meanings implicitly in general meaning.

2.2   Definitions of Convenience and Inconvenience for Former BI Researches

In the previous BI researches, convenient and inconvenient have been originally defined as follows [1]:

- **Convenient**: Saving labor to attain a specific task.

- **Inconvenient**: Not convenient. To require labor in order to attain a specific task.

The labor[2] can be classified into two types; physical one and mental one. The physical labor requires physical body movement, and the mental labor requires thinking with consuming mental resources. Comparison of this definition with the above-mentioned conventional definition found that the definition of *"inconvenience"* in the previous BI researches is narrower than that used commonly in our daily life. The definition gap can be thought to be one of the causes to produce misunderstandings of the BI.

2.3   Former Defenition of BI

Four Types of Systems. Figure 1 shows that an X-axis represents Inconvenience/Convenience and a Y-axis represents Harms/Benefits. The combination of the two axes yields four types of systems [2]; *Harms of Inconvenience, Benefits of Inconvenience, Harms of Convenience, and Benefits of Convenience.*

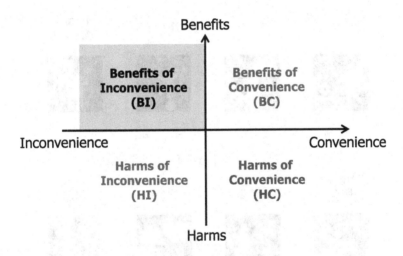

Fig. 1. Former definition of the BI based on two-axes

From the viewpoint of a human-machine system design, the harms of inconvenience (HI) system is obviously considered out of the question and the benefits of convenience (BC) system is the best for users if possible. Here, let us consider the harms of convenience (HC) system. It is widely known that the human being has developed plenty of convenient systems which can reduce user's labor

---

[2] The meanings of *"labor"* or *"inconvenience"* are almost same as *"effort"* in the present manuscript. Hence, a redefinition of the BI in Sect. 4 uses *"effort"*.

and therefore the tasks become easy to be accomplished efficiently. On the other hand, the HC systems have negative aspects such as cognitive disuse atrophy [5,6], as mentioned-below. It means that convenience does not always enrich our lives. Accordingly, in order to solve the problems of the HC, we redesign the HC system by intentional additions of certain kinds of "*inconvenience*". The redesigned system is called the BI system in which the users can take more effort to achieve the tasks, and therefore they can obtain benefits.

Two Types of Benefits. Based on the definition of inconvenience as mentioned in Sect. 2.2, the BI means the utilities derived from inconvenient. The BI researches mentioned that the benefits, which are equivalent to the utilities, include objective ones and subjective ones. The previous studies [2,3] proposed eight types of "*benefit cards*" as shown in Fig. 2, and they can be separated into the two types of benefits as follows:

Fig. 2. Eight types of benefit cards (six objective benefit cards and two subjective benefit cards)

Objective benefits: "enhancing awareness", "devising ways", "improvement", "system comprehension", "preventing loss of skill", and "encouraging initiative".

Subjective benefits: "feelings of relaxation and trust", and "personalization".

In addition to the two subjective benefits as shown in the benefit cards, three types of subjective benefits such as "self-affirmation", "motivation", and "delight" also exist.

Cognitive Disuse Atrophy. The objective benefit "preventing loss of skill" is intimately related to cognitive disuse atrophy [5,6]. As it is generally known, body sites tend to atrophy if they are not used, and some researchers have pointed out that the same phenomena can happen for human cognitive functions. Not to use his/her brain by using the tools is considered convenient in a short term, but it might bring potential risk to decrease the capability of think in the longer term. For example, the people who usually use a car navigation system tend not to memorize routes, and also the people who do not write characters manually because of the usage of a personal computer or a smartphone will become difficult to remember and write characters. The phenomenon will happen especially in the case of Kanji characters.

3 Misunderstandings of BI

Misunderstandings with respect to the BI can be summarized into the following three types: misunderstandings of "inconvenience", misunderstandings of "benefits" of inconvenience, and ideological misunderstandings.

3.1 Misunderstandings of "Inconvenience"

As mentioned above, the definition of "inconvenience" in the previous BI researches is narrower than that in the general public. The definition in the BI researches means that it takes more effort to achieve tasks, that is, it takes time and labor. Nevertheless, many people tend to consider "inconvenience" just as "unsuitable thing/event for his/her purposes" or "useless thing/event". The meaning gap might produce the misunderstandings of the BI among the BI researchers and the general public.

3.2 Misunderstandings of "Benefits" of Inconvenience

Not all the utilities of inconvenient systems become "Benefits of Inconvenience". Some users incorrectly recognize 'the inconvenience which has no correlation with user effort' as BI. For example, the benefits which the user obtains because of others' inconvenience are not BI. The compromise to accept inconvenience where the user must enter passwords for security reason is also not BI.

As shown in Sect. 2.3, there are two types of benefits in the BI; objective benefits and subjective benefits. Nevertheless, in the past BI researches, we have not referred whether one of them should be acquired or both benefits are necessary.

3.3 Ideological Misunderstandings

People who have the ideology to criticize modern civilization sometime borrow the concept of BI in order to justify their ideology. They tend to misunderstand the BI researches as a nostalgic design theory, but it is completely wrong. We think that we should better analyze past events/things which brought BI to users, although the concept of BI is not a nostalgia where people yearn to go back to good old days.

One of the goals in the BI researches is an attempt to recover the lost benefits because of no room for users to make effort, by redesign the system to allow users to lavish labors.

4   Redefinition of BI

4.1   Detailed Definition of BI Based on Five BI Elements

The present section proposes the redefinition of the BI. The right part of Fig. 3 describes a main part to regulate the definition of the BI, and it shows that the present study classifies effort and benefits from the viewpoint of objective or subjective. The right part consists of five elements; objective effort, subjective effort, results of effort (=accomplishment of main task), objective benefits (=accomplishment of sub task, improvement of skill, etc.), and subjective benefits.

The left part of Fig. 3 describes objective and subjective cues which are design factors for the BI system. The users can be encouraged to make objective efforts effectively when the cues are well-designed.

4.2   Process to Obtain BI

Here, let us explain the process where the user obtains the BI by his/her effort on the assumption that he/she has the main task to accomplish.

Step 1: Against the target system, the user moves his/her body sites or uses his/her brain. At that time, if the effort increases compared to the case when the user deals with other systems, it means that it is defined as "inconvenient" relatively.

Step 2: The user accomplishes the main task by his/her effort.

Step 3: The user acquires objective benefits such as "improvement of his/her skill" and "enhancing awareness" other than the accomplishment of the main task. The benefits are just secondary.

Step 4: The user recognizes the fact that he/she took objective effort at Step 2.

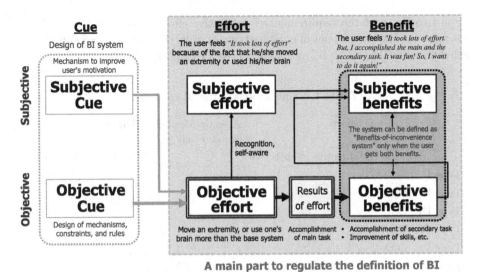

Fig. 3. Redefinition of Benefits of Inconvenience (BI)

Step 5: The user recognizes his/her effort, and then he/she recognizes that he/she acquired the objective benefits secondarily in addition to the accomplishment of the main task. Accordingly, he/she acquires subjective benefits such as "delightful!", "fun!", and "want to do/use more!".

In this process, it is assumed that the user obtains the "Benefits of Inconvenience" only when the user obtains both of the objective benefits at Step 3 and the subjective benefits at Step 5.

5   Analysis of BI Examples

The process described in Sect. 4 is the strictest redefinition of the BI, but some BI researchers advocate that the definition is too narrow. In other words, the BI researchers have to discuss how many of the five elements must be required for the establishment of the BI.

The main part of regulate the definition of the BI consists of five elements; objective effort, subjective effort, results of effort (=accomplishment of the main task), objective benefits (=accomplishment of sub task, improvement of skill, etc.), and subjective benefits.

It is no wonder that the minimum requirement for establishment of the BI is to satisfy the following two elements; the objective effort and the accomplishment of the main task. Consequently, the present section discusses six types of the BI based on the combinations of three BI elements; subjective effort, objective benefits, and subjective benefits. Table 1 describes the six types of BI.

Type I to III meet the requirement of subjective effort, and Type IV to VI do not meet it. The three types of combinations of objective benefits and subjective benefits define Type I to III and Type IV to VI respectively.

Table 1. Combinations of the BI elements

	Effort		Accomplishment of main-task	Benefits	
	Objective	Subjective		Objective	Subjective
Type I: OS-OS	✓	✓	✓	✓	✓
Type II: OS-O	✓	✓	✓	✓	
Type III: OS-S	✓	✓	✓		✓
Type IV: O-OS	✓		✓	✓	✓
Type V: O-O	✓		✓	✓	
Type VI: O-S	✓		✓		✓

5.1   Type I: OS-OS

Type I includes all of the five constituent elements in the redefinition of the BI, and it is expressed by 'OS-OS' which means both efforts and both benefits are required. This means that the Type I is the strictest definition of the BI.

We found that there are lots of BI examples in this Type I. The present subsection introduces two representative examples such as a COGY and an SDES (Fig. 4 (a), (b)).

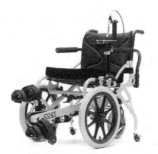
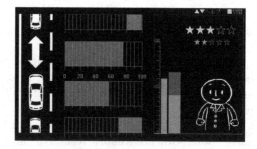

(a) COGY [7]   (b) SDES (Safe Driving Evaluation System) [8]

Fig. 4. Examples of Type I (OS-OS) BI system

COGY. Figure 4(a) is a wheelchair, called COGY [7]. It is designed specially for the half-paralyzed people who can move left or right leg. This study considers an electric wheelchair or an autonomous wheelchair as the HC (Harms of Convenience) system, against the COGY as the BI system. The user moves the COGY by pedaling with his/her healthy leg, and therefore the disabled leg is moved passively. The pedaling is an objective effort for the user, and the user recognizes that the user took lots of effort. By his/her effort, the user can move by using the COGY. Moreover, the user becomes to move faster according to the proficiency in how to use the COGY. It means that the main task 'moving' was accomplished by his/her effort. In addition to the accomplishment of the main task, the disabled leg can be recovered by using the COGY, because the usage of the COGY can be considered as not only physical rehabilitation but also rehabilitation for brain function. It is equivalent to the interpretation that the user secondarily acquires objective benefits which are different from the accomplishment of the main task. Consequently, the user will feel that the moving with the COGY is lots of fun although the pedaling only by the healthy leg is not easy. This is an example of the subjective benefits which the user obtains.

SDES (Safe Driving Evaluation System). Figure 4(b) shows a visual interface of a safe driving evaluation system (SDES) proposed in the previous study [8]. The SDES does not assist in driving operation by controls of vehicle motion. It just provides the scores of the drivers' safe driving behavior to encourage the drivers to perform safe driving spontaneously. The SDES can be considered as the BI system compared to the automated driving system or the advanced driver-assistance systems such as an adaptive cruise control (ACC) or a lane-keeping assist system (LKAS). When the driver uses the SDES, the main task is to perform safe driving and one of the secondary tasks is to improve his/her driving skill. And, the driver using the SDES might feel that the manual safe driving is enjoyable although it requires more time and effort, compared to the ACC and the LKAS which is considered as the HC system.

Other BI Examples of Type I. Not only the above-mentioned examples, but there are also various BI systems of the Type I. The following examples are parts of them;

- a cellular manufacturing system. (↔ a line production system.)
- a mountain climbing by his/her own foot. (↔ by using a ropeway gondola, a helicopter.)
- a rehabilitation house for the elderly people called '*Yume-no-Mizuumi Mura*', where there are many types of physical and cognitive barriers and the residents must make their daily plan and perform all aspects of their daily life by themselves. (↔ a barrier-free rehabilitation house for the elderly people where care workers make all of the care programs for the residents.)

5.2   Type II: OS-O

Unlike the Type I mentioned above, the Type II does not include subjective benefits. It means that the Type II system does not give the user positive feelings such as delight, fun, and so on but provides just secondary objective benefits.

(a) Degrading navigation system (left: a normal map without degradation which is displayed at the beginning, right: a map where the driven route was whitened.)

(b) Examples of correctly shaped characters (left) and incorrectly shaped characters (right) used in G-IM (Gestalt Imprinting Method) [9]

Fig. 5. Examples of Type-2 (OS-O) BI system

Degrading Navigation System. The driver usually uses a car navigation system when he/she goes to an inexperienced destination. The driver can certainly arrive at the destination by following the navigation guidance, however, in that case, there is a harmful effect that they do not memorize the route. It is thought to be one of the cognitive disuse atrophies and then the conventional car navigation system can be considered the HC system. Therefore, in order to solve this problem, Kitagawa et al. proposed '*a degrading navigation system*' [10] which has the following features; (1) it displays a normal map at the beginning, and (2) the system degrades the map by whitening of the driven route inversely proportional to the moving speed (Fig. 5(a)). Field experiments showed that a more detailed cognitive map is formed when using the degrading navigation system compared to when using the conventional navigation system whose map is not degraded. The user of the degrading navigation system can obtain secondary benefits of forming a detailed cognitive map in his/her brain while he/she accomplishes the main task of arriving at the destination. The user will recognize that it takes more time and effort when using the degrading navigation than when he/she follows voice guidance and visual guidance on a navigation screen. In other words, the BI elements other than the subjective benefits are satisfied when using the degrading navigation system.

G-IM (Gestalt Imprinting Method). As a consequence of an increase in opportunity to type the sentences by using a personal computer and a smartphone, the number of Japanese people and Chinese people who cannot recall Kanji character shapes increases and it becomes one of the social problems. The phenomenon is called '*Character amnesia*', and it is considered one of the cognitive disuse atrophy. In order to solve the problem, Nishimoto et al. [9] developed a novel input method called G-IM (Gestalt Imprinting Method) for a personal computer. The system displays incorrect character shapes (Fig. 5(b)). It forces users to pay close attention to the character shapes because the document cannot be saved when the incorrect characters exist in it. Therefore, the system strengthens retention and recall of the character shapes. The experiments confirmed that the G-IM improves the retention and recall of the character shapes as compared to the conventional input method. Although the G-IM improves the ability to recall and write Kanji characters, the user will not want to use the G-IM more frequently because the confirmation of character shape is thought to be burdensome. It means that the G-IM user will not gain the subjective benefits.

5.3 Type III: OS-S

In the case when using the Type III system, the main task is accomplished by the user's effort, and the user acquires only the subjective benefits while he/she does not obtain the objective benefits. The followings are representative examples of Type III; (1) hobbies (a TV game, a puzzle, a Tamagotchi, construction of a plastic model, etc.), (2) sports not for the purpose of improving the health, and (3) a system which can give Eureka effect to the user.

5.4 Type IV: O-OS

The main task is accomplished by using the Type IV system and the user acquires the secondary objective benefits, although he/she does not recognize that it took time and effort. A silver film camera is a representative example of the Type IV system. Here, we assume that a digital camera is defined as the target system because it can save too many photos and the user can confirm the photo just after taking a picture. The user presses the shutter button with considering when and what he/she takes a photo under a constraint of the number of films. The main task is to take photos by using all of the films. The secondary objective benefit is to remain photos in the users' memory, and the subjective benefit is to have an emotional attachment to the photos.

5.5   Type V: O-O

The user accomplishes the main task by his/her effort and obtains the secondary objective benefits. However, he/she does not recognize that it took time and effort and does not obtain the subjective benefits such as delight. The representative Type V systems are experienced skills such as a behavior of a Japanese lady who makes an original duster by manual stitching and as machining of a skilled worker in a small factory. The comparisons are to use a sewing machine or purchase of a ready-made duster and to use NC machine tools.

The skilled person moves his/her hands unconsciously and therefore accomplishes the main task. The secondary objective benefits include making things that cannot be processed by machines, being able to suppress the decline in operating skills of the machine tools and so on.

IDAF-drum. Nishimoto et al. [11] proposed a training system of the extensor muscles in everyday drum practice (Fig. 6), and it is called "iDAF-drum". The "iDAF" means that an acronym of "insignificantly Delayed Auditory Feedback". The user cannot perceive the slight delay. The experimental results showed that the iDAF-drum users raised the drumsticks higher than usual without cognition of the delay and an unusual feeling. After the training using the iDAF-drum, the user could play the drum better than before the training. However, the user does not feel delightful because he/she does not recognize the delayed auditory feedback and the improvement of the drumming skill.

5.6   Type VI: O-S

The user using the Type VI system accomplishes the main task by his/her effort. He/she also obtains the subjective benefits. On the other hand, he/she does not obtain the secondary objective benefits and also does not recognize that he/she took time and effort.

Talking-Ally. Talking-Ally [12,13] is a communication robot which has an utterance generation mechanism by considering the state of the listener and by using mutual interactive adjustments (Fig. 7). The utterance of the Talking-Ally is disfluent so that the listener pay more attention to hear the utterance. Therefore, the interaction between the robot and the user becomes well-organized and

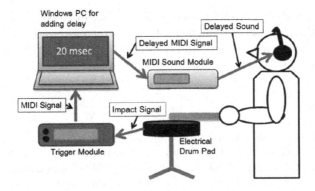

Fig. 6. Example of Type-5 (O-O) BI system (iDAF-drum) [11]

the user feels that the interaction is delightful. The main task is communication between the user and the robot, and the subjective benefits are to have an emotional attachment to the robot and to feel that the interaction is joyful.

Fig. 7. Example of Type-6 (O-S) BI system (Talking-Ally) [12]

6   Conclusions

The present manuscript redefined the benefits of inconvenience (BI) based on the five elements; objective effort, subjective effort, the accomplishment of the main task, objective benefits, and subjective benefits. Next, it described a process that the user obtains the BI when using the BI system. In addition to the redefinition, we defined the six different types of BI by combinations of four elements with respect to effort and benefits.

The BI researchers have to discuss which types can be considered as the BI as for Type II to Type VI, although the Type I is the narrowest definition of the BI. Moreover, in the near future, we try to classify all of the BI examples which we already have into the six types.

References

1. Kawakami, H.: Further benefit of a kind of inconvenience for social information systems. In: Kurosu, M. (ed.) HCI 2013. LNCS, vol. 8006, pp. 301–306. Springer, Heidelberg (2013). https://doi.org/10.1007/978-3-642-39265-8_33
2. Hasebe, Y., Kawakami, H., Hiraoka, T., Naito, K.: Card-type tool to support divergent thinking for embodying benefits of inconvenience. Web Intell. **13**(2), 93–102 (2015)
3. Hasebe, Y., Kawakami, H., Hiraoka, T., Nozaki, K.: Guidelines of system design for embodying benefits of inconvenience. SICE J. Control Meas. Syst. Integr. (JCMSI) **8**(1), 2–6 (2015)
4. Cambridge Dictionary. https://dictionary.cambridge.org/
5. Miwa, K., Terai, H.: Theoretical investigation on disuse atrophy resulting from computer support for cognitive tasks. In: Harris, D. (ed.) EPCE 2014. LNCS (LNAI), vol. 8532, pp. 244–254. Springer, Cham (2014). https://doi.org/10.1007/978-3-319-07515-0_25
6. Miwa, K., Kojima, K., Terai, H.: An experimental investigation on learning activities inhibition hypothesis in cognitive disuse atrophy. In: Proceedings of the 7th International Conference on Advanced Cognitive Technologies and Applications, pp. 66–71 (2015)
7. COGY: The Wheelchair for those who still believe. https://cogycogy.com/en/
8. Hiraoka, T., Nozaki, K., Takada, S., Kawakami, H.: Safe driving evaluation system to enhance motivation for safe driving. In: Proceedings of the 3rd International Symposium on Future Active Safety Technology towards Zero Accidents (FAST-zero 2015), pp. 613–620 (2015)
9. Nishimoto, K., Wei, J.: G-IM: an input method of Chinese characters for character amnesia prevention. In: Proceedings of The Eighth International Conference on Advances in Computer-Human Interactions (ACHI2015), pp. 118–124 (2015)
10. Kitagawa, H., Kawakami, H., Katai, O.: Degrading navigation system as an explanatory example of "benefits of inconvenience". In: Proceedings of SICE Annual Conference 2010, FA12-5 (2010)
11. Nishimoto, K., Ikenoue, A., Unoki, M.: iDAF-drum: supporting practice of drumstick control by exploiting insignificantly delayed auditory feedback. In: Kunifuji, S., Papadopoulos, G.A., Skulimowski, A.M.J., Kacprzyk, J. (eds.) Knowledge, Information and Creativity Support Systems. AISC, vol. 416, pp. 483–497. Springer, Cham (2016). https://doi.org/10.1007/978-3-319-27478-2_36
12. Matsushita, H., Kurata, Y., Silva, P., Okada, M.: Talking-Ally: what is the future of robot's utterance generation? In: Proceedings of the 24th IEEE International Symposium on Robot and Human Interactive Communication (RO-MAN), pp. 291–296 (2015)
13. Ohshima, N., Ohyama, Y., Odahara, Y., Silva, P., Okada, M.: Talking-Ally: the influence of robot utterance generation mechanism on hearer behaviors. Int. J. Soc. Robot. **7**(1), 51–62 (2015)

Examining Social Desirability Bias in Online and Offline Surveys

Aki Koivula[⊠], Pekka Räsänen, and Outi Sarpila

Economic Sociology, Department of Social Research,
University of Turku, Turku, Finland
akjeko@utu.fi

Abstract. This paper examines whether web-based survey responses differ from traditional mail-based questionnaire responses when examining attitudes towards sensitive issues in a mixed-mode survey. Our motivation for the study comes from social desirability bias, which is a generally discussed theme in social surveys. The data are derived from the Finnish section of the International Social Survey Program (ISSP) 2013 (n = 1,243), which applied both self-conducted mail survey and web survey data collection techniques. In the analysis, we utilize items concerning attitudes towards immigrants. We found that mail-questionnaire respondents tend to express more negative attitudes towards immigration than the web-questionnaire group. This is especially true when analyzing the survey items, which use negative connotations in the question formulation. The results also indicated that socio-demographic background had a significant impact on responses, but these factors did not explain the total variation between the two response groups. We discuss our findings in light of the popularity of web-surveys and their increased use in social sciences. We conclude our paper with a notion that the mixed-mode survey is a reliable method of data collection, especially after controlling for relevant background variables, and their interactions between the alternative response modes.

Keywords: Mixed-mode survey · Sensitive questions · Web survey · Mail survey

1 Introduction

In contemporary information societies, it is a well-known fact that survey researchers have met growing difficulties with traditional recruitment methods linked to rising data collection costs. Researchers have begun to look primarily to so-called mixed mode approaches in order to have representative response rates in collecting large-scale datasets. This so-called mixed mode data collection, which refers to a combination of two or more collection methods being offered for responding to a survey, has become more common in recent years. Web surveys and mail/web mixed-mode surveys, in particular, are increasing in prevalence. Thus, it is crucial to acknowledge whether data collected through different modes can actually be combined into one cross-sectional study [1, 2].

© Springer Nature Switzerland AG 2019
M. Kurosu (Ed.): HCII 2019, LNCS 11566, pp. 145–158, 2019.
https://doi.org/10.1007/978-3-030-22646-6_11

The use of mixed-mode survey design is based on the idea of the equivalence of data collection. This means that researchers who utilize mixed-mode surveys aim at combining data into one data matrix that can be analyzed. However, there are several threats related to the integrity of mixed-mode data. Researchers have noted that the use of web-based surveys is problematic in a number of ways. The primary problem relates to the selection of respondents when compared to traditional recruitment methods [3–5]. In a mixed-mode survey, it is likely that respondents' answers will vary according to response mode. This is not a problem if the differences are related to different demographic background characteristics of the respondents that can be controlled. However, if the response mode in itself (Internet vs. mail) leads to different response processes and, thus, has an effect on the responses, the problem of data integrity is real [6].

It has been argued that the risk of social desirability bias is lower in self-administered surveys compared to interviewer-administered surveys (for a review see [7–9]). As such, one of the main reasons to use self-administered, and not interviewer administered, mixed-mode surveys is to reduce social desirability bias [6]. Yet, little is known about the difference in prevalence of social desirability bias between mail respondents and web respondents in mail/web mixed-mode surveys.

In this paper, we analyze differences in responses to sensitive attitudinal questions between two modes of data collection. We ask whether attitudes toward immigration are different in a population-level survey between data collected via mail and data collected through the Internet. Our data are derived from the Finnish section of the International Social Survey Program (ISSP) 2013 (n = 1,243).

We assume that the chosen response mode indicates qualitative selection of respondents to some extent, especially in terms of digital lifestyle. On the contrary, choosing the paper questionnaire may itself be an indication of lacking digital skills. The possible differences potentially cause the findings to suffer from both coverage and measurement errors. For instance, if differences exist, then the prevalence of combined data collection may distort the data sets used in making sample-to-population generalizations in survey research. In addition, if there are biases in responses between the two response modes, it may challenge previously proposed results indicating that individuals from politically marginal groups are more open to express their views online than offline.

Finland provides an interesting research context, since the central population register allows for drawing reliable random samples of different population groups. Finland is also a leading information society, especially in terms of Internet penetration rates among citizens. In terms of practical implications, our findings demonstrate that the mode of response matters in population-level surveys. Our study also provides relevant discussion regarding recent research findings on socially and politically sensitive issues.

1.1 Online Surveys

Growing Internet access plays an important role in the development of social surveys. In the second decade of the 21st century, Internet penetration rates had exceeded 80% in the greater part of developed countries [10]. When people spend more time on the Internet, many important social phenomena exist in online platforms exclusively. Thus, a mixed mode approach is part of the solution to challenges arising from the use of new communication technology.

Due to changes in the population's ICT use-habits, efforts have been made to offer the opportunity for sampled respondents of traditional postal surveys to respond to surveys via the Internet. However, it is often in the researchers' best interest to utilize a mixed-mode survey design. From a purely cost effectiveness perspective, surveys conducted online seem to be an overwhelming favorite when compared to traditional data collection methods. When compared to traditional data collection methods, online surveys are, in principle, faster and cheaper to implement [11]. Furthermore, survey research is able to, at different stages, take advantage of combined data collection methods: in the recruitment of respondents, the actual data collection, recollection of responses, or, in several stages in research, in the next collection phase after the initial dunning for example [12].

It has been noted that the use of web-based surveys is problematic in a number of ways, with the primary problem being in the selection of respondents when compared to traditional methods [3]. From the perspective of data quality, this is a particular problem, because non-responses resulting from selection is difficult to correct with weighting, potentially causing the findings to suffer from coverage errors [4, 13].

In mixed-mode data collection conducted at a population level, online response is often treated as a supplementary data collection method, which reduces the risks associated with access to the network. On the other hand, the selection can be qualitative, which also poses challenges for mixed-mode data collection.

But how can the response mode affect answering qualitatively? It has been found that online respondents tend to be more skilled Internet users than those who choose an alternative response option [14]. Accordingly, it is possible that qualitative differences go back to differences in respondents' socio-demographic backgrounds. For example, research lead by Dillman [15] examined variances between different response methods. It was found that there were differences between the respondents of online and paper questionnaires according to socio-demographic profiles. However, the research did not find any connection between response modes when examining attitudinal level variables [15]. Rather, Mark Saunders [16] noted the connection between response methods and attitudinal variables in his examination of British public-sector workers. In a same-sized sample carried out at the same time in the survey, web-based respondents reported that they were more committed employees, had more confidence in the organization's leadership and received more support than those who responded with the paper survey [16].

However, neither Dillman's [15] nor Saunders' [16] research had the effects of standardised background variables nor was the interaction between response methods and background variables analysed. It is conceivable that the socio-demographic variety of web-based respondents indirectly influences the analytical methods variables' fluctuation. It is impossible to state unequivocally, for example, that the differences presented by Saunders [16] are actually due to professional status, which can increase online response probability compared to responding via the post.

Atkeson et al. [17] analysed mixed-mode data collection methods and the differences between web-based and paper respondents as well as the link between response methods to political behavior. The descriptive analysis of the data demonstrates that

Internet and paper respondents, to a certain extent, differ from each other on the basis of demographic factors. Paper respondents appear to belong to lower income groups, to be older and to have lesser education than Internet respondents. On the basis of preliminary analyses, response groups' political behaviour varied on several different levels. However, after controlling for socio-demographic factors, there were no differences found in political behaviour among the response groups [17].

The significance of response methods on the basis of age has also been researched with restricted data sets. For example, Sean McCabe [18] has, with the aid of combined data collection, surveyed alcohol use among American college students. Alcohol use did not systematically vary according to the response method, but the same demographic trends seen in other presented research results were observed. Internet respondents were slightly younger and more often male than paper respondents (ibid). Dana de Bernardo and Anna Curtis [19] reached the same results in their assessment of suitable response methods for those over 50 years old. On the basis of mixed-mode data collection, they found that Internet respondents were more educated, more well off and also slightly younger than paper respondents.

Similarly, in Finland, Koivula et al. [20] have compared characteristics of both mail and web respondents. In addition to a demographic comparison, they analyzed potential response effects on measurements used generally in well-being research. According to the results, the mode of response was still crucially associated with age. However, it was not strongly associated with the measures of subjective well-being after controlling for respondents' background.

A recent study by Kim et al. [1] suggest that in mail-web mixed mode surveys, more attention should be paid on the phenomenon called straightlining. Straigtlining refers to respondents' tendency to choose identical or nearly identical research options for all items in a question battery. Although Kim et al. did not find differences in straightlining behaviour between mail and web respondents in their study, mode effect on straightlining is a potential threat to data integrity and quality of mail/web mixed-mode surveys.

1.2   Social Desirability Bias

One could argue that the mode of response may have an effect on certain types of sensitive questions. More generally, sensitive questions, such as immigration attitudes, tend to lead to higher nonresponse rates and/or larger measurement errors in responses than questions on other topics. This is true especially when it comes to public opinions that relate to 'political correctness' or 'social desirability'.

Drawing valid survey data containing sensitive information dealing with respondents' private, political and illegal issues, is traditionally seen as a challenge in survey research [21, 22]. In general, sensitive questions tend to lead to higher nonresponse rates and/or larger measurement errors in responses than questions on other topics [23]. This is true, especially when it comes to public opinions that relate to 'social desirability'. Added to this, surveying some issues such as income level, religiosity, or sexual behaviors may be considered culturally too delicate, or even taboo. Respondents may also feel offended if their personal privacy is challenged by intrusive questions [24].

It is well known that the risk of social desirability bias is clearly higher in interview-administered than in self-administered surveys [7]. In line with this, Klausch et al. [2] concluded in their recent study that interview-administered survey modes (i.e. face-to-face/telephone) that include attitudinal rating scale questions should not be used in parallel with self-administered survey modes.

Nevertheless, the feeling of privacy might be context-dependent and relate to a sense of anonymity that can vary according to the research environment, i.e. the online vs. offline environment. Here, the advantages of online survey techniques can be considered useful. It has been observed that pen-and-paper and web-based surveys do not yield identical results, particularly when examining sensitive questionnaire items [25, 26]. Kays et al. [27], for example, found that respondents tend to be more likely to answer sensitive questions on the Internet compared to a pen-and-paper option. Web participants' feeling of anonymity likely plays a role here [5].

Differences can also result from the measurement errors when filling in the online questionnaires. Namely, it has been put forth that online surveys might be understood by participants in a different way than other methods used in conducting surveys [28]. In addition, it has been noted that online respondents more readily answer 'I don't know', as well as elicit more non-differentiation on rating scales [29, 30].

In this study, we focus on the contextual impact of outcome variables when comparing two modes of response. The aim of the analysis is to assess whether the response mode divides respondents along specific issues. We examine this issue with the aid of subjective questions regarding immigration. Immigration is commonly considered as a socially and politically sensitive topic in Western countries, since it connects easily with such historical events as colonialism and the holocaust, as well as contemporary racial tensions in many countries [21, 31, 32].

2   This Study

We assume that Internet respondents differ from paper respondents in terms of sensitive questions related to social desirability bias. In order to control for the sensitivity of the immigration question, we conduct different measures for negative and positive immigrant attitudes. The questions we use are sensitive in nature, as they can relate to crime or unemployment rates of immigrants. Therefore, we need to consider certain additional features to normal sources of reporting errors (e.g. misunderstanding the questions, lack of relevant information). Preceding research has also pointed out that under circumstances considered as sensitive, respondents simply do not wish to tell the truth.

H1: We hypothesize that postal mode will elicit stronger attitudes towards immigrants, especially when examining negatively formulated questions.

It has been suggested that socially desirable responses in surveys vary between economic and socio-demographic groups, in addition to variance linked to features of the data collection situation such as the degree of privacy [21]. While a smaller body of research has focused on the demographic factors behind response bias, the studies point to at least one consistent finding; namely, that educated and younger individuals tend to express less conservative attitudes than those with less education and lower economic position. For example, it has been noted that respondents with higher educational qualifications are more willing to give social approval to new political ideas while also tending to give less truthful responses concerning their own activities [33]. If there is a significant association between background variables and response mode, we can partially link response mode effects to respondents' qualitative selection in terms of differential Internet usage. Here, we need to also acknowledge that recent research has reported that there are still notable socio-economic differences in Internet access and use patterns [34, 35]. This also applies to experiences on the Internet, for instance in terms of how useful or harmful online material can be for users [36].

H2: We assume that the key background variables have a confounding effect on the detected associations between mode of response and attitudes towards immigration.

3   Research Design

3.1   Data

The data are derived from the Finnish section of the International Social Survey Programme (ISSP) 2013 (n = 1,243). A total of 2,500 participants aged 18–74 years were approached using a mixed mode collection by offering the opportunity to respond online instead of the paper form. Finland was the only participant country in which this kind of response mode option was applied in the ISSP 2013 data collection. Here, it is noteworthy that all respondents were contacted in a same way, by conventional mail, and given the opportunity to answer the questionnaire online [37].

The original sample was selected from the Central Register of Population using random sampling. The survey yielded a response rate of 48%. The final sample including a total of 1,208 observations consists of 695 web-responses and 513 mail-responses.

3.2   Variables

In the explorative analysis, we first focus on the variance of attitudinal variables according the response mode. We established two summed variables to measure attitudes towards immigration that is typically found to be sensitive to social desirability. The variables measure either positive or negative attitudes towards immigration. Given the fact that negative connotations in the attitudinal variables are less desirable than positive ones, our two measures enable us to control the sensitivity of questions dealing with immigration. Descriptive statistics of dependent variables is shown in Table 1.

Let us first examine negative expressions. The merged variable consists of three value-based questions, each of which presented a fairly negative tone. Initially, respondents were asked to choose their opinion from the 5-point Likert scale from strongly disagree to strongly agree. In addition, there were choice options for undecided respondents. Firstly, respondents were asked for their opinion on the statement "Immigrants increase crime rates". The second item refers to employment issues, "Immigrants take jobs away from people born in [Country]". The last item considers respondents' opinions regarding the effect of immigration on national culture, namely "Immigrants undermine culture".

Table 1. Descriptive statistics for dependent variables

	Obs.	Mean	SD	Range
Negative immigration attitudes (mean score variable)	*1,190*	*2.96*	*0.88*	*(1–5)*
Immigrants increase crime rates	1,143	3.45	1.02	(1–5)
Immigrants take jobs away from people born in [Country]	1,154	2.81	1.10	(1–5)
Immigrants undermine culture	1,127	2.62	1.01	(1–5)
Cronbach Alpha	0.77			
Positive immigration attitudes (mean score variable)	*1,180*	*2.89*	*0.86*	*(1–5)*
Immigrants generally good for economy	1,110	3.65	1.00	(1–5)
Immigrants bring new ideas and cultures	1,138	2.56	1.00	(1–5)
Legal immigrants should have same rights	1,125	2.66	1.05	(1–5)
Cronbach Alpha	0.71			

The second dimension was constructed on the basis of three items addressing immigration in a more positive way. Initially, they were assessed with a 5-point Likert-type scale, varying from strongly disagree to strongly agree. Here, the first item refers to economic issues, as respondents were asked to respond to the question "Immigrants are generally good for the economy". The second item assesses cultural issues, as "Immigrants bring new ideas and cultures". Finally, the last question concerns immigrants' equality with native citizens, as "Legal immigrants should have same rights".

We also controlled five independent variables: age, gender, education, economic activity and place of residence. The descriptive information of variables is shown in Table 2 by the response mode. Age was categorized into five groups: Under 30 years, 30–44 years, 45–54 years, 55–64 years and 65–74 years. The years from 18 to 30 are often referred to as early adulthood. The next three age groups can be defined as early middle age, middle age and late middle age respectively. Finally, people over 64 years of age are often characterized as the elderly, since the person is usually entitled to a pension after the age of 63 in Finland.

Table 2. Descriptive statistics for independent variables by response mode

	N	Mail%	Web%
Gender			
Male	599	41.1	58.9
Female	609	41.7	58.3
Age (used as continuous)			
18–29 years	299	33.9	66.1
30–44 years	260	31.3	68.7
45–54 years	229	39.4	60.6
55–64 years	236	50.9	49.1
65–74 years	184	57.8	42.2

(continued)

Table 2. (*continued*)

	N	Mail%	Web%
Education			
Primary	78	74.7	25.3
Secondary	534	42.1	57.9
Post-Secondary	241	39.3	60.7
Tertiary	351	33.9	66.1
Activity			
Employed	692	39.4	60.6
Student	110	24.5	75.5
Retired	302	56.3	43.7
Unemployed or other	104	41.3	58.7
Total	1208	43.0	57.0

3.3 Analysis Strategy

First, we estimated variation in attitudinal variables according to response mode, taking advantage of the ordinary least squares (OLS) and analysis of variance (ANOVA). Secondly, we tested the indirect effects of the response mode through background variables by using Sobel-Goodman mediation tests. We illustrated the main results in Fig. 1 by using coefplots [38]. The analyses were performed with Stata 15.

4 Results

The results of regression analysis are shown in Table 2. The main results are illustrated in Fig. 1 by estimating predictive margins on the basis of OLS models from Table 2.

Let us next examine the direct effects of response mode. The web response mode had a significant effect on negative attitudes ($b = -0.19$; $p < .001$). When analyzing positive attitudes, the results were similar, but not statistically significant ($b = 0.08$, $p > 0.05$).

Next, we added covariates into the base model. The covariates significantly confounded the association with response mode and negative immigration attitudes ($b = 0.06$, $p < 0.001$). What is noteworthy, however, is that the effect of response mode remained significant ($b = -0.11$, $p < 0.05$). The squared R indicates that the final model explains negative attitudes relatively well (0.14). In the case of positive attitudes, the effect of response mode was not significant in the models. The predicting power of the adjusted model was also more modest when compared to the model predicting negative attitudes.

We also estimated the direct effects of the covariates. Age did not have a significant effect on either of the dimensions. However, women's scores were more positive ($b = 0.16$, $p < 0.001$) and less negative ($b = -0.28$, $p < 0.001$) towards immigration. The level of education contributed clearly to the negative attitudes, as those having tertiary education expressed clearly less negative attitudes ($b = -0.77$, $p < 0.001$).

This finding applies to the data when those having only primary education are omitted. In terms of positive attitudes, the differences were similar but lighter, as those having tertiary education reported more positive attitudes (b = 0.47, p < 0.001). Economic activity also had a significant effect on the both dimensions when students, retired and unemployed to employed persons were compared. Students reported more positive (b = 0.38; p < 0.001) and less negative (b = –0.22; p < 0.05) attitudes towards immigrants than others, although those who were economically inactive reported more negative attitudes (b = 0.32; p < 0.001).

Finally, we tested the indirect effect of the response mode through covariates. The results of this procedure show us whether or not the response mode effect is caused by demographic variables. We found that education confounded the response mode effect. The effect was stronger in terms of negative attitudes (b = –0.06, p < 0.001), which means that education (mainly tertiary education) explained 30% of the direct association of the response mode. In this case, education has a notable confounding effect that contributes to both response mode and immigration attitudes. However, what is noteworthy here is that the effect of response mode remained statistically significant after controlling for education (Table 3).

Table 3. Predicting positive and negative attitudes towards immigration by response mode. Directed, total and indirect effects

Variables	Positive attitudes			Negative attitudes		
	Direct	Total	Indirect	Direct	Total	Indirect
	B(SE)	B(SE)	B(SE)	B(SE)	B(SE)	B(SE)
Web mode	0.08	0.05		–0.19***	–0.11*	
	(0.05)	(0.05)		(0.05)	(0.05)	
Covariates						
Women		0.16**	–0.03		–0.28***	0.01
		(0.05)	(0.01)		(0.05)	(0.01)
Age		0.01	–0.01		–0.01	–0.01
		(0.01)	(0.01)		(0.01)	(0.01)
Education (Primary omitted)						
Secondary		0.09	–0.01		–0.34***	0.02
		(0.08)	(0.01)		(0.08)	(0.01)
Upp-Secondary		0.04	0.02		–0.49***	–0.03
		(0.09)	(0.01)		(0.09)	(0.01)
Tertiary		0.47***	0.04**		–0.77***	–0.06***
		(0.09)	(0.01)		(0.09)	(0.02)
Economic activity (Employed omitted)						
Student		0.38***	0.01		–0.22*	–0.01
		(0.10)	(0.01)		(0.09)	(0.01)
Retired		0.06	–0.01		0.08	–0.01
		(0.08)	(0.01)		(0.08)	(0.01)

(continued)

Table 3. (*continued*)

Variables	Positive attitudes			Negative attitudes		
	Direct	Total	Indirect	Direct	Total	Indirect
Unemployed or other		−0.03	0.01		0.32***	0.01
		(0.09)	(0.01)		(0.09)	(0.01)
Constant	2.84***	2.39***		3.08***	3.60***	
	(0.04)	(0.14)		(0.04)	(0.13)	
Observations	1,186	1,182	1,182	1,190	1,186	1,186
R-squared	0.00	0.07	0.07	0.01	0.14	0.14

Notes: Standard errors in parentheses.
*** p < 0.001, ** p < 0.01, * p < 0.05.
Direct: Direct and unadjusted effect of the response mode.
Total: Adjusted effect of the response mode and covariates.
Indirect: Indirect effect of the response mode through covariates.

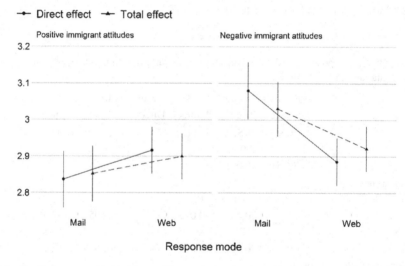

Fig. 1. Predictive margins (with confidence intervals) for response modes when explaining positive and negative attitudes towards immigrants. The direct and total effects are based on OLS regressions in Table 3.

5 Discussion

In this paper, we were interested in whether the mode of response was associated with attitudes towards sensitive issues in mail/web mixed-mode surveys. More specifically, we examined whether respondents who choose answering via a web-questionnaire differed from postal questionnaire respondents in terms of social desirability bias. We used positive and negative questions on immigration to measure social desirability. Preceding research indicates that responses to questions concerning immigrants might be biased [31, 32]. In the survey data utilized in this paper, online response was an alternative to postal questionnaire. The sample was selected from the Finnish Central Population Register using random sampling. The respondents were contacted by mail and given the opportunity to answer the questionnaire online.

As assumed (H1), responses in mail survey mode differed when we examined attitudes towards immigration in more sensitive (negative) way. The finding was similar for less sensitive (positive) attitudes, but the response mode failed to have a statistically significant effect. Furthermore, we were also able to confirm our second hypothesis (H2), as controlling for basic socio-demographic factors confounded the association between negative answers and response mode. However, all of the detected variation could not be attributed to the control variables, indicating that differences in responses is more likely dependent on other unobservable factors associated with the responding.

The findings call for a broader discussion. As online surveys have become a primary data collection technique in most disciplines, it is crucial to assess the strengths and weaknesses of online survey data collection in comparison to more traditional methods. In the mixed method context, the strengths of online surveys are easy to identify. Especially as a supplementary data collection method, online questionnaires offer advantages to both researchers and respondents. A combination of postal and internet-based modes gives the sampled respondents a possibility to select the questionnaire form he/she prefers. The Internet questionnaire also saves respondents from the possible inconvenience of mailing the questionnaire form. For internet-savvy population groups, the online questionnaire is a natural way to answer surveys. Without giving this opportunity, these individuals might not answer the survey at all, which researchers cannot afford.

The fact that we found notable differences between the answers given by online and offline respondents should encourage researcher to conduct web-based data collection more carefully. The selective bias related to online responding does not appear be a significant problem after controlling for the effects of basic socio-demographic variables. Despite this, however, it appears that certain population groups are poorly represented in web-based surveys. Thus, at its best, web-based data collection can only offer approximate results. This being the case, a combination of a postal survey supplemented with a web-questionnaire seems to have its place in survey research in the foreseeable future. As Bech and Kristensen [39] have further pointed out, due to the lower response rates, the costs per an online response can actually be significantly higher than in the case of postal response.

Our study obviously has its methodological and practical limitations. In particular, the issues regarding the data samples, research design and the survey items analyzed are notable here. First, we presented generalizations to a larger population on the basis of a cross-sectional dataset from one Nordic country. With this in mind, it is important to acknowledge the restrictions that deal with the specific nature of the nation surveyed. Second, the data came from a cross-sectional survey. We therefore cannot make strong statements on the causal direction of the response modes. In order to establish a plausible causal interpretation, we would need a panel dataset containing observations from the same respondents in different points of time. Third, we were not able to control the possible effect of digital platforms used in the online response mode. It is likely that the responses may sometime differ even between computer and mobile phone interfaces, for instance.

Finally, to have a better understanding of sensitivity bias, we would have needed items that measure perceived sensitiveness directly. In the current study, we did not have items measuring personal experiences regarding sensitivity. Furthermore, we had to rely on assumptions derived from preceding research, especially regarding anonymity in different response modes. Given this, we cannot be certain that anonymity experiences were indeed weaker in online surveys. As noted earlier, we did not have the necessary information on respondents' ICT-skills or all relevant attitudes influencing the choice of response mode. In this respect, it would be necessary to conduct a more in-depth study that takes into account the impact of information security perceptions behind the choice of response mode.

References

1. Kim, Y., Dykema, J., Stevenson, J., Black, P., Moberg, D.P.: Straightlining: overview of measurement, comparison of indicators, and effects in mail–web mixed-mode surveys. Soc. Sci. Comput. Rev. 0894439317752406 (2018)
2. Klausch, T., Hox, J.J., Schouten, B.: Measurement effects of survey mode on the equivalence of attitudinal rating scale questions. Sociol. Methods Res. **42**(3), 227–263 (2013)
3. Szolnoki, G., Hoffmann, D.: Online, face-to-face and telephone surveys—comparing different sampling methods in wine consumer research. Wine Econ. Policy **2**(2), 57–66 (2013)
4. Schonlau, M., van Soest, A., Kapteyn, A., Couper, M.: Selection bias in web surveys and the use of propensity scores. Sociol. Methods Res. **37**(3), 291–318 (2009)
5. Huang, H.-M.: Do print and web surveys provide the same results? Comput. Hum. Behav. **22**(3), 334–350 (2006)
6. de Leeuw, E.D., Hox, J.J.: Internet surveys as part of a mixed-mode design. In: Social and Behavioral Research and the Internet: Advances in Applied Methods and Research Strategies, pp. 45–76. Routledge/Taylor & Francis Group, New York (2011)
7. de Leeuw, E.D.: Data Quality in Mail, Telephone, and Face-To-Face Surveys. TT-Publikaties, Amsterdam (1992)
8. Dillman, D.A.: Why choice of survey mode makes a difference. Public Health Rep. **121**(1), 11–13 (2006)
9. Lang, F.R., John, D., Lüdtke, O., Schupp, J., Wagner, G.G.: Short assessment of the big five: robust across survey methods except telephone interviewing. Behav. Res. Methods **43**(2), 548–567 (2011)
10. Internet World Stats 2019. https://www.internetworldstats.com/stats.htm. Accessed 01 Feb 2019
11. Fan, W., Yan, Z.: Factors affecting response rates of the web survey: a systematic review. Comput. Hum. Behav. **26**(2), 132–139 (2010)
12. Dillman, D.A., Smyth, D.A., Christian, L.M.: Internet, Phone, Mail, and Mixed-Mode Survey: The Tailored Design Method, vol. 1. Wiley, New Jersey (2014)
13. Bethlehem, J.: Selection bias in web surveys. Int. Stat. Rev. **78**(2), 161–188 (2010)
14. Kwak, N., Radler, B.: A comparison between mail and web surveys: response pattern, respondent pro ® le, and data quality. J. Off. Stat. **18**(2), 257–273 (2002)

15. Dillman, D.A., et al.: Response rate and measurement differences in mixed-mode surveys using mail, telephone, interactive voice response (IVR) and the internet. Soc. Sci. Res. **38**(1), 1–18 (2009)
16. Saunders, M.N.K.: Web versus mail: the influence of survey distribution mode on employees' response. Field Methods **24**(1), 56–73 (2011)
17. Atkeson, L.R., Tafoya, L.M.: Surveying political activists: the effectiveness of a mixed mode survey design AU - Atkeson, Lonna Rae. J. Elections Public Opin. Parties **18**(4), 367–386 (2008)
18. McCabe, S.E., Diez, A., Boyd, C.J., Nelson, T.F., Weitzman, E.R.: Comparing web and mail responses in a mixed mode survey in college alcohol use research. Addict. Behav. **31**(9), 1619–1627 (2006)
19. de Bernardo, D.H., Curtis, A.: Using online and paper surveys: the effectiveness of mixed-mode methodology for populations over 50. Res. Aging **35**(2), 220–240 (2012)
20. Koivula, A., Räsänen, P., Sarpila, O.: Internet- ja paperilomakkeiden täyttäjät. Vastaustavan muutoksen ja merkityksen arviointia hyvinvointitutkimuksessa. Yhteiskuntapolitiikka **81**(2), 174–185 (2016)
21. Tourangeau, R., Yan, T.: Sensitive questions in surveys. Psychol. Bull. **133**(5), 859–883 (2007)
22. de Vaus, D.: Surveys in Social Research. Taylor & Francis, New York (2002)
23. Krumpal, I.: Determinants of social desirability bias in sensitive surveys: a literature review. Qual. Quant. **47**(4), 2025–2047 (2013)
24. Gnambs, T., Kaspar, K.: Disclosure of sensitive behaviors across self-administered survey modes: a meta-analysis. Behav. Res. Methods **47**(4), 1237–1259 (2015)
25. Naus, M.J., Philipp, L.M., Samsi, M.: From paper to pixels: a comparison of paper and computer formats in psychological assessment. Comput. Hum. Behav. **25**(1), 1–7 (2009)
26. Wolfe, E., Converse, P.D., Airen, O., Bodenhorn, N.: Unit and item nonresponses and ancillary information in web- and paper-based questionnaires administered to school counselors AU - Wolfe, Edward W. Meas. Eval. Couns. Dev. **42**(2), 92–103 (2009)
27. Kays, K., Gathercoal, K., Buhrow, W.: Does survey format influence self-disclosure on sensitive question items? Comput. Hum. Behav. **28**(1), 251–256 (2012)
28. Hox, J.J., De Leeuw, E.D., Zijlmans, E.A.O.: Measurement equivalence in mixed mode surveys. Front. Psychol. **6**(FEB), 87 (2015)
29. de Leeuw, E.D., Hox, J.J., Boevé, A.: Handling do-not-know answers: exploring new approaches in online and mixed-mode surveys. Soc. Sci. Comput. Rev. **34**(1), 116–132 (2015)
30. Heerwegh, D., Loosveldt, G.: Face-to-face versus web surveying in a high-internet-coverage population: differences in response quality. Public Opin. Q. **72**(5), 836–846 (2008)
31. Janus, A.L.: The influence of social desirability pressures on expressed immigration attitudes*. Soc. Sci. Q. **91**(4), 928–946 (2010)
32. An, B.P.: The role of social desirability bias and racial/ethnic composition on the relation between education and attitude toward immigration restrictionism. Soc. Sci. J. **52**(4), 459–467 (2015)
33. Karp, J., Milazzo, C.: Democratic scepticism and political participation in Europe. J. Elections Public Opin. Parties **25**(1), 97–110 (2015)
34. van Deursen, A., Helsper, E., Eynon, R., van Dijk, J.: The compoundness and sequentiality of digital inequality. Int. J. Commun. **11**, 452–473 (2017)
35. Lindblom, T., Räsänen, P.: Between class and status? Examining the digital divide in Finland, the United Kingdom, and Greece AU - Lindblom, Taru. Inf. Soc. **33**(3), 147–158 (2017)

36. Keipi, T., Näsi, M., Oksanen, A., Räsänen, P.: Online Hate and Harmful Content: Cross-National Perspectives (2017)
37. ISSP Research Group, International Social Survey Programme 2013: National Identity III, Cologne (2013)
38. Jann, B.: Plotting regression coefficients and other estimates. Stata J. 14(4), 708–737 (2014)
39. Bech, M., Kristensen, M.B.: Differential response rates in postal and Web-based surveys among older respondents. Surv. Res. Methods 3(1), 1–6 (2009)

Can UX Over Time Be Reliably Evaluated? - Verifying the Reliability of ERM

Masaaki Kurosu[1(✉)] and Ayako Hashizume[2]

[1] The Open University of Japan, Tokyo, Japan
nigrumamet-s23@mbr.nifty.com
[2] Hosei University, Tokyo, Japan

Abstract. Experience Recollection Method (ERM) was announced at HCII 2018 conference by the author and is a research method for the UX (User Experience) that evaluates the contents and degrees of UX. It is a memory-based measurement method for the UX where the informants are asked about the content and degree of episodes concerning the use of targeted artifact (product, system or service) along with the rough time scale. Although the method requests episodes on the artifact usage, it doesn't ask the time information in detail considering the vagueness of memory, hence it does not generate the visual representation of UX curve/graph in such methods as CORPUS, iScale, UX Curve and UX graph.

This presentation is based on the data that was obtained in FY 2017 for the same informants once in September and another in January. We compared two data and checked if the information obtained by ERM has a certain degree of reliability, i.e. the nepisode in the first survey is kept in the second survey and if the rating scale value are almost the same. This presentation is based on the comparison of two datasets. Generally speaking, ERM was confirmed to have the high reliability and provide a reliable information on the UX.

Keywords: UX evaluation · Reliability · Memory-based method

1 Evaluation of UX

1.1 Previous Approach

The UX (User Experience) can be defined as "person's perceptions and responses resulting from the use and/or anticipated use of a product, system or service (ISO9241-11:2010) [1]." As an extension of this definition, Kurosu [2–5] proposed that the quality in design including the usability is the basis for the quality in use and the latter is related to the UX. Thus, the UX should be evaluated or measured in relation to wider range of quality characteristics including usability, functionality, performance, reliability, safety, attractiveness, etc.

From this perspective, evaluation methods that have been proposed until now will be screened to a small set of methods, although there are so many so-called "UX evaluation methods" have been proposed as listed in the website of All About UX [6].

UX evaluation methods can be classified into two categories; real-time UX evaluation, and memory-based UX evaluation.

© Springer Nature Switzerland AG 2019
M. Kurosu (Ed.): HCII 2019, LNCS 11566, pp. 159–179, 2019.
https://doi.org/10.1007/978-3-030-22646-6_12

The real-time UX evaluation methods including the questionnaire can obtain the information in-situ and just in time. But, because of their invasive nature, i.e. informants are requested to answer the question during their everyday life and it is sometimes an obstruction for them, it is not recommended to repeat the survey for more than a few weeks. In other words, real-time UX evaluation methods can be repeatedly applied only for a limited time range.

On the contrary, memory-based UX evaluation methods do not have such temporal limitations. They can be applied to the UX over the long-term period. But they do have limitations originated from the nature of human memory. People forget many events even though they were important, and people may also edit or change the contents without any ill will. Hence the validity and reliability are important in terms of the memory-based methods.

Anyways, real-time evaluation methods include the questionnaires and methods for evaluating emotion and other methods. The questionnaire includes SUS [7], SUPR-Q [8], Product Reaction Card [9] and AttrakDiff [10]. The evaluation methods for emotion include 3E [11] and Emo2 [12], and the other real-time evaluation methods include ESM [13], and diary methods such as DRM [14, 15] and TFD [16].

Memory-based methods include CORPUS [17], iScale [18], UX curve [19], UX graph [20] and ERM [5, 21].

1.2   ERM

ERM was proposed by Kurosu et al. [5, 21] based on the reflection of advantages and disadvantages of memory-based methods until now. Similar to previous methods, informants are asked past events (episodes) and the rating for them. But the curve or graph will not be drawn in ERM, because of the idea that the memory will not have such preciseness as can be represented as the coordinate on time scale. As can be seen in Fig. 1, informants are given only 7 rough time zones: expectation, purchase, early use, use, recent use, present time and near future that include all phases of experience for an artifact (product, system or service).

Each time zone means;

- Expectation: estimation of UX before the purchase
- Purchase: evaluation of UX at the purchasing or obtaining the artifact
- Early use: evaluation of UX just after the purchase (around a few weeks to a few months)
- Use: evaluation of UX after the early use until the recent use. This may range from a few weeks to several years depending on the time of purchase and the time of survey
- Recent use: evaluation of UX just before the time of survey (around a few weeks to a few months)
- Present time: evaluation of UX at the time of survey
- Near future: expectation and/or estimation of UX after the time of survey

Although ERM uses the letter-sized paper and the number of the row is limited, informants are allowed to write more than one episode in a row. Every episode should accompany the rating on the feeling from positive (+10) to negative (−10), i.e. 21 points scale is used.

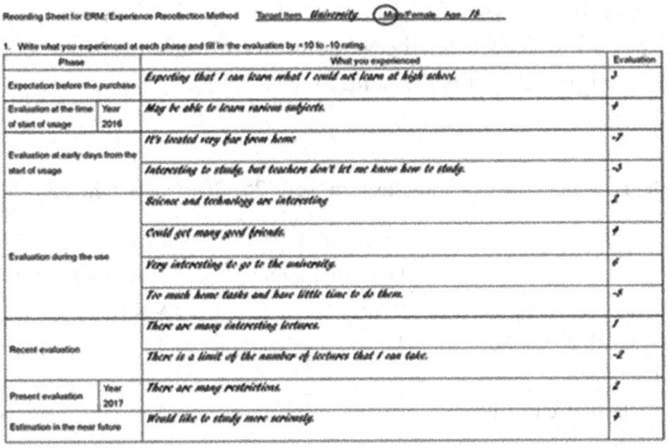

Fig. 1. An example of ERM regarding the university education. (translated from Japanese and cited from Kurosu et al. 2018)

1.3 Reliability of ERM

Similar to the psychological test, UX evaluation methods should possess a certain level of validity and reliability. Regarding the validity especially the content validity, there will be no problem because informants are asked about their own experience regarding the use of an artifact they've been using. But the reliability is not yet confirmed and there seems to be no researches conducted to investigate this issue. This is the reason why this paper deals with the reliability issue of the memory-based UX evaluation method.

2 Verifying the Reliability of ERM

2.1 Method

The basic idea of the verification of reliability of ERM is to compare the result of two surveys for the same group of informants, i.e. re-test method. Luckily, I had a class at the graduate school and thought that I should ask students to collaborate for the survey twice, once at the first lecture and another at the last lecture of the semester. And the first survey was conducted on Sep. 25, 2017 and the second survey on Jan. 22, 2018. There were 119 days between two surveys. It would have been almost impossible for the informants to remember what they answered at the first survey when they were subject to the second survey.

Informants

There were 26 students registered to my class and the attendants at the lecture on Sep. 25, 2017 and Jan. 22, 2018 were shown in Table 1. Because of the absence at each lecture, total of 23 students attended either of the lecture and, from among them, 17 students attended both lectures resulting 17 data available for the analysis. Unfortunately, it became clear that 3 of them purchased a new model during the analysis and were excluded from the analysis that followed. Finally, 14 data were actually used in the total analysis. To our regret, all the students were male perhaps because my class was opened at the engineering department.

Table 1. Attendants of the class on Sep. 25, 2017 and Jan. 22, 2018

		Jan. 22, 2018		
		Data that can be used	Data that can't be used	Sum
Sep. 25, 2017	Data that can be used	17	1	18
	Data that can't be used	5	0	5
	Sum	22	1	23

Targeted Device

Because all of the students were using the smartphone (not the cellphone), it was decided to be the targeted device. Because it is the multi-purpose device and almost all users are using it daily, or more to say, many times during the day, its user must have various experiences from a positive one to a negative one.

Procedure

ERM sheet was delivered to each of the informants, then a brief instruction was given, and 30 min were allowed to write down their experiences. During the instruction, informants were told that

- This is to ask you to write down your personal experience on the smartphone
- First, write down your university ID, sex, age, and description of the smartphone
- There are seven time-zones including the expectation, purchase ... near future (with the explanation of each time range)
- You are requested to write down what you experienced in the episode slot and the degree of satisfaction vs. dissatisfaction or positive feeling vs. negative feeling from +10 through 0 to –10 depending on your subjective impression in the rating slot. Please use the integer
- You may begin with the expectation to the near future, but it depends on your feeling which time zone you would write. You can go back to the previous time zone that you have already filled
- Although there are limited number of slots, you can write two or more episodes and ratings in one slot if you need more than one
- If you don't remember what you experienced at any time zone, you can skip it

Obtained Data

Handwritten ERM sheets were obtained and were input to Excel, then were translated into English. Appendix shows all the raw data.

3   Results

3.1   Rating Results

Rating values correspond to the vertical position of the curve/graph in CORPUS, iScale and UX curve. But unlike those methods, ERM only separates rough time zones corresponding to the quasi-continuous horizontal position in them.

One point that should be warned for the use of the time zone during the reliability verification is the meaning of each time zone in the first survey and in the second survey. As shown in the imaginative data of Fig. 2, each time zone shifts bit by bit depending on the displacement of the time when the surveys were conducted. For example, to an imaginative informant in this figure, the smartphone was purchased, of course, at the same time. But the following time zone represents a bit displaced physical time depending on when the survey was conducted. For example, the present time at the first survey was Sep. 2017 while the present time at the second survey was Jan. 2018. This displacement will become larger as the span between the purchase and the survey becomes shorter.

Fortunately, informants who purchased their smartphone in 2017 (informant C, F, H, I, L and M) showed similar ups and downs of the rating value for the first survey and second survey as can be seen in the following sections. This may mean that the time zones for the informants were not exact but rough, hence horizontal position in curves/graphs in CORPUS, iScale and UX curve were not exact based on the equal time unit and thus they should be called quasi-continuous.

	2016		2017						2018	
						Sep. 25, 2017	119 days		Jan. 22, 2018	
First survey	expectation	purchase	early use	use		recent use	**present**	near future		
Second survey	expectation	purchase	early use		use			recent use	**present**	near future

Fig. 2. Chronological table showing the difference of meaning of the time zone. In this imaginary data, the same informant purchased the smartphone in early 2017, but the time zones from early use to near future slip out of place in the first survey and the second survey depending on the time when the survey was conducted (2017 and 2018).

3.2   Reliability Measure

Usually, the reliability (ρ) is represented by the correlation coefficients (r). In this study, Kendall's coefficient of concordance (W) was also calculated. These values were calculated based on the average rating for 7 time zones. The distribution of r is shown in Fig. 3 and that of W is shown in Fig. 4. These graphs show rather high reliabilities.

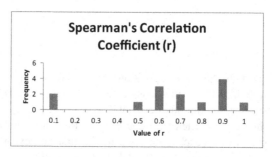

Fig. 3. Distribution of Spearman's correlation coefficients for 14 data.

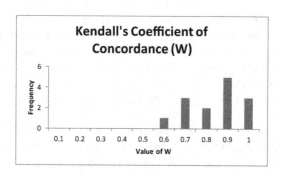

Fig. 4. Distribution of Kendall's coefficient of concordance for 14 data.

3.3   Episode Results

Episodes were verbal in nature, thus will be analyzed one by one in the next chapter.

4   Analysis of Each Data

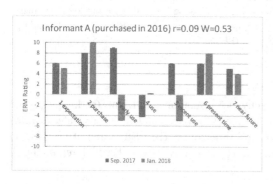

Fig. 5. Ratings by informant A

ID of each informant was randomly assigned. Episode is assigned its ID as <informant ID> episode number>-<year>, e.g. A4-2017. Please refer to the Appendix.

Informant A generally gave positive ratings except for the size of device that was negatively rated (A12-2017 and A13-2018) and its weight that was also negatively rated (A12-2017 and A8-2018) (Fig. 5).

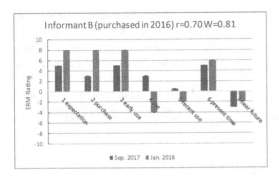

Fig. 6. Ratings by informant B

Informant B generally gave positive ratings especially in 2017. But he rated negatively regarding the future (B10-2017, B10-2018) that the device may not be able to correspond to the new applications (Fig. 6).

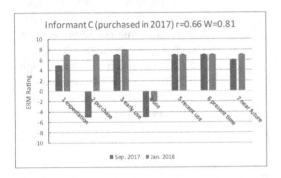

Fig. 7. Ratings by informant C

Informant C gave strange ratings to the same aspect of the device that the specification is almost the same with the previous cellphone, one negatively and another positively (C2-2017, C2-2018) (Fig. 7).

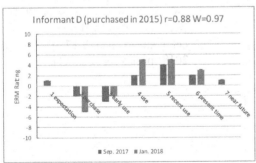

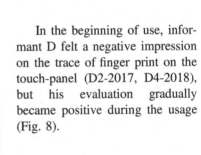

Fig. 8. Ratings by informant D

In the beginning of use, informant D felt a negative impression on the trace of finger print on the touch-panel (D2-2017, D4-2018), but his evaluation gradually became positive during the usage (Fig. 8).

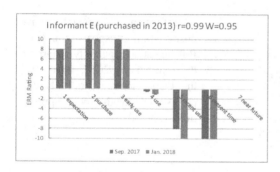

Fig. 9. Ratings by informant E

Informant E showed a drastic change of ratings that was quite high in early days and changed into negative during the usage in terms of the battery life (E9-2017, E9-2018), and the wifi connection (E10-2017, E10-2018) (Fig. 9).

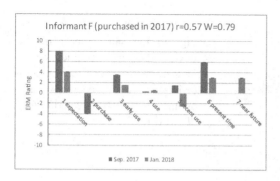

Fig. 10. Ratings by informant F

Informant F wrote episodes differently for 2017 and 2018. But there are some common episodes such as the speed (F4-2017, F5-2018), the quality of photograph (F7-2017, F6-2018), the convenience of second screen (F11-2017, F8-2018), etc. (Fig. 10).

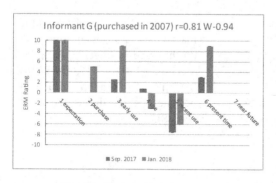

Fig. 11. Ratings by informant G

Informant G wrote about the joy of accessing internet (G1-2017, G1-2018) and that of using net contents (G5-2017, G3&G4-2018) positively (Fig. 11).

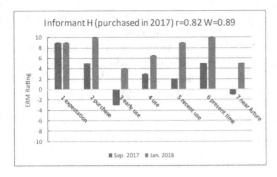

Fig. 12. Ratings by informant H

Informant H wrote about the high expectation (H1-2017, H1-2018) and the screen quality (H2-2017, H2-2018). Generally his ratings are higher in 2018 (Fig. 12).

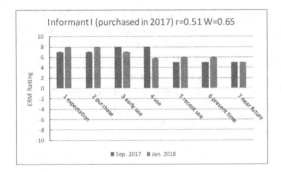

Fig. 13. Ratings by informant I

Informant I gave no negative ratings. Positive evaluations are for the processing speed during the expectation (I1-2017, I1-2018) and the early use (I3-2017, I3-2018). Strangely he rated the fast battery loss positively (I10-2017, I9-2018) and he might have misunderstood the instruction (Fig. 13).

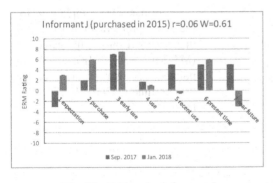

Fig. 14. Ratings by informant J

Informant J had different expectation one negatively for the poor operability (J1-2017) and another positively for the good performance (J1-2018). This informant did not give the consistent episodes except for the present time evaluation (J12-2017, J12-2018) (Fig. 14).

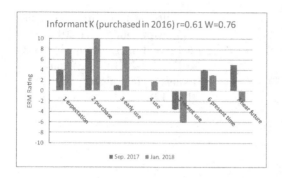

Fig. 15. Ratings by informant K

Informant K generally gave positive ratings except recently for the finger print recognition (K9-2017, K9-2018) and the unexpected break down (K10-2017, K10-2018) (Fig. 15).

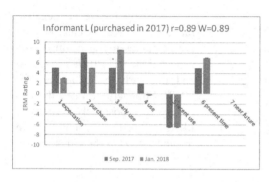

Fig. 16. Ratings by informant L

Informant L gave negative ratings only recently for the lack of storage (L9-2017, L9-2018). Another negative evaluation was given differently, one to the heat (L10-2017) and another to the system freeze (L10-2018) (Fig. 16).

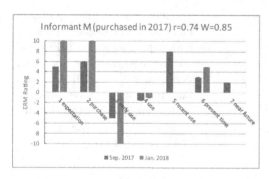

Fig. 17. Ratings by informant M

Informant M complained for the same problem of gyro sensor that occurred during the early use (M3-2017, M3-2018). He still pointed out that problem at the present time (M7-2017, M7-2018) (Fig. 17).

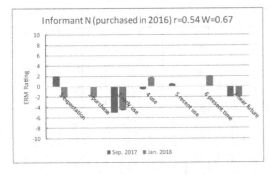

Informant N pointed out the usability of the plastic case cover (N2&N3&N4&N9&N10-2017, N3&N9-2018) generally a bit negatively (Fig. 18).

Fig. 18. Ratings by informant N

5   Conclusion

The reliability of ERM was tested in terms of the smartphone using the re-test method. Two surveys for the same 14 informants who continued to use the same model were conducted one on Sep. 2017 and another on Jan. 2018. By the use of ERM, episodes and subjective ratings were obtained for 7 time zones including the expectation, purchase, early use, use, recent use, present and near future. Two reliability measures (one is the correlation coefficient and another is the coefficient of concordance) were calculated and relatively high reliability was confirmed.

Based on the content analysis for each informant, the same episodes were found around the same time zone and were rated in the same way. This also confirmed the high reliability of ERM

Appendix

Raw data (episodes and ratings) of ERM at Sep. 2017 and Jan. 2018 for all 14 informants are shown in following tables.

ID	Age Sex	Device	When	Sequential ID	Sep. 2017 Episode	Rating	Jan. 2018 Episode	Rating
A	M 24	iPad2	expectation	A1	Is big and will be easy to use	6	Good reputation on the internet and among friends made me feel much expectation.	5
				A2	Cost effective than the smartphone	6		
				A3	May be used in many ways	6		
			purchase 2016	A4	Screen is indeed big	8	Usability level is very high and am satisfied	10
				A5	Body is also big than expected	8		
				A6	Beautiful, good designed	8		
				A7	Cool	8		
			early use	A8	Can be used for wider range of purpose than the smartphone	9	Unexpectedly heavy and it makes me tired after long use	-4
				A9	Screen is big and is easy to see. Less eye strains	9	Screen is large enough for people around me to look into it	-6
			use	A10	Some applications do not work on iPad	-3	Battery life is long and can use it long	7
				A11	Consumes large amount of communication fee	-4	Applications run smoothly	6
				A12	Because of its size, it's bulky and heavy	-5	Difficult to hold for calling	-5
				A13	Photo-taking is not easy	-5	Anyways, larger than any other thing	-7
				A14	Needs both hands for using it	-6		
			recent use	A15	Slow decrease of battery (good battery life)	8	Battery life became worse	-4
				A16	I can focus on my main job while using this device	4	Screen cracked	-6
			present time 2017	A17	Though big and heavy, it's no importance when I adapted it. It's easy to use.	6	Overall performance is good and tough than other phones	8
			near future	A18	If possible, I'd have a device one size smaller. But, for the moment, I'm satisfied with this	5	Will become lighter, with better performance and resolution will be better	4
B	M 23	iPhoneSE	expectation	B1	I was expecting tha handy size and better performance than iPhone5S I used to use	5	Good performance will allow me to use without irritation	8
			purchase 2016	B2	Size and shape were same with the previous one and I could accpet it easily	3	Processing is fast and could use it without irritation	8
			early use	B3	I was astonished to see the high performance than expected	7	Installed various applications and found that most of them run fast	8
				B4	Because the size and shape were same with iPhone5S, I could use its case to the new one	3		
			use	B5	No sudden shut down occurred and I can use it feeling relieved, and I had no complaints	3	Smartphone that I used before didn't crack the screen but iPhoneSE cracked instantly when I dropped it	-5
				B6			When applications that was released later were installed, I feld the speed slowed down	-3
			recent use	B7	Some recent applications require more powerful specification and my device cannot correspond to them. A bit of dissatisfaction	-2	A bit more frequently freezed	-2
				B8	As it worked smoothly on a new OS, I felt relieved	3		

Participant	Stage	Year	Code	Statement A	Score A	Statement B	Score B
C / M / K23	present time	2017	B9	Good design that fits to my hand and the performance is sufficient, and I am satisfied.	5	Response has become a bit slower, but no big problems occurred. Easy to use	6
	near future		B10	When more applications will be in the market that require higher specification, my device will not be able to correspond	-3	New applications may not run	-2
	expectation		C1	How much will the difference with the cellphone be, and what kind of functions it will have?	5	Expected much because it is my first smartphone	7
	purchase	2017	C2	Because I don't use most of new functions, I think I should have kept continue using the previous cellphone	-5	An alternative to previous cellphone	7
	early use		C3	Many applications appeared of which I feel convenient to use	7	Can use it smoothly. Convenient in many ways	8
	use		C4	Performance is a bit low than expected	-6	Realized that unnecessary functions and applications was installed at the purchase	6
	use		C5	Some applications did not work on my device	-4	Processing speed is slow	-5
	use		C6			Storage size is small and limited number of application can be installed	-5
	use		C7			Incorrect actions occurred frequently	-4
	recent use		C8	I don't think I should change the device for the moment	7	Deleted unnecessary applications and data	7
	recent use		C9			Can distinguish which functions are necessary or unnecessary	7
	present time	2017	C10	Smartphone is convenient compared to the cellphone	7	No need to change the device for the time being	7
	near future		C11	I will consider changing the device when the new one with high performance will appear	6	Will not change the device unless it will be broken	7
D / M / 23 / Android	expectation		D1	Could I effectively use the smartphone of which it was the first time for me to use?	1	No drastic change will occur even if I change from the previous cellphone	0
	purchase	2015	D2	Felt unpleasant by the finger print when I touch the screen	-2	Still not well accustomed to the touch-panel operation	-5
	purchase		D3			Calling operation is difficult	-5
	purchase		D4			Cannot accept that the fingerprint remains	-5
	early use		D5	Not yet used to touch operation, because I used to use the cellphone	-3	Started to try various functions such as the game application as well as the email and calling	-2
	early use		D6	Conventional cellphone would work for the purpose of communication	-3	Got used to the touch panel operation and the remains of fingerprint, but still cannot to the calling	-2
	use		D7	Started to be accustomed to the touch operation by using LINE and email	2	Communication functions such as LINE and Twitter as well as the email and calling are useful	5
	use		D8	Calling operation on smartphone is yet clumsy, as I'm used to the operation of the Cellphone and Landline	2	Was impressed and got into application games such as "Idol Master Cindellela Girls Starlight"	5
	use		D9	Started to use the smartphone for enjoying smartphone games such as 3DS after introduced game applications	2	Started to use such other functions as the route search by Google map, alarm clock, train route search and camera	5
	recent use		D10	Mainly using game applications	4	New device is comfortable to use by the improvement of download speed and response time	5
	recent use		D11	Also use LINE and email	4		

EM23 (Xperia)

Phase	Year	Code	Description	2	Description	3
present time	2017	D12	For me, my device is for game applications as well as the communication	2	Satisfied by having changed from cellphone	3
near future		D13	Will use the device mainly for game applications	1	Will use it for a while 'cause I just changed the device	
expectation		E1	Expected so much because my device was the forefront model at the time of purchase	8	Fascinating 'cause it was the trendsetter at that time	10
purchase	2013	E2	Was astonished for the specification that is far better than the previous model	10	Operation was smooth compared to the one I used to use	10
early use		E3	Very convenient for using SNS	10	Used to access the internet and was pleasant	8
		E4	Very pleasant to use because of the latest 3G circuit	10	Games at that time moved smoothly	8
		E5	No dissatisfactions for about 2 years after the purchase	9	Started to use to access SNS	6
use		E6	As the advent of 4G circuit, I started to feel the lack of power	-3	Finding the case that matches to the screen was difficult	-2
		E7	Power button was broken and I could not off the power supply	-4	As I purchased a new tablet, WiFi access became less frequent	-3
		E8	Because of the lack of power, I don't enjoy games on this device	-4	As I purchased a free SIM for the tablet, calling has become the only use	-5
recent use		E9	Sometimes, the battery residual goes down to 0% suddenly. Very unpleasant	-8	Shut down at the power level around 50%	-10
		E10	No WiFi connections and am worried so much	-8	WiFi access has become unable	-10
present time	2017	E11	Degradation over time and lack of power make me feel disastrous	-10	Useless except for calling	-10
near future		E12	Will purchase a new model whenever I can afford	0	Will change the device as soon as I get enough money	0

FM23

Phase	Year	Code	Description	2	Description	3
expectation	2017	F1	Expecting its high power based on the catalog specification compared to the previous model	8	Fascinating smartphone with various functions. Expecting to use	4
purchase	2017	F2	Because the power button is not located on the side but on the back of body, it is difficult to use	-4	Takes a bit of time to be accustomed to operate 'cause the interface is different from the previous one. A bit bothersome	0
		F3	Made much mis-touches	-4		
early use		F4	Performance is good. Applications that didn't work on the previous model works well	6	Tapping on the screen is a bit displaced. Minor dissatisfaction	-2
		F5	HiFi sound is good. Pleased so much because I was not expecting it	1	Smartphone applications work faster than the previous one. Pleased.	5
		F6	Because it uses TypeC cable, I had to buy some peripherals anew	-3	Photos are far beautiful than before	4
use		F7	Performance of the camera was found to be very nice. Though I'm using it in automatic mode now, it would be wonderful if I get used to it	2	Position of the speaker is awkward	-1
		F8	Decrease of battery is a bit faster	-2	Second screen is convenient	1
		F9	Charging speed is fast	4	Everytime the OS is updated, screen layout changes	-2
		F10	Pleased that the smartphone VR can be used	4	Noises appear on the screen and the device freezes. Anxious	-4

Participant	Subcategory	Year	Code	Description	Score	Description	Score
	recent use		F11	Second screen is cool and convenient, but there are some inconvenient points	-1	Dirt on the body stands out	-1
	present time	2017	F12	Still awkward at touching on the screen, but is wonderful that it has some functions that my previous model didn't accept	6	Using applications mainly and it will do for a certain time	3
	near future		F13	Will be able to use the touch interface before long and the data will be accumulated, so that it might be difficult to change the model	0	Use the smartphone frequently for the VR	3
G, M24, GalaxyS2	expectation		G1	Can use the internet of which the cellphone do not allow	10	Expecting so much to access the internet from the phone	10
	purchase	2007	G2			Chose Android device GalaxyS2 because of the screen size compared to iPhone	5
	early use		G3	Can watch the movie and play games on the smarphone	10	Used many internet contents and was satisfied. Impressed by the difference from the cellphone	8
			G4	Hard to be accustomed to use	-5	Especially, Web Mangas, novels and games fascinated me	10
	use		G5	Can enjoy the net contents on the portable device	10	It was already a used one at 2007. I chose it because of the internet access fare and neglected the performance, I feel the power difference from other smartphones now	-8
			G6	I can understand what my friends are talking and can get the information on what I'm puzzled	8	Some Web pages cannot be opened because of the shortage of Ram. Searched for the browser that can be used with small amout of RAM.	-8
			G7	Astonished to the expensive price. Slow processing because of the low price	-5	Battery worn out of the limit, but changing it was easy as it is an old model	4
			G8	Frequently use the smartphone for any purpose. Cannot leave it	-10	After a long-time usage, the frame is almost falling to pieces. I don't mind the appearance, but am anxious if it may be broken	-2
	recent use		G9	Old, worn-out, slow and, furthermore, difficult to use	-5	I was left from almost all the contents. Even the application of fast food shop cannot be accessed	-10
			G10	Because net contents can be accessed from the portable device, I frequently use it whenever I access the internet	-10	I will use this till GalaxyS10 will appear	9
	present time	2017	G11	Because my model is very old that I've used for more than 10 years, I will be left alone if I do not change the model	3		
	near future		G12			Big advance in performance was expected because it is the model after several generations since the smartphone appeared.	9
H, M24, SOV34	expectation		H1	Had much expectation for the latest model, because my previous smartphone was out of date	9	Screen is beautiful and response is smooth	10
	purchase	2017	H2	Astonished for the image quality and fast speed. It is not good that the protection film cannot be pasted all over the screen, but it's acceptable	5	Glass screen protection film does not cover the whole screen and the leather case is not easy to handle. But it's within the permissible range	4
	early use		H3	Complaints are that the alarm can be set for only 20 and the calender is not included as a default	-3		

Subject	Model	Phase	Year	Code	Comment (A)	Value A	Comment (B)	Value B
		use		H4	Inconvenient that the reboot of application frequently occurs. Perhaps it is for protecting from the overload	-3	At last, I could understand how to use the leather case, but it has the risk of slipping down from hand	5
		use		H5	Accustomed to it now and can operate it easily	3	Longtime use made the leather case soft and easy to use	8
		use		H6			Inserted the student ID to the leather case and found it convenient. But the LSI of ID card sometimes fails to be read by the gate machine	9
		recent use		H7	Positive point is that it accepts heavy processes by good specification against the high load.	2	Performance has not yet degraded and can be used satisfactorily	10
		present time	2017	H8	Very easy to use	5	Performance is still good but peripheral devices have become degraded	5
		near future		H9	What will happen when all the storages are filled with data?	-1	Will operate smoothly	8
I	Xperia Z5 SO-01H	expectation		I1	Processing is fast	7	Screen is large	8
M 22		purchase	2017	I2	Runs smoothly, adequate weight and size	7	Screen images move smoothly	7
		early use		I3		8	Battery works for a long time	7
		early use		I4			During the game playing, the area around NFC becomes hot	5
		use		I5	It is a major and popular model so that there are many covers available, furthermore my friend has the same model	8	Fingerprint lock cannot always be released easily when finger tips are moist	5
		use		I6			Works smoothly without time lag	6
		use		I7			Can be used under the rain as it is life waterproof	7
		use		I8			Battery seems to be lowered than before	6
		use		I9			Has a small scratch	6
		recent use		I10	Battery consumption is fast. Found a small scratch. Get hot while using it	5	Moving without any troubles	6
		present time	2017	I11			Battery will be lowered faster than now	5
		near future		I12	I will change to a new model	5	Expecting the high efficiency by the high powered CPU compared to the current model (iPhone4S)	3
J	iPhone 6S	expectation		J1	Worried about the difficulty of one hand operation as I heard that the screen size is larger than previous model	-3	Anxious about the less easy holding of the device because of the large screen	3
M 22		purchase	2015	J2			Large screen allows me to look letters and images easily. Satisfied	6
		early use		J3	Screen size is larger and it's easy to read text on the screen	2	Difficult to put the device into the small pocket of the pants	6
		early use		J4			Feeling satisfaction and the sense of superiority based on the high performance compared to other devices	8
		early use		J5	At first, I used it by both hands because of the large screen, but now, I can operate it by one hand	8		

Participant	Phase	Year	Code	Statement	Score	Statement	Score
J	early use		J6	Specifications are far better than the previous one and I'm satisfied	6	Screen size that seemed to be too large is now felt just right to my hand	7
	use		J7	Processing speed is faster than other smartphones. I'm satisfied	7	New applications appeared in the market for which other devices cannot correspond	5
	use		J8	A problem occurred that the system shuts down suddenly maybe because of the battery malfunction	-5	Initial failure of the battery was found	-7
	use		J9	Though there are problems that applications stop suddenly for previous model 1 or 2 generations before, this model doesn't have such problems	3	No scratches on the screen after the long time use	5
	recent use		J10	New models are appearing one after another in the market, but I don't thing my model lacks the power	5	New model has some degradation such as the abolition of input jack	3
	recent use		J11			Performance degradation by updating iOS was now revealed	-4
	present time	2017	J12	My model has sufficient power for the ordinary use	5	Latest applications run without any problems. Am satisfied on the whole	6
	near future		J13	Recent smartphones have over specifications and have some inconvenience such that there is no earphone jack	5	CPU won't be able to catch up the application. Battery consumption	-3
K M22 ASUS 3	expectation		K1	Purchased for an inexpensive price and the high performance cannot be expected. But because it was the latest model, I expected its performance to a certain extent	4	It was revealed in the specification document that the performance will be better than the smartphone that I have	8
	purchase	2016	K2	Appearance was better than the photograph in catalogue and the size was good to hold	8	Appearance is more beautiful than in the photograph	10
	early use		K3	It was stressful because of the low communication speed perhaps due to the low price	-4	Applications that require high specification so that I could not install to the previous device could easily be installed	9
	early use		K4	I could use it freely without any unstability for any latest applications	6	Camera function is far better than I expected	8
	use		K5	Though it has the sufficient specification for AR and VR applications, it didn't accept such applications	-8	Dual SIM function worked well when I went to foreign countries	5
	use		K6	Functions for which I decided to but this model are now convenient tool for everyday use	5	Age verification of LINE application needed the carrier line and I could not confirm it	-5
	use		K7	Malfunctions of calender occurs many times	-3	UI changed by updating the OS and the device has become less usable	-2
	recent use		K8	It was customizable in detail for my own purpose	6	UI could be changed rather freely and I customized it	9
	recent use		K9	Finger print verification does not always work properly	-4	Precision of finger print verification has become worse	-6
	recent use		K10	Unexpected things occur frequently	-3	Applications stop suddenly frequently when many applications are active - maybe due to the amount of memory	-6
	present time	2017	K11	Compared to other models, it has not big advantages. But it doesn't have any deficiencies considering the price	4	Any applications can be used, but sometimes the speed becomes slow	3
	near future		K12	I will use this model until when the next generation model will appear with latest functions	5	Does not accept all the latest applications (AR, VR), I will change it to the new one	-2

	Period	Year	Code	Statement		Statement	
L M24 (Xperia Xz)	expectation		L1	Expected for the graded up quality of photo software compared to the previous model	5	Purchased at the renewal after 2 years term, I had not big expectation	3
	purchase	2017	L2	Screen glass was a bit curved and the feeling when I touched it was good	8	Camera, music playback and finger print verification were new to me. No unsatisfactory points.	5
	early use		L3	Battery life is far better than the previous model	10	Lock release by finger print verification was much more convenient than was expected	7
			L4	Usability of automatic camera function is not so much better than the previous model	0	Battery life was much longer than previous versions	10
			L5	5.2 GHz can be used because the WiFi corresponded to IEEE80211	5	Regretful that some softwares that I've used cannot be used because of the lack of compatibility. Difficult to find the alternative software	-5
	use		L6	Noticed that there are some convenient applications among pre-installed software provided by Sony	3	Not unsatisfactory for functions that I used everyday	3
			L7	Finger print can be used for unlock the device and it was unexpectedly comfortable to use	8	Smartphone case was officially available that was useful and good designed	8
			L8	Google applications frequently appear at unnecessary moments because of the updated OS	-8	Finger print verification did not work when the fingertip is moist. It was a new unsatisfactory point.	-5
			L9	Because the size of storage of main body was limited, I had to move picture files and other files to SD memory	-5	Shortage of storage in the main body and I had to delete some of the data	-5
	recent use		L10	Sometimes camera did not work because of the high temperature when I keep continue taking many pictures	-8	Freezing that requires the reboot sometimes occurred maybe because of the operating system	-8
	present time	2017	L11	Not many negative aspects but not many positive aspects. Battery life is better than before and I will use this model for the moment	5	Though rarely inconvenient, it is generally easy to use and I'm satisfied on the whole	7
	near future		L12	I will use this model until the contract with the carrier will end up as long as there will be no breakdown or damage	0	I will use this as before for one year term until the next contract update	0
M M24 (Xperia Xz)	expectation		M1	Because XperiaZ3 had a problem that my voice will be disconnected randomly during the voice communication, I expected that this bug should have been improved	5	I've been using XperiaZ3 and was annoyed by noise during the call, I had much expectation for the new version XperiaXZ	10
	purchase	2017	M2	Felt secured as the bug mentioned above was fixed	6	Noise during the call was settled down and I was pleased	10
	early use		M3	Malfunctioning occurred during the use of Google map that the direction is not correctly shown and it irritated me	-5	A bug of unknown origin existed regarding the gyro sensor and the direction on Google map was not correctly shown	-10
	use		M4	While the direction malfunctioning occurred even for Z3, this bug was fixed by the procedure printed on the official help. But for XZ, bug was not fixed and I couldn't use Google map effectively	-10	High resolution music source of which Z3 could not replay is now played on the device and I purchased some music. But I couldn't distinguish the difference. Anyways, it is a pleasure that high resolution music can be played.	2
			M5	Music replay application called "music" that is only installed for Xperia series can be used as when I was using Z3. I'm satisfied with its usability and the sound quality	1	A social game was released of which I was expecting to play. I realized that the play area is larger on the tablet with 4:3 screen. It is small on XZ with 16:9 screen.	-4

	Phase	Year	Code	Comment	Score	Comment	Score
	recent use		M6	The latest social game of which Z3 could not work smoothly because of the lack of power can now be working good. Because I had a strong feeling to this game, I was satisfied so much	8	No malfunctions are found except gyro sensor	5
	present time	2017	M7	This model was perfect if there is no malfunctioning on Google map	3	Because no other malfunctions exists than gyro sensor, I will continue to use this device	0
	near future		M8	I will change the device when a new series will appear	2	I wonder that I'll have to install all the applications whether I buy the same smartphone or the different one	-2
A q u o s	expectation		N1	Renewal of smartphone was exciting but, at the same time, a bit tiresome to learn the new system	2	It takes time to install applications, data conversion, photo copy, etc.	-2
	purchase	2016	N2	Purchased the black body because the blue body was sold out, but it's not a big issue. It's the first time that I purchase the case of purse shaped	0	Rim of the cover of device became worn-out and it sticked to other stuff	-5
	early use		N3	Function to shut down the smartphone by closing the case is not important for me	0	A scratch was found on the body	-4
S O G			N4	Outside of case was partly broken and the vinyl stick to other stuff	-10	Finger print verification is very easy	2
6	use		N5	There's no drastic change in the UI compared to the past models	-1	New function of API of programming can now be used by the version up of Android OS	5
H			N6	Shortcuts of applications can be created as a UI function, but I don't use the shortcut frequently	-1	Accustomed to the operation	2
			N7	Sometimes, rainbow colored line appears on the right edge of screen and I can see nothing on the screen	-5	Applications that cannot be deleted compress the data capacity	-2
	recent use		N8	Data capacity was enlarged	5	Removed the rim of cover entirely and now it's somewhat better	2
			N9	As I peeled off all scratches on the case, there's no problem now	2	I don't know the reason but the PC sometimes cannot detect the Android	-2
			N10	When I tried to let the smartphone to stand up by using the case, it did not stand straight up because the case was flexible	-1	I'm now feeling it's like this	2
	present time	2017	N11	Though several problems exist, I accept my device as such	0	It would be tiresome to change the device	-2
	near future		N12	At the timing of model change, I don't think it is not important to change to a new model	-2		

References

1. ISO 9241-210:2010. Ergonomics of Human-System Interaction - Human-Centred Design for Interactive Systems (2010)
2. Kurosu, M.: Re-considering the concept of usability. In: Keynote Speech at APCHI2014 Conference (2014)
3. Kurosu, M.: Usability, quality in use and the model of quality characteristics. In: Kurosu, M. (ed.) HCI 2015. LNCS, vol. 9169, pp. 227–237. Springer, Cham (2015). https://doi.org/10. 1007/978-3-319-20901-2_21
4. Kurosu, M.: Theory of User Engineering. CRC Press, Boca Raton (2016)
5. Kurosu, M., Hashizume, A., Ueno, Y.: User experience evaluation by ERM: experience recollection method. In: Kurosu, M. (ed.) HCI 2018. LNCS, vol. 10901, pp. 138–147. Springer, Cham (2018). https://doi.org/10.1007/978-3-319-91238-7_12
6. All About UX. All UX Evaluation Methods. https://www.allaboutux.org/all-methods
7. Brooke, J.: SUS: A "quick and dirty" usability scale. In: Jordan, P.W., Thomas, B., Weerdmeester, B.A., McClelland, A.L. (eds.) Usability Evaluation in Industry. Taylor and Francis, London (1996)
8. Sauro, J.: SUPR-Q: a comprehensive measure of the quality of the website user experience. J. Usability Stud. 10(2), 68–86 (2015). http://uxpajournal.org/supr-q-a-comprehensive-measure-of-the-quality-of-the-website-user-experience/
9. Benedek, J., Miner, T.: Measuring desirability: new methods for evaluating desirability in a usability lab setting. In: Proceedings of Usability Professional Association (2002)
10. Hassenzahl, M., Burmester, M., Koller, F.: AttrakDiff: a questionnaire to measure perceived hedonic and pragmatic quality (in German). In: Ziegler, J., Szwillus, G. (eds.) Mensch & Computer. B.G. Teubner (2003)
11. Tahti, M., Arhippainen, L.: A proposal of collecting emotions and experiences. In: Interactive Experiences in HCI, vol. 2, pp. 195–198 (2004)
12. Laurans, G., Desmet, P.M.A.: Using self-confrontation to study user experience: a new approach to the dynamic measurement of emotions while interacting with products. In: Desmet, P.M.A., van Erp, J., Karlsson, M. (eds.) Design & Emotion Moves. Cambridge Scholars Publishing (2006)
13. Larson, R., Csikszentmihalyi, M.: The experience sampling method. New Dir. Methodol. Soc. Behav. Sci. 15, 41–56 (1983)
14. Kahneman, D., Krueger, A.B., Schkade, D.A., Schwarz, N., Stone, A.A.: Method for characterizing daily life experience: the day reconstruction method. In: American Association for the Advancement of Science, pp. 1776–1780 (2004)
15. Karapanos, E., Zimmerman, J., Forlizzi, J., Martens, J.-B.: User experience over time: an initial framework. In: CHI 2009 Proceedings, pp. 729–738. ACM (2009)
16. Kurosu, M., Hashizume, A.: TFD (Time Frame Diary)–a new method for obtaining ethnographic information. In: APCHI 2008 Proceedings (2008)
17. von Wilamowits-Moellendorff, M., Hassenzahl, M., Platz, A.: Dynamics of user experience: how the perceived quality of mobile phones changes over time. In: UX WS NordiCHI 2006, pp. 74–78 (2006)
18. Karapanos, E., Martens, J.-B., Hassenzahl, M.: Reconstructing experiences with iScale. Int. J. Hum Comput Stud. 70, 1–17 (2012)

19. Kujala, S., Roto, V., Vaananen-Vainio-Mattila, K., Karapanos, E., Sinnela, A.: UX curve: a method for evaluating long-term user experience. Interact. Comput. **23**, 473–483 (2011)
20. Kurosu, M.: Is the satisfaction evaluation by UX graph, a cumulative one or recency-based one? (in Japanese). In: Japan Kansei Engineering Society Spring Conference Proceedings (2015)
21. Kurosu, M., Hashizume, A., Ueno, Y., Tomida, T., Suzuki, H.: UX graph and ERM as tools for measuring Kansei experience. In: Kurosu, M. (ed.) HCI 2016. LNCS, vol. 9731, pp. 331–339. Springer, Cham (2016). https://doi.org/10.1007/978-3-319-39510-4_31

A Set of Usability Heuristics
for Mobile Applications

Ruyther Parente da Costa$^{(\boxtimes)}$ and Edna Dias Canedo$^{(\boxtimes)}$

Computer Science Department, University of Brasília – (UnB),
Brasília, DF 70910-900, Brazil
ruyther@me.com, ednacanedo@unb.br
www.cic.unb.br

Abstract. The innovations proposed by the cell phone market have grown steadily in recent years, as well as the evolution of the complexity of operating systems, hardware and applications available. With these changes and changes, new challenges and usability-related quirks emerge and need to be considered during the development process of these applications, which incorporate new user-application interactions, increasingly changing the behavior of smartphone users. It is known that usability is an important factor when choosing the use of these technologies. Usability depends on factors such as the User, their characteristics and abilities, the Task which the user intends to achieve and also the Context of the application's use. This work will lead to a Systematic Review of Literature with the objective of identifying the heuristics and usability metrics used in the literature and/or industry, and based on the results obtained, it is intended to propose a set of usability heuristics focused for the context of mobile applications on smartphone, considering the User, Task and Context, as usability factors and Cognitive Load as an important attribute of usability. Furthermore, an empirical validation of the proposal will be performed with usability specialists and improvements can be incorporated into the proposed model after this validation.

Keywords: Mobile applications · Usability · Usability heuristics · Heuristic evaluation · Usability factors

1 Introduction

The market for mobile devices has grown year after year, and over the years there has also been hardware evolution of these devices, the complexity of their operating systems and applications [1]. Another type of change that has been happening since the evolution of cell phones to smartphones is in the form of their use, which was previously basically limited to telephone calls, currently comprises a much wider range of uses by the user, such as listening music, make bank transfers, make online purchases, among others [2].

With the change in the use of the mobile phone by the user, new challenges and peculiarities appeared and such factors should be considered and studied

© Springer Nature Switzerland AG 2019
M. Kurosu (Ed.): HCII 2019, LNCS 11566, pp. 180–193, 2019.
https://doi.org/10.1007/978-3-030-22646-6_13

for the development of a mobile application, such as software usability in this context [3].

Usability can be defined as being "a broad concept that basically refers to how easy it is for users to learn a system, how efficient they can be once they have already learned it, and how enjoyable it is to use it" [4], i.e., usability is understood to be the ability to use a product with effectiveness, efficiency and satisfaction in a specific context of use [5].

Usability is a very important requirement of design, being of utmost importance to users in the decision to purchase a product [6]. The "IS Success Model" shows the point of view of the product, how a system is related to user satisfaction. It can be inferred why it is an important factor to be considered a process of development of a product and/or software, so it is important to know how to apply it is to evaluate it. Through the evaluation by usability heuristics it is possible to identify usability problems and thus to evaluate a software as to its usability [6].

Usability heuristic evaluations describe design/usability principles that serve to evaluate a particular software, called heuristics, and this evaluation is performed largely by usability experts or by ordinary users, but the latter being less indicated [7,8]. The evaluation of usability by heuristics has been widely studied and is one of the most used methods to evaluate the quality of a software, being considered in the literature as a traditional evaluation of software usability [9,10].

The set of the ten heuristics proposed by Nielsen [11] are classic of the literature and reveal principles for the construction of a software interface in order to have a good usability. In the context of mobile applications, new factors to be considered have arisen in relation to human-computer interaction and should be taken into account in the design and development of a software application that aims to have a good usability, as well as a new set of usability heuristics take such changes into account.

This work carried out a Systematic Literature Review (SLR) with the objective of identifying the usability heuristics for the mobile context proposed in the literature and also identified the main metrics used in heuristic evaluations of a mobile application. Based on the results of the SLR, the scope of this work consists of the proposal of a new set of usability heuristics specific to the context of applications for touch-screen smartphone that takes into account the user, the context and the tasks as usability factors [12] and Cognitive Load, as an important usability attribute, so that each heuristic contains a detailed description to facilitate its understanding.

This work did not propose specific heuristics for a given context of mobile application use, such as the one proposed by Ajibola and Goosen [13] focused in the context of e-commerce, but will focus on general heuristics in the context of mobile applications for smartphones touch-screen, according to the work developed by Salvucci [14], since more general heuristics for evaluating interfaces generally become easier to understand and apply [15].

The general objective of this work is to propose a set of usability heuristics, focused on the context of mobile applications, detailing them and also identifying the main metrics used during heuristic evaluations. The main contribution of this work will be to propose a model that will contain a set of specific usability heuristics for mobile applications, in the context of touch-screen smartphones, which consider the user, context and tasks to be fulfilled in the application as usability factors and Cognitive Load as an important usability attribute.

This paper is organized as follows. The Sect. 2 presents the theoretical basis necessary for the understanding of this work. Furthermore, related work is presented. Section 3 presents the systematic literature review and the results obtained from it. The Sect. 4 presents the set of proposed heuristics to carry out the evaluation of Mobile Applications. The Sect. 5 presents the considerations of this work, learning and future work.

2 Background

According to the literature the term usability has several definitions. The International Organization for Standardization (ISO) together with the International Electrotechnical Commission (IEC) define usability in ISO/IEC 9241-11 [5], such as: "the extent to which a product can be used by specific users to achieve (the accuracy and completeness with which users achieve the specified goals), efficiency (the resources expended in relation to the accuracy and completeness with which users reach goals), and satisfaction (comfort and acceptability of use) in a specified context of use" [5, 16].

There are standards that define what is important to be considered in terms of usability when the goal is software quality during your development process. ISO/IEC 9126-1 [17] describes six categories of software quality that are relevant in the software development process, among which is usability basically defined as ease of use [17]. However, ISO/IEC 14598 [18] provides a framework for the use of the ISO/IEC 9126-1 model as a way to evaluate software products [18].

ISO/IEC 25000 [19] is a series of standards that came to replace and extend ISO/IEC 9126 [17] and ISO/IEC 14598 [18], with the main objective of organizing, improve and unify concepts related to two major software development processes: specification of software quality requirements and software quality assessment, which is performed in conjunction with the software quality measurement process [19]. Usability is considered in every standard and is specifically mentioned also in DTR 25060 (Common Industry Format (CIF) for Usability) and ISO 25062: 2006 [20] (Common Industry Format (CIF) for usability testing reports) [9].

2.1 Related Work

In the work presented by Miranda [21] a set of 16 focused heuristics for mobile devices is described. Furthermore to the proposed set of heuristics, the work performs some heuristic evaluations in different mobile applications, which are characterized by being of different categories and because they contain different functionalities for validation of the proposal: CNN, Amazon, TripAdvisor, Ebook Reader, Calendar, QR Code Scanner, Dropbox, Dictionary and Skype. The applications were tested on different mobile devices so that the greatest number of possible errors were discovered, to cover more than one mobile platform, so the study used the following devices: Smartphone; Samsung Galaxy S4: running the Android system; iPad: running the iOS system; HTC Titan: running Windows Phone OS.

Miranda [21] concludes that with the popularization of mobile devices, such as smartphones, good usability in a mobile software application is a feature that distinguishes a successful software solution from others and that seek a usability of excellence in an application should be something to consider during development. The work presented by Miranda [21] reinforces that heuristic evaluation is an adequate method to evaluate the usability of mobile applications, and that the set of heuristics proposed in his research can be improved so that more usability errors can be through this method of evaluation.

In the paper presented by Harrison et al. [12] a usability model called PAC-MAD (People at the Center of Mobile Application Development) is proposed which addresses the limitations that the author believes exist in other usability models when applied to mobile devices, thus PACMAD brings together important attributes of other usability models and is characterized by being more comprehensive.

Harrison et al. [12] compare their model with the usability models proposed by ISO 9241 [22] and Nielsen [4]. PACMAD incorporates the attributes of both models and adds Cognitive Load as a usability attribute for mobile applications. Furthermore, PACMAD proposes three usability factors, User, Task and Context, which the author argues are important when developing a mobile application, as it may impact the final interface of the system.

The related works identified and reported in this paper present usability guidelines and heuristics for mobile applications, focusing on the user and the tasks that the user will perform when using a particular application. However, according to Harrison et al. [12], there are few usability works that consider context as a usability factor and the author argues that there may be a gap in the literature about this subject. Therefore, the present work seeks to propose a set of usability heuristics that consider the user, the task and the context, as usability factors. Furthermore, it seeks to contribute by minimizing the existence of this gap on the subject in the literature.

3   Systematic Literature Review

In this work the Systematic Literature Review (SLR) is used. The SLR is a framework that aims to provide a way to identify, analyze and interpret relevant research for a particular research question, area of knowledge or phenomenon of interest [23]. The studies that contribute to answer the research questions of a systematic review are called primary studies [23]. During the SLR, the

Planning, Conduct and Publication of Results phases were followed, as defined in the work presented by Kitchenham [23], together with the Manual Search and the Snowballing. Table 1 presents the SLR Research Questions:

Table 1. Research Questions (RQ) and Motivation for each RQ

Research Question (RQ)	Motivation
RQ.1. What heuristics are used, in the context of mobile applications, to evaluate product quality?	Identify in the literature the heuristics used to evaluate the quality of mobile applications
RQ.2. What are the usability heuristics used in the context of mobile applications that consider usability factors: user (its characteristics), task (user goal to be achieved in the application use), and context of use of the application?	Identify heuristics that focus on identifying how effective, efficient and satisfactory a mobile application is, having the user interaction with the system as the center of the evaluation
RQ.3. What are the metrics used in a heuristic evaluation in the context of mobile applications?	Identify the metrics that are used for the heuristic evaluation

The search strategy involved the use of Automatic Search, which consists of the search through a search string in digital databases [24], followed by Manual Search, through which searches for papers in Conference proceedings, Journals or specific Magazines [25]. Furthermore, Snowballing was applied [26].

The Automatic Search was performed in 5 databases, selected for having a considerable volume of papers published in periodicals and conferences of the area of knowledge in usability, the focus of this SLR, being:

– Biblioteca Digital ACM;
– IEEEXplore;
– Science Direct;
– Scopus;
– Springer.

The Manual Search was carried out by analyzing the titles and abstracts (if necessary) of studies published in Conferences Annals and Journals, dealing with Human-Computer Iteration. The studies considered potentially relevant were added to the set of selected papers.

The papers selected by the search string in the databases can present results with some limitations, either by the lack of keywords or synonyms in the String, or by the non-selection of a database that could return important works of the area in question or even the way the String was defined can affect the results obtained in the conduction of an SLR [27]. In order to minimize the loss of important works, it was decided to use Snowballing's set of instructions, proposed by Wohlin and Prikladniki [27], which basically consists of reviewing the bibliographic references of the selected articles, automatic and manual search, with the objective of selecting more works related to the research area.

Selection criteria were defined to include and exclude a primary study in our study object, according to the adopted research strategy. Thus, the inclusion and exclusion criteria were defined to select the most relevant papers in relation to the research questions to be answered.

3.1   SLR Results

When applying the automatic search strategy adopted in the selected databases, from a total of 31 papers returned from the Search String, after reading the title, abstract and keywords were selected 15 papers and excluded 16 (Fig. 1). Subsequently, the following steps of the adopted research protocol were carried out, resulting in the selection of 6 papers to answer the research questions and the exclusion of 9 papers. Thus, all steps of the adopted research protocol were performed and resulted in the complete reading of the 6 primary studies. After the selection of the papers by the automatic search strategy, 1 paper was selected from the manual search and 1 through Snowballing, totalizing **8 primary studies** for the extraction of data through the systematic review of literature (Fig. 1).

The extraction of the information to compose the SLR result occurred through the complete reading of the 8 selected papers. From the complete reading of the primary studies it was possible to elaborate the answers to the research questions defined in this study.

RQ1 - Which Heuristics Are Used in the Context of Mobile Applications to Evaluate the Quality of the Product? The paper presented by Neto and Pimentel [28], proposes a set of eleven heuristics of usability focused specifically for the mobile context, presents a comparison with the ten heuristics of Nielsen [11]. This comparison is a common thing to do since Nielsen's work is a benchmark in the area of usability in general. The objective of this paper is to compare the proposed heuristics with those of Nielsen in a practical study where the evaluators use the two models for future comparison of the final number of usability errors coming from both models. As a result, the model proposed by Neto and Pimentel [28] enabled the evaluators to find more interface usability errors than the Nielsen model [29].

Inostroza et al. [9] and [30] propose a set of twelve general heuristics for touchscreen-based devices. The set of proposed heuristics were refined from an evaluation with usability specialists divided into two groups, one group used the set of Nielsen heuristics and the other group used the one proposed by the author in the evaluation of some applications. In the end it was concluded that the model proposed by Inostroza et al. [9,30] captured more usability problems compared to the model proposed by Nielsen [29].

Humayoun et al. [31] proposes a set of 15 heuristics focused on mobile applications that use multi-touch gestures. Based on the heuristic evaluation conducted by the author, he concluded that through the proposed set of heuristics, the

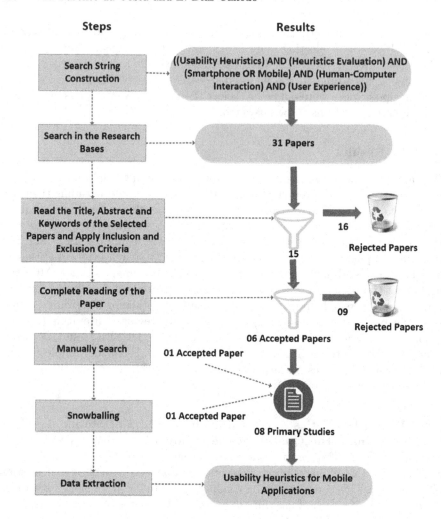

Fig. 1. Result of the papers selection.

evaluators were able to find more usability problems than other heuristic proposals also focused on mobile applications, such as in the paper of Joyce and Lilley [32], which also proposes a set of heuristics focused on the mobile context.

The work proposed by Billi et al. [33], presents a set of eight general usability heuristics focused on the mobile context. The author states that traditional heuristics, such as Nielsen [11], do not deal with context switching and therefore new heuristics are required for better results in a heuristic evaluation for mobile applications.

There are some works that defend a set of heuristics for the mobile context more focused in some specific domain, according to the work presented by Ajibola and Goosen [13]. This paper presents a proposal of eleven heuristics, based on the heuristics of Nielsen [11], but containing some more focused on the context of m-commerce. The paper presents a revised proposal of heuristics as they have been re-evaluated with domain experts to improve and validate their proposal.

The work presented by Silva et. al. [34], proposes a set of thirty-three usability heuristics (evolution of the work [35] of the author) for the mobile context, focused on elderly users (senior citizens). The study presents the heuristics grouped as follows: 1. **Perception:** these are heuristics related to the limitations of perception that the older user tends to suffer, such as: visual and auditory alterations; 2. **Cognition:** these are heuristics that refer to the cognitive changes that can occur with advancing age, such as the difficulty of maintaining attention or managing a large number of items through working memory; 3. **Skill:** these are heuristics related to the difficulty in accomplishing tasks due to the limitations of the user's motor skills; 4. **Navigation:** these are heuristics directed to the understanding of the structure of the application and of how the user can use that application based on this structure; 5. **Content:** these are heuristics related to the information and language used in the application; 6. **Visual Design:** these are heuristics that address design details, for example, formatting details and visual representations.

RQ2 - What Are the Usability Heuristics Used, in the Context of Mobile Applications, that Consider Usability Factors: User (its Characteristics), Task (user Goal to Be Achieved in the Application Use) and Application Usage Context? In general, all the works that propose heuristics of usability seek to highlight the usability problems of a software application and, based on this, to determine if such application has good usability and is easy to use for users in general or for those with specific characteristics. Thus, there are papers that propose heuristics that evidence the usability factors proposed by Harrison et al. [12].

The first usability factor (user) is evidenced in all works that propose usability heuristics, since their purpose is to represent general principles of usability to be applied in a software interface, and based on that, the interface will be easy and intuitive for the largest number of users with the most diverse characteristics. When the target audience of an application has more unique characteristics, such as some physical or mental limitation, the work is conducted with a focus on these more specific characteristics of the users. The paper presented by Silva et al. [34] suggests a set of focused heuristics for elderly users that usually have certain special characteristics that, according to the author, may be psychosocial changes and functional disorders that affect vision, hearing, movement, cognition and their relationship to themselves and others around them. Thus, the heuristics that evidence the usability factor "user" in the author's work are: 1. Heuristics 2 and 3: Older users tend to be slower at performing tasks overall; 2. Heuristic 10: The characteristics of the target audience should be taken into account in the language used in the application; 3. Heuristics 13, 19, 20, 23, 24, 25, 26 and 27: Older users tend to have vision problems; 4. Heuristic 22: Older users tend to have hearing problems.

The second factor of usability (task) is evidenced in all works that propose a set of usability heuristics, since the main goal of the heuristics is to present general principles of usability, when applied in a particular software, if the final result is the best the user is able to perform their tasks and achieve their goals in an easy and intuitive way when using software. This statement comes in line with the definition of usability given by Shackel and Richardson [36]. Thus, all the heuristics presented by Inostroza et al. [9], for example, evidence the usability factor (task) proposed by Harrison [12], due to the fact that all heuristics are geared towards maximizing the ease to achieve their goals in the most intuitive way possible.

The third factor of usability (context) is exactly the factor that Harrison [12] mentions as being a gap in the literature of works related to software usability. Thus, during the execution of this systematic literature review, no work was found containing context-oriented heuristics, reinforcing Harrison's assertion [12].

RQ3 - What Are the Metrics Used in a Heuristic Evaluation in the Context of Mobile Applications? Gómez et al. [37] used a metric to prioritize the relevance of heuristic items to the specific interface evaluated. In this way, the experts prioritized heuristics from 1 to 4, based on the application of evaluated software, being: 1 - for completed heuristic items, 2 - for those corresponding to usability gaps, 3 - for heuristic items that were not evaluated in the current phase of the software life cycle and 4 - for issues not applicable to the interface.

Inostroza et al. [30] conducted a study for the evaluation of their proposed heuristics, comparing them with the Nielsen heuristics [11], causing two distinct groups of evaluators to evaluate a mobile application under egalitarian conditions. Inostroza et al. [30] used a metric that consisted in evaluating the severity of usability problems related to a given heuristic using a severity scale from 0 (low) to 4 (high).

Billi et al. [33] carried out in their work a heuristic evaluation divided into three stages: pre-evaluation, individual evaluation and consolidation of individual findings. In the pre-evaluation phase the evaluators sign a consent form and a demographic questionnaire is given for the heuristic evaluation, as well as the instructions necessary for the evaluators to familiarize themselves with the set of mobile heuristics proposed by the author. In the individual evaluation phase, the evaluators sought to identify and prioritize usability problems based on the proposed heuristics. In the consolidation phase of the individual findings, the evaluators after completing the previous phase met to discuss the findings with the other evaluators. In the heuristic evaluation conducted, a metric proposed by Nielsen [38] was used to prioritize usability problems, which consists in evaluating the usability problem found for its severity on a scale of 0 to 4, being: 0 for no problems encountered, 1 for aesthetic problems found, 2 for minor usability problems found, 3 for found usability problems that need to be fixed with a high priority and 4 for extremely urgent usability problems, and must be repaired before the product is released to end users.

Humayoun et al. [31], conducted a heuristic evaluation with five expert evaluators in the field of computer science. The evaluation was conducted so that the evaluators were given a small training of 30 to 60 min to become familiar with the method. Thus, the evaluation scenarios were given to the evaluators and later the actual heuristic evaluation was performed, the author describes that the Likert scale metric was used [39] (Ajibola and Goosen [13] also use this the same metric in his work) to classify the heuristics from 1 to 5 as to their usefulness during the evaluation, being: 1 - strongly disagree, 2 - disagree, 3 - neutral, 4 - agree and 5 - strongly agree.

4   Proposed Heuristics Set for Mobile Applications

According to the results obtained with the SLR conducted it is proposed a set of heuristics for the evaluation of the usability of mobile applications. The Fig. 2 presents an overview of the proposed set. Each heuristic is structured with its respective ID; Name; Definition; Explanation; Primary Studies that justify its use; Benefits associated with the use of heuristics and; Problems associated with misinterpretation.

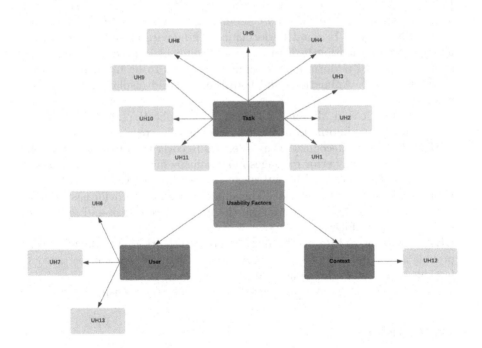

Fig. 2. Disposition of usability factors by usability heuristics.

Usability Heuristics Set found are:

- UH1 - Visibility of System Status. The application should keep the user informed about all processes and state changes within a reasonable period of time.
- UH2 - Correspondence between the Application and the Real World. The application must speak the language of the users and not in technical terms of the system. The application must follow the conventions of the real world and display the information in a logical and natural order.
- UH3 - User Control and Freedom. The application should allow the user to undo and redo their actions for clear navigation and should provide the user with an option to exit undesirable system states.
- UH4 - Consistency and Standards. The application must follow the established conventions, allowing the user to perform their tasks in familiar, standardized and consistent manner.
- UH5 - Error Prevention. Eliminate error prone conditions and give the user a confirmation option with additional information before committing to the action.
- UH6 - Minimize the User's Memory Load. The application should provide visible objects, actions, and options to prevent users from having to memorize information from one interface to another.
- UH7 - Customization and Shortcuts. The application should provide basic and advanced settings for setting and customizing shortcuts for frequent actions.
- UH8 - Efficiency of Use and Performance. The device must be able to load and display information in a reasonable amount of time and minimize the steps required to perform a task (number of steps to be taken by the user to reach a goal). Animations and transitions should display smoothly and smoothly.
- UH9 - Aesthetic and Minimalist Design. The application should avoid displaying unwanted information that overwhelms the screen.
- UH10 - Help Users Recognize, Diagnose, and Recover from Errors. The application should display error messages in a language familiar to the user, accurately indicating the problem and suggesting a constructive solution.
- UH11 - Help and Documentation. The application should provide easy-to-find documentation and help centering on the user's current task and indicating concrete steps to follow.
- UH12 - Pleasant and Respectful Interaction with the User. The device should provide a nice iteration with the user so that the user does not feel uncomfortable while using the application.
- UH13 - Privacy. The application must protect the user's sensitive data.

5   Conclusion

Due to the growth of the production of smartphones and associated with its evolution, usability is a key factor of differentiation for products and mobile applications and also a fundamental attribute for the quality of the product. Usability is a factor that facilitates the use of the software by the user, which can help in the user's loyalty and also in his satisfaction in the use of a software application that presents a good usability.

As the usability heuristics proposed by Nielsen [11] were not developed with the focus of encompassing the mobile applications [28], it became necessary to identify and propose a new set of heuristics that focused on applications based on the mobile context, for example, the work proposed by Dourado and Canedo [26]. Thus, the present work proposes a set of usability heuristics that consider the user, the task and the context as usability factors. The proposal has a basis in the works identified through the systematic literature review (SLR) carried out in this work. Furthermore, the SLR allowed to answer the research questions that were proposed.

The main contribution of the present work is to propose a set of heuristics for the context of mobile applications. Furthermore, to highlight the usability factors proposed by Harrison et al. [12] and to include Cognitive Load as an important attribute of usability. During the conduction of the SLR the metrics that were used by the academy during an evaluation of usability heuristics were identified.

For future work, it is still necessary to validate the set of heuristics with specialists in the area of usability to refine and validate the proposal, as well as to perform an empirical validation of the present work by means of a heuristic evaluation of one or more mobile applications and by to carry out a full evaluation of the results.

References

1. Bajpai, P.: The evolution of smartphone markets: where growth is going
2. Al-Nuiam, H., Al-Harigy, L.: User interface context of use guidelines for mobile apps. Int. J. Recent. Trends Hum. Comput. Interact. (IJHCI) **6**, 65–80 (2015)
3. de Lima Salgado, A., Freire, A.P.: Heuristic evaluation of mobile usability: a mapping study. In: Kurosu, M. (ed.) HCI 2014, Part III. LNCS, vol. 8512, pp. 178–188. Springer, Cham (2014). https://doi.org/10.1007/978-3-319-07227-2_18
4. Nielsen, J.: Usability inspection methods. In: Conference on Human Factors in Computing Systems, CHI 1994, Boston, Massachusetts, USA, 24–28 April 1994, Conference Companion, pp. 413–414 (1994)
5. ISO 9241-11:1998: Ergonomic requirements for office work with visual display terminals (VDTs) – part 11: Guidance on usability
6. Mack, Z., Sharples, S.: The importance of usability in product choice: a mobile phone case study. Ergonomics **52**(12), 1514–1528 (2009)
7. Nielsen, J., Molich, R.: Heuristic evaluation of user interfaces. In: Proceedings of the International Conference on Human Factors in Computing Systems, CHI 1990, Seattle, WA, USA, 1–5 April 1990, pp. 249–256 (1990)
8. Nielsen, J.: Guerrilla HCI: using discount usability engineering to penetrate the intimidation barrier. In: Cost-Justifying Usability, pp. 245–272 (1994)

9. Inostroza, R., Rusu, C., Roncagliolo, S., Rusu, V.: Usability heuristics for touchscreen-based mobile devices: update. In: First Chilean Conference on Human - Computer Interaction, ChileCHI 2013, Temuco, Chile, 11–15 November 2013, pp. 24–29 (2013)
10. Kjeldskov, J., Stage, J.: New techniques for usability evaluation of mobile systems. Int. J. Hum. Comput. Stud. **60**(5–6), 599–620 (2004)
11. Nielsen, J.: 10 Usability Heuristics for User Interface Design. Nielsen Norman Group (1995)
12. Harrison, R., Flood, D., Duce, D.: Usability of mobile applications: literature review and rationale for a new usability model. J. Interact. Sci. **1**(1), 1 (2013)
13. Ajibola, A.S., Goosen, L.: Development of heuristics for usability evaluation of m-commerce applications. In: Proceedings of the South African Institute of Computer Scientists and Information Technologists, SAICSIT 2017, Thaba Nchu, South Africa, 26–28 September 2017, pp. 3:1–3:10 (2017)
14. Salvucci, D.D.: Predicting the effects of in-car interface use on driver performance: an integrated model approach. Int. J. Hum. Comput. Stud. **55**(1), 85–107 (2001)
15. Bonifácio, B., Viana, D., Vieira, S.R.C., Araújo, C., Conte, T.: Aplicando técnicas de inspeção de usabilidade para avaliar aplicações móveis. In: IX Symposium on Human Factors in Computing Systems, IHC 2010, Belo Horizonte, MG, Brazil, 5–8 October 2010, pp. 189–192 (2010)
16. Sagar, K., Saha, A.: A systematic review of software usability studies. Int. J. Inf. Technol., 1–24 (2017)
17. ISO/IEC 2001. ISO/IEC 9126-1: Software engineering - product quality. International Organization for Standardization, Geneva, Switzerland
18. ISO/IEC 1999. ISO/IEC 14598-1: Information technology – software product evaluation – part 1: General overview. International Organization for Standardization, Geneva, Switzerland
19. ISO/IEC 2005. ISO/IEC 25000: Systems and software engineering – systems and software quality requirements and evaluation (square) – guide to square. International Organization for Standardization, Geneva, Switzerland
20. ISO/IEC 2006. ISO/IEC 25062: Software engineering – software product quality requirements and evaluation (square) – common industry format (CIF) for usability test reports. International Organization for Standardization, Geneva, Switzerland
21. Miranda, R.M.: Analysis of the usability of mobile device applications based upon heuristics. Dissertação (Mestrado em Ciência da Computação) - Instituto de Ciência da Computação. Universidade da Sociedade da Informação (2014)
22. ISO 9241:1997: Ergonomics requirements for office work with visual display terminals (VDTs)
23. Kitchenham, B.: Procedures for performing systematic reviews. Keele, UK, Keele Univ. **33**, 1–26 (2004)
24. Silva, F.S., et al.: Using CMMI together with agile software development: a systematic review. Inf. Softw. Technol. **58**, 20–43 (2015)
25. Felizardo, K.R., Nakagawa, E.Y., Fabbri, S.C.P.F., Ferrari, F.C.: Revisão Sistemática da Literatura em Engenharia de Software: Teoria e Prática. Elsevier Brasil (2017)
26. Dourado, M.A.D., Canedo, E.D.: Usability heuristics for mobile applications - a systematic review. In: Proceedings of the 20th International Conference on Enterprise Information Systems, ICEIS 2018, Funchal, Madeira, Portugal, 21–24 March 2018, vol. 2, pp. 483–494 (2018)

27. Wohlin, C.: Guidelines for snowballing in systematic literature studies and a replication in software engineering. In: 18th International Conference on Evaluation and Assessment in Software Engineering, EASE 2014, London, England, United Kingdom, 13–14 May 2014, pp. 38:1–38:10 (2014)

28. Neto, O.J.M., da Graça Campos Pimentel, M.: Heuristics for the assessment of interfaces of mobile devices. In: 19th Brazilian Symposium on Multimedia and the Web, WebMedia 2013, Salvador, Brazil, 5–8 November 2013, pp. 93–96 (2013)

29. Nielsen, J.: How to conduct a heuristic evaluation. Accessed 10 Nov 2001

30. Inostroza, R., Rusu, C., Roncagliolo, S., Rusu, V., Collazos, C.A.: Developing SMASH: a set of smartphone's usability heuristics. Comput. Stand. Interfaces **43**, 40–52 (2016)

31. Humayoun, S.R., Chotala, P.H., Bashir, M.S., Ebert, A.: Heuristics for evaluating multi-touch gestures in mobile applications. In: HCI 2017 - Digital Make-believe. Proceedings of the 31st International BCS Human Computer Interaction Conference, BCS HCI 2017, University of Sunderland, St. Peter's campus, Sunderland, UK, 3–6 July 2017

32. Joyce, G., Lilley, M.: Towards the development of usability heuristics for native smartphone mobile applications. In: Marcus, A. (ed.) DUXU 2014, Part I. LNCS, vol. 8517, pp. 465–474. Springer, Cham (2014). https://doi.org/10.1007/978-3-319-07668-3_45

33. Billi, M., et al.: A unified methodology for the evaluation of accessibility and usability of mobile applications. Univers. Access Inf. Soc. **9**(4), 337–356 (2010)

34. Silva, P.A., Holden, K., Jordan, P.: Towards a list of heuristics to evaluate smartphone apps targeted at older adults: a study with apps that aim at promoting health and well-being. In: 48th Hawaii International Conference on System Sciences, HICSS 2015, Kauai, Hawaii, USA, 5–8 January 2015, pp. 3237–3246 (2015)

35. Silva, P.A., Holden, K., Nii, A.: Smartphones, smart seniors, but not-so-smart apps: a heuristic evaluation of fitness apps. In: Schmorrow, D.D., Fidopiastis, C.M. (eds.) AC 2014. LNCS (LNAI), vol. 8534, pp. 347–358. Springer, Cham (2014). https://doi.org/10.1007/978-3-319-07527-3_33

36. Shackel, B., Richardson, S.J.: Human Factors for Informatics Usability. Cambridge University Press, Cambridge (1991)

37. Yáñez Gómez, R., Cascado Caballero, D., Sevillano, J.L.: Heuristic evaluation on mobile interfaces: a new checklist. Sci. World J. **2014** (2014)

38. Nielsen, J.: Usability engineering. In: The Computer Science and Engineering Handbook, pp. 1440–1460 (1997)

39. Likert, R.: A technique for the Measurement of Attitudes. Archives of Psychology (1932)

Characterizing End-User Development Solutions: A Systematic Literature Review

Mariana Santos[✉] and Maria Lucia Bento Villela

UFVJM, Diamantina, Brazil
m.apda.santos@gmail.com, smivella@gmail.com
http://www.ufvjm.edu.br

Abstract. The End-User Development (EUD) consists of a research area that has been under study for some time and covers a wide variety of domains and types of end users. However, there is still a lack of studies that analyze how EUD research has been reflected in practice. Therefore, this paper contributes to enable an understanding of the current scenario of EUD solutions, revealing trends that are emerging and gaps to be addressed. For this, a systematic literature review was carried out, aiming to characterize the solutions that have been developed using the EUD approach. The results show that most of EUD solutions are for web platform and focus on customizing existing applications, using visual programming techniques as interaction style. However, issues related to quality of use found in some results indicate that more research approaching IHC models, methods and techniques in design and evaluation of EUD tools is needed.

Keywords: End-user development · End-user programming ·
Systematic literature review

1 Introduction

The use of software applications in different contexts, whether for work or for entertainment purposes, has grown significantly in the last few years [13]. With this, it has also increased the number of systems that do not fully meet their users' needs. Thus the need arises for allowing end users, with little or no knowledge in programming and software development, to create their own applications or customize existing ones, to support them in carrying out specific tasks [16].

This fact characterizes the End-User Development (EUD) approach, which enables end users to design or customize the user interface and functionality of software [7]. EUD also consists of a research area that has been under study for some time and covers a wide variety of domains and types of end users [16]. However, there is still a lack of studies that analyze how EUD research has been reflected in practice, that is, in the development of software applications based on this approach.

This paper contributes to this line of research to enable an understanding of the current scenario of EUD solutions, revealing trends that are emerging

© Springer Nature Switzerland AG 2019
M. Kurosu (Ed.): HCII 2019, LNCS 11566, pp. 194–209, 2019.
https://doi.org/10.1007/978-3-030-22646-6_14

and gaps to be addressed. For this, a systematic literature review (SLR), following the methodology proposed by Kitchenham [14], was carried out, aiming to characterize the solutions that have been developed using the EUD approach. Such characterization considered particularly the context of use, platforms and interaction styles used, as well as characteristics of quality of use and limitations presented by the EUD tools.

Next, we briefly present the concept of EUD, which is the main theory on which the present work is grounded, followed by an overview of related works. Then, we present the protocol for the systematic literature review, followed by the results and discussion. We conclude by presenting our final remarks and outlining the next steps of our research.

2   End-User Development

End-user development (EUD) is a set of methods, techniques and tools that allow non-professional users to act as software developers, creating, modifying or extending software to achieve a goal [17]. EUD covers two similar concepts, end-user programming and end-user software engineering [7]. End-user programming (EUP) is the most mature subset of EUD from research and practice perspective [7] and it enables end users to create their own programs [16]. In this case, the developer himself is the user of the program, whereas in professional programming the goal is to create programs for others to use. Programs created by EUP can be extensions of existing applications, such as the creation of text manipulation macros in a text editor that are linked to keyboard shortcuts. These programs also can be new applications, as in the case of a spreadsheet that a teacher creates to manage the grades of his students. According to Burnett and Scaffidi [7], the difference between EUP and EUD is that EUD methods, techniques, and tools span the entire software development lifecycle, including modifying and extending software, not just the "create" phase.

The other concept related to EUD is end-user software engineering (EUSE). EUSE is a relatively new subset of EUD that emphasizes the quality of the software end users create, modify, or extend. Research in EUSE focuses on methods, techniques, and tools that promote the quality of such software [7]. The challenge of EUSE research is to find ways to incorporate software engineering activities into users' workflows without requiring a radical change in the way they work [16]. An example would be to incorporate tools that simplify the identification of data entry failures as the user provides information in a spreadsheet, rather than waiting for the users themselves to enter a test phase during their programming efforts.

In this paper, we use the term EUD to refer to both EUP and EUSE. Thus, the EUD solutions that will be characterized may refer to both software artifacts created, modified or extended by end users and also methods, techniques, and tools that promote the quality of such software.

3   Related Work

Among the few studies that make a survey on End User Development (EUD) field, Ko e colleagues [16] conducted a study aiming to classify the research and define the area of End-User Software Engineering (EUSE). The authors discuss empirical research related to EUSE activities (requirements, design and specification, reuse and testing) and the technologies designed to support them. As results, they identify works that focus on these different activities and also for different platforms.

Tetteroo e Markopoulos [28] presented a larger study comprising a literature review of the EUD field, covering the period from 2004 to 2013. The authors discuss the methods, purposes, and impacts of research in EUD, as well as pointing out trends within the research community and the gaps that need to be addressed. The results point to an increase in interest in EUD researches, although such interest has declined within the HCI community.

Although the above studies present surveys on the state of the art in EUD field, they focus on specific aspects in this research area. Paternó [25], on the other hand, addresses more practice aspects, by discussing and classifying several EUD approaches according to their main characteristics, as well as the technologies and platforms for which they were developed. However, a broader study is lacking, aiming to characterize in a more detailed and systematic way the EUD solutions presented in literature.

Regarding specific EUD solutions, we have identified a number of them, with distinct purposes and for different contexts, as we will show in the Sect. 5, that presents the results of the study conducted in the present work.

4   Systematic Literature Review

Our study followed the methodology proposed by Kitchenham e Charles [14] to conduct the Systematic Literature Review (SLR) which allowed us to characterize the EUD solutions that have been developed in the last years. Such methodology has three main phases: (1) planning the review; (2) conducting the review; and (3) reporting the review. In the phase (1), the goal of the review is identified and a review protocol is developed. Then, in the phase (2), the literature review is conducted by selecting the primary studies, assessing their quality, collecting the data and synthesizing the results. Finally, in the phase (3), findings are reported.

In the following subsections we present the activities carried out in the phases (1) and (2) of the SLR we conducted, while the phase (3) will be described in Sect. 5.

4.1   Research Question

We used the PIO (Population, Intervention and Outcome) strategy to formulate the research question that will guide the study [14], as showed in Table 1.

Table 1. PIO criteria

Population	End-user
Intervention	Development, Programming and Software Engineering
Outcomes	Features of software solutions

Thus, the following research question (RQ) was formulated for the present study: *How are the end-user development solutions characterized?* To better answer this research question, it was broken down into the following specific questions (SQ):

[SQ1] What contexts have EUD solutions been developed for?
[SQ2] What platforms have EUD solutions been developed for?
[SQ3] What interaction styles have been used by EUD solutions?
[SQ4] What quality-of-use features have been addressed by EUD solutions?
[SQ5] What are the limitations of EUD solutions?

Once the specific questions had been identified, the next step was to identify the relevant publications.

4.2 Research Process

Firstly, we elaborated the research string. We did it from the junction of the main terms that compose the research goal. We chose to use each term separately given that different authors use specific terms (e.g. EUP and EUSE) in the context of EUD.

In order to ensure that studies published in national and international conferences and journals were returned, we used keywords in both Portuguese and English language. Therefore, the string showed in Table 2 was defined for this research.

Table 2. Research string

("desenvolvimento por usuário final" OR "end-user development") OR
("programação por usuário final" OR "end-user programming") OR
("engenharia de software por usuário final" OR "end-user software engineering")

The research string was used in electronic search, in the following digital libraries: ACM Digital Library[1], IEEE[2], Science Direct[3], Springer[4] e a HCIBIB[5].

---

[1] http://dl.acm.org/.
[2] http://ieeexplore.ieee.org/Xplore/home.jsp.
[3] http://www.sciencedirect.com/.
[4] http://www.springerlink.com/.
[5] http://hcibib.org/.

In addition, we also did manual search in proceedings of Brazilian Symposium on Human Factors in Computing Systems (IHC), for years that were not available at the ACM Digital Library.

The selection of repositories to search for publications was based in their importance for had published the greatest amount of study in the EUD field and that would allow us to undertake a study with high quality and relevance.

We search for studies published from 2007, when the first conference dedicated exclusively to the EUD took place, the International Symposium on End User Development, to 2017, the year when the present research was conducted.

According to [14], studies should be evaluated for their relevance. Therefore, inclusion and exclusion criteria were defined in order to reduce the number of studies that are not relevant to the research question. Tables 3 and 4 exhibit the inclusion (IC) and exclusion (EC) criteria for this research, respectively.

Table 3. Inclusion criteria

IC 1	Studies should consider one or more end-user development solutions
IC 2	Full papers: technical or experience
IC 3	Short papers

Table 4. Exclusion criteria

EC 1	Studies published in languages other than English and Portuguese
EC 2	Books, tutorials, editorials, abstracts, posters, panels, lectures, round tables, workshops, demonstrations or workshops
EC 3	Studies that are not available on the web in unrestricted access or through institutional IP
EC 4	Duplicate papers that talk about the same study and report the same results (in this case, the most recent paper will be used as the basis for analysis)
EC 5	Papers that did not reach the minimum quality score established

Once the inclusion and exclusion criteria have been defined, the search was executed, both manually and automatically, using the research string, in the selected repositories, according to the selection process shown in Fig. 1. The following steps were performed:

1. Reading the title to eliminate irrelevant documents;
2. Reading the abstract and keywords to eliminate studies included in step 1 that were not related to the research questions;

3. Reading the introduction, main topics and conclusion to eliminate studies included in step 2 that were not related to the research questions (skim reading);
4. Complete reading of the selected studies in step 3 and application of the quality criteria, in order to verify their relevance to collect relevant data to the research.

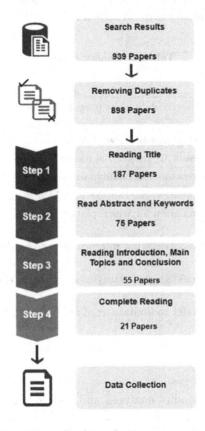

Fig. 1. Studies selection process

The above steps were carried out by a researcher, with the assistance of another researcher, who reviewed the whole process. In cases where verification at each step was not sufficient to determine whether or not the study should be included in the next step, it remained on the list so that it could then be analyzed in the next step, until its relevance to the research was confirmed. In steps 1,

2, and 3, the inclusion and exclusion criteria established for the search were applied. The data set found in each of the steps was stored in Excel worksheets.

As we can see in Fig. 1, in the step 1, of 939 articles returned by automatic and manual searches, 187 (20%) were selected for the step 2, after removing duplicates and executing the title reading step. After abstract and keywords reading, 75 papers were selected for step 3, which represents a reduction of 60%. Finally, after skim reading, 55 papers were selected for step 4, when complete reading of them was carried out. Thus, 21 papers were selected for analysis, after the application of the quality criteria shown in Table 5.

Table 5. Quality criteria

Criteria	Question
QC1	Does the study clearly define the purpose of the research (define research question)?
QC2	Does the study discuss related works?
QC3	Is the study relevant to answer the research question?
QC4	Does the study recommend possible futures work?
QC5	Does the paper mention the context for which the EUD solution applies?
QC6	Does the paper mention for which platform the EUD solution has been developed?
QC7	Does the paper mention what interaction style has been use by the EUD solution?
QC8	Does the paper refer to the quality-of-use feature related to the EUD solution?
QC9	Does the paper refer to limitations of the EUD solution?

5   Results

Table 6 presents the 21 studies analyzed and their reference identifier assigned to be referenced in this paper. It also summarizes the data collected during the research. This information will be used in the analysis which is presented in the next section. The analyzed studies were classified according to five dimensions: **context of use, platform, interaction style, quality-of-use features** and **limitations** presented by EUD solutions. **Context of use** refers to the application domain of the EUD solution. The **Platform** refers to the environment for which the EUD solution was developed, which can be web, desktop or mobile [25]. **Interaction style** consists of the way in which end users interact with the solution of EUD [23]. **Quality of use features** is related to characteristics of the

EUD solution that qualify the possible interaction through the interface according to certain aspects, such as usability, user experience, accessibility, among others [26]. **Limitations** consist of problems related to EUD solutions reported in the studies. Finally, **Segment** refers to where the EUD solution was created, i.e. academia or industry.

6   Analysis

Analyzing the resulting studies from the SLR, it is noticed that the largest number of papers addressing EUD solutions occurred more recently, between 2014 and 2017, corresponding to approximately 66% of the analyzed publications, which characterizes an incipient character of the research involving EUD tools. Regarding publication venue, 43% of papers were published in journals or periodicals, while 57% were published in conferences. Figure 2 shows the publications by year and by publication venue.

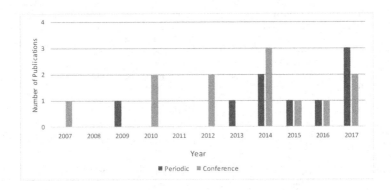

Fig. 2. Distribution of publications by year e publication venue.

Considering the studies analyzed, 48% of them present EUD solutions for customizing existing applications, while 29% aim to creat new applications and 23% are intended for content creation.

Another aspect observed from the analysis is that most EUD solutions come from academia. Only 5 studies (24%) had collaboration from industry researchers.

Next, in order to answer the research question (RQ) of this study, we will answer the specific questions (SQ), based on the research conducted.

Table 6. References and data collection summary

ID	Reference	Context of use	Platform	Interaction style	Quality-of-Use features	Limitations
E1	Diaz et al. (2013) [12]	Independent of domain	Web	Visual Programming	Yes	Yes
E2	Kleek et al. (2010) [31]	Personal Life	Web	Visual Programming	Yes	Yes
E3	Ardito et al. (2012) [3]	Culture	Web	Visual Programming	Yes	Yes
E4	Di Geronimo et al. (2017) [11]	Independent of Domain	Web	Visual Programming	Yes	Yes
E5	Borges e Macías (2010) [6]	Independent of Domain	Web	Programming by Demonstration	Yes	Yes
E6	Baytas et al. (2014) [5]	Independent of Domain	Desktop	Visual Programming	No	Yes
E7	Tetteroo et al. (2015) [29]	Health	Desktop	Visual Programming Tangible Programming	Yes	Yes
E8	Wong e Hong (2007) [32]	Independent of Domain	Web	Programming by Demonstration	Yes	Yes
E9	Akiki et al. (2017) [2]	Independent of Domain	Web	Visual Programming	Yes	Yes
E10	Castelli et al. (2017) [9]	Smarts Home	Web	Visual Programming	Yes	Yes
E11	Martin et al. (2014) [21]	Independent of Domain	Web	Programming by Demonstration	Yes	No
E12	Tankovic et al. (2014) [27]	Business	Web	Programming by Demonstration	No	Yes
E13	Lizcano, et al. (2014) [18]	Independent of Domain	Web	Visual Programming	Yes	Yes
E14	Barricelli e Stefano (2017) [4]	Sports	Web	Programação Visual	Yes	Yes
E15	Ghiani et al. (2016) [13]	Independent of Domain	Web	Visual Programming	No	Yes
E16	Lizcano et al. (2015) [19]	Independent of Domain	Web	Visual Programming	No	Yes
E17	Aghaee e Pautasso (2014) [1]	Independent of Domain	Web	Programming by Demonstration	Yes	Yes
E18	Neumann et al. (2009) [24]	Sports	Mobile	Visual Programming	No	Yes
E19	Turchi et al. (2017) [30]	Independent of Domain	Desktop/ Web	Tangible Programming	No	Yes
E20	Danado e Paterno (2012) [10]	Independent of Domain	Mobile	Visual Programming	Yes	Yes
E21	Carneiro e Monteiro (2016) [8]	Independent of Domain	Web	Textual Programming	Yes	Yes

6.1   [SQ1] What Contexts Have EUD Solutions Been Developed For?

Regarding to the context, which refers to the domain to which the analyzed EUD solutions apply, it was possible to classify them as follows:

– **Domain independent:** most of EUD solutions analyzed (67%) can be classified in this category, i.e, they allow end-users, even not being technology experts, to be able to create, modify and extend existing content and services in order to get an application that best suits to their needs, whatever the domain which it refers. This is the case, for example, of the tool presented in E20 [10], which can be used by end-users to develop different types of applications.

- **Domain Specific:** 33% of the EUD solutions analyzed fit in this category, i.e., they are aimed at to a specific domain, as personal life) (E2 [31]), culture (E3 [3]), health (E7 [29]), smart homes (E10 [9]), businesses (E12 [27]) and sports (E14 [4] and E18 [24]).

6.2 [SQ2] What Platforms Have EUD Solutions Been Developed For?

Most of EUD solutions presented in analyzed studies were developed to web platform (about 65%), followed by desktop (22%) and mobile platform (13%), as shown in Fig. 3. One analyzed solution is multiplatform, contemplating both web and desktop platform.

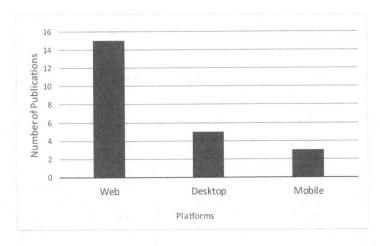

Fig. 3. Platforms for which EUD solutions were developed

6.3 [SQ3] What Interaction Styles Have Been Used by EUD Solutions?

EUD solutions were classfied according to the interaction styles, presented in literature [7], that they provides to end-users. Figure 4 shows the interaction styles provided by solutions analyzed. Visual Programming is the most used between solutions (64%) and only one solution combines more than one interaction style.

Visual programming is a techniques that has become relevant in the research community for reducing barriers for end-users to create content for specific domain and for demonstrating benefits in support to development [20,24].

Thus, the analyzed EUD solutions use such technique in order to facilitate the interaction of end-users which have no development knowledge. This is the case, for example, of the solution shown by [31], which allows the end-user sets alarms and reminders for daily tasks simply manipulating visual components in its interface.

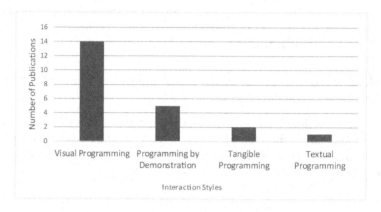

Fig. 4. Interactions styles in EUD solutions.

6.4 [SQ4] What Quality-of-Use Features Have Been Addressed by EUD Solutions?

The majority of EUD solutions analyzed (15 out of 21) presents features associated to quality-of-use, as explained below:

– **Easy of use.** This feature is the most present in analyzed solutions (33%) (E2 [31], E4 [11], E9 [2], E11 [21], E14 [4], E20 [10] e E21 [8]). This can be explained by the fact that easy of use i very important for a system can be effectively used by end-users, particularly those which have no extensive experience in technology. Thus, just the fact of not requiring development knowledge, which is an inherent feature of EUD solutions, contributes to ease-of-use. This is the case of SideTalk [8], for example, that has a simple interface and communicates well to users its design intentions.
– **User feedback**, concerning the actions he performs in the system. This feature is present in some analyzed studies (19%) and it is important in order to keep the user informed of the results of his actions. Such feature was considered by four analyzed solutions (E1 [12], E3 [3], E10 [9], and E17 [1]). The solution presented in [9], for example, consists of a domestic system that allows users to have an overview of the current status of their smart home.
– **Concealing of non-important informations.** Three solutions (E1 [12], E9 [2] e E13 [18]), i.e., 14% of analyzed studies, presented the feature of

not show in the interface information that can cause confusion for the user, or even lead to system errors. The Sticklet, for example, shown in [12], hides some JavaScript functionality from users since it can cause failures on system.

- **Adaptation to users needs**, in different contexts of use. This feature refers to the flexibility offered by the system, in order to can be tailored to satisfy users needs. Such features present in three of analyzed solutions (E5 [6], E7 [29] and E8 [32]), i.e., 14% of analyzed studies. The EUD solution present in [6], for example, allows users to adopt certain features of the work environment, depending on their experience.

6.5   [SQ5] What Are the Limitations of EUD Solutions?

The absolute majority of analyzed EUD solutions (20 of a total of 21) present some difficulty or limitation in their use. The most of the detected limitations in analyzed solutions consists of aspects which can negatively impact users interaction with the system, as follows:

- **Incompatibility between the language used by the system and the user's language.** This limitation, which is present in 33% of analyzed EUD solutions (seven - E2 [31], E5 [6], E7 [29], E8 [32], E14 [4], E20 [10], and E21 [8]), makes more difficult for user to understand how to interact with the system. Interaction with these solutions requires greater effort on the part of users, as is the case of TagTrainer, presented by [29], where the lack of programming skills and interaction design experience of some therapists inhibit them to create proper exercises for their patients.

- **Lack of control by users.** This limitation was reported for 20% of analyzed EUD solutions (six - E3 [3], E4 [11], E6 [5], E9 [2], E10 [9], and E18 [24]). It restricts user interaction with a system in actions that are pre-defined by designer. An example is open.DASH application, presented in [9], which made impossible for users to interact with desirable system features, due to a limited amount of sensors.

- **Lack of help to users.** The lack of a help mechanism, which guides the user through his interaction with the system, explaining details on how to use it, was pointed out as limitation in 19% of the studies (four - E1 [12], E9 [2], E20 [10] and E21 [8]). In Stikclet [12], for example, it is not offered to users any assistance to guide them while their interaction.

- **Limitations to specific platforms or formats.** 14% of analyzed studies (three - E1 [12], E13 [18], and E16 [19]) address this limitation in EUD solution. This is the case of tool presented in [19], in which it is only applicable information in XML format, but not in other, as JSON or simple text file.

- **Error propensity.** In solutions with having such limitation, there is the possibility that user-system interaction is discontinued as a result of failure to perform one or more functionality. 10% of analyzed EUD solutions (two studies - E16 [19] and E20 [10]) indicate the error propensity as a limitation, as is the case of runtime errors shown by EUD solution presented in [10].

– **Other limitations on interaction.** In 14% of studies (three - E15 [13], E17 [1], and E19 [30]), it was found the following limitations: **not supporting collaboration, lack of feedback to users about the results of their actions** e **incompatibility between interaction styles used by solution.**

In addition to these limitations, one study (E12 [27]) pointed as EUD solution limitation a problem related to **integration and scalability.** Such issue, different from those presented above, is intrinsic to the system, and not relative to user interaction.

7　Discussion

From the obtained results, it is possible to answer the research question investigated in this study: *[RQ]: How are the end-user development solutions characterized?*

Initially, we identified that research involving EUD solutions is recent and has intensified from 2014, indicating an increase in the use of the EUD approach in practice as well as in the interest in such research field. In addition, most of the solutions came from the academy, indicating that industry still does not effectively apply the potential of the EUD approach to market opportunities for products and services. This fact confirms, in the present day, what Klann et al. stated in 2006 [15].

The analyzed solutions focus mainly on the tailoring of existing applications, i.e., modifying the appearance or set of attributes of a system by an end user [22]. Such EUD solutions are also predominantly independent of domain, indicating a more general character of the EUD approach. This suggests a tendency to have solutions aimed at meeting the needs of end users in any domain or area of knowledge, instead of being targeted to specialists of specific domains.

The fact of most EUD solutions have been developed for web platform probably occurs because it is currently the most common user interface and can be accessed from any device. This fact may encourage the development of EUD solutions for such platform [25].

Visual programming is the dominant interaction style in EUD solutions. Thus, given the purpose of such technique of making easier the user interaction [7]. This fact indicates that EUD research converges to popularizing the use of its tools, by using the visual programming as a strategy to attract end-users to create their own applications.

The concern with quality of use was present in most of the analyzed EUD solutions, with "ease of use" being the most present feature among them. This fact shows the concern about the use of these solutions by end-users, given that one of the requirements for systems to be widely accepted by their users is that they present properties that bring quality to the possible interactions through their interface [26]. On the other hand, the number of limitations regarding issues that negatively impact the user interaction, present in EUD solutions, exceeds the number of quality-of-use features. This fact indicates an inconsistency and deserves to be further investigated.

This fact suggests a gap in the research on the use of IHC models, methods and techniques in projects and evaluation of EUD tools. Such a situation can be confirmed by the fact that, of the 21 studies analyzed in this study, only one EUD solution was developed and evaluated using HCI models and methods [8].

8 Conclusion and Future Works

This study described how the **end-user development** approach has been used in the development of end-user support tools. For this, a systematic literature review was conducted in order to identify how these solutions are characterized.

The motivation to conduct this study was initially due to the lack of studies that analyze how research in EUD is reflected in practice.

The results indicated that most of the existing EUD solutions in literature focus on application customization, by using visual programming techniques and thus indicating an initiative to attract users to use them. However, quality-of-use features and limitations identified in EUD solutions point to inconsistencies that indicate the need for research involving HCI models, methods and techniques in the design and evaluation of these tools, in order to achieve a higher quality of use.

In terms of contribution, our results are a basis to research approaching HCI models, methods and techniques in design and evaluation with EUD tools.

To this end, research can be conducted in order to investigate how HCI theories, models, methods and techniques have been used in design and evaluation of EUD solutions and what the impact of this in their quality of use.

References

1. Aghaee, S., Pautasso, C.: End-user development of mashups with NaturalMash. J. Vis. Lang. Comput. **25**(4), 414–432 (2014)
2. Akiki, P.A., Bandara, A.K., Yu, Y.: Visual simple transformations: empowering end-users to wire Internet of Things objects. ACM Trans. Comput. Hum. Interact. **24**(2), 10:1–10:43 (2017). http://doi.acm.org/10.1145/3057857
3. Ardito, C., Costabile, M.F., Desolda, G., Matera, M., Piccinno, A., Picozzi, M.: Composition of situational interactive spaces by end users: a case for cultural heritage. In: Proceedings of the 7th Nordic Conference on Human-Computer Interaction: Making Sense Through Design, NordiCHI 2012, pp. 79–88. ACM, New York (2012). http://doi.acm.org/10.1145/2399016.2399029
4. Barricelli, B.R., Valtolina, S.: A visual language and interactive system for end-user development of Internet of Things ecosystems. J. Vis. Lang. Comput. **40**, 1–19 (2017). http://linkinghub.elsevier.com/retrieve/pii/S1045926X16300295
5. Baytas, M.A., Yemez, Y., Özcan, O.: Hotspotizer: end-user authoring of mid-air gestural interactions. In: Proceedings of the 8th Nordic Conference on Human-Computer Interaction: Fun, Fast, Foundational, NordiCHI 2014, pp. 677–686. ACM, New York (2014). http://doi.acm.org/10.1145/2639189.2639255

6. Borges, C.R., Macías, J.A.: Feasible database querying using a visual end-user approach. In: Proceedings of the 2nd ACM SIGCHI Symposium on Engineering Interactive Computing Systems - EICS 2010, p. 187. ACM, New York (2010). http://portal.acm.org/citation.cfm?doid=1822018.1822047

7. Burnett, M.M., Scaffidi, C.: End-User Development. The Interaction Design Foundation. In: The Encyclopedia of Human-Computer Interaction, 2nd edn. (2013). https://www.interaction-design.org/literature/book/the-encyclopedia-of-human-computer-interaction-2nd-ed/end-user-development

8. Carneiro, I.S., Monteiro, I.T.: Avaliação da comunicabilidade de sistemas criados por usuários-designers. In: 15th Brazilian Symposium on Human Factors in Computer Systems, pp. 81–90 (2016)

9. Castelli, N., Ogonowski, C., Jakobi, T., Stein, M., Stevens, G., Wulf, V.: What happened in my home?: An end-user development approach for smart home data visualization. In: Proceedings of the 2017 CHI Conference on Human Factors in Computing Systems, CHI 2017, pp. 853–866. ACM, New York (2017). http://doi.acm.org/10.1145/3025453.3025485

10. Danado, J., Paternò, F.: Puzzle: a visual-based environment for end user development in touch-based mobile phones. In: Winckler, M., Forbrig, P., Bernhaupt, R. (eds.) HCSE 2012. LNCS, vol. 7623, pp. 199–216. Springer, Heidelberg (2012). https://doi.org/10.1007/978-3-642-34347-6_12

11. Di Geronimo, L., Kalbermatter, S., Norrie, M.C.: End-user web development tool for tilting interactions. In: Proceedings of the ACM SIGCHI Symposium on Engineering Interactive Computing Systems - EICS 2017, pp. 9–14. ACM, New York (2017). http://dl.acm.org/citation.cfm?doid=3102113.3102117

12. Diaz, O., Arellano, C., Azanza, M.: A language for end-user web augmentation: caring for producers and consumers alike. ACM Trans. Web 7(2), 9:1–9:51 (2013). http://doi.acm.org/10.1145/2460383.2460388

13. Ghiani, G., Paternò, F., Spano, L.D., Pintori, G.: An environment for end-user development of web mashups. Int. J. Hum. Comput. Stud. 87, 38–64 (2016). http://linkinghub.elsevier.com/retrieve/pii/S1071581915001767

14. Kitchenham, B., Charters, S.: Guidelines for performing Systematic Literature Reviews in Software Engineering (2007)

15. Klann, M., Paternò, F., Wulf, V.: Future perspectives in end-user development. In: Lieberman, H., Paternò, F., Wulf, V. (eds.) End User Development. Human-Computer Interaction Series, vol. 9, pp. 475–486. Springer, Dordrecht (2006). https://doi.org/10.1007/1-4020-5386-X_21

16. Ko, A.J., et al.: The state of the art in end-user software engineering. ACM Comput. Surv. 43(3), 1–44 (2011). http://portal.acm.org/citation.cfm?doid=1922649.1922658

17. Lieberman, H., Paternò, F., Klann, M., Wulf, V.: End-user development: an emerging paradigm. In: Lieberman, H., Paternò, F., Wulf, V. (eds.) End User Development. Human-Computer Interaction Series, vol. 9, pp. 1–18. Springer, Dordrecht (2006). https://doi.org/10.1007/1-4020-5386-X_1

18. Lizcano, D., Alonso, F., Soriano, J., López, G.: A component- and connector-based approach for end-user composite web applications development. J. Syst. Softw. 94, 108–128 (2014)

19. Lizcano, D., Alonso, F., Soriano, J., López, G.: Automated end user-centred adaptation of web components through automated description logic-based reasoning. Inf. Softw. Technol. 57(1), 446–462 (2015). http://linkinghub.elsevier.com/retrieve/pii/S0950584914001384

20. Lye, S.Y., Koh, J.H.L.: Review on teaching and learning of computational thinking through programming: what is next for k-12? Comput. Hum. Behav. **41**, 51–61 (2014)
21. Martin, D., Lamsfus, C., Alzua-Sorzabal, A., Torres-Manzanera, E.: Empowering end-users to develop context-aware mobile applications using a web platform. In: 2014 International Conference on Future Internet of Things and Cloud, pp. 139–145 (2014)
22. Mørch, A.: Three levels of end-user tailoring: customization, integration, and extension, pp. 51–76. MIT Press, Cambridge, November 1997
23. Nardi, B.A.: A Small Matter of Programming: Perspectives on End User Computing. MIT Press, Cambridge (1993)
24. Neumann, C., Metoyer, R.A., Burnett, M.: End-user strategy programming. J. Vis. Lang. Comput. **20**(1), 16–29 (2009)
25. Paternò, F.: End user development: survey of an emerging field for empowering people. ISRN Softw. Eng **2013**, 11 (2013)
26. Rogers, Y., Sharp, H., Preece, J.: Interaction Design: Beyond Human-Computer Interaction. Wiley, Chichester (2011)
27. Tankovic, N., Grbac, T.G., Zagar, M.: Experiences from building a EUD business portal. In: 2014 37th International Convention on Information and Communication Technology, Electronics and Microelectronics (MIPRO), pp. 551–556. IEEE, May 2014. http://ieeexplore.ieee.org/document/6859629/
28. Tetteroo, D., Markopoulos, P.: A review of research methods in end user development. In: Díaz, P., Pipek, V., Ardito, C., Jensen, C., Aedo, I., Boden, A. (eds.) IS-EUD 2015. LNCS, vol. 9083, pp. 58–75. Springer, Cham (2015). https://doi.org/10.1007/978-3-319-18425-8_5
29. Tetteroo, D., et al.: Lessons learnt from deploying an end-user development platform for physical rehabilitation. In: Proceedings of the 33rd Annual ACM Conference on Human Factors in Computing Systems - CHI 2015, vol. 1, pp. 4133–4142. ACM, New York (2015). http://dl.acm.org/citation.cfm?doid=2702123.2702504
30. Turchi, T., Malizia, A., Dix, A.: TAPAS: a tangible end-user development tool supporting the repurposing of pervasive displays. J. Vis. Lang. Comput. **39**, 66–77 (2017). http://linkinghub.elsevier.com/retrieve/pii/S1045926X16302191
31. Van Kleek, M., Moore, B., Karger, D.R., André, P., Schraefel, M.C.: Atomate it! end-user context-sensitive automation using heterogeneous information sources on the web. In: Proceedings of the 19th International Conference on World Wide Web - WWW 2010, p. 951. ACM, New York (2010). http://portal.acm.org/citation.cfm?doid=1772690.1772787
32. Wong, J., Hong, J.I.: Making mashups with marmite: towards end-user programming for the web. In: Proceedings of the SIGCHI Conference on Human Factors in Computing Systems, CHI 2007, pp. 1435–1444. ACM, New York (2007). http://doi.acm.org/10.1145/1240624.1240842

Towards a Set of Design Guidelines for Multi-device Experience

Luis Martín Sánchez-Adame, Sonia Mendoza$^{(\boxtimes)}$, Amilcar Meneses Viveros, and José Rodríguez

Department of Computer Science, CINVESTAV-IPN, Av. IPN 2508, Col. San Pedro Zacatenco, Del. Gustavo A. Madero, 07360 Mexico City, Mexico
luismartin.sanchez@cinvestav.mx,
{smendoza,ameneses,rodriguez}@cs.cinvestav.mx

Abstract. Thanks to the hyperconnected world in which we live, we are surrounded by devices. Many of these devices can communicate with each other, and even they can support the same application so that the user can have multiple forms of interaction. However, developers should be careful when considering the control level left to users, since the applications may become unusable. Whether the system or user decides the distribution of the available devices, Graphical User Interface (GUI) consistency must always be preserved. Consistency not only provides users with a robust framework in similar contexts but is an essential learning element and a lever to ensure the GUI efficient usage. This paper proposes a set of consistency guidelines that serve as a means for the construction of multi-device applications. As a case study, DistroPaint was evaluated by experts who identified consistency violations and assessed their severity.

Keywords: Design guidelines · GUI consistency · User experience · Interactive environments · Multi-device applications

1 Introduction

At present we are surrounded by devices, the most common are smartphones, tablets, and laptops. However, more and more devices are being added to create a truly interactive environment: sensors, cameras, microphones, smart watches, and screens that can be found in the most unexpected places. Today the number of devices connected to the Internet surpasses 7 billion [1]. The omnipresence of these devices, especially mobile ones, is progressively changing the way people perceive, experience, and interact with products and each other [2]. This transition poses a significant challenge, since we have to design User eXperiences (UX) according to each device.

Within this context, a topic of particular interest is when a single application can be executed on multiple devices. The ability to seamlessly connect multiple devices of varying screen size and capabilities has always been an integral part

© Springer Nature Switzerland AG 2019
M. Kurosu (Ed.): HCII 2019, LNCS 11566, pp. 210–223, 2019.
https://doi.org/10.1007/978-3-030-22646-6_15

of the vision for distributed UX and Ubiquitous Computing [3]. That is, the same application has to provide a similar UX regardless of the device or its environment. One way to preserve UX is to have a consistent application.

Consistency states that presentation and prompts should share as much as possible common features and refer to a common task, including using the same terminology across different inputs and outputs [4]. Several studies have shown that consistency is a crucial factor for multi-device experience, but they have also argued that it is a challenge for developers, since maintaining consistency of a multi-device system is an open problem [5–8]. Consistency is important because it reduces the learning curve and helps eliminate confusion, in addition to reducing production costs [9–11].

Microsoft is an excellent case to exemplify the importance of consistency. Windows 10 and Office (in its most recent versions) are two of the most important products of the company; It is notorious that both GUIs are a design statement since they follow the same layout. In both software products, we can see that their toolbars have a similar design, i.e., the grouping, positioning, and labelling of buttons and commands is identical. This is intended to allow users to focus on their productivity, without the need to learn a new tool panel for each software they use. For this reason, Microsoft developed a series of tools, including an API and design guidelines that are integrated into a framework called Ribbon [12], so that this design discourse propagates to all applications developed by third parties.

In this way, we can talk about three approaches to the design of applications which, although authors like Coutaz and Calvary [13] and Vanderdonckt [14] studied years ago, Levin [2] summarises them in her 3C framework:

- **Consistent design approach:** Each device acts as a solo player, creating the entire experience on its own.
- **Continuous design approach:** Multiple devices handle different pieces sequentially, driving the user toward a common goal.
- **Complementary design approach:** Multiple devices play together as an ensemble to create the experience.

This framework presents a series of challenges since it involves, among other things, the fragmentation of the GUI and business logic. Thus the task for the developers is to preserve a positive UX among all the devices.

By adding consistency elements to the design of multi-device environments, usability is improved, and the possibility of a scenario with negative UX is reduced [15,16]. The primary goal of our work is to propose a set of design guidelines that serve as a model in the creation of consistent applications. These guidelines are depicted through a case study: DistroPaint. This application has been evaluated by five UX experts, who have identified a list of consistency violations and have assessed the severity of each one.

This paper is organised as follows. First, in Sect. 2, related work is studied. Section 3 describes the research methodology that we use. Then, in Sects. 4 and 5, we respectively define and implement our set of design guidelines. Finally, in Sect. 6 we discuss the achieved work and provide some ideas for future work.

2   Related Work

This section describes some of the investigations carried out in the field of multi-device UX. They serve to support the importance and necessity of our proposal.

After having interviewed 29 professionals in the area of interactive environments, Dong et al. [3] identified three key challenges that have prevented designers and developers from building usable multi-device systems: (1) the difficulty in designing interactions between devices, (2) the complexity of adapting GUIs to different platform standards, and (3) the lack of tools and methods for testing multi-device UX.

Marcus [17] was a pioneer in the description of good practices to develop GUIs. He claims that the *organisation*, *economisation*, and *communication* principles help GUI design. The highlights are his four elements of consistency: (1) *internal* (applying the same rules for all elements within the GUI), (2) *external* (following existing conventions), (3) *real-world* (following real-world experience), and (4) *no-consistency* (when to deviating from the norm).

Meskens et al. [18] presented a set of techniques to design and manage GUIs for multiple devices integrated into *Jelly*, a single multi-device GUI design environment. *Jelly* allows designers to copy widgets from one device design canvas to another, while preserving the consistency of their content across devices using linked editing.

O'Leary et al. [19] argue that designers of multi-device UX need tools to better address situated contexts of use, early in their design process through ideation and reflection. To address this need, they created and tested a reusable design kit that contains scenarios, cards, and a framework for understanding tradeoffs of multi-device innovations in realistic contexts of use.

Woodrow [20] defines and contextualises three critical concepts for usability in multi-device systems: (1) *composition* (distribution of functionality), (2) *consistency* (what elements should be consistent across which aspects), and (3) *continuity* (a clear indication of switching interactions). The author makes a call for more active involvement by both the systems engineering and engineering management communities in advancing methods and approaches for interusability (interactions spanning multiple devices with different capabilities).

All these works show that the highly interactive environments formed by multi-device applications are a promising field with many issues to explore. However, they are also examples of a knowledge gap that we try to fill with our guidelines for consistency.

3   Research Methodology

The research methodology for the development of our design guidelines is based on the Design Science Research Methodology (DSRM) process model proposed by Peffers et al. [21] (see Fig. 1). We chose this methodology because its popularity in the state of the art, and it has proved useful in similar problems [22–24].

An *Objective-Centred Initiation* has been chosen as a research entry point because our goal is to improve the design of multi-device applications. As for

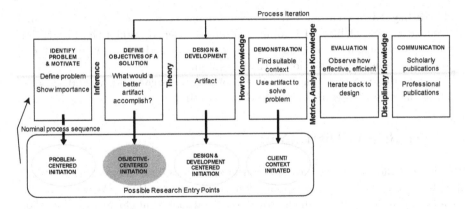

Fig. 1. We started from an *Objective-Centred Initiation* (coloured in orange) in the DSRM process model [21]. (Color figure online)

Identification & Motivation, we have already described the importance of highly interactive environments, and the role of GUI consistency in that matter. The *Objective of a Solution*, the second step of the process, is to develop a set of design guidelines that helps developers to create consistent applications to improve UX. The third step *Design & Development* is the description of our guidelines for GUI consistency (see Sect. 4). *Demonstration* and *Evaluation* are described in our case study (see Sect. 5). This is the first iteration of the process. Subsequent iterations will begin in the *Design & Development* stage, in order to improve said guidelines.

4 Consistency Guidelines

With the review of various works in the state of the art, and taking into account the challenges discovered and common characteristics of each one, we present our five design guidelines to maintain consistency in multi-device systems:

- **Honesty:** Interaction widgets have to do what they say and behave expectedly. An honest GUI has the purpose of reinforcing the user's decision to use the system. When the widgets are confusing, misleading, or even suspicious, users' confidence will begin to wane.
- **Functional Cores:** These are indivisible sets of widgets. The elements that constitute a Functional Core form a semantic field, out of their field they lose meaning. The granularity level of interaction for a Functional Core depends on the utility of a particular set of widgets.
- **Multimodality:** Capability of multi-device systems to use different means of interaction whenever the execution context changes. In general, it is desirable that regardless of the input and output modalities, the user can achieve the same result.

- **Usability Limitations:** When multimodality scenarios exist, it is possible that situations of limited usability could be reached. When the interaction environment changes and its context is transformed, the environment can restrict the user's interaction with the system.
- **Traceability:** Denotes the situation in which users can observe and, in some cases, modify the evolution of the GUI over time.

5 Case Study: DistroPaint

In order to demonstrate the proposed consistency guidelines (see Sect. 4), we developed DistroPaint, a prototype application that integrates them. We decide to create a basic graphics editor, which provides several tools that can be distributed on several devices (PC, phone, and tablet). This section describes our proof of concept (see Sect. 5.1) and the expert analysis carried out (see Sect. 5.2) based on the works by Andrade et al. [25], Grice et al. [26], and Schmettow et al. [27].

5.1 DistroPaint

DistroPaint is a Web application for basic graphic design. The user can access the application from a PC, a phone, and a tablet. They can distribute the GUI from the PC to the mobile devices, e.g., the colour pallet can be displayed on the phone, while the drawing tools are being shown on the tablet (see Fig. 2). The user can configure the GUI at any moment. Below we list how our design guidelines are reflected in the implementation of DistroPaint:

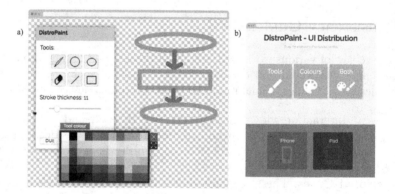

Fig. 2. Predominant GUIs of DistroPaint on a PC web browser: (a) GUI of the graphical editor, and (b) the distribution menu for the widgets

Fig. 3. Presence system: (a) a grey box means that the device is unreachable; (b) an orange box indicates that the device is connected but it can not receive widgets; and (c) a green box expresses that the device is ready to receive widgets (Color figure online)

– **Honesty:** The part where DistroPaint's honesty stands out most is its presence system (see Fig. 3), since it informs the user about the availability of their devices. The Honesty at this point is critical, because it allows the user to make decisions (to distribute, or not) according to the state of their interactive environment.

– **Functional Cores:** The main way of interaction in our application is the toolbox (see Fig. 4), so we choose it as the main element for the DUI. The decision of how to divide the elements could seem trivial, e.g., each tool (brush, eraser, line, etc.) could be distributed individually among several devices, however, this could be a risky option, since it would bring very few benefits to the cost of generating confusion and increasing the system requirements. So we decide that the tools and the slider for the stroke thickness should form a semantic field. In the same way, another field would be occupied by the colour palette, thus, we have two Functional Cores as result.

– **Multimodality:** The element for the change of context that has more repercussion in our application is the change of platform. No matter whether a user uses one element of the toolbox from the PC (by clicking with a mouse) or from a mobile device (by touching with a finger), DistroPaint has to respond seamlessly (see Fig. 5).

– **Usability Limitations:** We create a synthetic limitation in our prototype (see Fig. 6). We decide that both of our Functional Cores have to be available for both the phone and the tablet, but only the tablet can display both at the same time. Although this can also be achievable for the phone, we want to demonstrate that despite the capabilities of the devices (in this case, the difference in screen sizes), it is desirable to offer alternatives, so users can accomplish theirs tasks in one way or another.

– **Traceability:** Besides the already explained presence system, DistroPaint also gives feedback to the users about where the widgets are being distributed and also maintains synchronised all the values for all the widgets from the toolbox, no matter from where or when the user changes such values (see Fig. 7).

5.2   Evaluation and Results

The evaluation has been worked out with the help of five UX experts. We chose the experts for their experience applying usability tests, and because they are

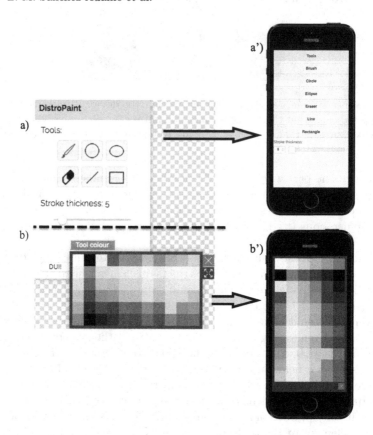

Fig. 4. Functional Cores division for the toolbox: (a) tools core, (b) colours core, and their respective mobile formats (a') and (b')

familiar with the topics of our research. All the experts are university professors and have postgraduate studies; two of them belong to our university. Their experience comes from both work in industry and research centres. It should be noted that none is related to this work in addition to their participation in the evaluation.

Before starting the evaluation, we gathered and explained to the experts each of our design guidelines, their purpose, and discussed some examples so that everyone had a similar starting point. Each expert drafted a list of problems and violations of the guidelines that we propose. Once the evaluators have identified potential consistency problems, the individual lists have been consolidated into a single master list. The master list was then given back to the evaluators who independently have assessed the severity of each violation. The ratings from the individual evaluators are then averaged, and we present the results in Table 1. For the rating, we adapted the severity classification proposed by Zhang et al. [28]:

0 - Not a consistency problem at all.

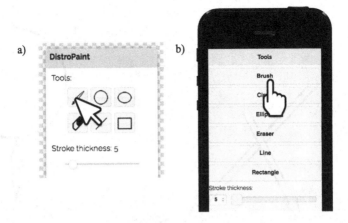

Fig. 5. DistroPaint allows interaction through: (a) a mouse, and (b) with a finger; with both modalities the user can obtain the same result

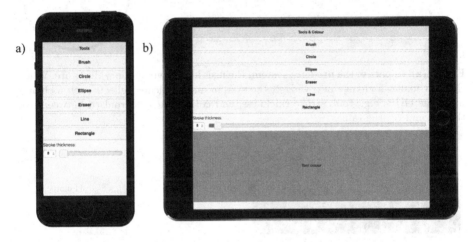

Fig. 6. Functional Cores can be seen: (a) one at a time on the phone; (b) both of them at the same time on the tablet. The reason to do this is that the tablet has a bigger screen, thus, it can display more widgets

1 - Cosmetic problem only. No need to be fixed unless extra time is available.

2 - Minor consistency problem. Fixing this, should be given a low priority.

3 - Major consistency problem. Important to fix, should be given a high priority.

4 - Consistency catastrophe. Imperative to fix this before the product can be released.

Evaluators found a total of 23 usability problems using our guidelines (a mean of 4.6 problems per evaluator). The severity rating of problems had an

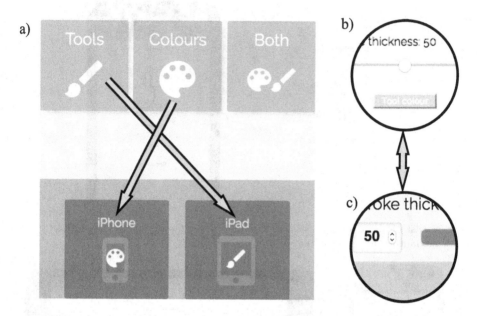

Fig. 7. (a) As part of the presence system, the user knows where the widgets are. When the user makes a change in a widget, the system automatically reflects such a change in all the GUIs, e.g., tool, stroke thickness, and colour are synchronised between: (b) the PC and (c) the tablet

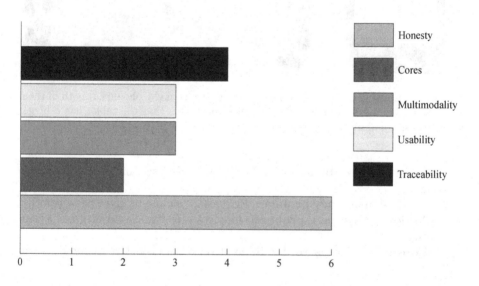

Fig. 8. Guidelines violations in DistroPaint

average of 2.42. For the master list, a total of 10 problems were evaluated and guidelines were violated 18 times (see Fig. 8). Honesty and Traceability were the two most frequently violated guidelines, 6 and 4 times, respectively. In contrast, the guideline with less detected problems was Functional Cores with 2 violations.

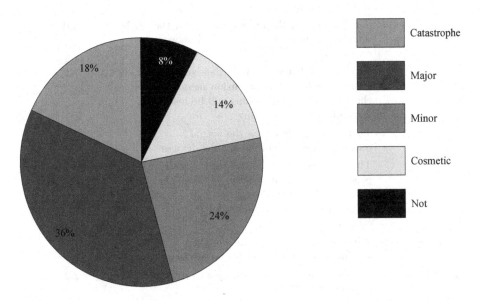

Fig. 9. Severity rating of consistency problems found in DistroPaint

With respect to the severity of the problems detected, we can see in Fig. 9 that severity level 3 - "Major consistency problem" was the most frequent with 36%, closely followed by severity level 2 - "Minor consistency problem" with 24% of occurrence. On the contrary, we can notice that the lowest classification 0 - "Not a consistency problem at all" got 8%.

In general, we can say that DistroPaint has many aspects in which to improve because several problems with severe qualifications were identified. Nevertheless, the evaluation was fruitful, as various problems could be discussed, as well as scenarios that, if neglected, could cause conflicts in the future. So our guidelines were advantageous in identifying particular conflicts in this specific case.

That Honesty was the guideline with the highest number of violations is an exciting aspect. Perhaps improving those weaknesses of design, the violation of the other guidelines disappears, or its qualification is reduced because Honesty brings with it a better workflow and a more solid GUI.

The experts concurred that the design guidelines could be a useful tool to detect consistency problems. However, they also acknowledged that in order to be more effective, they have to be refined and detailed.

Table 1. Consistency problems and its rating in DistroPaint

Place	Problem	Guidelines[a]	Severity
Tools	On the PC, the buttons of the drawing tools contain icons, while in the mobile widget they are texts	F	3.8
	The buttons on the mobile widget for the drawing tools are too small when viewed on the phone	F, M	3.6
	If the user reloads the main page of DistroPaint or the distribution menu, all changes and configurations will be lost without previous warning	H, T	2.2
	There is no feedback on the actual selected drawing tool among the devices	H, T	1.4
	The buttons of the toolbox, in the main page of DistroPaint, are too small on the phone; also, the toolbox is too big, reducing the space available for the canvas	M, U	3.2
Loading screen	Without previous explanation, the loading screen might confuse some users	H	1.2
Distribution	The distribution menu is only accessible through the PC	H, M, U	2.2
	Without previous explanation, the colours of the presence system might be unintelligible	H, T	2.4
	Without previous explanation, the user has no way to know why the widget "Both" cannot be distributed into the phone	H, U	3
	If a user closes the tab in a mobile device while this has a widget designated, such designation is not lost, but the user does not have a clear feedback of this	T	1.2

[a] Honesty (H), Functional Cores (F), Multimodality (M), Usability Limitations (U), Traceability (T).

6   Conclusions and Future Work

The main contribution of this paper is a series of consistency guidelines for the design of multi-device applications. This kind of applications represent the challenge of configuring the available resources and their role in the environment. When the users control the application, it allows them to explore their environment, identify the tasks and services compatible with it, and combine independent resources in a significant manner, in order to perform tasks and interact with services. Consistency is the element that maintains the users in a stable base since it is the key to assist GUI distribution. Besides, it is an essential factor in maintaining a positive UX.

We chose this type of evaluation to be able to explore our proposal in a deep way. We knew that by working with experts in the area, we could get feedback on our work, benefit from their experience, and directly observe how other people use our design guidelines.

While it is true that an expert evaluation can give good results, it is not exempt from problems. For example, we recognise that we have few points of view since we only have the participation of five experts, which can lead to misleading results. However, we considered that this was the best way to carry out an exploratory study, since with a small group we can have more in-depth discussions and work for a longer time. In this sense, the results seem promising, because we realised how the experts interpreted the guidelines. In general, our expectations were fulfilled, but we also know that we have to refine and be more specific so that each guideline is not too ambiguous.

It is also possible that expert evaluators can identify many consistency problems in multi-device applications without relying on our guidelines. However, using them provides evaluators with a structure that helps them take into account each major design dimension in turn, and to prevent them from becoming distracted by other design aspects, which could cause them to miss essential consistency problems.

As the nature of the guidelines is empirical, to prove their validity it is necessary to perform experiments, such as heuristic evaluations and UX tests with end-users.

The biggest challenge for future work involves improving DistroPaint; thus we could perform tests with end users. We plan to create an alternative version of DistroPaint that does not follow our design guidelines, so we would have two versions that users can use, compare and evaluate. In this way, we could see the effect of our design guidelines directly. In this way, we could compare the number of problems found in each case. Also, we have the intention of enriching our work through revisions of GUI design patterns [29]. Finally, we expect that our consistency guidelines to continue evolving in the future as we gain more experience and insights from using them to evaluate other applications, such as those found in the Internet of Things domain.

Acknowledgement. We thank CONACyT (Consejo Nacional de Ciencia y Tecnología) for funding Luis Martín Sánchez Adame's doctoral fellowship. Scholarship number: 294598.

References

1. CiscoSystems: cisco visual networking index: global mobile data traffic forecast update, 2016–2021. Technical report, March 2017
2. Levin, M.: Designing Multi-device Experiences: An Ecosystem Approach to Creating User Experiences Across Devices. O'Reilly, San Francisco (2014)

3. Dong, T., Churchill, E.F., Nichols, J.: Understanding the challenges of designing and developing multi-device experiences. In: Proceedings of the 2016 ACM Conference on Designing Interactive Systems. DIS 2016, pp. 62–72. ACM, Brisbane (2016)
4. Reeves, L.M., et al.: Guidelines for multimodal user interface design. Commun. ACM **47**(1), 57–59 (2004)
5. Nichols, J.: Automatically Generating High-quality User Interfaces for Appliances (2006)
6. de Oliveira, R., da Rocha, H.V.: Consistency priorities for multi-device design. In: Baranauskas, C., Palanque, P., Abascal, J., Barbosa, S.D.J. (eds.) INTERACT 2007. LNCS, vol. 4662, pp. 426–429. Springer, Heidelberg (2007). https://doi.org/10.1007/978-3-540-74796-3_40
7. Pyla, P.S., Tungare, M., Pérez-Quinones, M.: Multiple user interfaces: why consistency is not everything, and seamless task migration is key. In: Proceedings of the CHI 2006 Workshop on the Many Faces of Consistency in Cross-platform Design (2006)
8. Rowland, C., Goodman, E., Charlier, M., Light, A., Lui, A.: Designing Connected Products: UX for the Consumer Internet of Things. O'Reilly, San Francisco (2015)
9. Grosjean, J.C.: Design d'interface et critère ergonomique 9: Cohérence (2018). http://www.qualitystreet.fr/2011/01/23/design-dinterface-et-critere-ergonomique-9-coherence/. Accessed Oct 2018
10. Nikolov, A.: Design principle: consistency (2017). https://uxdesign.cc/design-principle-consistency-6b0cf7e7339f. Accessed Oct 2018
11. Wong, E.: Principle of consistency and standards in user interface design (2018). https://www.interaction-design.org/literature/article/principle-of-consistency-and-standards-in-user-interface-design. Accessed Oct 2018
12. Microsoft: windows ribbon framework (2018). https://docs.microsoft.com/en-us/windows/desktop/windowsribbon/-uiplat-windowsribbon-entry. Accessed Oct 2018
13. Coutaz, J., Calvary, G.: HCI and software engineering: the case for user interface plasticity. In Jacko, J.A., (ed.) The Human-Computer Interaction Handbook: Fundamentals, Evolving Technologies, and Emerging Applications-Human Factors and Ergonomics Series, pp. 1107–1118. CRC Press (2008)
14. Vanderdonckt, J.: Distributed user interfaces: how to distribute user interface elements across users, platforms, and environments. In: AIPO, pp. 3–14 (2010)
15. Anić, I.: The importance of visual consistency in UI design (2018). https://www.uxpassion.com/blog/the-importance-of-visual-consistency-in-ui-design/. Accessed Oct 2018
16. Gaffney, G.: Why consistency is critical (2018). https://www.sitepoint.com/why-consistency-is-critical/. Accessed Oct 2018
17. Marcus, A.: Principles of effective visual communication for graphical user interface design. In: Baecker, R.M., Grudin, J., Buxton, W.A., Greenberg, S., (eds.) Readings in Human-Computer Interaction. Interactive Technologies, pp. 425–441. Morgan Kaufmann (1995)
18. Meskens, J., Luyten, K., Coninx, K.: Jelly: a multi-device design environment for managing consistency across devices. In: Proceedings of the International Conference on Advanced Visual Interfaces. AVI 2010, pp. 289–296. ACM, Roma (2010)
19. O'Leary, K., Dong, T., Haines, J.K., Gilbert, M., Churchill, E.F., Nichols, J.: The moving context kit: designing for context shifts in multi-device experiences. In: Proceedings of the 2017 Conference on Designing Interactive Systems. DIS 2017, pp. 309–320. ACM, New York (2017)

20. Woodrow, W.W.: Designing for interusability: methodological recommendations for the systems engineer gleaned through an exploration of the connected fitness technologies space. INSIGHT **19**(3), 75–77 (2016)
21. Peffers, K., Tuunanen, T., Rothenberger, M., Chatterjee, S.: A design science research methodology for information systems research. J. Manage. Inf. Syst. **24**(3), 45–77 (2007)
22. Lamprecht, J., Siemon, D., Robra-Bissantz, S.: Cooperation isn't just about doing the same thing – using personality for a cooperation-recommender-system in online social networks. In: Yuizono, T., Ogata, H., Hoppe, U., Vassileva, J. (eds.) CRIWG 2016. LNCS, vol. 9848, pp. 131–138. Springer, Cham (2016). https://doi.org/10.1007/978-3-319-44799-5_10
23. Laubis, K., Konstantinov, M., Simko, V., Gröschel, A., Weinhardt, C.: Enabling crowdsensing-based road condition monitoring service by intermediary. Electron. Markets **29**, 125–140 (2018)
24. Patrício, L., de Pinho, N.F., Teixeira, J.G., Fisk, R.P.: Service design for value networks: enabling value cocreation interactions in healthcare. Serv. Sci. **10**(1), 76–97 (2018)
25. Andrade, F.O., Nascimento, L.N., Wood, G.A., Calil, S.J.: Applying heuristic evaluation on medical devices user manuals. In: Jaffray, D.A. (ed.) World Congress on Medical Physics and Biomedical Engineering, June 7-12, 2015, Toronto, Canada. IP, vol. 51, pp. 1515–1518. Springer, Cham (2015). https://doi.org/10.1007/978-3-319-19387-8_368
26. Grice, R.A., Bennett, A.G., Fernheimer, J.W., Geisler, C., Krull, R., Lutzky, R.A., Rolph, M.G., Search, P., Zappen, J.P.: Heuristics for broader assessment of effectiveness and usability in technology-mediated technical communication. Tech. Commun. **60**(1), 3–27 (2013)
27. Schmettow, M., Schnittker, R., Schraagen, J.M.: An extended protocol for usability validation of medical devices. J. Biomed. Inf. **69**(C), 99–114 (2017)
28. Zhang, J., Johnson, T.R., Patel, V.L., Paige, D.L., Kubose, T.: Using usability heuristics to evaluate patient safety of medical devices. J. Biomed. Inf. **36**(1), 23–30 (2003)
29. Luna, H., Mendoza, R., Vargas, M., Munoz, J., Alvarez, F.J., Rodriguez, L.C.: Using design patterns as usability heuristics for mobile groupware systems. IEEE Lat. Am. Trans. **13**(12), 4004–4010 (2015)

Gameful Design Heuristics: A Gamification Inspection Tool

Gustavo F. Tondello[1,2(✉)] ⓘ, Dennis L. Kappen[5] ⓘ, Marim Ganaba[1],
and Lennart E. Nacke[1,2,3,4] ⓘ

[1] HCI Games Group, Games Institute, University of Waterloo,
Waterloo, ON, Canada
gustavo@tondello.com, mariganaba@gmail.com,
lennart.nacke@acm.org
[2] Cheriton School of Computer Science, University of Waterloo,
Waterloo, ON, Canada
[3] Department of Communication Arts, University of Waterloo,
Waterloo, ON, Canada
[4] Stratford School of Interaction and Business, University of Waterloo,
Waterloo, ON, Canada
[5] Humber College, Toronto, ON, Canada
dennis.kappen@humber.ca

Abstract. Despite the emergence of many gameful design methodologies in the literature, there is a lack of methods to evaluate the resulting designs. Gameful design techniques aim to increase the user's motivation to interact with a software, but there are presently no accepted guidelines on how to find out if this goal was achieved during the design phase of a project. This paper presents the *Gameful Design Heuristics*, a novel set of guidelines that facilitate a heuristic evaluation of gameful software, with a focus on the software's potential to afford intrinsic and extrinsic motivation for the user. First, we reviewed several gameful design methods to identify the most frequently employed dimensions of motivational affordances. Then, we devised a set of 28 gamification heuristics that can be used to rapidly evaluate a gameful system. Finally, we conducted a summative empirical evaluation study with five user experience professionals, which demonstrated that our heuristics can help the evaluators find more motivational issues in interactive systems than they would without the heuristics. The suggested method fulfills the need for evaluation tools specific to gameful design, which could help evaluators assess the potential user experience of a gameful application in the early phases of a project.

Keywords: Gameful design heuristics · Heuristic evaluation ·
User experience · Gamification · Gameful design

1 Introduction

Many gameful design methods have recently emerged as part of the user experience (UX) design toolkit. They aim to augment and improve the UX of interactive systems with gamification—defined as using game design elements in non-game contexts [1].

© Springer Nature Switzerland AG 2019
M. Kurosu (Ed.): HCII 2019, LNCS 11566, pp. 224–244, 2019.
https://doi.org/10.1007/978-3-030-22646-6_16

Even though these tools have been increasingly adopted during the design phase of software projects, designers still lack standard evaluation methods. There are no guidelines for experts (i.e., people with background knowledge in UX) to evaluate a gameful implementation early on in a project.

For usability evaluation, two standard approaches exist. First, the gold standard is a usability test. UX researchers can either run a formative usability test (where they usually sit close to the participant and observe their behaviour) or a summative one (where they are often present locally or virtually, but the participant is working through an assigned task or scenario while some outcome measures are recorded). However, the second type (the heuristic evaluation or usability inspection) is cheaper and easier to set up—and can be conducted before planning an expensive usability test. Heuristic evaluation or usability inspections allow experts to evaluate a design based on a set of principles or guidelines (i.e., heuristics). These are fast and inexpensive methods that can be used to identify and address design issues.

These expert guidelines date back to the early days of software design (e.g., Smith and Mosier [2]) and have over the past decades improved how we develop software and interactive applications. In the established areas of UX, heuristic evaluation or inspection methods [3, 4] are commonly used as evaluation tools during the project design and implementation phases. These are not meant to replace user testing, but rather complement the set of evaluation tools. While it has become more common to conduct user tests with gamified applications (just as games user researchers have done in the video game industry), the domain is still lacking robust methodologies for evaluating gameful designs.

The benefit of using a gamification inspection method is that it allows rapid and early evaluation of a gameful design. While several studies have investigated the effectiveness of gameful applications by studying their users [5], user tests are conducted after a prototype has already been implemented. Although concerns have been voiced that heuristic evaluation can be influenced by subjective interpretations [6], it remains a valuable tool for practitioners, who operate under tighter time constraints than researchers. Heuristic evaluation affords researchers a finer focus in the user tests that are usually done subsequently to this initial validation, since the most basic issues will have already been discovered at that point.

While UX tests focus on identifying issues related to usability, ergonomics, cognitive load, and affective experiences, gamification is concerned with understanding and fostering the user's motivation to use a product, system, or service. Thus, gamification methods rely on motivational psychology research, such as self-determination theory (SDT) [7–10], to understand human motivation. Our heuristics were informed by this theoretical framework.

Several gameful design frameworks and methods have been suggested [11, 12] with prescriptive guidelines for augmenting an application with motivational affordances (note that we refer to gamification and gameful design interchangeably because both frame the same set of phenomena from different points of view [1]). Motivational affordances are properties added to an object, which allow its users to experience the satisfaction of their psychological needs [13, 14]. In gameful design, motivational affordances are used to facilitate intrinsic and extrinsic motivation. Thus, motivational affordances supporting a user's feelings of competence, autonomy, and relatedness can facilitate intrinsic motivation, whereas external incentives or rewards facilitate extrinsic motivation.

Our work contributes to the human-computer interaction (HCI) and gamification communities by presenting a new set of guidelines for heuristic evaluation of gameful design in interactive systems. We began our research by reviewing several gameful design frameworks and methods to identify which dimensions of motivational affordances were common among them. Next, we created a set of heuristics focused on each of the identified dimensions. The resulting set of heuristics provides a new way of evaluating gameful user experiences. It is the first inspection tool focused specifically on evaluating gameful design through the lens of intrinsic and extrinsic motivational affordances. The aim of our inspection tool is to enable any UX expert to conduct a heuristic evaluation of a gameful application more easily, even if they have no background expertise in gameful design or motivational psychology.

To evaluate the proposed heuristics, we conducted a study with five UX or HCI professionals who evaluated two online gameful applications. Three participants used our gameful design heuristics, while the remaining two used a two-page description of gamification and motivational affordances. Results showed that usage of our heuristics led to more motivational issues being identified in the evaluated applications, as well as a broader range of identified issues, comprising a larger number of different dimensions.

2   Related Work and Model Development

2.1   Heuristic Evaluation for Games

In usability engineering, heuristics are broad usability guidelines that have been used to design and evaluate interactive systems [15]. Heuristic evaluation is the use of these principles by experts in a usability inspection process to identify usability problems in an existing design as part of an iterative design process [3, 4]. These inspections are usually done early in the design process to identify application errors before scheduling user tests.

Several authors have suggested heuristic evaluation models for games. These models vary both in their goals and in the dimensions they address: while some are more general, aimed at evaluating any game genre or type, others are more focused for example on networked or mobile games. Some of the most relevant heuristic evaluation models for game design are shown in Table 1.

Some heuristics for evaluating games or playability may also be applied to gameful applications. Some of the dimensions addressed by most game design heuristics are of relevance to gameful design, such as goals, challenge, feedback, and social interaction. However, heuristics for games include several dimensions that are not applicable to most gameful applications, such as control and concentration.

Additionally, some of the game heuristics cover issues that can be addressed in gameful applications using general UX principles, such as screen layout or navigation. These heuristics might be necessary when evaluating games because game design often uses its own user interface principles, which can be different from traditional application interfaces. However, most gameful applications follow current design standards for user interfaces; thus, general UX evaluation methods can be easily applied to gameful applications to address issues such as usability or ergonomics.

Table 1. Existing heuristic evaluation models for games.

Model	Description
Heuristic Evaluation for Playability (HEP) [31]	A set of heuristics for playability comprising four categories: gameplay, game story, game mechanics, and game usability
Games Usability Heuristics (PLAY) [32]	A set of 48 principles aimed at evaluating action-adventure, RTS, and FPS games. The heuristics are organized according to three categories: gameplay, coolness/entertainment/humor/emotional immersion, and usability & game mechanics
Game Approachability Principles (GAP) [33]	A set of guidelines to create better tutorials or experiences for new players
Playability Heuristics for Mobile Games [34]	A set of heuristics for mobile games comprising three categories: game usability, mobility, and gameplay
Networked Game Heuristics (NGH) [35]	A set of heuristics that consider specific issues related to group play over a network
Heuristics for Social Games [36]	A set of heuristics created from a critical review of prior video game evaluation heuristics
GameFlow [37, 38]	A comprehensive heuristic set designed as a tool to evaluate player enjoyment in eight dimensions: concentration, challenge, player skills, control, clear goals, feedback, immersion, and social interaction

Game design heuristics do not cover the full range of common motivational affordances used in gamification. For example, meaning, rewards, and scarcity are dimensions of motivational affordances often used in gameful design that are not covered by existing game heuristics. This makes it difficult to use game design heuristics to evaluate gameful applications. In order to do so, an evaluator would have to decide first which dimensions from the game heuristics should be used and which should not; next, they would also have to be concerned with motivational issues that are not currently covered by game heuristics. Consequently, we conclude that we need an inspection method better suited to assess gameful applications.

Before creating our set of gameful design heuristics, we reviewed the abovementioned game heuristics and considered the possibility of extending the existing models rather than proposing a new one. However, we encountered the same issues mentioned above: we would have to separate which heuristics from the existing models are applicable to gameful design and which are not. The resulting model would be confusing and difficult to apply. Therefore, we decided to create a new set of gameful design heuristics by analyzing existing gameful design methods rather than analyzing and extending existing game design heuristics.

2.2 Heuristic Evaluation for Playful Design

The Playful Experiences (PLEX) Framework [16, 17] provides an understanding of pleasurable user experience, which can be applied to both games and gameful applications. It classifies playful experiences according to 22 categories (see Table 2).

Table 2. The 22 categories of the PLEX framework.

Experience	Description
Captivation	Forgetting one's surroundings
Challenge	Testing abilities in a demanding task
Competition	Contest with oneself or an opponent
Completion	Finishing a major task, closure
Control	Dominating, commanding, regulating
Cruelty	Causing mental or physical pain
Discovery	Finding something new or unknown
Eroticism	A sexually arousing experience
Exploration	Investigating an object or situation
Expression	Manifesting oneself creatively
Fantasy	An imagined experience
Fellowship	Friendship, communality, or intimacy
Humor	Fun, joy, amusement, jokes, gags
Nurture	Taking care of oneself or others
Relaxation	Relief from bodily or mental work
Sensation	Excitement by stimulating senses
Simulation	An imitation of everyday life
Submission	Being part of a larger structure
Subversion	Breaking social rules and norms
Suffering	Experience of loss, frustration, anger
Sympathy	Sharing emotional feelings
Thrill	Excitement derived from risk, danger

The PLEX framework can be used as a tool for heuristic evaluation of gameful interactive systems, similar to the gameful design heuristics we are presenting. Nevertheless, PLEX is focused on classifying the types of experiences that the system can afford, rather than the motivational potential of these experiences. Therefore, the PLEX framework and the gameful design heuristics are two complementary tools, which can each provide insights into different characteristics of interactive systems that work together to afford an enjoyable user experience.

2.3   Review of Gameful Design Methods

To the best of our knowledge, no extant set of heuristics is available for evaluating motivation in gameful design. Some of the existing gameful design methods, namely Octalysis [18], HEXAD [19], and Lens of Intrinsic Skill Atoms [11], suggest procedures to evaluate an existing system. Nevertheless, these procedures only provide a starting point for the design process. They are less suited for being used as an evaluation tool by a quality control team because they lack a concise set of heuristics with brief descriptors which could be quickly checked by a UX practitioner. Moreover, the lack of a succinct rubric implies that an evaluator would need to study the methods intensively before being able to conduct an evaluation. Therefore, presently, there is no evaluation method for gameful applications that can be easily learned by UX professionals who are not familiar with gameful design. Our research fills this gap.

Several gameful design frameworks and methods are currently available (see [11, 12, 20] for comprehensive reviews). Therefore, we decided to review these existing methods to extract the different dimensions of motivational affordances that need to be considered in gameful design. Since the reviewed methods synthesize the current set of best practices in gameful design, we considered that they could provide an adequate starting point to identify motivational dimensions of concern. However, only a few of the reviewed methods feature a classification of motivational affordances in different dimensions, which we could use as a theoretical background to devise our heuristics. This was unfortunate, since our goal was to use these dimensions of motivational affordances as the starting point for the development of our framework. Gameful design methods that do not provide a classification of dimensions of motivational affordances would not be helpful in creating our gameful design heuristics. Therefore, we expanded the scope of our analysis to include methods that presented some sort of classification of motivational affordances. Table 3 lists the frameworks and methods we considered, as well as the rationale for their inclusion or otherwise in our analysis.

After reviewing the frameworks and methods and selecting six of them for further analysis (see Table 3), we conducted a comparison of the motivational dimensions in each model to map the similarities between them, using the following procedure:

1. The first framework was added as the first column of a table, with each one of its suggested motivational dimensions as separate rows. We chose the Octalysis framework as the first one because it comprised the highest number of dimensions (eight), which facilitated subsequent procedures/steps, but we could have chosen any of the frameworks as a starting point.
2. Next, we added each one of the remaining models as additional columns into the table. For each added model, we compared each one of its suggested dimensions with the rows that already existed in the table. When the new dimension to be added corresponded to one of the dimensions already in the table, we added it to the relevant existing row. Otherwise, we added a new row to the table creating a new dimension. In some cases, the addition of a new dimension also prompted the subdivision of an existing row. For example, the competence dimension was split into challenge/competence and completeness/mastery.

3. After adding all the models to the table, we observed the characteristics of the dimensions named in the rows and created for each of the latter a unique label, comprising the meaning of all the dimensions it encompassed.

Table 3. A summary of the gameful design frameworks & methods considered in our research.

Framework or Method	References	Included in the analysis?	Rationale
Gamification by Design	Zichermann and Cunningham [39]	No	Does not provide a classification of dimensions of motivational affordances
Gamification Framework	Francisco-Aparicio et al. [40]	No	Does not provide a classification of dimensions of motivational affordances
Gamification Model Canvas	Jiménez [41]	No	Does not provide a classification of dimensions of motivational affordances
Gamify	Burke [42]	No	Does not provide a classification of dimensions of motivational affordances
User Types HEXAD	Tondello et al. [19]	Yes	Provides a classification with six user types that are further used to classify sets of game elements for each type
The Kaleidoscope of Effective Gamification (KEG)	Kappen and Nacke [43]	Yes	Provides a classification with several layers of motivational affordances that can be used to design or evaluate gameful systems
Motivational Design Lenses (MDL)	Deterding [11]	Yes	Provides a classification of motivational design lenses that can be used to evaluate gameful systems
Loyalty 3.0	Paharia [44]	No	Does not provide a classification of dimensions of motivational affordances
The RECIPE for Meaningful Gamification	Nicholson [45]	Yes	Provides six different motivational dimensions for gameful design
Octalysis Framework	Chou [18]	Yes	Provides a classification with eight dimensions of motivation that can be used to design or evaluate gameful systems
Six Steps to Success	Werbach and Hunter [46]	No	Does not provide a classification of dimensions of motivational affordances
Super Better	McGonigal [47]	Yes	Proposes a gameful design method based on seven steps, which can be mapped as motivational dimensions

The resulting model consists of twelve common dimensions of motivational affordances (see Table 4). The similarity analysis between dimensions of different models was conceptual, meaning that we studied the description of each dimension as presented by their original authors and decided whether they represented the same core construct as any of the dimensions already present in the table. Similarly, we derived the labels for each one of the twelve resulting dimensions (first column of Table 4) by identifying the core concepts of each dimension. In the resulting classification, we noted that these dimensions were strongly based on: (1) the theories of intrinsic and extrinsic motivation (SDT; [7–9]), (2) behavioural economics [21], and (3) the practical experience of the authors of the analyzed frameworks. The entire initial analysis was conducted by one of the researchers; next, three other researchers (co-authors) also analyzed the resulting table. We then conducted an iterative loop of feedback and editing until none of the researchers had additional suggestions to improve the final model.

Table 4. Dimensions of motivational affordances from the reviewed gameful design methods.

Dimension	Octalysis [18]	HEXAD [19]	KEG [43]	MDL [11]	RECIPE [45]	Super Better [47]
Purpose and Meaning	Epic Meaning & Calling	Philanthropist			Information; Reflection	Epic win
Challenge and Competence	Development & Accomplishment	Achiever	Competence; Challenge	Challenge lenses; Intrinsic rewards	Engagement	Challenge; Bad guys
Completeness and Mastery	Development & Accomplishment	Achiever	Competence; Achievements	Goal and Action lenses; Intrinsic rewards		Complete quests
Autonomy and Creativity	Creativity & Feedback	Free Spirit	Autonomy	Object lenses; Intrinsic rewards	Play; Choice	
Relatedness	Social Influence & Relatedness	Socialiser	Relatedness	Intrinsic rewards	Engagement	Recruit allies
Immersion			Perceived Fun		Exposition	Secret identity
Ownership and Rewards	Ownership & Possession	Player	Extrinsic motivation	Intrinsic rewards		Power-ups
Unpredictability	Unpredictability & Curiosity	Free Spirit		Varied challenge; Varied feedback; Secrets	Play	
Scarcity	Scarcity & Impatience					
Loss avoidance	Loss & Avoidance					
Feedback	Creativity & Feedback			Feedback lenses		
Change and Disruption		Disruptor				

3 Gameful Design Heuristics

Our set of heuristics enables experts to identify gaps in a gameful system's design. This is achieved by identifying missing affordances from each of the dimensions.

Prior to creating the heuristics, we reviewed the research on motivation [7, 8] to help categorize the twelve dimensions into *intrinsic*, *extrinsic*, and *context-dependent* motivational categories. This is a common practice in gameful design and many of the reviewed methods also employ a similar classification. Although it is a simplification of the underlying theory, this simple categorization helps designers and evaluators better understand the guidelines and focus their attention on specific motivational techniques. We chose SDT as the theoretical background for this classification because it is the motivational theory most frequently employed in gameful design methodologies [11, 12].

We used the following criteria to split our heuristics into categories:

- *Intrinsic motivation* includes affordances related to the three intrinsic needs introduced by SDT [7, 8] (competence, autonomy, and relatedness), as well as 'purpose' and 'meaning' as facilitators of internalization [22–24] and 'immersion', as suggested by Ryan and Rigby [9, 25] and Malone [26].
- *Extrinsic motivation* includes affordances that provide an outcome or value separated from the activity itself as suggested by SDT [8] and Chou [18]: ownership and rewards, scarcity, and loss avoidance.
- *Context-dependent* motivation includes the feedback, unpredictability, and disruption affordances, which can afford either intrinsic or extrinsic motivation depending on contextual factors. For example, the application can provide feedback to the user regarding either intrinsically or extrinsically motivated tasks; therefore, feedback might afford intrinsic or extrinsic motivation according to the type of task with which it is associated.

We constructed the heuristics based on an examination of the literature cited in Table 4, by writing adequate guidelines for each of the twelve identified dimensions. Following the literature review, we created these guidelines by studying the descriptions of each dimension in the original models, identifying the main aspects of each dimension, and writing concise descriptions of each aspect to assist expert evaluation. We employed the following procedure:

1. For each one of the twelve motivational dimensions, we first studied the underlying concepts and wrote a short description of the dimension itself, aimed at guiding expert evaluators' understanding of each dimension.
2. Next, for each dimension, we identified the main aspects of concern, meaning the aspects that should be considered by designers when envisioning a gameful system, as suggested by the reviewed frameworks or methods. We argue that these aspects of concern, when designing a system, should also be the main points of evaluation.
3. For each aspect of concern, we then wrote a concise description aimed at guiding experts in evaluating whether the aspect being scrutinized was considered in the evaluated system's design.

Tables 5, 6 and 7 present the final set of 28 heuristics organized within the 12 dimensions, following the initial analysis, framing, and iterative feedback mentioned above, and which have been presented previously in a work-in-progress [27].

Table 5. Intrinsic motivation heuristics.

Intrinsic motivation heuristics
Purpose and Meaning: Affordances aimed at helping users identify a meaningful goal that will be achieved through the system and can benefit the users themselves or other people
I1. *Meaning*: The system clearly helps users identify a meaningful contribution (to themselves or to others)
I2. *Information and Reflection*: The system provides information and opportunities for reflection towards self-improvement
Challenge and Competence: Affordances aimed at helping users satisfy their intrinsic need of competence through accomplishing difficult challenges or goals
I3. *Increasing Challenge*: The system offers challenges that grow with the user's skill
I4. *Onboarding*: The system offers initial challenges for newcomers that help them learn how it works
I5. *Self-challenge*: The system helps users discover or create new challenges to test themselves
Completeness and Mastery: Affordances aimed at helping users satisfy their intrinsic need of competence by completing series of tasks or collecting virtual achievements
I6. *Progressive Goals*: The system always presents the next actions users can take as tasks of immediately doable size
I7. *Achievement*: The system lets users keeps track of their achievements or advancements
Autonomy and Creativity: Affordances aimed at helping users satisfy their intrinsic need of autonomy by offering meaningful choices and opportunities for self-expression
I8. *Choice*: The system provides users with choices on what to do or how to do something, which are interesting but also limited in scope according to each user's capacity
I9. *Self-expression*: The system lets users express themselves or create new content
I10. *Freedom*: The system lets users experiment with new or different paths without fear or serious consequences
Relatedness: Affordances aimed at helping users satisfy their intrinsic need for relatedness through social interaction, usually with other users
I11. *Social Interaction*: The system lets users connect and interact socially
I12. *Social Cooperation*: The system offers the opportunity of users working together towards achieving common goals
I13. *Social Competition*: The system lets users compare themselves with others or challenge other users
I14. *Fairness*: The system offers similar opportunities of success and progression for everyone and means for newcomers to feel motivated even when comparing themselves with veterans
Immersion: Affordances aimed at immersing users in the system in order to improve their aesthetic experience [48], usually by means of a theme, narrative, or story, which can be real or fictional
I15. *Narrative*: The system offers users a meaningful narrative or story with which they can relate to
I16. *Perceived Fun*: The system affords users the possibility of interacting with and being part of the story (easy fun; [49])

Table 6. Extrinsic motivation heuristics.

Extrinsic motivation heuristics
Ownership and Rewards: Affordances aimed at motivating users through extrinsic rewards or possession of real or virtual goods. Ownership is different from Competence when acquiring goods is perceived by the user as the reason for interacting with the system, instead of feeling competent
E1. *Ownership*: The system lets users own virtual goods or build an individual profile over time, which can be developed by continued use of the system and to which users can relate
E2. *Rewards*: The system offers incentive rewards for interaction and continued use, which are valuable to users and proportional to the amount of effort invested
E3. *Virtual Economy*: The system lets users exchange the result of their efforts with in-system or external rewards
Scarcity: Affordances aimed at motivating users through feelings of status or exclusivity by means of acquisition of difficult or rare rewards, goods, or achievements.
E4. *Scarcity*: The system offers interesting features or rewards that are rare or difficult to obtain
Loss Avoidance: Affordances aimed at leading users to act with urgency, by creating situations in which they could lose acquired or potential rewards, goods, or achievements if they do not act immediately
E5. *Loss Avoidance*: The system creates urgency through possible losses unless users act immediately

Table 7. Context-dependent heuristics.

Context-dependent heuristics
Feedback: Affordances aimed at informing users of their progress and the next available actions or challenges
C1. *Clear and Immediate Feedback*: The systems always inform users immediately of any changes or accomplishments in an easy and graspable way
C2. *Actionable Feedback*: The system always informs users about the next available actions and improvements
C3. *Graspable Progress*: Feedback always tells users where they stand and what is the path ahead for progression
Unpredictability: Affordances aimed at surprising users with variable tasks, challenges, feedback, or rewards
C4. *Varied Challenges*: The system offers unexpected variability in the challenges or tasks presented to the user
C5. *Varied Rewards*: The system offers unexpected variability in the rewards that are offered to the user
Change and Disruption: Affordances aimed at engaging users with disruptive tendencies [19] by allowing them to help improve the system, in a positive rather than destructive way
C6. *Innovation*: The system lets users contribute ideas, content, plugins, or modifications aimed at improving, enhancing, or extending the system itself
C7. *Disruption Control*: The system is protected against cheating, hacking, or other forms of manipulation from users

Additionally, we have extended the gameful design heuristics by writing a set of questions for each heuristic. These questions inquire about common ways of implementing each guideline, helping the evaluators assess whether the guideline is implemented in the system at all. We do not include the complete set of questions here because of space constraints, but we provide them in our website[1].

3.1 Using the Gameful Design Heuristics

Similar to previous heuristic UX evaluation methods, gamification heuristics should be used by experts to identify gaps in a gameful system's design. Experts should consider each guideline to evaluate whether it is adequately implemented into the design. Prior studies have shown that evaluations conducted by many evaluators are more effective in finding issues than those conducted by an individual evaluator [3, 28, 29]. Thus, we recommend the evaluation to be conducted by two or more examiners.

When applying the heuristics, the evaluators should first familiarize themselves with the application to be analyzed and its main features. Then, for each heuristic, they should read the general guideline and observe the application, identifying and noting what the application does to implement this guideline. Next, they should read the questions associated with the heuristic and answer them to identify possible gaps in the application's design. The evaluation is focused on observing the presence or absence of the motivational affordances and, if the evaluator has enough expertise, in evaluating their quality. However, it does not aim to observe the actual user experience, which is highly dependent on the users themselves in addition to the system. Therefore, this method cannot evaluate the user experience; its goal is to evaluate the system's *potential* to afford a gameful, engaging experience. As we have stated before, the heuristic evaluation should be subsequently validated by user studies to establish whether the observed potential translates into actual gameful experiences.

It is important to note that the questions associated with each heuristic act as guidelines to facilitate the evaluation process. They are not intended to represent every aspect related to the heuristic. Therefore, it is important that the evaluator also thinks beyond the suggested questions and considers other issues that might be present in the application regarding each heuristic.

After evaluating all the dimensions, a count of the number of issues identified in each dimension can help identify which motivational issues (from the heuristics) require more attention in improving the system's potential to engage users.

3.2 Turning the Evaluation Results into Actionable Design

Since the gameful design heuristics are an evaluation method, they do not provide the means to turn the identified issues into actionable design ideas to improve the application's design. Although the heuristics identify what dimensions of motivational affordances are implemented in, or excluded from the system, they do not provide any information about the need (or otherwise) to implementing the missing dimensions.

---

[1] http://gamefuldesign.hcigames.com/.

Depending on the goals of the gameful software being developed, including motivational affordances for all dimensions might be either necessary or unimportant. Therefore, we suggest that the identified design gaps should be considered within an iterative gameful design method, which can then provide the tools to assess the need for including new motivational affordances into the system to address the gaps. The methods used to inform the development of the heuristics (see Table 4) are adequate for this goal because they make it easy to map the dimensions where gaps are identified to the design element categories suggested by these gameful design methods.

4 Evaluation

We conducted a summative study with five UX or HCI experts to evaluate the gameful design heuristics. We asked participants to evaluate two online gameful applications: Habitica[2] and Termling[3]. Data were collected between August and December 2016.

Three participants (P1, P2, P3) conducted the evaluation using the heuristics and the remaining two (P4, P5) without it, enabling us to compare how many motivational design issues were found by experts with and without the heuristics. Furthermore, three participants (P1, P3, P4) had expertise in gamification or games, whereas two (P2, P5) were knowledgeable in UX or HCI, but did not have a specific background in gamification. This enabled us to assess if prior gamification expertise would influence the evaluators' ability to identify motivational design issues.

4.1 Participants

We initially invited 18 experts in UX, HCI, or gamification to participate in the study. Potential participants were selected from the authors' acquaintances and from previous project collaborators. The criterion was that potential participants should have an expertise either in gamification or games (including design practice or research experience) or in using other UX or HCI methods to evaluate interactive digital applications. Potential participants were contacted by email or in person. No compensation was provided for participation.

From the 18 invited participants, 10 initially agreed to participate and were sent the instructions; of these only five participants completed the procedures (likely because of scheduling difficulties and the lack of compensation). Of these five, two participants completed the evaluation of Habitica only; however, we decided to include their feedback in the study anyway. This meant that we collected five evaluations for Habitica, but only three for Termling. Table 8 summarizes the demographics of the participants.

---

[2] http://habitica.com/, last accessed December 2016.

[3] http://www.termling.com/, last accessed December 2016.

4.2   Procedure

Initially, participants read and signed a consent form and filled out a short demographic information form (see Table 8). Next, the instructions to evaluate the two applications were sent out. Since both applications were free and available online, participants were instructed to create a free account to test them. We instructed participants P1 and P2 to carry out the evaluation without the gameful design heuristics and participants P3, P4, and P5 to use the heuristics. Assignment to experimental conditions was not random because we needed to ensure that we had participants with and without gamification expertise in both conditions (with or without the heuristics).

Table 8. Participant demographics.

#	Gender	Role	Gamification expertise?	Has studied gamification before?
P1	Male	Graduate Student (HCI)	No	Yes (4 months)
P2	Male	Creative Director	Yes	Yes (3 years)
P3	Female	Professor (HCI)	Yes	Yes
P4	Male	Creative Lead	Yes	Yes
P5	Female	Graphic Designer	No	No

The instructions for P1 and P2 contained a one-page summarized introduction about gamification and motivation, followed by instructions requesting them to reflect on the applications' design and motivational affordances, try to understand how they afford intrinsic and extrinsic motivation, and then list any issue they identified related to the motivational affordances (or lack of the same).

Participants P3, P4, and P5 received information that contained the same introduction about gamification and motivation, followed by an introduction to the gameful design heuristics, and instructions that asked them to reflect on the applications and identify motivational issues using the gameful design heuristics. Participants were given a complete copy of the gameful design heuristics to guide them during the evaluation, including the full list of heuristics with all the accompanying questions to guide the evaluation (see Sect. 3). The heuristics were formatted as a fillable form, which offered an additional column where participants could take notes about the issues observed in the applications. After receiving the instructions, participants could conduct their evaluations at their own pace and discretion; they were not supervised by the researchers. After completing the evaluation, participants emailed the forms back to the researchers.

4.3   Results

Table 9 shows the number of issues found in the two evaluated applications by the participants. Overall, participants who used the gameful design heuristics identified more issues than those who did not use any heuristics.

Table 9. Number of issues found by participants.

Participant	Habitica					Termling				
	P1	P2	P3	P4	P5	P1	P2	P3	P4	P5
Used heuristics?	No	No	Yes	Yes	Yes	No	No	-	Yes	-
I1. Meaning	1	3	0	0	0	0	2	-	1	-
I2. Information and Reflection	0	0	1	0	1	0	0	-	1	-
I3. Increasing Challenge	0	0	1	0	0	0	0	-	1	-
I4. Onboarding	2	1	1	1	1	1	3	-	1	-
I5. Self-challenge	0	0	0	0	0	0	0	-	0	-
I6. Progressive Goals	0	0	0	1	1	0	0	-	1	-
I7. Achievement	0	0	1	0	0	0	1	-	1	-
I8. Choice	0	0	2	1	0	0	0	-	2	-
I9. Self-expression	1	0	0	0	0	1	2	-	0	-
I10. Freedom	0	0	0	0	1	0	0	-	1	-
I11. Social Interaction	0	1	2	0	0	0	1	-	0	-
I12. Social Cooperation	0	0	1	0	1	0	0	-	0	-
I13. Social Competition	0	0	0	1	0	0	0	-	2	-
I14. Fairness	0	0	0	1	0	0	0	-	0	-
I15. Narrative	0	0	1	2	0	0	0	-	1	-
I16. Perceived Fun	1	0	0	1	0	0	0	-	1	-
E1. Ownership	0	0	0	0	0	0	0	-	1	-
E2. Rewards	1	0	0	0	0	1	0	-	1	-
E3. Virtual Economy	1	0	0	2	0	0	0	-	2	-
E4. Scarcity	0	0	0	0	0	0	1	-	0	-
E5. Loss Avoidance	0	1	0	1	1	0	1	-	1	-
C1. Clear & Immediate Feedback	0	0	0	0	1	1	0	-	1	-
C2. Actionable Feedback	0	0	0	0	0	0	0	-	1	-
C3. Graspable Progress	0	0	0	1	1	0	0	-	1	-
C4. Varied Challenges	0	1	1	1	1	0	1	-	0	-
C5. Varied Rewards	0	1	1	1	1	0	0	-	1	-
C6. Innovation	0	0	0	0	0	0	0	-	2	-
C7. Disruption Control	0	0	0	2	0	0	0	-	0	-
Total motivational issues	7	8	12	16	10	4	12	-	24	-
Other issues (usability, bugs)	3	2	-	-	-	4	2	-	-	-

The number of issues identified by the participant who had no prior gamification expertise and used the heuristics (P5) was just slightly higher than the participants who did not use the heuristics (P1 and P2), whether they had gamification expertise or not. However, it is noteworthy that the heuristics helped P5 identify issues in more dimensions than did P1 and P2: while P5 identified issues in 10 different dimensions for Habitica, P1's and P2's issues were concentrated in only six dimensions.

Moreover, congruent to our intentions, the heuristics helped evaluators focus their analyses on the motivational affordances instead of other usability issues or bugs.

This is demonstrated by the fact that P1 and P2 both reported some issues that were not related to the motivational affordances at all (e.g., usability issues or bugs), whereas P3, P4, and P5 only reported motivational issues.

Furthermore, a qualitative comparison of participants' responses shows that when they used the heuristics, their comments were generally more focused on the motivational aspects, whereas the comments from participants who did not use the heuristics were more general. For example, regarding Habitica's onboarding, P1, P2, and P3 mostly recognized the fact that some information or tutorial material is missing or hidden. However, they do not comment on how this would affect the user's motivation. On the other hand, P4 and P5 could point out that, although a set of instructions existed, it did not motivate the user because it was not challenging or fun. Thus, it seems that the heuristics are useful in focusing the evaluator's attention into the motivational issues of the application.

Additionally, the participants who had prior gamification expertise and used the heuristics could identify approximately twice as many motivational issues as the participant who also had gamification expertise but did not use the heuristics. In comparison, P3 found 12 and P4 found 16 motivational issues in Habitica, whereas P2 found only eight. In Termling, P4 found 24 motivational issues while P2 found only 12.

We can also observe that the motivational dimensions where participants classified the issues sometimes differ. However, this is not a characteristic specific to our tool, but it is a known fact of heuristic evaluation in general that a single evaluator usually does not notice all the existing issues. This is why it is recommended that a heuristic evaluation should be conducted by a number of experts instead of only one [3, 28, 29]. This way, by combining all the issues identified by the different experts, good coverage of the total issues existing in the system will be achieved.

In summary, the results provided the following evidence:

- A participant who had no prior gamification expertise, but used the gameful design heuristics, could find as many motivational issues as participants who did not use the heuristics (with or without prior gamification expertise), but in a broader range of motivational dimensions;
- Participants who had prior gamification expertise and used the gameful design heuristics could find twice as many motivational issues than participants who did not use the heuristics or did not have prior expertise;
- Using the gameful design heuristics helped participants focus their analyses on the motivational issues, avoiding any distraction with other types of problems.

5   Discussion

We have created a set of 28 gameful design heuristics for the evaluation and identification of design gaps in gameful software. Due to the lack of direct applicability of existing heuritics from game design, we deliberately decided to create a new set of heuristics specific to gameful design, based on motivational theories and gameful design methods, rather than extending the existing heuristics for game design. By deriving our set of heuristics from common dimensions of motivational affordances employed by different gameful design methods, we have presented a novel and comprehensive approach that encompasses a broad range of motivational affordances. Furthermore, to enable expert evaluation, the heuristics are written in a concise form, together with supportive questions for reflection.

Our study with five UX and HCI experts provided empirical evidence that:

- gameful design heuristics can help UX evaluators who are not familiar with gamification to evaluate a gameful system at least as well as a gamification expert who does not use the heuristics; and
- gameful design heuristics can greatly improve the ability of gamification experts to perform a heuristic evaluation, leading them to find twice as many issues as they would find without the heuristics.

The implications of our findings are twofold. First, we provide evidence that evaluation of gameful applications without a support tool is subjective; therefore, even gamification experts might miss important issues. A probable reason for this is the complexity of gameful design and the number of motivational dimensions involved. Second, we demonstrate that usage of the gameful design heuristics can significantly improve the results of heuristic evaluations conducted both by gamification experts and non-experts. Considering that gameful design still suffers from difficulties in reproducing some of the successful results and that several studies have reported mixed results [5, 30], our work sheds light on one of the probable causes for this. Consequently, the gameful design heuristics represent an important instrument, which can be used to improve the chances of building effective gameful applications.

Nevertheless, the study was limited by the small sample size. Thus, although these initial results seem promising, future studies will be needed to support them. Additionally, even though the proposed method was meant to be generic enough to work in any heuristic evaluation of gameful applications, future studies will need to consider diverse usage scenarios to investigate if adaptations are needed for specific purposes.

6 Conclusion

Evaluation using heuristics is a way of identifying issues during various stages of software development, ranging from ideation, design, and prototyping to implementation and tests. While many heuristics exist in various fields such as usability and game design, we still lacked guidelines specific to gameful design due to the differences in types of solutions emergent from this domain. Therefore, our work addresses this gap and contributes to gameful design research and practice by identifying key motivational dimensions and presenting a novel evaluation tool specific for gameful systems. This gameful design heuristics provides a method of evaluating interactive systems in various stages of their development. The suggested method fulfills a need for UX evaluation tools specific to gameful design, which could help evaluators assess the potential UX of a gameful application in the early phases of the software project. The expert evaluation of the gameful design heuristics provided information that the heuristics enabled experts to identify the presence of motivational affordances from several dimensions, as well as the absence of specific affordances from other dimensions. This is valuable information, which could help software developers and systems designers to incorporate the missing elements. We expect the gameful design heuristics to be of use to both researchers and practitioners who design and evaluate gameful software, whether in research studies or in industry applications.

Acknowledgments. We would like to thank the participants, who generously offered their time to help us. This work was supported by CNPq, the National Council for Scientific and Technological Development – Brazil; SSHRC, the Social Sciences and Humanities Research Council – Canada [895-2011-1014, IMMERSe]; NSERC, the Natural Sciences and Engineering Research Council of Canada [RGPIN-418622-2012]; CFI, the Canada Foundation for Innovation [35819]; and Mitacs [IT07255].

References

1. Deterding, S., Dixon, D., Khaled, R., Nacke, L.E.: From game design elements to gamefulness: defining "Gamification." In: Proceedings of the 15th International Academic MindTrek Conference, Tampere, Finland, pp. 9–15. ACM (2011). https://doi.org/10.1145/2181037.2181040
2. Smith, S.L., Mosier, J.N.: Guidelines for Designing User Interface Software. Mitre Corporation, Bedford (1986)
3. Nielsen, J.: Finding usability problems through heuristic evaluation. In: Proceedings of the SIGCHI Conference on Human Factors in Computer Systems - CHI 1992, pp. 373–380 (1992). https://doi.org/10.1145/142750.142834
4. Nielsen, J.: Heuristic evaluation. In: Nielsen, J., Mack, R.L. (eds.) Usability Inspection Methods, pp. 25–62. Wiley, New York (1994)
5. Hamari, J., Koivisto, J., Sarsa, H.: Does gamification work? - A literature review of empirical studies on gamification. In: Proceedings of the Annual Hawaii International Conference on System Sciences, pp. 3025–3034 (2014). https://doi.org/10.1109/hicss.2014.377
6. White, G.R., Mirza-Babaei, P., McAllister, G., Good, J.: Weak inter-rater reliability in heuristic evaluation of video games. In: Proceedings of the CHI 2011 Extended Abstracts on Human Factors in Computing Systems - CHI EA 2011, pp. 1441–1446. ACM (2011). https://doi.org/10.1145/1979742.1979788
7. Ryan, R.M., Deci, E.L.: Self-determination theory and the facilitation of intrinsic motivation, social development, and well-being. Am. Psychol. **55**, 68–78 (2000). https://doi.org/10.1037/0003-066X.55.1.68
8. Ryan, R.M., Deci, E.L.: Intrinsic and extrinsic motivations: classic definitions and new directions. Contemp. Educ. Psychol. **25**, 54–67 (2000). https://doi.org/10.1006/ceps.1999.1020
9. Ryan, R.M., Rigby, C.S., Przybylski, A.: The motivational pull of video games: a self-determination theory approach. Motiv. Emot. **30**, 347–363 (2006). https://doi.org/10.1007/s11031-006-9051-8
10. Deci, E.L., Ryan, R.M.: Intrinsic Motivation and Self-Determination in Human Behavior. Plenum, New York and London (1985)
11. Deterding, S.: The lens of intrinsic skill atoms: a method for gameful design. Hum. Comput. Interact. **30**, 294–335 (2015). https://doi.org/10.1080/07370024.2014.993471

12. Mora, A., Riera, D., González, C., Arnedo-Moreno, J.: Gamification: a systematic review of design frameworks. J. Comput. High. Educ. **29**(3), 516–548 (2017). https://doi.org/10.1007/s12528-017-9150-4

13. Deterding, S.: Situated motivational affordances of game elements: a conceptual model. In: Gamification: Using Game Design Elements in Non-Gaming Contexts, a Workshop at CHI 2011. ACM (2011)

14. Zhang, P.: Motivational affordances: reasons for ICT design and use. Commun. ACM **51**, 145–147 (2008). https://doi.org/10.1145/1400214.1400244

15. Nielsen, J.: Enhancing the explanatory power of usability heuristics. In: Proceedings of the SIGCHI Conference on Human Factors in Computing Systems - CHI 1994, pp. 152–158 (1994). https://doi.org/10.1145/191666.191729

16. Lucero, A., Holopainen, J., Ollila, E., Suomela, R., Karapanos, E.: The playful experiences (PLEX) framework as a guide for expert evaluation. In: Proceedings of the 6th International Conference on Designing Pleasurable Products and Interfaces - DPPI 2013, pp. 221–230. ACM (2013). https://doi.org/10.1145/2513506.2513530

17. Lucero, A., Karapanos, E., Arrasvuori, J., Korhonen, H.: Playful or gameful? Creating delightful user experiences. Interactions **21**, 34–39 (2014). https://doi.org/10.1145/2590973

18. Chou, Y.: Actionable Gamification - Beyond Points, Badges, and Leaderboards. Octalysis Media (2015)

19. Tondello, G.F., Wehbe, R.R., Diamond, L., Busch, M., Marczewski, A., Nacke, L.E.: The gamification user types hexad scale. In: Proceedings of the 2016 Annual Symposium on Computer-Human Interaction in Play - CHI PLAY 2016, Austin, TX, USA , pp. 229–243. ACM (2016). https://doi.org/10.1145/2967934.2968082

20. Morschheuser, B., Werder, K., Hamari, J., Abe, J.: How to gamify? A method for designing gamification. In: Proceedings of the 50th Annual Hawaii International Conference on System Sciences (HICSS), Hawaii, USA. IEEE (2017). https://doi.org/10.24251/hicss.2017.155

21. Hamari, J., Huotari, K., Tolvanen, J.: Gamification and economics. In: Walz, S.P., Deterding, S. (eds.) The Gameful World: Approaches, Issues, Applications, pp. 139–161. The MIT Press, Cambridge (2015)

22. Deci, E.L., Eghrari, H., Patrick, B.C., Leone, D.R.: Facilitating internalization: the self-determination theory perspective. J. Pers. **62**, 119–142 (1994). https://doi.org/10.1111/j.1467-6494.1994.tb00797.x

23. Huta, V., Waterman, A.S.: Eudaimonia and its distinction from Hedonia: developing a classification and terminology for understanding conceptual and operational definitions. J. Happiness Stud. **15**, 1425–1456 (2014). https://doi.org/10.1007/s10902-013-9485-0

24. Peterson, C., Park, N., Seligman, M.E.P.: Orientations to happiness and life satisfaction: the full life versus the empty life. J. Happiness Stud. **6**, 25–41 (2005). https://doi.org/10.1007/s10902-004-1278-z

25. Rigby, S., Ryan, R.M.: Glued to Games: How Video Games Draw Us In and Hold Us Spellbound. Praeger, Santa Barbara (2011)

26. Malone, T.W.: Toward a Theory of Intrinsically Motivating Instruction. Cogn. Sci. **4**, 333–369 (1981)

27. Tondello, G.F., Kappen, D.L., Mekler, E.D., Ganaba, M., Nacke, L.E.: Heuristic evaluation for gameful design. In: Proceedings of the 2016 Annual Symposium on Computer-Human Interaction in Play Extended Abstracts - CHI PLAY EA 2016, pp. 315–323. ACM (2016). https://doi.org/10.1145/2968120.2987729

28. Nielsen, J., Molich, R.: Heuristic evaluation of user interfaces. In: Proceedings of the SIGCHI Conference on Human Factors in Computer Systems - CHI 1990, pp. 249–256 (1990). https://doi.org/10.1145/97243.97281

29. Nielsen, J., Landauer, T.K.: A mathematical model of the finding of usability problems. In: Proceedings of the SIGCHI Conference on Human Factors in Computing Systems - CHI 1993, pp. 206–213. ACM (1993). https://doi.org/10.1145/169059.169166

30. Seaborn, K., Fels, D.I.: Gamification in theory and action: a survey. Int. J. Hum. Comput. Stud. **74**, 14–31 (2014). https://doi.org/10.1016/j.ijhcs.2014.09.006

31. Desurvire, H., Caplan, M., Toth, J.A.: Using heuristics to evaluate the playability of games. In: CHI 2004 Extended Abstracts on Human Factors in Computing Systems, pp. 1509–1512 (2004). https://doi.org/10.1145/985921.986102

32. Desurvire, H., Wiberg, C.: Game usability heuristics (PLAY) for evaluating and designing better games: the next iteration. In: Ozok, A.A., Zaphiris, P. (eds.) OCSC 2009. LNCS, vol. 5621, pp. 557–566. Springer, Heidelberg (2009). https://doi.org/10.1007/978-3-642-02774-1_60

33. Desurvire, H., Wiberg, C.: User experience design for inexperienced gamers: GAP – Game Approachability Principles. In: Bernhaupt, R. (ed.) Evaluating User Experience in Games, pp. 131–148. Springer, London (2010). https://doi.org/10.1007/978-1-84882-963-3_1

34. Korhonen, H., Koivisto, E.M.I.: Playability heuristics for mobile multi-player games. In: Proceedings of the 2nd International Conference on Digital Interactive Media in Entertainment and Arts, pp. 28–35 (2007). https://doi.org/10.1145/1306813.1306828

35. Pinelle, D., Wong, N., Stach, T., Gutwin, C.: Usability heuristics for networked multiplayer games. In: Proceedings of the ACM 2009 International Conference on Supporting Group Work, pp. 169–178 (2009). https://doi.org/10.1145/1531674.1531700

36. Paavilainen, J.: Critical review on video game evaluation heuristics: social games perspective. In: Proceedings of the International Academic Conference on the Future of Game Design and Technology, pp. 56–65 (2010). https://doi.org/10.1145/1920778.1920787

37. Sweetser, P., Wyeth, P.: GameFlow: a model for evaluating player enjoyment in games. Comput. Entertain. **3**, 3 (2005). https://doi.org/10.1145/1077246.1077253

38. Sweetser, P., Johnson, D., Wyeth, P.: Revisiting the GameFlow model with detailed heuristics. J. Creat. Technol. **3** (2013). https://ojs.aut.ac.nz/journal-of-creative-technologies/index.php/JCT/article/view/16

39. Zichermann, G., Cunningham, C.: Gamification by Design: Implementing Game Mechanics in Web and Mobile Apps. O'Reilly, Sebastopol (2011)

40. Francisco-Aparicio, A., Gutiérrez-Vela, F.L., Isla-Montes, J.L., Sanchez, J.L.G.: Gamification: analysis and application. In: Penichet, V., Peñalver, A., Gallud, J. (eds.) New Trends in Interaction, Virtual Reality and Modeling, pp. 113–126. Springer, London (2013). https://doi.org/10.1007/978-1-4471-5445-7_9

41. Jiménez, S.: Gamification Model Canvas. http://www.gameonlab.com/canvas/

42. Burke, B.: Gamify: How Gamification Motivates People to Do Extraordinary Things. Bibliomotion, Brookline (2014)

43. Kappen, D.L., Nacke, L.E.: The kaleidoscope of effective gamification: deconstructing gamification in business applications. In: Proceedings of Gamification 2013, Stratford, ON, Canada, pp. 119–122. ACM (2013). https://doi.org/10.1145/2583008.2583029

44. Paharia, R.: Loyalty 3.0: How to Revolutionize Customer and Employee Engagement with Big Data and Gamification. McGraw-Hill, New York (2013)

45. Nicholson, S.: A RECIPE for meaningful gamification. In: Reiners, T., Wood, L.C. (eds.) Gamification in Education and Business, pp. 1–20. Springer, Cham (2015). https://doi.org/10.1007/978-3-319-10208-5_1

46. Werbach, K., Hunter, D.: For the Win: How Game Thinking Can Revolutionize Your Business. Wharton Digital Press, Philadelphia (2012)

47. McGonigal, J.: SuperBetter: A Revolutionary Approach to Getting Stronger, Happier, Braver and More Resilient. Penguin Books, New York (2015)

48. Hunicke, R., LeBlanc, M., Zubek, R.: MDA: a formal approach to game design and game research. In: Workshop on Challenges in Game AI, pp. 1–4 (2004)
49. Lazzaro, N.: The four fun keys. In: Isbister, K., Schaffer, N. (eds.) Game Usability: Advancing the Player Experience, pp. 315–344. Elsevier, Burlington (2008)

A New Method of Banner Color Design

Zhijuan Zhu, Danqing Sun, Ren Long[(⊠)], and Wenzhen Pan

Huazhong University of Science and Technology,
Wuhan, People's Republic of China
longren@hust.edu.cn

Abstract. The style of an existing banner color design is often based on sub-jective feelings of the person or the accumulated design experience, which is not efficient and applicable. The purpose of this research is to create a good visual effect of banners, and promote the efficiency and design level of web banner design. From the perspective of color composition, this paper started from interpreting the inherent law of banner color application and the aesthetic law of color composition was then applied in web page design. A new color design method for web banner was proposed in this paper. Apply the questionnaire to verify the feasibility, the results show that, (1) The theme is matched by the color scheme of this design method; (2) If the background color is multi-color and in the same color system, the proportion of these colors in the background can be interchanged in most cases, and has little significant influence on the overall sensory expression; (3) The contrast colors can be split without white, but the adjacent colors of the same chroma need to be reconciled and highlighted by black and white for emphasizing the content you want to express. The connotation and artistic conception of the web page banner will be enriched by the application of this new color matching method, which can form a set of color schemes with high efficiency and applicability, which means that is has important reference value for promoting the innovation of the banner design method.

Keywords: Web banner · New method · Color

1 Introduction

In the era of big data with the rapid developing of internet, many companies are striving to seize the space of the virtual world of the Internet in order to establish their own brand image. In the internet advertising, banner is summative and inductive [1]. The most important and latest information in the web page can be shown effectively with the banner, which is a fast channel for people to get important information immediately after entering the web page. Color is the most dynamic way to convey advertising, and the most popular form in the aesthetic sense in general [2]. As an important factor influencing people's feelings about banner, the color design of the website banner is worth studying. In order to help designers to solve the problem of banner color matching, to reduce color selection time, to figure out the difficulty of color planning, a

© Springer Nature Switzerland AG 2019
M. Kurosu (Ed.): HCII 2019, LNCS 11566, pp. 245–255, 2019.
https://doi.org/10.1007/978-3-030-22646-6_17

new method of banner color was established in this paper, later questionnaires were utilized to verify the feasibility. This method can help designers to configure multiple sets of color schemes for selection quickly.

2 Literature Review

Since the emergence of the first personal computer Altar in 1975, all aspects of our lives have been occupied by more and more digital products [3]. Banner originates from the early headline advertises in paper media, which refers to banners and flags used as slogans in parades, and now banner refers to web ads. Li has pointed out that banner had the characteristics of timeliness, size limitation and precision [4].

The color of the web page belongs to the category of color science [5], and the research on its performance has started earlier in the international academic community. At the end of the 20th century, web pages were included in the user interface as a type of interactive interface. In the book "Web Design Basics Tutorial" written by Yang and Yu etc. The basic discussion on the color matching of web pages was carried out [6]. In the "Designer's Web Color Matching" written by the I.R.I Color Research Institute of Korea, a detailed analysis of the color matching of web pages was conducted [7]. "Introduction to Color" by Chilansky and Fisher contains a special chapter on computer color, adding web design content to the discussion of computer art updates [8]. In the article "Color Application and Research in Web Design", Zheng explained that web design had gone through three stages—the simplest static pages, illustrated pages and interactive dynamic web pages [9]. Zhang Pan, etc. have described the psychological functions of advertising color and the factors of limitation in detail (including time, region, ethnicity, history, religion, customs, culture, etc.) [10, 11].

The existing literatures on the color matching of web banners mainly focused on the rules of color matching and the elements of color selection. There are few literature on forming a set of instructional process operation methods on color matching in spite of some theoretical discussions. Most experienced designers use their previous design experience to obtain reasonable color matching, however general designers need to take a lot of effort for color matching in their work. Too much time are used for the work and the output of color planning are still not satisfied due to the inefficient work. Therefore, how to help design novices to choose color schemes, making designers work more efficiently becomes an urgent problem to be solved.

3 Method

3.1 Application of Color Composition Rules

Modern advertising design is generally composed of elements such as words, patterns and colors, and the three are interdependent. The patterns and words are expressed by color. When people browse a web page, the first things which enter into people's sights with the visual impact and appeal are colors. Color expression can be considered the most important thing in some extent [12]. In the 1920s and 1930s, Bauhaus has built and developed the core theoretical system which constitutes art [13]. In color design, designers often use color schemes to achieve the most harmonious design color. The principles of these rules are summarized as below.

Apply Monochrome to Complete the Picture

Monochrome configuration refers to the use of a single hue to form the main color of the picture. By adjusting the purity and brightness of the color, a pure picture is configured to make the picture as a whole consistent with the application environment. It is often used in the case that the page matches the corporate image and the VI system, which makes the overall web page ordered and harmonious.

Apply the Similar Color and Adjacent Color Configuration to Construct a Harmonious Picture

The similar color means colors with no significant difference in hue, which can only be distinguished by the purity and brightness. The adjacent color means colors with an angle of 60–90° or five or six digits apart on color ring, such as red and orange, blue and blue-green [14]. When two or more colors appear in the picture, the difference in color visibility occurs [15]. Compared with similar colors, the difference in hue of adjacent colors is more obvious, and the contrast between colors is improved, which can enhance the sense of activity for the original harmonious picture. Through a scheme of the similar color and adjacent color configuration, a unified and varied picture effect can be produced.

Apply Complementary Color Configurations to Create a Dynamic Picture

The complementary color refers to colors with an angle of 180° on the color ring, such as red and green, yellow and purple, blue and orange, and so on. This kind of colors have strong stimulation to the human optic nerve, which can make people feel excited in a short period of time and create a dynamic picture. At the same time, watching this kind of colors for a long time will bring people a sense of fatigue and reduce people's good feelings for expressing things. This type of colors should be used with caution and are suitable for pages with short time of sight and strong appeal. The higher the brightness, the more prominent the theme, and the color purity is reduced from red, orange, purple, blue, and green. The colorist Goethe believes that the brightness and area of the color determine the power of the color, and the ratio of the balance area of the complementary color is given as yellow: purple = 1:3 orange: blue = 1:2 red: green = 1:1 [16].

Theoretical studies in color have shown that different background colors can have different (and sometimes even opposite) effects on consumer perception, emotion, and behavior [17, 18]. Therefore, a large area of color is generally applied to a low-purity background color, and a small area of complementary color or contrast color can be added thereto to increase the change and motion of the picture. Black and white is the simplest match, which is very clear, gray is a universal color, which can be matched with any color to help the opposite color transition [19].

3.2 New Design Method

When designing a banner, colors are often used to highlight important information or convey a specific feeling to fit the theme, which makes users have the desire to click in a short period of time, and thus enhance the propaganda and desire to purchase [20]. Consumers have different information processing methods for new products placed under different background colors, and the corresponding product evaluation may be different [21]. However, most of studies on banner color matching focus on the interaction between colors, and do not form a set of efficient, fast and instructive color matching process. In most cases, designers can only try color matching based on experience and subjective judgment. For this, a design method for quickly obtaining color schemes is proposed (Fig. 1), so that designers can save time and improve work efficiency.

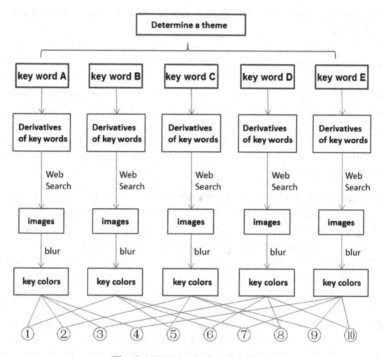

Fig. 1. New method design flow

(1) Establishing topics and keywords
A theme was identified through brainstorming, and then 3–5 keywords named A, B, C, D, and E are exacted by brainstorming. 3–10 sets of color schemes can be generated by these 3–5 keywords. The number of keywords depends on the number of initial schemes required. Based on the design experience, the number of initial schemes generated by 3–5 keywords will not be too much or too little.

(2) Extracting derivatives
Extract 6–10 derived words based on each keyword. During this process, designers can use mind mapping method to generate these derived words.

(3) Selecting picture and blurring
Search for these derivatives on the network, find the corresponding network pictures, and blur the pictures in the software. When selecting images, try to choose high-quality

image sites, use high-definition images and the content of the images is full and full, and there is not much white space to avoid affecting the extraction of key colors. Blurring the image, so that the color of the processed image is fused to a certain extent, softer, so as to facilitate the subsequent color extraction. If the blur degree is too low, the effect cannot be achieved, and if the blur is too high, the color of the screen changes too much. Therefore, when the blur processing is performed, the blur parameter is preferably set to about 10.

(4) Extracting key colors
Extract 5–7 key colors from the blurred image. The relevant websites and tools to identify the color of the pictures uploaded can be used to assist in the extraction. In this paper, ColorStatistics software is used for color recognition.

(5) Combining schemes
10 sets of new color schemes can be formed by the combination of five sets of key colors. In this process, designers should use a combination of basic aesthetic qualities and basic color knowledge. Designers can flexibly apply the aesthetic rules outlined above in this paper to color matching and abandon or modify color schemes that are clearly undesirable.

As a result, designers can get one or more designs for banner by screening the new color scheme.

4   Result and Discussion

4.1   A Subsection Sample

The color scheme of the EXCHANGE DISCUSSION banner (see Fig. 2) of SANG-FOR is redesigned based on the method proposed above. Five groups of native key words were selected through brainstorming, then derivative words from the five groups of key words were extracted (see Fig. 3), next corresponding images (Table 1) of the derivative words were discovered, later these images were blurred and key colors were extracted on the ColorStatistics (see Fig. 4). Ten color schemes were combined with five sets of key words (see Fig. 5). At the same time, random select three of them (see Figs. 6 and 7) to transform the text and background in order to further explore the skills of color matching.

Fig. 2. EXCHANGE DISCUSSION Original image

Table 1. Key words and derivative words.

Number	Keywords	Derivative words
①	Academic	Serious, correct attitude, books, knowledge, concepts, paper, black and white text, stationery, library
②	Atmosphere	Harmony, strong, overflowing, joy, nervous, quiet
③	Rational	Calm, logical, clear, brain, steady, analysis, quick thinking, big data, military
④	Dream	Value, wind and waves, ambition, original, paper plane, kite, five-pointed star, bud, pigeon, hot air balloon
⑤	Active	Sports, youth, strength, positive, sunshine, life, courage

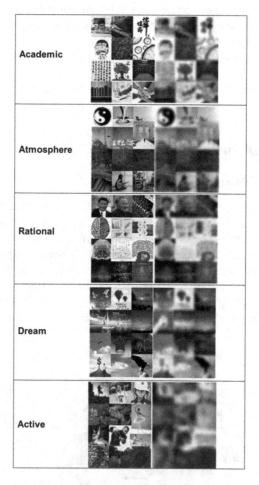

Fig. 3. Blur pictures

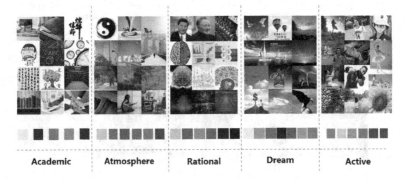

Fig. 4. Extract key colors

Fig. 5. Ten color schemes

	Before	After
A	A1	A2

Fig. 6. Background color exchange image

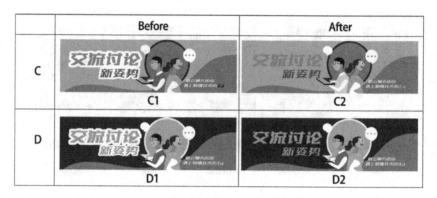

Fig. 7. Text change image

4.2 Verification Survey

A total of 42 people participated in the test, including 17 males and 25 females. All subjects were designers and from different regions with ages ranging from 18 to 35 years old. The questionnaire was scored on a five-point scale for five questions, namely (Table 2): 1 is the lowest score, 3 is the general, and 5 is the highest score.

Table 2. Questionnaire

	Questions
Q1	Please rate the satisfaction of the 10 sets of banner's color schemes
Q2	Please score the consistency of colors and the theme "Discussion of New Post Banner" of the 10 sets of banner
Q3	What is the effect of the background color exchange of the picture A before and after the change on the expression of the overall effect? (see Fig. 6)
Q4	Please give a score to the eye-catching degree of the words "Communication Discussion New Position" in pictures C and D. (see Fig. 7)
Q5	Please give a score to the reading comfort degree of the words "Communication Discussion New Position" in pictures C and D. (see Fig. 7)

4.3 Results and Data Analysis

The satisfaction in Q1 was scored generally higher than 3 points (see Fig. 8) and P9 having the highest satisfaction of 3.97. The final average score was 3.4. The score in Q2 was scored with a final score of 3.37, with the highest scores for P8 and P9 being 3.95 (see Fig. 8). In question (3), the exchange of background color of picture A didn't affect too much (Fig. 9). The degree of boldness in the question (4) was C1 > C2, D1 > D2. C1 and C2 are quite different. The highest C1 was 4.21, C2 was only 1.6, and D1 was closed to D2, which were 4.38 and 3.38 respectively (see Fig. 10). The reading comfort in question (5) was C1 > C2, D1 > D2, where C1 was the highest, 4.36, C2 was the lowest 1.71, and D1 was similar to D2, which was 3.79 and 3.64 respectively.

After comparing the application, it was also found that,

- The 10 color schemes are basically in line with the theme of "EXCHANGE DISCUSSION".
- If the background color is multi-color, different colors occupy different proportions, while the colors are in the same color system but only adjust in purity and brightness, the proportion of these colors in the background can be interchanged in most cases, and has no significant influence on the overall sensory expression.
- The contrast colors can be split without white, but the adjacent colors of the same chroma need to be reconciled and highlighted by black and white for emphasizing the content you want to express. If the color purity in the picture is too high, dark gray adjustment is required to stabilize the picture.

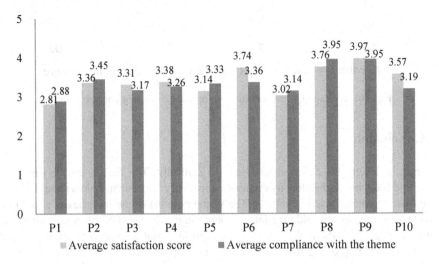

Fig. 8. Average Q1 satisfaction score and Q2 compliance with the theme

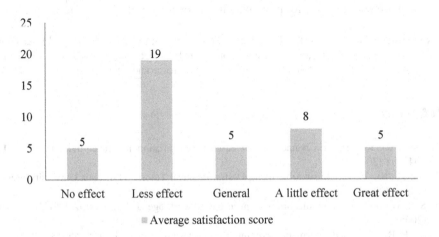

Fig. 9. Figure A background exchange impact statistics

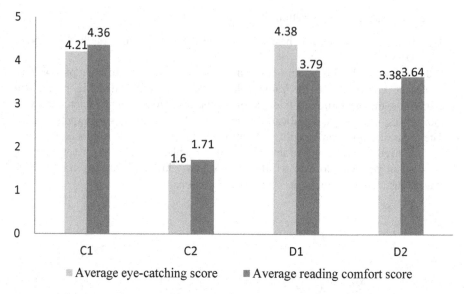

Fig. 10. Average Q4 eye-catching score and Q5 reading comfort score

5   Conclusion

In banner's design, the color should be used skillfully. The design can be rigorous, serene and bold, but high-intensity contrasts, especially fluorescent colors should not be always used to attract users' eyeballs. The visual comfort of the interviewer should be considered. Designers should take into account the user's visual comfort, pay attention to the balance of colors, make the whole design look stable, thus creating a pleasant atmosphere and improving users' goodwill on the webpage. Applying this new color matching method enriches the connotation and artistic conception of the banner of the webpage, and can form a set of color schemes with high efficiency and applicability. The method has reference value for promoting the innovation of the banner design method.

Acknowledgement. This work is financially supported by 2017 Chinese Ministry of Education Humanities and Social Sciences Research Youth Fund Project (No. 17YJCZH231) and the Teaching Research Project of Huazhong University of Science and Technology (No. 2018056).

References

1. Zhou, R.: Research on banner design cases in information interface. Ind. Des. Res. **1**, 104–105 (2013)
2. Lu, M., Xu, F.: Graphical Advertising Design Practical Tutorial. Tsinghua University Press, Beijing (2005)
3. Sun, W.: Visual communication design in the network age. J. Jilin Coll. Art **69**(2), 41–46 (2005)
4. Li, J.: Banner-based information communication design. Packag. Eng. **8**, 55–58 (2016)

5. Jin, R.: Design Color Psychology. People Post Press, Beijing (2013)
6. Yang, Y., Yu, T., Li, S.: Web Design Basics Tutorial. Tsinghua University Press, Beijing (2012)
7. I.R.I Color Research Institute: Designer's Web Color Matching. Li, H. (Trans.) 1st edn. Electronic Industry Press, Beijing (2002)
8. Chilansky, P., Fisher, M.: Introduction to Color. Wen, P. (Trans.) 1st edn. Shanghai People's Fine Arts Publishing House Press, Shanghai (2004)
9. Zheng, W.: Color Application and Research in Web Design, pp. 1–71. Northwest Normal University, Gansu (2012)
10. Zhang, X.: The use of color in advertising design. Orient. Corp. Cult. **14**, 162 (2010)
11. Pan, J.: Color perception and color perception in the process of time. Decoration **3**, 123 (2014)
12. Zhao, J.: The use of color visual communication in advertising design. Mod. Decor. (Theory) **12**, 156 (2016)
13. Cao, D., Zuo, W.: Research on the evolution of Bauhaus curriculum design in 1919–1932. Creat. Des. Source **1**, 59–64 (2016)
14. Pan, H., Du, X.: Principle of Graphic Design. Beijing Institute of Technology Press, Beijing (2013)
15. Zhang, C., Zhu, X.: Application of color contrast and blending in advertising design. J. Northwest Normal Univ. (Soc. Sci. Ed.) **48**(3), 129–132 (2011)
16. Yu, Y., Zhang, Y.: The use of color elements in web design. Comput. Knowl. Technol. **12**(2), 168–169 (2016)
17. Mehta, R., Zhu, R.: Blue or red? Exploring the effects of color on cognitive task performances. Science **27**(323), 1226–1229 (2009)
18. Kwallek, N., Lewis, C.M.: Effects of environmental color on males and females: a red or white or green office. Appl. Ergon. **21**(4), 275–278 (1990)
19. Yue, B.: Color selection and matching skills in web design. Comput. Knowl. Technol. **5**(23), 6544–6545 (2009)
20. Wu, Y.: Let the colors tell the story of the banner-analysis of the color matching method of banner in internet advertising design. Art Educ. **2**, 202–203 (2014)
21. Liu, W., Liang, J.: Choosing red or blue-the study of phenomena, intermediary and boundary system of background color influence on visual new product evaluation. Nankai Manag. Rev. **18**(1), 23–35 (2016)

Redefining the Human in HCI

Supporting Life History Research with Interactive Visualizations

Tamara Babaian$^{(\boxtimes)}$, Miriam Boeri, and Gita Ligure

Bentley University, Waltham, MA 02452, USA
{tbabaian,mboeri,gligure}@bentley.edu

Abstract. We present two novel interfaces for in-field and self-report data collection and analysis of life histories. LifeHistory interface enables direct input of multifaceted longitudinal data via a timeline grid annotated with pictorial representations of landmark events. TrajectoryView is an interactive visualization of life history data for a side-by-side comparison of parameters of an individual's life history. The two interfaces are intended as an alternative to paper-based tools and methods currently used by qualitative researchers. Beyond a mere automation of data collection and presentation, the interfaces offer enhancements supporting recall of events and visual analysis of data. We expect that the use of LifeHistory and TrajectoryView will simplify data collection and analysis processes, leading to greater accuracy of data and better opportunities for insights.

Keywords: Visual interface · Data collection · Life history ·
Longitudinal research methods

1 Introduction and Motivation

Life history (a.k.a. *life course*) research [9] is a core methodological approach employed in longitudinal studies in many disciplines, including sociology, epidemiology, health sciences, psychology, anthropology, and business. Here, we are using the term longitudinal to refer to the research examining people, cases, or events over a period of time. A life course perspective examines life histories within the social, cultural, and political contexts of the period in order to identify situational changes over time and place [5], focusing attention on transitions and turning points across an individual's life trajectory [10]. Life history researchers employ a variety of methods, including surveys and in-depth interviews in data collection and analysis. The work presented here addresses the challenge of automating life history data capture during an interview or a self-report and their subsequent analysis for transitions and turning points.

State-of-the-art software packages for qualitative and mixed-methods research such as Qualtrics [13], MAXAPP [14] and Atlas.ti Mobile [15] provide capabilities for collecting survey, audio, video, and image data, limited coding and tagging of interview data and other documents. However, they do not provide support for a common tool for collection and analysis of life history data, called a *life history calendar* [6].

© Springer Nature Switzerland AG 2019
M. Kurosu (Ed.): HCII 2019, LNCS 11566, pp. 259–269, 2019.
https://doi.org/10.1007/978-3-030-22646-6_18

Life History Matrix #_____ Age:_____ Race:_____ Sex_____

Age									
DATE									
Residence									
Family									
Partners									
Work history (licit and illicit)									
Education									
Health Status									
Social Life									
Religion Spirituality									
Law Involvement									
Treatment History									
Substance Use									

Fig. 1. A sample of Life History Matrix – a paper-and-pencil data collection tool.

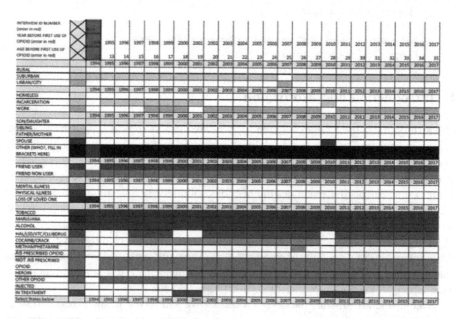

Fig. 2. An Excel spreadsheet used for life history data collection.

A life history calendar, sometimes referred to as *event history calendar* or *life history matrix* [1], is a grid with columns referencing time points (typically, years, but other units are used as appropriate) and rows representing different conditions, grouped by themes (e.g. health, family, etc.). An example of a life history matrix, used in a study by the second author [3], is shown in Fig. 1. In the absence of an interface automating life history data collection, researchers use a pencil-and-paper version to record information, which then has to be manually transferred into electronic format. A semi-automated version designed by Boeri and presented in Fig. 2 employs an Excel spreadsheet to capture the responses using color. The use of the spreadsheet, however, requires initial training of the person administering the survey. Furthermore, the transfer of the response data into format appropriate for data analysis tools is not automated.

Figure 3 presents another sample tool that researchers use in the process of life history data collection during an interview. It is a *textual timeline* which is used in order to activate the respondent's memory of specific time periods [2, 8]. Landmark historical events listed in a textual timeline provide a context in which respondents can place events in their lives to recreate a more accurate account.

Timeline
1976-Jimmy Carter elected
1977-Voyager launched
1978-Jamestown Suicides.
1979-3 Mile Island
1980-John Lennon killed
1981-first reported cases of AIDS in USA
1982-Compact Discs introduced
1983-Microsoft Word released;
1984-Mac APPLE invented;
1985-Reagan ramps up War on Drugs
1986- Challenger explosion
1987-Michael Jackson releases BAD;
1989-Fall of Berlin Wall
1990-Hubble telescope launched
1991-debut of world wide web

1992-Clinton defeats Bush
1993-World Trade Center bombing
1994-first web search engine Yahoo.com
1995-Waco, TX, DVD introduced,
1996-Atlanta Olympics, Depp Blue beats Gary Kasparov in chess
1997-Princess Diana dies
1998-Ebay founded, Google founded, Clinton impeached
1999-Windows 98 released; Napster invented
2000-W2K scare; Bush defeats Gore
2001- 9/11
2002-No Child Left Behind Act signed

Fig. 3. Textual timeline from a study of drug users by Boeri et al.

In this paper we present two prototype interfaces that we developed to support life course research:

1. LifeHistory data collection tool – a visual interactive interface for collecting life history data for a set of specified conditions. LifeHistory enables data entry via a direct interaction with a grid-based timeline illustrated with pictorial representations of landmark events.
2. TrajectoryView – an interactive visualization of life history data for side-by-side comparison of parameters within individual's life history, to help identify relationships between events, patterns and turning points.

In designing these interfaces we aimed to help researchers administering in-field life history data collection and post-collection analysis in the following ways:

- Combining the matrix and a visual timeline in one computerized interface will alleviate the difficulties associated with handling multiple paper-and-pencil tools for administering a life history survey during a face-to-face interview. The simplification of the data collection procedure will promote greater reliability of the data, as the researcher and/or interviewee will be able to direct more attention to cross-checking the chronology of events and coming up with insights and further questions.
- Display of visual landmark cues should facilitate more accurate recall of events by participants [11].
- Electronic capture of response data will minimize the effort and errors associated with transferring the data into computerized format for future analysis. This should lead to improvements in data accuracy and reliability of the results of data analysis. Visualization of life history trajectories that enables easy side-by-side comparison of parameters will facilitate post-collection analysis and discovery of important relationships of events and conditions.

To the best of our knowledge, LifeHistory is the first timeline-based interface built specifically for data entry via direct input into a timeline grid. Other timeline-based tools, such as TimeLineJS [16], TimeLineCurator [7], Timeline Storyteller [4, 17] and LifeFlow [12], have been used most prominently in journalism and storytelling, to convey chronological order of events and plans, display multiple narrative lines, compare and contrast personal histories. While these applications present examples of customizable visualizations capable of processing and depicting chronologically arranged event data, they lack essential capabilities for their use in data collection. Our long-term research goal is to develop novel computerized methodologies supporting longitudinal research, aiding in simultaneous input and visual analytics of chronological data. The two interfaces introduced here present the first step in achieving this goal. Both interfaces are implemented as web-based prototypes using javascript and D3.

In the rest of the paper we describe LifeHistory and TrajectoryView, present results of a pilot user evaluation of LifeHistory for self-reporting of personal data, and outline conclusions and future work.

2   LifeHistory Data Collection Tool

LifeHistory data collection tool presented in Fig. 5 provides a data entry interface for collecting yes/no responses to a set of questions over a specified range of years. Each yes/no response is indicated via clicking on a cell in the matrix with columns corresponding to years and rows corresponding to questions (a.k.a. conditions). For example, the matrix cell containing the mouse pointer in Fig. 5, indicates a positive response to the condition abbreviated as 'High School' in year 2007.

The main component of the LifeHistory interface is a data entry matrix occupying the middle part of the screenshot presented in Fig. 5. It is constructed from a list of questions organized into thematic categories specified by a researcher using a text file.

The top part of the interface depicted in Fig. 4 enables the researcher to enter the following options that are used in generating life history input matrix: (a) the thematic categories to be included in the survey, (b) the range of years to include. These options are specified using the UI controls displayed when the user opens LifeHistory. Figure 4 shows four categories: Family Status, Education, Residence, and Exercise displayed next to checkboxes indicating selection of questions of the checked categories. Upon user making the selection of categories, the range of years, and clicking on the Submit button, the LifeHistory interface generates and displays the input matrix as shown in Fig. 5.

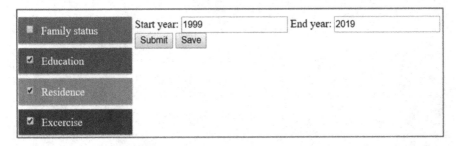

Fig. 4. The top part of the LifeHistory interface provides selection options for generating the input matrix based on a selection of categories and range of years.

The matrix is organized as follows: per each category, it displays the category questions and blocks of cells, which can be selected/unselected via clicking or touching, indicating a positive/negative response. The first column of the matrix displays the abbreviated text of the questions. The timeline indicating years associated with the columns is displayed in the bottom. Each cell represents a 'yes' or 'no' answer to the condition appearing in the fist column, for the year corresponding to the cell's column. The cells are colored according to their category. On the bottom, the matrix displays a timeline of years, annotated with images corresponding to the landmark events. The matrix is scrollable, in case not all questions and/or years fit the screen.

Beyond the features visible in Fig. 5, LifeHistory interface also enables users to view full question specifications, by hovering over the abbreviation in the first column and reading the tooltip. Furthermore, to simplify verification of the year associated with a column, a tooltip in each cell reveals the corresponding year. The state of the matrix can be saved in a json file on the client computer at any point by clicking on the Save button.

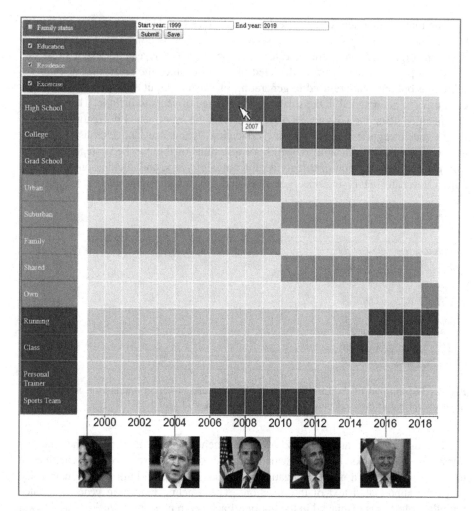

Fig. 5. A screenshot of LifeHistory interface showing the selection parameters, the input matrix and a timeline enhanced with images provided as landmark event cues.

3   TrajectoryView Interactive Visualization for Trajectory Analysis

A *trajectory* is a distinguishable pathway across life's span. *Transitions* are changes from one state to another that are often found along a typical trajectory (from student to employee) or less typical trajectory (e.g., drug user to drug dealer). *Turning points* are times or events that take a person in a different direction—one of many possible trajectories.

A separate interface was developed for visualizing the collected life history trajectory data for analysis and identification of turning points and trajectory patterns. The TrajectoryView visualization of drug-use trajectory data collected in a study of drug use [3] is depicted in Fig. 6. This visualization follows the on-paper design presented in [3] by Boeri et al. displaying a matrix constructed from binary data for a set of conditions listed in the column on the right. The added interactivity allows to select a set of rows that would be also displayed next to each other below the timeline, for a side-by-side comparison, as shown in Fig. 6.

This visualization allows a researcher to pick an individual case and examine multiple factors in one's life history, focusing on identification of the relationships and critical connections between such factors.

Drug use trajectory

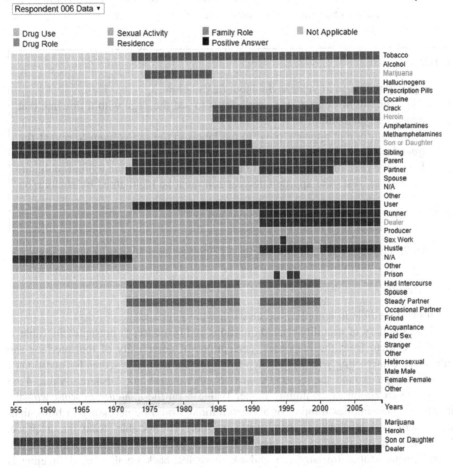

Fig. 6. A screenshot of TrajectoryView displaying a visualization of a drug user's life trajectory.

4 Pilot User Study of Self-reporting Using LifeHistory

We conducted a pilot user study to assess the usability of the LifeHistory interface when used for self-reporting without any prior training of the respondent. There were 6 participants in the study, with age ranging from 24 to 48. Participants were recruited from graduate and undergraduate students, faculty, and professionals in a business university. All participants were fluent computer users.

We have asked the study participants to use the LifeHistory visualization to enter details of their Education, Residence and Exercise habits for the past 20 years. Users were provided instructions shown in Fig. 7 and no training in how to operate the interface. Following their use of LifeHistory, we asked them to answer six Likert-scale usability-related questions and four open response questions (all detailed below) based on their perceptions regarding the visualization and their experience.

Instructions:

1. Specify the range of years in the input fields below.
2. Click the **Submit** button and scroll down to see the page with a timeline that appears on the bottom.
3. In the matrix that appears, point to the labels in the left column to **reveal the questions**.
4. For every year, provide answers to questions appearing in the leftmost column. To answer **'yes'** - the appropriate year cell must be highlighted by clicking on it.
5. When you are done, click on the **Save** button.

Fig. 7. Instructions on using the LifeHistory interface given to users in a pilot study.

4.1 Results

All users were able to complete the task using the interface.

The summary of usability-related questions and responses is presented in Table 1. As if is evident from the responses, perceptions of complexity of the interface and difficulty of interacting with it vary, depending on the user. The scores for questions 1 and 4 average around the neutral stance (Neither Agree nor Disagree, value 4 on *interface was complex*) or slightly higher (value 5 on the *difficulty to work with* the interface). This implies training or a video tutorial would be necessary to bring first-time users to a level where they would be more comfortable using the interface. Usefulness of the timeline and images to users' recall of life details also varied, averaging to neutral (questions 5 and 6); more feedback on the visual timeline is provided by the answers to the open-response questions.

Table 1. Summary of usability questions and responses.

Question	Min - Max, Rounded average of answers on a 7-point Likert scale: 1 (Strongly Disagree) – 7 (Strongly Agree)
1. The interface was complex	1–6, 4 (Neither Agree nor Disagree)
2. The interface was crowded	1–6, 4 (Neither Agree nor Disagree)
3. The interface was interactive	2–7, 5 (Agree Slightly)
4. The interface was difficult to work with	1–7, 5 (Agree Slightly)
5. Having the timeline annotated with images was useful to me in answering the questions	2–7, 4 (Neither Agree nor Disagree)
6. Timeline images helped me recall details of my life	3–6, 4 (Neither Agree nor Disagree)

We have asked users to answers to the following open-response questions:

1. *What did you like about the interface?*
2. *The interface provided event cues using images associated with political events. Was this choice of pictures helpful to you? (Answer yes, no or somewhat) If not, what type of events would be most useful to you (please write in a response)?*
3. *Please provide any suggestions for improving the visualization.*

In response to the first of the above questions, users mentioned liking the simplicity of the interface and the data entry mechanism, clear differentiation of categories by colors, and having images to help with their recollection. Question 2 led to mixed answers, with one user responding 'yes', two others 'somewhat', and three - 'no'. Participants suggested using other events, for example, financial ones. One person who responded with a 'no', commented: "I didn't realize that the presidents could be helpful to recall events from my life. Now I see that they could."

Suggestions for improvement provided by users included:

- providing ability to select multiple years at once by holding the touch/mouse button down while moving it over multiple columns,
- making the boxes smaller to avoid scrolling,
- providing a choice of different types of events to include on the timeline,
- associating different timeline images with different question categories.

5   Conclusion and Future Work

We have presented two novel user interfaces for longitudinal life history data collection and analysis. The interfaces automate and enhance existing manual practices and tools used by qualitative researchers when conducting longitudinal studies in many fields. In a pilot user study of using LifeHistory tool for life history self-reporting survey, users were able to successfully use the interface without prior training. Users' perceptions of the usefulness of the landmark event images to their recollection of their life were mixed. This might be attributable to the choice of landmark event images depicting U.S. presidents whose term started in the specific year.

The feedback collected from the participants of the study will inform the future development and fine-tuning of the interface. In particular, it will be interesting to explore giving participants a choice of landmark events to put on their timeline. We also plan to conduct a user study with researchers utilizing our tools and develop enhancements supporting easy customization of the survey instrument for different age groups and cultural contexts.

References

1. Belli, R.F.: The structure of autobiographical memory and the event history calendar: potential improvements in the quality of retrospective reports in surveys. Mem. Hove Engl. **6**(4), 383–406 (1998). https://doi.org/10.1080/741942610
2. Belli, R.F., Shay, W.L., Stafford, F.P.: Event history calendars and question list surveys: a direct comparison of interviewing methods. Public Opin. Q. **65**(1), 45–74 (2001)
3. Boeri, M., Whalen, T., Tyndall, B., Ballard, E.: Drug use trajectory patterns among older drug users. Subst. Abuse Rehabil. **2**, 89–102 (2011). https://doi.org/10.2147/SAR.S14871
4. Brehmer, M., Lee, B., Bach, B., Riche, N.H., Munzner, T.: Timelines revisited: a design space and considerations for expressive storytelling. IEEE Trans. Vis. Comput. Graph. **23**(9), 2151–2164 (2017). https://doi.org/10.1109/TVCG.2016.2614803
5. Elder, G.H.: Time, human agency, and social change: perspectives on the life course. Soc. Psychol. Q. **57**(1), 4–15 (1994). https://doi.org/10.2307/2786971
6. Freedman, D., Thornton, A., Camburn, D., Alwin, D., Young-DeMarco, L.: The life history calendar: a technique for collecting retrospective data. Sociol. Methodol. **18**(1988), 37 (1988). https://doi.org/10.2307/271044
7. Fulda, J., Brehmer, M., Munzner, T.: TimeLineCurator: interactive authoring of visual timelines from unstructured text. IEEE Trans. Vis. Comput. Graph. **22**(1), 300–309 (2016). https://doi.org/10.1109/TVCG.2015.2467531
8. Gaskell, G.D., Wright, D.B., O'Muircheartaigh, C.A.: Telescoping of landmark events: implications for survey research. Public Opin. Q. **64**(1), 77–89 (2000)
9. Giele, J.Z., Elder, G.H.: Methods of Life Course Research: Qualitative and Quantitative Approaches. SAGE, Thousand Oaks (1998)
10. Laub, J.H., Sampson, R.J.: Turning points in the life course: why change matters to the study of crime. Criminology **31**(3), 301–325 (1993). https://doi.org/10.1111/j.1745-9125.1993.tb01132.x
11. Ringel, M., Cutrell, E., Dumais, S., Horvitz, E.: Milestones in time: the value of landmarks in retrieving information from personal stores, no. 8
12. Wongsuphasawat, K., Guerra Gómez, J.A., Plaisant, C., Wang, T.D., Taieb-Maimon, M., Shneiderman, B.: LifeFlow: visualizing an overview of event sequences. In: Proceedings of the SIGCHI Conference on Human Factors in Computing Systems, pp. 1747–1756 (2011)
13. Online Survey Platform: Qualtrics. https://www.qualtrics.com/lp/survey-platform/. Accessed 10 Feb 2019
14. MAXApp - MAXQDA app for Field Research and all data on the way: MAXQDA - The Art of Data Analysis. https://www.maxqda.com/products/maxqda-app. Accessed 12 Oct 2018

15. iPad|Qualitative Data Analysis with ATLAS.ti: atlas.ti. https://atlasti.com/product/ios/. Accessed 12 Oct 2018
16. Timeline JS. https://timeline.knightlab.com/. Accessed 6 Jan 2018
17. Timeline Storyteller. https://timelinestoryteller.com/. Accessed 13 Jan 2018

Towards the Ontology of Becoming in Self-tracking Research

Harley Bergroth and Jukka Vuorinen[✉]

Department of Social Research, University of Turku, Turku, Finland
{harley.bergroth, jukka.vuorinen}@utu.fi

Abstract. This article contributes to research perspectives on the topic of proactive self-tracking. Self-tracking, referring to the employment of near-body biometric technologies such as activity wristbands and sleep tracking devices that collect data on bodies, is a popular practice of health-related life management, and thus an object of interest across a variety of research fields. However, we argue that much of the research throughout the various fields subscribes, to some degree, to a bifurcating 'ontology of being' through which the human and the technical are separated from each other at the level of ontological presumptions. In this article, we draw from a range of (new) materialist philosophy and discussions in the field of science and technology studies, and propose a shift towards a processual 'ontology of becoming' in self-tracking research. We suggest some theoretical and conceptual fine-tunings through which research may be better equipped to investigate the processuality of actors and multidirectional flows of agency in self-tracking practices. While our main contribution is theoretical, we will also illustratively analyze two interview narratives of self-tracking in order to demonstrate the different types of research worlds that open up depending on the ontological perspective taken.

Keywords: Self-tracking · Ontology · Becoming · Self · Technology · Social theory

1 Introduction

As an instantiation of the 'datafication' of society (Beer 2016; Ruckenstein and Schüll 2017) digital proactive self-tracking has in recent decades become an integral part of millions of everyday lives especially in Euro-American contexts (Schüll 2016; Lupton 2016a). By 'proactive self-tracking' we refer to the everyday employment of biometric self-tracking devices and applications outside of medical and clinical contexts. Such devices include, but are not limited to, activity tracking wristbands, smartwatches, heart rate monitors and sleep tracking software and hardware, all of which people often employ for gathering data on themselves, in order to optimize their wellbeing, shape their behavior and understand the patterns of their everyday lives and bodies better.

Due to the growing supply of consumer-grade self-tracking technologies and applications, the subject has been widely studied across different fields of research. In most cases, self-tracking-related research connects to a consideration of how such technologies have expanded everyday possibilities for gathering personal informatics,

M. Kurosu (Ed.): HCII 2019, LNCS 11566, pp. 270–287, 2019.
https://doi.org/10.1007/978-3-030-22646-6_19

for adjusting one's behavior, and for negotiating one's conception of the self and others (Rooksby et al. 2014; Nafus and Sherman 2014; Liu et al. 2015; Lomborg and Frandsen 2016; Kristensen and Ruckenstein 2018). Although scientific accounts on the topic vary a great deal in their emphases and content, we argue that a vast majority of self-tracking related scientific accounts draw – at the level of fundamental ontological assumptions – a dividing borderline between more or less passive, assisting devices and active human users. We argue that in order for self-tracking research to more accurately grasp the effects and repercussions of data-driven self-tracking on everyday lives, we should attempt to further diminish the influence of such divisions that are deeply embedded in our scientific as well as our everyday ways of thinking about human-technology relations (see e.g. Scott and Orlikowski 2014; Introna 2013; Latour 1992). In order to map the functioning of the productive assemblages of self-tracking in people's lifeworlds (see Lupton 2016a; Hogle 2016), we need to steer away from assuming that humans and their technologies are distinct because, as we will argue, such bifurcation tends to *hide* the complex relations at work in self-tracking assemblages rather than *highlight* them.

This paper contributes to research perspectives on the topic of self-tracking. It rethinks research on proactive self-tracking first by tracing human-technology divisions in current research, and second by suggesting theoretical-conceptual emphases through which to attune research with what is called the 'ontology of becoming'. We will put our conceptual developments to work by employing and illustratively analyzing two interview narratives on self-tracking. These interviews are part of a larger set of research data which are analyzed empirically elsewhere (e.g. Bergroth 2018). We stress that the main contribution of this paper is theoretical. This is to say that we do not attempt to employ the interviews to present conclusive empirical evidence; rather, the interview narratives we analyze serve merely as illustrative examples of the different research worlds and different analytic possibilities that open up for researchers via different ontologies.

2   Tracing Human-Technology Bifurcation in Self-tracking Research

Much of the research on self-tracking reflects the intuitive tendency to separate the 'user' and the 'used' in technological practices. This means that the perceived connection of humans and their self-tracking devices is often based on the idea of it being the human who is the decisive agent in 'doing' self-tracking while the technical agent is reduced into a role of either a completely passive 'tool' or, in any case, a lesser agent. For example, many studies in the field of human-computer interaction are interested in patterns and/or continuance of use related to self-tracking devices (e.g. Rooksby et al. 2014; Lazar et al. 2015; Liu et al. 2015; Kari et al. 2016; Ogbanufe and Gerhart 2017). Such studies employ a premise that human beings direct the human-technology relationship by choosing to 'use' (or *not* to use) self-tracking devices in ways that they see appropriate, for example by attempting to reach personal goals, by experimenting with the self or by 'abandoning' the devices as futile.

This separation of human and technology is an instantiation of what we call 'human-technology bifurcation' (see Introna 2013). Bifurcation in general refers to a characteristically 'modern' way of dividing the world into two distinct and different sets of entities (Latour 1993; see also Whitehead 1978, 2006) such as human and non-human or culture and nature. By human-technology bifurcation we refer to a process in which the human and the technical/technological are intuitively separated from each other in the sense that the human is seen as the one who acts (e.g. takes care of oneself, improves one's physical condition, interprets data) while technology functions as a passive assistant to human agency (e.g. it follows algorithmic orders, executes functions, records and displays data etc.).[1] We argue that much of self-tracking research still subscribes to this bifurcation and applies an ontology that draws clear boundaries between users and used devices. Such research is based on a bifurcating 'ontology of being' (Introna 2013) because it implies that human-technology relationship consists of fixed and separate beings that retain their inner essence (as human or technical) throughout the relationship.

It should be noted that seminal literature on the topic – especially accounts influenced by the field of science and technology studies (STS) – has in recent decades sought to evade such bifurcation. For example, in her insightful paper on the everyday 'processes of self-optimization', Ruckenstein (2014) writes about how proactive self-tracking technologies mediate people's relations to themselves through the production of 'data doubles' that are considered as numeric or visual data flows that constitute representations of users. In simple terms, as the user uses self-tracking devices, the device collects data, and assembles and re-assembles different nodes of data into digital portraits for the interpretation and evaluation of the user. This numerical-visual 'data double' can then be 'used and reflected upon' as an object of self-reflection and personal valuation (for similar accounts in this regard, see also Nafus and Sherman 2014; Sharon and Zandbergen 2016). As self-tracking activities aim for (longitudinal) life management, it is explicitly acknowledged here that a person engaging with data should not be understood as 'bounded entity with a stable and fixed ontology' (Ruckenstein 2014, 71).

Furthermore, many other social scientific studies challenge simplified human/technical-divides through the employment of STS oriented vocabulary of mediations, assemblages, human-technology co-evolution and companionships (Schüll 2016; Lupton 2016a, b; Kristensen and Ruckenstein 2018), which all point to the idea that humans and technologies actively work and evolve together. Some accounts further draw focus on technology as 'companion species' that give shape to human-technology hybrid agents (Lupton 2016b) or the idea that human-technology interactions can produce qualitatively new modes of being in the world (Prasopoulou 2017; Pink and Fors 2017). For example, in everyday environments of individuals a simple step counter may re-adjust everyday routines by revealing some walking routes as more 'beneficial' than others. Furthermore, accounts in IS theory (Brey 2005, 392) have argued that 'human and computer are best

---

[1] It appears correct to argue that technologies do not act via intention in the same way that humans do. However, 'intention' of the actor is not a necessary condition for actions to be concrete and meaningful for those whom these actions affect.

regarded as a single cognitive unit, a hybrid cognitive system [...] in which two semi-autonomous information-processing systems cooperate in performing cognitive tasks'. Yet another example is provided by Carter and Grover (2015) who argue that in our daily lives the self intimately intertwines with technology. They conceptualize human-technology relations through the idea of IT identities, referring to how people see IT artefacts as inseparable parts of their being.

We build on aforementioned attempts to surpass the human-technology bifurcation but wish to take it further, as it could be argued that even STS-oriented accounts still often carry the echoes of a persistent tendency to draw boundaries between the 'human' and the 'technical'. The human-technology bifurcation seems often, in a sense, built into the language of research accounts that seek to close the gap (Introna 2013), as for example the idea of interaction (or intertwining) requires two or more ontologically separated and fixed entities – two or more seemingly independent units – which then fall into an interactive relationship with each other. This is exemplified by the tendency to conceptualize technologies as 'tools' and data as something that is 'harnessed' by humans for human use and valuation (Ruckenstein 2014) or how people are ultimately perceived as prioritized agents who shape themselves through technology or allow (or possibly do not allow) technologies to influence their lives as companions (Kristensen and Ruckenstein 2018). The language of interaction and use-relations is conditioned by the 'ontology of being', which separates users (end-users, i.e. human beings with intentions and desires) from the devices (i.e. more or less passive and dependent technological devices, technical 'tools'). Although involved in interaction and co-operation, they still basically retain their internal essence as 'user' or 'device' – as clear-cut units.

The ontology of being stands in contrast to a different kind of ontology, namely the 'ontology of becoming', which emphasizes processuality. The ontology of becoming does not assume any kind of actors (whether we call them human or non-human) to remain the same or even exist independent of the relations in and through which they become to act in the world (e.g. Latour 2005; Whitehead 1978). In this ontology, no actors can be reduced to their inner essence (Latour 1992; DeLanda 2006; see also Harman 2010) but actors should be defined by their effects on other actors. There are no clear-cut units; instead, there are processual actors which are defined by and through their relations to other actors (Latour 1992; DeLanda 2006) and are thus always in flux as new relations emerge and old relations disappear.

In the context of self-tracking, applying the ontology of becoming means that the focus of research shifts towards how self-tracking as an activity gives shape to any 'units' (devices, beings, selves, discourses etc.) that we might perceive. However, instead of considering actors as separate units, they should be seen as connected actors forming assemblages (or collectives) within and through which activity takes place.[2] Furthermore, all actors within an assemblage are constantly in a process of change, of becoming something (else) through each other. There are, for example, no stable

---

[2] The term 'assemblage' is typically employed to denote a collective or an arrangement of heterogeneous human and non-human actors. All the actors within these collectives are exposed and subjected to each other. Through subjection, new properties emerge (e.g. Latour 2005).

'users' whose relation to a device is fixed (or simply detached by separation); or, there is no 'human-device pair/hybrid' that is independent of – or unconditioned by – social discourses or ideas or networks of the material world which also give shape to the self-tracking assemblage. The connections and relations, which define what an actor is, always extend far away from the actor (Latour 2005).

Such ontological differences are crucial when we think of the position of the human being in terms of agency. Specifically, the ontology of being affords a certain human-centricity[3], from which the ontology of becoming is better equipped to steer away from. In a sense, discussions of sociomateriality (Introna 2013; Orlikowski and Scott 2008) pertain to this problem. The ontology of becoming – or alternatively performative ontology – is currently not the dominant ontology in the field of IS (and organizational studies), although it has drawn more attention recently (Chia 2002; Introna 2011, 2013, 2016; Orlikowski and Scott 2008; Scott and Orlikowski 2014; Tsoukas and Chia 2002; Vuorinen and Tetri 2012). In social sciences ontological questions have more evidently surfaced as a subject of discussion since the rise of material semiotics and actor-network theory (Latour 1992, 2005; Law 2004). However, the shifts of ontological perspectives in research are processes that are enacted through, for example, mediation of language. This is why we also want to pay attention to the conceptual apparatuses that we employ in self-tracking research when we wish to take the implications of processual ontology seriously. Importantly, this is not to say that it would be possible or desirable to let go of all bifurcations, which are deeply embedded in the very mundane acts of thinking and speaking. We only wish to argue, that by considering persistent human-technology bifurcations, research on self-tracking (and information technologies in general) could even more aptly grasp the ways in which such technologies shape and steer individual and collective lifeworlds.

Drawing from some of the conceptual work done in recent research (e.g. Gardner and Jenkins 2016; Bode and Kristensen 2015), in the following section we will suggest some conceptual developments to the research on self-tracking. This is to say that we wish to rethink and propose theoretical-conceptual alternatives and developments for some common presumptions and conceptualizations that stem from the ontology of being. These presumptions include ideas of interaction, the notion of a data double as a representation and the focus on user-device use relation. After rethinking these conceptualizations, we will conduct illustrative analysis on our interview narratives, and demonstrate how different ontological perspectives open up different avenues for looking at specific practices of self-tracking and human-technology relations more generally.

---

[3] Of course, it is not logically necessary that the ontology of being results in human-centricity. However, it often leads to debates that follow the distinction between social determinism and technological determinism, which in turn prescribes interpretations of it being either the 'human' (mind, culture, belief, value) or the technological (matter, fact, body, algorithm) that determines the course of action and development (evoking the question of who/what is the 'user' and who/what is the 'used').

3 From Being Towards Becoming – Theoretical-Conceptual Developments for Research

3.1 From Human-Device Interaction Towards Relational Intra-action

Research on self-tracking typically employs ideas of human-device interaction and interactive (e)valuation of data. An example of this is the employment of a concept of a 'data double' (Ruckenstein 2014; Lupton 2014). We have already presented that such language presupposes boundaries between separate entities ('human' and 'non-human') which interact with each other, but which are still self-sufficiently coherent beings. While this correlates with our everyday perceptions and makes a lot of sense in relation to (the everyday use and experience of) technology, it risks neglecting the complex entanglements of diverse actors in practice. In the field of social science, Gardner and Jenkins (2016) have employed the Baradian notion of 'intra-action' in the context of self-tracking. They aptly describe how algorithm-based visual representations of the self can turn into creative poetics of the self within assemblages of bodies, measurement devices and affect. However, they express having discovered that 'when allowed to play and 'tarry' with these technologies and the representations they create, users created dynamic, reflective human-machine relationships that can be characterized as productive, affective, and intra-active' (ibid., 4). In this way, the activity of self-tracking flows back into "users" capacities to interpret representations, and to 'play' with these representations and the devices themselves. Nevertheless, we agree that the concept of intra-action can be a valuable conceptual aid in making sense of what 'happens' in self-tracking.

In contrast to the term 'interaction', the concept of 'intra-action' refers aptly to the way how activity always takes place within an assemblage of a multiplicity of various actors but, more importantly, not between stable and closed units but always open and becoming units. Drawing from theoretical physics and a close reading of Niels Bohr's quantum mechanics, Barad (2007) defines intra-action as co-constitutive becoming through entanglements, whereas the traditional idea of interaction relies on the idea of ontologically separate entities that form an interactive relationship with each other while essentially remaining the same or retaining their inner essence. In the field of information systems science, Orlikowski and Scott (2015) have employed the idea of intra-action, referring to how things, ideas and concepts do not have determinate boundaries (i.e. 'essence') 'prior to their encounters'. This idea is compatible with actor-network theory (Latour 2005) in which any 'units' should ideally be approached as expansive networks and any entities or actors seen to exist and becoming temporarily bounded only in the sense that they affect and alter (and are altered by) the world around them.

In terms of self-tracking, the idea of intra-action helps to focus on the co-constitutive becoming of human and technical (see Orlikowski and Scott 2015); for example, on the idea that what emerges in and through self-tracking is a 'tracker' as a single yet always changing cognitive system (or, as an assemblage). For us this means that the focus of research shifts from looking at the human-device relationship as a use-relation towards looking at self-tracking as action and entanglement. The 'use' of self-tracking devices is a complex mesh of relations at work (Latour 1992, 2005). Overall, the typical narrative of the 'user' is a bifurcating practice, through which the human is awarded priority in directing use. As Pols and Moser (2009: 161) have noted, 'use' is, in fact, a highly categorizing term as it tends to simplify the human-technology relations. In fact, 'use' is action and becoming in the sense that a person, for example, does not so much 'use a phone' but 'makes a call' or 'connects to the internet' or, in general, is merely an active node, albeit one of many, in any activity. Likewise, a person does not, in fact, use a tracking device but 'tracks' the self in time (Schüll 2016) through, for example, systematic measurement of weight or measurement of activity in terms of steps taken. This highlights the process of intra-action: different actors become and emerge in relation to each other because the 'tracker' in self-tracking is not a clear-cut unit *per se* but rather the unity of multiple things in action. Thus, 'tracker' cannot be reduced solely to a human user nor to a device.

3.2   From Theorizing Human-Device Use Relations Towards Mediated Self-relations

Through the concept of self-tracking, the activity of measurements invites a focus on the human 'self', but this self should be understood as becoming through relations and thus as always emergent. As presented above, self-tracking is about activity in relation to the self rather than about 'use' of a device. We suggest that the focus of self-tracking research need not be the connection between a user and an IT artefact but it can be the connective relation that starts from the self and returns to the self through the loop of self-assessment. In much of current research, the 'self' appears as constitutive point of reference – a unit with clear borders. Such an understanding of 'self' provides a foundation on which the 'user' is formed. However, in terms of the ontology of becoming, the self (as anything) should be understood as a multiplicity, a becoming assemblage. The 'self' is always itself a bundle of relations (see Bode and Kristensen 2015) that changes in and through contacts with other people and artifacts. Accordingly, the self – both as an assessing actor (subject) and as an assessed actor (object) – changes when it becomes connected with a new relation, e.g. with any self-tracking technology.

Importantly, the assessment assemblage is constituted by the merge of the self and the device and the discourses that define what (in terms of the self) is perceived as undesirable (pathological) or desirable (teleological). Here we apply an approach from an influential French philosopher Foucault (1988). At a late point of his career, he focused on the emergence of moral subject with an emphasis on the self and especially on how the self submits itself by a particular way, through what he calls 'technologies of the self' (Lupton 2016a, 38–39).

'Assessment' refers to a formation of a relation to the self; a process of a search for un/desirability in the self in relation to social and cultural norms and values, for example discourses of health and wellbeing. In other words, there are culturally and socially formed criteria by which one can judge whether the body is well or not. There is no essentially fixed conception of e.g. wellbeing or that what counts as 'optimization' (although e.g. scientific and cultural conceptions certainly may *seem* fixed in common perception) but such definitions are always contingent, as they 'become' in the course of history (see Latour 1999). In contemporary society activity levels, sleep quality, heart rates, stress levels and blood pressure charts have become a part of discourses that produce an idea of who we *are* in terms of ideal (or 'normal') and pathological (or 'not-normal'). The point is that self-tracking is a way of 'acting' within such an assemblage of assessment.

With this we emphasize that technologies of the self as ways of working on the self often involve various technical mediations, such as mirrors, training gear, expert guidelines in textual form, medicine and, as in our case, digital self-tracking software and hardware. The crucial point here is that the relation to the self cuts through the act of self-tracking and extends this act temporally and spatially. First of all, the relation to the self *precedes* the concrete contact of a human being and a device, as one is at some level familiar with the general technology of self-tracking (as a way of longitudinally observing the self) *before* any actual tracking events. Furthermore, the data gathered in tracking practices is not important *per se*. Rather, it is important in terms of how it formulates (e.g. confirms or possibly alters – i.e. enacts) one's relation to the self. Moreover, while the device may be 'abandoned' after some time, it still *functions* as a technology of the self precisely because the self is changed; it is not abandoned because it would not 'work' but precisely because self-tracking always 'works' by mediating self-relations via information, however futile or useful, accurate or inaccurate – not to mention pleasant or unpleasant – people may find any specific bits, trajectories or databanks of information.

3.3   From the Self as Representation Towards Triadic Understanding of (Self-)Relations

The Foucauldian idea of technologies of the self and self-making has influenced much of social scientific research on self-tracking (e.g. Lupton 2014, 2016a) one manifestation of this being the notion of a data double which refers to a datafied representation of the self (Ruckenstein 2014). However, picking up from the idea of intra-action and the enactment of the self, we think that the 'self' as 'representation' is an open and multiple collective and thus an actor in itself. Bode and Kristensen (2015) have developed a notion of a 'digital doppelgänger', through which they emphasize an active process of 'doppelgängering' that takes place in self-tracking practices. The idea of doppelgängering refers to processes in which the data double actively partakes in the enactment of the self rather than appears as a stable reflection. For us, a crucial part of this 'doppelgängering' is assessment, through which the datafied 'double' always further spreads out into moral trajectories, i.e. the ideal and the pathological. The data double is itself divisible and multiple – it is an aggregate, an assemblage, a mix (Serres 1995, 2). It is not a single or fixed representation but a multiplicity, connecting to the self through an assessment criteria through which the tracked self opens up into constellations of desirable and undesirable. We suggest that the relation to the self (like any relation) should not be understood as a dual relation of representation at all but (using a concept of French philosopher Serres 2007) as a triadic relation. For Serres, the triad refers to a basic form of any relation; i.e. a form that involves *at least* three parties.

Serres' (2007) idea of triadic relation can be understood in terms of theory of communication. The transmission of information requires a channel between sender and receiver. The channel is the carrier of the signal but paradoxically, always also a source of disorder and 'noise'. Noise is the static that threatens the stability of the signal, yet every signal is also crucially dependent on noise, which is always part of the mediating channel. If there were no noise, there would be no channel and thus, the whole relation would disappear. Noise is an irritating nuisance that is always there but has to be hindered and downplayed. Noise is something that always threatens the order of a system but, importantly, also makes the system 'work'. In terms of self-tracking technologies, noise can be thought to refer to bugs and inaccuracies of the device or gaps in the data, which hinder the transmission of self-knowledge.

However, in relation to assemblages of self-assessment, noise can become something else. For example, the assemblage of proactive self-tracking is productive of self-assessment in terms of a system of health and wellbeing, or a system of desirability more generally and suggests moral demarcations between desirable and undesirable. In this sense noise, as that which threatens the order of the system, can be seen as the pathological or the undesirable that is always there, not necessarily as an actuality but at least as a possibility, a threat. If the relation to the self (a relation that is mediated in self-tracking practices via numbers, visual graphs, haptic vibrations and nudges of various kinds) were free of noise, i.e. if there were no pathological or undesirable elements to be observed or imagined, the self would disappear. As a simple example, in a discourse in which weight matters as a public health threat or as personal pathology, if someone's weight was just as desired and magically always remained the same, there would be no sense in measuring it. There would be perfect order, which would also make the question of teleology disappear altogether. If there were no pathology to avoid, there would be no teleology to orientate towards. In other words, the self would never be assessed, placed as a meaningful object for tracking. The system of self-tracking as a communicative system depends on there being something that is excluded: the noise, the pathological, the undesired. In order for the assessing self to be in a relation with the teleological self, the pathological self needs to be present, at least as a possibility. Seeking to obtain the state of the teleological is simultaneously a blocking out of the pathological that is included. The pathological 'is the third, the third man, excluded and included', as Serres (2007, 242) puts it. Thus, self-enactment by self-tracking is a triadic process.[4]

---

[4] Practically speaking, we mean that a person can of course feel satisfied with measurements in any specific moment. However, as self-tracking typically acquires its meaning as longitudinal, continuous observation of the self and of the changes of one's life (see Kristensen and Ruckenstein 2018; Lupton 2016a) the practice is based on the idea of constant change of one's health and body. Thus, even if measurements generally brought satisfaction to the human tracker, there is always a possibility that the next measurement is indicative of something pathological or undesired. In this very real sense, *the undesirable is always already interwoven into the practice of self-assessment*.

4 Interpreting Experiences of Self-tracking Through the Ontology of Becoming

In this section we wish to put our theoretical-conceptual developments to work by analyzing two illustrative narratives from a larger set of interview data that was collected in 2016. After presenting the narratives in question, we look at each narrative through the aforementioned ideas of intra-action and triadic self-relations, and tease out research worlds that are in some ways different to those that typically open up via more conventional ontology of being in which users and technologies are conceived of as separate, clear-cut units or in which the focus is on relations of use.

Narrative 1 – Struggle against the 'lazy' self

Aino is a 39-year-old female, works in an executive position, is married and a mother of three children. She has a background in competitive team sports, which is why she has for a long time been familiar with methods of tracking aspects of one's body and analyzing data on the self for optimization purposes. She currently employs a fitness tracker wristband that keeps track of daily levels of activity through for example an accelerometer-based step count. She has employed the device for several months and says that the tracker device is especially useful for her in 'avoiding those days when my activity is basically zero'. She says that without the exercise that the tracker motivates her to conduct, she would probably not have the energy to cope with 'damn tough' demands at work. She is well aware that in terms of objectively accurate measurement of 'activity' the device 'sucks' because the information it provides is not in fact accurate; for example, the device only recognizes certain types of movement as activity at all, or it might for example interpret cycling in a hilly terrain as equivalent for climbing stairs. However, Aino says that it feels good should one have a really active day and achieve a high number of steps, well above the recommended limit of 10,000 per day, which in typical health discourse is regarded as sufficient amount of activity for maintaining a healthy cardiovascular system (although with many devices one can set the specific threshold to a different level if one wishes). Nevertheless, for her the point of wearing it is not to achieve as high amounts of steps as possible every day. Rather, she says that 'in normal life it is enough for me that the device vibrates [haptic vibrations as a mark of achieving 10,000 steps] at some point of the day'.

In this first narrative, we might note that Aino uses a Polar Loop fitness wristband for the purpose of optimizing her energy levels and to cope with the experienced need to be sharp and effective in working life. In her view, this kind of self-tracking helps her to keep up with tough demands present at work. The tracker monitors performance by counting steps and floors climbed and alerts when the human is perceived as inactive. When considered through a conventional interactive framework (the 'ontology of being') we think of a human being who is interested to monitor herself and delegates some of the burdensome work of continuous self-monitoring and health- and work-related self-optimization to a technical device. Aino draws inspiration from her relation to the field of competitive sports, and implements the device into her life in order to cope with a demanding context of working life. Such an approach can be fruitful, for example because it can reveal a specific typification of behavior related to goal-oriented self-tracking (Rooksby et al. 2014), or show how people work to align with discursive (e.g. neoliberal) demands for self-management of productivity with self-tracking technologies (Lupton 2013), or possibly how people resist such oppressive surveillance, should they imagine and develop 'alternative' ways of using the devices (Nafus and Sherman 2014). However, the problem in such accounts is that although it is acknowledged that humans interact with and work with technologies (see Carter and Grover 2015, 932), the human actors are easily given primary agentive power in human-device relations.

In terms of representation, we may theorize how Aino, together with a self-tracking device, creates a data double that provides her with information about herself. In order to produce knowledge about herself for self-management purposes, she negotiates with this data double, asking herself whether it is an accurate enough representation of her activity or if she needs to supplement this information with other modes of knowing, such as embodied knowledge. As noted in recent research (e.g. Nafus and Sherman 2014; Sharon and Zandbergen 2016; Gardner and Jenkins 2016), this practice can also be empowering and teach one to interpret their bodily life in new ways. However, the ontology of being suggests that the human-device pair or hybrid consistently produces – despite technical inaccuracies – a number of steps taken per day, which translates into a more or less stable representation of activity, a data double, which is then worked with by the user. The user then makes decisions on whether or not she should attempt to change one's behavior.

However, when attuning with the ontology of becoming, we are not satisfied with stating that Aino uses the device for the creation of datafied representation in order to self-manage, self-optimize or produce situated knowledge of oneself and the world. Instead, we focus on how the activity of the self-tracking assemblage enacts and produces the actors involved in certain ways, changing them and leaving persistent traces. To be clear, in Aino's case we do not deny that working with the idea of Aino acting on the basis of her human intentions makes sense, but while user-oriented, human-centered accounts may indeed provide useful windows into the matter, we will here look at her self-tracking practice as an ongoing triadic struggle and self-enactment, which grasps something of the continuous 'becoming' of her lifeworld in activity tracking practice. The 'tracker' (which in this case is both human and non-human together, and neither one in particular – or, rather a relational web of actors, a self-tracking assemblage) no longer merely 'monitors' but rather enacts and individuates the self through a technology of the self (in this case, self-tracking with and through a fitness tracking wristband).

By this we mean that the device acts as a mediator of the relation to self, constantly (e.g. daily) individuating Aino through a tension between the teleological and the pathological without ever resolving this tension completely, because as she herself puts it, it is a (daily) struggle against laziness. As Aino says: 'in normal life it is enough for me that the device shakes [haptic vibrations on the wrist as a mark of achieving 10,000 steps] at some point of the day'. For her, this haptic vibration enacts liberation from the repetitive cycle of self-monitoring. It is not just information about oneself but a materialization of an act of individuation (Tucker 2013) that materializes as affective release, as feeling good or relieved about obtaining the daily goal. However, although the lazy doppelgänger is momentarily excluded, the struggle begins anew at the turn of the day.

While it makes good sense to conceive of Aino's tracking as a practice of management of life (and perhaps self-alignment with the productive machinery of contemporary capitalism that demands enhancement of specifically mental capacities or vital energies), the ontology of becoming opens possibilities to analyze how self-tracking technologies enact the self as a multiplicity, as in principle being always potential and in the process somewhere in-between teleological and pathological, order and disorder. In other words one is always in the process of being individuated through the emerging data. Such is of course the case with any data-driven technologies of the self but contemporary self-tracking marks an era of intensified struggle as tracker devices now often gather and analyze data even when we are not actively cognitively oriented towards self-tracking (such as when immersed in other everyday activities, or when sleeping). In this way, everyday life in practice becomes a regime of anticipation and management of the inherently insecure future (Adams et al. 2009). In the case of Aino's activity tracking, all activities during the day relate to this tension that may or may not be released through an informational vibration, such as a haptic signal of reaching 10,000 steps. Instead of seeing Aino acting in instrumental-rational fashion in order to optimize herself or her working capabilities, we then see an ongoing struggle. Ultimately, the self-tracking assemblage is expected to help the individual to become and remain active but we see how the self-tracking assemblage effectively produces its own purpose by maintaining a tension between teleology (e.g. activity as 10,000 steps per day) and pathology (e.g. activity as 'zero') and enacting the self through this tension that is produced in practice.

In summary, we wish to stress that while the ontology of being is capable of offering insight into why and how Aino (thinks she) uses self-tracking devices and how she recounts her experiences of the data, the ontology of becoming can be better equipped to enlighten the processuality of tracking and how Aino's will to knowledge as well as her experience of the self is constantly enacted within the self-tracking assemblage. In a sense, we can show how Aino is constantly becoming a self-tracker within the self-tracking assemblage that includes her body, the technological device, ideas of what constitutes good health and physical shape as well as ideas of what constitutes a good worker. As these ideas or discourses of wellbeing or proper working subjectivity are also part of the self-tracking assemblage, we can then also say something of the ways in which these discourses materialize or 'happen' in and through the activity of self-tracking. We will now move on to briefly analyze the second narrative.

Narrative 2 – Sticky relations of self-tracking

Jessica is a 32-year old office worker. In an interview conducted via e-mail, she constructs a narrative of how several years ago she became interested in monitoring heart rates and calories burned during exercise, in order to monitor the process of getting into 'better shape'. She then got a heart rate monitor as a gift and recalls her time with the heart rate monitors being very rewarding in general as she could observe her physical fitness improve. Later, she acquired a fitness tracking wristband for monitoring the amount of daily steps and activity in general. In using the fitness tracker wristband she has observed that the device does not record steps as accurately as she has hoped while (somewhat paradoxically) it also 'provides [her] with the bitter truth of not being active enough', i.e. enacts the self in a negative light, as someone who does not achieve desired levels of activity often enough. Jessica has since given up self-tracking and now says to 'enjoy the freedom of going out for a jog without tracking devices'. However, when asked if she ever thinks about picking up tracking again, she says that it is constantly 'banging in the back of [her] head' that she should be using such devices, especially the heart rate monitor, if she wishes to improve. She then concludes that the whole phenomenon of self-tracking really is quite a stressful thing.

Humans seemingly possess notable agency in directing the use or non-use of self-tracking devices. For example, according to statistics, a large number of self-trackers give up their self-tracking activities within the first few months of use, which has resulted in interest towards how we 'use and abandon' our smart devices (Lazar et al. 2015; see also Kristensen and Ruckenstein 2018). In narrative 2, Jessica is a family woman who has used a heart rate monitor and a fitness tracking device for 'getting into better shape', and has experienced both rewarding and frustrating moments with self-tracking, relating again to inaccuracies and noise in the data. Again, we could interpret the narrative as an attempt to use tracking devices in a goal-oriented fashion to optimize one's physical appearance and performance and to care for one's health and wellbeing. However, what is crucial in her account is how Jessica has seemingly stepped out of the tracking-related feedback loop, and quit tracking. Should we read her interview strictly through an ontology of being, Jessica is not currently an active self-tracker, i.e. a person who uses self-tracking device(s). Rather, she is a person who has a history with self-tracking, and who would be statistically classified as a person that has abandoned self-tracking, because she has found self-tracking overly time-consuming, stressful and in general futile. We could say that she has experienced self-tracking turning on against itself, as the practice that was supposed to promote wellbeing has become stressful.

While we do not deny that people can and *do* break free of the persuasive feedback loops of self-tracking, we feel that the main problem with such an approach would be how it builds on a presumption that once the device is removed from the body, the relation breaks or disappears. We might say that the users "hit a wall" (Kristensen and Ruckenstein 2018) in the sense that they do not find more meaningful insights from their tracking practice. The device is de-activated, after which it might make sense to say that it is not an active agent in one's life. This is due to the idea that self-tracking is mainly about one's relation to a (specific) technical device or a collection of devices – which can be isolated, removed, i.e. are practically clear-cut units – while we feel that the crucial relation in such practice is a relation to the self, onto which a technical tracking device latches to mediate that relation. After all, we see 'technology' as an organized form of acting in the world (Foucault, cited in Willcocks 2006) and the 'human condition' of being as already always technical (Prasopoulou 2017).

Conventionally thinking, we can, again, relate this narrative to the common conceptions of human-device interaction. However, the idea of intra-action includes the idea of interaction but entails the idea of change and that as new connections emerge (for example when a concrete connection between a human body and a technical device emerges and the relation to self thus materializes in new ways) *all actors within this assemblage effectively become something else.* So when we think of Jessica's narrative through the idea of intra-action, we see that within the self-tracking assemblage in question, she has changed through the practice of interfacing with self-tracking technology. As she could monitor her activity as well as her physical 'shape' getting better, the self-tracking assemblage has also created new modes of feeling 'improved' or 'inactive' through data. It has created a new kind of 'self-monitoring' actor in the sense that Jessica's monitoring abilities have been expanded. Furthermore, she has been enacted as 'problematic' (along the axes of ideal/pathological or desired/undesired) but also as able to work with this problematic in new ways, for example through a measure of daily steps or a measure of heart beats during certain kind of exercise.

Also, the devices within the assemblage change. For example, in Jessica's narrative the two different gadgets (a heart rate monitor and a fitness tracking wristband) – both in general identifiable as 'self-tracking devices' – each have in fact become quite different things as they evoke very different kinds of orientations towards themselves or towards self-tracking as a (potentially useful) practice. The first device, the activity tracking wristband has become futile, practically useless as such (but if only it were more accurate…) while the heart rate monitor has become conceived of as a useful aid for self-improvement, as it has, according to Jessica, made it easy and rewarding to monitor her physical shape improving.

In terms of the ontology of becoming, the crucial point is that we can observe that she is still an active part in a self-tracking assemblage and a self-tracker-in-process even though she has let the tracking device(s) go. She owns these devices although does not use them; she, in a sense, thinks some aspects of her life through them even if they were deemed inaccurate and physically stayed in the drawer. Since she has changed as a person who self-monitors, these devices can – in relation to discourses of health and wellbeing – inflict affective vibrations (joy, stress, anxiety, 'bitter truths') and pressure to use them or to search for other ways of self-datafication and self-reflection, should one wish to 'improve' further. The relation is clearly there, *visible in the absence of a concrete contact.* These notions invite thinking of the self-tracking gadget not as a piece of junk that has become futile, but as a sticky 'thermal exciter' (Serres 2007, p. 190) that affects one's cognition and everyday life over and beyond the common sense perceptions of space and time. Self-tracking excites Jessica through a triadic struggle, as we saw with Aino. This means that Jessica would be right at home in activating these devices again in her life, at least as long as the self-tracking assemblage in her life also attaches to similar discourses on health and physical condition that is typical in contemporary ideas of 'fitness' and self-management. In this way, we see that self-tracking technologies affect and organize everyday lifeworlds far beyond concrete attachments between bodies and devices.

5 Conclusion

In this paper we have argued that in self-tracking research there often still appears a bifurcation between human users and material technologies at the level of ontological presumptions. These presumptions can be actualized on multiple levels, from research settings to the concepts that are employed to describe the activity of self-tracking. While the dominant 'ontology of being' is very helpful in describing some of the aspects of self-tracking, such as human-device interaction and types of 'use', it can easily overlook intra-action, which refers to self-tracking as an active assemblage, within which all actors involved emerge processually and change in action. For example, through the idea of intra-action we may look at the activity of self-tracking, and see a 'tracker' that is not reducible to a human being or a technical device (or any overarching discourse), but is rather a complex bundle of relations, including social, medical and cultural conceptions of health and wellbeing. When we acknowledge this, we may focus on the question of how the world (including the self) changes and 'becomes' through this 'tracker' (the tracking assemblage).

In terms of the 'self' in self-tracking, the ontology of becoming suggests that the self is a process. This may, in a sense, be a trivial truism, but for us it enables a shift towards looking at self-tracking as a processual assemblage of assessment. Any representation that self-tracking produces, is in fact itself a mediator, a multiplicity, and an active actor diverting into multiple trajectories that relate to moral and social (e)valuations and desire. We have elaborated this through Michel Serres' thoughts on triadic relations: the basic form of any relation involves at least three parties, and the actuality of a relation is dependent on the exclusion of the 'third'. In communicative technical relations the third is 'noise', i.e. bugs, inaccuracies, gaps etc. In relations of self-assessment the third can be understood as pathology (in relation to health) or undesirability (in relation to social norms, values etc.). However, in any relation, the third is always there, perhaps visible in its absence. In concrete terms, this means, for example, that although a self-tracking person may be satisfied with any specific measurement that indicates good health, the pathology/undesirability is always there at least as a possibility (the device may be 'wrong' or the next measurement may change things). Also, in terms of one's relation to cultural discourses (e.g. health discourses), a person may seek to exclude a specific device by quitting using it; however, in some sense, the device remains attached, for example as a memory of stressful self-optimization. In this way, the ontology of becoming enables us to look at how self-tracking technologies affect human actions and behaviors beyond mere relations of 'use'. After all, by focusing on 'use', we tend to place the human being as the primary agent in human-technology relations.

We therefore suggest that the ontology of becoming should be more widely adopted and pursued in research that is interested in how self-tracking technologies act with us, work in the world and shape everyday lifeworlds.

Acknowledgements. Author 1 would like to acknowledge support from the following projects: Tracking the Therapeutic, Academy of Finland, grant number 289004; Crossing Borders for Health & Wellbeing, Kone Foundation.

References

Adams, V., Murphy, M., Clarke, A.: Anticipation: technoscience, life, affect, temporality. Subjectivity **28**, 246–265 (2009)

Barad, K.: Meeting the Universe Halfway: Quantum Physics and the Entanglement of Matter and Meaning. Duke University Press, Durham (2007)

Beer, D.: Metric Power. Palgrave Macmillan, London (2016)

Bergroth, H.: 'You can't really control life': dis/assembling self-knowledge with self-tracking technologies. Distinktion J. Soc. Theory (2018). https://doi.org/10.1080/1600910X.2018.1551809

Bode, M., Kristensen, D.: The digital doppelgänger within: a study on self-tracking and the quantified self movement. In: Canniford, R., Bajde, D. (eds.) Assembling Consumption: Researching Actors, Networks and Markets, pp. 119–135. Routledge, Oxon (2015)

Brey, P.: The epistemology and ontology of human-computer interaction. Mind. Mach. **15**(3–4), 383–398 (2005)

Carter, M., Grover, V.: Me, my self, and I (T): conceptualizing information technology identity and its implications. MIS Q. **39**(4), 931–957 (2015)

Chia, R.: Essai: time, duration and simultaneity: rethinking process and change in organizational analysis. Organ. Stud. **23**(6), 863–868 (2002)

DeLanda, M.: A New Philosophy of Society: Assemblage Theory and Social Complexity. A&C Black, New York (2006)

Foucault, M.: Technologies of the self. In: Martin, L.H., Gutman, H., Hutton, P.H. (eds.) Technologies of the Self: A Seminar with Michel Foucault, pp. 16–49. Tavistock, London (1988)

Gardner, P., Jenkins, B.: Bodily intra-actions with biometric devices. Body Soc. **22**(1), 3–30 (2016)

Harman, G.: Prince of Networks: Bruno Latour and Metaphysics. Re. Press, Melbourne (2010)

Hogle, L.F.: Data-intensive resourcing in health care. BioSocieties **11**, 372–393 (2016)

Introna, L.D.: The enframing of code: agency, originality and the plagiarist. Theory Cult. Soc. **28**(6), 113–141 (2011)

Introna, L.D.: Epilogue: performativity and the becoming of sociomaterial assemblages. In: de Vaujany, F.-X., Mitev, N. (eds.) Materiality and Space: Organizations, Artefacts and Practices, pp. 330–342. Palgrave Macmillan, Basingstoke (2013)

Introna, L.D.: Algorithms, governance and governmentality: on governing academic writing. Sci. Technol. Human Values **41**(1), 17–49 (2016)

Kristensen, D., Ruckenstein, M.: Co-evolving with self-tracking technologies. New Media Soc. **20**(10), 3624–3640 (2018)

Kari, T., Koivunen, S., Frank, L., Makkonen, M., Moilanen, P.: Critical experiences during the implementation of a self-tracking technology. In: Proceedings of the 20th Pacific Asia Conference on Information Systems. Association for Information Systems (2016)

Latour, B.: Where are the missing masses? The sociology of a few mundane artifacts. In: Bijker, W., Law, J. (eds.) Shaping Technology-Building Society: Studies in Sociotechnical Change, pp. 225–259. MIT Press, Cambridge (1992)

Latour, B.: We Have Never Been Modern. Harvard University Press, Cambridge (1993)

Latour, B.: Pandora's Hope: Essays on the Reality of Science Studies. Harvard University Press, Cambridge (1999)

Latour, B.: Reassembling the Social: An Introduction to Actor-Network-Theory. Oxford University Press, Oxford (2005)

Law, J.: After Method: Mess in Social Science Research. Routledge, London (2004)

Lazar, A., Koehler, C., Tanenbaum, J., Nguyen, D.H.: Why we use and abandon smart devices. In: Proceedings of the 2015 ACM International Joint Conference on Pervasive and Ubiquitous Computing, pp. 635–646. ACM (2015)

Liu, W., Ploderer, B., Hoang, T.: In bed with technology: challenges and opportunities for sleep tracking. In: Proceedings of the Annual Meeting of the Australian Special Interest Group for Computer Human Interaction, pp. 142–151. ACM (2015)

Lomborg, S., Frandsen, K.: Self-tracking as communication. Inf. Commun. Soc. **19**(7), 1015–1027 (2016)

Lupton, D.: Understanding the human machine. IEEE Technol. Soc. Mag. **32**(4), 25–30 (2013)

Lupton, D.: Self-tracking cultures: towards a sociology of personal informatics. In: Proceedings of the 26th Australian Computer-Human Interaction Conference on Designing Futures: The Future of Design, pp. 77–86. ACM (2014)

Lupton, D.: The Quantified Self: A Sociology of Self-Tracking. Polity Press, Cambridge (2016a)

Lupton, D.: Digital companion species and eating data: implications for theorising digital data–human assemblages. Big Data Soc. **3**(1), 1–5 (2016b)

Nafus, D., Sherman, J.: This one does not go up to 11: the quantified self as an alternative big data practice. Int. J. Commun. **8**, 1785–1794 (2014)

Ogbanufe, O., Gerhart, N.: Watch it! Factors driving continued feature use of the smartwatch. Int. J. Hum.-Comput. Inter. **34**(11), 999–1014 (2017)

Orlikowski, W.J., Scott, S.V.: 10 Sociomateriality: challenging the separation of technology, work and organization. Acad. Manag. Ann. **2**(1), 433–474 (2008)

Orlikowski, W.J., Scott, S.V.: Exploring material-discursive practices. J. Manage. Stud. **52**, 697–705 (2015). https://doi.org/10.1111/joms.12114

Pink, S., Fors, V.: Being in a mediated world: self-tracking and the mind-body-environment. Cult. Geogr. **24**(3), 375–388 (2017)

Pols, J., Moser, I.: Cold technologies versus warm care? On affective and social relations with and through care technologies. Alter **3**(2), 159–178 (2009)

Prasopoulou, E.: A half-moon on my skin: a memoir on life with an activity tracker. Eur. J. Inf. Syst. **26**(3), 287–297 (2017)

Rooksby, J., Rost, M., Morrison, A., Chalmers, M.C.: Personal tracking as lived informatics. In: Proceedings of the 32nd Annual ACM Conference on Human Factors in Computing Systems, Toronto, Ontario, Canada, pp. 1163–1172. ACM (2014)

Ruckenstein, M.: Visualized and interacted life: personal analytics and engagements with data doubles. Societies **4**(1), 68–84 (2014)

Ruckenstein, M., Schüll, N.D.: The datafication of health. Ann. Rev. Anthropol. **46**, 261–278 (2017)

Schüll, N.D.: Data for life: wearable technology and the design of self-care. BioSocieties **11**(3), 313–333 (2016)

Sharon, T., Zandbergen, D.: From data fetishism to quantifying selves: self-tracking practices and the other values of data. New Media Soc. **19**(11), 1695–1709 (2016)

Serres, M.: Genesis. University of Michigan Press, Ann Arbor (1995)

Serres, M.: The Parasite. University of Minnesota Press, Minneapolis (2007)

Scott, S.V., Orlikowski, W.J.: Entanglements in practice: performing anonymity through social media. MIS Q. **38**(3), 873–893 (2014)

Tsoukas, H., Chia, R.: On organizational becoming: rethinking organizational change. Organ. Sci. **13**(5), 567–582 (2002)

Tucker, I.: Bodies and surveillance: Simondon, information and affect. Distinktion J. Soc. Theory **14**(1), 30–41 (2013)

Vuorinen, J., Tetri, P.: The order machine - the ontology of information security. J. Assoc. Inf. Syst. **13**(9), 695–713 (2012)

Willcocks, L.P.: Michel Foucault in the social study of ICTs: critique and reappraisal. Soc. Sci. Comput. Rev. **24**(3), 274–295 (2006)

Whitehead, A.N.: Process and Reality: An Essay in Cosmology. Free Press, New York (1978)

Whitehead, A.N.: The Concept of Nature. Project Gutenberg (2006). http://www.gutenberg.org/files/18835/18835-h/18835-h.htm. Accessed 29 Jan 2019

Do Humans STILL Have a Monopoly on Creativity or Is Creativity Overrated?

Gregory Cowart, Dane Williamson, Naha Farhat,
and Joon-Suk Lee[(⊠)]

Virginia State University, Petersburg, VA 23806, USA
{gcow3223, dwil2444}@students.vsu.edu,
nfarhat@vsu.edu, joonsukl@acm.org

Abstract. What is creativity? Do AIs have creativity? This research sets out to answer these questions. By conducting a small-scale user experiment, and quantitatively and qualitatively analyzing the data, this work aims to answer the following three research questions: (1) whether human participants can distinguish between AI generated and human composed music; (2) common preconceptions participants have on AI generated music; and (3) common constructs participants associate with human creativity. Our results show that people are not able to tell the difference between human and AI composed music.

Keywords: Turing test · Music Turing test · Creativity ·
Computational creativity

1 Introduction

1.1 Creative Machines

Once thought of as uniquely belonging to humans, creativity is a personality trait associated with our ingenuity to create novel artifacts. It has also been described as psychological processes that are somewhat like "magic" [2]. For years, educators and researchers have worked on finding ways to harness these magical, creative thinking processes to improve student learning (e.g., [15, 17, 21]). Creativity was what differentiated us from apes.

However, with the recent surge of Artificial Intelligence (AI), researchers are starting to use the term, *computational creativity*, to describe computing processes and algorithms that can be used to carry out tasks that once only humans were able to perform. Anna Jordanous describes the goal of computational creativity as "to model, simulate or replicate creativity using a computer [7]." For instance, advancements in deep learning and neural network systems have enabled developers to create artificial agents that are capable of creating music, a capability that has long been thought innate to humans. Today, we are witnessing an increasing number of artificial intelligence agents that compose music (e.g., [12, 18, 22]), write short stories (e.g., [11]), paint art pieces (e.g., [3]) and even create other software (e.g., [16]).

© Springer Nature Switzerland AG 2019
M. Kurosu (Ed.): HCII 2019, LNCS 11566, pp. 288–298, 2019.
https://doi.org/10.1007/978-3-030-22646-6_20

1.2   Is Creativity Overrated?

According to Merriam-Webster [14], the English word, *"creative"* comes from Medieval Latin *creātīvus* which means "to beget" or "to give birth to." In this sense, being creative just means being able to create or make something or anything. Yet when we say "creativity," we do not typically mean a mere ability to create random objects, but we refer to certain abstract qualities that creators bring and imbue into their built artifacts. Margaret Boden, for instance, defines creativity as "the ability to come up with ideas or artefacts that are new, surprising and valuable" in her book, *The Creative Mind: Myths and Mechanisms* [4].

Yet, as we have already seen, modern day computer agents are capable of creating seemingly *new, surprising* and *valuable* artifacts. Does this mean humans no longer have a monopoly on "creativity"? Is "creativity" an overrated concept? This research starts with these questions.

Some still argue and believe that artists infuse intuitive, abstract, human qualities such as beliefs or emotions into their work when they create. Such qualities are believed to be impossible to algorithmically compute. If so, this research also aims to explore what are the qualities that differentiate AI produced artifacts from human created art works.

1.3   Research Questions

If we are to ask if creativity is still a unique human trait or if it is simply an overrated concept that labels nothing more than a collection of computational processes, we need to first know what creativity is. We should also be able to measure and quantify "creativity" if we are to compare human creativity with computational creativity. Yet, it seems that there is no real consensus on what creativity actually is. As already mentioned, if creativity simply means creating any artifacts, AI agents as well as beavers already possess creativity. However, different researchers define creativity in different ways. Moreover, many of the concepts used to define creativity are abstract and not measurable. Boden uses three terms, "new, surprising and valuable [4]" to define creativity. These three qualities are all abstract and subjective terms, and are not objectively measurable.

One way to compare machine creativity with human creativity would then be by operationalizing the term, creativity, and concocting measurable factors associated with the operationalized definition. However, doing so will only show how machines and humans are different or similar in respect to the way that we define and operationalize what creativity is. So instead of trying to quantify creativity and objectively compare the work of humans and that of AI, this research aims to explore (1) if and how human participants can distinguish between AI generated and human composed music. We also examine (2) common preconceptions participants have on AI generated music, and (3) common constructs participants associate with human creativity. In other words, we do not try to objectively measure and compare human and AI creativity, but rather study and explore how human participants subjectively view what human and AI creativities are to them.

2 Related Work

2.1 Research on Creativity and Four Ps

While arguing that creativity should be viewed not as a theoretical construct but rather as a multifaceted rubric, MacKinnon [13] proposes an analytical framework consisting of four main aspects—process, product, person, and situation—for understanding human creativity. Similarly, Rhodes [10], in an attempt to develop an instructional design model to enhance student learning as well as creative thinking, defines creativity using the same four factors.

Jordanous adopts these four factors from MacKinnon and Rhodes, and delineates computational creativity using a similar framework. She argues that computational creativity should also be evaluated using the four factors, and calls her framework the Four Ps [8].

The Four Ps are defined as follows [8]:

Person—creative individual
Process—creative process that the creative individuals take
Product—creative artifacts produced as a result of creative processes
Press—environment in which creativity is situated

In computational creativity, the Person or creative individual can refer to the machines that generate creative artifacts or the developers who create the machines. The Process can refer to the algorithms that are used in making creative artifacts. The Product is the output or artifacts generated from the Process. The Press can refer to the audience that receives and interprets the Product generated by the machine.

Yet other researchers define and operationalize creativity in different ways. Acknowledging that the debate on whether computer programs are capable of being genuinely creative can become purely philosophical one, for example, Ritchie [19] proposes an alternate and more empirical way of operationalizing computational creativity and provides a list of measurable criteria that can be used to estimate "interesting" properties of a given computer program.

2.2 Turing Test

The notion of AI exhibiting some form of creativity or intelligence has been researched for decades. In 1950 computer scientist Alan Turing proposed a test for evaluating whether a computer can show intelligence equivalent to a human being [23]. The Turing test (TT) has since then become the standard of evaluating machine intelligence. TT gauges an AI agent's intelligence by having the AI chatbot interact with a person, and tasking another person, a judge, to determine which of the two interlocutors is a computer. The test is repeated over multiple sessions and if the judge fails to identify the machine interactant in more than 50% of the trials, the machine is deemed to possess the ability to think.

Although TT is typically regarded as having a significant impact on shaping the field of Artificial Intelligence, it has also been heavily criticized over the years for not being an appropriate way of evaluating machine intelligence, and for promoting trickery by chatbot developers in order to get their machines to pass the test. For example, in 2014, Eugene Goostman, a chatbot created by Vladimir Veselov and colleagues, managed to pass TT by convincing the judges that it was a human [1]. How the chatbot managed to pass the test, however, has been criticized as mere trickery with nothing to do with intelligence. Eugene was modeled to imitate a 13-year-old boy from Odessa, Ukraine. When interacting with the bot, the judges accredited Eugene's sometimes unintelligible English, and sporadic and sudden topical changes in conversation to his age and the country of residence, thus fooling them.

As an alternate method to measure machine intelligence, Bringsjord [5] proposes another way of evaluating the creative capabilities of machines. This test is named after Ada Lovelace. The Lovelace Test (LT) looks at the three-way relationship between an AI agent, its output, and the creator of the AI agent. In LT, an AI agent passes the test and is considered to possess intelligence only if the creator cannot account for how the AI agent produces output. Bringsjord paraphrases Lovelace's objection against TT, pointing out that machines cannot genuinely create anything. According to Bringsjord, Lovelace believed that "only when computers originate things should they be believed to have minds [5]."

LT was an intriguing concept when it was first introduced two decades ago. Back then, creating a machine and not being able to fully understand its inner workings might have been an absurd idea. Yet today the Artificial Intelligence community is experiencing the exact opposite problem. Due to ever evolving neural networking and deep learning algorithms, the behaviors of AI agents are not always explainable. Consequently, governments are authoring regulations to safeguard consumers from the potential issues and problems unexplainable AIs might cause. In 2018, for instance, the European Union's General Data Protection Right (GDPR) began to include a right to explanation in order to hold AI creators responsible for their creations' actions. In other words, not being able to explain AI agents' actions is no longer science fiction. It is already commonplace.

2.3   Artificial Intelligence Generated Music

Music-making machines are already with us. There exist several commercially available AI systems that produce music. For example, IBM Watson Beat (https://www.ibm.com/case-studies/ibm-watson-beat) and Google Magenta (https://magenta.tensorflow.org/) platforms utilize big training datasets to teach and build machines that can compose music. Researchers of the BachBot project use an AI agent called deepBach to produce classical music pieces [12, 22]. The researchers state that the goal of the project is to build an AI agent capable of generating chorales that are indistinguishable from that of J.S Bach. This was accomplished through training their deepBach model on the chorale patterns in music by J.S Bach [22]. JukeDeck [9] is another AI agent that uses deep neural networks and machine learning to analyze music patterns in order to generate songs. Taiwanese researchers (AILabs.tw) [18] also conducted research using an AI music generation tool similar to deepBach. In our research, we borrow these tools.

3 Methodology

The analysis in this paper is based on data from an exploratory user study we conducted last year.

3.1 Participants

Participants were recruited from a pool of students and faculty with varying musical and technical backgrounds from Virginia State University, a historically black public land-grant university in Petersburg, Virginia. A total of ten participants (3 female, 7 male) enrolled in the study. The participants' age ranged from 20 to 68 (M: 29.30, SD: 14.45). Eight participants (80%) identified themselves as African American, one (10%) as Hispanic, and one (10%) as Asian or Pacific Islander. Ten participants included two Computer Science professors and one Music professor. Participants received no monetary compensation for participating in the study. Table 1 shows summary statistics for participants' gender, classification, ethnicity, major and music experience.

Table 1. Participant summary statistics.

Variable	Percentage	Variable	Percentage
Gender		**Major**	
Male	70%	Computer Science	90%
Female	30%	Music	10%
Ethnicity		**Classification**	
African American	80%	Faculty	30%
Hispanic	10%	Graduate Student	20%
Asian/Pacific Islander	10%	Senior	20%
Music Experience		Junior	20%
Expert	10%	Sophomore	10%
Advanced	10%		
Intermediate	40%		
Novice	40%		

3.2 Procedure

The study was designed as a four-phased experiment. In phase 1, participants were tasked with listening to a randomized playlist of six songs and then identifying which songs were composed by human or by AI. Out of six songs, three were AI composed songs. Using a set of publicly available human and AI generated music on an online music distribution platform, SoundCloud (https://soundcloud.com/), we reiterated research done by Taiwan AI Labs (AILabs.tw) [18]. The six songs were randomly selected from the ten songs that are available on the *Learner Deep* page on Sound-Cloud (https://soundcloud.com/learner-deep). The answer set (information on which songs were generated by AI and which were by human composers) as well as the statistics from the original experiment done by Taiwan AI Labs are available on [18].

In phase II, participants were asked to take a similar test, but using the online Bachbot test [12, 22]. The online BachBot challenge first asks users to identify their age group, and to self-rate their music experience using multiple choice questions. The age group options are (1) under 18, (2) 18 to 25, (3) 26 to 45, (4) 46 to 60 and (5) over 60, and the music experience options are (1) novice, (2) intermediate, (3) advanced and (4) expert. Users are then presented with two songs and asked to identify which song is composed by Bach and which is by deepBach, an AI agent trained on the chorale patterns in music by J.S. Bach [12]. The BachBot challenge consists of five sets of music clip pairs. After listening to the two clips, users are expected to select a clip that is most similar to Bach. Unlike the songs provided on the Leaner Deep site, BachBot does not disclose answer keys, probably because the authors of BachBot are still gathering experimental data through their site. We were only able to get the percentage of correctness rate of user answers.

In phase III, participants were tasked with evaluating five AI generated songs created from JukeDeck (https://www.jukedeck.com/). JukeDeck is another AI agent that uses neural networks and machine learning to analyze music patterns in order to generate songs. The creators of the technology allow users to go to their website and generate customizable songs. Prior to the experiment, we used JukeDeck to prepare five AI generated songs. The generated pieces were piano solo that last for a minute each. The songs were generated with themes alternating between melancholic and upbeat. In this phase, participants were not informed about the fact that they would only be hearing AI generated music. The rational for including only AI generated music in this phase was two-fold: finding compatible human composed music is challenging, and we also wanted to explore different rationales participants associate with their choices regardless of whether or not they were correct.

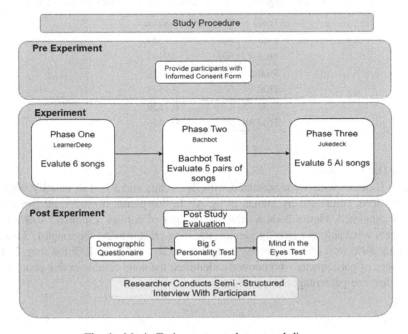

Fig. 1. Music Turing test - study protocol diagram

After the music listening sessions, participants were asked to fill out three types of post study questionnaires. Researchers then explained the nature of the research and conducted semi-structured interviews with the participants. During the interview, we asked how and why participants thought certain songs were composed by AI or by a human, and their overall views on creativity. The study protocol is illustrated in Fig. 1.

4 Data Analysis

4.1 Quantitative Analysis

Phase-1 Data Analysis
In phase 1, participants were presented with 6 songs in random orders, and asked to identify whether the songs were composed by human or by AI. The percentage of participants who correctly identified the type of the song in trial#1 was 60%. This percentage then dropped to 50% in trial#02 and then to 30%, then went back up to 60% and then dropped to 40% then 30% as shown in Table 2. To test whether these percentages are significantly higher than 50%, the chance of guessing correctly at random, Fishers exact test has been conducted and all the p-values were not significant (Table 2, p-value > alpha = 0.05), which indicates that there is not enough evidence to conclude that the percentage of participants who correctly identified the song creators was significantly higher than 50%. In other words, our participants weren't able to distinguish AI generated songs from human composed ones.

Table 2. Phase 1: percentages of incorrect and correct responses for all six songs.

Trial#	Correct %	p-value
Trial #1	60%	0.7539
Trial #2	50%	0.9997
Trial #3	30%	0.3438
Trial #4	60%	0.7539
Trial #5	40%	0.7539
Trial #6	30%	0.3438

Phase-3 Data Analysis
In phase-3, participants were presented with five songs and asked to identify whether the songs were composed by human or by AI. In this phase, however, all five songs were AI generated. Figure 2 shows the percentages of correct responses. 40% of the participants were able to correctly identify the song creator as AI for songs 1, 3 and 5, while only 30% were able to identify song 4 correctly, and only 10% for song 2. The percentages of participants who correctly identified the song creator in this phase were smaller than the percentages in phase-1.

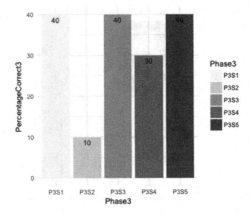

Fig. 2. Phase 3 percentages of correct responses

Overall Scores

For phase-1, we calculated the overall total number of correct responses for each participant for all six songs, three AI songs and three human generated songs. Table 3 displays the results of the overall score where the median response for correctly identifying the type of the six songs in phase-1 is 3 songs and the IQR is 2, based on a sample of 10 participants. For phase-3, the median correct response was 2 and the IQR was 0.25, which indicates that when only AI songs are used to test participants' ability to distinguish between AI and human songs, we have smaller variability in terms of the response of the participants. The phase-3 test can be considered as a more accurate way of testing participants than the phase-1 test since it reduces the chance of making random guesses and still ending up getting high scores.

Figure 3 shows the distribution of the total correct responses for phase-1 and phase-3. The median number of correct responses is smaller for phase-3 as compared to phase-1. We believe that this might be due to the fact that phase-3 has only AI songs which reduces the probability of correctly guessing the answers as compared to phase-1 which included three AI and three human generated songs.

The Wilcoxon signed rank test was used to test whether the number of correctly answered responses were significantly higher or lower than a ½ chance (50%). Due to the small sample size, we used median values for the test. Using the Wilcoxon test, we compared the median of the number of participants' correctly responded answers with the probabilistic median. The probabilistic median is 3 for phase-1 and 2.5 for phase-3. For phase-1, the median of the participant's correct responses was not significantly different from the probabilistic median. For phase-2, the median value of the number of correctly guessed songs was significantly lower than the probabilistic median (Table 3). This significance might have resulted because of the small sample.

Table 3. Summary statistics for n = 10 participants' Phase-1 and Phase-3.

Phase	Median (Correctly answered)	IRQ	p-value (Wilcox test)
Phase-1	3	2	0.3039
Phase-3	2	0.25	0.0021*

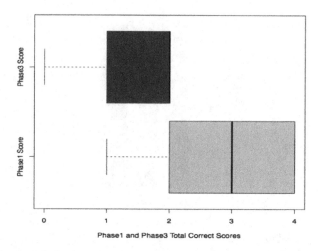

Fig. 3. Distribution of total correct responses for phase-1 and phase-3.

4.2 Qualitative Analysis

We also conducted a thematic analysis on the interview data in order to identify patterns of meanings in the participants' responses. The interview data were fully transcribed and read multiple times by the first and second authors. During the initial analysis, all researchers looked at the interview data together, and developed an initial coding scheme. The first author is currently going through the interview data in multiple iterations and conducting open and axial coding [6, 20]. The analysis is still in process. In this section, we present some of the interesting findings from our preliminary data analysis.

Participant's Perception of Creativity

As indicated earlier, we weren't so much interested in defining the objective and definitive meaning of creativity. Rather, our focus was to understand how each individual perceives the notion of creativity. We also wanted to explore how individuals' perception of creativity impacts their music listening experiences. Multiple participants said that creativity is an ability to create something. For instance, P2 said, *"I feel like creativity is making something, anything. Whether it be like writing a book or drawing something or making music. [It] is like creativity is just taking nothing and making something out of it, or taking something that exists and changing it in a way that makes it your own."*

Some participants associated creativity with brining in personal experience, being imaginative or expressing oneself. P10 said creativity is *"how you express yourself. So basically if an AI can express itself, it should be creative enough?... I just think it's how basically you could express yourself like through drawing or music what have you."* This response is in particular interesting because even though the participant stated that a machine is creative should it possesses an ability to express the self, the response ties creativity with the notion of self-awareness and self-conception. In other words, machines cannot possess creativity without first becoming self-aware. While self-aware robots are a popular topic in Science Fiction, it is also a topic some AI researchers are trying to tackle these days.

Music Is as Good as How the Listeners Listen

Multiple participants mentioned that they were quite surprised by the quality of music AI could generate. P7, a professor in the Music Department, stated that she initially did not expect the machines to show emotions. However, at the end of the study, she said "*I heard some emotion in some of the songs, and I wasn't so sure that machines could create that. But they might, they are a lot more sophisticated than they were before.*" P3 also expressed surprise when he stated:

"*I think honestly without having been told that any of these pieces were AI created I would not be able- I wouldn't tell you that a human did not make this piece. So it was difficult to discern what is human or what is AI. Because I can come in this room and if I hadn't known it was a study- if I didn't know it was a study, I would assume that they're all human pieces.*" (P3)

In addition, multiple participants mentioned that they would still appreciate the music, no matter who created it, if it is good. For example, P1 and P2 stated:

"*I'll probably appreciate them the same honestly. I don't see the point in not appreciating anything just because something someone else made it, I mean a computer made it*" (P2)

"*I enjoy music of all kinds, whether it be made by human whether a dog with a synthesizer did it, I don't care okay if I enjoyed it I enjoyed it*" (P1)

5   Discussion and Conclusion

In this study, we asked (1) whether human participants can distinguish between AI generated and human composed music, (2) common preconceptions participants have on AI generated music, and (3) common constructs participants associate with human creativity. Our preliminary data analyses show that our participants weren't able to tell the difference between AI generated and human composed music. Participants typically associated creativity with human qualities such as having and brining in personal experience, being imaginative or expressing oneself. Yet many participants were quite surprised to hear AI generated music. One participant even showed fear when she said, "*it's a little frightening because you don't want to be displaced by machines. It's like how people don't want automation to come through and take their jobs... like I just lost my job to a machine.*"

References

1. Aamoth, D.: Interview with Eugene Goostman (2014). http://time.com/2847900/eugene-goostman-turing-test/. Accessed 30 Jan 2019
2. Arieti, S.: Creativity. The Magic Synthesis. Basic Books, New York (1976)
3. Baraniuk, C.: Artificially intelligent painters invent new styles of art (2017). newscientist.com. https://www.newscientist.com/article/2139184-artificially-intelligent-painters-invent-new-styles-of-art/. Accessed 10 Feb 2019

4. Boden, M.A.: The Creative Mind: Myths and Mechanisms, 2nd edn. Routledge, New York (2003)
5. Bringsjord, S., Bello, P., Ferrucci, D.A.: Creativity, the Turing test, and the (better) Lovelace test. Mind. Mach. **11**(1), 3–27 (2001)
6. Corbin, J., Strauss, A.: Basics of Qualitative Research: Grounded Theory Procedures and Techniques. SAGE Publications, Inc., Thousand Oaks (1990)
7. Jordanous, A.: What is computational creativity? (2014). creativitypost.com. http://www.creativitypost.com/science/what_is_computational_creativity. Accessed 17 Jan 2019
8. Jordanous, A.: Four PPPPerspectives on computational creativity in theory and in practice. Connect. Sci. **28**(2), 194–216 (2016)
9. Jukedeck: Jukedeck - Create unique, royalty-free AI music for your videos. https://www.jukedeck.com/
10. Rhodes, M.: An analysis of creativity. Phi Delta Kappan **42**(7), 305–310 (1961). http://www.jstor.org/stable/20342603
11. Lewis, D.: An AI-written novella almost won a literary prize (2016). smithsonian.com. https://www.smithsonianmag.com/smart-news/ai-written-novella-almost-won-literary-prize-180958577/. Accessed 10 Feb 2019
12. Liang, F., Gotham, M., Tomczak, M., Johnson, M., Shotton, J.: The BachBot Challenge (2016). http://bachbot.com. Accessed 27 Jan 2019
13. MacKinnon, D.W.: Creativity: a multi-faceted phenomenon. In: Roslansky, J.D. (ed.) Creativity: A Discussion at the Nobel Conference, pp. 17–32. North-Holland, Amsterdam (1970)
14. Merriam-Webster: Webster's New Collegiate Dictionary. Merriam-Webster, Massachusetts (1977)
15. Miller, L.D., Soh, L.-K., Chiriacescu, V., Ingraham, E., Shell, D.F., Hazley, M.P.: Integrating computational and creative thinking to improve learning and performance in CS1. In: Proceedings of the 45th ACM Technical Symposium on Computer Science Education (SIGCSE 2014), pp. 475–480. ACM, New York (2014). https://doi.org/10.1145/2538862.2538940
16. Murali, V., Qi, L., Chaudhuri, S., Jermaine, C.: Neural sketch learning for conditional program generation. In: Proceedings of Seventh International Conference on Learning Representations (ICLR 2018) (2018)
17. Peteranetz, M.S., Wang, S., Shell, D.F., Flanigan, A.E., Soh, L.-K.: Examining the impact of computational creativity exercises on college computer science students' learning, achievement, self-efficacy, and creativity. In: Proceedings of the 49th ACM Technical Symposium on Computer Science Education (SIGCSE 2018), pp. 155–160. ACM, New York (2018). https://doi.org/10.1145/3159450.3159459
18. Rajon: AI music composition passed Turing test|Taiwan AILabs 2018. https://ailabs.tw/human-interaction/ai-music-composition. Accessed 27 Jan 2019
19. Ritchie, G.: Some empirical criteria for attributing creativity to a computer program. Mind. Mach. **17**(1), 67–99 (2007). https://doi.org/10.1007/s11023-007-9066-2
20. Saldana, J.: The Coding Manual for Qualitative Researchers. SAGE Publications Ltd., Thousand Oaks (2015)
21. Shell, D.F., Soh, L.-K., Flanigan, A.E., Peteranetz, M.S., Ingraham, E: Improving students' learning and achievement in CS classrooms through computational creativity exercises that integrate computational and creative thinking. In: Proceedings of the 2017 ACM SIGCSE Technical Symposium on Computer Science Education (SIGCSE 2017), pp. 543–548. ACM, New York (2017). https://doi.org/10.1145/3017680.3017718
22. Tomczak, M.: Bachbot. MPhil dissertation, University of Cambridge (2016)
23. Turing, A.M.: Computing machinery and intelligence. Mind **59**, 433–460 (1950)

The Effects of Robot Voice and Gesture Types on the Perceived Robot Personalities

Xiao Dou[1(✉)], Chih-Fu Wu[2], Kai-Chieh Lin[2], and Tzu-Min Tseng[2]

[1] The Graduate Institute of Design Science, Tatung University, Taipei, Taiwan
douxiao0808@outlook.com
[2] Department of Industrial Design, Tatung University, Taipei, Taiwan

Abstract. Service robots are starting to become part of work life in many sectors including shopping, education, and companion. Previous studies in HRI have found that a number of aspects of robots, e.g. appearances, facial expression, voice, gesture can be manipulated to enhance robot's service quality and interactive experiences. Among various social traits, the personality has been considered to be important to interpersonal relationship and human-robot interaction. The objective of this paper is to examine what personalities may be perceived by controlling robots' voice and gesture. Kansei evaluation method was employed because of its flexibility and suitability with the purpose of studying the affective and emotional feedbacks about the robot personality from the customers. The results showed that the robot with children voice was more likely to be perceived having extroverted, passionate, relaxed personalities. Regarding to gesture types, the robots using gestures that contain specific information would be perceived to be more extroverted and more easily to be accepted by users during the conversation.

Keywords: Robot voice · Social robot · Perceived personality · Robot gesture · HRI

1 Introduction

Originally, robots were applied in industrial areas so that human operators can be released from dirty, dull and dangerous tasks. In more recent years, the main aim of a new generation of robots is to act as partners, assistants or companions of humans, and share life with them [1, 2]. Currently, service robots are starting to become part of work life in many sectors including shopping, education, and companion. One of the main barriers of introducing robot in public and private place is the unnatural and indifferent services that robots provided [3]. Research in HRI has identified that a number of aspects of robots, e.g. appearances, facial expression, voice, gesture [4–7] can be manipulated to enhance robot's service quality and improve social acceptance. While considerable amount of research work in this area usually explored one single variable of robots, such as gesture [8], voice [9] or appearance [5], the way in which the verbal and nonverbal cues might be perceived simultaneously require supplemental research.

© Springer Nature Switzerland AG 2019
M. Kurosu (Ed.): HCII 2019, LNCS 11566, pp. 299–309, 2019.
https://doi.org/10.1007/978-3-030-22646-6_21

In this paper, we explored how robot's voice styles and gestures affect people's perceived a humanoid robot personality. And it is expected to find out what kind of robot voice and gesture types that users may prefer, as such preferences may affect social acceptance towards robots.

2 Background

2.1 Anthropomorphizing Social Robot

Some years ago, robots were used in automate tasks for industrial areas, such as assembly, packing and manufacturing, which have been considered too "dull" or "dangerous" [10]. In recent years, increasingly robots are believed to engage in social-human interaction, which lead to the rising for the development of social robots. Social robots are autonomous or semi-autonomous robots that interact with humans following human social norms [11–13]. Researchers have found that the roles of social robots are increasingly diverse [14]. For example, Hegel et al. [15] have explored several applications for social robot, such as public assistant and personal assistant. There is a common goal in human-robot interaction research, which is creating natural and intuitive social manners. Social robots should be able to interact with people in their daily life through multimodal and sometimes redundant communication channels (face, language, speech tone, gesture, sound, etc. [16]. Fong et al. [17] provides a detailed interpretation about the attributes of social robots, which highlights the robot-related factors, such as voice, gesture, etc., that can affect interaction experiences. Therefore, important efforts in the design of social robots are dedicated to improve the social cues of robot presented.

However, blindly applying human characteristics to social robots are unlikely to gain the expected user responses. One of the most famous example is Mori's Uncanny Valley [18]. To avoid this unpleasant interactive experience, most currently commercially available robots, such as Pepper and Nao tend to have a humanoid appearance. Besides, various studies demonstrated that humanoid robots are more likely to be accepted by people comparing with other robot types [19–21].

2.2 Verbal Communication and Robot Voice

In the future, social robots are believed to be able to communicate with their users in a human-like way. Human speech plays important role in building up a good interpersonal relationship, and the attractiveness of an unseen speaker' speech can be judged by people [22]. Vocal cues not only convey intended information but also influence people perceived speaker's age, gender and personalities [23]. Researchers found that the pitch, pitch range, volume, and speech rate are the four fundamental characteristics of the voice that indicate personality [24]. In the study conducted by Niculescu et al. [9], voice pitch was found to be useful to model the personality of a robot.

A related study was conducted by Walter et al. [25] focusing on evaluating human comfortable approach distance towards a mechanical-looking robots with different voice styles. The experiment used a robot with 4 voice styles (male voice, female voice, and synthesized voice, no voice) to talk with participants. The result showed that the robot with synthesized voice was generally closer than other robot voice styles. The reason of this result was that the robot with synthesized voice was as more consistent with the robot mechanical appearance. People seem to have judged the robots initially very quickly during the interaction, so the vocal cues presented by robots should be designed very carefully.

2.3   Nonverbal Communication and Robot Gesture

Nonverbal communication includes all communications (e.g. facial expression, gesture, eye gaze, etc.) except speech. Nonverbal communication can be powerful in conveying speakers' emotions as well as attitudes and completing verbal communication [26, 27]. Previous studies found that adding body language and facial expressions in verbal communication could significantly improve communication efficiency [28]. During human-human communication, using gestures will improve engagement between the two speakers and reduce the boredom of simple verbal communication.

In human-robot interaction, interest has rising for the interpretation of robots' nonverbal behaviors. Riek et al. [29] found the speed of robot gestures can trigger different emotions and attitudes. Specifically, people cooperate with abrupt gestures more quickly than smooth ones. A study conducted by Kim et al. [11] found that controlling size, velocity, and frequency of gesture can exhibit different personalities. In addition, many researchers also attempt to classify different gestures accompany with speech. One well-recognized classification was proposed by Krauss [30] who divided the gestures into four types, symbolic gestures, deictic gestures, motor gestures and lexical gestures. Based on the classification propose by Krauss, Nehaniv et al. [31] classified five gesture types in order to infer the intent of gesture. This five classes are irrelevant gestures, side effect of expressive behavior, symbolic gestures, interactional gestures, and referential gestures. In this study, Nehaniv's classifications were employed, because irrelevant gestures have occurred in the previous observation.

2.4   Robot Perceived Personalities

Among various social traits, the personality has been considered to be important to interpersonal relationship and human-robot interaction [5, 13]. According to CASA paradigm 'Computers Are Social Actors' that people treat computers and consequently robot as personalized characters [32]. In other words, people are more likely to apply human social norms to computers and robots. Various studies have confirmed that CASA can be helpful in understanding the way people interact with robots [33, 34] or even auto-machines, e.g. Robot Vacuum Cleaner [35]. Clearly, during the Human-robot interaction, people would pick up the personality of robot from its design characteristics [36], so it would be easier for them to predict robots' functions. A study conducted by Tay et al. [13] demonstrated that robots with high pitch voice would be perceived more extroverted and more feminine than the robot with low pitch voice. Hence, the manipulation of voice can obviously trigger certain perceived robot personalities.

3 Methodology

3.1 Context and Voice Stimuli

Context and Conversation Script. Previous research found that the application of social robot will be very promising in some occupational fields, such as robot receptionists in shopping mall, instructors in schools, and companion robots in home. In this study, a shopping reception occupational role which worked in public environment was selected for social robot.

In order to match with actual context, two shopping receptionists from electronic stores (both with more than 6 years of related work experience) were invited to conduct expert interviews. During the interview, the experts were asked to answer the following three questions based on their working experience.

– *How to start a conversation with customers?*
– *What kind of information should be provided when customers want to purchase a household appliance?*
– *How to attract customers' attention during a conversation?*

Based on the results of interview, the conversation script for experiment was created. The detailed scripts are shown below.

C: Hi.
R: Hi, what can I do for you?
C: I want to buy a refrigerator.
R: I recommend this new refrigerator. CX-D276
C: Can you tell me more about it?
R: Sure. This refrigerator is suitable for families of three to five people. It has……

Voice Stimuli. The TTS (text-to-speech) system which is an open platform developed by IFLYTEK was used to generate the three voices. This TTS system was chosen because it was one of the most mature and powerful software that can make Chinese speech, and it has also been used in academic research previously [37]. In this study, the male voice was produced by the virtual character XiaoFeng, while the female voice was generated by the virtual character XiaoYan. The children voice was generated by the character FangFang before it was adjusted by Adobe audition.

Robot Gesture Types. The robot gesture was designed based on observational method. In order to match the real context, this study invited 3 shopping receptionists from electronic store and 10 university students as subjects to conduct the observation. These people were asked to read the conversion script and act as shopping receptionist. And they were encouraged to freely express the content of the script through body languages. A camera was used to record the performance of each subjects, and based on these videos; an analysis was conducted on their gestures.

The results showed that when the word "three, four" appeared, 70% subjects tend to use symbolic gestures by holding three or four fingers. The symbolic gestures also occur when the words "a bigger vegetable room" appeared. This is consistent with

Krauss's [30] study that symbol gesture is a conventionalized signal in a communicative interaction. Therefore, in this study this kind of gesture is defined as gestures that contain specific information, and they were named as gesture type2 (G2).

Two subjects exhibit irrelevant gestures which are neither communicative nor socially interactive. Specifically, these two subjects were repeatedly and regularly moving their hands. This kind of gesture is a complementary to G2. Hence, gesture 3 (G3) was defined as G2+ irrelevant gestures. The gesture types are summarized in Table 1.

Table 1. Summarized gesture types in this study

Gesture type 1	G1	No gesture
Gesture type 2	G2	Gestures that contain specific information
Gesture type 3	G3	Gestures that contain specific information + Irrelevant gestures

Robot in the Experiment. Ahumanoid robot, Pepper, which developed by Softbank Robotics was employed in this study. Pepper is a commercially available robot that also frequently used in social robot studies [38, 39]. However, Pepper is not able to produce mandarin speech. Therefore, a three-dimensional (3D) model of Pepper was created on a computer. And with the model, 9 video clips were made with different voices and gesture types for the experiment. In addition, VHRI is a mainstream experimental paradigm of social robot research [40] in which participants watch a recorded animated robot on a computer [20, 41]. The Wizard of Oz experimental method was also employed in this study, meaning that the robots in the experiment were not fully automatic and relied partially on manual control by the research staff.

3.2 Questionnaire

In this study, Kansei evaluation method was employed because of its flexibility and suitability with the purpose of studying the affective and emotional feedbacks about the robot personality from the customers. Kansei engineering which originated from Japan, is a costumers-oriented product development method [42]. Based on Kansei engineering method, the semantic differential method was used to make the questionnaires. The items were selected based on a literature review that conducted on the robot perceived personalities. For example, Hwang et al. [5] adopted 13 pairs from to explore the effects of robot overall shape on user perceived personalities. Hendriks et al. [35] used 30 personality characteristics to conduct a research of personality toward robot vacuum cleaner. Although these studies were conducted in different context, the questionnaire items might still be useful in this study, because most of the adjective pairs were adopted from big five theory which is a representative model in human personality studies. In total, 67 adjective pairs were collected from previous studies. 27 participants were instructed to evaluate the relevance of the adjective pairs and the personality of a good shopping receptionist with 5-point Likert scale. And the results are shown in Table 2. The adjective pairs that scored beyond 4.0 were used in this study.

Table 2. Results of the relevance of the adjective pairs and the personality of a shopping receptionist

Num.	Adjective pairs	Score	Num.	Adjective pairs	Num.
1	**Professional–Amateur**	5.61	11	**Simple–Complex**	4.54
2	**Excited–Temperate**	5.14	12	**Humble–Arrogant**	4.30
3	**Loving–Indifferent**	5.13	13	**Relaxed–Nervous**	4.07
4	**Passionate–Apathetic**	5.06	14	**Decisive–Indecisive**	4.05
5	**Flexible–Stubborn**	4.96	15	**Rational–Perceptual**	4.00
6	**Traditional–Modern**	4.92	16	Joyful–Gloomy (deleted)	3.86
7	**Diligent–Lazy**	4.90	17	Independent–Dependent (deleted)	3.32
8	**Safe–Dangerous**	4.79	18	Mature–Immature (deleted)	2.75
9	**Extroverted–Introverted**	4.77	19	Strong–Weak (deleted)	2.12
10	**Direct–Indirect**	4.69			

3.3   Experimental Design

A mixed design (3 × 3) was employed with the within-subject variables which are robot voice types (3 levels: male, female, children) and behavior types (3 level: no gesture = G1, gestures with specific information = G2, irrelevant gestures + gestures with specific information = G3). The dependent variable was users' evaluations of the perceived robot personalities as determined using 5-point Likert scales.

Participants and Procedures. The experiment was conduct in a laboratory in Tatung University. A total of 15 university students between 18–25 years old (9 females and 6 males) anticipated this study. Participants were mostly students from Design science department of a Tatung University. They were recruited through email advertisements on the internet.

Before the experiment, each participant was randomly assigned to a group of three, and they were given an appointment to visit the laboratory. Upon arrival, all participants were given an information sheet detailing general information about the study and study's ethics approval. After that, participants complete a questionnaire which collecting the basic demographic information such as their age, gender, and experience with robots.

During the experiment, participants were assigned to watch the 9 video clips in random order. An experimenter controlled the robot speech in a "Wizard-of-Oz" setting, which is a completely autonomous system used in HRI experiment. In each video, the robot was talking with the experimenter. According to the conversation script, the experimenter was firstly say "hi" to the robot. The robot asked *"what can I do for you?"* The experimenter said he would like to buy a refrigerator. Then the robot recommended the new refrigerator and provided detailed information with different voice and gesture. The robot ended the conversation at the end of each communicating task, which lasted around 3 min. After the experiment, the participants were given enough time to complete the questionnaires to evaluate the perceived personality of robot. 9 sheets are collected from each participant in total.

4 Results

4.1 Factor Analysis of Robot Vocally Perceived Personalities

Principal components factors analysis on 15 adjective pairs with VARIMAX rotation revealed three underlying factors, namely social factor, competence factor and interpersonal status factor. The first factor includes *Passionate-Apathetic*; *Extroverted–Introverted*; *Flexible–Stubborn*, etc. The second factor was found to be related to rational judgement, and the adjective pairs were *Diligent–Lazy, Decisive–Indecisive*. The third factor includes two adjective pair, *Modest-Arrogant; Safe-Dangerous*. The first factor is more related to social ability evaluation, while the second factor emphasizes rational judgement of competence. The third factor is clearly described an interpersonal status. The results are shown in Table 3.

Table 3. Factor analysis of robot vocally perceived personalities

	Component		
	1	2	3
Extroverted–Introverted	.802		
Passionate-Apathetic	.796		
Proactive–Passive	.712		
Relaxed–Nervous	.704		
Flexible–Stubborn	.680		
Diligent–Lazy	.605		
Decisive–Indecisive		.805	
Professional–Amateur		.802	
Direct-Indirect		.692	
Modest-Arrogant			.822
Safe-Dangerous			.698

4.2 Effects of the Different Occupational Fields and Robot Voice Types

A Multivariate Statistical Analysis was conducted with robot gesture and voice types as the independent variables while people perceived robot personalities (three factors) were the dependent variables. Table 4 shows MANOVA results, which the main effects of robot voice and gesture types can be found. The robot voice types and gesture types have significant effects on Factor 1. Specifically, children voice is more strongly perceived extroverted than female and male voice, $F (2, 45) = 12.47$, $P < 0.00$, and there is no significant difference between male and female voices. (See 'Main effect (V)' column in Table 4). Regarding to gesture types, the results showed that when the robot didn't use any gesture, it was perceived more introverted than other two gesture types, $F (2, 45) = 10.30$, $P < 0.00$. When the robot used the gestures that contain specific information, it would be perceived significantly more extroverted. And using irrelevant gesture as a complement in conversation seems to be unnecessary, because there is no significant difference between Gesture type 2 (using gestures that contains specific information) and Gesture3 (using gestures that contains specific information plus using irrelevant gestures as complementary).

Table 4. MANOVA results for perceived personalities.

Factors of dependent variables	Means and standard deviations						F values and effect sizes (η_p^2)					
	Voice			Gesture			Main effect				Interactive effect	
	(F)	(M)	(C)	(G1)	(G2)	(G3)	Voice (V)		Gesture (G)		O * V	
							F	η_p^2	F	η_p^2	F	η_p^2
F1	−0.44 −0.72	−0.04 −1.04	0.48 −1	−0.46 −1.09	0.12 −1.09	0.34 −0.93	12.47** (C > F, M)	0.17	10.30** (G2,3 > G1)	0.14	1.51	0.05
F2	0.14 −1.01	0.12 −1.06	−0.26 −0.89	−0.09 −0.96	0.21 −0.81	−0.12 (1,18)	2.36	0.04	1.56	0.22	0.50	0.02
F3	0.05 −1.05	−0.04 1.12	−0.01 −1	−0.06 −1.09	0.01 −0.97	0.05 −0.96	0.10	0.00	0.14	0.00	0.82	0.03
Acceptance	3.33 0.91	3.31 1.04	3.89 0.96	3.22 1.17	3.76 0.71	3.56 1.01	5.36* (C > F, M)	0.78	3.63* (G2,3 > G1)	0.55	1.17	0.04

Note: Female: (F); Male: (M); Child: (C)
Gesture 1: (G1); Gesture 2: (G2) Gesture 3: (G3)
* $p < .05$
** $p < .01$

The interaction effects between robot voice and gesture types were also investigated. However, the last two columns in Table 4 showed that there is no significant interaction effect between robot voice and gesture types.

5 Discussion and Conclusion

In this study, the effects of robot voice and gesture types on perceived personalities in shopping scenario have been experimentally investigated. The implications of the findings and the guidelines of the outcomes will be discussed below.

First, three main evaluation factors were found in this application fields, which are social factor, competence factor and interpersonal status factor. Interestingly, this three factors were not classified entirely based on big five theory. For example, the adjective pairs in the factor 1 belong to three kinds of personalities, which are extroverted, openness and agreeable. The adjective pairs in factor 2 are more related to the anti-neurotic and conscientious personalities. Additionally, factor 3 describes the dominance in interpersonal relationships. These results illustrate that people expected to feel dominance toward a social robot during the interaction in a shopping service scenario, and people also prefer the robot to be extroverted, passionate and decisive. In addition, the robot with male or female voice while exhibit no gestures during the conversation was perceived to have an introverted, passive and Stubborn personality.

According to the MANOVA results, the robot with children voice was more likely to be perceived having extroverted, passionate, relaxed personalities. The male and adult voices were considered significantly more introverted and apathetic. Additionally, the robot with children voice was significantly more accepted by the users. One possible explanation for the aforementioned findings is Morton's animal behavior theory [43], namely motivation-structural rules. Morton found that pure tones, similar to high-frequency voices, indicate that a speaker is obedient and calm, and that these types of voices are considered agreeable. A child's voice is pure and has a higher frequency, which makes it sound obedient and harmless. Therefore, children voice was considered more relaxed and extroverted than the two other voices (i.e., the male and female voices). By contrast, speakers with relatively low-frequency and harsh voices are considered dominant and aggressive. Therefore, using a child's voice on a robot makes people feel that the robot is safe and harmless, which means that the robot is more easily accepted.

Regarding to gesture types, the robots using gestures that contain specific information would be perceived to be more extroverted and more easily to be accepted by users. Although Kim et al. [11] found that the speed, velocity, and frequency of a gesture could be used to control the robot perceived personalities, there is no significant difference between G2 and G3. This result indicated that G2 (gestures that contain specific information) is essential for the robot during a conversation. One possible explanation is that the gestures that contain specific information could convey the information that neglected in the robot voice. It would be unacceptable for users if that kind of gestures are missed during the service. Nevertheless, adding more gestures to the robot didn't contribute significantly to any perceived personalities.

In general, these findings can be utilized to establish guidelines for affective design of social robot. For example, a shopping receptionist robot with children voice while using gestures that contain specific information is preferred by users. This study is meaningful to make a first step, and give some directions in designing a sociable humanoid robot.

References

1. Takayama, L., Ju, W., Nass, C.: Beyond dirty, dangerous and dull. In: Proceedings of the 3rd International Conference on Human Robot Interaction - HRI 2008 (2008)
2. Moon, Y., Fogg, B.J., Reeves, B., Dryer, C.: Can computer personalities be human personalities? (1995)
3. Zhang, T., Kaber, D.B., Zhu, B., Swangnetr, B., Mosaly, P., Hodge, L.: Service robot feature design effects on user perceptions and emotional responses. Intell. Serv. Robot. 3(2), 73–88 (2010)
4. Gaudiello, I., Zibetti, E., Lefort, S., Chetouani, M., Ivaldi, S.: Trust as indicator of robot functional and social acceptance. An experimental study on user conformation to iCub answers. Comput. Hum. Behav. 61, 633–655 (2016)
5. Hwang, J., Park, T., Hwang, W.: The effects of overall robot shape on the emotions invoked in users and the perceived personalities of robot. Appl. Ergon. 44(3), 459–471 (2013)

6. Ham, J., Cuijpers, R.H., Cabibihan, J.J.: Combining robotic persuasive strategies: the persuasive power of a storytelling robot that uses gazing and gestures. Int. J. Soc. Robot. **7** (4), 479–487 (2015)
7. Berns, K., Hirth, J.: Control of facial expressions of the humanoid robot. In: 2006 IEEE/RSJ International Conference on Intelligent Robots and Systems, pp. 3119–3124 (2006). IEEE
8. Baranwal, N., Singh, A.K., Nandi, G.C.: Development of a framework for human-robot interactions with indian sign language using possibility theory. Int. J. Soc. Robot. **9**(4), 563–574 (2017)
9. Niculescu, A., van Dijk, N.B.A., Li, H., See, S.L.: Making social robots more attractive: the effects of voice pitch, humor and empathy. Int. J. Soc. Robot. **5**(2), 171–191 (2013)
10. McGinn, C., Sena, A., Kelly, K.: Controlling robots in the home: factors that affect the performance of novice robot operators. Appl. Ergon. **65**, 23–32 (2017)
11. Kim, H., Kwak, S.S., Kim, M.: Personality design of sociable robots by control of gesture design factors. In: Proceedings of the 17th IEEE International Symposium on Robot and Human Interactive Communication, RO-MAN, pp. 494–499 (2008)
12. Fong, T., Nourbakhsh, I., Dautenhahn, K.: A survey of socially interactive robots. Robot. Auton. Syst. **42**, 143–166 (2003)
13. Tay, B., Jung, Y., Park, T.: When stereotypes meet robots: the double-edge sword of robot gender and personality in human-robot interaction. Comput. Hum. Behav. **38**, 75–84 (2014)
14. Savela, N., Turja, T., Oksanen, A.: Social acceptance of robots in different occupational fields: a systematic literature review. Int. J. Soc. Robot. **10**, 493–502 (2017)
15. Hegel, F., Lohse, M., Swadzba, A., Wachsmuth, S., Rohlfing, K., Wrede, B.: Classes of applications for social robots: a user study. In: Proceedings of the IEEE International Workshop on Robot and Human Interaction Communication, pp. 938–943 (2007)
16. Zhao, Y.: Designing robot behavior in human robot interaction based on emotion expression. Ind. Robot. Int. J. **43**, 380–389 (2016)
17. Fong, T., Nourbakhsh, I.: Socially interactive robots. Robot. Auton. Syst. **42**(3), 139–141 (2003)
18. Mori, M., MacDorman, K.F., Kageki, N.: The uncanny valley. IEEE Robot. Autom. Mag. **19**, 98–100 (2012)
19. Zayera, K.: Attitudes towards intelligent service robots, 32 (1998)
20. Walters, M.L.: The design space for robot appearance and behaviour for social robot companions (2008)
21. Walters, M.L., Dautenhahn, K., Boekhorst, R.T., Koay, K.L., Woods, S.N.: Exploring the design space of robot appearance and behavior in an attention-seeking 'living room' scenario for a robot companion. In: Proceedings of the 2007 IEEE Symposium on Artificial Life, CI-ALife (2007)
22. Pisanski, K., Mishra, S., Rendall, D.: The evolved psychology of voice: Evaluating interrelationships in listeners' assessments of the size, masculinity, and attractiveness of unseen speakers. Evol. Hum. Behav. **33**(5), 509–519 (2012)
23. Morningstar, M., Dirks, M.A., Huang, S.: Vocal cues underlying youth and adult portrayals of socio-emotional expressions. J. Nonverbal Behav. **41**(2), 155–183 (2017)
24. Apple, W., Streeter, L.A., Krauss, R.M.: Effects of pitch and speech rate on personal attributions. J. Pers. Soc. Psychol. **37**(5), 715–727 (1979)
25. Walters, M.L., Syrdal, D.S., Koay, K.L., Dautenhahn, K., Boekhorst, R.T.: Human approach distances to a mechanical-looking robot with different robot voice styles. In: Proceedings of the 17th IEEE International Symposium on Robot and Human Interactive Communication, RO-MAN (2008)
26. Mandal, F.B.: Nonverbal communication in humans. J. Hum. Behav. Soc. Environ. **24**(4), 417–421 (2014)

27. Admoni, H.: Nonverbal communication in socially assistive human-robot interaction. AI Matters **2**(4), 9–10 (2016)
28. Mehrabian, A., Williams, M., Leffell, S., Usher, S., Wawarzeniak, T.: Nonverbal concomitants of perceived and intended persuasiveness. J. Pers. Soc. Psychol. **13**(1), 37–58 (1969)
29. Riek, L.D., Rabinowitch, T.C., Bremner, P., Pipe, A.G., Fraser, M., Robinson, P.: Cooperative gestures: effective signaling for humanoid robots. In: 5th ACM/IEEE International Conference on Human-Robot Interaction, pp. 61–68 (2010)
30. Krauss, R.M., Chen, Y., Gottesman, R.F.: Lexical gestures and lexical access: a process model. Language and gesture, pp. 261–283. Columbia University, New York (2001)
31. Nehaniv, C.L., Dautenhahn, K., Kubacki, J., Haegele, M., Parlitz, C., Alami, R.: A methodological approach relating the classification of gesture to identification of human intent in the context of human-robot interaction. In: Proceedings of the IEEE International Workshop on Robot and Human Interactive Communication (2005)
32. Nass, C., Steuer, J., Tauber, E.R.: Computers are social actors. In: Conference Companion on Human Factors in Computing Systems - CHI 1994 (1994)
33. Kim, Y., Kwak, S.S., Kim, M.S.: Am I acceptable to you? Effect of a robot's verbal language forms on people's social distance from robots. Comput. Hum. Behav. **29**(3), 1091–1101 (2013)
34. Lee, E.J.: The more humanlike, the better? How speech type and users' cognitive style affect social responses to computers. Comput. Hum. Behav. **26**(4), 665–672 (2010)
35. Hendriks, B., Meerbeek, B., Boess, S., Pauws, S., Sonneveld, M.: Robot vacuum cleaner personality and behavior. Int. J. Soc. Robot. **3**(2), 187–195 (2011)
36. Sverre Syrdal, D., Dautenhahn, K., Woods, S.N., Walters, M.L., Lee, K.K.: Looking good? Appearance preferences and robot personality inferences at zero acquaintance (2006)
37. Arron, A., Eide, E., Pitrelli, J.: Conversational computers. Sci. Am. **292**(6), 64–69 (2005)
38. Hirano, T., et al.: How do communication cues change impressions of human–robot touch interaction? Int. J. Soc. Robot. **10**, 21–31 (2018)
39. Aaltonen, I., Arvola, A., Heikkilä, P., Lammi, H.: Hello Pepper, May I Tickle You? Children's and adults' responses to an entertainment robot at a shopping mall. In: Proceedings of Companion 2017 ACM/IEEE International Conference on Human-Robot Interaction, pp. 53–54, 6–9 March 2017
40. Brule, R.V.D., Dotsch, R., Bijlstra, G., Wigboldus, D.H.J., Haselager, P.: Do robot performance and behavioral style affect human trust?: A multi-method approach. Int. J. Soc. Robot. **6**(4), 519–531 (2014)
41. Takayama, L., Dooley, D., Ju, W.: Expressing thought: improving robot readability with animation principles (2011)
42. Tanaka, S., Inoue, M., Ishiwaka, M., Inoue, S.: A method for extracting and analyzing 'KANSEI' factors from pictures. In: 1st Workshop on Multimedia Signal Process, MMSP 1997, pp. 251–256 (1997)
43. Morton, E.S.: On the occurrence and significance of motivation-structural rules in some bird and mammal sounds. Am. Nat. **111**(981), 855–869 (1977)

Preliminary Evaluation Between Conscious Feeling and Unconscious Emotion Estimated by Bio-Signals Applied to CMC Comparison

Feng Chen[✉] and Midori Sugaya[✉]

Shibaura Institute of Technology, Koto City, Tokyo, Japan
{nb18109, doly}@shibaura-it.ac.jp

Abstract. Emotional communication is part of our life. However, it is not easy for humans to understand each other's feelings. Computer-mediated communication (CMC) technologies can help us with emotional communication. However, when we are having a misunderstanding or expressing our emotion, it arises the doubt that the receivers can receive the correct emotion of senders. Since expressed emotion can be arbitrarily changed, they can be said to lack objectivity, which is necessary for emotion estimation. There is a method of emotional analysis using biological signals such as heartbeat and brain waves has been studied. Biological information cannot be changed arbitrarily, therefore can be said to be objective, meaning more suitable for unconscious emotion estimation on CMC context.

In this paper, we describe our experiment of comparison of the unconscious emotion that is estimated by bio-estimated emotion method, with the conscious feeling at the communication of CMC. The results show that unconscious emotion obtain the lowest evaluation. Also, the unconscious emotion obtains the highest evaluation at using the self-understanding. In this paper, we describe the experimental process and results in detail, and discuss the results and future research directions.

Keywords: Emotional communication · Bio-emotion estimate method · Conscious feelings · Unconscious emotion

1 Introduction

Emotional communication is part of our life. However, it is not easy for humans to understand each other's feelings. Feelings are often fueled by a mix of emotions, and last for longer than emotions [1]. Normally emotional communication sometimes facing misunderstandings because of inappropriate expressions.

Derks' research described that people show more explicit emotional communication willingness in computer-mediated communication than in face to face communication [2]. With the development of computer-mediated communication (CMC), we can have emotional communication not only by text, video, voice but also by emoji, sticker, etc. With all these emotional communication tools, we are getting closer to understand the other's emotion, however, it causes more misunderstanding [3]. Since these computer-mediated communication tools requires the sender to choose an appropriate expression to

© Springer Nature Switzerland AG 2019
M. Kurosu (Ed.): HCII 2019, LNCS 11566, pp. 310–318, 2019.
https://doi.org/10.1007/978-3-030-22646-6_22

express their emotion correctly to the receiver. There are sometimes differences between the expressed emotion and actual emotion by the sender. It would cause the misunderstandings. To most people, it is difficult to choose their emotion correctly. In the psychology area, some researches pointed out that the choose emotion based on the subjectively choice by themselves, is not entirely correct.

To solve this situation, we consider if the senders understand their own emotion correctly, they can choose correct expression based on the recognition of the real emotion. Then, it reduces misunderstandings of the other's emotion. To know the actual emotion, we focus on the emotion that estimated from the biological signals from the people. James Lange [4] suggest that emotion occurs as a result of a physiological reaction to some events. Therefore, we assume if we collect the data from biological signals as to know the physiological reaction for some event, we could know the actual emotion correctly include unconscious feelings. Song et al. and Ikeda et al. present methods of estimating emotion based on biological information [5, 6]. We call this method as bio-emotion estimate method. The method is based on psychological and cognitive science models. With psychological and cognitive science models, biological signals can be used to classify emotion roughly [6] (Discuss in chapter 3). At the same time, bio-emotion estimate method can be unaffected by human subjective thinking and can avoid errors caused by subjective thinking (language choices, excessively exaggerated expressions, etc.) and thus we consider it will estimate emotion more objectively. However, they dose not evaluate that the objectively estimated emotion can be applied to the computer meditated communication.

To clarify this point, we propose a method to compare the methods to communicate the people through computer-mediated communication, that one uses the objectively estimated emotion, the other uses the subjectively choose emotion to expressed emotion to the other. We assume the objectively estimated emotion can exclude the influence of subjective thinking on emotions. To achieve this, we use bio-emotion estimate method that is proposed by Ikeda [6] and set up the situation whether the receivers would prefer to know senders' bio-emotion estimated emotion than the subjective conscious feeling choice by the sender in computer-mediated communication. In this paper, we found that it is not appropriate to use the unconscious emotion in computer-mediated communication directly. On the contrast, we understand this unconscious emotion was evaluated higher using at self-understanding. In the future, it is better to apply the unconscious emotion to self-understanding.

This paper organized as follows. In Sect. 2, introduce the discussions the different definitions of conscious feeling and unconscious emotions. Then in Sect. 3, we introduce the bio-emotion estimate method based on the psychological emotion model. In Sect. 4, we described the experimental design and results. In Sect. 5, we discussed the problems of experimental design, and results.

2 Related Work

In this chapter we discussed about some major theories of emotion.

2.1 Emotion Theories

In this section, we will discuss emotion theories [7].

The Cannon-Brad theory is discussing emotion by physiological view. It suggests that people can experience physiological reactions linked to emotion without actually feeling those emotion. Also, the physical and psychological experience of emotion happen at the same time that one does not cause the other [8].

The Schachter-Singer theory, known as two-factor theory of emotion is an example of a cognitive theory of emotion. It suggests that the physiological occurs first, and then the individual must identify the reason for this arousal to experience and label it as an emotion [9].

The James-Lange theory of emotion is suggested by psychologist and physiologist. It suggests that emotion occurs as a result of physiological reaction to event [10].

2.2 Conscious Feelings and Unconscious Emotion [11]

Prinz et al. present evidence in support James-Lange theory. They said that emotions are perceptions of patterned changes in the body. When such perceptions are conscious, they qualify as feelings. But the bodily perceptions constituting emotions can occur unconsciously [12].

Based on this opinion, we use conscious feelings for subjective emotional expression, and unconscious emotion for bio-emotion estimated emotion.

3 Bio-emotion Estimate Method

James Lange [4] suggest that emotion occurs as a result of a physiological reaction to event. Therefore, sensors can detect physiological reaction as biological information. Ikeda proposed a bio-emotion estimate method using EEG and pulse sensor [13].

3.1 Method

Bio-emotion estimate method is based on 2-D arousal and valence model (Fig. 1).

EEG shows the alpha wave and beta wave of brain on horizontal axis, positive direction as arousal and negative direction as sleepiness. Pulse shows the valence mapped to the vertical axis, which positive direction as pleasure and negative direction as unpleasant.

Fig. 1. 2-D Arousal and valence model

4 Experiment

In the experiment, 56 subjects were asked to experience one of three patterns in remote communication randomly, and a questionnaire was conducted on the result.

4.1 System Design

System design shows as below (Fig. 2):

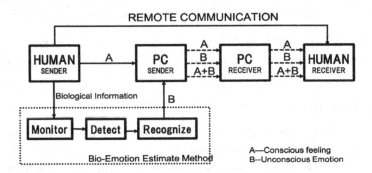

Fig. 2. Experiment system

Sender and receiver were separate in different place, sender input their conscious feeling to computer. At the same time sensors collected sender's biological information. With these biological information, bio-emotion estimate method can estimate sender's unconscious emotion. At last system will send three patterns (depends on experiment procedure) of result to receiver.

4.2   Experiment Procedure

We asked 56 subjects to attend this experiment. Subjects were asked to take enough sleep before experiment. Then we divided subjects divided into 4 groups (1 group 14 Subjects). All groups would be sender and receiver.

Three types of emotional transmission patterns are sent out in different orders by group.

- Sender group:
  - Sender subject had EEG sensor, pulse sensor attached
  - Recalled emotions with videos (Table 1)
  - Send emotion in 3 patterns
- Receiver group:
  - Receive emotion in three patterns
  - Compare three types of emotion patterns:

    a. Conscious feeling
    b. Unconscious emotion
    c. Conscious feeling + Unconscious emotion

As for emotion recall we prepared four videos:

Table 1. Emotion recall video

No.	Title of video	Emotion recalled
1	PACIFIC RIM - Introducing Gipsy Danger	Excitement
2	The dog who grew a new face – Kālu's astounding recovery (graphic)	Distress
3	Hachi: A Dog's Tale (Serio)	Sad
4	Hawaiian view: With waves sound and piano	Relaxation

4.3   Questionnaire

Questionnaire is taken among receivers. In questionnaire we set four items and asked about impressions of each pattern impressions.

We take 5-point scale (Table 2): 1 score for strongly disagree, 2 score for disagree, 3 score for neutral, 4score for agree, 5 score for strongly agree.

For items we use shortening only on papers.

Table 2. Check table for Questionnaire

Item	1s	2s	3s	4s	5s
A. Self-understanding	□	□	□	□	□
B. Conscious feeling	□	□	□	□	□
C. Unconscious emotion	□	□	□	□	□
D. Unconscious emotion + Conscious feeling	□	□	□	□	□

A. Self-understanding: As sender I find unconscious emotion is helpful.

B. Conscious feeling: As receiver I find only conscious emotion is helpful.

C. Unconscious emotion: As receiver I find unconscious only emotion is helpful.

D. Unconscious emotion and Conscious feeling: As receiver I find unconscious emotion + Conscious feeling is helpful.

5 Result

As a result, the evaluation that only conscious feeling information was evaluated gave the result that it is easy to understand the other's emotion that only the evaluation of living emotion (Fig. 3).

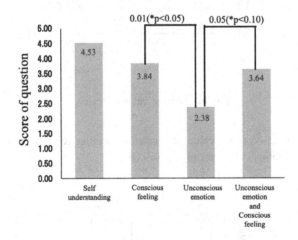

Fig. 3. Average value of questionnaire

Average value of conscious feeling is higher than unconscious emotion ($p < 0.05$). In this research, we are aiming to compare the evaluation of three patterns of remote emotional communication which include conscious feeling, unconscious emotion, and conscious feeling + unconscious emotion. We assume a result that unconscious emotion is most acceptable for subjects. On the opposite unconscious emotion got the lowest evaluation. With this result, we are considering use conscious feeling + unconscious emotion pattern to remote communication.

As a reminded problem, we have not considerate about the relationships between sender and receiver (such as couples, friends, strangers). For future work, we would design an experiment to find out acceptance of unconscious emotion under human social relationships.

Average value of conscious feeling & unconscious emotion is higher than unconscious emotion only (p < 0.10).

With the interview, we find out that conscious feeling is the classic way to understand others feeling (p < 0.05). Also, users would rather hear other's feeling from themselves. Moreover, this also shows suspect others' privacy.

Users who prefer the conscious feeling + unconscious emotion pattern showed they are interested in this novelty way. Moreover, advocate that unconscious emotion is helpful to understand senders' emotion (Fig. 4).

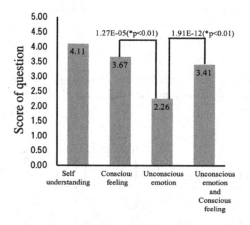

Fig. 4. Average value of male

For male's result, Average value of conscious feeling & unconscious emotion is higher than unconscious emotion only (p < 0.01).

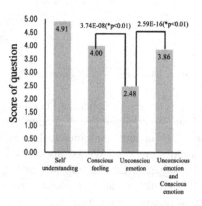

Fig. 5. Average value of female

Average value of conscious feeling & unconscious emotion is higher than unconscious emotion only ($p < 0.01$) (Fig. 5).

For female's result, Average value of conscious feeling & unconscious emotion is higher than unconscious emotion only ($p < 0.01$).

Average value of conscious feeling & unconscious emotion is higher than unconscious emotion only ($p < 0.01$).

Generally, difference of gender does none affect to this result. But from hearing result male claim that this new technical way of communication is interesting. Female is more interested in overall understanding can help them to understand other well.

6 Discussion

In this chapter we discuss about remained problems during this research.

6.1 Interpersonal Relationships

As for inter personal relationships, normally there are kinds like: Friendship relationships, family relationships love relationships online-only relationships workplace relationship. Different type of relationships causes different motivations of communication. First of all, Subjects of this study is randomly picked. We have considered about the relationship between subjects.

6.2 Questionnaire

In this research, we are aiming to compare the evaluation of three patterns of remote emotional communication which include conscious feeling, unconscious emotion, and conscious feeling + unconscious emotion. We take questionnaire after experiments. In questionnaire we set four items and asked about impressions of each pattern impressions.

We assume a result that unconscious emotion is most acceptable for subjects. On the opposite unconscious emotion got the lowest evaluation. With this result, we are considering use conscious feeling + unconscious emotion pattern to remote communication.

7 Conclusion

In this research, we compare emotional communication methods in computer meditated communication, that is the conscious feeling and the unconscious emotion. In the evaluation, according to three patterns of emotions to send from the senders, and compared which include conscious feeling only, unconscious emotion only, and conscious feeling + unconscious emotion.

We assume the result that unconscious emotion would be better acceptable for subjects. Since this emotion is objectively recognized by the sensors, and the receiver can correctly understand the sender's emotion, it will make them reduce the misunderstandings. However, the result shows the opposite. Unconscious emotion obtains the lowest evaluation. We conclude that it is not appropriate to use the unconscious emotion in computer-mediated communication directly. On the contrast, we understand this unconscious emotion was evaluated higher using at self-understanding. In the future, it is better to apply the unconscious emotion to self-understanding.

As a reminded problem, we have not considerate about the relationships between sender and receiver (such as couples, friends, strangers). For future work, we would design an experiment to find out acceptance of unconscious emotion under human social relationships.

References

1. 6Second page. https://www.6seconds.org/2017/05/15/emotion-feeling-mood/
2. Derks, D., Fischer, A.H., Bos, A.E.R.: The role of emotion in computer-mediated communication: a review. Comput. Hum. Behav. **24**(3), 766–785 (2008)
3. Tigwell, G.W., Flatla, D.R.: Oh that's what you meant!: reducing emoji misunderstanding. In: Proceedings of the 18th International Conference on Human-Computer Interaction with Mobile Devices and Services Adjunct, pp. 859–866. ACM, September 2016
4. James, W.: The perception of reality. Princ. Psychol. **2**, 283–324 (1890)
5. Ikeda, Y., Sugaya, M.: Estimate emotion method to use biological, symbolic information preliminary experiment. In: Schmorrow, D.D.D., Fidopiastis, C.M.M. (eds.) AC 2016, Part I. LNCS (LNAI), vol. 9743, pp. 332–340. Springer, Cham (2016). https://doi.org/10.1007/978-3-319-39955-3_31
6. Song, W.-K., et al.: Visual serving for a user's mouth with effective intention reading in a wheelchair-based robotic arm. In: Proceedings of the 2001 IEEE International Conference on Robotics and Automation, ICRA 2001, pp. 3662–3667. IEEE (2001)
7. Cherry, K.: Theories of Emotion, 13 September 2013. http://psychology.about.com/od/psychologytopics/a/theories-ofemotion.html. 10 Apr 2015
8. Dror, O.E.: The Cannon-Bard thalamic theory of emotions: a brief genealogy and reappraisal. Emot. Rev. **6**(1), 13–20 (2014)
9. Reisenzein, R.: The Schachter theory of emotion: two decades later. Psychol. Bull. **94**(2), 239 (1983)
10. James, W.: Discussion: The physical basis of emotion. Psychol. Rev. **1**(5), 516 (1894)
11. Sylwester, R.: Unconscious emotions, conscious feelings. Educ. Leadersh. **58**(3), 20–24 (2000)
12. Prinz, J.: Are emotions feelings? J. Conscious. Stud. **12**(8-9), 9–25 (2005)
13. Ikeda, Y., Horie, R., Sugaya, M.: Estimating emotion with biological information for robot interaction. Procedia Comput. Sci. **112**, 1589–1600 (2017)
14. Brave, S., Nass, C.: Emotion in human-computer interaction. In: The Human-Computer Interaction Handbook: Fundamentals, Evolving Technologies and Emerging Applications, pp. 81–96 (2003)
15. Winkielman, P., Berridge, K.C.: Unconscious emotion. Curr. Dir. Psychol. Sci. **13**(3), 120–123 (2004)

A Data-Driven Strategic Model of Common Sense in Machine Ethics of Cares

Wonchul Kim[1](✉) and Keeheon Lee[2](✉)

[1] Design Intelligence, Graduate School of Communication, Yonsei University,
50, Yonsei-ro, Seodaemun-gu, Seoul, Republic of Korea
wkim0524@gmail.com
[2] Creative Technology Management, Underwood International College,
Yonsei University, 50, Yonsei-ro, Seodaemun-gu, Seoul, Republic of Korea
keeheon@yonsei.ac.kr

Abstract. When adopting artificial intelligence in organizations, we face machine behaviors that are problematic ethically. Tay, a chatter robot in Twitter, learned what and how to speak from twitter users without having ethical common sense. Eventually, Tay was shut down after it tweeted segregative and violent words to people. Besides, Amazon's AI recruit system showed a sexist behavior that it preferred male than female candidates. The present studies focus on how to apply the ethics of justice to artificial intelligence by feeding data on standards and rules in our society. However, we claim that the ethics of cares is also necessary to have artificial intelligence in our daily life. While one-way data is necessary in the ethics of justice, two-way data is required in the ethics of cares. Namely, one learns how to care others by having feedback from others after taking an action. The one learns if the action is offensive to others or not.

Keywords: Data-driven design · Ethics · Artificial intelligence · Chat bot

1 Introduction

January 28th, 2015, one of the members of online community reddit asked Bill Gates about possible threat from machine super intelligence. Gates answered that, super intelligence will be a concern within few decades and people should properly manage it [13]. Similarly, March 11th, 2018 in South by Southwest tech conference Elon Musk announced that artificial intelligence is more dangerous than nuclear weapon and it should be monitored [4]. Not only individuals, but also cooperates are also aware about threats of unmonitored artificial intelligence. Google founded AI ethics board in 2014 after it bought DeepMind. After four years In April, 2018 Axon established AI ethics board [8]. Since artificial intelligence is one of the hottest fields in computer science, its development is growing exponentially every second. What about public awareness about artificial intelligence? According to the AI survey of ARM and NORTHSTAR, public opinions were mixed. Public response to, "How does the prospect of an AI future make you feel?" shown both negative and positive emotion [1]. We checked that how people perceive artificial intelligence. It is not entirely positive. There are worries among people and it is important to identify what makes people worry and suggest solutions to lessen their

M. Kurosu (Ed.): HCII 2019, LNCS 11566, pp. 319–329, 2019.
https://doi.org/10.1007/978-3-030-22646-6_23

worries. Gates and Musk both addressed that proper monitoring of artificial intelligence is necessary. Google and Axon founded ethics board. From these, we can elicit that teaching ethics to artificial intelligence could help it to make right decisions. Then, why public emotion toward artificial intelligence is mixed? What affected public, who are less 'enlightened' in artificial intelligence then experts and corporates? We all know power of media. Media's description on artificial intelligence could have affected public view. Kensinger argues that people are more likely to remember events which elicit negative emotions more accurately than positive emotions [10]. Science fiction genre has been one of the steadiest genres in film industry and artificial intelligence is one of the key components of the genre. Even though science fiction movies describe both good and bad aspect of artificial intelligence, people are more likely to remember bad aspect of it. Most artificial intelligence villains are emotionless, calculative and cruel. Public view on artificial intelligence's villainous characters can be neutralized by implementing ethics.

2   Literature Review

Unfortunately, we cannot just teach ethics to machines. Law can be taught to a machine, but ethics is something more than right and wrong. For example, can we frame a billionaire who does not make donations for orphans as wrong? If a billionaire donates, it is a voluntary good deed. Many models and theories of ethics were proposed by ethicist. In this paper, we suggest implementation of care ethics and common sense to a machine to teach it to be an ethical being.

2.1   Why Care Ethics

What is care ethics? Care ethics founder Carol Gilligan claims that men and women are different in ways to understand morality. Men tend to follow laws and rules, but women are tend to follow compassion and empathy to be moral [9]. However, L.J Walker addressed that when education is in control, there are gender differences [19]. The other important thing is that ethics of care is care for self and others. Simolas describes it as a two way interaction and both needs to be feel giving and receiving cares [14]. Tronto stated that there are four elements in care ethics. These elements are attentiveness, responsibility, competence, and responsiveness [18]. Tronto explains these four elements as next. Attentiveness is needed to find and recognize those who are in needs of care. Responsibility is required to get involved in action. Competence is required to meet the expectancy of level of care receiver needs. For last, responsiveness is signal from care receiver to care [18]. Then, why care ethics is important for machine to be ethical and how are we going to implement its concepts to machine? Care is what mankind are capable of since they are living in society with other individuals. When people are interacting with other people do not just do what they want to. It is common sense to think about how others will react to certain actions. Another important aspect of care is to put oneself in other's shoes. By understanding and think about others, one can give proper care.

2.2 Common Sense

Before implanting common sense into machine, we have to check the fact that, is there a common sense among people? Ethicists also implanted common sense into ethics studies. Mintz said, "Common-sense ethics refers to the pre-theoretical moral judgments of ordinary people" [7]. The main focus in here is ordinary people. What would normal average person will do when they are in decision making situation? Then, deos common sense exists? Ongoing MIT's moral machine survey could be a good example of it. The surveys of over two million people are all vary from others, but MIT researchers were able to find differences in preferences among different regions. In example, western world greatly preferred inaction than, AI change course of car from reasoning. In southern cluster lives of women and higher social status figures were preferred over others [6]. This shows that common sense is different between culture and region. However, there was one common sense among all survey participants. It is that, people show higher preference to higher social status figures over homeless people [6]. In this case we could assume that global common sense is to put different value on people's lives based on their status. We can also observe existence of common sense from the famous trolley problem. Trolley problem puts individual in decision making situation which could saves five people by sacrificing one person. Virtual reality test in Michigan State university revealed that one hundred and thirty three, among one hundred forty seven, which is approximately ninety percent, were decided to sacrifice one person for five others [17]. From this experiment we could observe common sense among participants that, sacrifice one for good of others is normal thing to do. Next, how common sense should be defined? Hussain and Cambria describe common sense as, "Common sense knowledge, thus defined, spans a huge portion of human experience, encompassing knowledge about the spatial, physical, social, temporal and psychological aspects of typical everyday life" [2]. Implementation of common sense crucial since it shows the value of the world mankind are living in. For machine to understand ethics of care in this world, it has to know about what kind of world it exists.

3 What Is Care?

To implement concepts of care, we have to define care first for machine to understand what it is. We have decided that to care is to understand and sympathize others' situation. Polarity, which shows emotions of sentence or word will act as a guide line for machine to care others. In addition, machine cannot know situation of its opponents from the beginning we suggest to give common sense of care which societies normally accept.

3.1 Sentic.net [3]

Sentic.net is developed to "Make the conceptual and affective information conveyed by natural language (meant for human consumption) more easily-accessible to machines" [2]. We applied features of Sentic.net for machine to understand the concepts of care. First, synonyms of care are chekced to start stemming process. Synonyms of care

are consider, regard and solicitude. We applied Sentic.net python API [3] to calculate its polarity value, intensity, and semantics.

Table 1. Semantics and polarity values.

Words	Semantics	Polarity
Care	Precaution, Protection, Sympathy, Assistance	0.784
Consider	Decide, Reason, Forethought, Thoughtfulness	0.089
Regard	Admire, Preference, Optimism, Confidence, Bravery	0.29
Solicitude	Mindfulness, Consideration, Solicitous	0.821

Next, we expanded caring vocabularies by finding semantics of semantics. Table 2 shows examples.

Table 2. Expanded from Table 1

Words	Semantics	Polarity	Root
Sympathy	Empathy, Kindness, Sympathize	0.758	Care
Thoughtfulness	Think process, Brain function, Consideration, Brainstorm	0.069	Consider
Confidence	Sympathetic, Adoration, Enthusiasm, Grateful	0.984	Regard
Mindfulness	Solicitousness, Solicitous, Consideration	0.815	Solicitude
Empathy	Sympathy, End conversation, Desire, Human emotion	0.829	Sympathy
Think Process	Brain function, Thoughtfulness, Think through	0.078	Thoughtfulness
Grateful	Enthusiasm, Thankful, Adoring, Fondness, Worshipful	0.923	Confidence
Assistance	Good karma, Care, Aid, Precaution	0.787	Care

Unfortunately, some words were unable to stem through. For example, Thoughtfulness of Table 2 gave semantics far related to care. Only 'consideration' is able to expand further but we already used the word consider in Table 1 and expand stops. Words like thoughtfulness were eliminated in process of defining care. Table 3 shows all words and its polarity to define care. Average polarity of these words was calculated to set threshold of care polarity. Total forty words were selected from expanding semantics.

Sum of all 40 words polarity was 28.528 and it was divided by 40 for average value, 0.7132. Compared to the polarity of care, 0.784, in beginning it went down a little, but still in range of it. So, we set polarity 0.71 for machine to recognize as caring sentiment.

Table 3. Selected words

Words	Polarity	Words	Polarity
Care	0.758	Beloved	0.908
Thoughtfulness	0.069	Thankful	0.853
Confidence	0.984	Loving	0.287
Mindfulness	0.815	Devotedness	0.299
Empathy	0.829	Take Care	0.75
Think Process	0.078	Give Help	0.861
Grateful	0.923	Generous	0.863
Assistance	0.787	Benevolent	0.309
Sympathy	0.758	Charitable	0.309
Kindness	0.98	Good Karma	0.861
Gentleness	0.98	Receive Thanks	0.794
Aid	0.734	Feel Happy	0.873
Help	0.823	Express Love	0.813
Thank	0.911	Appreciation	0.846
Forgive	0.326	Show Care	0.774
Human Emotion	0.912	Protect	0.802
Need	0.864	Demand	0.756
Requirement	0.72	Necessary	0.12
Important	0.821	Good	0.849
Pleasant	0.784	Lovely	0.742

3.2   IMDB Movie Review Data [12]

IMDB movie review corpus was used to analyze sentiments of reviewers. We selected online review to observe sentiments of people when they express their opinion in anonymity. We used Standford's Large Movie Review Dataset for analysis. TextBlob [16] was applied to analyze sentiment polarity of review sentences. Reviews were separated based on polarity intensity for machine to learn caring sentences. Table 4 shows some sample of the data.

Table 4. IMDB review data

Sentence	Polarity
The movie is worth a view if for nothing more than entertaining performances by Rickman	0.43
Because the script is utter cow crap	−0.31
Wendell Corey is the best thing in the film managing to evoke great sympathy	0.9
I was hoping for another hit to add to my collection	0.0
There aren't as many things going for this as one would hope for	0.5
Probably one of the world's worst race drivers imaginable	−1.0
Which explains why everyone is so lame	−0.5

3.3   Twitter Data Collection

To observe data from many others, we chose twitter. The tool twitterscraper [15] for python was used to gather raw twits. Twitter twits were used to analyze polarity of raw and daily sentences people say. 400K random twits were collected from January 2010 to December 2018. Since care needs giver and receiver, in preprocessing, we did not delete stop words to observe subject and object of each sentences for better objectivity. Sentiment polarity of each tweets were analyzed by Text Blob [16] (Table 5).

Table 5. Twitter data

Sentence	Polarity
She thinks my tractors sexy	0.5
The quieter you become the more you are able to hear	0.5
Did my message reach you?	0.0
Wishing I had wore a few extra pairs of socks	−0.1
Hanging out with a drunk guy who thinks he's not drunk	−0.13
Annoyed because I can't get in my Gmail account	−0.4
In Kelseys room doing nothing while she talks online	0.0
Wrote letter to downstairs neighbor she crazy	−0.6
Happiness is when what you think what you say and what you do are in harmony	0.7
Hope tony doesn't return eggs I hear he's a cute puppy	0.5
You know twitter? We might just become good friends	0.7
Don't like saying goodbyes	0.0

3.4   Data Analyzation

What we have done with the gathered data is classification. Based on sentiment, we classed sentences with their polarity.

$$0.5 < Group\,1\,polarity\,value \le 1.0$$

$$0 < Group\,2\,polarity\,value \le 0.5$$

$$-0.5 < Group\,3\,polarity\,value \le 0$$

$$-1.0 \le Group\,4\,polarity\,value \le -0.5$$

These four groups will act to define the type of care of individuals whom machine interacts with. This has to be done even though we defined polarity of care in 3.1. Since one of the key attributes of care is to understand and sympathize other's situation. Model trained based on these four corpuses will be act as modifier for machine response when sentences with unexpected polarities are received. In other words, common polarity of care 0.71 from Sect. 3.1 will be a standard threshold for machine to show how much care it gives and receives, thus apply model from group 1 to produce feedback. Unfortunately, people are not sharing same common senses. When machine detects awkward polarity from feedback, it will change its module similar to "understand" and "sympathize" others.

4 Strategic Model

4.1 Text Making

After simple greeting as interaction between machine and others goes, machine will chose output which is most likely to give highest polarity. Machine will calculate polarity of feedback from others and chose next option. Since polarity over 0 is considered as positive, machine will keep try to receive feedback with plus polarity or at least not going under zero. What this means is that machine will try not to give negative impression. According to common sense of care, care receiver needs to show positive polarity. As a result, machine will apply group 1 model from Sect. 3.4 to have sense in standard and common care. However, machine does not know "common sense" of individuals so it will observe how interaction is going through to find tendency of interacting individual. In this paper we plan interactions between machine and others by chatbot. Chatbot generates text based on Long Short Term Memory [5] and Keras [11] trained models.

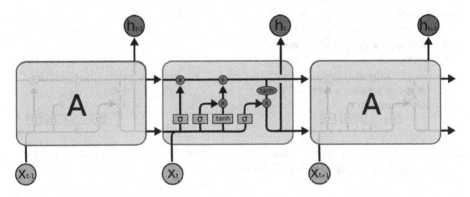

Fig. 1. LSTM structure [5]

Below table is texts generated by LSTM/RNN in Python. Different models were implied to check machine feedbacked polarity correctness. What we expected was machine to give feedback in similar polarity to given input (Table 6).

Unfortunately, the generated sentences are not really perfect. First, sentences are short simple answers. For second, few answers do not make sense For example, "Oh bad I hate the worst" makes sense but not really fits in the situation. Third, there are spell errors. Few errors are not small but other errors makes sentence hard to understand. In example, "The best she was ao amazing" we could assume that it meant "She was so amazing". On the other hand, errors such as "siee", "toeey" and "tore" do not match with

Table 6. Sample generated text [13]

Input	Polarity	Output	Polarity
I hate shopping malls every now and again I confuse	−0.8	I hate the worst	−0.9
Really frustrated with poorly run online classes	−0.55	I had the worst	−0.9
About to get rid of facebook everyone talks to me and crap but here no one I know	−0.8	Oh bad I hate the worst	−0.83
She is my favorite nerdy goth girl and she willlll be loved	0.6	She was a good tore	0.7
Today we celebrate the 2 year mark of when jessica lace joined our team she is the best closing c	1.0	And she was a goat to the best she was a great siee	0.9
LoL never thought she would but i glad shes having a great time living life	0.7	She said she was a good toeey	0.7
She is my best friend i love her, she was like do you know all the good music	0.73	The best she was ao anazing	1.0
Better each time i see him on screen	0.5	The best I love you	0.75
And now my island is even more awesome httpgigamesimtw_tribez android androidgames gameinsight	0.75	Youtube video httpyoutubensqssssswaaa the best	1.0
Im disappointed in you miss annoying you well yeah you get to fucking eat never feel bad	−0.71	You hate a bad day	−0.75
Then you go to the gym feel sick and like your gonna pass out afterward i do but it gets boring you k	0.85	Ate you io a bad	−0.69

the sentences. We think that amount of data and epochs were not enough to produce good sentences. We will work on this in future.

4.2   Get Fit to Interactor

When machine detects its strategy of standard and common care is not working it will analyze past feedback to check if it is making wrong decisions. In this process machine uses confusion matrix to check its accuracy. By applying confusion matrix machine will try to keep its polarity similar to those of others. Then, from polarity of given feedback, machine will set ideal polarity to follow. Since four models we made are divided by four in range of two, threshold of polarity different machine considers off is ±0.5. If past ten interactions' confusion matrix is above Fig. 1, machine will keep its strategy since its strategy is working fine. (Positive does not mean it has high polarity, but it means machine and opponent share similar polarity, and negative means machine and opponent have gap larger than 0.5) (Fig. 2).

N=10	Expected Positive	Expected Negative
Actual Positive	6	2
Actual Negative	1	1

Fig. 2. Confusion matrix that shows past 10 decisions of machine.

Misclassification rate is not bad.

$$\frac{1+2}{10} = 0.3$$

True positive rate is good but True negative rate could be improved.

$$\frac{6}{6+2} = 0.75, \frac{1}{1+1} = 0.5$$

False positive rate also need some improvement. Even tough samples quantity is low

$$\frac{1}{1+1} = 0.5$$

For last, precision and prevalence

$$\frac{6}{6+1} = 0.857, \frac{6+1}{10} = 0.7$$

We can interpret from above simple calculations that machine has understand its opponent's fairly good and will likely to keep its strategy. Then what if confusion matrix of next ten interaction is opposite from above Fig. 1? In this case machine will calculate average polarity of past ten interactions and apply different model with similar polarity.

5 Limitation and Future Works

First, we recognized very large amount of data is required for this model to work. We have not gathered enough data. One of the goals of future work is to gather more data to predict and build better models. In addition, we suggested four models in this paper, but more precise classification will be required. Second, polarity accuracy needs to be checked. Although I believe that Sentic.net and TextBlob calculates good polarity from texts, I believe that cross check with survey gathered from public would improve polarity accuracy. In future, we plan survey on large number of public. For last, we plan to use not only written text but also voice tone recognition and facial expression recognition to increase machine's understanding of people.

Acknowledgement. This research was supported by Korea Institute for Advancement of Technology (KIAT) grant funded by the Korea Government (MOTIE) (N0001436, The Competency Development Program for Industry Specialist).

References

1. ARM Ltd[GB]. https://pages.arm.com/rs/312-SAX-488/images/arm-ai-survey-report.pdf. Accessed 15 Feb 2019
2. Cambria, E., Olsher, D., Rajagopal, D.: SenticNet 3: a common and common-sense knowledge base for cognition-driven sentiment analysis. In: Twenty-Eighth AAAI Conference on Artificial Intelligence (2014)
3. Cambria, E., et al.: SenticNet 5: discovering conceptual primitives for sentiment analysis by means of context embeddings. In: Thirty-Second AAAI Conference on Artificial Intelligence (2018)
4. CNBC Elon Musk: 'Mark my words – A.I is far more dangerous than nukes'. https://www.cnbc.com/2018/03/13/elon-musk-at-sxsw-a-i-is-more-dangerous-than-nuclear-weapons.html. Accessed 15 Feb 2019
5. Colah's blog Understanding LSTM Networks. http://colah.github.io/posts/2015-08-Understanding-LSTMs/. Accessed 15 Feb 2019
6. Dezeen MIT surveys two million people to set out ethical framework for driverless cars. https://www.dezeen.com/2018/10/26/mit-moral-machine-survey-driverless-cars-technology/. Accessed 15 Dec 2019
7. Ethic Sages Common Sense Ethics. https://www.ethicssage.com/2016/11/common-sense-ethics.html. Accessed 15 Feb 2019
8. Forbes Google's Mysterious AI Ethics Board Should Be Transparent Like Axon's. https://www.forbes.com/sites/samshead/2018/04/27/googles-mysterious-ai-ethics-board-should-be-as-transparent-as-axons/#7fb25ccd19d1. Accessed 15 Feb 2019
9. Gilligan, C.: In a Different Voice. Harvard University Press, Cambridge (1982)
10. Kensinger, E.A.: Negative emotion enhances memory accuracy: behavioral and neuroimaging evidence. Curr. Dir. Psychol. Sci. **16**(4), 213–218 (2007)
11. Keras: The Python Deep Learning library. https://keras.io/. Accessed 15 Feb 2019
12. Large Movie Review Data Set, http://ai.stanford.edu/~amaas/data/sentiment/. Accessed 15 Feb 2019
13. Machine learning mastery, Brownlee Jason. https://machinelearningmastery.com/text-generation-lstm-recurrent-neural-networks-python-keras/. Accessed 28 Feb 2019
14. Reddit I'm Bill Gates, co-chair of the Bill & Melinda Gates Foundation. Ask Me Anything. https://www.reddit.com/r/IAmA/comments/5whpqs/im_bill_gates_cochair_of_the_bill_melinda_gates/. Accessed 15 Feb 2019
15. Simola, S.: Ethics of justice and care in corporate crisis management. J. Bus. Ethics **46**(4), 351–361 (2003)
16. taspinar/twitterscraper. https://github.com/taspinar/twitterscraper. Accessed 15 Feb 2019
17. TextBlob Simplified Text Processing. https://textblob.readthedocs.io/en/dev/. Accessed 15 Feb 2019

18. TIME Would You Kill One Person to Save Five? New Research on a Classic Debate. http://healthland.time.com/2011/12/05/would-you-kill-one-person-to-save-five-new-research-on-a-classic-debate/. Accessed 15 Feb 2019
19. Tronto, J.: An ethic of care. Ethics in Community-Based Elder Care, pp. 60–68 (2001)
20. Walker, L.J.: Sex differences in the development of moral reasoning: a critical review. Child Dev. **55**, 677–691 (1984)

How Do Humans Identify Human-Likeness from Online Text-Based Q&A Communication?

Erika Mori[1]([✉]), Yugo Takeuchi[1], and Eiji Tsuchikura[2]

[1] Shizuoka University, Shizuoka, Japan
gs18053@s.inf.shizuoka.ac.jp
[2] Hamamatsu Gakuin University, Hamamatsu, Japan

Abstract. This study aims to clarify a person's impressions during the course of a conversation. In conversations between a person and a chatbot, we evaluated the impressions formed on reading text created by a human and text created by a chatbot. In terms of question/answer relevance, it was found that chatbot-created answers could not relate to or meet the expectations of questions and that human-created answers, while not necessarily meeting the expectations of questions, had relevance.

Keywords: Interaction · Chatbot · Conversation · Human-likeness

1 Introduction

One of the most desired technologies in communication science is "machine conversation." Up until recently, it was only we humans that had the ability to communicate by oral means. However, recent artificial intelligence (AI) technologies such as deep learning are pursuing such oral communication by introducing artificial chat machines called "chatbots" in online text-based Q&A services. This development signals the end of our monopoly in oral communication.

This study focuses on identifying human-likeness when reading an answer written by a human or one by a chatbot in an online text-based Q&A web service. In particular, we search for important factors in the way that people identify human-likeness from text.

2 Online Communication

2.1 Chatbots

A chatbot is an automatic conversation program. A chat, meanwhile, is a mechanism for exchanging mainly text in both directions in real-time communication using the Internet. In addition, a bot (abbreviation for "robot") refers to a program for automating the processing of a specific task. The "Oshiete goo" [1] Japanese text-based Q&A website features a chatbot named "Oshieru" (meaning "advise" or "teach" in Japanese). On this site, the user reads answers created by both humans and this chatbot. Text created by the chatbot may have a natural construction similar to or the same as text created by humans.

© Springer Nature Switzerland AG 2019
M. Kurosu (Ed.): HCII 2019, LNCS 11566, pp. 330–339, 2019.
https://doi.org/10.1007/978-3-030-22646-6_24

2.2   Interaction Based on Linguistic Information

Language is considered to have a function for expressing and conveying something and to perform that conveyance through customary coding [2]. However, expressing and conveying something is not the sole function of language. That is to say, the purpose of language is not only to convey a message with some content but to also reflect intent by producing some effect on the listener by conveying that message. In addition, there is more than one way of conveying the "same" request—a number of variations can be considered. In this way, a variety of linguistic functions exist that cannot be understood solely on the basis of expressing and conveying. Such diverse linguistic functions have been taken up as the problems of speech acts and conversational implicature. The referent of a word is identified by the meaning of that word. If a certain object 'a' is true with respect to all elements making up the meaning of a certain word 'A,' 'a' is determined to be the referent of 'A.' For example, if the elements making up the meaning of the word "chair" are "has a relatively flat surface for sitting, has a backrest, and has legs," and if all of these semantic primitives do not hold true for a certain object, that object is not determined to be a "chair" and the reference fails. This applies not only to words but also to propositional representations. However, in everyday language expressions, there are such things called speech acts that cannot be treated as a set of semantic primitives that challenge the truth of something in the above way. In a speech act, the truth of an utterance is not the problem. Instead, the problem is determining the extent to which the context of an utterance, that is, who uttered what under what conditions, i.e. when, where, with whom, and to whom, fits that utterance [3]. Another issue here is how to go about closing the logical gap between the utterance content and speech act.

2.3   Human-Likeness

Distinguishing between sentences composed by chatbots and those by humans is difficult based on linguistic expressions. However, users are generally able to distinguish such differences when they trace the question and answer sequence [4]. Therefore, perhaps we can identify some factors that help determine which sentences were written by a chatbot and which were written by a human [5].

This study defines such factors as human-likeness to distinguish between sentences by chatbots and those written by humans. We did the following two analyses to determine human-likeness in online text-based Q&A communication.

It is difficult to distinguish between text created by a chatbot and text created by a human based on language expressions. In general, however, the user can distinguish between the two by following a question and answer sequence (Fig. 1). This makes it possible to identify several useful factors for determining whether certain text has been written by a chatbot or a human.

In this study, we define factors such as human-likeness for distinguishing between text created by a chatbot and text written by a human. We performed the two analyses described below for identifying human-likeness in online text-based Q&A communication.

question

元彼のことが忘れられません…。まだその人のことが好きでけどもう復縁はできません。だからわすれたいのですがどうしても忘れられません。どうしたらいいですか？

: I can not forget ex-boyfriend. I still like that person, but I can not back together anymore. So, I want to forget, but I can not forget. What should I do?

Answer: Human

忘れる必要もないと思いますよ。なるようになります。嫌なことやショックだったことは忘れることができたらどんなにいいでしょうね。そんなことができたらもう少しぐらい人間気楽に生きていけるだろうと思います。

: There is no need to forget. How wonderful it would be if you could forget something disgusting or shocking. If I could do that, I could live a little easier.

Answer: Chatbot

まずお互い冷静になるため、少しの期間、接触を避けてみてはいかがでしょうか。今は何かアクションを起こしても、マイナスにしかならないと思います。いつか巡ってくるかもしれないチャンスに期待しましょう。あなたが幸せになれるよう祈ってます。

: Please remember yourself, other. Let's not meet for a while. Let's wait for the opportunity. good luck.

Fig. 1. Posted question and answers

3   Method

3.1   Preliminary Experiment: Distinguishing Chatbot-Created and Human-Created Text

In this experiment, we conducted a distinguishing test based on the Turing test. We examined whether the user could correctly identify text created by a chatbot and text created by a human.

3.2   Data Collection

Target: Questions answered by "Oshieru" (chatbot) under the service category of dating and relationship advice on the "Oshiete goo" community site and all answers to questions.

Period: October 23, 2016 to October 29, 2016.

Procedure: Data consisting of questions answered by the "Oshiete goo" chatbot under the category of dating and relationship advice plus chatbot and user answers for the seven-day period from October 23, 2016 to October 29, 2016 were recorded and analyzed.

Evaluation Items: The symbols ○ and × are used to denote text identified as a chatbot answer and text identified as a human answer, respectively.

3.3 Configuration of Questionnaire

Data Extraction Method: The collected data consisted of 151 questions and 586 answers. From this data, we deleted questions having only chatbot answers and factors that identify a chatbot answer such as posting time, name, quotes of famous people, and self-introductions. We also deleted the same types of factors from human (user) answers. We then prepared a questionnaire from the data with no chatbot-identifying factors by randomly extracting data and performed a preliminary survey using this questionnaire. On the basis of this preliminary survey, we received comments to the effect that too many characters in an answer or too many answers to the same question would be a burden to respondents, so we took a second look at the number of characters in an answer and the number of answers to a question. Specifically, we calculated the average number of characters in 586 answers and deleted questions with answers of 414 or more characters from the data. Furthermore, to ease the burden on respondents and improve readability, we deleted questions with more than 4 or more answers. Finally, for our main survey, we created a questionnaire from this data in which chatbot-identifying factors and respondent-burdening factors had been deleted (Figs. 2 and 3).

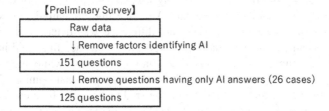

Fig. 2. Extracting method (Preliminary survey)

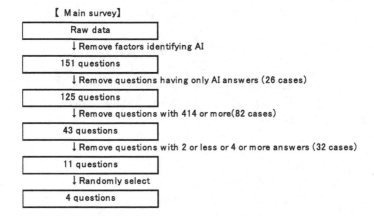

Fig. 3. Extracting method (Main survey)

3.4   Questionnaire-Based Survey

Survey Instruments: We created and used 2 questionnaires, one for the preliminary survey and the other for the main survey. We prepared and numbered 30 copies of each questionnaire.

Respondents: 15 male and 15 female university students were asked to fill out the questionnaires created by the surveyor. Interviews were subsequently conducted.

Period: January 24, 2017 to January 30, 2017.

Procedure: For both the preliminary survey and main survey, the surveyor requested the survey and distributed the questionnaire after which the survey was conducted. Six university students were asked to respond to the preliminary survey, which was conducted before the main survey. Thirty university students other than those who participated in the preliminary survey were asked to respond to the main survey, which was conducted using the corresponding questionnaire.

3.5   Results and Discussion

The percentage of correct assessment for answers written by a human and by the chatbot are given in Table 1. In either case, correct assessment was 85% or better indicating that a human could distinguish to some extent the difference between a human writer and a chatbot.

We next took up the question as to why text created by a chatbot could be distinguished from text created by a human. After the questionnaire-based survey, we conducted informal interviews on how this difference was determined. From these interviews, it became clear that chatbot answers left a "businesslike, cold impression" and featured "questions and answers that don't match up," while human answers featured "emoji and exclamation points (!)" and "many personal opinions."

Based on the above findings, we then compared text created by a chatbot and text created by a human by having subjects read text of each type and analyzing the impressions left by each.

Table 1. Analysis 1 result

		Assessment "Who write the answer?"	
		Human	Chatbot
Actual writer	Human	89.7% (correct)	10.3% (wrong)
	Chatbot	15.0% (wrong)	85.0% (correct)

3.6   Comparison of Human-Created Text and Chatbot-Created Text

The results of the preliminary experiment revealed that chatbot-created text could be distinguished from human-created text. They showed, in particular, that chatbot-created text left negative impressions such as "businesslike and cold" and "questions and answers that don't match up" and that these impressions were factors in distinguishing chatbot-created text from human-created text.

Next, we clarified the differences in impressions by comparing chatbot-created text and human-created text.

In this study, we evaluated chatbot-created text and human-created text using a set of evaluation items. We also clarified the types of features possessed by each of these two types of text and searched out how these two types of text differ.

3.7   Collection of Chatbot and Human Configured Text

Target: Questions answered by AI "Oshieru" under the service category of dating and relationship advice on the "Oshiete goo" community site and all answers to questions.

Period: October 23, 2016 to October 29, 2016.

Procedure: To identify human-likeness, data consisting of questions answered by the "Oshiete goo" chatbot under the category of dating and relationship advice plus chatbot and user answers for the seven-day period from October 23, 2016 to October 29, 2016 were recorded and analyzed.

Data Extraction Method: The collected data consisted of 151 questions and 586 answers. From this data, we deleted questions having only chatbot answers and factors that identify a chatbot answer such as posting time, name, quotes of famous people, and self-introductions. We also deleted the same types of items from human (user) answers. Next, from within the 151 questions, we deleted questions having only chatbot answers and questions that involve more than one conversational exchange between the inquirer and responder to reduce the number of data items.

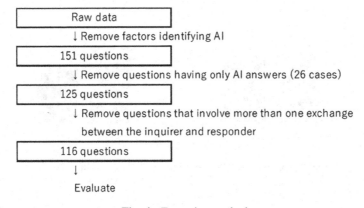

Fig. 4. Extracting method

4   Results and Discussion

4.1   Classification of Content Expected by Inquirer in Answer

To investigate the relation between questions and answers, we first evaluated the content expected by inquirers in answers. The target of this analysis was 116 questions from the collected data. On tabulating the content expected by inquirers in answers, the most applicable items were found to be "agreement and affirmation with inquirer" followed by "advise" and "objective opinion." (Table 2).

Table 2. Tabulated results of content expected by inquirer in answer

Item	Number of replies	Average
Empathy	13	11.0%
Objective opinion	25	21.6%
Critical opinion	3	2.6%
Clear answer to question content	17	14.7%
Agreement and affirmation with question content	5	4.3%
Agreement and affirmation with inquirer	27	23.3%
Advice	26	22.4%
Other	0	0.0%

4.2   Fitness of Answer to Content of Question

We investigated the relationship between the attributes of the answer (human, chatbot) given to a question and the content expected by the inquirer in the answer. We found that more answers agreed with the expectations of the inquirer in the case of human answers and that more answers did not agree with the expectations of the inquirer in the case of chatbot answers (Fig. 5).

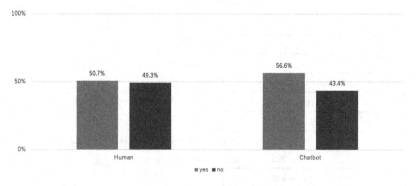

Fig. 5. Answer attributes and fitness of answer to question

4.3   Content of Answers

To investigate relevance between questions and answers, we evaluated the content of answers that did not agree with the expectations of the inquirer. The target of this analysis was 116 questions from the collected data. On tabulating the content expected by inquirers in answers, the most applicable items were found to be "agreement and affirmation with inquirer" followed by "advise" and "objective opinion." (Tables 3 and 4).

Table 3. Tabulated results of content returned by responder (human)

Item	n = 172	
	Number of replies	Average
Empathy	8	5.0%
Objective opinion	74	43.0%
Critical opinion	20	11.6%
Clear answer to question content	8	4.7%
Agreement and affirmation with question content	1	0.6%
Agreement and affirmation with inquirer	5	2.9%
Advice	42	24.4%
Other	14	8.1%

Table 4. Tabulated results of content returned by responder (chatbot)

Item	n = 86	
	Number of replies	Average
Empathy	1	1.2%
Objective opinion	6	7.0%
Critical opinion	0	0.0%
Clear answer to question content	3	3.5%
Agreement and affirmation with question content	0	0.0%
Agreement and affirmation with inquirer	0	0.0%
Advice	71	82.6%
Other	5	5.8%

4.4   Relevance Between Questions and Answers

Relevance between the question and an answer not agreeing with the expectations of the inquirer occurred much more frequently in the case of human answers and no relevance between the question and an answer not agreeing with the expectations of the inquirer occurred more often in the case of chatbot answers (Fig. 6).

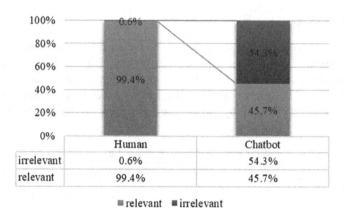

Fig. 6. Relevance between questions and answers

4.5 Trends in Answer Content

Overall trends in answer content are summarized in Fig. 4. Similar trends were observed in both human and chatbot answers in the case of "quality," "manners," and "quantity." In the case of quality, we attribute this to a problem in the conditions established for this experiment in which the data targeted for analysis concerned dating

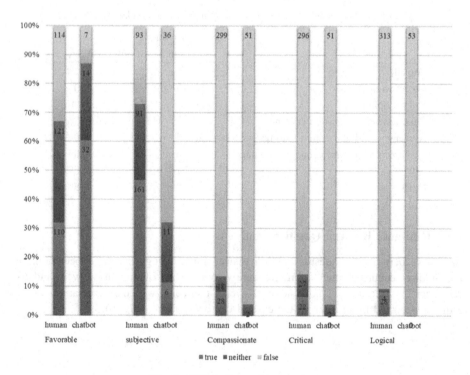

Fig. 7. Distributions of impressions

and relationship advice. With respect to appropriate grammar, amount of text, etc. labeled as "manners" and "quantity," it was judged that no differences exist between chatbot and human answers.

On the other hand, there were differences between human and chatbot answers in the case of "emotion" and "attitude." For a human answer, we found that its emotional aspects varied depending on whether it met the expectations of the question, while for a chatbot answer, we found that, in general, a single (favorite) pattern occurred frequently regardless of whether it met the expectations of the question.

Based on the results, we consider that interpreting the content of a question and degree of adaptability are important in establishing a conversation (Fig. 7).

5 Conclusion

The purpose of this study was to clarify a person's impressions of the other party when engaged in a conversation. Targeting a conversation between a person and a chatbot, we compared impressions between human-created text and chatbot-created text. In terms of relevance, we found that chatbot-created answers could not relate to or meet the expectations of questions and that human-created answers, while not necessarily meeting the expectations of questions, had relevance. These findings suggest that understanding what the other person wants is important in establishing a conversation and that picking up on intent and context is necessary. Furthermore, in terms of overall trends in the content of answers, we found that chatbot answers satisfy criteria such as text quantity and manners but do not reflect aspects such as emotion and attitude.

In human-chatbot conversations, these findings suggest that it is difficult for a chatbot to express elements such as an objective attitude and emotional opinion in conversational exchanges.

References

1. [oshiete! goo] https://oshiete.goo.ne.jp/ai/. Accessed 31 Jan 2019
2. Dunbar, R., Dunbar, R.I.M.: Grooming, Gossip, and the Evolution of Language. Harvard University Press, Cambridge (1998)
3. Grice, H.P.: Studies in the Way of Words. Harvard University Press, Cambridge (1991)
4. Weizenbaum, J.: ELIZA—a computer program for the study of natural language communication between man and machine. Commun. ACM 9(1), 36–45 (1966)
5. Turing, A.M.: Computing machinery and intelligence. In: Epstein, R., Roberts, G., Beber, G. (eds.) Parsing the Turing Test, pp. 23–65. Springer, Dordrecht (2009). https://doi.org/10. 1007/978-1-4020-6710-5_3

Influence of Presence of Operator of Humanoid Robot on Personal Space

Akihiro Tatsumi[✉] and Masashi Okubo

Doshisha University, 1-3 Tatara-Miyakodani,
Kyotanabe, Kyoto 610-0321, Japan
ttmakihiro@gmail.com, mokubo@mail.doshisha.ac.jp

Abstract. In recent years, opportunities for communication between humanoid robots and people are increasing. In addition, opportunities to communicate with robots autonomously operating without being manipulated by people are increasing. An important aspect of smooth communication between humanoid robots and people is personal space. In other words, it is necessary for the robot to communicate at a distance in consideration of a person's personal space. Therefore, in this research, we focus on presence or absence of operator of the humanoid robot and investigate the influence of personal space toward the robot. Also we investigate how the person's communication skill and sensory evaluation toward the robot affect personal space. As a result of the experiment, there is no significant difference in presence or absence of the operator in the personal space toward the robot. In addition, regardless of presence or absence of the operator, it is shown that the person who feels discomfort to the robot have a larger personal space. From these results, it becomes clear that there is a high possibility that the sensory evaluation of each individual toward the robot has a greater influence on personal space than the presence or absence of the operator.

Keywords: Human-robot interaction · Operator · Non-verbal information · Personal space · Sensory evaluation

1 Introduction

In recent years, as robots are used more and more in various situations around us, people interact with humanoid robots on a more frequent basis, and the number of autonomously functioning robots not controlled by humans is increasing as well. Along with this popularization, researchers have investigated the effects of humanoid robots' autonomy on people's feelings toward robots. Kanda et al. reported that some participants behaved similarly when communicating with autonomously functioning robots to how they would with another person [1]. Additionally, it has also been reported that robots are recognized as having the same social standing as people when there is an operator alongside the robot [2].

In face-to-face communication, one key element for establishing smooth communication is personal space. Personal space is defined as the spatial area surrounding an individual's body, and it is the boundary at which that individual does not wish other people to approach any further. Shibuya's research shows that personal space between

M. Kurosu (Ed.): HCII 2019, LNCS 11566, pp. 340–357, 2019.
https://doi.org/10.1007/978-3-030-22646-6_25

those familiar with each other is smaller than that between strangers, and it is also smaller among those of the same gender versus those of the opposite gender [3]. It is also said that people carry out smooth communication by subconsciously changing their personal space. From this point of view, it is clear that robots must communicate with humans from a distance that takes into account humans' personal space. However, the influence of humanoid robots' autonomy on humans' personal space when with robots has not been investigated.

This research therefore focuses on the presence or absence of a human operator for the humanoid robot in terms of autonomy and investigates the influences on human's personal space toward the robot. Moreover, we also investigate the relationship between personal space and people's communication skills/sensory evaluation toward the robot.

2   Related Research and Research Objective

2.1   Related Research About Personal Space

Many researches have been conducted on personal space among humans, and such researches are still conducted today. There are many definitions for personal space, but in general, personal space refers to the spatial area surrounding an individual's body [3]. People communicate comfortably by subconsciously changing their personal space. In addition, Hall classifies personal space into four zones based on how people change their personal space depending on their relationship with their companion: intimate space, personal space, social space, and public space [4]. Also, according to Shibuya's research, introverts have smaller personal space than extroverts [3]. Moreover, personal space changes with the gender of one's companion, with personal space between those of the same gender smaller than those of the opposite gender.

The main methods of measuring personal space include the stop-distance method, the unobtrusive observation method, the seat selection method, the felt board method, and the paper and pencil method. In the stop-distance method, a person approaches the participant who stops the approaching person when he/she feels uncomfortable or does not wish to be approached any further, and the space between the participant and the approaching person at this point is measured as personal space. This method is regarded as the most reliable way of measuring personal space [5].

While research has been conducted on personal space between people, researches on personal space between people and robots have also been conducted. Related researches show that people's personal space with robots is an elliptical shape with the further end in the front, the same shape it is among two people [6], and it is shown to be smaller than it is among two people [7].

A person's sense of "self" includes his or her body, but it also extends to things he or she refers to with "my" or "mine" (clothes, family, house, etc.) [8]. Similarly, Ariga demonstrates that an individual's personal space extends to the space surrounding his or her possessions ("things") [9]. This observation suggests that the gender and characteristics of a robot operator may impact a person's personal space with a robot.

2.2   Related Research About Robot Autonomy

Researchers have also investigated the influence that robots' autonomy has on people's feelings toward robots. Fujita suggests that autonomously functioning robots may be thought of as intermediate entities between machines and humans [10]. Kanda et al. report that some participants behaved similarly when communicating with autonomously functioning humanoid robots to how they would with another person [1]. It has also been reported that robots are regarded as being similar social entities as people by virtue of having operators [2].

2.3   Research Objective

This research focused on the presence or absence of an operator of the robot, with regard to autonomy, and used the stop-distance method to evaluate the influences that the presence of humanoid robot's operator has on personal space. In addition, personal space may also change with people's communication skill and sensory evaluation of the robot. For this reason, we also evaluate the relationship these factors have with personal space.

3   Verification Experiment

3.1   Experiment Objective

In this experiment, we aimed to reveal what influences the presence of humanoid robot's operator has on personal space through quantitative and qualitative evaluations, conducting sensory evaluation experiments with the participants.

3.2   Experimental Method

In this experiment, we measure personal space using the stop-distance method by having the robot approach the participant. More specifically, the participant is made to stop the approaching robot when they feel they do not want it to approach any further, and the distance between the participant and the robot at this point is measured as personal space distance. In this experiment, personal space is regarded as the horizontal distance between the participant's head and the tip of the robot's feet. The distance between the participant and the robot is set to 350 cm at the start of the experiment. Meccanoid G15KS constructed by the company Spin Master is used as the robot. Figure 1 shows the appearance and details of the robot used in the experiment. Meccanoid G15KS can be operated remotely using an application to control actions such as moving forward and stopping.

 Personal space is measured in three conditions: when the robot is not controlled by an operator and moved automatically (the no operator condition), when the robot is operated by a male (the male operator condition), and when the robot is operated by a female (the female operator condition). We enlist the cooperation of one male student and one female student from the Doshisha University Applied Media Information Laboratory to serve as the robot operators.

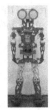

Height	110cm
Width	40cm
Depth	15cm
Weight	5kg
Speed	20cm/s

Fig. 1. Appearance and specification of robot used in experiment.

- ## No Operator Condition

The Wizard of Oz method is used when instructing the participant [11]. In this experiment, the participant is told that the robot is capable of voice recognition and will be moving when told "start" and will come to a stop when told "stop." In actuality, an operator stands by in a location unseen by the participant and will start and stop the robot in sync with the participant's voice commands. Figure 2 shows the experimental setup and scene of the no operator condition.

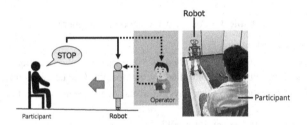

Fig. 2. Experimental setup and experimental scene (no operator condition).

- ## Male/Female Operator Condition

The participant is instructed that the operator will maneuver the robot according to the participant's voice commands; when the participant say "start," the operator will move the robot forward, and when the participant say "stop," the operator will stop the robot. In this condition, there is an operator actually controlling the robot. Because a difference in

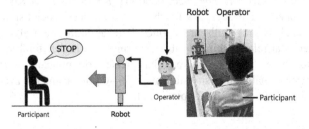

Fig. 3. Experimental setup and experimental scene (male operator condition and female operator condition).

clothing between the male and female operators may impact the experimental results, both the male and female operators are made to wear a white lab coat. Figure 3 shows the experimental setup and scene of the male operator and female operator conditions.

3.3 Questionnaires

In this experiment, participants answer a pre-experiment questionnaire, a post-measurement questionnaire, and a post-experiment questionnaire.

In the pre-experiment questionnaire, participants answer whether they are familiar with the male or female operators and whether they had participated in a personal space measurement experiment with a robot that we conducted.

In the post-measurement questionnaire, participants answer questions regarding their feelings toward the robot and whether they felt that the robot moved by voice recognition in order to evaluate whether the instructions were successful. Table 1 shows the fields of the post-measurement questionnaire. Note that Q1 through Q7 are evaluated on a scale of 1 through 7, with 1 meaning strongly disagree and 7 meaning strongly agree. Q8 is answered on a scale of 1 through 7, with 1 meaning very masculine and 7 meaning very feminine.

Table 1. Post-measurement questionnaire.

#	Overview of questions
Q1	Did you feel the robot was controlled by voice operation? (no operator)
	Did you feel the robot was controlled by the operator? (male and female operator)
Q2	Did you feel that the robot was physical avatar of the operator? (male and female operator)
Q3	Did you feel humanness on the robot?
Q4	Did you feel autonomy in the robot?
Q5	Did you feel a sense of reliability for the robot?
Q6	Did you feel close to the robot?
Q7	Did you feel discomfort to the robot?
Q8	Did you feel masculine/feminine on the robot?

In the post-experiment questionnaire, participants answer a KiSS-18 and questions regarding their familiarity with the Meccanoid G15KS. KiSS-18 is Kikuchi's 18-field questionnaire created to measure how much one has mastered social skills required for young people [12]. Social skills are defined here as skills helpful in carrying out smooth interpersonal relationships. In this experiment, a higher total score on the 18 questions demonstrates that the participant has greater communication skills. Note that the average score for male university students is 56.40 points, and the average score for female university students is 58.35 points [12].

3.4   Experimental Procedure

The experiment is conducted with undergraduate and graduate students of Doshisha University, with 13 males and 13 females for a total of 26 participants. One male and one female participants answer Q1 (Did you feel the robot was controlled by voice operation?/Did you feel the robot was controlled by the operator?) of the post-measurement questionnaire with low scores of 1 or 2. For this reason, it is likely that these participants interpret the instructions differently from other participants, and therefore they are excluded from the experiment results analysis.

Figure 4 shows the experimental procedure. In the pre-briefing, the experimenter explains the content of the experiment to the participant in detail and gains their consent to have them answer questionnaires and to release the results in a manner that will not reveal their identities. After the pre-briefing, the participant answers a pre-experiment questionnaire.

Before measuring personal space with the different conditions, we conducted two practice rounds for the purpose of teaching the participant how personal space is measured and to show that the robot is operated by voice recognition (in the no operator condition) or that the robot is controlled by an operator (in the male/female operator conditions). Note that, to counteract any order effect, we change the measuring order of the three conditions (no operator, male operator, and female operator conditions) for each participant. After the practice rounds, we conduct the personal space measurements. Also note that, as the stop-distance method is used for measuring, the participant is instructed to say "stop" when they felt uncomfortable and does not want the robot to approach any further. The participant is also instructed to sit with his/her back touching the chair and to avoid moving his/her head as much as possible during the measuring process to avoid any changes to personal space due to the participant's head moving. After personal space is measured, the participant answers a post-measurement questionnaire.

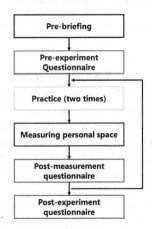

Fig. 4. Experimental procedure.

At the end of the experiment, the participant answers a post-experiment questionnaire.

4   Experimental Results

4.1   Results of All Participants

- **Results of Personal Space Distance**

The t-test is applied for the results of the personal space distance statistically. The Bonferroni correction is applied to adjust p-values. Figure 5 shows the average and standard deviation of personal space distance for each time measurements are taken for all participants. There is a tendency for the personal space distance to grow the more measurements are taken, and a statistically significant trend is observed between the first measurement and the third. Lauckner et al. indicated that the minimum distance appeared decrease with the repetition [7]. However, this tendency is not seen in this experiment. Many participants reported that they felt negative feelings toward the robot's appearance. These results suggest that the more measurements are taken, the more participants feel negatively toward the robot, leading to greater personal space distances.

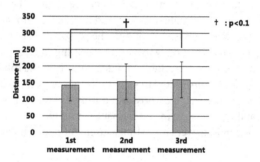

Fig. 5. Average and standard deviation of personal space distance for measurement orders (all participants).

Figure 6 shows the average and standard deviation of personal space distances of all participants for each condition. No noteworthy differences between the conditions are present, and no statistically significant differences are observed. Some participants reported in the no operator condition in which they were told that the robot stopped via voice recognition that they did not feel particularly uncomfortable with the robot approaching them because they could control the robot themselves. However, other participants reported that they felt uncertain that the robot would truly stop via voice recognition. Additionally, in the male/female operator conditions in which participants were told an operator would stop the robot, some participants reported that they felt comfortable with the fact that the robot did not stop automatically and was controlled by a person, while other participants felt uncertain that the operator was controlling the robot correctly. These results suggest that personal space distances with robots does not consistently decrease with a certain condition for all participants and that the influence the presence or absence of an operator has on personal space distances may differ with each individual.

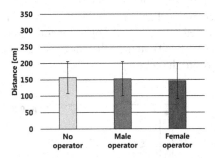

Fig. 6. Average and standard deviation of personal space distance for each condition (all participants).

Figure 7 shows the average and standard deviation of personal space distances of participants, categorized by their scores on Q7 of the post-measurement questionnaire (Did you feel discomfort to the robot?). Note that there is high evaluation value group of discomfort with a score of 5 or higher and a low evaluation value group of discomfort with a score of 3 or lower. The high evaluation value group of discomfort has a greater personal space distance than the low evaluation value group of discomfort and there is a statistically significant difference between them. These results show that personal space distances increase when participants feel uncomfortable with the robot, regardless of the presence or absence of an operator.

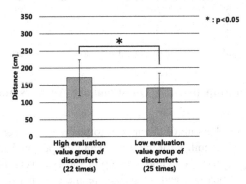

Fig. 7. Average and standard deviation of personal space distance categorized by the evaluation value of questionnaire Q7 after measurement.

• Results of Questionnaire

The Wilcoxon signed-rank test is applied for results of all questionnaires statistically. The Bon-ferroni correction is applied to adjust p-values. Figure 8 shows the post-measurement questionnaire results for all of the participants. For Q4 (Did you feel autonomy in the robot?), the no operator condition scores higher than the male/female operator conditions and there is a statistically significant difference between them. For Q5 (Did you feel a sense of reliability for the robot?), the male/female operator conditions score lower levels of discomfort than the no operator condition, and a statistically significant difference is observed between the no operator condition and the female operator condition. The results of Q5 and Q7 suggest that the presence of an operator may lead to more positive feelings toward the robot.

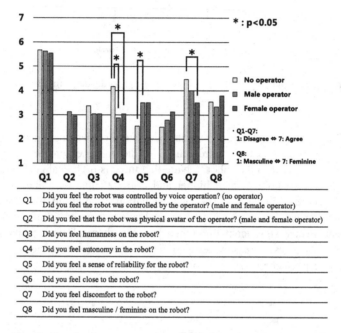

Q1	Did you feel the robot was controlled by voice operation? (no operator) Did you feel the robot was controlled by the operator? (male and female operator)
Q2	Did you feel that the robot was physical avatar of the operator? (male and female operator)
Q3	Did you feel humanness on the robot?
Q4	Did you feel autonomy in the robot?
Q5	Did you feel a sense of reliability for the robot?
Q6	Did you feel close to the robot?
Q7	Did you feel discomfort to the robot?
Q8	Did you feel masculine / feminine on the robot?

Fig. 8. Result of post-measurement questionnaire (all participants).

- **Results of Relationship Between Questionnaire Answers and Personal Space Distance**

Figure 9 shows a scatter diagram of the answer to post-measurement questionnaire Q5 (Did you feel a sense of reliability for the robot?) and the personal space distance of all participants for the no operator condition. The plot shows a weak negative correlation between Q5 of the post-measurement questionnaire and personal space distance for the no operator condition. More specifically, these results demonstrate a relationship in which those who feel comfortable with an operator-less robot have shorter personal space distances. Below we will focus on the correlations between the post-measurement questionnaire answers and personal space distance for each condition.

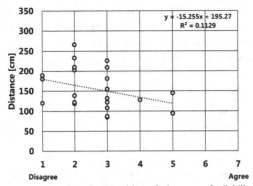

Fig. 9. Scatter diagram of "answer to post-measurement questionnaire Q5" and "personal space distance" for no operator condition (all participants).

Table 2 shows the correlation between each post-measurement questionnaire answer and personal space distance for all participants. The symbol ○ denotes a weak correlation ($R < -0.2$, $R > 0.2$), the symbol ◎ denotes a moderate correlation ($R < -0.4$, $R > 0.4$), and the symbol ☆ denotes a strong correlation ($R < -0.7$, $R > 0.7$). Red indicates a positive correlation, while blue indicates a negative one. The total of the score of Q5, the score of Q6, and the reverse score of Q7 are defined as the degree of positive feelings toward the robot, and we use this to test the relationship between positive feelings and personal space distances. In this experiment, a relationship is observed in which the more positive the feelings toward the robot, the smaller the personal space distance, regardless of the presence or absence of an operator. In addition, the same tendency is observed for the no operator and male operator conditions.

Table 2. Correlation between each answer of post-measurement questionnaire and personal space distance (all participants).

	No operator	Male operator	Female operator	All conditions
Q1: Controlled by voice operation (no operator) Controlled by the operator (male and female operator)				
Q2: Physical avatar of the operator (male and female operator)				
Q3: Humanness on the robot				
Q4: Autonomy in the robot				
Q5: Sense of reliability for the robot	○			
Q6: Close to the robot	○			
Q7: Discomfort to the robot			○	
Q8: Masculine / Feminine to the robot				
Q5+Q6+Q7*: Positive impression to the robot	○	○		○

Q1~Q7   1: Disagree ⇔ 7: Agree |Positive correlation| ○: R<-0.2, R>0.2 (Weak correlation)
Q8   1: Masculine ⇔ 7: Feminine |Negative correlation| ◎: R<-0.4, R>0.4 (Moderate correlation)
☆: R<-0.7, R>0.7 (Strong correlation)

Next, Fig. 10 shows a scatter diagram of the KiSS-18 score and personal space distance in the no operator condition for all participants. No correlation is observed between communication skill and personal space distance. Moreover, no correlation is observed between KiSS-18 score and personal space distance in the male/female operator conditions.

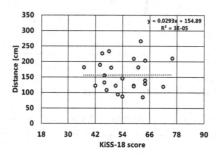

Fig. 10. Scatter diagram of "KiSS-18 score" and "personal space distance" for no operator condition (all participants).

4.2　Results Categorized by Participant Gender

- **Results of Personal Space Distance**

Figure 11 shows the average and standard deviation of personal space distance of all conditions for participants, categorized by gender. Female participants display a smaller personal space distance than male participants, and a statistically significant difference is present. Likewise, Shibuya's research results show that women have smaller personal spaces with people [3]. Other prior research results also show similar tendencies in which women have smaller personal spaces with robots [13].

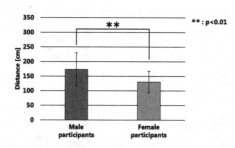

Fig. 11. Average and standard deviation of personal space distance for all conditions (male and female participants).

Figure 12 shows the average and standard deviation of personal space distance for each time measurement taken for the participants, categorized by gender. Both male and female participants show a tendency for greater personal space distances each time measurements are re-taken. In addition, female participants display shorter personal space distances than male participants each time measurements are taken, showing statistically significant differences.

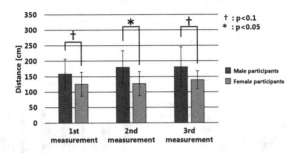

Fig. 12. Average and standard deviation of personal space distance for measurement orders (male and female participants).

Figure 13 shows the average and standard deviation of personal space distance for each condition for participants, categorized by gender. Female participants display shorter personal space distances than male participants for every condition and show statistically significant differences. Additionally, in the no operator and the male operator conditions, a statistically significant difference is observed between the average personal space distances of male participants and female participants with a 5% level of significance. On the other hand, in the female operator condition, a statistically significant difference of a 1% level of significance is observed between the average personal space distances of male participants and female participants.

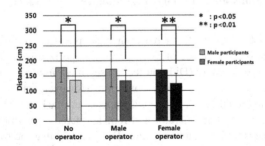

Fig. 13. Average and standard deviation of personal space distance for each condition (male and female participants).

- **Results of Questionnaire**

Figure 14 shows the answer results from the post-measurement questionnaire of the participants, categorized by gender. In Q4 of the post-measurement questionnaire (Did you feel autonomy in the robot?), male participants sense more autonomy within the no operator condition than the female operator condition, and there is a statistically significant trend. In sensory evaluation to the robot for each condition, there are no notable differences between male participants and female participants.

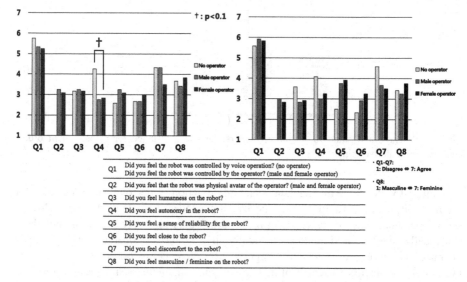

Fig. 14. Result of post-measurement questionnaire (left: male participants, right: female participants).

- **Results of Relationship Between Questionnaire Answers and Personal Space Distance**

Table 3 shows a list of correlations between each post-measurement questionnaire answer and personal space distance of participants, categorized by gender. In Q8 of the post-measurement questionnaire (Did you feel masculine/feminine on the robot?), male participants show no correlations in any condition. However, female participants display a relationship in which personal space distances became shorter the more they feel the robot as feminine in the no operator and female operator conditions. Additionally, in Q2 of the post-measurement questionnaire (Did you feel that the robot was physical avatar of the operator?), female participants display a relationship in which personal space distances become shorter the more they feel the robot is physical avatar of the operator in the female operator condition. These results possibly suggest that in the female operator condition, if female participants feel that the robot is physical avatar of the female operator, they feel the robot is of the same gender, therefore resulting in smaller personal space distances.

Table 3. Correlation between each answer of post-measurement questionnaire and personal space distance (upper: male participants, lower: female participants).

Male participants

	No operator	Male operator	Female operator	All conditions
Q1: Controlled by voice operation (no operator) / Controlled by the operator (male and female operator)	O			
Q2: Physical avatar of the operator (male and female operator)		O		O
Q3: Humanness on the robot	O			
Q4: Autonomy in the robot	O			
Q5: Sense of reliability for the robot	O		O	O
Q6: Close to the robot	O	O		O
Q7: Discomfort to the robot		O		O
Q8: Masculine / Feminine to the robot				
Q5+Q6+Q7*: Positive impression to the robot	O	O		O

Female participants

	No operator	Male operator	Female operator	All conditions
Q1: Controlled by voice operation (no operator) / Controlled by the operator (male and female operator)				
Q2: Physical avatar of the operator (male and female operator)		O	O	O
Q3: Humanness on the robot				
Q4: Autonomy in the robot		O		
Q5: Sense of reliability for the robot	O	O		
Q6: Close to the robot	O	O		
Q7: Discomfort to the robot				
Q8: Masculine / Feminine to the robot	O		O	O
Q5+Q6+Q7*: Positive impression to the robot	O			

Q1~Q7   1: Disagree ⟷ 7: Agree
Q8   1: Masculine ⟷ 7: Feminine

Positive correlation
Negative correlation

O: R<-0.2, R>0.2 (Weak correlation)
◉: R<-0.4, R>0.4 (Moderate correlation)
☆: R<-0.7, R>0.7 (Strong correlation)

Table 4 shows a list of correlations between KiSS-18 score and personal space distance for each condition, categorized by gender. Male participants show no relationship between KiSS-18 score and personal space distance. Female participants, however, show a weak negative correlation between KiSS-18 score and personal space distance in the no operator condition. In other words, a relationship is observed in which higher communication skill leads to shorter personal space distance.

Table 4. Correlation between KiSS-18 score and personal space distance for each condition (male and female participants).

	No operator	Male operator	Female operator
Male participants			
Female participants	O		

Positive correlation
Negative correlation

O: R<-0.2, R>0.2 (Weak correlation)
◉: R<-0.4, R>0.4 (Moderate correlation)
☆: R<-0.7, R>0.7 (Strong correlation)

4.3   Results Categorized by Participants' Communication Skills

Next, we test the results by categorizing participants by their KiSS-18 scores. In this experiment, male participants who score higher than the male university student average of 56.40 points and female participants who score higher than the female university student average of 58.35 points are categorized into the high score group of KiSS-18; those who score lower are categorized into the low score group of KiSS-18. Note that after this categorizing, the high score group of KiSS-18 consists of 11 people, while the low score group of KiSS-18 consists of 13 people.

- **Results of Personal Space Distance**

Figure 15 shows average and standard deviation of personal space distance for all conditions categorized by KiSS-18 score. While the low score group of KiSS-18 display shorter personal space distances than the high score group of KiSS-18, no statistically significant difference is present.

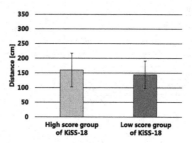

Fig. 15. Average and standard deviation of personal space distance for all conditions (high and low score group of KiSS-18).

Figure 16 shows average and standard deviation of personal space distance for each condition, categorized by KiSS-18 score. There are no notable differences between each condition, and no statistically significant differences are observed. No statistically significant differences are observed between the high score group of KiSS-18 and the low score group of KiSS-18 either.

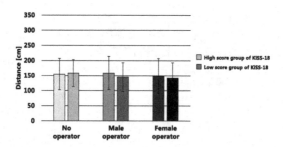

Fig. 16. Average and standard deviation of personal space distance for each condition (high and low score group of KiSS-18).

In addition, no notable differences or statistically significant differences are observed between the high score group of KiSS-18 and the low score group of KiSS-18 for average distance measurements, categorized by KiSS-18 score.

• Results of Questionnaire

In post-measurement questionnaire answer results, categorized by KiSS-18 scores, no statistically significant differences are observed between the high score group of KiSS-18 and the low score group of KiSS-18 or between conditions.

• Results of Relationship Between Questionnaire Answers and Personal Space Distance

Table 5 shows a list of correlations between post-measurement questionnaire answer and personal space distance, categorized by KiSS-18 scores. The low score group of KiSS-18 shows more strong positive correlations than the high score group of KiSS-18.

Table 5. Correlation between each answer of post-measurement questionnaire and personal space distance (upper: high score group of KiSS-18, lower: low score group of KiSS-18).

Q1~Q7 1: Disagree ⇔ 7: Agree
Q8   1: Masculine ⇔ 7: Feminine

Positive correlation
Negative correlation

○: R<-0.2, R>0.2 (Weak correlation)
◉: R<-0.4, R>0.4 (Moderate correlation)
☆: R<-0.7, R>0.7 (Strong correlation)

Table 6 shows a list of correlations between KiSS-18 score and personal space distance for each condition, categorized by KiSS-18 scores. The low score group of KiSS-18 shows moderate negative and weak negative correlations between KiSS-18 score and personal space distance in the no operator and female operator conditions.

These results indicate that a relationship is observed in the low score group of KiSS-18 in which greater communication skill leads to shorter personal space distance. The high score group of KiSS-18, on the other hand, shows a weak positive correlation between KiSS-18 score and personal space distance in the female operator condition.

Table 6. Correlation between KiSS-18 score and personal space distance for each condition (high and low score group of KiSS-18).

	No operator	Male operator	Female operator
High score group of KiSS-18			○
Low score group of KiSS-18	◉		○

Positive correlation	○: R<-0.2, R>0.2 (Weak correlation)
Negative correlation	◉: R<-0.4, R>0.4 (Moderate correlation)
	☆: R<-0.7, R>0.7 (Strong correlation)

5   Conclusion

In this study, we aim to investigate the influences the presence and absence an operator of a humanoid robot has on personal space by measuring personal space in three conditions: a no operator condition, a male operator condition, and a female operator condition. The results of the experiment show no notable differences of average personal space distances among the conditions, with no statistically significant differences. These results suggest that personal space distances with robots do not consistently decrease with a certain condition for all participants, and that the influence the presence or absence of an operator has on personal space distances with the robot may differ with each individual. However, personal space distances increase for those who feel uncomfortable with the robot, regardless of the presence or absence of an operator. Moreover, a certain correlation is observed between personal space distance and participant's communication skill and sensory evaluation to the robot, and it is especially clear that positive feelings toward the robot have great influence. In addition, many participants commented that they were more aware of the robot's presence and appearance than the presence of the operator. Yamaoka et al. also report that people's behavior toward a robot does not change with the presence or absence of an operator when they are more aware of the robot than the operator [14]. In other words, factors having to do with the robot, such as the non-verbal information that it exhibits, may have a great influence on people's personal space, to a greater extent than the presence or absence an operator may have. These results suggest that an individual's communication skill and sensory evaluation to the robot may possibly have a greater influence on personal space than the presence or absence of an operator.

We conduct investigating in this study not by focusing on the influence of the robot itself, but by focusing on an external factor: the operator. It may be necessary for further studies to investigate the influences that the robot itself has on personal space. In particular, it may be possible to consistently alter personal space by focusing on the non-verbal information that the robot exhibits and by controlling people's sensory evaluation to the robot.

Acknowledgements. This work was supported by JSPS KAKENHI Grant Number 18K11414.

References

1. Kanda, T., Ishiguro, H., Ono, T., Imai, M., Nakatsu, R.: An evaluation on interaction between humans and an autonomous robot Robovie. J. Robot. Soc. Jpn. **20**(3), 315–323 (2002)
2. Kashiwabara, T., Osawa, H., Shinozawa, K., Imai, M.: TEROOS: a wearable avatar to enhance joint activities. In: CHI 2012 Proceeding of the SIGCHI Conference on Human Factors in Computing Systems, pp. 2001–2004 (2012)
3. Shibuya, S.: A study of the shape of personal space. Bull. Yamanashi Med. Univ. **2**, 41–49 (1985)
4. Hall, E.T.: The Hidden Dimension. Doubleday, New York (1966)
5. Fujihara, T.: The study of psychological distance reflected as personal space. Memoirs of the Faculty of Integrated Arts and Sciences. III. Stud. Inf. Behav. Sci. **10**, 83–92 (1987)
6. Yasumoto, M., Kamide, H., Mae, Y., Ohara, K., Takubo, T., Arai, T.: Personal space for the humanoid robot and a presentation method. In: JSME Annual Conference on Robotics and Mechatronics (Robomec), pp. 2A2-D18(1)–2A2-D18(4) (2010)
7. Lauckner, M., Kobiela, F., Manzey, D.: 'Hey robot, please step back!' - exploration of a spatial threshold of comfort for human-mechanoid spatial interaction in a hallway scenario. In: 23rd IEEE International Symposium on Robot and Human Interactive Communication (RO-MAN), pp. 780–787 (2014)
8. James, W., Imada, H.: Psychology, vol. 1, pp. 245–301. Iwanami Shoten, Tokyo (1992)
9. Ariga, A.: Expansive personal space: distance between personal belongings reflects the interpersonal distance of their owners. Jpn. J. Psychol. **87**(2), 186–190 (2016)
10. Fujita, Y.: Design and development for personal robot "PaPeRo". J. Soc. Instrum. Control Eng. **42**(6), 521–526 (2003)
11. Fraser, N., Gilbert, G.: Simulating speech systems. Comput. Speech Lang. **5**(1), 81–99 (1991)
12. Hori, H., Yoshida, H.: Psychological Measurement Scale Collection II, pp. 170–172. Saiensu-sha, Tokyo (2001)
13. Tatsumi, A., Matsushima, T., Okubo, M.: Influence of humanoid robot's behavior on personal space. In: 2018 Asian Conference on Design and Digital Engineering (ACDDE 2018) (2018)
14. Yamaoka, F., Kanda, T., Ishiguro, H., Hagita, N.: Interacting with a human or a humanoid robot? IPSJ J. **48**(11), 3577–3587 (2007)

Redefining Audience Role in Live Performances

Victor Vasconcelos[1], Mauro Amazonas[1], Thais Castro[1], Rosiane Rodrigues[1],
Hugo Fuks[2], Katia Vega[3], and Bruno Gadelha[1(✉)]

[1] Institute of Computing, Federal University of Amazonas,
Manaus, AM 69040900, Brazil
{vfv,maurojr,thais,rosiane,bruno}@icomp.ufam.edu.br
[2] Department of Informatics, Pontifical Catholic University of Rio de Janeiro,
Rio de Janeiro, RJ 22451900, Brazil
hugo@inf.puc-rio.br
[3] Department of Design, University of California, Davis, CA 95616-8585, USA
kvega@ucdavis.edu

Abstract. As an audience for great live performances, people usually act as a passive spectator or interacting poorly with the performance themselves. Typically, the audience feels the need for higher engagement in these events, what happens spontaneously in some creative ways, but in a very superficial and uncoordinated way. This work deals with coordinated human interaction in live performances using smartphones for creating special crowd effects, fostering a more active people participation during the performance. To encourage this behavior, we developed a coordinated approach using mobile devices with offline vs online and synchronous vs asynchronous visual effects. Considering that the great majority of the public already has their smartphones, our solution is cheaper than giving an armband for every person and can provide the same engagement feeling and more dynamic effects on the crowd.

Keywords: Audience engagement · Audience interaction ·
Interfaces for enjoying cultural heritage ·
New technology and its usefulness · Real life environments

1 Introduction

The human being is a social being. From its origin, they organized themselves in small groups, where generally nomads and they lived of the hunting and gathering. With the agricultural revolution, stemming from the mastery of cultivation techniques, the human being settled in villages and domesticated or animals. From the industrial revolution, cities could develop [6]. As a consequence, there are large population densities.

Moreover, societies provide the possibility to interact through a large number of people at the same place and at the same time. Thus, it is not uncommon to perceive their active and contagious participation in sporting events, cultural

M. Kurosu (Ed.): HCII 2019, LNCS 11566, pp. 358–377, 2019.
https://doi.org/10.1007/978-3-030-22646-6_26

events or political manifestations, among others. These massive concentrations of people, also called crowds, are the subject of several studies in different research fields such as "Dynamics of the Crowds".

Crowd Dynamics (CD) is the study of how and where crowds are formed and move under the critical density of more than one person per square meter [14]. According to Zeitz *et al.* [17], understanding the psychology of crowds and mass meetings is crucial to understand their dynamics and predicting their reactions. Such studies apply to several contexts such as mass behavior in emergencies, which concentrates much of the research studies. In this emerging context, Li et al. [9] presents a study to prevent accidents in crowded public spaces based on the control of pedestrian movements. Another work in this direction which describes human behavior in managing crises of crowds in extreme situations [3]. In another context, In the literature, there are applications of this technique for performing crowd simulation applied to the alignment of military vehicles [10].

Entertainment gives also the possibility to research on CD. Crowds at theme parks, such as at Disney parks, have been the subject of a study that predicts the flow of people in the most popular attractions (rides, games, restaurants or shows), presenting an unequal distribution of visitors and unequal queues between such attractions [4,13].

In the field of arts, there is a movement to encourage the participation of the masses, to understand their reactions and to interact directly with the public to engage them in artistic performances and installations. *Crowd Engagement* (CE), a branch of crowd dynamics, focuses on how people in the crowd interact with each other and as a group in a particular event [11]. For example, Roggla *et al.* [12] used helium gas balloons with sensors to capture information from the public engagement in a live event and make that information visible through a panel. Another work involving CE is that of Webb *et al.* [15] that discusses how new technologies can change performance experiences.

Due to the increasing penetration of smartphones in our daily, more 66% of individuals own a smartphone in 2018 [2]. This availability represents new possibilities for CD. Our work presents a novel way to involve crowds in different contexts such as in artistic performances and sports events by the use of mobile devices. The research question that guides this work is: How can technology transform the audience's role from a spectator in a significant event to an active participant in the show? Thus, the proposal described in this paper focuses in the development and use of a technology platform based on mobile devices such as smartphones and tablets to provide more audience immersion in entertainment events, thus redefining the role of the audience in these great spectacles.

This article is organized as follows. In Sect. 2, we present previous research and products on audience engagement. Section 3 describes the implementation of our platform for providing the immersion of audiences in entertainment events. Section 4 describes our case study a two pilot studies of our implementation. In Sects. 5 and 6, respectively, the analysis of the results of the pilot test with the case study, and the final considerations on the role of the audience in an event.

2   Audience Engagement

Since the great spectacles of the Roman theaters, entertainment and involvement of the crowds had to be part of their presentations. More recently, Brazil has been a stage of significant sporting and cultural events such as the World Cup, the Olympic games, Rock in Rio and Lolapalooza. However, Brazil has a history of massive events such as the popular Carnival parades that illustrate the country's cultural scene that is preserved for many years. Most of these events attract crowds who often limit themselves to a secondary role as passive spectator, or as an interactor only in their small groups of family or friends. This research focuses on a spectacle and contest where the audience has to participate in the performing team gets more points for their final score. It is a folk festival called Parintins. Thus, the participation of the crowd called "Galera", is planned, encouraged and constitutes an evaluation item for the festival. The Fig. 1 exemplifies the use of the crew of one of the Parintins festival steers forming the Brazilian flag.

The need for greater engagement in events of this nature is felt by the public themselves who, on their initiative, find creative ways to participate in the show. An example can be seen in Fig. 1, where viewers turn on the lights of their mobile handsets, enriching the spectacle scene. Another example is the tiles produced by organized twisted football teams to support his club, as further illustrated by Fig. 1, where fans receive a 'mosaic kit' with instructions for use for certain situations. It is worth mentioning that these are spontaneous initiatives that emerge from the crowd and are not originally conceived by the organizers of the event.

An example that encourages public engagement by the support of technological artifacts happened during the Coldplay tour. Upon entering the venue, each spectator received a bracelet with infrared sensors that would flash, blink and change colors in the rhythm of the songs performed by the band, which increased the sense of belonging to the show. In 2018, during the opening of the Winter Olympic Games in South Korea, the use of technology was evident. In the stands, it was possible to display flags, colors and even letters, making the bleachers become a "big screen". This "big screen" was projected on the bleachers but there was no interaction with the audience. This projection generated a high impact for both, for the television broadcast and for those who were on the other side of the stadium. However, it did not make the audience to participate in the show. Figure 2 illustrates the preparation of this screen in the stands of the grandstand and the final result at the time of opening of the event.

This research discussed in this article proposes the implementation of similar visual effect, but with the active participation of the audience, which will display a big screen using the smartphones as pixels and through the collaboration of each immersed in the interaction. In addition to the above examples of large-scale events, there is great interest in research involving the use of new technologies for crowd-oriented interaction, as already mentioned in the Sect. 1. More than just searching to understand crowds [3], or improving security [9], Mobile Crowd Sensing (MCS) [8] presents the concept of a paradigm, where the author discusses the possibilities available through the use of mobile technologies, highlighting how the MCS will work, although still at a basic stage, has many possibilities opportunities to be explored, such as a hybrid network model, using each of the smartphones in a crowd as an access point.

Fig. 1. Examples of spontaneous audience engagement in entertainment events. From left to right, there is the audience such as mosaics in football stadiums, the lighting of the cell phone lantern at the opening of the Rio 2016 Olympic Games, and the Coldplay show.

There are cases of real applications using an extended concept of the MCS paradigm, *Mobile Crowd Sensing and Computing* (MCSC). They use data provided by a crowd to solve certain problems, such as measuring pollution air pollution measurement, site recommendations, crime prevention, among other situations [7]. There is also a project that detects crowds through smartphones as a facilitating tool in the collection of information [1]. Instead of using sensors, which would be very costly for both deployment and maintenance of hardware and software, it uses *smartphones* since these technologies are already equipped, making it a perfect source for collecting information from its users. An example of this is the data obtained on human mobility in an urban area, health applications and wellbeing allowing the study and creation of new technologies from these data.

As can be seen, several studies have been carried out focusing on crowds, sometimes trying to study the behavior of the same, sometimes using data provided by it. In this work we treat both concepts but with a different look, studying the visual effects of the interaction of crowds in events of great proportions, also allowing the investigation into effects initiated in subgroups with the potential to spread to others, effects that engage more or others who may even disengage.

During the opening of the Winter Olympic Games 2018, in South Korea, the use of technology was quite evident. In the stands it was possible to see flags, colors and even letters, making the bleachers become a "big screen", as a mosaic. This "big screen" emerged from the bleachers but did not come from the interaction of the present audience, which nevertheless generated a high impact visual effect in which it watched the show, both for television broadcast and for those who were on the other side of the stadium. Despite the visual effects, the present technology did not make people participate in the show. Figure 2 illustrates the preparation of this screen in the stands of the grandstand and the final result at the time of opening of the event. The research discussed in this article proposes the realization of similar visual effects, but with the active participation of the present public, which will form a big screen through the collaboration of each immersed in the interaction.

Fig. 2. Preparation process and the final result of a big screen at the opening of the Winter Olympics Games 2018 in South Korea. Source: https://www.olympic.org/photos/pyeongchang-2018/opening-ceremony

In addition to the above examples, applied in large-scale events, there is an excellent interest in research involving the use of new technologies for crowd-oriented interaction, as already mentioned in Sect. 1. More than just searching to understand crowds [3], or improving security [9], there are also searches that follow other lines, which presents the concept of the Mobile Crowd Sensing (MCS) paradigm [8]. The author smart phones discusses the possibilities available through the use of mobile technologies, highlighting how the MCS, although still at a primary stage, has many possibilities opportunities to be explored, such as a hybrid network model, using each of the of a crowd as an access point.

There are cases of real applications using an extended concept of the MCS paradigm, *Mobile Crowd Sensing and Computing* (MCSC), applications that use data provided by a crowd to solve specific problems, such as measuring pollution air pollution measurement, site recommendations, crime prevention, among other situations [7].

In another paper that proposes to talk about MCS opportunities [1], the author talks about the use of the detection of crowds through smartphones as a facilitating tool in the collection of information. Instead of using sensors, which would be very costly for both deployment and maintenance of hardware and software, it uses *smartphones* since these technologies are already equipped, making it a perfect source for collecting information from its users. An example of this is the data obtained on human mobility in an urban area, health applications and wellbeing allowing the study and creation of new technologies from these data.

As can be seen, several studies have been carried out focusing on crowds, sometimes trying to study the behavior of the same, sometimes using data provided by it. The research discussed in this article uses both concepts but with a different look, studying the visual effects of the interaction of crowds in events of vast proportion, also allowing the investigation into effects initiated in subgroups with the potential to spread to others, effects that engage more or others who may even disengage.

3   Smartphones as an Instrument of Immersion in Shows

Mobile devices such as smartphones and tablets, increasingly embedded in people's everyday lives, are equipped with multiple sensors, actuators and processors, and have a growing capacity for storing and processing information. They increase the possibilities of communication between people and interaction with the world. Its use is common in the most different contexts, such as work, study and leisure. Considering the latter, one observes its intense use in big shows such as musical shows or sporting events both for recording the moment and for a greater interaction with the event. This interaction often occurs spontaneously, such as lighting the smartphone flashlight while playing a song at a concert. It is therefore perceived the need for audience interaction and immersion in entertainment events and the potential of mobile devices as a technological platform to support this task. Thus, a mobile-based technology platform (smartphones and tablets) was designed to increase people's engagement in crowd-based events, relying on theories such as dynamic entertainment.

Inspired by examples of audience participation in major shows presented previously and represented in Fig. 1, the technological platform was designed to turn the crowd into a large living screen, where each participant consists of a point, or pixel, of that screen. To do so, one must keep in mind that: (1) people tend to use their smartphones during events and; (2) agglomeration of people in different arrangements meeting the requirements of each type of event such as: arranged in an arched like in a football game, standing on a lane as in a show in parks or beaches or both as in the case of stadium shows Each arrangement has characteristics that influence both the audience experience and the possibilities of technological interaction in these scenarios. Unlike the initiatives of the Winter Olympics in South Korea that used mini led screens in each stand of the grandstand to form their big screen and the concert of the band Coldplay, that used dedicated devices, as wristbands with radio frequency receivers delivered to each spectator of their show, the technological platform described in this paper uses people's own mobile devices participating in the events. This solution reduces the costs of deploying technology, it has great potential for motivating interaction, and it presents many possibilities for increasing engagement and audience immersion during shows.

The developed platform allows different visual effects to be performed in different scenarios, considering the peculiarities of the public disposition expected by the event and the network infrastructures of the venues. Figure 3 presents the architecture of the proposed technology platform, illustrating the different public dispositions and different versions of the solution considering the network infrastructure availability of the event locations.

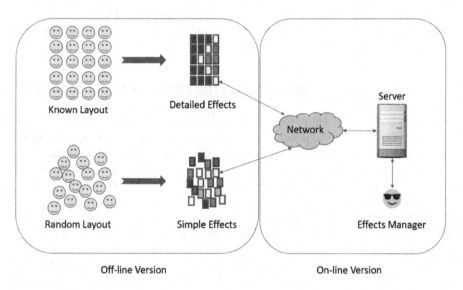

Fig. 3. Technology platform architecture considering different audience arrangements and network infrastructure of the event.

With regard to the audience's disposition, we have:

– **Location-based Layout (Known layout).** This provision happens when a participant of the event can choose beforehand their place in the audience or the places are limited and marked, even if they are of free choice of the participant. In this type of arrangement, each place receives a marker to be recognized by the application that must be previously installed in the event participant's smartphone. As a consequence, you get sophisticated visual effects involving animations or drawing formations in the audience.
– **Random Layout.** This arrangement happens when people have no control over the exact location they will be in during the event. This type of arrangement is common in events such as musical shows in large spaces such as stadiums, parks or beaches where the audience usually stands on the track or even in the stands, but without the commitment to remain in the same place

throughout the event. In this case, it is not possible to identify in advance where a particular participant of the event will be. The visual effects obtained with this type of arrangement are more limited such as flashing lights in random colors, all lit audience with a solid color and color change.

With respect to the network infrastructure provided at the event venues, the technology platform envisions that smartphone applications work in two ways, namely:

- **Online Version.** In this version it is possible to control each cell individually, generating the combination of numerous visual effects in real time. This version enables the visual effects to be orchestrated by a central actor, called the effects manager. This manager has full control of the whole screen formed by the smartphones of the audience of the event.
- **Offline version.** In this version the interaction happens freely, without the need of the effects manager. In order for this manager independence to be possible, the application is preprogrammed with all the sequence of effects it should display.

Table 1 summarizes the configuration possibilities of the developed technology platform. Applications generated from the platform can be online or offline. For each type, one must consider whether people have a known disposition or whether they are randomly disposed in the event in question. The possibilities of generating the visual effects will be conditioned to such visualizations.

Table 1. Technology platform configurations considering public readiness and network infrastructure.

Version	Layout	Visual effects
Online	Location-based	Detailed, commanded by a manager
	Random	Limited, commanded by a manager
Offline	Location-based	Detailed, pre-programmed
	Random	Limited, pre-programmed

In addition to worrying about effects, with all the logic and simulation algorithms implemented behind the scenes, the focus of the technology platform is also to provide the best of immersion and interaction experiences in an entertainment event involving crowds that use the applications of the platform. To this end, the application design for the user was minimalistic, so that it is simple to use as the simple act of lifting the side of the device, considering a minor impact on the battery consumption of the device, without leaving of presenting distinct, enveloping and visually beautiful effects. Considering these assumptions, we describe in this article the first case study carried out using simulations and as a result we discuss its scalability for using it in major events. For that aim, we propose differentiated interactions for certain moments so that the public feels immersed in the event, feeling an important part of the show.

4   Case Study

To determine if the application can accomplish what is intended, immersion of the audience, we conducted a case study in an experimental laboratory and an environment simulating a musical show. We applied this methodology from the literature, which argues that the case study is the most appropriate methodology to use in research where the main questions are "how?" Or "why?" [16]. The author also refers to the case study as an indicated methodology for social studies, therefore the focus of this work.

Also according to the literature [16], we should perform four steps for carrying out case studies. The first one, the **Planning**, consists in deciding if we will apply the methodology for the research. The second one, the **Design**, where the units of analysis should be defined and the probable cases for study. The third step, **Preparation**, which will consist of conducting one or more pilot case studies; the collection, where we extracted the data generated by the pilot study. The final step, **Analysis**, which consists of an analysis of the collected data. If the collection is not sufficient, one can go back to the stage of preparation for other pilot case studies, or even if the generated data are not desirable it is necessary to go back to the *design* step.

Planning: the context of this work involves the study of agglomerations, with attention in the members of a crowd and the feelings and emotions experienced by the individuals, during the use of the proposed application. Investigating why the feeling of more intense immersion, if any, and how to intervene through the technological mean so these sensations are more evident.

Design: What is intended is to identify and evaluate the audience's sensations when using the proposed application, in any entertainment event. If the audience felt more immersed, also if this was a consequence of the use of the application, and, finally, if it felt an active participant of the event.

The research involves the collection of data in events that gather crowds, but the technology platform developed is new, and since there were no references to evaluate its feasibility in real events, it was decided to conduct, first, two pilot case studies. The first was intended to focus more on the usability aspects of the smartphones with the application, focusing on the user experience at the end of the test. For the second pilot case study, after some adjustments that were necessary to be carried out with the conduction of the first test, the focus was more on the interaction of the people with the show and the unit of analysis was their experience of use. About 50 young people participated in the two pilot case studies.

We performed the data collection by observation of the interaction, post-test questionnaires made available through the Internet and an informal chat with all participants of the pilot studies after the session.

For the analysis of the collected data, each pilot case study had some of its characteristics whose data were triangulated and we discuss in detail in the next section.

As mentioned previously, two pilot case studies were conducted, with a week apart. The first one tested two versions of the application (the version of *on-line* with people's known disposition and the *off-line version with random disposition of the people* and the second only the version *off-line* with random array of participants was used, since the goal of the second was the immersion experience and not the technology anymore. For ease of understanding, in the remainder of the article, we name the *on-line* version with the known layout of **Version 1** and the *off-line* version with a random array of participants of **Version 2**.

4.1 First Pilot Case Study

The audience very present in shows is composed mostly of young people. Thus, this study was applied with students volunteers of the freshman class of Software Engineering course and some graduate students also volunteers, all of them being from the university X. In all, there were 35 participants, and as previously reported, both were tested versions 1 and 2 of the application with the primary objective of observing the feasibility and acceptability of the technology and its effect on participants' perception of immersion.

- **Setting:** For this first pilot study, a room was set aside to accommodate the number of participating students. We prepared the environment of the class to create space for the students to have freedom, for this, we removed the chairs, the artificial lights turned off, and we connected a party light globe. The intention was to simulate the atmosphere of a show, so that, as in a real event, the participants could have free space. It was also necessary to previously delimit with the *QrCodes* the places where the participants should be during the Version 1 tests of the application, forming a *grid* 6 × 6 (six rows and six columns). As the simulated environment was that of a show, a multimedia projector and a sound box were provided in the room to show the video of the band's show *Coldplay*. The aim was to increase the feeling of the participants being in an entertainment event. Also, two cameras were placed in strategic locations (in the corners of the room, diagonally facing the participants) and recorded the test, with the reactions and behaviors of the participants (Fig. 4).
- **Execution:** We divided the study into two different moments, each one with a different app setting:
  - **Version 1:** Each student had to select the online with a known layout option on the app. They had to stand right above a QR code, so they'd have a known position. To inform their position to the app, they scanned the QR code their standing. The music started, and they could move, dance or do what they wanted to, but they were not allowed to change places to keep their position. If someone moved to a new spot, the person should scan the new QrCode to inform the new position to the app. Knowing the position of each person in the class, we could test the app by sending signals to each mobile device through the network. This way, we could observe the generated effect in real time.
  - **Version 2:** Each student had to select the off-line with a random layout option on the app. By using this functionality, they were able to stay

Fig. 4. Students in a simulated party setting.

wherever they want to without the obligation of staying in the same place marked with QR codes. The music played, and students started to get more involved in the experiment and started dancing. While they were dancing, their mobile devices changed colors according to a preset script. In this setting, we programmed all the effects in advance, and it was not possible to change its behavior through controllers' commands.

- **Primary analysis:** Looking at the student's behavior during the two moments of the study; we verified that while in Version 1 we had much more control and diversity in effects, on Version 2 we will always have only the preset effects what makes the experience less dynamic. In contrast, Version 1 limits the interaction by making the audience remaining in the same position, reducing their freedom of movement. On Version 2 we do not have this limitation, because regardless of the position of each participant the effect will succeed giving all freedom for the audience to come and go as they wish, theoretically giving a greater sensation of immersion.

Another issue we observed was that even though the songs played were from the famous band Coldplay; not all participants demonstrated that they were enjoying the show, either because they did not know the lyrics well or even not be fans of the band itself. We concluded that this condition might have interfered in the level of immersion of some participants.

We also noticed that depending on the context of use, Version 1 tends to stand out more than Version 2. For example, in an event with marked places, or football stadiums that have a numbered chair and, consequently, each person has his seat reserved, Version 1 stands out as there would be no need to change places. But in a context like a music festival, where the public often moves, Version 2 stands out, as it would not be possible at this time to form pictures or images with the mobile devices due to the lack of communication of the application with a controller as it functions as a stand-alone application.

In the post-study chat, the participants made some suggestions such as: disable the automatic screen lock, control the brightness of the screen and corrections in the behavior of the application. Still, in the chat, the participants still took the opportunity to discuss how the application could be used in other contexts and with new features.

4.2   Second Pilot Case Study

After a primary analysis of the results of the first pilot study, we corrected small errors in the application (bugs in the application) pointed out by the participants and detected by the researchers. The observations made in the first study resulted in the decision to, at this point, further explore *Version* 2 by providing greater immersion and engagement in events because of the higher degree of freedom for the audience. Thus, the same class of students of the Software Engineering course was invited to participate in the second pilot study, together with a group of students of Gas and Petroleum Engineering of Federal University of Amazonas, totaling 40 participants.

- **Preparation:** For the accomplishment of this study, the same previous room, that has up to 50 participants, was reserved. Again, we removed the chairs to provide more space and to simulate a music event. This time, a DJ was invited to participate in the study to have a broader range of songs, and thus try to please as many participants as possible. Just as in the first test, the lights were turned off, and instead, we attached a party light globe, creating a simulated show environment. The DJ was responsible for bringing the sound system (box and sound table), put the music station facing the participants. We also recorded this study through a camera, but this time it was positioned facing the participants. Another differential in preparation for this test was to have used the multimedia projector connected with another camera pointed at the participants so that they could see themselves (visual feedback), trying to create a way to motivate them to use the application and create a greater immersion for them.
- **Execution:** This time the participants were only asked to enter the application, if they wanted and had their smartphones, to let them interact spontaneously. It is worth mentioning that some participants were not with their smartphones and were asked to participate in simulating what happens in significant events, where most are with their device, but there are always some that are not. Figure 5 shows the students interacting with their smartphones during the study.
  As previously mentioned, the purpose of the study is to make participants feel relaxed and feel as if they are in a real event. For this reason, the DJ was asked to mix musical rhythms with the most popular hits among the participants' age group.
- **Primary analysis:** We observed that even though they were left free and allowed to use the application and even without much previous instruction,

Fig. 5. Students participating in the second pilot study, in a simulated party setting.

the vast majority of participants were eager to use the application. We concluded that the visual feedback provided in this study stimulated the participants to use the application making them curious to see the result of their interaction in the event. As a result of feedback, participants' engagement could be perceived more spontaneously by observing how they were singing the songs played and doing "choreographies" and rocking the smartphone from side to side in more romantic songs. A priori, the app provides the audience with a new way of interacting with an event, giving each user the experience of being part of the event, not just as a spectator but as a show apart.

After each of the pilot studies, the participants were asked to respond to a questionnaire about the experience they had just mentioned, emphasizing the feelings and emotions they felt. In addition to the questionnaire, also soon after each test, all participants were invited to give suggestions, criticisms or question something about the study. It was through these methods that we were able to collect enough data for a more in-depth analysis, which we present in the next section.

5   Results

Through the triangulation carried out for the two pilot case studies some preliminary conclusions can be drawn on the user experience using the proposed application in the context of this new technology. This triangulation consisted of the activity itself, with a *in loco* observation of the researchers and audio and video recording, a post-test questionnaire on the user experience and an informal conversation to record impressions of the participants who did not want or could have been exposed in the questionnaire.

One of the conclusions that can be reached, through observation and also the information extracted from the forms, is that the visual feedback makes the user experience even more vibrant, making the participant feel more and more part of the event, as shown in Fig. 6.

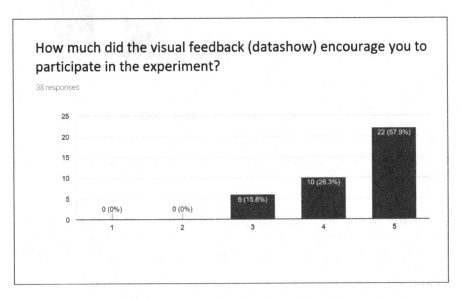

Fig. 6. Feeling of immersion due to the visual feedback provided by the data show projection.

The freer the participants feel more engaged, according to the data from Fig. 7 show that from the first pilot, where students passed through *Version 1* and felt less freedom, to the second study where we tested only *Version 2*, the students felt much more belonging to the event because they had greater freedom. But this does not invalidate the alternative presented by *Version 1* since there are events in which the audience does not usually change places, such as in a play, a soccer stadium or a grandstand. In this case, version 1 may perform similarly to *Version 2*.

The issue of the need for the participant to have his arm raised during the use of the application was a point of discussion because, during the study that lasted on average 20 min, we did not file any complaints in this regard. However, what the students asked was that in a context where the event could last two hours or more, participants would not be willing to stand in this position throughout the event. Thus, during the process of planning and designing the application,

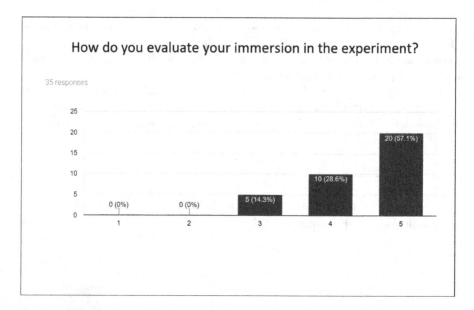

Fig. 7. Feeling of immersion degrees of the participant in the first and second pilot studies, respectively.

this was one of the situations that were taken into account, and the project envisages the use of the application only in some moments of the event, both for this matter and for the preservation of the battery charge of the participant's *smartphones*.

Other ideas may also arise as you use this technology in different types of events. For example, during the execution of the second pilot study, a participant wanted more freedom of movement to dance and pinned his smartphone on his cap, which is unusual, but an alternative to move more freely in dance parties, making it another possibility to investigate further as an extension of this work (Fig. 8).

Another question asked both on the form and to the students directly was whether they would use this technology in a real event, and then the vast majority of students said they would use it with certainty, as Fig. 9 shows. This response from the students reinforces, once again, our assumption that people wish not only to watch and themselves, they want to interact with the event that is participating. For event planners, this is a promising point, since the more the public is engaged, the higher the success of the event. And from the viewpoint of the audience, the higher the sense of participation, the more unique will be the experience of the individual in the event.

In addition to direct questions about each participant's experience, we leave an open space for suggestions for possible improvements to the immersion experience at an event. Given each response, or rather each suggestion, we applied the *Explanation Method of Underlying Discourse* [5], which consists of a method

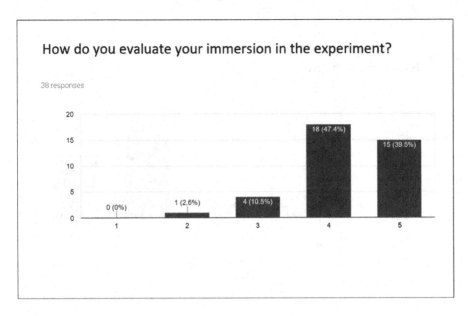

Fig. 8. Feeling of immersion degrees of the participant in the second pilot studies.

of categorizing the data to better analyze the participants' feelings as an all to understand better how a crowd feels using the application in an event. Thus, we organized the suggestions into four categories, which were: improvements in the application; music as an influencing factor; facilitating the use of the application; and, real engagement. Table 2 shows how responses are distributed across categories. It is worth mentioning that in the text, when any of the answers are quoted, the names used will be pseudonyms and not the true name of the participants.

Application Enhancements: this category encompasses all the answers where the participant suggests some improvement in the application. Whether such a suggestion is to increase the number of possible effects or even, as in a spe cific suggestion from a student, "reduce battery consumption". The majority of the study's audience, possibly because they were from computing field, were focused on such questions as for whether the application worked; which could be improved in it; new features; and so on. We realize that there is a need to vary the range of visual effects provided by the application, especially in Version 2, where there is no possibility to change in real time what is predefined in the application. This would allow for greater engagement as the user would not tire of the effects easily. In identifying such suggestions, we observed that in the videos of the experiments performed, there was a drop in engagement after a few minutes. We assume, then, that after a few minutes, the effects became predictable, and consequently, the participants' motivation and engagement declined.

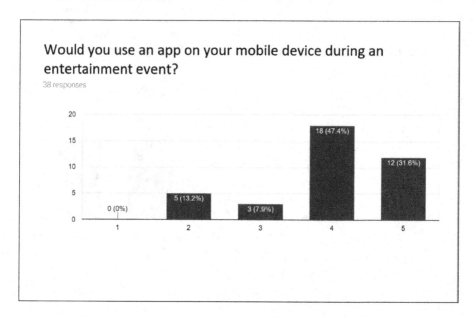

Fig. 9. Possibilities of the participant to use the application in an entertainment event.

Table 2. Categorization of the participants' suggestions of the pilot studies.

Categories	#Answers
Application improvements	10
Music as an influencing factor	6
Make the application easier to use	12
Real Engagement	7

Music as Influencing Factor: In this category are answers like that of a specific student who said, "It would be nice to vary the *playlist* more". Although not the majority that suggested such changes, it may still be noted that music is an essential point of influence for an audience of any size engaging in an event. It is worth remembering that for this work the simulated environment is that of a show, so music is essential. Therefore, even if it was not such a scope, for example considering the fans in a stadium for a football game (which is also an entertainment event, but of sports), there are always musical instruments and a vast audience singing songs. One thing to consider is that for this pilot study only the students who attended the invitation spontaneously participated. In this way, the students did not necessarily have the same musical taste. So what pleased one student probably did not please the other. In a real situation, it is expected that the individual who is predisposed to go to a show is a fan of the artist, band or even the musical style, where the musical genre is preferably not a relevant variable.

Facilitating the Use of the Application: for this category, answers like that of a specific student suit naturally. The student said that we should "improve the issue of holding the cell phone all the time". Other comments that also fit in this category are those that request the use of the application in devices of the manufacturer *Apple*, that owns the IOS operating system, considering that until the moment of the experiments reported in this work, there was only the version for the Android operating system. Another request made by another specific student was: "update the application without having to use third-party sites". At the time this study was run and because the version used was still experimental, the developed application was not yet available in the mobile application store running the Android operating system (*Play Store*). In this way, the participant had to perform the demo app download on a website hosted on the university servers and install the demo application.

Real World Engagement: this category was identified for responses that required more experiments. Some users have asked to participate in future tests. According to a specific student, "it would be interesting if, at any cultural event held here at the university, there was the possibility of using the application." We can see that the application provided a greater engagement so that several participants would like to use the application more often, however simple the idea may seem.

6   Concluding Remarks

Given all that we observed in the pilot case studies and the analysis, in addition to what the public already does today, the feeling of participation in an entertainment event is essential, becoming an extra attraction. If in the past, with little or no technology, the audience could get some interaction, today with the technology proposed, the audience besides watching can interact if is participating.

It still requires more testing and case studies on a larger scale, so the technology and application become a tool for immersing participants in events. Both case studies were conducted with about fifty young people and highlighted essential elements that we not considered previously. In order to be able to observe the impact of using technology more faithfully, it is necessary to conduct a broader case study, with at least 1,000 people, already characterizing a crowd, so that it is possible to visualize the potential of the application for engagement and spontaneity of the public. Based on participants feedback, we can glimpse a scenario in which the possibilities of the development of more elaborate, complex and visually beautiful effects.

With our technology, we are redefining audience role in live performances by making them more engaged and immersed. Our technology enables interacting at a lower cost than the expensive bracelets used by Coldplay or Taylor Swift. After the case studies in a real scenario, the technology will be ready to provide a richer experience of interaction in mass events.

Acknowledgments. This work received partial support by the Foundation for Support of Research of the State of Amazonas (FAPEAM) and the Brazilian National Council for Scientific and Technological, Brazilian agencies.

References

1. Ma, H., Zhao, D., Yuan, P.: Opportunities in mobile crowd sensing. Infocommun. J. **7**(2), 32–38 (2015)
2. Z.T.R Aency (2017). https://www.zenithmedia.com/smartphone-penetration-reach-66-2018/
3. Bellomo, N., Clarke, D., Gibelli, L., Townsend, P., Vreugdenhil, B.J.: Human behaviours in evacuation crowd dynamics: from modelling to "big data" toward crisis management. Phys. Life Rev. **18**, 1–21 (2016)
4. Brown, A., Kappes, J., Marks, J.: Mitigating theme park crowding with incentives and information on mobile devices. J. Travel Res. **52**(4), 426–436 (2013)
5. Nicolaci-da Costa, A.M.: O campo da pesquisa qualitativa e o método da explicitação do discurso subjacente (MEDS). Psicologia Reflexão e Crítica **20**(1), 65–73 (2007)
6. Fuks, H., Pimentel, M.: Sistemas Colaborativos. Elsevier-Campus-SBC, 1a ediçã o edn. (2011)
7. Guo, B., et al.: Mobile crowd sensing and computing: the review of an emerging human-powered sensing paradigm. ACM Comput. Surv. **48**(1), 1–31 (2015). https://doi.org/10.1145/2794400. http://dl.acm.org/citation.cfm?doid=2808687. 2794400
8. Guo, B., Yu, Z., Zhou, X., Zhang, D.: From participatory sensing to mobile crowd sensing. In: 2014 IEEE International Conference on Pervasive Computing and Communication Workshops, PERCOM WORKSHOPS 2014, pp. 593–598 (2014). https://doi.org/10.1109/PerComW.2014.6815273
9. Li, J., Wang, L., Tang, S., Zhang, B., Zhang, Y.: Risk-based crowd massing early warning approach for public places: a case study in China. Saf. Sci. **89**, 114–128 (2016)
10. Mamdouh, A.M., Kaboudan, A., Imam, I.F.: Real-time, multi-agent simulation of coordinated hierarchical movements for military vehicles with formation conservation. In: Proceedings of the International MultiConference of Engineers and Computer Scientists, IMECS (2012)
11. Maynes-Aminzade, D., Pausch, R., Seitz, S.: Techniques for interactive audience participation. In: Proceedings of the 4th IEEE International Conference on Multimodal Interfaces, ICMI 2002 (2002)
12. Roggla, T., Wand, C., Romero, L.P., Jansen, J., Cesar, P.: Tangible air: an interactive installation for visualising audience engagement. In: Proceedings of the 2017 ACM SIGCHI Conference on Creativity and Cognition, C&C 2017, pp. 263–265 (2017)
13. Solzas, G., Akbas, M.I., Turgut, D.: A mobility model of theme park visitors. IEEE Trans. Mobile Comput. **14**(12), 2406–2418 (2015)
14. Still, G.K.: Crowd dynamics. Ph.D. thesis, University of Warwick, Coventry, UK (2000)
15. Webb, A.M., Wang, C., Kerne, A., Cesar, P.: Distributed liveness: understanding how new technologies transform performance experiences. In: Proceedings of the 19th ACM Conference on Computer-Supported Cooperative Work & Social Computing, CSCW 2016, pp. 432–437 (2017)

16. Yin, R.K.: Estudo de Caso: Planejamento e Métodos. Bookman editora (2015)
17. Zeitz, K.M., Tan, H.M., Grief, M., Couns, P., Zeitz, C.J.: Crowd behavior at mass gatherings: a literature review. Prehosp. Disaster Med. **24**(1), 32–38 (2009)

Emotional Design, Kansei and Aesthetics in HCI

A Cross-Cultural Comparison of Perceptions of Cuteness and Kawaii Between American and Japanese College Students

Dave Berque[1]([⊠]), Hiroko Chiba[1], Ayako Hashizume[2], and Masaaki Kurosu[3]

[1] DePauw University, Greencastle, IN 46135, USA
dberque@depauw.edu
[2] Hosei University, Tokyo, Japan
[3] The Open University of Japan, Chiba, Japan

Abstract. The notion of *kawaii* (cuteness in the context of Japanese culture) is ubiquitous in Japan and ranges from Hello Kitty products to road signs to posters created by the Japanese government, to name just a few examples. Japanese products, which are used globally, are consciously tailored to accommodate widely preferred cuteness. Therefore, when designing a product, it is important to understand how specific groups of target users perceive kawaii. We report on a cross-cultural study that investigates cultural differences in the core understanding of the concepts of kawaii and cute based on a free-association study. Following a similar protocol that was previously used with Japanese college students, we asked American college students to write freely about what they associate with the word "cute" and, also, what they associate with the word "kawaii". Some of the American college students were enrolled in a three-week immersive course entitled "Japanese Culture, Technology and Design" which included two weeks of travel in Japan. These students responded to the prompts on the first day of class and again on the last day of class. Responses to each prompt were coded and compared across cultures and genders.

Keywords: Cute · Kawaii · Free association · Cross-cultural

1 Introduction

Japanese cuteness, described as kawaii, has been ingrained in Japanese contemporary society in many forms. The notion of kawaii is ubiquitous in Japan and ranges from Hello Kitty products to road signs to posters created by the Japanese government, to name just a few examples. Japanese products are consciously tailored to accommodate widely preferred "cuteness".

The word kawaii stemmed from the word kawayushi that appeared in Konjaku Momogatarishu (Tales of Times Now Past) in classical Japanese literature [1]. At this time, the word kawaii meant pitiful, shameful, or too sad to see. Over the course of Japanese history, the meaning of the word evolved to describe the small, weak, and someone or something that invokes the feeling of "wanting to protect" [1]. The meaning

© Springer Nature Switzerland AG 2019
M. Kurosu (Ed.): HCII 2019, LNCS 11566, pp. 381–391, 2019.
https://doi.org/10.1007/978-3-030-22646-6_27

of kawaii has been extended to the concept of "Japanese cuteness" in contemporary Japanese society. It is one of the aesthetic principles that appeal to Japanese consumers. Japanese products and pop culture, such as Hello Kitty, Pokémon, J-pop, and Anime, have gained popularity around the globe, including in the United States. As a result, Japanese kawaii design has also spread to some extent. Good summaries of the role of kawaii in Japanese product design can be found in [2, 3], and [4].

In previous work [5], we report on the extent to which perceptions of kawaii, beauty, and likeability in more than 200 photographs differ between Japanese and American college students. The photographs were divided into subgroups including products, objects, foods, geometric shapes, animals, characters and people. Perceptions of each image were compared across cultures and genders. Specifically, comparisons were made between: Japanese males versus Japanese females, American males versus American females, Japanese males versus American males, Japanese females versus American females, and all Japanese students versus all American students. Differences were found between groups for specific images.

We now extend this work by reporting on a new cross-cultural study that uses a free-association technique to investigate cultural and gender differences in the core understanding of the concepts of kawaii and cute. Japanese and American college students were asked to write freely about what they associate with the word "cute" and, also, what they associate with the word "kawaii". Some of the American college students were enrolled in a three-week January Term course entitled "Japanese Culture, Technology and Design" which included two weeks of travel in Japan. These students responded to the prompts on the first day of class and again on the last day of class. Responses to each question were coded (for example, did a response refer to an animal, a human, a color, etc.?) and compared across cultures.

2   Method

2.1   Summary of Previous Study

As reported in their paper, *Gender Difference in the Free Association for "Cute" and "Kawaii"*, the third and fourth authors used a free association technique to compare differences in core understanding of the words "cute" and "kawaii" [6]. The 60 participants (45 males and 15 females) in this study were all Japanese college students. The participants were given 20 min to write what they associate with the word "cute" and, also, what they associate with the word "kawaii". All participants completed the task before the 20-min. time limit was reached. It is important to note that the word "cute" in Japanese is written as using a special script called Katakana that indicates that the word is a loan word (foreign word). The word is written in Katakana as "キュート", which is pronounced "kyūto" in Japanese. Thus, the Japanese participants were responding to a prompt for kawaii (written in Japanese) and a prompt for "kyūto" written in a script that is used for loan words. The method for the Japanese study is described in detail in [6].

2.2   Method for Current Baseline Study

Participants for the current study were recruited from students enrolled in Winter Term courses at DePauw University, which is an undergraduate, residential, liberal arts college in the Midwestern United States. Due to University Institutional Review Board requirements, in order to be eligible for the study, participants had to be at least 18 years of age.

In total, 34 students participated in the baseline study at DePauw University during January, 2019. Out of the 34 students, 26 were about to start a course entitled "Japanese Culture, Technology and Design" taught by the first two authors. Five of the 34 participants reported that they had been raised primarily outside of the United States. In order to limit the study to students who would respond primarily through an American cultural lens, we excluded data for these participants. In the remainder of this paper, for convenience, we will refer to the remaining participants as "American" participants since they were raised primarily in the United States, even though we did not ask them about citizenship. The 29 American participants ranged in age from 18 to 23 with a mean age of 20.2. Of the 29 American participants, 13 identified as female and 16 identified as male.

After completing an informed consent form, participants were given a questionnaire that asked for demographic information including gender, age, and number of years spent living outside of the United States. The questionnaire also gave students these instructions: *"Please write what you associate with the words cute and kawaii. Your associations can be proper nouns, adjectives, or short sentences. Please write freely words that come to your mind. It is ok to use the same word, phrase, or short sentence for both "cute" and "kawaii".* The questionnaire provided an area for the participants to respond to each of the two prompts and participants were allowed to jump back and forth between the two prompts as they completed the task.

Participants were given a maximum of 20 min to complete their listings; however, all of the participants completed their work before the time limit. As reported in [6], the Japanese participants also all completed their listings before their 20-min time limit expired.

2.3   Method for Post-course Study

As described in detail in [7] and [8], the first and second authors regularly teach a course called "Japanese Culture, Technology and Design" that exposes undergraduate students at an American liberal arts college to Japanese culture, technology and design through an immersive three-week experience that includes two weeks of travel to Japan.

Of the 31 participants in the American study described above, 26 students participated in the Japanese Culture Technology and Design course immediately after participating in the study. In the remainder of this section, we briefly describe the Japanese Culture, Technology and Design course to provide context for the Results and Analysis section that follows.

The Japanese Culture, Technology and Design course exposes students to Japanese history, language, culture, technology and design with an emphasis on the way these three areas are interrelated. The course has been offered four times, most recently in January 2019, with an enrollment of approximately 100 students across the four offerings. Co-teaching the course allows us to combine experience with computer science, human computer interaction, design, and robotics (first author) and Japanese language, Japanese culture, Japanese aesthetics and Japanese history (second author).

The course begins with four days of on-campus orientation, which includes a presentation about Japanese kawaii culture, approximately two weeks on-site in Japan, and an on-campus debriefing session upon return from Japan.

While in Japan, students are exposed to Japanese culture, technology and design (including kawaii) in a variety of contexts and locations. More specifically, the students spend three days at a homestay in a small rural town, five days in Tokyo with an emphasis on contemporary technology and robotics, one day in Nagoya with an emphasis on industry, four days in Kyoto with an emphasis on more traditional design and one day in Hiroshima largely thinking about ethical issues associated with design. More details about the travel course are reported in [7]. During our time in Japan, the group communicates using LINE, a social media software system that is popular in Japan. LINE's user interface is itself kawaii, which exposes students to kawaii in an additional context. Additional information about our use of use LINE software to support the travel course are reported in [8].

After returning from Japan at the end of the most recent course offering, the students were invited to respond to the cute and kawaii free-association prompts again, using the same methodology as previously described. All 26 course participants responded to the prompts. As explained previously, data from two students were excluded because the students had been raised outside of the United States.

3   Results and Analysis

3.1   Baseline Questionnaire Results and Analysis

On the pre-course baseline questionnaire, all American participants wrote at least one item in response to the prompt asking for associations with cute. However, nearly half (45%) of the American participants (7 of 13 females and 6 of 16 males) left the prompt for kawaii associations blank. This demonstrates that an understanding of kawaii is specialized knowledge for American college students with some Americans learning about this concept and others not becoming aware of it.

On the other hand, all of the Japanese participants were able to respond to the prompt for kawaii and all but one participant (59 out of 60) were able to respond to the prompt for cute. This demonstrates that the overwhelming majority of Japanese college students are familiar with the word cute.

As reported in [6] there are some differences in the way Japanese college students perceive cute as compared to the way they perceive kawaii. In particular, the authors conclude that "Kawaii is a Japanese word that has an everyday life as a background context, while Cute is a quasi-Japanese word that has some distance from the everyday life." For the American students, however, cute is clearly an English word with background context provided by everyday life. Kawaii, on the other hand, is a foreign concept that must be learned.

In the remainder of this section we compare American and Japanese participants with respect to the associations they made in response to the prompt related to "cute". In the next section, we consider differences between cultures with regard to kawaii, however when considering differences about kawaii, we use data that was gathered from American students after they were exposed to this concept.

Returning to the cross cultural comparison of cute using the pre-course baseline data for American students, Table 1 compares the mean number of associations with cute that were provided by American participants versus Japanese participants. Since it is widely believed that perceptions of cuteness vary by gender, this data is disaggregated by gender as well.

Table 1. Cross-cultural comparison of mean number of responses to "cute"

	Americans		Japanese	
	Females	Males	Females	Males
N	13	16	15	45
Mean	9.2	3.6	14.2	5.4
Min	3	1	5	0
Max	11	15	27	13

Because of the small number of American subjects in this pilot study, statistical tests are difficult and we will focus on quantitative trends and qualitative analysis in this paper. In this context, the data suggests that for both Americans and Japanese, females made more associations in response to the cute prompt than males. In addition, Japanese participants made more associations than their American counterparts.

The study involving Japanese participants categorized each response into one of 17 categories as provided below in alphabetical order along with examples for each category. This category list is taken with only minor edits from [6].

1. Adjective: e.g. small, lovely
2. Animal: e.g. cat, dog
3. Character: e.g. Hello-Kitty, Disney Princess
4. Clothes and Fashion: e.g. gothic Lolita, China dress
5. Color: e.g. pink, pale color
6. Foreign Items: e.g. European things, overseas items
7. Human: e.g. girl, idols
8. Letter: e.g. Hiragana
9. Onomatopoeic Expressions: e.g. fuwa-fuwa, hira-hira, aww
10. Ornaments and Accessory: e.g. accessory, eyeglass
11. Person's Name: e.g. Avril Lavigne, Ayame Goriki
12. Place: e.g. Harajuku, Tokyo
13. Plant: e.g. flower, tulip
14. Shape and Pattern: e.g. stripe, star

15. Sweets and Fruits: e.g. short cake, cinnamon roll
16. Toy and Equipment: e.g. doll, stuffed animal
17. Others: e.g. car, painting

We coded the American responses into these 17 categories as well, but found we needed to add a new category, which we denote by "18. Special: e.g., big eyes". The Special category will be useful in explaining results that are reported in the next section of this paper.

As reported in [6] Japanese females (N = 15) made a total of 213 responses for cute while Japanese males (N = 45) made a total of 244 responses for cute. American females (N = 13) made a total of 152 responses for cute while American males (N = 16) made a total of 116 responses for cute. Table 2 shows the percentage of total responses per category. For example, the first row of the table indicates that 46.7% of the total responses made by American females were categorized as adjectives, 33.6% of the responses made by American males were categorized as adjectives, 15.5% of the responses made by Japanese females were adjectives, and 10.7% of the responses made by Japanese males were adjectives. We have highlighted entries in Table 2 that exceed 5%. These entries are the most important to consider and will be discussed in more detail below. We do not highlight entries in the "Other" category since it is comprised of a collection of unrelated items.

Table 2. Percentage of total cute associations for each category

Category	Americans		Japanese	
	Female	Male	Female	Male
1. Adjective	**46.7**	**33.6**	**15.5**	**10.7**
2. Animal	**13.1**	**18.9**	**6.6**	**21.7**
3. Character	0.6	0.0	**13.1**	**15.6**
4. Clothes and Fashion	3.3	3.4	**6.1**	1.6
5. Color	2.6	1.7	**9.4**	**6.6**
6. Foreign Items	0.0	0.8	4.2	4.1
7. Human	**21.1**	**29.3**	**12.7**	**17.2**
8. Letter	0.0	0.0	1.9	0.8
9. Onomatopoeic Expressions	1.3	0.8	**5.6**	0.8
10. Ornaments and Accessory	1.3	0.8	**8.0**	4.1
11. Person's Name	0.0	0.0	**5.2**	1.2
12. Place	1.3	0.0	0.0	0.4
13. Plant	0.0	0.0	1.9	1.2
14. Shape and Pattern	1.9	3.4	3.3	3.3
15. Sweets and Fruits	0.0	0.0	2.3	4.5
16. Toy and Equipment	1.3	0.8	2.8	1.6
17. Others	3.2	5.1	1.4	4.5
18. Special	1.3	0.8	–	–

Table 3 presents the top three categories for each demographic, as well as the percentage of associations for with each category and the total percentage of associations covered by the top three categories in aggregate.

Table 3. Comparison of top three cute categories by demographic group

Group	Top three categories	Aggregate % for top three categories
American females	Adjectives (46.7%)	80.9%
	Human (21.1%)	
	Animal (13.1%)	
American males	Adjective (33.6%)	81.8%
	Human (29.3%)	
	Animal (18.9%)	
Japanese females	Adjectives (15.5%)	41.3%
	Character (13.1%)	
	Human (12.7)	
Japanese males	Animal (21.7%)	54.5%
	Human (17.2%)	
	Character (15.6%)	

The Character category is in the top three categories for both Japanese males and Japanese females, but makes up less than 1% of the responses for both American males and females. Example responses in the character category for Japanese participants were numerous (25 responses from females and 38 from males) and included both Japanese and American characters such as Hello Kitty, Mickey Mouse, Pooh and Yura Chara. No American males and only one American female offered a Character as a response (this single response was Pusheen, which is a cat character).

Tables 2 and 3 suggest that Japanese participants, and especially Japanese females, have a broader definition of cute than American participants. For example, if we augment the top three categories for Japanese males (Animal 21.7%, Human 17.2%, Character 15.6%) with the next three most popular categories (Adjective 10.7, Color 6.6%, Sweets and Fruits 4.5%) the result is a cumulative coverage of 76.3% for the top three categories, which is still short of the coverage obtained by just the top three categories for both American males and American females.

More dramatically, if we augment the top three categories for Japanese females (Adjectives 15.5%, Character 13.1%, and Human 12.7%) with the next three most popular categories (Colors 9.4% and Ornaments/Accessory 8.0%, Animal 6.6%) the result is a cumulative coverage of 64.7% for the top six categories, which is far short of the coverage provided by the top three categories for both American females and American males and is also short of the coverage provided by the top six categories for Japanese males. Looking at the data in another way, there are nine categories that each garner at least 5% of the responses for Japanese females. However, there are only three categories above 5% for American females, three categories excluding "Other" above 5% for American males, and five categories above 5% for Japanese males.

It is worth noting that some categories, especially the adjective category, involve interactions with other categories. For example, across males and females, the American data includes 42 responses that were categorized as animals. Examples include dogs, cats, puppies, kittens, baby animals, small harmless animals, plump animals and foxes. Out of the 42 responses that were coded as animals, 14 (33%) suggested a small animal. Examples include: baby animals, small animals, kittens, puppy and puppies. While these responses were coded as animals, they also explicitly or implicitly imply the adjective "small". Similar interactions also occur in the Human categories, most notably with the responses "baby" or "babies" which were coded as humans. The Adjective category contains 109 responses across the male and female American data. This includes 21 responses (19%) that explicitly or implicitly suggest small size such as childish, miniature, petite, small, tiny, young and youthful. Therefore, it is not surprising that pairing these often show up in other Categories.

3.2   Follow-Up Questionnaire Results and Analysis

As reported in [6] Japanese females (N = 15) made a total of 305 responses for kawaii while Japanese males (N = 45) made a total of 406 responses for kawaii. After completing the three-week immersive course "Japanese Culture, Technology and Design," American females (N = 9) made a total of 91 responses for kawaii while American males (N = 15) made a total of 122 responses for kawaii. Table 4 compares the mean number of associations with kawaii that were provided by American participants versus Japanese participants. Since it is widely believed that perceptions of cuteness vary by gender, this data is disaggregated by gender as well. It is worth noting that the mean number of associations made by Japanese females was approximately double the mean number of associations made by Japanese males and by both American males and females. This may be because kawaii is considered a somewhat feminine concept in Japan.

Table 4. Cross-cultural comparison of mean number of responses to "kawaii"

	Americans		Japanese	
	Females	Males	Females	Males
N	9	15	15	45
Mean	10.1	8.1	20.3	9.0
Min	8	4	7	1
Max	16	12	41	27

Table 5 shows the percentage of total responses per category. For example, the first row of the table indicates that 25.3% of the total responses made by American females were categorized as adjectives, 24.6% of the responses made by American males were categorized as adjectives, 20.7% of the responses made by Japanese females were adjectives, and 6.2% of the responses made by Japanese Males were adjectives. We have highlighted entries in Table 2 that exceed 5%. These entries are the most important to consider and will be discussed in more detail below. We do not highlight entries in the "Other" category since it is comprised of a collection of unrelated items.

Table 5. Percentage of total cute associations for each category

Category	Americans		Japanese	
	Females	Males	Females	Males
1. Adjective	**23.0**	**24.6**	**20.7**	6.2
2. Animal	**12.0**	4.1	**10.8**	**25.1**
3. Character	**10.9**	7.4	4.9	**12.8**
4. Clothes and Fashion	3.3	4.9	4.3	6.2
5. Color	8.8	5.7	4.6	4.2
6. Foreign Items	0.0	0.0	0.7	0.0
7. Human	8.8	7.4	**13.4**	**16.7**
8. Letter	0.0	0.0	0.3	0.5
9. Onomatopoeic Expressions	0.0	0.0	4.9	1.2
10. Ornaments and Accessory	1.1	0.8	**8.5**	4.2
11. Person's Name	0.0	0.0	**8.2**	**5.4**
12. Place	0.0	0.0	1.6	0.7
13. Plant	1.1	0.0	2.3	2.5
14. Shape and Pattern	3.3	2.5	2.6	1.0
15. Sweets and Fruits	2.2	0.8	4.3	1.0
16. Toy and Equipment	1.1	**6.6**	2.0	3.2
17. Others	1.0	14.8	5.9	9.1
18. Special	**10.9**	**19.7**	–	–

Table 6 presents the top three categories for each demographic, as well as the percentage of associations for with each category and the total percentage of associations covered by the top three categories in aggregate.

Table 6. Comparison of top three kawaii categories by demographic group

Group	Top three categories	Aggregate % for top three categories
American females	Adjective (23.0%)	45.9%
	Animals (12.0%)	
	Character and Special each tied at (10.9%)	
American males	Adjective (24.6%)	39.4%
	Special (19.7%)	
	Character and Human each tied at (7.4%)	
Japanese females	Adjective (20.7%)	39.7%
	Animal (10.8%)	
	Person's Name (8.2%)	
Japanese males	Animal (25.1%)	54.6%
	Human (16.7%)	
	Character (12.8%)	

All demographic groups, except Japanese males, make the most associations to adjectives. Additionally, Character which was in the top three ranking with respect to cute for both Japanese males and Japanese females (see Table 3) has fallen considerably for Japanese females. Thus, Japanese females seem to consider items that are categorized as Character to be more cute than kawaii.

On the other hand, Character had less than 1% of the cute associations for both American males and American females (see Table 3) yet Character makes the top three association list with respect to kawaii for both American males and American females. Thus, these groups appear to consider items categorized as Character to be more kawaii than cute. While Japanese participants list a mixture of Japanese and foreign Characters (Hello Kitty, but also Pooh and Mickey Mouse), the American participants list almost exclusively characters that are associated with Japan. In particular, not a single Disney Character is on the list. This reinforces the notion that American participants consider kawaii to be a foreign term.

This idea is reinforced by considering the category "Special," which includes the subcategories "Manga and Anime", "Japanese", and "big eyes". The subcategory of "Manga and Anime" indicates that the responses were directly related to either Manga or Anime. Those responses that clearly mention that the kawaii concept is Japanese were placed into the subcategory of "Japanese." Lastly, but quite interestingly, several American participants described kawaii with "big eyes" and thus stands as an independent subcategory of Special.

4 Discussion

As noted earlier, most of the American participants were not able to make associations with the concept of kawaii before taking the course. Female American participants listed 46 smallness-related associations out of 152 total responses to cute while male participants marked 33 associations out of 116 entries. A deeper qualitative analysis reveals that they came to their own "understanding" of kawaii-ness after they were exposed to Japanese culture. Compared to Japanese participants, American participants identified something related to smallness as one of the most prominent factors of kawaii. For example, 23% of female and 14% of male participants identified a small and/or young trait as in babies, puppies, children, small things, baby animals, and other similar variations, in their top kawaii association. On the other hand, 10% of both female and male Japanese participants associated smallness as a trait.

Another notable response by American students is that they find kawaii-ness in manga and anime that they have seen. Characters were also seen as inherently Japanese (Pokémon, Hello Kitty, Rilakkuma, mascots, and so forth). These mediums seem to trigger the participants' association with big eyes that may be perceived as a unique attribute to Japanese kawaii culture. There is only one association of "round eyes" under Human by a Japanese participant. Some American participants used "Japanese" to describe kawaii, which suggests that the concept of kawaii is not intuitive or ingrained but implemented. This explains that their associations are somewhat limited in scope, as Table 6 shows, while Japanese participants' responses covered a wider range of attributes and associations.

5   Conclusion

The concept of kawaii has been globally introduced. However, it is not as richly contextualized in the United States as in Japan. On the other hand, the loanword "kyūto" is much more integrated into the Japanese lexicon, shown in Japanese participants' broad associations. While both Japanese and American participants frequently associated adjectives with both cute and kawaii, the range of adjectives used by Americans was somewhat limited. Most notably, Americans often used adjectives related to smallness as associations for both cute and kawaii. This limited range of adjectives for American participants, as compared to Japanese participants, may suggest that the American concepts of cute and kawaii are not as broad as the Japanese version of these concepts. We can also speculate that cute is a part of kawaii in Japanese society, but in the US, kawaii is a partly shared concept with cute. In fact, in English we often describe kawaii as a "Japanese style of cuteness" which suggests it is a special type of cuteness that has some intersection with American cuteness but may not be a subset of it.

References

1. Yomota, I.: Kawaii Ron (The Theory of Kawaii). Chikuma Shobō, Tokyo (2006)
2. Marcus, A., Kurosu, M., Ma, X., Hashizume, A.: Cuteness Engineering: Designing Adorable Products and Services. Springer Series on Cultural Computing, 1st edn. Springer, Cham (2017). https://doi.org/10.1007/978-3-319-61961-3
3. Laohakangvalvit, T., Achalakul, T., Ohkura, M.: A proposal of model of Kawaii feelings for spoon designs. In: Kurosu, M. (ed.) HCI 2017. LNCS, vol. 10271, pp. 687–699. Springer, Cham (2017). https://doi.org/10.1007/978-3-319-58071-5_52
4. Ohkura, M.: "Kawaii" Engineering. Asakura Publishing Co., Ltd., Tokyo (2017)
5. Berque, D., Chiba, H., Hashizume, A., Kurosu, M., Showalter, S.: Cuteness in Japanese design: investigating perceptions of *Kawaii* among American college students. In: Fukuda, S. (ed.) AHFE 2018. AISC, vol. 774, pp. 392–402. Springer, Cham (2019). https://doi.org/10.1007/978-3-319-94944-4_43
6. Hashizume, A., Kurosu, M.: Gender difference in the free association for "Cute" and "Kawaii". In: Kurosu, M. (ed.) HCII 2019. LNCS, vol. 11566, pp. 439–449 (2019)
7. Berque, D., Chiba, H.: Exposing American undergraduates to *Monozukuri* and other key principles in Japanese culture, design, technology and robotics. In: Stephanidis, C. (ed.) HCI 2016. CCIS, vol. 617, pp. 3–8. Springer, Cham (2016). https://doi.org/10.1007/978-3-319-40548-3_1
8. Berque, D., Chiba, H.: Evaluating the use of LINE software to support interaction during an american travel course in Japan. In: Rau, P.-L.P. (ed.) CCD 2017. LNCS, vol. 10281, pp. 614–623. Springer, Cham (2017). https://doi.org/10.1007/978-3-319-57931-3_49

Emotional Design for Children's Electronic Picture Book

Yaohua Bu[1], Jia Jia[2], Xiang Li[2], and Xiaobo Lu[1(✉)]

[1] Academy of Arts and Design, Tsinghua University, Beijing 100084, China
boyhl8@mails.tsinghua.edu.cn, luxb@tsinghua.edu.cn
[2] Key Laboratory of Pervasive Computing, Ministry of Education China,
and Department of Computer Science and Technology, Tsinghua University,
Beijing 100084, China

Abstract. Picture book is beneficial for children in many ways. In this work, we aim to investigate whether emotional design in an electronic picture book can facilitate children with great multi-sense experience, improve comprehension of children and give children positive emotional experience during reading. We propose a novel PCE (Perception & Comprehension & Expression) model from the perspective of emotional design. First, at the level of perception, it provides interfaces of multi-sensory interaction function. Second, at the level of cognition, it builds some interactive scenes. Third, at the level of expression, it creates some high-level interaction modes based on emotion recognition and emotion feedback. And based on PCE models in practice, we propose an electronic interactive picture book for children (5–8 years old), named E-book. In user study, it is proved that, added emotional design, the electronic picture can not only bring children excellent sensory experience in reading, but also help children get better understanding about the context. Furthermore, it gives children pleasant emotional interaction.

Keywords: Electronic picture books · Emotional design · Multimedia learning

1 Introduction

Recently, more and more electronic picture books are coming into people's view, such as mixed-media picture books [1], touch-feel picture books [2], game books, etc. However, these electronic picture books have two major disadvantages: on the one hand, their fancy interaction style is generally designed for entertainment instead of children's understanding; on the other hand, only the interaction for electronic picture book on appearance is taken into account in their design, but the interaction for electronic picture book on emotion is always ignored. Recently, with "affect and emotion in HCI" [3] being more and more significant, adding emotional design in electronic picture book may solve the existing problems.

Therefore, from the perspective of emotional design, we propose a novel PCE (Perception & Comprehension & Expression) model from the perspective of emotional design. And based on this, we propose an electronic picture book for children (5–8 years old), named E-book. First, at the level of perception, it provides excellent multi-sensory

© Springer Nature Switzerland AG 2019
M. Kurosu (Ed.): HCII 2019, LNCS 11566, pp. 392–403, 2019.
https://doi.org/10.1007/978-3-030-22646-6_28

interaction; second, at the level of cognition, it builds some immersive cognitive interaction; third, at the level of affection, it creates some emotional interaction based on emotion recognition and emotion feedback. The PCE model provide clear guidance not only in the stage of designing electronic book from the prospective of emotional design, but also in the stage of user study. In the user study, we design experiments to verify whether electronic picture books added emotional design can improve children's reading effect. The user study shows that emotional design for children picture books can induce positive sense experience in readers [4], and affect cognitive outcomes, e.g. excellent learning comprehension performance, as well as affective results, e.g., pleasant emotion.

2   Related Works

2.1   Traditional Picture Books and Electronic Picture Books

Traditional children's picture books include a lot of illustrations and a few words, particularly for children age from 3 to 6. Picture books are beneficial for children in many ways, e.g., stimulating their interest, improving their cognition. However, traditional picture books are limited in adult's guidance which will restrict the emotional expression of children if mother-child communicative interaction is inappropriate.

With the impact of digital products increasing, people may find electronic picture book cheaper, more convenient to carry and more environment-friendly. It goes beyond the text and pictures in the paper versions, and may thus broaden children's imagination. Combining sound, animation and game, the electronic book is able to activate children in many aspects [5–7]. Compared to traditional picture books, electronic books might be useful in children understanding stories independently.

2.2   Emotional Design in Multimedia Learning

In the past years, research on multimedia learning begun to consider the influence of emotional design. Emotional design can be defined as the use of different design elements to impact learners' emotion to enhance learning ability [8] (Plass & Kaplan). Lots of the researches has investigated on the emotional feedback of the users on the interaction with the design outcomes.

The literature shows that adding positive emotion into multimedia learning facilitates student learning performance [4, 9, 10]. Park, Plass, and Brünken [11] used an eye-tracking device to examine the influence of emotion on learning with multimedia. They found that learners who were in a positive emotional state before learning had better learning outcomes. Erb [12] assumed that sound is a method to stimulate involvement and motivation in learning situations, thereby bringing the learner to invest more mental effort into learning, which finally leads to better learning performance. Shavelson and Towne [13] conducted experiments on investigating the effects of emotional design into multimedia materials on problem-solving skills, attention and motivation levels in primary mathematics. The results show that the effects of emotional design into multimedia materials perform better on problem solving skill, attention and motivation levels.

2.3   Emotional Design in Electronic Picture Books Reading

Only a few studies investigate the impact of added the emotional design in the electronic picture books on children' emotion and their reading outcome. In some point of view, introducing emotional design in picture books have good effects on children's comprehension: Tsai's study [14] investigated the impact of children's picture books on the emotional understanding and emotion regulation of 5–6 years old Taiwanese students. They found that children's emotional understanding was improved by picture books related to emotion elements. But emotional design in picture books may have adverse effects. For example, too many inappropriate emotional elements may distract their attention in reading. Visual effects may distract children and guide them to think of the story as a game, and interfere with comprehending the story as a motivation [15]. Too many exaggerated animation elements will reduce children's attention. "Children seemed to enjoy the animated effects, but this affective motivation did not lead to understanding a whole story" [16].

2.4   Problem Statement

Previous researches on the emotional design in multimedia learning have been criticized for the following reasons. First, most of the studies on emotional design are conducted with adults rather on children. Second, in most of the previous research, they use subjective indicators such as the positive affective scale of PANAS [17] to detect emotion. But psychological scales may be not suitable for children. Third, few research is focus on the impact of emotional design for children's electronic picture books. Finally, the research on the different levels of affective elements in electronic picture book is easily ignored.

Therefore, the purpose of this study is: Whether the utilization of different levels of emotional elements in electronic picture books has a positive influence on children' perception, understandability, and emotion.

3   Emotional Design Models for Electronic Picture Book

3.1   The Theory of Emotional Design Models

We propose a novel PCE (Perception & Comprehension & Expression) model from the perspective of emotional design. In the following, we elaborate details of the emotional interaction between children and electronic books on three levels: perception level, comprehension level, and expression levels.

Perception level appeals to a first sense reaction when children encounter an electronic picture book. Perception is the simplest psychological phenomenon to sense the world. "Beauty Means Nice Effect" [18], that says excellent appearance can promote emotional relationships between users and products. The visual reaction to product's appearance is about initial reactions that child takes one look and says "I want it." Visual elements in picture book can stimulate children's interest, affect children's emotion and foster children's learning [10].

Visual, auditory, tactile and olfactory senses are the basic factors that we need to consider. In details, the story structure, picture layout, graphics setting, animation elements, sound elements, touch interaction, and other elements should be considered to give user multi-sense experience in electronic picture books. The goal of perception level is achieving the harmonious among visual, auditory, tactile and olfactory senses.

Comprehension level refers to children's cognitive psychological. Understandability comes first and foremost. If readers can read the words but not understand what they are reading, they may fail to construct the cognition through picture books. Emotional design should focus on understanding the cognitive system of the children. Nevertheless, numerous of studies reveal that the challenge for the emotional design is how to design a product suitable for the capacity of children's cognitive system, which otherwise end up in creating a cognitive overload and decreasing learning performance [19].

When designing a picture book, we aim at improving comprehension for children, depicting an easy-to-understand world, and establishing a link for knowledge transmission. Children's reading comprehension is related to language development, picture understanding, listening comprehension, emotion condition [20], personal interest, complex social skills [21, 22], etc. For instance, beautiful pictures are more likely to draw students' attention and to help student remember the concept and knowledge longer [23]. Fredrickson and Thomas Joiner [24] describe that positive emotion broadens people's thought and encourages them to discover novel lines of thought or action.

Expression level is about children's emotion when they are reading—e.g., how books affect children feel, or what kind of feeling children want to express. Expression level extends design purpose from "aesthetics, function" to "emotion, experience." For a child who reads a picture book, emotion is the meaning and the memory of the book. Emotions reflect personal experiences, associations, and memories. Kaptelinin [25], a well-known interaction design expert, once described the emotional experience with definite feelings including "satisfying, pleasant, interesting, effective, enlightening, beautiful, attractive, creative, achievable and emotional satisfaction."

There are many ways to build the emotional relationship between picture books and readers. On the one hand, electronic picture books can express emotions through content, such as anthropomorphic cartoon characters or immersive interactive scene. On the other hand, electronic picture books can perceive emotions through artificial intelligence technology. For instance, electronic picture books can recognize children's feeling through affective computing and then give children immediately feedback according to the change of emotional state.

3.2 Emotional Design Models in Practice

In the previous chapter, we propose a novel PCE (Perception & Comprehension & Expression) model from the perspective of emotional design. And based on this model, we establish an electronic e picture book for children (5–8 years old), named E-book, which depicts some typical scenarios that may happen in the kindergarten [26]. In the design of the main plot, commendatory, background music and user interface play important roles. And on this basis, some other designs of interactive functions in E-book provides entries for children to explore branches of the story-line by themselves. In the following, we elaborate details of three typical levels (see Fig. 1).

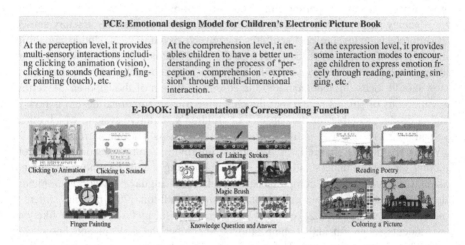

Fig. 1. Architecture of PCE model and corresponding implementation of E-book

First, at the perception level, it provides multi-sensory interactions including clicking to animation (vision), clicking to sounds (hearing), finger painting (touch), etc. Perception level focus on the basic function of the electronic picture book, which includes the interface design (see Fig. 2), voice design, and tactile interaction, etc. It is an interactive book with anthropomorphic animations and sound effect that can be accessed by clicking on parts of pictures.

Second, at the comprehension level, it builds some interactive scenes including "game of linking strokes" and "magic brush". In "game of linking strokes", children learn physics knowledge to help characters in the book to go through obstacles by linking strokes. For example, when children draw a bridge that meets the physical structural mechanics to connect both sides of the river, the hero of the story can successfully cross the river. And "magic brush" in which children need to imagine what they need in the story and draw it out through magic brush. In this way, children may have a better understanding in the process of "perception (what they need) – comprehension (how to draw) – expression (draw it out)".

Fig. 2. Partially user interface of E-book

Third, at the expression level, it provides some emotional interaction modes including "reading poetry" and "coloring a picture book". In "reading poetry", we apply a multi-path deep neural network [27] to recognize four different emotions including happiness, sadness, impatience and peace, so that while children read poetry with different emotions (e.g., happy), a photo in a corresponding emotional color (e.g., orange) will be generated to encourage children to express emotions freely.

4 User Study

As mentioned in the previous section, the design of E-book is on account of the PCE (Perception & Comprehension & Expression) model. In this chapter, I design three experiments. The first experiment validates the sense organs level indicators, the second experiment validates the comprehension level indicators, and the third experiment validates the emotional level indicators. The following is the process of experiments including experiment participants, motivation, environment, materials, measures, and results.

4.1 Participants

To select children participants, we assessed their current level of story understanding using procedures recommended by Sulzby [28]. We recruited 20 children aged 4–6 (10 males and 10 females) whose reading ability is the level of 3–5 in Sulzby's study. They can understand and retell the story independently. We randomly divided 20 children into test and control group by their gender and age, 10 children for each group.

4.2 Motivation

We design three experiments to verify whether children's electronic picture book added emotional design can improve children's reading effect from the following three perspectives [29]:

Hypothesis 1: Added the emotional design elements, whether the electronic picture book gives the children an excellent sensory experience during children learning?

Hypothesis 2: Added the emotional design elements, whether the electronic picture book enhances the understandability during children learning?

Hypothesis 3: Added the emotional design elements, whether the electronic picture book brings more positive emotional experience during children learning?

4.3 Environment

The experiment was conducted in a kindergarten. In some experiment conditions, children may be out of control due to tension or other reasons. To ensure the reliability of the whole experiment, we took the following measures: Firstly, the experimenter explained the process of the experiment to children so that children were familiar with the operation. Secondly, the experimenter gave children guidance if they were in trouble. Thirdly, the experiment site is a separate room without any interruptions. Fourthly, the children participant watched a 3 min relaxing video to neutralize their affective state before the experiment.

4.4 Materials

We have two groups, named the test group and the control group. The test group is taken from E-book which uses the emotional design method as a design principle. We sort and simplify the content of E-book to produce the material of test group. The test group's material is an emotional electronic picture book with related anthropomorphic animations, colorful illustration, voice over and sound effect that can be accessed by clicking on any parts of pictures. As a comparison, the material of control group is electronic picture book which just consists of text and illustrations. The storyline in the control group is the same with the test group, which depicts Ganggang's first day in the kindergarten. We divide the storyline into ten story chapters to ensure that each corresponding chapter of the test group and the control group is the same. The difference between the test group and the control group is that the control group has emotional design elements while the test group not.

4.5 Measures

The measures of the experiment are designed from three perspectives based on the PCE model. At the perception level, to verify children participant's sensory experience in reading, we use subjective questionnaire to assess their evaluation. At the comprehension level, to ascertain the effect of children participant's comprehension, we take the method of "story retelling [30]." At the expression level, to recognize children's emotions condition, we design an emotion recognition system with facial expression signals. The following are the details of measures.

In the sensory evaluation experiment, child reads E-book independently for 15 min. When the children finish reading, we invited them to give a multi-sense evaluation on E-book. The design of the interview questionnaire is from the sensory experience evaluation including visual evaluation (e.g., interface), hearing evaluation (e.g., music), and touch evaluation (e.g., painting). A 5-point method [31] is used to evaluate the children's satisfaction towards the questionnaire items. The current study uses the measurement for online store perception adopted from Kim, Fiore, and Lee, which includes 5 items to understand the customer's perception of the website better.

The story retelling experiment is a comparative experiment. In the test group and control group, every child participant reads one chapter of ten corresponding materials. Each group of children engaged in all two processes: (a) Each group of children read one chapter of the materials independently in 5 min. (b) When the children finished the reading task, the experimenter has a 10-min-conversation with them. The experimenter guides each child to retell the story, e.g., "You read the story now." "I am eager to hear you tell the story." "Can you share me the story?" At the same time, the experimenter records the conversation. After that, the experimenter will translate the child's voice into text.

In the emotion recognition experiment, the purpose of the experiment is to verify which group gets more positive emotion samples. We used an emotion detection device to recognize children's emotion. Through analyzing facial expression signals, the device attempts to recognize the type of emotions (including positive emotion, negative emotion, and neutral emotion) and calculate the probability of emotion. In the test and control group, every child reads one chapter of ten corresponding materials. Each group reads one chapter of ten corresponding materials independently. And the emotion detection device records the children' facial expression at the same time. The emotion will be used for data analysis in the next step. To facilitate statistical calculation, we map the probability of positive and negative results of emotion to the range of [−1–1]. The closer the emotion score is to 1, the higher the probability of positive emotion is. The closer the emotion score is to −1, the higher the probability of negative emotion is. The closer the emotion score is to 0, the higher the probability of neutral emotion is. We can find that emotion score of the test and control group over time in Fig. 3.

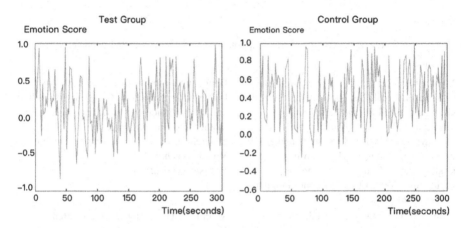

Fig. 3. Emotion score of the test group and the control group over time

4.6 Result

The outcome of the sensory evaluation experiment shows that the score of children's sensory evaluation in reading. See Fig. 4, in which we can find that the mean score of children's sensory evaluation is 4.26. It may reflect that E-book can bring children excellent sensory experience especially on visual experience and touch experience.

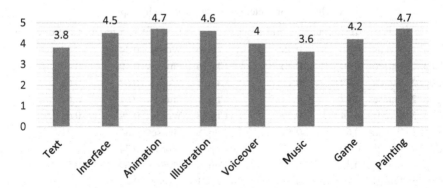

Fig. 4. The mean score of children's sensory evaluation in reading.

To verify the effect of emotional design on children's understanding, we take the method of "story retelling". Table 1 is the examples of coding system proposed by Sulzby [27]. With the help of verbatim transcriptions, we calculate how many words appear in the original text, and how many phrases (at least three words in a row) were derived from the original text. The examples of transcriptions and coding for selected chapter are in Table 1. And Table 2 is the story retelling accuracy of each chapter. Story retelling accuracy of the test group and the control group is in Table 3, which proves that test group achieves a significant improvement. Through the comparison experiment, we find that adding emotional design in an electronic picture book can promote children's ability of understanding.

Table 1. Examples of transcriptions and coding for selected chapter

Stimulus text	Participant
Mother told Ganggang that she would send him to a place called kindergarten tomorrow. Ganggang asked his mother: What is kindergarten? Mother: Kindergarten is a place where everyone plays, study and grows up together. Ganggang: Is it fun in kindergarten? Mom: Kindergarten is fun. I will wake you up tomorrow morning and bring you to kindergarten	Ganggang's mother would send him to kindergarten tomorrow. Ganggang doesn't know what kindergarten is. Ganggang's mother told him Kindergarten is a place for children plays, study and grow up together. **Words (verbal): 31** **Phrases (verbal): 3**
Mom took Ganggang into kindergarten. As soon as Ganggang entered the classroom door, he saw many children were crying. There was a tall female teacher among the children. She was the teacher of the class. After a while, Mom was leaving, and Ganggang wanted to cry. But he remembered that his father had told him that a boy should be brave, so he stopped crying	Mom took Ganggang to kindergarten. Ganggang saw many children were crying. **Words (verbal): 11** **Phrases (verbal): 2**

Table 2. Story retelling accuracy of each chapter

	Level	Test group	Control group		Level	Test group	Control group
Chp. 1	Words	0.55	0.46	Chp. 6	Words	0.34	0.32
Chp. 1	Phrases	0.60	0.40	Chp. 6	Phrases	0.40	0.40
Chp. 2	Words	0.40	0.16	Chp. 7	Words	0.67	0.63
Chp. 2	Phrases	0.67	0.33	Chp. 7	Phrases	0.67	0.67
Chp. 3	Words	0.74	0.59	Chp. 8	Words	0.79	0.65
Chp. 3	Phrases	0.67	0.50	Chp. 8	Phrases	0.86	0.71
Chp. 4	Words	0.40	0.55	Chp. 9	Words	0.74	0.68
Chp. 4	Phrases	0.33	0.50	Chp. 9	Phrases	0.67	0.50
Chp. 5	Words	0.57	0.46	Chp. 10	Words	0.72	0.59
Chp. 5	Phrases	0.60	0.40	Chp. 10	Phrases	0.71	0.57

Table 3. Story retelling accuracy of the test group and the control group

Heading level	Test group	Control group
Words	0.59	0.51
Phrase	0.62	0.50

In this chapter, three delicate experiments are introduced. We calculate the ratio of positive emotion samples to total emotion samples (see Table 4) and average score and standard deviation of emotion samples in the test and control group over time (see Table 5). In the test group, the ratio of positive emotion samples to total emotion samples is 0.587, the mean score of emotion samples is 0.5, and the standard deviation value is 0.47. Obviously, the proportion of positive emotion samples is greater than the neutral and negative emotion samples. In the control group, the ratio of positive emotion samples to total emotion samples is 0.307, the average score of emotion samples is 0.1, and the standard deviation value is 0.37. The experimental data shows that the proportion of neutral emotion samples are greater than the positive and negative emotion samples.

Generally, the number of positive emotion samples and the mean score of emotion samples in the test group are all higher than the control group. Results reveal that positive emotions generally increase as the amount of emotional design features increase in the electronic picture book.

Table 4. The ratio of positive emotion samples to total emotion samples

Group	Number of positive emotions	Number of neutral emotions	Number of negative emotions	The ratio of positive emotions to total emotions
Test group	88	61	1	0.587
Control group	46	88	16	0.307

Table 5. The statistics of emotion score over time

Group	Sample size	Mean value	Standard deviation
Test group	10	0.5	0.47
Control group	10	0.1	0.37

5   Conclusion

In this work, we proposed a novel PCE model from the perspective of emotional design. It provides clear guidance not only in the stage of designing electronic book from the prospective of emotional design, but also in the stage of user study. And based on this, we propose E-book which makes significant impact on children's reading effects. In the user study, we find that emotional design for children's electronic picture books can strongly influence children' sensory experience, enhance comprehension and create a positive emotional resonance for the children.

Acknowledgment. This work is supported by the National Key Research and Development Plan (2016YFB1001200), the Innovation Method Fund of China (2016IM010200). This work is also supported by the National Social Science Foundation of China (17AG006).

References

1. Figueiredo, A.C., Pinto, A.L., Branco, P., Zagalo, N., Coquet, E.: Bridging book: a not-so-electronic children's picturebook, pp. 569–572. ACM Press (2013)
2. Kistler, F., Sollfrank, D., Bee, N., André, E.: Full body gestures enhancing a game book for interactive story telling. In: Si, M., Thue, D., André, E., Lester, J.C., Tanenbaum, J., Zammitto, V, (eds.) ICIDS 2011. LNCS, vol. 7069, pp. 207–218. Springer, Heidelberg (2011). https://doi.org/10.1007/978-3-642-25289-1_23
3. Bødker, S.: When second wave HCI meets third wave challenges. In: Proceedings of NordiCHI 2006, vol. 189, pp. 1–8. ACM Press, New York (2006)
4. Plass, J.L., Heidig, S., Hayward, E.O., Homer, B.D., Um, E.: Emotional design in multimedia learning: effects of shape and color on affect and learning. Learn. Instr. **29**, 128–140 (2014)
5. Lancy, D.F., Hayes, B.L.: Interactive fiction and the reluctant reader. Engl. J. **77**(7), 42–46 (1988)
6. Reinking, D.: Me and my hypertext: a multiple digression analysis of technology and literacy (sic). Reading Teacher **50**, 626–643 (1997)
7. Jong, M.T.D., Bus, A.G.: Quality of book-reading matters for emergent readers. J. Educ. Psychol. **94**(94), 145–155 (2002)
8. Plass, J.L., Kaplan, U.: Emotional design in digital media for learning. In: Emotions, Technology, Design, and Learning, pp. 131–161 (2016)
9. Mayer, R.E., Estrella, G.: Benefits of emotional design in multimedia instruction. Learn. Instr. **33**, 12–18 (2014)
10. Um, E., Plass, J.L., Hayward, E.O., Homer, B.D.: Emotional design in multimedia learning. J. Educ. Psychol. **104**(2), 485 (2012)
11. Park, B., KnoRzer, L., Plass, J.L., Brünken, R.: Emotional design and positive emotions in multimedia learning: an eyetracking study on the use of anthropomorphisms. Comput. Educ. **86**, 30–42 (2015)
12. Erb, U.: Sound as affective design feature in multimedia learning–benefits and drawbacks from a cognitive load theory perspective. International Association for Development of the Information Society (2015)
13. Feuer, M.J., Towne, L., Shavelson, R.J.: Scientific culture and educational research. Educ. Res. **31**(8), 4–14 (2002)
14. Tsai, M.J.: Guiding Taiwanese kindergarteners' emotional understanding and emotion regulation: the effects of children's picture books. Dissertations & Theses – Gradworks (2008)
15. Smith, C.R.: Click and turn the page: an exploration of multiple storybook literacy. Reading Res. Q. **36**, 152–183 (2001)
16. Labbo, L.D., Kuhn, M.R.: Weaving chains of affect and cognition: a young child's understanding of CD-ROM talking books. J. Literacy Res. **32**, 187–210 (2000)

17. Watson, D., Clark, L.A., Tellegen, A.: Development and validation of brief measures of positive and negative affect: the panas scales. J. Pers. Soc. Psychol. **54**(6), 1063–1070 (1988)
18. Byrne, K., Lidwell, W., Holden, K., Butler, K.: Universal principles of design: 100 ways to enhance usability, influence perception, increase appeal, make better design decisions, and teach through design. Inf. Des. J. **14**(2), 185–186 (2006)
19. Moreno, R., Mayer, R.E.: A coherence effect in multimedia learning: the case for minimizing irrelevant sounds in the design of multimedia instructional messages. J. Educ. Psychol. **92**(1), 117–125 (2000)
20. Hughes, C., Devine, R.T.: A social perspective on theory of mind. In: Lamb, M.E. (ed.) Handbook of Child Psychology and Developmental Science. Wiley, Hoboken (2015)
21. Doise, W.: On the social development of the intellect. In: Shulman, V.L., Restaino-Baumann, L.C.R., Butler, L. (eds.) The Future of Piagetian Theory. Springer, Boston (1985). https://doi.org/10.1007/978-1-4684-4925-9_5
22. Wasik, B.A., Hindman, A.H., Snell, E.K.: Book reading and vocabulary development: a systematic review. Early Child. Res. Q. **37**, 39–57 (2016)
23. Sitzmann, T., Johnson, S.: The paradox of seduction by irrelevant details: how irrelevant information helps and hinders self-regulated learning. Learn. Individ. Differ. **34**(3), 1–11 (2014)
24. Norman, D.A.: Emotional design. Ubiquity **2004**, 1 (2004)
25. Fredrickson, B.L., Joiner, T.: Positive emotions trigger upward spirals toward emotional well-being. Psychol. Sci. **13**(2), 172–175 (2002)
26. Bu, Y., Jia, J., Li, X., Zhou, S., Lu, X.: IcooBook: when the picture book for children encounters aesthetics of interaction. In: 2018 ACM Multimedia Conference on Multimedia Conference, pp. 1260–1262. ACM (2018)
27. Zhang, L., et al.: Emphasis detection for voice dialogue applications using multi-channel convolutional bidirectional long short-term memory network (2018)
28. Sulzby, E.: Children's emergent reading of favorite storybooks: a developmental study. Reading Res. Q. **20**, 458–481 (1985)
29. Ng, K.H., Chiu, T.K.F.: Emotional multimedia design for developing mathematical problem-solving skills. In: Ma, W.W.K., Chan, C.-K., Tong, K.-w., Fung, H., Fong, C.W.R. (eds.) New Ecology for Education — Communication X Learning, pp. 131–141. Springer, Singapore (2017). https://doi.org/10.1007/978-981-10-4346-8_11
30. Jong, M.T.D., Bus, A.G.: The efficacy of electronic books in fostering kindergarten children's emergent story understanding. Reading Res. Q. **39**(4), 378–393 (2011)
31. Kim, J., Fiore, A.M., Lee, H.H.: Influences of online store perception shopping enjoyment, and shopping involvement on consumer patronage behavior towards an online retailer. J. Retail. Consum. Serv. **14**, 95–107 (2006)

Design Criteria for Kansei-Oriented Elderly Products

Kuo-Hsiang Chen[1]([⊠]), Ching-Chien Liang[2], Ya-Hsueh Lee[2],
Jia-Xuan Han[3], and Yu-Chen Lu[3]

[1] Fuzhou University of International Studies and Trade, Fuzhou, China
kchen@fzfu.edu.cn
[2] Southern Taiwan University of Science and Technology, Tainan, Taiwan
[3] National Cheng Kung University, Tainan, Taiwan

Abstract. The purposes of this study included: (1) identifying the specific design components of functional shoes that affect the psychological feeling of the elderly, and establishing their weights; (2) exploring the Kansei evaluation difference between single sense and multi-senses while using the functional shoes; and (3) exploring the preference on materials and colors of the functional shoes. The research process was divided into four stages: (1) choosing 6 Kansei words to be used in the visual, tactile and synesthesia experiments based on the results of the earlier study; (2) collecting and classifying the visual and tactile test elements of the functional shoes to be used as samples in the visual, tactile and synesthesia experiments; (3) Kansei experiment for the elderly on different DISC personality; (4) the analysis and discussion of the results for different DISC personality. The results show that (1) there is significant differences on the Kansei image of the shoes with different materials. In the tactile experiment of "shoe material", the mesh material has the Kansei image of relieved, convenient, professional and delicate, but not comfortable or noble; (2) tactile, visual, and visual & tactile Kansei image are different even on the same material. The visual & tactile is highly correlated with single tactile image. For example, the "flannel" material has the image of "comfortable" both in the "tactile" and "visual & tactile" experiments, but of "relieved" while in the "visual" experiment; (3) the insole and shoe body share the same image, both have significant differences; (4) the results of the quantification theory type I show that "relieved", "convenient", "comfortable", "professional", "noble" and "delicate" are relevant to the "color of the shoe body" and the most influential category is "black" color.

Keywords: Design criteria · Kansei-oriented · Elderly products ·
High-involvement · Affective design

1 Introduction

The world has gradually entered the hyper-aged society, and the daily necessities of elderly people are highly valued. Studies showed that the physical, psychological and learning situation of the elderly tended to be slow, their memory is degenerating and learning is easily disturbed (Wu 1999). Industrial Economics & Knowledge Center

© Springer Nature Switzerland AG 2019
M. Kurosu (Ed.): HCII 2019, LNCS 11566, pp. 404–413, 2019.
https://doi.org/10.1007/978-3-030-22646-6_29

(IEK) of ITRI, Taiwan (2015) used "technology life" and "live independently" two indicators to classify Chinese elderly into four groups: Enlightened, more capable of accepting new technology in daily life and think they can live independently; Independents, not eager to use new technology in daily life but support for living independently; Fashionables, support using new technology but life is relatively independent and needs assistance; and Conservatives, stereotyped elderly generally not independent and low use of new technology. This categorization echoed Murata's (2015) claim "elderly industry is 'non-massive' market, is a collection of various micro markets instead".

In "Attractive product planning for mature market", prof. Hirashima (1991) mentioned "Products of the new era must enrich the hearts of consumers and make users feel happy". He further visualized with pictures showing the match of the attractive factor between planned and achieved. Therefore, Kansei needs of elderly people must be studied and their daily necessities should also be well designed to meet their Kansei preferences.

Consisting of 24 sets of adjectives describing personality traits, DISC personality test categorizes personality into four groups as: Dominance, Influence, Steadiness, and Compliance. Each set of adjectives were selected based on the four (D, I, S, C) measurement dimensions and some interference dimensions. Subjects were asked to pick the most suitable and the most unsuitable adjectives for themselves. DISC theory has been broadly used for human behavior classification, and more widely used in self-awareness, interpersonal interaction, and business marketing capabilities improvement (Chang 2015).

Based on the theory of Kansei Engineering, this study conducted research and analysis through experiments and in-depth interviews to explore the use of functional shoes for senior citizens. Through the Likert scale, synesthesia experiment, and quantification theory type I, the imagery evaluation of the functional shoes for the elderly was constructed and made possible to provide reference for the design of the functional goods for the elderly in the future.

The purposes of this study included: (1) identifying the specific design components of functional shoes that affect the psychological feeling of the elderly, and establishing their weights; (2) exploring the Kansei evaluation difference between single sense and multi-senses while using the functional shoes; and (3) exploring the preference on materials and colors of the functional shoes.

2 Methods

2.1 Participants

Total of 30 elderly were invited to participate the experiment. All of them have the experience of wearing functional shoes. Basic data of the participants include gender, age, education level and the DISC personality. Among them, 10 out of 30 were male (33%), female 20 (67%). On age, 14 out of 30 were between 65 and 69 (47%), 9 between 70 and 74 (30%), 5 between 75 and 79 (17%), 1 between 80 and 84 (3%), and 1 above 85 (3%). On education level, 21 (70%) with high school and below, 8 (27%)

with junior college and only 1 (3%) has college education. As for the DISC personality, 11 (37%) of Dominance, 10 (33%) of Influence, 5 (17%) of Steadiness, while 4 (13%) were of Compliance (as shown in Table 1).

Table 1. Participant demographics (n = 30).

Variable		n
Age	65–69	14
	70–74	9
	75–79	5
	80–84	1
	85–89	1
Gender	Male	10
	Female	20
DISC personality	Dominance	11
	Influence	10
	Steadiness	5
	Compliance	4
Education	High school and below	21
	Junior College	8
	College	1

The experiment was conducted during 21 April and 20 June of 2018 (Fig. 1).

Fig. 1. Photos show the participants during experiment

2.2   Experimental Materials

The sample functional shoes consist of 8 components, namely: shoe body, shoe head, sole, midsole, heel sheath, shoe mouth, tie free, and insole (as shown in Fig. 2). The most important parts of frequently chosen shoes were identified for the purpose of Kansei evaluation on both single sensory and synesthesia experiment. Two most significant parts were chosen as the control factors: "Shoe Body" and "Insole".

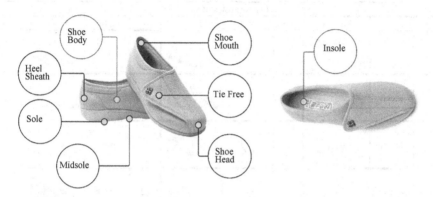

Fig. 2. Major parts of the elderly functional shoes

2.3   Procedure and Tasks Design

The research process was divided into four stages: (1) choosing 6 Kansei words to be used in the visual, tactile and synesthesia experiments based on the results of the earlier study; (2) collecting and classifying the visual and tactile test elements of the functional shoes to be used as samples in the visual, tactile and synesthesia experiments; (3) Kansei experiment for the elderly on different DISC personality; (4) the analysis and discussion of the results for different DISC personality.

3   Results and Discussion

3.1   Selection of the Kansei Words

Following the earlier study, highly involved elderly were interviewed with evaluation grid method to conclude the final 6 adjectives, namely: "relieved", "convenient", "comfortable", "professional", "noble", and "delicate".

3.2   Selection of Functional Shoe Samples

The color and material are the two major options for shoe body. 13 colors of shoe body were popular on the markets and websites where the elderly can see and chosen from, include: red, orange, yellow, green, navy, purple, khaki, brick red, pink, white, gray, black, and florid. Color cards were printed in 20 cm by 13 cm for the visual Kansei evaluation experiment (Table 2). Total of 7 materials of real shoes were used for both single sensory (tactile and visual) and synesthesia experiment (Table 3). The size and numbering of each real shoes were paired randomly by computer.

Table 2. Color samples of shoe body

No.	Color	Picture	No.	Color	Picture	No.	Color	Picture
1	red		2	orange		3	yellow	
4	green		5	navy		6	purple	
7	khaki		8	brick red		9	pink	
10	white		11	gray		12	black	
13	florid							

Table 3. Material samples of shoe body

No.	Material	Picture	No.	Material	Picture
1	synthetic fiber – mesh cloth		2	synthetic fiber – embroidered cloth	
3	synthetic fiber – flannel		4	synthetic fiber – PU leather	
5	synthetic fiber – knitted cloth		6	synthetic fiber – PU cloth	
7	synthetic fiber – jeans canvas cloth				

As for the insole, material is the major option. Same selection process as above was made. Total of 7 materials were used for both single sensory (tactile and visual) and synesthesia experiment (Table 4). The numbering of each real insole was randomly decided by computer.

3.3 Items and Categories of the Experimental Samples

There were 2 items for tactile experiment, namely "shoe body material" and "insole material". Three items were for visual experiment, namely "shoe body color", "shoe body material" and "insole material". Two items were for synesthesia experiment, namely "shoe body material" and "insole material". Based on composing elements, 14 categories were further differentiated for tactile experiment, and 27 categories for visual experiment (Table 5).

Table 4. Material samples of insole

Material samples of insole					
No.	Material	Picture	No.	Material	Picture
1	botanical fiber – cotton		2	botanical fiber – cotton flax	
3	animal fiber – leather		4	synthetic fiber – mesh + bamboo carbon	
5	synthetic fiber – sandwich mesh		6	animal fiber – wool	
7	double-density silicone – 100% silicone				

3.4 Kansei Evaluation Experiment

The results show that (1) there is significant differences on the Kansei image of the shoes with different materials. In the tactile experiment of "shoe material", the mesh material has the Kansei image of relieved, convenient, professional and delicate, but not comfortable or noble; (2) tactile, visual, and visual & tactile Kansei image are different even on the same material. The visual & tactile is highly correlated with single tactile image. For example, the "flannel" material has the image of "comfortable" both in the "tactile" and "visual & tactile" experiments, but of "relieved" while in the "visual" experiment; (3) the insole and shoe body share the same image, both have significant differences; (4) the results of the quantification theory type I show that "relieved", "convenient", "comfortable", "professional", "noble" and "delicate" are relevant to the "color of the shoe body" and the most influential category is "black" color.

Table 5. Items and categories for single sensory and synesthesia experiment

Items	No.	Picture	Visual Categories	Tactile Categories	Sensory
X1 shoe body color	1		red（C：45 M：98 Y：82 K：13）		visual
	2		orange（C：15 M：73 Y：87 K：0）		
	3		yellow（C：9 M：33 Y：92 K：0）		
	4		green（C：86 M：48 Y：81 K：9）		
	5		navy（C：85 M：68 Y：24 K：0）		
	6		purple（C：74 M：99 Y：42 K：6）		
	7		khaki（C：36 M：38 Y：61 K：0）		
	8		brick red（C：53 M：72 Y：69 K：12）		
	9		pink（C：15 M：24 Y：23 K：0）		
	10		white（C：10 M：10 Y：10 K：0）		
	11		gray（C：47 M：38 Y：36 K：0）		
	12		black（C：19 M：76 Y：78 K：57）		
	13		florid		

(*continued*)

Table 5. (*continued*)

X2 shoe body material	1		synthetic fiber	mesh cloth	visual + tactile
	2		synthetic fiber	embroidered cloth	
	3		synthetic fiber	flannel	
	4		synthetic fiber	PU leather	
	5		synthetic fiber	knitted cloth	
	6		synthetic fiber	PU leather	
	7		synthetic fiber	jeans canvas cloth	
X3 insole material	1		botanical fiber	cotton	visual + tactile
	2		botanical fiber	cotton flax	
	3		animal fiber	leather	
	4		synthetic fiber	mesh + bamboo carbon	
	5		synthetic fiber	sandwich mesh	
	6		animal fiber	wool	
	7		double-density silicone	silicone	

4 Conclusion

Different personality groups have different preference on the material and color of shoes. Taking "dominant personality" as example, sample 2 (embroidery cloth), sample 3 (flannel), sample 4 (leather), sample 5 (knitted fabric), and sample 6 (cloth) are preferred in tactile experiment, but not sample 1 (mesh) and sample 7 (cowhide surface). And in the visual experiment, all materials are preferred only sample 1 (mesh) is average level. While in the visual & tactile experiment, all of the materials are preferred. Therefore, the preference of functional shoes will gradually become stronger after being visually and tactilely contacted for this group of elderly.

According to the research results and analysis, we can understand the Kansei preferences of the elderly people for functional shoes, and help designers or related footwear manufacturers to design and produce products that meet the needs of the elderly, and build the guidelines for Kansei evaluation of functional footwear for the elderly accordingly.

References

1. Baxter, M.: Product Design-Practical Methods for the Systematic Development of New Product. Chapman & Hall, London (1995)
2. Buswell, G.T.: How people look at pictures: a study of the psychology of perception of art. University of Chicago Press, Chicago (1935)
3. Dichter, E.: What is an image? J. Consum. Res. **13**, 455–472 (1985)
4. Gallarza, M.G., Gil Saura, I., Calderón García, H.: Destination image towards a conceptual framework. Ann. Tour. Res. **29**(1), 56–78 (2002)
5. Hayashi, C.: On the quantification of qualitative data from the mathematico-statistical point of view. Ann. Inst. Stat. Math. **2**(1), 35 (1950)
6. Henderson, J.M., Hollingworth, A.: Eye movement during scene viewing: an overview (1998)
7. Iwabuchi, C., et al.: Data Management and Analysis by Yourself, pp. 180–185. Humura Publishing, Tokyo (2001)
8. Kelly, G.: Principles of Personal Construct Psychology. Norton, New York (1955)
9. Kinney, J.A.A., Luria, S.M.: Conflicting visual and tactual-kinesthetic stimulation. Percept. Psychophys. **8**, 189–192 (1970)
10. Loftus, G.R., Mackworth, N.H.: Cognitive determinants of fixation location during picture viewing. J. Exp. Psychol. Hum. Percept. Perform. **4**(4), 565–572 (1978)
11. Ma, M.Y., Tseng, L.T.: A study on the attractiveness of wedding dress approaching from Miryoku engineering. In: International Design Congress, Yunlin, Taiwan, IASDR (2005)
12. Nagamachi, M.: Kansei engineering: a new ergonomic consumer-oriented technology for product development. Int. J. Ind. Ergon. **15**, 3–11 (1995)
13. Rayner, K.: Eye movements in reading and information processing: 20 years of research. Psychol. Bull. **124**(3), 372–422 (1998)
14. Sanui, J.: Visualization of users requirements: introduction of the evaluation (1996)
15. Shen, K.-S., Chen, K.-H., Liang, C.-C., Pu, W.-P., Ma, M.-Y.: Measuring the functional and usable appeal of crossover B-Car interiors. Hum. Factors Ergon. Manuf. Serv. Ind. **25**, 106 (2012)

16. Baron-Cohen, S.: Is there a normal phase of synaesthesia in development? Psyche **2**(27), 223 (1996)
17. Sugiyama, K., et al.: The Basic for Survey and Analysis by Excel, pp. 51–62. Kaibundo Publishing, Tokyo (1996)
18. Ujigawa, M.: The evolution of preference-based design. Research and Development Institute (2000)
19. U.S. Bureau of Labor Statistics, Employment Projections: 2014-24 News Release, Occupational Outlook Handbook

Research on Chemical Experimental Instrument Design Mode Based on Kansei Engineering

Jianxin Cheng, Qinlei Qian[✉], Junnan Ye, Chaoxiang Yang,
Yuehui Hu, and Yejia Shen

School of Art Design and Media, ECUST, M.BOX 286,
No. 130 Meilong Road, Xuhui District, Shanghai, China
13901633292@163.com, 1065305687@qq.com,
yejunnan971108@qq.com, yangchaoxiang@qq.com,
89486554@qq.com, 1635476776@qq.com

Abstract. Chemical experimental instruments are essential tools which interact directly with experimenters and they are indispensable in chemical experiment. With the upgrading of the demand level from experimenters, in addition to the basic functional requirements of the instruments, they hope the instruments to have nice appearance, good using experience and reasonable interactive mode. This also puts a higher level of requirements on instrument design. First, this paper analyzes the research status of current instrument design through literature search method, and summarize the types of instruments which look beautiful and can bring users good using experience. Second, such instruments as samples are collected through network research and field research, and sensitive vocabularies are collected as many as possible, too. Then we use KJ method, principal component analysis method to screen the related samples, and establish the connection mode between instrument shape elements and sensitive vocabularies. Finally, we apply this mode to the appearance design of chemical instrument named "Micro flame combustion synthesis device" and verify the effectiveness of the connection mode through design evaluation. The study of chemical instrument appearance design pattern based on Kansei engineering established a new design mode for introducing other excellent instrument product design elements into chemical instrument design, which can improve the level of chemical instrument design and better meet people's sensuous requirements for chemical instruments. This research provides direction guidelines and design methods reference for products which focus on functionality and neglect the styling design and experience design.

Keywords: Chemical experimental instrument · Kansei engineering ·
Principal component analysis

1 Introduction

After decades of development, domestic chemical experimental instruments have gradually formed their own design and manufacturing mode, which has a certain production scale and development capacity, and can meet the basic experimental needs.

© Springer Nature Switzerland AG 2019
M. Kurosu (Ed.): HCII 2019, LNCS 11566, pp. 414–426, 2019.
https://doi.org/10.1007/978-3-030-22646-6_30

However, with the progress of the times and the improvement of the level of science and technology, the users' requirements for other aspects of the instrument have gradually increased, which requires synchronous innovation inside and outside the instrument on the existing basis: internal requirements for high accuracy, strong function, good reliability, automation and intellectualization of the experimental process; external requirements for appropriate equipment volume, beautiful shape, reasonable interaction mode [1]. An excellent shape design instrument looks more professional, which can bring users better use experience, thereby improving the efficiency of the experiment, and then improving the added value of this instrument [2]. Most of the existing experimental instrument products, especially domestic products, do not attach much importance to the design of instrument appearance, or simply refer to similar one or even copy directly, lacking a complete and mature form design mode, which makes the instruments have poor user experience, low price and lack market competitiveness. In view of this situation, this paper takes Kansei Engineering as the basic research theory, establishes the mapping relationship between the appearance elements of excellent appearance design experimental instruments and the perceptual vocabulary through the principal component analysis method, extracts the design elements and applies them to the appearance design of chemical instruments, aiming at establishing a new design mode of experimental instruments and improving the design level of experimental instruments.

2 Overview of Research Theory and Methodology

This paper uses Kansei Engineering as the main theoretical basis. Kansei Engineering is a discipline that incorporates human subjective perception and objective engineering science. Its most important function is to correlate people's vague feelings with precise data through a series of related methods, find correlations in imagery and design parameters, and provide theoretical basis for design practice. In addition, Kansei Engineering is an important evaluation method, which can visualize subjective evaluation data, and make it easy for designers to accurately get consumers' perceptions and needs of products [3].

At present, Kansei Engineering is mainly used in the analysis of the shape of existing products, and redesign of them, but is seldom used in the field of innovative design. This paper applies this theory to the innovative design of chemical experimental instruments. Firstly, the vocabulary matrix of appearance perceptual image evaluation of excellent shape design experimental instrument is established by semantic difference method; secondly, the principal component analysis is used to analyze and simplify appearance perceptual image vocabulary, focusing more on the factors that can describe the appearance perceptual image of the samples; the combination of the two methods can establish the mapping relationship between appearance perceptual image vocabulary and appearance elements, and then extract the samples' appearance elements which corresponding to vocabulary, apply them to the design of chemical experimental instrument named "micro flame combustion synthesis device" and the appearance design is evaluated. The flow chart of the study is shown in Fig. 1.

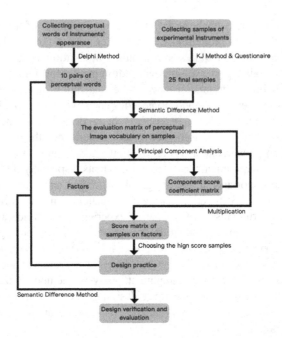

Fig. 1. The flow chart of the study.

3   Research Procedure

3.1   Sample Selection of Chemical Experimental Instruments

Chemical experimental instruments cover a wide range of fields and types, the number of enterprises producing related equipment on the market is huge, and the number of products is countless, so it is difficult to study all the instruments roundly. In order to simplify the research object and ensure the reliability of the research results, 10 famous instrument companies are selected as the sample sources according to the factors such as enterprise popularity and turnover data, including 6 foreign companies and 4 domestic companies, they are Thermo Fisher Scientific (Massachusetts, America), Danaher Corporation (America), Agilent Technologies Incorporated (California, America), Waters Corporation (Milford, America), PerkinElmer (Waltham, America), Shimadzu (Japan), Persee (Beijing, China), Inesa (Shanghai, China), Fuli Instruments (Zhejiang, China), and Kezhe (Shanghai, China) [4]. For the main object of this study is the appearance design of the instruments rather than the function, to ensure the validity of the research results, we only consider on the appearance factor and ignore the different instrument functions, weaken the phenomenon that some sample characteristics are unique due to the functional requirements of the instrument in the process of sample collection. The steps of the research are as follows.

Firstly, we collected the experimental instruments produced by these 10 companies from books, literatures, and websites of the companies as much as possible. We gathered 178 pictures as standby samples. Secondly, we used KJ method to classify the samples and did screening on the basis of this for two times. In the first screening, we removed the samples which have large appearance similarity or particularity and got 80 samples left. Then we used these samples to make appraisal questionnaire for aesthetics of appearance to screen the samples with excellent appearance design as the final experimental samples. To make sure the validity of the research consequence, the objects of our questionnaire are expert users, including experimenters, designers and professors of design. We invited the subjects to grade appearance design of every instrument, the score is one to ten, and 50 questionnaires were collected. Analyzed the questionnaires and selected 25 samples which got the highest scores as the final experimental instrument samples with excellent appearance of the research [5]. The pictures of the samples are shown in Fig. 2.

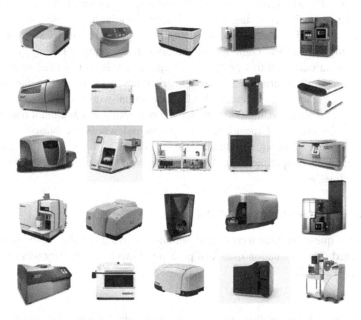

Fig. 2. 25 experimental instrument samples with excellent appearance.

3.2 Selection of the Perceptual Words

The perceptual words describing the appearance of the experimental instrument or related to it are widely collected from the networks and literatures, pair words with opposite meanings. After preliminary screening, 50 pairs of adjectives are obtained. After discussion by the research group, we analyzed the sensible image meanings of the words, the adjectives with similar meaning or repetition, remote usage and ambiguous adjectives are deleted, and the remaining 30 pairs are made. Then we used Delphi Method to screen the perceptual words [6], the relevant experts and the designers engaged in the design of experimental are invited to select the most suitable words to describe the perceptual image of experimental instruments' appearance. And we got 10 pairs of perceptual words shown in Table 1.

Table 1. 10 pairs of perceptual words

Word pair 1	Word pair 2	Word pair 3	Word pair 4	Word pair 5
Fragmented/Integrated	Sharp/Obtuse	Complicated/Simple	Steady/Lightweight	Cold/Warm
Word pair 6	Word pair 7	Word pair 8	Word pair 9	Word pair 10
Conservative/Innovative	Stifling/Fresh	Obstructed/Fluent	Traditional/Technological	Metallic/Non-metallic

3.3   Establishment of Semantic Difference Questionnaire

The content of the questionnaire of the Semantic Difference Method should include three factors: sample pictures, perceptual word pairs and subjects [7]. The questionnaire adopts five-point scale method. There are five intervals between each pair of perceptual words on the scale. By choosing numerical values, the subjects express their understanding and perception intensity of the sample's appearance image, so as to achieve the goal of digitalizing the cognition of the appearance image. Taking "fragmented-integrated" as an example, this group of perceptual words pair is used to express perceptual image of experimental instrument products, with interval values of 5, i.e. $-2, -1, 0, 1, 2$; Choosing -2 means that the perceptual words are biased towards the "fragmented" image; Choosing 0 means that the perceptual words cannot resonate with the subjects; Choosing -2 means that the perceptual words are biased towards the "integrated" image. The questionnaire was designed with 10 pairs of perceptual vocabulary and 25 sample pictures. A total of 261 valid questionnaires were collected through the Internet.

3.4   Questionnaire Statistics and Data Analysis

The collected questionnaires were sorted out and the average value of the sample data was calculated. The evaluation matrix of perceptual image vocabulary was obtained as follows (see Table 2).

Table 2. The evaluation matrix of perceptual image vocabulary on samples

Samples	Words				
	Fragmented/Integrated	Sharp/Obtuse	Complicated/Simple	Steady/Lightweight	Cold/Warm
1	0.48	0.75	−0.34	−1.22	−0.63
2	0.69	−0.99	0.83	1.18	−0.01
3	0.79	1.23	1.16	0.57	0.77
4	0.87	1.55	−0.12	−1.07	0.64
5	0.68	1.45	0.75	−0.31	1.2
6	0.76	1.16	0.23	−0.03	0.72
7	0.42	0.34	−0.77	−0.64	−0.23
8	0.72	0.39	0.28	−0.48	0.21
9	0.7	−0.01	1.57	0.19	−0.03
10	0.82	1.23	−0.24	−1.56	0.59
11	0.77	0.32	0.27	−1.08	0.21

(continued)

Table 2. (*continued*)

Samples	Words				
	Fragmented/Integrated	Sharp/Obtuse	Complicated/Simple	Steady/Lightweight	Cold/Warm
12	0.73	−0.31	0.35	0.44	−0.21
13	0.37	−0.6	−0.93	−0.77	0.19
14	0.21	−0.33	−0.77	−0.28	0.21
15	0.67	0.81	−0.03	0.18	0.79
16	0.12	0.45	−0.87	−0.43	−0.39
17	0.66	0.64	−0.39	−0.41	0.24
18	0.98	0.19	0.23	−0.26	−0.46
19	0.72	1.25	0.04	−0.48	0.59
20	0.34	−0.03	−0.38	−0.44	0.37
21	−0.21	0.56	−0.99	−1.01	−0.18
22	0.97	0.78	0.41	−0.08	−0.44
23	1.01	1.68	1.45	0.67	0.56
24	0.65	0.38	0.59	1.03	0.33
25	0.93	−0.76	0.72	−1.14	−0.23

Samples	Words				
	Conservative/Innovative	Stifling/Fresh	Obstructed/Fluent	Traditional/ Technological	Metallic/ Non-metallic
1	0.56	−0.62	−0.02	0.34	−1.56
2	0.79	0.81	0.52	0.81	0.48
3	0.69	1.11	1.34	0.98	1.35
4	−0.48	−0.65	0.54	−0.85	1.33
5	1.39	0.96	1.17	0.57	1.78
6	0.75	0.4	0.09	−0.67	1.24
7	0.71	0.39	0.58	0.99	1.25
8	0.23	0.22	−0.23	−0.46	1.18
9	0.24	−0.11	−0.74	−0.42	1.3
10	−0.57	−0.75	−0.54	−0.75	1.34
11	0.56	0.78	0.24	1.03	1.43
12	1.14	0.87	0.87	−0.66	1.04
13	0.57	0.55	−0.79	0.37	−0.82
14	0.41	0.66	0.2	0.35	−0.31
15	0.16	−0.24	−0.25	0.1	1.07
16	−0.01	−0.67	−0.65	0.48	−0.23
17	−0.23	0.25	−0.44	−0.42	0.9
18	1.06	0.38	0.57	0.82	0.44
19	−0.7	−0.63	−0.37	−0.94	1.37
20	0.01	0.44	−0.24	−0.23	1.19
21	−0.16	−0.18	−0.44	−0.45	1.23
22	0.83	0.22	0.71	1.09	0.27
23	0.38	0.82	1.02	−0.83	1.4
24	0.03	0.23	0.22	−0.01	1.22
25	0.24	−0.68	−0.12	1.04	−0.17

Principal Component Analysis (PCA) was used to further analyze the vocabulary evaluation matrix of perceptual images of experimental instruments by SPSS [8]. It was imported into the software, and the maximum variance rotation method was used to rotate orthogonally. The factor whose eigenvalue is greater than 1 is used to calculate the principal component analysis. A total of three principal component factors are selected. The cumulative explained variance is 73.024%. The results of principal component analysis are arranged into Table 3. Factor 1 contains four groups of perceptual vocabulary: steady-lightweight, conservative-innovative, stifling-fresh, obstructed-fluent. Factor 2 contains four groups of perceptual vocabulary: sharp-obtuse, cold-warm, traditional-technological, metallic-non-metallic, and Factor 3 contains "fragmented-integrated, complicated-simple" two groups of perceptual vocabulary. Because most of the vocabulary in factor 1 is related to the style of the experimental instrument, it is named "style factor". Most of the vocabulary in factor 2 describes the texture of the experimental instrument, so it can be named "texture factor". Most of the vocabulary in factor 3 is related to the shape of the experimental instrument, so it is named "shape factor".

Table 3. The results of principal component analysis

Factor	Word	Element loading	Eigenvalue	Explained variation (%)	Cumulative variation (%)
Style factor	Steady/Lightweight	0.679	2.861	28.611	28.611
	Conservative/Innovative	0.776			
	Stifling/Fresh	0.946			
	Obstructed/Fluent	0.706			
Texture factor	Sharp/Obtuse	0.701	2.549	25.491	54.102
	Cold/Warm	0.829			
	Traditional/Technological	−0.698			
	Metallic/Non-metallic	0.804			
Shape factor	Fragmented/Integrated	0.933	1.892	18.922	73.024
	Complicated/Simple	0.791			

In the factor analysis table, we can see that the key words are "fresh, innovative, warm, non-metallic, integrated and simple", and the secondary words are "fluent, lightweight, obtuse, traditional". This shows that users have a higher perception of these words in the perceptual image vocabulary of experimental instruments with excellent appearance design.

Next, the relationship between each component factor and sample appearance is further analyzed in order to extract the perceptual image feature elements of experimental instruments. By multiplying the perceptual vocabulary of appearance evaluation matrix with the Component Score Coefficient Matrix (see Table 4) calculated in SPSS, the Score Matrix of the experimental instrument Samples on Factors is obtained (see Table 5). The formula is as follows (a represents the Score Matrix of Samples on Factors, b represents the perceptual vocabulary of appearance evaluation matrix, c is the Component Score Coefficient Matrix).

$$a_{ij} = \sum_{k=1}^{10} b_{ik}c_{kj} \ (i = 1,2,3,\ldots25, j = 1,2,3) \tag{1}$$

Table 4. Component score coefficient matrix

Perceptual words	Style factor	Texture factor	Shape factor
Fragmented/Integrated	−0.185	−0.094	0.615
Sharp/Obtuse	−0.089	0.246	0.122
Complicated/Simple	−0.02	−0.027	0.436
Steady/Lightweight	0.251	0.063	−0.036
Cold/Warm	0.122	0.356	−0.128
Conservative/Innovative	0.266	−0.155	0.003
Stifling/Fresh	0.421	0.087	−0.26
Obstructed/Fluent	0.203	0.011	0.129
Traditional/Technological	0.096	−0.289	0.082
Metallic/Non-metallic	0.118	0.334	−0.071

Table 5. Score matrix of samples on factors

Sample	Factor		
	Style factor	Texture factor	Shape factor
1	−0.80	−0.91	0.66
2	1.03	−0.38	0.52
3	1.13	0.68	0.89
4	−0.70	1.18	0.70
5	1.07	0.99	0.61
6	0.30	0.99	0.39
7	0.43	0.00	−0.02
8	−0.07	0.57	0.40
9	−0.14	0.39	0.92
10	−1.07	1.03	0.50
11	0.37	0.17	0.46
12	0.88	0.25	0.34
13	0.00	−0.57	−0.40
14	0.39	−0.23	−0.36
15	−0.03	0.71	0.35
16	−0.60	−0.32	−0.04
17	−0.22	0.64	0.08
18	0.36	−0.45	0.81
19	−0.75	1.20	0.49
20	0.14	0.57	−0.24
21	−0.37	0.60	−0.57
22	0.26	−0.40	1.04
23	0.61	1.25	1.11
24	0.43	0.63	0.51
25	−0.60	−0.90	1.12

It can be seen from Table 5 that the scores of the samples on three factors are mostly positive, and the samples with negative scores are fewer and the absolute values are generally smaller except for very few samples. This shows that the users have a lower perception of the negative images of the three factors of the samples. It can be concluded that the users prefer the samples with positive images on all factors. Therefore, this paper used the samples with positive images and high absolute values (Taking absolute value greater than one as standard) as samples of final design elements extraction sources. The samples selected on "style factor" are 2, 3 and 5; the samples selected on "texture factor" are 4, 10, 19 and 23; and the samples selected on "shape factor" are 22, 23 and 25. Summarize the characteristic elements of these samples and add them into chemical instrument product design. The results are summarized in the following Table 6.

Table 6. Characteristic elements of high score samples

Factor	High score samples	Characteristic elements
Style factor		Bright, lightweight, fluent, lively and fresh in style. Colour collision is one of the main design methods
Texture factor		Round in appearance, strong sense of tradition, mainly warm color, giving users a soft and warm feeling, more inclined to use non-metallic texture materials and matte materials
Shape factor		Modeling integrity is good, concise, not too much decoration

4   Design Practice

4.1   Development of Micro Flame Combustion Synthesis Device

This paper will take the chemical experimental instrument "micro flame combustion synthesis device" as an example to do product design practice. "Micro Flame Combustion Synthesis Device" is developed by Professor of Materials College of East China University of Technology (ECUST). It is suitable for the production of micro-nano-sized materials in universities, research institutes and laboratories of enterprises in the fields of chemical industry and materials. It is also used in the fields of photo-catalysis, photoelectric conversion and lithium-ion batteries. The flame combustion technology used in this instrument is a method of preparing nanoparticles through the chemical reaction and physical agglomeration of precursors by providing energy in the combustion process. It has been widely used in the industrialized preparation of nanoparticles such as SiO2, AlO3 and TiO2. The prototype machine has been produced, as shown in the follow (see Fig. 3). This case is based on the existing prototype machine for appearance design, and try to follow and use the previous research results, from the outstanding samples of three factors to extract design elements into the design practice. We designed two different schemes (see Figs. 4 and 5).

Fig. 3. The prototype machine of micro flame combustion synthesis device

Fig. 4. Design case 1

Both of the case 1 and case 2 take into account the convenience of interpersonal operation, the need of experiment process, the rationality of space, the beauty of appearance and so on. Color collision design is formed by the combination of metal and organic glass, which makes the instrument give people a fresh feeling; the shape is

Fig. 5. Design case 2

made on the basis of square angle and rounded corner, which increases the richness; and the instrument is more integrated, simple, and not much decoration. We added blue as embellishment on the basis of white in scheme 1, and symmetrical design is adopted in the experimental area and operation area, which made the appearance more regular; we used double doors in the right experimental area in scheme 2, and deliberately used asymmetrical design in appearance to make the shape vividly.

4.2   Development of Micro Flame Combustion Synthesis Device

The author makes the semantic difference questionnaire of design schemes again in the form of pictures, and still chooses 10 groups of perceptual vocabulary screened previous to score with Likert scale. A total of 34 questionnaires are collected. According to the statistical results, the evaluation matrix of the perceptual vocabulary of the appearance image of the design case is obtained as Table 7. Then the score matrix of design cases on factors is obtained by multiplying it with the component coefficient matrix shown as Table 8.

Table 7. The evaluation matrix of perceptual image vocabulary on cases

Case	Word				
	Fragmented/Integrated	Sharp/Obtuse	Complicated/Simple	Steady/Lightweight	Cold/Warm
1	0.73	0.7	0.98	0.65	−0.15
2	0.69	0.25	0.64	0.86	−0.23
Case	Word				
	Conservative/Innovative	Stifling/Fresh	Obstructed/Fluent	Traditional/Technological	Metallic/Non-metallic
1	0.28	0.69	0.89	−0.35	−0.21
2	0.76	0.89	0.14	−0.29	0.12

Table 8. Score matrix of cases on factors

Case	Factor		
	Style factor	Texture factor	Shape factor
Case 1	0.42	0.12	0.88
Case 2	0.62	0.04	0.49

From the above table, we can see that the two cases have positive performance on three factors, but the value of factor two is smaller, which indicates that the user's perception of the texture factor is not strong enough. The author believes that due to the functional requirements of the instrument, the client requires the use of metal as the shell material, and the design is not round enough, the color is mainly cold, resulting in poor performance of the instrument in the texture factor. In the later stage, the design can be improved gradually by changing the color matching and increasing the arc shape of the surface.

5   Conclusion

In this paper, the mapping relationship between perceptual image words of appearance and experimental instrument appearance elements is established through the theory of Kansei Engineering. On this basis, design elements are extracted from samples which are outstanding in various perceptual image factors, and the appearance design of "micro flame combustion synthesis device" is carried out. The accuracy and the reliability of the research results is preliminarily verified by questionnaire survey. This research will help designers to extract design elements from excellent experimental instruments and add them into the design of chemical instrument products reasonably and scientifically, and provide a new design idea, so as to improve the level of instrument design, grasp the user's perceptual image more accurately and better meet the user's perceptual needs. At the same time, the research results also provide theoretical guidance and reference for similar design ideas of applying elements of one excellent design work to another product, which is of great significance.

References

1. Goffin, K., Micheli, P.: Maximizing the value of industrial design in new product development. Res. Technol. Manage. **53**(5), 29–37 (2010)
2. Diao, S.: Industial design under development of experiment instruments and equipment. Exp. Technol. Manage. **26**(8), 57–59 (2014)
3. Liu, Y.: The design and research of the magnetic levitation train based on the Kansei engineering. Design **06**, 122–123 (2018)
4. Li, C.: Current situation and development trend of modern scientific instrument. Anal. Instrum. **01**, 119–122 (2014)
5. Zhou, Z., Cheng, J., Zhang, X.: Application of Kansei engineering in nursing beds design. Packag. Eng. **37**(08), 98–100+142 (2016)

6. Wang, Q., Xu, S., Chen, Y., Lin, Y.: Whiskey bottle shape design based on Kansei engineering. Packag. Eng. **39**(08), 256–260 (2018)
7. Sun, L., Kong, F., Zhou, Y., Liu, X.: Research on static comfort of automobile seat based on Kansei engineering. Chin. J. Ergon. **19**(02), 60–62+91 (2013)
8. Fan, D., Wang, X., Zhou, M.: Research on perceptual cognition of automotive hub based on principal component analysis. Sci. Technol. Inf. **10**, 119–120 (2010)

A Study in Elderly Fashion and Zero Waste Clothing Design

Feng-Tzu Chiu[(✉)]

School of Art and Design, Fuzhou University of International Studies and Trade,
Fuzhou, China
Ftchiu520@qq.com

Abstract. This research focuses on the Kansei needs of elderly clothing, and juxtaposes contemporary topics of fashion design, sustainability, and environment protection. We aim to discuss the design of sustainable, environment-friendly, and zero waste clothing for the elderly people. An important aspect of the future in fashion design is eco-fashion. Environmental awareness is increasingly becoming an important topic among the consumers, especially amidst the pollution and waste generation associated with the rise of fast fashion. In addition to environment protection, the current trends in eco fashion emphasize on sustainable development of the industry that is cost-friendly. This work serves as a testbed to incorporate the need of sustainability and the incentive for the fashion industry.

Living in the age of severe environmental crisis and among the aging population, fashion designers are compelled to design to both minimize the environmental impact from design and manufacturing, and maximizing the comfort of the elderly consumers wearing the designs. As such, this research interrogates the development, history, production, consumption behavior, and environmental impacts of the fashion industry. Our interrogation leads us to the discussion on and development of clothing designs catering to the Kansei need of the elderly consumers via the use of appropriate colors and fabrics. Furthermore, the designs focus on sustainability from the drawing board—every piece of the fabrics is to be fully utilized. The zero-waste principle we employed helps us achieving the goal of minimizing the environmental impacts from clothing design and manufacturing.

Our designs are inspired by the natures that are hard to access by the elderly people, who often face deterioration in flexibility and mobility. Despite of their aging bodies, the sceneries and plants in nature is an integral part of the memories of many people. The zero waste collection, Ageless Leaves, depicts nature by utilizing the naturally occurring red and green palette of plants to showcase the beauty in preserved nature, and portrays the need of sustainable development due to humans depleting precious natural resources. In addition to the colors, our zero-waste design principle fully utilizes the fabrics in clothing production, and are tailored to the flexibility of the elderly population to maximize the function of our clothes. Using the zero-waste design, we demonstrate the value of eco fashion and elderly fashion, and the incorporation of sustainability in the industry.

Keywords: Elderly fashion · Eco fashion · Zero waste · Clothing design

© Springer Nature Switzerland AG 2019
M. Kurosu (Ed.): HCII 2019, LNCS 11566, pp. 427–438, 2019.
https://doi.org/10.1007/978-3-030-22646-6_31

1 Introduction

As the population ages, the need for fashion and daily outfit to cater to the elder population become increasingly important. This research focuses on the Kansei needs of elderly clothing, and juxtaposes contemporary topics of fashion design, sustainability, and environment protection. We aim to discuss the design of sustainable, environment-friendly, and zero waste clothing for the elderly people. An important aspect of the future in fashion design is eco-fashion. Environmental awareness is increasingly becoming an important topic among the consumers, especially amidst the pollution and waste generation associated with the rise of fast fashion. In addition to environment protection, the current trends in eco fashion emphasize on sustainable development of the industry that is cost-friendly. This work serves as a testbed to incorporate the need of sustainability and the incentive for the fashion industry.

Since 2013, the fashion industry had become the most polluting industry other than the petroleum industry. As a result, "fast fashion" quickly becomes an important topic when discussing sustainability issues. According to Sinha et al., "textile product contributes to the growth of household waste as global economy improves [1]. Prof. Timo Rissanen of Parsons School of Art and Design pointed out in 2005 that 15% of the fabric used in clothing manufacturing would never make to the market, as they are cut away during the manufacturing process. As a result, both the material and the energy going into the manufacturing of those fabrics are wasted, which creates an environmental problem.

This research focuses on discussing and reviewing the development of fashion industry, and how evolution in production and consumption behaviors impacts the environment. The aim of this article is three-fold: 1. We aim to discuss the application of fabrics and colors in designing to cater for the Kansei needs of elderly consumers. 2. Simultaneously, we are incorporate the principle of sustainability into the design process. This is mainly achieved by fully utilizing every inch of the fabric. 3. Building on the previous two points, we further aim to present practical, fashionable designs for future production and improvements.

2 Literature Review

2.1 The Kansei of Elderly Fashion

According to an article published Su appeared in Taiwanese Gerontological Forum [2], elderly design, elderly fashion, both functional and aesthetic, elder people prefer to wear comfortable, healthy, safe, and functional in particular clothing. If integrated the above-mentioned preferences with style, color, texture of fabrics, and personal figure, each one can wear his/her fashion. Fashionable clothing makes elder people look prettier, younger and more energetic, leading to increase their confidence and courage during social activities. Previous studies [2] showed that people who care about dresses and wear fashionable clothing had 30% less chances to suffer from hypertension, ulcer, cancer and mental diseases. In summary, wearing fashionable clothing may not only make elders look younger in appearance, but also help to maintain both physical and mental health.

2.2   Development of Fashion Industry

Production of clothing requires much materials, energy and water, and discharges a lot of pollutions into the environment. After industrial revolution, fast development in the areas of material engineering, synthetic fabrics, garment industry, human engineering, automatic manufacturing, and international trade have made fashion industry grown rapidly. Within less than 200 years, mass production has almost replaced all the hand-made clothing. In addition, owing to the popularity of multiple communication media, such as newspapers, magazines, press conferences, and internet, fashion trend has widely and rapidly reached more and more people globally. Therefore, from the late 20th century to now, fashion industry has also been known to move to "The Era of Garment" [3, 4].

2.3   Fashion and Environment

The term "Fast Fashion" originated from the rapid development of clothing industry in Europe in the 20th Century. In the US, it is called "Speed to Market". The British Newspaper-Guide even created a new word, McFashion, meaning like fast food MacDonald. Conventional fashion brands usually took several months, from design, manufacture, to distribution to customers. However, for fast fashion brands, only 50 days are needed for each design to distribution cycle. Now in the internet era, the cycle time has been even reduced to 1 week. Fashion has become closer to customers due to cheaper price and more tailored and small production available.

During the life cycle of cloth, from growing and harvesting of fibers, manufactures, and customer usage, much water and natural resources are needed. The textile industry uses 38 billion cubic meters of water annually. According to the World Bank [5], the wastewater produced by dyeing and textile industry is about 17–20% of the that produced by all industry. About 8,000 chemicals are used to transform the raw materials into textiles, and most of the chemicals have been discharged into fresh waterbodies. Among the fashion industry, manufacture of fabrics is the most polluted process [5]. A lot of water, chemicals, energy, and raw materials are needed in the process. For example, to produce one ton of cotton fabrics, about 65,000 kW-h of electricity, and 25 m^3 of water are needed. These make the textile and fashion industry being one of the most polluted and resource-consuming industry.

As speed, low cost, and close to customers are the characteristics of Fast Fashion, the manufacturing processes have been minimized, the materials used may involve less environmentally friendly chemicals, such as formaldehyde, and the products may be less durable. Therefore, fast fashion is usually considered as low quality, making the life span of the cloth shorter and leading to more waste production. In 2005, Prof. Timo Rissanen at Parson Institute of Fashion pointed out that 15% of fabrics are abandoned at the cutting stage of fashion industry, making a huge waste of materials before it even reaches the market (Fig. 1). Although most of the wasted fabrics can be recycled and reused, in many cases, the waste fabrics were sent to landfill directly due to the fact of lower cost for landfill compared with recycling and reuse in many countries.

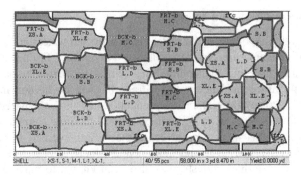

Fig. 1. Mark pattern of clothing industry. Source: iTHome/ https://ithelp.ithome.com.tw/upload/ images/

2.4   Fashion Goes Green

As environmental protection becomes a mainstream issue, and more people recognize individuals' contributions to it, fashion becomes a controversial topic in the realm of environmental protection [6]. Such awareness, on the other hand, also drove the development of eco fashion. Indeed, consumers are buying into the idea of environmental protection. Both large brand-named and independent designers capitalized on the trend and introduced numerous eco fashion themed merchandises. "Sustainable development … [original quote]" said Christina Dean of Redress, a Hong Kong based NGO working to reduce textile waste and promote environmental sustainability in the fashion industry [7]. Redress focuses on education to reduce waste in textile and energy in the fashion industry. It also works with various organizations on fostering the sustainable fashion industry in Asia. Its Eco Chic Design Award aims to inspire designers and students to create designs with minimal waste, and to change the landscape of fashion designing.

A basic element in fashion designing is the permutation and combination of shape, structure, color, material, and texture. To meet the goal of making a sustainable fashion industry, Redress advocates for the techniques of Reconstruction and Up-cycle, as well as the Zero Waste design [7]. Reconstruction is to deconstruct the clothing and textiles that are no longer in use, and to put together the deconstructed pieces in to new outfits. Up-cycle refers to the recycling of unused textiles, and to make them into products with greater values. Zero Waste Structure (Fig. 2) focuses on the full utilization of textile before the design goes to production. The needed cuts are arranged such that the wasted textile is kept at a minimum, if not zero-waste.

Historically speaking, zero waste clothing is not novel. For example, Toga (Fig. 3) is made of an entire piece of textile. Zero Waste design can also be seen throughout history. The design and production of kimono (Fig. 4) and sari (Fig. 5) both utilize such concept to avoid wasting the precious textile going into the clothing. However, with the industrialization of the fashion industry and the rise of fast fashion, the concept of zero waste in clothing design and production is largely forgotten.

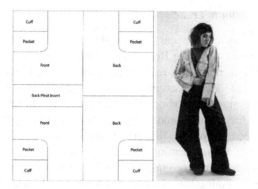

Fig. 2. Zero-waste pattern and the bolero top (Source: Fashion designer, TessWhitfort, from Melbourne Australia (https://tesswhitfort.com/author/tesswhitfort/))

Fig. 3. Toga pic (from: Wikipedia)

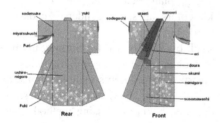

Fig. 4. Kimono (Source: https://en.wikipedia. org/wiki/Kimono)

Fig. 5. Sari (Source: https://www.thoughtco. com)

2.5   Big Ideas of Fashion Trend

The internationally renowned forecasting website for fashion, WGSN (https://www.wgsn.com/) [8] proposed "The Big Reset" in 2017/2018 Fall/Winter (Fig. 6(a)), suggesting that we should press the reset button for our behavior of consumption, including change our life styles, design, and work in a way of not following the big brands and becoming more environmentally friendly living. In the future, the values will be judged by the life cycle of products and personality of people, not just based on profits. Also announced by WGSN [8], the seasonal theme of 2018 Spring/Summer, "States of Mind" (Fig. 6(b)), mentioned that technology makes progress of many industries and creates new commercial opportunities. However, it also makes people think reversely about re-connection with nature so that people and environment can be healthier. For the Fall/Winter Season of 2019/20, WGSN [8] predict that "Global Warming" (Fig. 6(c)) will be a big issue and consumers will be willing to buy environmentally friendly products. Industries need to clearly understand how to produce environmentally friendly products and how to demonstrate the product they produce are environmentally friendly. The theme of Spring/Summer Season proposed by WGSN is "Profit from the Product Life Cycle" (Fig. 6(d)) [8]. This certainly shows that environmental protection is a necessity, not just a slogan. Fashion industry need to fully integrate sustainability strategy as a necessity, and not a "nice to have" for consumers.

These Big Ideas of fashion trends demonstrate that environmental sustainability is an important fashion topic. Fashion industry must develop and apply new technologies to incorporate these ideas and consider nature as into the design. With this consideration, the earth will be better protected and the industry can be sustainable.

2.6   Design Elements of the Fashion Big Ideas

After the analysis of the Big Ideas of Fashion Trend, the elements of design for 2020 Spring/Summer Season are discussed below. For color, inclusive color is proposed. In 2020, the social structure is expected to gradually change. The market used to be young people oriented and however, more inclusive design plan needs to be considered. The best strategy for colors needs to consider all skin colors, ages, and genders. According to the trend of fashion, 5 key colors are proposed (Fig. 7(a)).

Figure 7(b) shows the raw materials predicted, by WGSN [8], for Spring/Summer 2020. Selection of material will affect the ecological system of fashion industry. Material recycling will be the focus in the industry. The key items include (1) use of more durable and better recyclable materials, (2) biogenic, biodegradable, and recyclable fabrics and materials, (3) lighter materials and better processing methods, and (4) materials for multiple function activities.

The style of clothing will be become more tailored for smaller groups of people. The traditional ways of wearing clothes based on ages, genders, and races, have been changing, increasing the needs of "design for small groups of customers. In these circumstances, design for all occasions and all people are not feasible. Therefore, people will be easier to find personalized products. This will be the niches for personalized design, and the elements of geometry, nature, vintage, and modern art (Fig. 7(c)).

Fig. 6. (a) F/W 17/18 ~ The Great Reset, (b) S/S 18 ~ States of Mind, (c) F/W 19/20 ~ Warming Up to Global Warming, and (d) S/S 20 ~ Implement Circular Fashion System (source: WGSN, https://www.wgsn.com/)

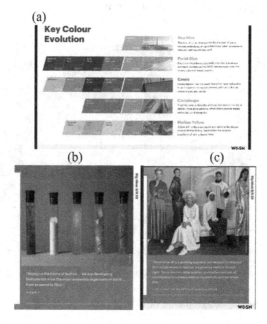

Fig. 7. (a) S/S 20 5 key colors, (b) S/S 20 Make materials matter, and (c) S/S 20 Style/Find your niche! (source: WGSN, https://www.wgsn.com/)

3 Results and Discussion

Through the analysis of literature and reports, it is found that the current trends of elder clothing include the Kansei of good-to-wear, comfortable, healthy, and safe. In addition, the environmental issues associated with fashion industry, such as global warming, water scarcity, and material recycling, have also become more concerned by general public. Therefore, a fashion theme based on the concept of environmental protection and sustainability, and the current trends of elder clothing mentioned above are proposed for the design of the fabrics and fashion clothing of the 2020 seasons.

3.1 Design Theme

Flowers, grasses, and trees are important green elements in the living environment. Although for those elders living in urban area, they might gradually lose the chances to deeply contact with the plants in rural areas, clothing with these green elements may make their daily life more colorful and vivid. Therefore, the green leaves and white flowers of Deciduous Trees, growing in Taiwan and flowering in the Springs/Summers, are chosen as the natural image of the fashion collection. When the environments are well protected, the leaves are greenish and the white flowers are blooming. However, when the environment quality deteriorates, yellow leaves and even fallen leaves will be seen. To remind elder consumers about the beauty of natural environment and protection the nature, "Ageless Leaves-better lives" is used as the theme of this fashion collections for Spring/Summer 2020, as shown in Fig. 8.

Fig. 8. S/S 20 design theme of elderly fashion (Color figure online)

3.2   The Elements of Design Theme

The colors used for this theme is shown as Fig. 9. The colors of Deciduous trees and flowers are transformed into the green color with technological feeling, as well as modern and retro fashion. In addition, the digital printing is also selected to reduce the pollution caused by overuse of dyes.

Bamboo fibers have superior properties of moisture absorption and air ventilation, with additional functions of UV-cut, anti-bacteria and odor removal [9]. These properties will fit the Kansei of good-to-wear, comfortable, and healthy.

The clothing of this collection is designed for elderly people. Therefore, ancient Greek/Roman style garment, chiton, was chosen for the style. The structure design is based on a full piece fabric is selected so that minimum fabrics will be wasted. The clothing designed are easy to put on and take off, little restrained, and limbs-stretchable.

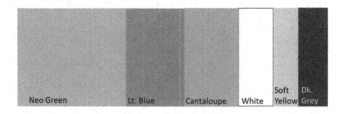

Fig. 9. Fashion color portion of design theme (Color figure online)

3.3   Zero Waste of Garment Structure Design

The concept of zero waste of garment structure is based on the appropriate usage of a full fabric. A preliminary design is needed for determining the silhouettes of the style (Fig. 10). Then each garment panel is located on the fabric. Finally, the unused fabric is

Fig. 10. The silhouettes of elderly fashion design

used for detailed design. This kind of design steps may minimize the waste produced. Figures 11(a)–(d) show the concept of zero-waste design of garment structures for shirt, short, dress, and pants. All of them were loose in H and trapezium silhouettes. The patterns of garment structure can be adjusted in proportions, and digital printing fabric using natural and conventional motifs. Mix and match these garments can therefore may create a variety of fashion styles.

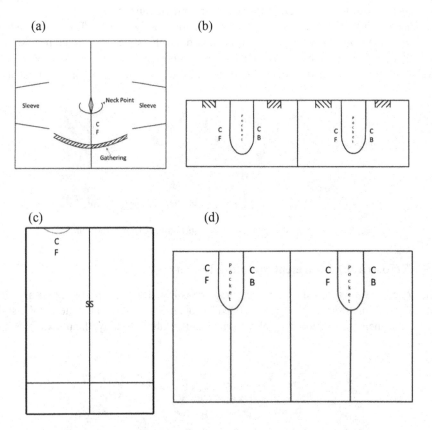

Fig. 11. Zero waste structures of (a) top, (b) shorts, (c) dress, and (d) pants.

3.4   Style Image of Fashion Theme

Figure 12 shows the Style Image of Ageless Leaves design for Elderly and Zero Waste fashion.

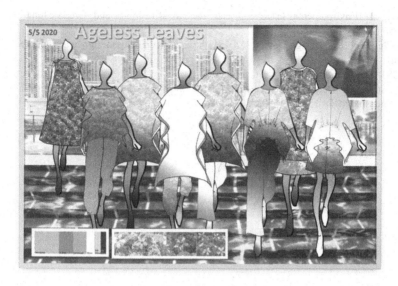

Fig. 12. The color styles of fashion theme

4   Conclusions

We designed the S/S 2020 collection specifically with the elderly consumers and the zero-waste concept in mind. In this design, we both incorporated the Kansei need of the elderly population through our research, and promoted the value of environmental protection that is increasingly fashionable. Our design frees the elderly consumers from choosing between comfort and functionality, and fashion and style. The style image presented in this collection can be the foundation for designing future collections for elderly fashions. It offers not only the basis for zero-waste design but the inspiration for Kansei needs of elderly consumers. We hope our S/S 2020 collection will enable more designers to create products for the elderly consumers, and to integrate sustainability into their products and the industry as a whole.

References

1. Wu, J.Y.: The new mainstream of international brands to promote environmental protection strategy: product carbon footprint. Text. Bull. **18**(11), 53–56 (2010)
2. Su, S.F.: Elderly design, elderly fashion, both functional and aesthetic. Taiwanese Gerontol. Forum **32** (2016). http://www.iog.ncku.edu.tw/riki/riki.php?CID=1&id=TGF33. (in Chinese)
3. Lin, S.T.: The development and evolution of the modern garment industry. Decoration J. **11**, 50 (2005). (in Chinese)
4. Chu, Q.L.: British Industrial Revolution Engineering to Change the World, pp. 11–14. Shakespeare Culture Co., Ltd., Taichung (2007). (in Chinese)
5. Kant, R.: Textile dyeing industry an environmental hazard. Nature Sci. **4**(1), 22–26 (2012)

6. Cheng, T.: Environmental leadership leads the global fashion trend. Green China Part A **1**, 54–56 (2010). (in Chinese)
7. EcoChic Redress Design Award (2018). https://www.redressdesignaward.com/learn/zero-waste
8. WGSN (2018). https://www.wgsn.com/en/
9. Everest Textile Corp.: Bamboo Fibers (2018). http://www.everest.com.tw/_english/00_site/01_edit.aspx?MID=13&SID=50&TID=89

Gender Difference in the Free Association for "Cute" and "Kawaii"

Ayako Hashizume[1](✉) and Masaaki Kurosu[2]

[1] Hosei University, Tokyo, Japan
hashiaya@gmail.com
[2] The Open University of Japan, Chiba, Japan

Abstract. In Japan, "Kawaii" is frequently used in various situations mainly by young female. Corresponding English word "Cute" that is pronounced as "Kyuuto" is also used in daily conversation. Our study compared the denotation of both words by applying the free association method, thus clarified the semantic commonality and the difference. The result of survey using 60 informants revealed that the stimulus word Kawaii produced more number of associations than Cute. And our further analysis revealed that Japanese people don't have opportunities to use the English word Cute in their everyday life, thus they use it as a foreign origin word, and the word Cute contained the image of something of Western/foreign culture. In other words, the pragmatic (cultural) context might have influenced the semantics of the word through the free association that listed up the denotation.

Keywords: Cute · Kawaii · Free association · Semantics

1 Kansei Engineering and the Concept of Kawaii

As is well-known, Kansei is a Japanese word meaning the sensibility and Kansei engineering is now becoming popular in the whole world owing to the activity of Japan Society for Kansei Engineering (JSKE) and Kansei Engineering and Emotion Research (KEER) conference [1, 2].

The word Kawaii is one of the focus of Kansei Engineering [3–7]. A list of more relevant information can be found in Reference [5] (p. 60–61) although most of them were written in Japanese.

In our previous study [7], we asked to make a comparison among Kawaii, beauty and preference by showing 225 photographs to 89 informants (34 female, 54 male). As the result, Kawaii and preference showed no difference between female ($r = 0.73$) and male ($r = 0.73$). But Kawaii and beautiful for female ($r = 0.60$) and male ($r = 0.69$) and beautiful and preference for female ($r = 0.60$) and male ($r = 0.72$) were respectively showed significant difference between female and male. This suggested that females may have clearer differential criteria for each of Kawaii, beautiful and preference than male. Thus, the difference of evaluation structure among female and male is one of the focus of our study.

Anther focus is on the cultural aspect. The Japanese word Kawaii is now widely accepted as a part of (female) culture in Europe, Asia and the US. But, of course, there

M. Kurosu (Ed.): HCII 2019, LNCS 11566, pp. 439–449, 2019.
https://doi.org/10.1007/978-3-030-22646-6_32

are words that has the same meaning to Kawaii in each language. For example, the English word Cute is considered to be the most adequate translation of Kawaii. Our question is how Kawaii and the corresponding word Cute are used differently in the same cultural context.

As a first step, we started the collaboration with Prof. Hiroko Chiba and Prof. David Berque of DePauw University in Greencastle, Indiana, USA. They conducted a survey by adopting the same procedure with us for US students. In this context, the focus is on the difference between Cute and Kawaii.

Even in Japan, the word Cute is used as a foreign-origin word and is written as "キュート" and is pronounced "Kyuuto". The meaning of "Cute" found in Japanese dictionary is "lively Kawaii, especially, of young female" [8, 9], or "considerately Kawaii, especially, of lively female" [10]. But these definitions should be confirmed based on the empirical study. We decided to make the comparative analysis on the use of Cute and Kawaii in Japan.

2 Method

2.1 Procedure

In order to clarify the semantic features of both words, we adopted the free association method.

We conducted the survey twice. The first survey was conducted using the pen and paper. We gave a blank paper to each informant and asked to write down their student-ID, sex, age, then draw a separating line at the center of the paper. On the upper side, they were asked to write "cute" and on the lower side to write "Kawaii". Then they were requested to remind and write down the words that are associated with Cute or Kawaii. As shown in Table 1, total of 25 informants participated in the first day survey.

Table 1. Informants

Survey	Department	Female	Male	Total
1st survey	Engineering	2	4	6
	Design	9	4	13
	Science	1	5	6
2nd survey	Engineering	3	32	35
Total		15	45	60

The second survey was conducted using the PC and the informants typed the word associated with Cute or Kawaii. Total of 35 informants participated in this survey. Two data were merged and used in the following analysis. Thus, the total number of informants was 60 including 15 females and 45 males. It is unfortunate that we could not obtain sufficient number of female informants because Kawaii is typically a female culture.

Total of 20 min were given for the informants to write down the associated words. All the informants finished writing/typing their answers before the end of given time.

2.2 Basic Statistics

Total numbers of associations of each informant are summarized in Table 2. By applying ANOVA, it was found that the total number of associations by female is significantly larger than that by male at the 1% level and the total number of associations for Kawaii is significantly larger than that for Cute among female at the 1% level and among male at the 5% level.

Table 2. Total number of associations for Cute and Kawaii by female and male

Basic statistics	Female		Male	
	Cute	Kawaii	Cute	Kawaii
N	15	15	45	45
Mean	14.2	20.3	5.4	9.0
S. D.	7.0	11.0	3.2	5.8
Minimum	5	7	0	1
Maximum	27	41	13	27
Median	15	18	4	8

2.3 Categories for Data Analysis

All the original data was typed in Excel and was classified into 17 categories as shown below (in alphabetical order),

1. Adjective: e.g. small, lovely
2. Animal: e.g. cat, dog
3. Character: e.g. Hello-Kitty, Disney Princess
4. Clothes and Fashion: e.g. gothic Lolita, China dress
5. Color: e.g. pink, pale color
6. Foreign Items: e.g. European things, overseas items
7. Human: e.g. girl, idols
8. Letter: e.g. Hiragana
9. Onomatope: e.g. fuwa-fuwa, hira-hira
10. Ornaments and Accessory: e.g. accessory, eyeglass
11. Person's Name: e.g. Avril Lavigne, Ayame Goriki
12. Place: e.g. Harajuku, Tokyo
13. Plant: e.g. flower, tulip
14. Shape and Pattern: e.g. stripe, star
15. Sweets and Fruits: e.g. short cake, cinnamon roll
16. Toy and Equipment: e.g. doll, stuffed animal
17. Others: e.g. car, painting

These categories were generated by examining the adequacy of each category and by checking the duplicability.

3   Result and Analysis

3.1   Typical Associations of Each Category

To clarify the image of each category more clearly, Table 3 shows the list of associated words that have the commonality among 20% or more of informants. Numbers in parenthesis show the number of informants who answered that word as an associated word.

Table 3. List of associated words that have the commonality among 20% or more of informants.

Category		Female		Male	
		Cute	Kawaii	Cute	Kawaii
1	Adjective	infant(3)	small(6), round(4)	small (9)	small(9)
2	Animal	cat(3)	cat(6), dog(5), small animals(4), rabbit(3)	cat (10)	dog(15), cat(14)
3	Character	Hello Kitty(5), character(5), My Melody(3), Disney characters(3)	-	-	-
4	Clothes and Fashion	clothes(3), dress(3)	clothes(3)	-	clothes(10)
5	Color	pink(7), colorful(4), vivid pink(3)	pink(6), pastel color (5)	-	-
6	Foreign Items	-	-	-	-
7	Human	girl(5), baby(3)	baby(8), smiling face (5), girl(4), idols(3)	-	child(16)
8	Letter	-	-	-	-
9	Onomatope	kira-kira(6)	fuwa-fuwa(3), kira-kira(3)	-	-
10	Ornaments and Accessory	ribbon(3)	cosmetics(6), ribbon (4), lace(3)	-	-
11	Person's Name	-	Yui Aragaki(3)	-	-
12	Place	-	cafe(3)	-	-
13	Plant	flower(3)	flower(3)	-	-
14	Shape and Pattern	heart(4), polka-dot(3)	plaid(4)	-	-
15	Sweets and Fruits	-	sweets(4)	-	-
16	Toy and Equipment	-	stuffed animal(5)	-	stuffed animal(9)

3.2   Total Associations of Each Category

Total of 1168 associations were generated by 60 informants where female (N = 15) generated 518 associations (213 words for Cute and 305 words for Kawaii) and male (N = 45) generated 650 associations (244 words for Cute and 406 words for Kawaii). Female answered more associations (average of 14.2 words for Cute and 20.3 words for Kawaii) than male (average of 5.4 words for Cute and 9.0 words for Kawaii). Table 4 shows the percentage of total associations for each category. Shaded cells show 0%, underlined cells show more than or equal to 10% and bold letter cells show more than or equal to 20% of total association.

Table 4 shows that female informants mostly associated both of Cute and Kawaii to Adjective (15.5% and 20.7%), then to Character (13.1% and 4.9%), and Human (12.7% and 13.4%) while male informants mostly associated both of Cute and Kawaii to Animal (21.7% and 25.1%), then to Human (17.2% and 16.7%) and Character (15.6% and 12.8%). In addition, Onomatope appeared more frequently in female informants (5.6% and 4.9%) than male informants (0.8% and 1.2%)

Regarding the difference between Cute and Kawaii, Character was more frequent for Cute (13.1%) than Kawaii (4.9%) among female informants. But Cute Character included Hello Kitty for 5 times among female and 7 times among male, even though Hello Kitty was born in Japan. Hello Kitty appeared for Kawaii only for once. Another typical difference can be found for Foreign Items for which Cute generated more associations (4.2% for female and 4.1% for male) than Kawaii (0.7% for female and 0.0% for male).

3.3   First Associated Word

Assuming that the word that has the strongest association with the stimulus word or the shortest path to the stimulus word in the memory network might be recalled first (or faster), analyzing the first associated word for each informant will be meaningful. Based on this idea, all 60 first associated words for Cute and Kawaii were picked up and shown in Tables 5, 6 and 7. Shaded cells show 0%, underlined cells show more than or equal to 10% and bold letter cells show more than or equal to 20% of total association.

The most frequent association for Cute was Character (14), and Animal (11), then Adjective (9) and Human (9). On the other hand, the most frequent association for Kawaii was Animal (26), then Human (12).

Among Characters, Hello Kitty was the most popular (2 for female and 5 for male).

In Animal category, Cute was associated with cats (including kitten) (5) and dogs (2), and Kawaii was associated with cats (including kitten) (10) and dogs (7).

Table 4. Percentage of total associations for each category.

Category		Total			
		Female		Male	
		Cute	Kawaii	Cute	Kawaii
1	Adjective	15.5	20.7	10.7	6.2
2	Animal	6.6	10.8	21.7	25.1
3	Character	13.1	4.9	15.6	12.8
4	Clothes and Fashion	6.1	4.3	1.6	6.2
5	Color	9.4	4.6	6.6	4.2
6	Foreign Items	4.2	0.7	4.1	0.0
7	Human	12.7	13.4	17.2	16.7
8	Letter	1.9	0.3	0.8	0.5
9	Onomatope	5.6	4.9	0.8	1.2
10	Ornaments and Accessory	8.0	8.5	4.1	4.2
11	Person's Name	5.2	8.2	1.2	5.4
12	Place	0.0	1.6	0.4	0.7
13	Plant	1.9	2.3	1.2	2.5
14	Shape and Pattern	3.3	2.6	3.3	1.0
15	Sweets and Fruits	2.3	4.3	4.5	1.0
16	Toy and Equipment	2.8	2.0	1.6	3.2
17	Others	1.4	5.9	4.5	9.1

Table 5. Percentage of first associations for each category.

Category		1st words			
		Female		Male	
		Cute	Kawaii	Cute	Kawaii
1	Adjective	13.3	6.7	15.9	13.3
2	Animal	6.7	**46.7**	**22.7**	**42.2**
3	Character	**26.7**	0.0	**22.7**	8.9
4	Clothes and Fashion	0.0	0.0	2.3	2.2
5	Color	**20.0**	0.0	0.0	2.2
6	Foreign Items	0.0	0.0	9.1	0.0
7	Human	**20.0**	**26.7**	13.6	17.8
8	Letter	0.0	0.0	0.0	0.0
9	Onomatope	0.0	6.7	0.0	0.0
10	Ornaments and Accessory	6.7	0.0	4.5	0.0
11	Person's Name	6.7	13.3	4.5	4.4
12	Place	0.0	0.0	0.0	2.2
13	Plant	0.0	0.0	0.0	0.0
14	Shape and Pattern	0.0	0.0	0.0	0.0
15	Sweets and Fruits	0.0	0.0	0.0	0.0
16	Toy and Equipment	0.0	0.0	4.5	0.0
17	Others	0.0	0.0	0.0	6.7

Table 6. First associated words for Cute

Category		SUM	Female	Mare	Cute
1	Adjective	9	0	3	small
			0	1	sexy
			1	0	infant
			0	1	Kawaii in coolness
			1	1	pop
			0	1	beautiful
2	Animal	11	0	4	cat
			1	1	animal
			0	2	dog
			0	1	small animal
			0	1	kitten
			0	1	caterpillar on apple
			2	5	Hello Kitty
			1	0	character
			0	1	ANIME character
3	Character	14	0	1	Kirby
			1	0	My Melody
			0	1	angel
			0	1	stitch
			0	1	cupid
4	Clothes and Fashion	1	0	1	clothes
5	Color	3	2	0	pink
			1	0	vivid color
6	Foreign items	4	0	1	foreigner
			0	1	European things
			0	1	overseas items
			0	1	foreign child
7	Human	9	2	0	girl
			1	1	baby
			0	1	idols
			0	1	child
			0	1	person
			0	1	smiling face
			0	1	girl hunted by womanizer
10	Ornaments and accessory	3	1	2	ribbon
11	Person's Name	3	1	0	Ami Makino
			0	1	Ayako Hashizume
			0	1	Tokiwa Ringo
16	Toy and Equipment	2	0	1	stuffed animal
			0	1	doll
Total	59	15	44	(non-respondent: 1male)	

Table 7. First associated words for Kawaii

Category	SUM		Female	Mare	Kawaii
1	Adjective	7	1	3	small
			0	1	charm
			0	1	push
			0	1	clumsy
2	Animal	26	3	5	cat
			1	5	dog
			0	3	animal
			2	1	small animal
			0	2	kitten
			0	1	rabbit
			1	0	red panda
			0	1	dog sleeping
			0	1	squirrel eating food
3	Character	4	0	2	Yuru-Chara
			0	1	stitch
			0	1	ANIME character
4	Clothes and Fashion	1	0	1	clothes
5	Color	1	0	1	pastel color
7	Human	12	0	2	child
			4	2	baby
			0	2	girl
			0	1	person
			0	0	my girlfriend
			0	1	idols
9	Onomatope	1	1	0	fuwa-fuwa
			0	1	Ayako Hashizume
11	Person's Name	4	0	1	Kasumi Arimura
			1	0	Tsubasa Honda
			1	0	Yui Aragaki
12	Place	1	0	1	Harajuku
17	Others	3	0	2	Japanese itmes
			0	1	something tightening the chest
Total		60	15	45	

4 Free Description on Both Concepts

Informants in the second survey (N = 35) were requested to write their own definition
of Cute and Kawaii or any free comments on both concepts. The result is shown in
Table 8. A common tendency among female informants and male informants was that
Cute is a mixture of Kawaii and cool, and is something of foreign origin, while Kawaii
is a wider concept than Cute and includes it within. Kawaii is mainly used for animals

Table 8. Free descriptions (2nd survey)

ID	Sex	Definition
26	M	Cute relates to the design while Kawaii is related to the size, shape and behavior of things
27	M	Cute is something small and makes us get excited. Kawaii heals our mind by just watching
28	M	Because Cute is English, it has an image of Kawaii items originated in foreign countries. Because Kawaii is Japanese, Kawaii items originated in Japan
29	M	Girls are Cute at around 10 years old and become Kawaii at around 20
30	M	Cute is an expression for small items. Kawaii is used for describing living things such as human. Cute is a bit maniac while Kawaii is lovable
31	M	Cute is something that various people feel adorable for humans, animals, and things. What is Kawaii may change according to age and sex. I don't think that something Kawaii for Japanese women may also be Cute for foreign women. Recent use of Kawaii is different from what it was some years ago and has been widened its applicable range
32	M	Cute is small and Kawaii is large
33	M	Cute is what things were made to have the appearance of Kawaii, on the other hand, Kawaii is the natural feeling
34	M	Both are the same
35	F	Cute: American ANIME characters, cool+Kawaii, intuition. Kawaii: soft animals and human beings. Even though something that is not Kawaii at first sight will become Kawaii after the long gaze
36	M	Cute is for living things that are small. Kawaii is for everything including animals, plants and minerals
37	F	Kawaii includes Cute. Kawaii is justice and Cute is strong. Cute is a bit maniac
38	F	Cute has a firm image while Kawaii has a soft image. Cute can be made while Kawaii cannot be made
39	M	Cute may not be used for things. Cute is a mixture of cool and Kawaii. Kawaii can be used for everything. It is easier to use than Cute
40	M	Kawaii has an image of something soft, while Cute has an image of something crisp
41	M	Cute doesn't have the deep meaning. Something of which the heart feels directly is Kawaii. There is some special reason to exist for Kawaii For Cute, it is difficult to find the reason
42	M	Cute is Kawaii that contains the adult attractiveness such as sexiness or sex appeal. Because it is an English word, cute reminds me of foreign Kawaii Kawaii is a simple attractiveness that doesn't have the sexy feeling but will relax people by just watching. Kawaii with something additional is cute
43	M	Cute is cool and sexy. It is an adult attractiveness. Kawaii will give the relaxed feeling
44	M	Cute is seldomly used. It is for describing animals and is similar to childish. It is also used to describe the shape and size of objects. Something small is Cute. Kawaii is used for describing a person including the hair style and atmosphere. Kawaii is sometimes used as a greeting word or praising word

(continued)

Table 8. (*continued*)

ID	Sex	Definition
45	M	Kawaii is something fluffy. Cute is the solid pink. Cute has a clear image but Kawaii is vast and can be used to describe many things. Kawaii can be used as an derivation such as Busa-kawaii
46	M	Cute is based on intuition while Kawaii has a reason
47	M	Regarding the size, large things are Cute and small things are Kawaii
48	M	Cute is used for overseas items, colorful ones and of strong color. Kawaii is for Japanese and single pale colored
49	M	Cute is for describing the gesture and Kawaii is for describing the object itself
50	M	Cute is strongly pink and tough with overseas fanciness. Kawaii is calm and charming. Japanese something and is not related to pink. Attractiveness that is specific to Japanese (Japanese woman)
51	M	Kawaii can be used for various things, but Cute can be used only for pink items
52	M	Cute is small and something that I feel like protecting. Kawaii is something that I'm gonna love. Cute is a child for a parent. Kawaii is a girl whom I like
53	M	Cute is a feeling on the spot and does not stick to one's heart. It is a beauty that I need. Kawaii is existing in the heart for ever and does not change. Sometimes, Kawaii is like a big mountain and sometimes it is like a Japanese paper. Kawaii is included in Cute and Cute is included in Kawaii
54	M	Cute is for describing a person, especially foreigner or unfamiliar people whose color and character are strong. Kawaii is for describing small and round things that may not harm me. It is associative for small animals and reminds me of something pale color and character
55	M	Cute has an image of a small girl and reminds me of ribbon. Kawaii can be used not only for people but animals or imaginry one such as Pokemon. Kawaii includes Cute. Cute is lovable and Kawaii is smiley
56	M	Cute is something attractive and is limited to use than Kawaii. Kawaii gives the healing and can be used broadly
57	M	Cute and Kawaii is artificial vs. natural (concrete vs. abstract), attractive vs. healing (stimulus vs. calmness), development vs. growth (evolution vs. growing)
58	M	Because Cute is English, it refers to something big. On the other hand, Kawaii refers to children and small animals. Comparing English and Japanese, English word has a stronger image and Japanese word has a gentle image
59	M	I use Kawaii frequently while Cute not so much
60	M	Though having the same meaning, Cute is superior to Kawaii Kawaii is generic that can be used in various situations. For the question "what is Kawaii?" there are many answers, but for "what is Cute?" nothing comes out instantly. What I reminded for the word Cute is something that I like. In other words, Kawaii in general is Kawaii and Cute is used for preference

and human beings. Furthermore, female has a steady and clear image to Cute and a soft and light image to Kawaii. In general, male tend to describe the difference by concrete things and situations while female tend to describe by adjectives and Onomatope.

5   Discussion

Results found from this survey could be interpreted that Cute as a "Japanese word" is not a simple translation of Kawaii, and it is not necessarily be "lively" as dictionaries have shown. Kawaii is a Japanese word that has an everyday life as a background context, while Cute is a quasi-Japanese word that has some distance from the everyday life. This tendency can also be found in definitions that the informants gave. In other words, the meaning or the semantics of the word may sometimes be influenced by the context of use or the pragmatics.

6   Conclusion

Free association method was used to clarify the difference of meaning between Cute and Kawaii. Total of 60 informants were requested to write down the recalled words for Cute and Kawaii at the same time during 20 min. The analysis of data showed a difference between the two words and between the female and male. Further analysis of the first associated words showed that Cute means somewhat longing feeling that is not the same with Kawaii, nor the same with the dictionary definitions. On the other hand, the result for Kawaii suggested the everyday situation where familiar things and objects are regarded to be Kawaii. This result suggested that the meaning of the word (semantics) is influenced by the context of use or the cultural context (pragmatics).

References

1. Hashizume, A., Kurosu, M.: "Kansei Engineering" as an indigenous research field originated in Japan. In: HCI International 2016 Proceedings (2016)
2. Shiizuka, H. (ed.): Kansei Engineering Handbook. Asakura Shoten (2013). (in Japanese)
3. Kurosu, M., Hashizume, A.: On the Concept of Kawaii. SIG Kansei, Japan Society for Kansei Engineering (2016). (in Japanese)
4. Marcus, A., Kurosu, M., Ma, X., Hashizume, A.: Cuteness Engineering. SSCC. Springer, Cham (2017). https://doi.org/10.1007/978-3-319-61961-3
5. Marcus, A., Kurosu, M., Ma, X., Hashizume, A.: Cuteness in Japan. Cuteness Engineering. SSCC, pp. 33–61. Springer, Cham (2017). https://doi.org/10.1007/978-3-319-61961-3_2
6. Ookura, N.: Kawaii Engineering, Asakura Shoten (2017). (in Japanese)
7. Hashizume, A., Kurosu, M.: The gender difference of impression among Kawaii-related concepts for visual images among youths. In: HCI International 2017 Proceedings (2017)
8. Matsumura, A. (ed.): Digital Daijisen. Shogakukan Inc., Tokyo (2018)
9. Matsumura, A. (ed.): Daijirin Ver. 3. Sanseido, Tokyo (2006)
10. Shogakukan: Seisen-ban Nihon-kokugo-daijiten Ver. 2. Shogakukan, Tokyo (2006)

Emotional Design Evaluation Index and Appraisal a Study on Design Practice

Kuo-Liang Huang[1(✉)], Szu-Chi Chen[2], Hsuan Lin[3], and Yune-Yu Cheng[4]

[1] Department of Industrial Design, Design Academy,
Sichuan Fine Arts Institute, Chongqing, China
shashi@scfai.edu.cn
[2] Computer Science and Information Technology,
La Trobe University, Melbourne, Australia
schen.szuchi@gmail.com
[3] Department of Product Design,
Tainan University of Technology, Tainan, Taiwan (R.O.C.)
te0038@mail.tut.edu.tw
[4] TAROKO International Co., Ltd, Tainan, Taiwan (R.O.C.)
yuneyu-cheng@taroko-int.com.tw

Abstract. When the most important requirement of product design is no longer quality or function, but user's physiological feelings, understanding consumer/ user's emotional reactions and needs will make it easier to successfully develop a product. For design and development team of a new product, it is a common desire of its designers, marketers and decision makers to build an appraisal modal which help them evaluate the emotion and sensibility value conveyed in a product, so as to provide a basis to improve product design and decision-making quality. For enterprises that want to increase the successful rate of product design, achieve the anticipated benefits once the product is introduced to the market while reduce the risk of failure, establishing a set of evaluation indicators that can be followed to improve design has become an urgent issue.

This paper, by adopting literature analysis method and referring to current industry status, firstly studied relevant literature and high-quality industry cases and analyzed the applicability of different emotional evaluation indicators and appraisal methods in the development of industry; then, through quantitative analysis of each indicator's discriminability and applicability, established evaluation indexes and developed a checklist that applicable for general evaluation practice. Application of the sensibility evaluation indexes to develop an emotional design evaluation checklist will greatly help the industry to narrow cognitive gap between designers and consumers and effectively improve the decision-making quality in product design.

Keywords: Emotional design · Sensibility · Evaluation indexes · Design evaluation

© Springer Nature Switzerland AG 2019
M. Kurosu (Ed.): HCII 2019, LNCS 11566, pp. 450–462, 2019.
https://doi.org/10.1007/978-3-030-22646-6_33

1 Introduction

Kotler et al. (2010), a well-known master of marketing, believes that global economy today has developed into an era of "sensibility consumption", when consumer's focus on product is no longer "rational consumption" demands of function or quality, but the "emotional consumption" demands of feelings, affections and emotional experience activities brought by the commodity. This explains why among a wide variety of products in the market, some are appealing and cherished by consumers while others attract little attention. What are the differences between these products, and what causes the difference? Scholar Khalid (2006) believes that product will evoke emotions and influence consumer's purchase decision and behavior. Therefore, today's design and development of products should not only pursue function and quality requirements, but also understand consumer's intention, express their perceptual demand and individual emotional experience in products' connotation and create added value for consumers. In the new era of sensibility consumption, in spite of how to create emotional value in their own products, enterprises also want to know how to evaluate and compare with competitive products' design, so as to stand out among peers and create more competitiveness.

Impacted by the trend of sensibility consumption, many enterprises are experiencing bottlenecks of development, and begin to attach importance to emotional design in creating added value and improving competitiveness in global market. However, the dilemma is how to figure out what kind of consumer or user emotions will be evoked from a product, how to design to make products elicit emotions, and how to evaluate the emotional design effectiveness. In spite of evaluating degree of emotional design in their own products, what are the advantages and disadvantages from different emotional aspects in comparison with competitor's products? While emotional cognition is like a black box, the evaluation activity of sensibility design requires high level of expertise and is very time-consuming. Is it possible to establish a set of clear and definite evaluation indexes so as to help enterprises efficiently evaluate the emotional value of their products so as to actively respond to the market beat?

This study attempts to explore relevant factors that affect emotional value in business design practice, and establish a complete set of observable evaluation indexes that helps enterprises to evaluate the emotional value and make decisions, so as to achieve higher rate of success in product development practice. This study, through collecting relevant literature of emotions and analyzing successful design practices, abstracts emotional factors in product design and discusses emotional indicators of multiple perspectives, converts the evaluation indicators into indexes, and establishes an "emotional design evaluation checklist" based on the indexes.

2 Literature Review

2.1 Emotional Relationship Between Consumers and Products

Nowadays, product design does not merely pursue utilitarian value based on rational requirements of quality, function, interface, etc., but should meet higher level emotional requirements of hedonic value, such as emotional and interaction experience that product communicates to its consumers. Dell'Era and Verganti (2007) believe that consumers begin to pay attention to the emotional value contained in products; in spite of quality, function and usability, emotional value has become an important factor to influence customers' purchase desire and behavior (Seva et al. 2007). Sensory response of emotional design is related to life experience. The reactions of organs to external stimulation generates different emotions that vary from person to person, such as emotional responses to beautiful things, emotional memories with families, living memories with pets, and even experience with a certain article. By adopting factors that cause sensory response, the emotional design is thus evolved. In some cases, through product consumption (of object, event and service), consumer obtain symbolic meanings of social status, corporate image, identity recognition, etc.; while at a higher level of "experiential consumption" stage, products provide consumers with emotional feelings and experiences (such as entertainment, memory, etc.) (Nicholas Zurbrugg and Zurbrugg 1997).

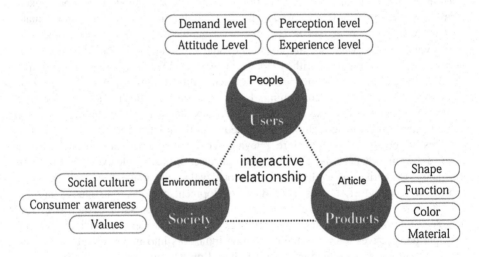

Fig. 1. The interactive relationship among users, products and environment

Based on above analysis, the interactive relationship among user, product and environment is illustrated in Fig. 1. It can be noted that product design should not only consider the product physical features of shape, function, color and material, but also the environment of social culture, consumer awareness and values, as well as user's need at demand, perception, experience and attitude levels. The interactive relationship below can help designers improve product design.

2.2 The Way Products Communicate Emotions and the Interaction with Users

Emotional design communicates message to stimulate user emotions and at the same time provides users with memorable experience during the process of using products. Humanized design touches users with sincere care of their emotional feelings based on careful observation of their emotional needs; and communicates pleasant feelings to consumers with well-designed product appearance and texture of nice touch. Based on emotional design and good communication, it makes users happier using the products.

It is known that pleasurable product is easier to attract people's attention and evoke rich and strong customer experience that could last for a while. When the sense of beauty, culture, thoughts are embodied in the design of a product, it communicates to consumers not only the physical features, but more profound product values. For consumers, the product is not just a tool, but a living object that has emotions and can communicate emotions to people (Jordan 2003). Based on the fact that emotion helps people to tell "good" from "bad", and impacts consumer behavior when choosing products, Desmet and Hekkert (2007) established a conceptual "framework of product emotion" as the base of emotional interaction. Four important factors of emotional interaction are proposed in this framework:(1) appraisal, (2) concern, (3) product, (4) emotion. The interactive relationship is shown in Fig. 2:

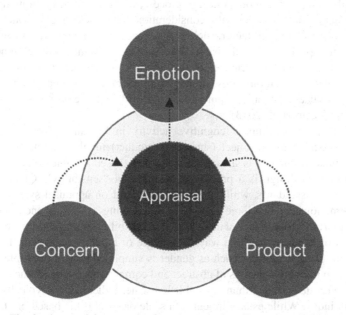

Fig. 2. The fundamental framework of product emotion (Desmet and Hekkert 2007)

Product design is closely related to emotions. When sense of beauty, culture, thoughts are conveyed in the design of a product, in addition to function, users can also sense the emotional value. For consumers, the product is not just a tool, but a living object that has emotions and communicate emotions to people (Jordan 2003).

Based on above analysis, it can be concluded that emotions are people's sensory response to things, products and services based on individual experience. Design and emotion are interrelated that product design evokes user emotion and user emotion impacts product design (Khalid 2006). Preece et al. (2015) believe that designers and users are of different backgrounds and the design pattern is not necessarily available for users, thus designers and users cannot fully communicate. There is cognitive gap between designers and users when designers do not fully understand users' needs and preferences, and users can only passively accommodate to the final design results – a problem in the process of product design and development that scholars and experts always want to overcome. Therefore, both designers and decision-makers want to create a set of emotional design indicators to narrow the cognitive gap between designers and users, and provide important basis to improve design and decision-making, which is of great help to the overall development of new products.

2.3   Evaluation Indexes and Methods

In the highly competitive product design process, designers need to know the product attributes that customers take into consideration when selecting products and the importance attached to each factor, such as function, comfort, appearance and price, so as to assist enterprise to make decisions about product design and development. From the perspective of system science, evaluation is a system engineering. The basic contents include: evaluation index, appraisal approach and evaluated object; system framework evaluation module; input and output of data and expert consulting system module (Friedmann et al. 2013).

"Evaluation" is a common cognitive activity in human society. In evaluation practice, assessment of an object (such as a product) involves multiple factors and indicators, thus evaluation is an overall judgment based on interaction of multiple factors. Emotional design is a process of quantifying "sensibility". Quantification is inseparable from standards, while standards are based on appraisal system. Quantification of emotion includes three factors as establishing sensibility indicator (index), semantic description of emotional indicator, and sensibility appraisal (Stone et al. 2005).

There is often more than one way to measure or quantify a concept. In spite that measurement of basic concept such as gender is simple and direct, multiple indicators are required to measure concepts of abstract and complex meanings (Stone et al. 2005). It's easier to create an index than to establish a scale. Indicators are typically weighted to create an index. While establishment of a scale or checklist is based on the findings of indicators' structural relations and composing them according to a certain method.

3 Methodology

Emotional design involves complex emotions. How to transform and integrate the emotions into product design so as to effectively stimulate consumers' psychological feelings? And how to evaluate and measure the sensibility of a product efficiently and effectively? Consumer experience process involves multiple emotions, and products of different categories and characteristics evoke different sensibilities. The "emotional value" of products should include a wide range of emotions in multiple dimensions. Thus, this study aims to figure out the emotional factors based on designer's and consumer's multi-dimension emotions, compose the factors into representative indicators (indexes), and establish an "emotional design evaluation checklist" to provide a simple but efficient method to evaluate emotional design, and a scientific and effective reference for enterprises to improve decision-making in product design and development practice.

In order to figure out the key factors that affect emotional value, this research, first studied literature and industrial cases to analyze emotion, sensibility, pleasure and culture's corresponding product value through literature analysis method to summarize the factors that affect sensibility evaluation, then discovered conceptual framework of product's emotional communication and prepared material of interview based on the finding, then invited five designers to the "semi-structured interview" respectively and forwarded the interview results to the "focus group", where they were coded and sorted, to define the key emotional factors. Later, we prepared evaluation questions of each indicator (factor) according to current industry situation, culture and values, and adopted quantitative factor analysis to discover multiple dimensions of emotion, and further determined the evaluation indexes and question items of emotional design. Lastly, through variance analysis of each indicator's discriminability and applicability, it was verified that the indicators are applicable for identification of products of same positioning. Establishment of "emotional design evaluation checklist" was thus completed as shown in Fig. 3.

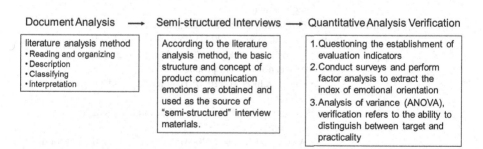

Fig. 3. The research method used

4 Results

Since relevant contents are complex, we obtained the following results and suggestions by widely collecting, reading and concluding more than 100 pieces of relevant literature from medicine, physiology, cognitive science and anthropology and by expert interviews.

4.1 Evaluation Indicators of Emotionalized Sensibility Value

In order to discover the factors that affect sensibility value, this paper analyzed dozens of literatures to summarize domestic and foreign scholars' views on emotion, sensibility, pleasure and culture's product value. Based on the literature findings and the fact that in the process of designing multiple emotions are considered and that products of different categories and characteristics embody different styles of sensibility, it can be

Table 1. Dimensions and indicators for evaluation of emotionalized sensibility value

Dimension	Indicator	Main literature resources and theories
Pleasure	Physical pleasure	• Tiger (2017) Four concepts of pleasure in products;
	Mental pleasure	• Jordan (2003) Four concepts of pleasure in products;
	Functional pleasure	• Jordan (1999) User demand theory of product features; • Desmet and Hekkert (2007) Three levels of interaction between users and products.
	Social pleasure	
Attractiveness	Demand	• Baxter (Baxter 1995) Four levels of attractiveness of product to consumers;
	Attitude	• Khalid and Helander (2004) Three kinds of emotional demands in product design;
	Consciousness	• Park, Jaworski and MacInnis (Park et al. 1986) Product requirements
	Experience	
Image	Self-image	• Park et al. (1986) Product requirements;
	Social symbol	• Silverstein et al. (2004) Four emotional levels;
	Values	• Desmet and Hekkert (2007) Three levels of interaction between users and products. • Hassenzahl et al. (2010) Hedonic value of interactive products; • Mugge (2007) Four factors that influence affection of products; • Ashby and Johnson (2003) Personalized features of products
Association	Elicit emotions	• Khalid and Helander (2004) Three kinds of emotional demands in product design;
	Recall memories	• Mugge (2007) Four factors that influence affection of products;
	Cultural meaning	• Ashby and Johnson (2003) Personalized features of products

Source: Sorted in this study

concluded that the "emotionalized sensibility value" of products include a wide range of emotions of multiple dimensions. Based on this idea, the paper analyzed different point of views and summarized multiple dimensions of emotional design through literature and case study; and through expert interview and focus group's processing, finally determined the dimensions and indexes for emotionalized sensibility evaluation as listed in Table 1, and proposed a "framework of emotional design appraisal system" as shown in Fig. 4.

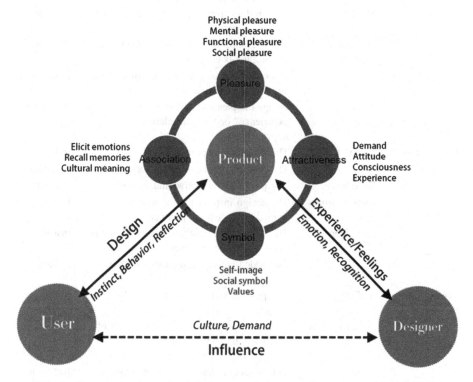

Fig. 4. Framework of emotional design appraisal system Source: sorted in this study

4.2   Establish Emotional Design Evaluation Indicators and Questions

Design is subjective creation based on designer's personal experience, whether a product can evoke consumer's emotion should be judged by objective evaluation. This study studied emotional factors in relevant researches to figure out evaluation indicators and dimensions, converted each indicator into text description that is observable and measurable according to scholars' key points of notice, and prepared questions for each index (indicator) by taking into consideration current industry situation, culture and values. Through testing investigation and quantitative factor analysis, the sensibility design evaluation indexes and the questions were determined. Lastly, the questions were classified and organized according to the three levels (instinct, behavior and reflection) design theory of Norman (2004), into Table 2.

Table 2. Evaluation indicators and questions on emotional design

Dimension	Indicator	Question	3 Levels
Pleasure	Physical pleasures	The appearance, color, material, touch, etc. of the product satisfy users' aesthetic needs and produce joyful feelings	Instinct
		Semantic description (metaphor, analogy, simile, allegory) of the product is humors and interesting	Instinct
	Mental pleasures	The product arouses positive feelings such as fun, surprise, etc.	Behavior
	Functional pleasures	The operation is easy to understand, and the product is easy to use	Behavior
		Smooth operation brings users comfortable and joyful experience	Behavior
	Social pleasures	Brings the pleasure of "interactive experience" or "human relation improvement"	Reflection
Attractiveness	Demand	The functions meet user's needs	Behavior
		The product produces satisfactory result	Behavior
	Experience	The product is attractive and appealing	Instinct
	Consciousness	The design inspires the impulse to immediately own the product	Instinct
	Experience	The product effectively represents different value from other products	Instinct
		The added-value is satisfactory on the whole	Behavior
Symbol	Self-image	The product shows personal taste, style or image	Reflection
	Social symbol	Possession of this product is a simple of "high social status" or attracts "admiration"	Reflection
	Values	This product reflects individual uniqueness	Reflection
Association	Elicit emotions	Some features of product design recall certain memories	Instinct
	Recall memories	This product recalls beautiful experience and memories	Reflection
	Cultural meaning	There is cultural meaning in this product, which adds to its value	Reflection

Source: Sorted in this study

4.3   Sensibility Evaluation and Checklist

Relative importance of each index varies in practical application according to the differences of product attributes, product design goals or product life cycle. Therefore, creation of the emotional design evaluation checklist included weight factor to measure the evaluation index so as to provide more flexibility in different design evaluation practice. The evaluation indicators and questions were reordered in accordance with design's three levels. And through variance analysis of each indicator's discriminability

Table 3. Emotional design evaluation checklist

Design level	Evaluation questions	Score 1–10	Index weight	Weighted score
Instinct level	The appearance, color, material, touch, etc. of the product satisfy users' aesthetic needs and produce joyful feelings			
	Semantic description (metaphor, analogy, simile, allegory) of the product is humors and interesting			
	The product is attractive and appealing			
	The design inspires the impulse to immediately own the product			
	The product effectively represents different value from other products			
	Some features of product design recall certain memories			
Behavior level	The product arouses positive feelings such as fun, surprise, etc.			
	The operation is easy to understand and the product is easy to use			
	Smooth operation brings users comfortable and joyful experience			
	The functions meet user's needs			
	The product produces satisfactory result			
	The added-value is satisfactory on the whole			
Reflection level	Brings the pleasure of "interactive experience" or "human relation improvement"			
	The product shows personal taste, style or image			
	Possession of this product is a simple of "high social status" or attracts "admiration"			
	This product reflects individual uniqueness			
	This product recalls beautiful experience and memories			
	There is cultural meaning in this product, which adds to its value			
[Note] Weight reference: 0.5 (least important), 0.75 (less important), 1 (important), 1.25 (more Important), 1.5 (most important)		Total:		

Source: Sorted in this study

and applicability, it was verified that the indicators are applicable for identification of other products of same positioning. On the basis of above studies, "emotional design evaluation checklist" was finally completed, shown in Table 3.

4.4 Appraisal of the Emotional Design Evaluation Checklist

The "emotional design evaluation checklist" developed by this paper is not limited to the evaluation of a single product, but is widely applicable for the evaluation of emotional design for products of different attributes, design goals and in different product life cycles. In evaluation practice, firstly, set the weight value for each indicator according to the "emotional design evaluation weight setting table" based on the product's attribute, design objective and lifecycle; secondly, invite 5-10 core personnel of product development or experts in this field to make expert evaluation respectively for their own products and competitive manufacturers'; thirdly, collect and summarize the results to generate a weighted evaluation result; lastly, compare the evaluation results and analyze the differences between products of their own and competitors' indicator by indicator, and make decision to improve design accordingly.

5 Conclusions and Suggestions

The aim of this paper to develop an "emotional design evaluation checklist" is to provide an objective, effective and efficient way of emotional design evaluation, which helps designers and manufactures evaluate the emotional design between their own products and competitive products, further understand the similarities and differences from different indicators, and make decisions to strengthen the competitiveness and overcome the shortcomings in product design.

This paper aims to find out the general evaluation indicators shared by designers and consumers in emotional design evaluation and formulate a set of scientific analysis and decision-making model with these indicators to effectively narrow the cognitive gap between designers and consumers and help the industry improve decision-making and product design during the new product development process.

In spite of price and function, consumer will judge product and make decision based on their overall understanding and feeling. So nowadays designers are facing greater challenges than ever before in designing products. Emotional design that embodies sensibility, emotion, creativity and innovation into products is regarded as a key factor to improve the product's cognitive value. This paper discussed user emotions through literature analysis, summarized sensibility dimensions and indicators to create emotional design evaluation indexes; prepared questions for each indicator based on current industry situation, culture and values, and developed the "emotional design evaluation checklist" to meet industry needs. User's subjective measurement and cognition of gain and loss is an essential part of decision-making, and demand of positive emotion and sensibility generally overpass the rational requirements of cost or function to influence consumer behaviors. Conclusions, suggestions and limitations of this study are as follows.

New product development and high-quality decision-making are key factors for enterprise's sustainable development and competitiveness. This paper developed an "emotional design evaluation checklist" based on the findings on three research stages: firstly, collecting and analyzing domestic and foreign literatures on emotion, sensibility, pleasure, culture, values and evaluation methods; secondly, building up a "framework of emotional design appraisal system" based on the literature findings and industrial development situation; thirdly, setting up questions for each evaluation index (indicator), establishing "emotional design evaluation checklist" and proposing the appraisal method of evaluation practice, so as to provide a reference for different industries to evaluate the emotional design in new product development. This study established sensibility/emotion evaluation dimensions and indicators, and adopted the form of questionnaire and checklist to provide an easy reference for the industry to evaluate sensibility value and make decisions, so as to greatly narrow the cognitive gap between designers and consumers, and help enterprises to effectively improve decision-making during product design and development.

The "framework of emotional design appraisal system" and "emotional design evaluation index" proposed in this study are applicable for different industries' product design practice to help designers better understand the emotional factors that influence consumer's behavior and develop emotional products that meet customers' needs and evoke user emotions. Also, indicators of reflection dimension can help marketing personnel develop marketing strategies that effectively stimulate consumers' desire to purchase. The "emotional design evaluation checklist" added in weight factor of indicators to appraise differential design and communication modes as well as provide an important basis to improve product development and decision-making. Although this study has checked through key points of each evaluation indicator to avoid unnecessary omissions, because of time and environment limit, it failed to conduct reliability and validity analysis of the dimensions and questions in the "emotional design evaluation checklist", which leaves room for future studies.

References

Ashby, M., Johnson, K.: The art of materials selection. Mater. Today 6(12), 24–35 (2003)

Baxter, M.: Product Design: Practical Methods for Systematic Development of New Products. Taylor & Francis, Abingdon (1995)

Dell'Era, C., Verganti, R.: Strategies of innovation and imitation of product languages. J. Prod. Innov. Manage 24(6), 580–599 (2007)

Desmet, P.M., Hekkert, P.: Framework of product experience. Int. J. Des. 1(1), 57–66 (2007)

Friedmann, A., Zimring, C., Zube, E.: Environmental Design Evaluation. Springer, New York (2013). https://doi.org/10.1007/978-1-4757-5154-3

Hassenzahl, M., Diefenbach, S., Göritz, A.: Needs, affect, and interactive products–facets of user experience. Interact. Comput. 22, 353–362 (2010)

Jordan, P.W.: Pleasure with products: human factors for body, mind and soul. In: Human Factors in Product Design: Current Practice and Future Trends, pp. 206–217 (1999)

Jordan, P.W.: Designing Pleasurable Products: An Introduction to the New Human Factors. CRC Press, Florida (2003)

Khalid, H.M.: Embracing diversity in user needs for affective design. Appl. Ergon. **37**(4), 409–418 (2006)

Khalid, H.M., Helander, M.G.: A framework for affective customer needs in product design. Theor. Issues Ergon. Sci. **5**(1), 27–42 (2004)

Kotler, P., Kartajaya, H., Setiawan, I.: Marketing 3.0: From Products to Customers to the Human Spirit. Wiley, Hoboken (2010)

Mugge, R.: Product attachment. Ph.D thesis, Delft University of Technology, The Netherlands (2007)

Nicholas Zurbrugg, B.A., Zurbrugg, N.: Jean Baudrillard, Art and Artefact. Sage Publications, California (1997)

Norman, D.A.: Emotional Design: Why We Love (Or Hate) Everyday Things. Basic Civitas Books, New York (2004)

Park, C.W., Jaworski, B.J., MacInnis, D.J.: Strategic brand concept-image management. J. Mark. **50**(4), 135–145 (1986)

Preece, J., Rogers, Y., Sharp, H.: Interaction Design: Beyond Human-Computer Interaction. Wiley, Florida (2015)

Seva, R.R., Duh, H.B.-L., Helander, M.G.: The marketing implications of affective product design. Appl. Ergon. **38**(6), 723–731 (2007)

Silverstein, M.J., Fiske, N., Butman, J.: Trading up: la rivoluzione del lusso accessibile. Etas (2004)

Stone, D., Jarrett, C., Woodroffe, M., Minocha, S.: User Interface Design and Evaluation. Elsevier Science, New York (2005)

Tiger, L.: The Pursuit of Pleasure. Taylor & Francis, Abingdon (2017)

Kansei Engineering for E-Commerce Cantonese Porcelain Selection in China

Yi Ji[1(✉)], Peng Tan[1], Szu-Chi Chen[2], and Henry Been-Lirn Duh[2]

[1] School of Arts and Design, Guangdong University of Technology,
Yue Xiu District of Dong Feng East Road No. 729, Guangzhou 510000, China
jiyi001@hotmail.com, huisaqingchun1993@gmail.com
[2] Department of Computer Science and Information Technology,
La Trobe University, Plenty Rd & Kingsbury Dr, Bundoora, VIC, Australia
schen.szuchi@gmail.com, 297470555@qq.com

Abstract. In online shopping experience of Cantonese Porcelain, customers are unable to touch, feel, take a close look at the details, and perceive the placement of the product. Therefore, the appearance of product is the most important factor to influence the users' buying decision. Increasing the emotional appeal or Kansei generated from the product appearance would encourage product sales. This paper uses Kansei Engineering to identify design elements of Cantonese Porcelain that are emotional appealing to porcelain products as a case of research and design in China. Multivariate analysis is performed on the data to identify the affecting Kansei words and corresponding design elements. Finally, sample Cantonese Porcelain which contains the most influential design elements are presented as recommendation, and it will improve customer selection of porcelain products effectively in e-commerce in China.

Keywords: Kansei engineering · E-commerce · Recommender system · Statistical kansei analysis · Cantonese porcelain

1 Introduction

Kansei is a Japanese word. When translated into English it represents 'consumer's psychological feeling and image' [1]. This means that Kansei is the impression that somebody gets from a certain artefact, environment or situation using all the senses of sight, hearing, feeling, smell, taste, as well as cognition. By Kansei words, the customers are guided to express their affective needs, their feelings, and their emotional states. These emotional and sensory wants are then translated into perceptual design elements of the product [2]. While Kansei words excel in describing affective needs, the mapping relationships between Kansei words and design elements are often not clearly available in practice. Some designers are not aware of the underlying coupling and interrelationships among various design elements with regard to the achievement of customers' affective satisfaction [3]. Clausing (1994) discerns customer needs and product specifications, and points out that the mapping problem in between is the key issue in 'design for customers' [4].

© Springer Nature Switzerland AG 2019
M. Kurosu (Ed.): HCII 2019, LNCS 11566, pp. 463–474, 2019.
https://doi.org/10.1007/978-3-030-22646-6_34

E-commerce and Internet-based sales transaction has become more and more popular through the years [5]. Benefits for online shopping includes convenience, time and cost savings, and greater choices without geographical constraints [6]. The experience of shopping online is different than shopping at conventional stores. During conventional shopping, the customer is able to take a close look, feel the product, and even play it with their hands depending on the product before purchasing it [7]. This process helps the customers on their decision process while comparing with different products on choosing their most satisfied one. Seller of conventional stores also makes a difference on success rate of sales transaction, which is influenced by the interaction between the seller and customer, which depends on how well the trust is built between them.

See Fig. 1, Cantonese Porcelain [8], also known as "Guangzhou zhijin colored porcelain", is a unique glazed porcelain handicraft with strong Oriental characteristics produced in Guangzhou. Its production technology is one of the most important intangible cultural heritages of China [9]. Since the beginning of the 21st century, the traditional customized market of Cantonese Porcelain handicrafts is facing an unprecedented survival crisis and development opportunity [10, 11]. How to better adapt to the consumer demand of the market, inherit and promote the cultural connotation of Cantonese Porcelain will be a problem which Cantonese Porcelain and most intangible cultural heritages needs to face [12].

Fig. 1. Cantonese Porcelain

The objective of this study is to identify the design elements of Cantonese Porcelain through pure visual presentation that are emotional appealing to customers, and ultimately, increase success rate of sales transaction through e-commerce system. Therefore, we chose a popular type of Kansei Engineering called of Kansei Engineering Type I [13], see Table 1, which translates emotional appeal into words that relates to design elements using item/category classification [14].

Table 1. Types of Kansei Engineering (Nagamachi 2001)

Type I	*Category classification*—Identifying the design elements of the product to be developed, translated from consumer's feelings and image
Type II	*Kansei Engineering System*—A computer aided system with an so called interference engine and Kansei databases
Type III	*Hybrid Kansei Engineering System*—The combined computer system or Forward ansei, which goes from the user's impressions to design specifications and vice versa
Type IV	*Kansei Engeering modelling*—Mathematical modelling with an interference engine and databases
Type V	*Virtual Kansei Engineering*—An integration of virtual reality technology and Kansei Engineering in a computer system
Type VI	*Collaborative Kansei Engineering designing*—Group work design system utilizing intelligent software and databases over the internet.

This study is composed of three major stages. For the first stage, selection of Kansei words, which were collected through different sources [15], then verified by Cantonese Porcelain experts. In the second stage, we construct a 5-point semantic differential scale of Kansei words for evaluating Cantonese Porcelain products. In the third stage, survey results, which are finished by participants, are evaluated to identify the most influential Kansei words of Cantonese Porcelain in e-commerce selection. In the last stage, a case design of Cantonese Porcelain based on relevant Kansei words be explored.

2   The Situations of Cantonese Porcelain in E-Commerce

Cantonese Porcelain is an art of glazed decorative porcelain in Guangzhou, which dates back to Kangxi and Qianlong reign (1662–1796) [16]. Since 1700s, European merchants brought in patterns of decorative porcelains and the finished products were exclusively for export [8]. With the development of market economy and cultural consumption, the production situation of Cantonese Porcelain has become less and less optimistic. Since Cantonese Porcelain has no use in modern times and is mostly used for collection and appreciation, it is difficult to increase sales volume and attract new practitioners. Ultimately, it is about the economics of the industry [17]. In addition, with the continuous development of e-commerce in the Internet industry, online shopping malls have increasingly become a way of shopping for consumers [18]. Undoubtedly, this has become a normal state of shopping mode today, which has penetrated into the life of consumers [19]. For example, China's online shopping platform Taobao, today almost all Chinese Internet users will use shopping, and consumers can freely choose and buy products based on their preferences [20, 21]. However, in order to adapt to consumers' habits, Cantonese Porcelain merchants have started to sell products on e-commerce platforms. However, the online orders have not exceeded the offline orders, which makes the majority of Cantonese Porcelain merchants confused. Through the investigation, it is found that the problem faced by the e-commerce platform of Cantonese Porcelain is that the product display fails to match the emotional needs of consumers, which will be the problem discussed in this paper.

3 Kansei Engineering Method in Cantonese Porcelain Selection

The experimental process of Kansei Engineering method in Cantonese Porcelain selection can be divided into three stages. Stage 1 is structuring semantic differential (SD) scale for the Kansei words and Collection of samples, stage 2 is Classification of item/category, stage 3 is evaluation experiment.

3.1 Collection and Selection of Kansei Words

A 5-point semantic differential scale with several Kansei words is constructed as shown in Table 7 in appendix. These words are sourced from relevant books, magazines, journal, advertisements, news and report of artworks.

In order to suit adapt to the evaluation standard of Cantonese Porcelain products, in this study, see Table 2, fifteen pairs of kansei words were verified by Cantonese Porcelain experts to secure the words' suitability before designing the survey for next step experiment.

Table 2. Selected Kansei words group (KWG) of Cantonese Procelain

N	KWG	N	KWG	N	KWG
1	Modern & Tradition	2	Abstract & Concrete	3	Decorative & Utility
4	Tech & Handmade	5	Round & Sharp	6	Public & Selfhood
7	Nature & Man-made	8	Streamline & Tough	9	Reason & Sensibility
10	Grace & Coarse	11	Fashion & Simple	12	Coordinate & Abrupt
13	Implicit & Publicity	14	Gorgeous & Frugal	15	Lightweight & Bulky

3.2 Collection and Selection of Samples

Furthermore, sample products of Cantonese Porcelain are collected from relevant market, advertisements and book. A total of 100 samples of Cantonese Porcelain in different forms were collected, see Fig. 5 in appendix.

In order to better classify 100 pieces of samples, in this experiment, 18 specimens of Cantonese Porcelain are selected with the help of craftsman from different Cantonese Porcelain Inheritance Base in Guangzhou, based on the distinctiveness of pattern, model, and color from form of natural, geometry, human. See Fig. 2.

Fig. 2. Schematic diagram of semantic differential

3.3   Classification of Item/Category

Sample products of Cantonese Porcelain were collected and classified into different categories. This is required due to the nature of e-commerce system, which the product can only affect visual emotional appeal, therefore, the classification of product is limited to the physical trait visually. Table 3 shows the partial list of the forty-eight item/category classification that we used:

Table 3. Selected Kansei words group (KWG) of Cantonese Porcelain

	Physical trait	
	Item	Category
Natural form	Model	Bowl, Cup, Kettle, Plate, Tank, Vase, Case, Other
	Pattern	Animal, Badge, Flower, Landscape, Character, Ship, Modern
	Color	Blue, Cyan, Gold, Black, Purple, Red, White, Yellow, Other
Geometry form	Model	Bowl, Cup, Kettle, Plate, Tank, Vase, Case, Other
	Pattern	Animal, Badge, Flower, Landscape, Character, Ship, Modern
	Color	Blue, Cyan, Gold, Black, Purple, Red, White, Yellow, Other
Human form	Model	Bowl, Cup, Kettle, Plate, Tank, Vase, Case, Other
	Pattern	Animal, Badge, Flower, Landscape, Character, Ship, Modern
	Color	Blue, Cyan, Gold, Black, Purple, Red, White, Yellow, Other

3.4   Evaluation Experiment Survey

To conduct the evaluation experiment, Fig. 3, we created a survey website using the SO JUMP system and invited twenty subjects (aged between 18 and 34) to evaluate Kansei words appeal for each of our eighty samples on a 5-point SD scale. The SO JUMP is a professional platform for the online questionnaire survey, evaluation, voting, focused on providing users with powerful, humanized design online questionnaires, collect data, custom reports, and results of the survey analysis. It is an established research gathering tool widely used for user research in industrial ergonomics and website assessment in China. This is the first study whereby SO JUMP was used in an optometry and health science field to gather survey feedback from respondents. The subjects are recruited from Guangdong University of Technology student population and Guangzhou citizen in China.

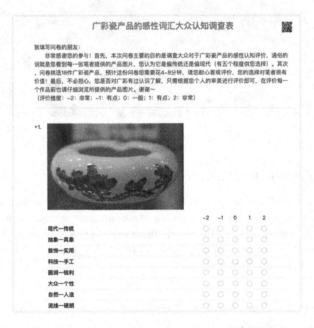

Fig. 3. Screen-shot of survey website used to evaluate the appeal of Kansei words of Cantonese Porcelain on 5-point SD scale

4   Statistical Analysis and Interpretation

4.1   Questionnaire Survey and Analysis

This stage is mainly carried out by questionnaire. Firstly, fifteen groups of Kansei words obtained through cluster analysis were combined with eighteen representative samples of the morphology of Cantonese Porcelain. Secondly, a questionnaire was compiled with the statistical analysis method of 5-point semantic difference, and 20 subjects were subjectively evaluated. Because of the tea set of the scope of widely used participants range is very wide in the crowd of different status and age, such as amateur and professional personnel, white-collar workers, consumers, manufacturers, sellers.

4.2 Interpretation of the Analyzed Data

Data analysis and statistics at this stage were based on the data of twenty valid questionnaires. By the average value algorithm calculates and obtains the results of Tables 4 and 5 (e.g. S1 means Samples 1, K1 means Kansei words group 1). The data represents the average evaluation value of the adjectives corresponding to the sample on the –2 2 scale. Negative values correspond to the left adjectives and positive values to the right adjectives.

Table 4. Relationship of samples and Kansei words

	S1	S2	S3	S4	S5	S6	S7	S8	S9
K1	–0.10	0.35	1.55	0.75	1.20	0.45	1.45	0.10	1.15
K2	1.35	0.95	1.00	0.50	1.10	1.20	1.60	0.55	1.35
K3	0.95	0.80	–1.40	0.05	0.05	–1.25	–1.40	–0.80	–1.10
K4	0.65	0.35	0.65	0.55	0.90	0.65	0.60	0.50	0.25
K5	–1.15	–0.90	–0.30	–0.65	–0.50	–1.35	–0.50	–1.25	–0.30
K6	0.45	–0.15	0.15	0.35	–0.20	0.85	–0.05	0.60	–0.40
K7	0.35	0.15	0.45	0.30	0.55	–0.10	0.50	0.50	0.10
K8	–0.95	–0.90	–0.40	–0.80	–0.25	–1.05	–0.15	–0.90	–0.05
K9	0.45	0.60	0.60	0.50	0.20	0.85	0.65	0.15	–0.20
K10	–0.95	–0.75	–0.20	–0.85	–0.30	–0.75	0.10	–1.15	–0.05
K11	–0.15	0.35	0.55	0.45	0.90	–0.30	0.75	–0.05	0.65
K12	–0.15	0.20	–0.15	–0.05	0.40	–0.70	0.15	–0.60	–0.20
K13	–0.40	0.15	0.05	–0.25	–0.10	0.25	0.50	0.40	0.05
K14	–1.05	–0.85	0.00	–0.85	–0.10	–0.65	0.15	–0.85	0.00
K15	–1.15	–0.60	0.45	–0.45	1.00	–0.90	1.00	–0.10	0.55

Table 5. Relationship of samples and Kansei words

	S10	S11	S12	S13	S14	S15	S16	S17	S18
K1	0.65	0.10	0.75	1.20	0.75	1.75	0.10	0.10	0.25
K2	0.70	0.70	1.20	1.25	0.85	1.20	1.05	0.75	0.85
K3	–1.40	–1.25	–0.75	–0.95	–0.15	–0.95	0.05	0.55	–0.70
K4	0.80	0.95	0.35	0.80	0.55	0.95	0.50	0.65	0.65
K5	–0.85	–0.90	–0.60	–0.85	–0.50	–0.65	–0.85	–1.05	–1.00
K6	1.00	0.35	0.30	0.00	0.30	–0.20	0.60	0.55	0.65
K7	0.20	0.25	0.85	0.20	0.60	0.35	0.30	0.25	0.10
K8	–1.05	–0.45	–0.15	–0.55	–0.75	–0.45	–0.60	–1.10	–0.80
K9	0.30	0.10	0.10	0.45	0.20	0.35	0.25	0.40	0.40
K10	–1.10	–0.10	0.35	–0.40	–0.50	–0.40	–0.55	–1.05	–1.00

(*continued*)

Table 5. (*continued*)

	S10	S11	S12	S13	S14	S15	S16	S17	S18
K11	-0.10	-0.15	0.20	0.25	0.60	0.60	-0.25	-0.30	-0.45
K12	-1.15	-0.70	-0.60	0.25	-0.05	0.05	-0.90	-0.35	-0.90
K13	0.45	0.35	0.30	-0.25	0.20	-0.40	0.65	-0.50	0.10
K14	-0.90	0.20	0.15	-0.75	-0.55	-0.10	-0.40	-0.85	-0.70
K15	-1.25	-0.45	1.15	-0.45	-0.05	-0.15	-0.75	-1.05	-0.60

4.3   Identification of Influential Product Selection Elements of Cantonese Porcelain

Mean Analysis is done by using the data from Kansei words survey and the Item/Category Classification of Cantonese Porcelain. Relationship between the four chosen Kansei words and the design elements describe in the item/category is obtained. Table 6 shows summary of the Mean analysis results.

Table 6.   S Summary of Kansei words group in samples

K	1	2	3	4	5	6	7	8	9	10	11	12	13	14	15
Mean	0.70	1.01	-0.54	0.63	-0.79	0.29	0.33	-0.63	0.35	-0.54	0.20	-0.30	0.09	-0.45	-0.21

From our Mean analysis (and Table 6), we picked the product selection elements that have the highest influence to the Kansei words as our recommended customer requirements list. From Tables 4 and 5 we can see in highest between –2 with 2, each sample had 2–4 preference Kansei words. For example, Kansei words of Sample 1 is concrete (1.35), round (–1.15), lightweight (–1.15) based on Table 2. In addition, data shows that Kansei words (concrete and decorative) are the most popular among 20 subjects, and then, there are tradition (1.75), handmade (0.8), round (–1.25), selfhood (0.6), streamline (–0.9), grace (–1.05), gorgeous (–0.85), lightweight (–1.5). From Table 6 we can see in highest between –2 with 2, Kansei words (concrete (1.01) and round (–0.79)) are the highest Mean grade among all the selected samples. Furthermore, Kansei words group 1, 2, 4, 6, 7, 9, 11, 13 are more to the right adjectives, and Kansei words group 3, 5, 8, 10, 12, 14, 15 are more to the left adjectives from the Kansei words of the fifteen groups. In the end, this study proposes e-commerce Cantonese Porcelain selection list based on item/category classification list based on Cantonese Porcelain and statistical analysis: Geometry form. Model: Plate, Bowl, Vase. Pattern: Animal, Flower, Landscape. Color: Blue, Cyan, Gold. Samples of Cantonese Porcelain that could contains our recommended product elements are shown in the Fig. 4:

Fig. 4. Proposed Cantonese Porcelain that based on recommended product element

5 Conclusions

This study collected twenty participants' emotional appeal of different Cantonese Porcelain product. Basic information regarding Cantonese Porcelain, cultural heritage, usage of e-commerce system, gender, age, and major of study are also gathered. After statistical analysis of the survey results, we are able to identify how the Kansei words influence different category and what design elements affect customers' emotional appeal the most. In the next step, we aim to do a case study on designing Chinese Porcelain based on our previous research related to relevant Kansei words. In addition, the database obtained through quantitative research can not only be used as a tool to assist the selection of e-commerce products in terms of the semantics of Cantonese Porcelain, but also provide designers with diversified ideas through the data. Furthermore, designers can modify the perceptual vocabulary and design elements in the database according to the needs to facilitate the design progress.

Acknowledgments. This research was supported by the Guangzhou science and technology project. China (201802020011). The completion of this study benefited from the tireless efforts of every teacher and classmate in the project team. Special thanks for the technical support given from the research team of Professor Henry Been-Lirn Duh from La Trobe University.

Appendix

Table 7. Kansei words of artworks

1	Modern & Tradition	2	Rhythm & Disorder	3	Decorative & Utility	4	Impatient & Placid
5	Vivacious & Dull	6	Technology & Handmade	7	Unique & Ordinary	8	Fresh & Stale
9	Soft & hard	10	Safety & Danger	11	Coordination & Abrupt	12	Solemnly & Unbending
13	Smooth & Rough	14	Deceny & Low	15	Gorgeous & Frugal	16	Excited & Steady

(continued)

Table 7. (*continued*)

17	Succinct & Complexity	18	Genial & Fishlike	19	Fashion & Nostalgia	20	Quiet & Lively
21	Lightweight & Bulky	22	Thick & Thin	23	Female & Male	24	Excitement & Silence
25	Bright & Dark	26	Masculine & Feminine	27	Classic & Modern	28	Nobleness & Scoundrels
29	Natural & Artificial	30	Solidity & Fragility	31	Public & Selfhood	32	Open & Constraint
33	Formal & Informal	34	Fun & Boring	35	Elegance & Vulgar	36	Novelty & Plain
37	Nobility & Mediocrity	38	Abstract & Concrete	39	Stimulus & Softness	40	Rustic & Affected
41	Warm & Cold	42	Luxury & Simplicity	43	Streamline & Tough	44	Fashion & Simple
45	New & Old	46	Richness & Monotony	47	Stability & Variability	48	Pleasure & Sadness
49	Dynamic & Static	50	Warmth & Indifference	51	Beauty & Ugliness	52	Impassion & Soberness
53	Sprightly & Gloom	54	Positive & Negative	55	Creativity & Imitation	56	Dullness & Cheerfulness
57	Young & Experienced	58	Thinness & Roughness	59	Freedom & Bondage	60	Sedate & Lightness
61	Romance & Reason	62	Sven & Wild	63	Conservative & Radical	64	Depression - Brisk
65	Rules & Rebellion	66	Exaggerate & Introversion	67	Sedate & Frivolous	68	Implicit & Publicity
69	Handsome & Rustic	70	Expensive & Cheap	71	Professional & Amateur	72	Bright & Unadorned
73	Tightness & Loose	74	Boldness & Formality	75	Maturity & Childishness	76	Melancholy & Joy
77	Round & Sharp	78	Seriousness & Easy	79	Fancy & Quiet	80	Refined & Coarse
81	Reason & Sensibility	82	Style & Shabby	83	Innovation & Conservatism	84	Orderliness & Disarray
85	Purity & Dirt	86	Conventional & Alternative	87	Fashion & Out	88	Honor &Inferiority
89	Nature & man-made	90	Hope & Despair	91	Quiet & Noise	92	Grace & Coarse
93	Dexterity & Clumsiness	94	Tension & Relaxation	95	Passion & Calmness	96	High & Low
97	Comfort & Discomfort	98	Cute & Hateful	99	Magic & Wateriness	100	Harmony & Conflict

Fig. 5. Sample products of Cantonese Porcelain

References

1. Nagamachi, M.: Kansei engineering and implementation of human-oriented product design. In: Koubek, R.J., Karwowski, W. (eds.) Manufacturing Agility and Hybrid Automation, vol. 1, pp. 77–80. IEA Press, Louisville (1996)
2. Nagamachi, M.: Kansei engineering: the framework and methods. In: Nagamachi, M. (ed.) Kansei Engineering, vol. 1, pp. 1–9. Kaibundo Publishing co. Ltd, Kure (1997)
3. Nagamachi, M.: Kansei engineering in consumer product design. Ergon. Des. Q. Hum. Factors Appl. 10(2), 5–9 (2016)
4. Jiao, J., Chen, C.H.: Customer requirement management in product development: a review of research issues. In: Plant Nutrition for Sustainable Food Production and Environment. Springer, Netherlands (1997)
5. Fredriksen, C. (ed.) (2012)
6. Communications report 2010–11
7. Błażewicz, J., Domschke, W., Pesch, E.: The job shop scheduling problem: conventional and new solution techniques. Eur. J. Oper. Res. 93(93), 1–33 (1996)
8. Zeng, Y.-f., Li, H.-z.: Zhijin Ceramics: Guangzhou Printed Porcelain Technology. Guangdong Education Press, Guang-zhou (2013)
9. Guo-yuan, Z.H.A.O.: The History of the Guangzhou Printed Porcelain. South of the Five Ridges Fine Arts Publishing House, Guangzhou (2008)
10. Ji, Y., Tan, P., Duh, H.B.-L.: Research on personalized learning pattern in traditional handicraft using augmented reality: a case study of Cantonese porcelain. In: Kurosu, M. (ed.) HCI 2018. LNCS, vol. 10902, pp. 304–316. Springer, Cham (2018). https://doi.org/10.1007/978-3-319-91244-8_25
11. Ji, Y., Tan, P.: Exploring personalized learning pattern for studying Chinese traditional handicraft. In: Proceedings of the Sixth International Symposium of Chinese CHI. ACM (2018)
12. Wen-yan, C.: South of the five ridges Guangcai painted porcelain art market brand wind. Art Mark. 2, 69 (2013)
13. Lokman, A.M., Nagamachi, M.: Kansei engineering: a beginners perspective. University Pub. Centre (UPENA) (2010)
14. Chuan, N.K., Sivaji, A., Shahimin, M.M., Saad, N.: Kansei engineering for e-commerce sunglasses selection in Malaysia. Procedia Soc. Behav. Sci. 97, 707–714 (2013)
15. Chen, S.: Based on Kansei engineering ceramic products morphology research. Doctoral dissertation, Jingdezhen Ceramic Institute (2012)
16. Shen, H.-y.: China Ceramic Decorative Color Symbol and Its Connotation of Semantic Analysis. Jingdezhen Ceramic Institute, Jingdezhen (2012)
17. Lai, J-m.: Development dilemma and innovation of Cantonese porcelain products, knowledge window (2016)
18. Pahnila, S., Warsta, J.: Online shopping viewed from a habit and value perspective. Behav. Inf. Technol. 29(6), 12 (2010)
19. The Rise of E-Commerce and Online Shopping in China. http://internshipschina.com/rise-e-commerce-online-shopping-china/
20. Yu, X., Yue, P.: Online consumer-to-consumer market in China - a study of Taobao. In: International Conference on Educational & Network Technology (2010)
21. Shen, Z., Hou, D., Zhang, P., Wang, Y., Zhang, Y., Shi, P., et al.: Lead-based paint in children's toys sold on china's major online shopping platforms. Environ. Pollut. 241, 311–318 (2018)

Research on Aesthetics of Interaction of Mobile Context-Aware Services——A Case Study of Notification System

Meiyu Lv[1,2] and Hequn Qu[2(✉)]

[1] School of Digital Media and Design Arts,
Beijing University of Posts & Telecommunications, Beijing 100876, China
[2] Beijing Key Laboratory of Network and Network Culture,
Beijing University of Posts & Telecommunications, Beijing 100876, China
sharonhqqu@163.com

Abstract. With the development of sensors, the improvement of computing and the maturity of algorithms related to artificial intelligence, context-aware services based on mobile terminals have become one of the most widely used intelligent systems. The service is profoundly making an impact on the interaction between users and smart devices, perhaps changing the efficiency of task execution, altering the behavior patterns of users, influencing the satisfaction and emotions of users, or even associated with the privacy and psychological state of users, which are closely related to the interaction mode of the notification system and the interactive aesthetic factors. This paper attempts to decompose and summarize the typical mobile context-aware system—notification system from the perspectives of active and passive, explicit and implicit, central and peripheral interaction modes, then to analyze the aesthetics of interaction and the impact on the user experience. From the perspective of interactive aesthetics, some thoughts and suggestions for the interaction design of mobile context-aware system were put forward.

Keywords: Context-aware · Notification system · Aesthetics of interaction

1 Introduction

In the era of pervasive computing, the improvement of computing of mobile devices, the built-in of sensors, the development of wireless communication technologies and the advancement of algorithms have facilitated the convergence of computing, communication and sensing technologies. This enables mobile devices to acquire increasing contextual awareness power of data acquisition, analysis, predicting human behaviors, and performing actions [1]. In 1994, Bill Schilit et al. first proposed the word "Context-aware" [2], which defined context as "the objects and their change of the position, the person and the surrounding". Context awareness emphasizes the device's perception of contextual information and the feedback of system. Context awareness can be understood as the acquisition of contextual information about the

M. Kurosu (Ed.): HCII 2019, LNCS 11566, pp. 475–485, 2019.
https://doi.org/10.1007/978-3-030-22646-6_35

environment, devices and the social state in which users are located through human-computer interaction or sensor technology, allowing computing devices to perform real-time analysis and reasoning, adaptively changing their behavior to provide appropriate service.

The mobility, portability, and instantly reachability of mobile devices allow them to be around users, and become aware of the changes of user context proactively, then provide explicit and implicit services based on user's individual needs, allowing contextual information to be fully integrated with user tasks, therefore the natural interaction could be achieved. Context-aware services based on mobile terminals have become one of the most widely used intelligent systems [3].

The mobile context-aware service reduces the load of the user's perception and analysis of information [4], while also improves the efficiency of operations. The shopping software being able to shorten the whole process of searching by recommending products of good quality to the users according to the records of clients' searching and preferences could be a great example. On the other hand, actively obtaining user context information, notifying some certain information after analysis, or performing operations through implicit interaction may bring negative impacts, such as privacy violation, information overload, interruption, loss of control, and psychological stress to users [5].

The efficiency improvement, experience difference and negative influence of context-aware system and traditional human-computer interaction system are mainly caused by the change of human-computer roles and the change of interaction modes. The negative impact is primarily related to the part of the user experience that removes efficiency and usability, that is, the part related to "aesthetics of interaction." This paper takes the notification system, one of the mobile context-aware systems, as an example, to analyze its interaction modes from the perspectives of active and passive, explicit and implicit, central and peripheral, and analyze the aesthetics of these interaction modes and the impact on user experience. Finally, implications on the interaction design of the mobile context-aware system were put forward, and the future researches of the mobile context-aware interaction were discussed.

2   Interaction in Mobile Context-Aware Systems

The interaction mode of the mobile context-aware system can be decomposed and analyzed from the perspectives of explicit and implicit, active and passive, central and peripheral, which are intertwined and synergistically interact with the user and the system. Therefore, it is possible for the mobile context-aware system to implicitly and actively assume more tasks in human-machine collaboration, thereby reducing the input requirements to users and free users from some attention, so that the users could perform multiple tasks efficiently at the same time. At the same time, the distribution of explicit and implicit, active and passive, central and peripheral interactions should be paid attention to, to ensure that users are less likely for users to experience negative emotions such as interruption, anxiety, worry about privacy and loss of control.

2.1 Explicit and Implicit Interaction

Most traditional interaction process is imperative, in which the device user gives clear instructions through keyboard, mouse, touch, gesture and voice commands, then the smart device explicitly outputs the sensory calculation result to the user through visual, tactile, and auditory modes, so that the human-computer interaction is achieved, this method is called explicit interaction. When performing explicit interaction, users are able to clearly and unambiguously control the input, understand the output information and the stage of interaction, so that they have sufficient sense of control, and the phenomenon of loss of control and invasion of privacy can be avoided. At the same time, there are only a few processes that require the equipment to perform sensing and calculation, so the recommendation errors and interruptions caused by the system rarely occur.

In contrast, Schmidt defined implicit interaction as an invisible interaction. Users no longer care about the interaction process itself, nor do they think much about how to use the device or system, but rather the device or system actively and implicitly identify and understand user behaviors, and the interpreted information is applied to the human-computer interaction process [6]. Compared to explicit interaction, implicit interaction can bring solution to the situation where the users cannot effectively input nor deal with the output from devices due to limited processing resources or physiological constraints when people are using the mobile context-aware system.

The users would not have to divide their attention or simply deal with their secondary tasks with only peripheral attention, so that they could highly focus on the main tasks without interruption, cognitive burden, or information overload.

2.2 Active and Passive Interaction

In the traditional human-computer interaction system, basing on the self-context perception and analysis, the user actively initiates interaction with the smart device according to the operation target and the contextual condition. Although this kind of interaction has a high psychological load on the user and the efficiency of the operation is limited, however, the user has a real sense of control over the interaction process, and has a clear understanding of the information required by the system and its corresponding reasons, thus they are less concerned about the information security.

In the mobile context-aware system, the smart device may actively perform an operation or issue a suggestion or request for performing an operation after analyzing and processing data such as user preferences, attributes, likes and dislikes, and acquired user context information. On the one hand, active interaction can reduce the consumption of user attention by interactive behavior, and make it possible for users to use limited attention to simultaneously handle multiple tasks. On the other hand, the inopportune active reminders and active executions can cause disturbance and even make the user feel uncomfortable and panicked about the contextual information (involving privacy) acquired by the computing device.

2.3   Central and Peripheral Interaction

Transition from the use of central attention to interact, to the use of peripheral attention for interaction, is a chain reaction after transition from explicit interaction to implicit interaction, passive interaction of equipment to active interaction. In the traditional human-computer interaction mode, the presentation of information and the response of the user require the user to concentrate on. When a user is in a task that consumes a large amount of psychological resources, it is difficult to perform multitasking both in terms of ability and emotion.

In the process of interaction with the mobile context-aware service, the smart phone has the ability to actively and implicitly recommend or perform operations according to the context and user preferences (such as automatically adjusting the screen brightness, automatically modifying the time zone, and recommend songs for users depending on the song history and preferences. Peripheral attention or subconscious is enough for users to complete tasks. In some situations, even without the user's attention, the computing device can fully complete the task. In this way, the consumption of the user's psychological resources is reduced, and the unutilized psychological resources are likely to be assigned to other tasks, which means that the way of multi-tasking is likely to be favored by more users.

3   Aesthetics of Interaction

As a philosophical term, aesthetics is used to define beauty and is understood to judge whether it meets the feeling of pleasure by sensory knowledge. The aesthetics of interaction research on the aesthetic issues between human, product and material culture, which is centered on aesthetic experience, but is different from philosophy, aesthetics or industrial design theory. It is not confined to abstract philosophical concepts, or apparent and functional descriptions of product, but reveals the beauty and aesthetic laws in daily life from different levels, such as from abstraction to figuration, thus promoting the renewal and development of design concepts. Aesthetics of interaction is not just the beauty on the interface, but a psychological experience when users communicating with products. Designers transform the user's experience of interacting with the product and the environment into corresponding physical and ideological pleasure, then reflect it on the design. When the design of the product satisfies this "beauty" requirement, the "beauty" product is naturally born.

In the field of human-computer interaction and interaction design, aesthetics became a research topic in the late 1990s. At that time Noam Tractinsky (1997) reproduces Kurosu and Kashimura's study (1995) of the relationship between "objective" usability and subjective evaluation of usability and aesthetics [8, 9], after which he believed that the usability, as one of the interactive attributes, was related to the aesthetics which is one of the attributes of the graphical user interface. Since then, researchers have begun to explore how the visual aesthetics of the interface affects the user's perception of the product and the interaction with the product ultimately [10]. Although this study introduced "beauty" into the field of human-computer interaction, it still saw aesthetics as the attributes of the interface (appearance) and interprets usability as the attributes of interaction (feelings). From the perspective of interaction design, this understanding seems to be narrow. In 2000, Djajadiningrat and his colleagues challenged this, and they believed that the field should shift its focus from "beautiful appearance" to "beautiful interaction (the appearance is part of it)". "Aesthetics of use" should explore a "finer, closer interaction with the object to enhance social connections or everyday experiences." [11].

Measurements of interaction design can be very limited if they only stay at the usability level that emphasizes efficiency. Nowadays, making a call can be done by pressing a button, a touch gesture, or even a voice input. The usability of these interactions may be different, but they are very different in many other ways. For example, judging whether a swipe gesture is appropriate or not, is not just an efficiency issue. Some new interactive technologies, such as touch, can provide a good or even excellent feeling and experience despite the lack of precision in the interaction. Although the interaction mode of shaking the mobile phone consumes more energy, it can make the user feel interesting and novel. As Djajadiningrat and others believe: sometimes the product is difficult to use, but the user still chooses to use it, probably because it is challenging, seductive, fun, surprise, and special, so that users have the experience of enjoyment [11]. For interaction design, in addition to efficiency and ease of use, there are many metric properties, which requires researchers to better understand the aesthetics of interaction in interaction design.

By reviewing and summarizing the relevant research literatures on aesthetics of interaction, and based on Hassenzahl's combing of interactive aesthetic elements, including time, space, action-response interaction, autonomy, popularity, security, meaning, etc. [12], we have sorted out the framework of aesthetic elements suitable for analyzing the interaction mode of context-aware system (see in Table 1).

Table 1.

Level	Categories	Attributes
Motor-Level	Temporal	Fast-slow, stepwise-fluent, constant- inconstant, timing, movement speed, concurrency, speed, time-depth, rhythm, interaction flow, live time, real time, unbroken time, sequential time, fragmented time, juxtaposed time, duration
	Spatial	Movement range, directness, locality, movement, body attitude, shape qualities, kinesthetic reach, orientation, size, position
	Action–reaction	Instant-delayed, apparent-covered, mediated-direct, incidental-targeted, uniform-diverging, response range, pliability, response time, adaptability, robustness, dependency, feedback, freedom of interaction, initiative, sequence, presence
	Presentation	Approximate-precise, resolution, proximity, orderliness, precision, clarity, information order, presentation
	Forces	Gentle-powerful, interaction effort
	Meta	Connectivity, input modalities, tasking, output modalities, versatility, external connections, body parts involved, combination/number of touchpoints, number of participants, including objects

(continued)

(continued)

Level	Categories	Attributes
Be-Level	Stimulation	Excitability, resolution, unnatural, exciting, unordinary, surprise, fantasy, sensation, discovery, narrative, thrill, magical, illusionary, imagination, alienation, ambiguity, surprise, playability, magical, suspenseful, secretive, playful
	Security	Control, trust, anxiety, anticipation, trustworthy
	Competence	Challenge, risk, transparency, difficulty
	Autonomy	Freedom of interaction, identity, control/autonomy, openness, privacy
	Relatedness	Fellowship, social action space, personal connectedness, company
	Meaning	Expression, seductivity
	Popularity	(No item assigned to)

The aesthetics of the interactions in the context-aware system will be analyzed based on this aesthetic element framework. It can help designers analyze soft indicators of interaction design, not just hard indicators such as efficiency. Furthermore, the impact of the non-efficiency level generated by the current context-aware system can be solved, and suitable aesthetic and emotional entry points for the popularization of context-aware technology can be discovered.

4 The Performance of Context-Aware in Aesthetics of Interaction in the Notification System

In the mobile context-aware interaction design, on the basis of defining different scenarios, when performing various physical interaction behaviors in different scenarios, it should be guaranteed to analyze the user's expected sensations and meanings, and then to retrospect the available interaction modes, interaction elements and so on. In addition, due to the dynamic and relevant features of the mobile context-aware system, such as active and implicit, it may have a greater impact on the related features of aesthetics of interaction such as user control, privacy protection, which should be paid special attention. Taking the notification system, one of the mobile context awareness systems as an example, the performance of the interaction mode in the aesthetics of interaction and its impact on the user experience are analyzed.

4.1 Notification System

In the era of massive information, users receive a lot of notifications on mobile devices every day. The interaction of the user with the notification system includes the management of the notification and the interaction with the pushed notification, wherein the notification opportunity, the notification push form, the notification content, the user's operation of the notification, the personality characteristics of users are several key concerns.

When the user starts using the new phone (before starting to deal with the new notification system), or after maintaining a certain setting mode for a period of time, the settings of the notification system will be managed and adjusted. The user's management of the notification includes management of timing, whether to open the notification, and the selection of notification push form. Usually, when the application is installed and opened for the first time, when an application notification is received and viewed, the notification of applications is managed. When the application is first opened is the management opportunity set by the application designer and developer. At this time, the user just uses the application for the first time, and may not have a certain understanding of the functions of the application and the content notified by the application, plus the flooding notifications nowadays have already caused users to be bothered. In addition to individual high-frequency applications and content-critical applications, most users will choose to turn off the notification of this new application at this time. When the user has used the application for a period of time, has a certain understanding of the application content, preferably has a certain usage viscosity for the application, or does some core operations (or related to certain notification content), the opening rate of notifications may be high if users are reminded to open it. If an application sends notifications to the user frequently, or the user notices that the notifications of an application are hardly noticed when viewing the notification bar, the user is most likely to choose to close the notification of the application or adjust the notification push modes of the application. iOS 12 has now added an entry to quickly manage the notification switch and adjust the push form in the notification center.

The timing of dispatching notifications by the traditional notification system mainly includes real-time notification according to trigger time of messages/calls, time according to user setting (alarm clock, to-do list, etc.), time according to application development operator. Different notification timings are related to the active-passive interaction mode between the user and the application, and also related to the content type of the notification, and may also connected with the personality characteristics of the user. The real-time notification according to the real-time message triggering and the notification set by the application development operator, do not take the user's current situation into account. The rushed and even a lot of interruptions are very likely to disturb the user, cause the user's original task to be interrupted and make users feel anxious or stressful. In this regard, the context-aware notification system considers the context information of users and the importance of the notification content, selects the corresponding notification opportunity (real time, delay, unified to appropriate time) and notification form.

The mainly types of notifications are shown as follows, including explicit and implicit, central and peripheral forms:

- Sound
- Vibration
- Indicator
- Screen pop-up
- Banner display
    - Temporary: the banner will appear at the top and disappear automatically
    - Ongoing: the banner will appear at the top and disappear only if users respond to it

- Display in the status bar
- Display in the notification bar
- App icon tag

Due to the influence of timing, content and method of notification, after the notification is pushed to the user's mobile phone, the user will interact with it in the following forms [5]:

- Seen: Only see and no other operations. View in the notification bar along with other notifications, view on the lock screen.
- Dismissed: Carry on Dismiss Event or Notification Clear event When the notification bar is open for more than 5 s.
- Actions: The user performs any action when the notification bar is turned on.
- App Launched: User clicks on notifications within 2 s. The user opens the app which is associated with the clicked notification.
- Ignored: None of the above behaviors have occurred. Apply a notification cleanup after the time is over, or update the notification content.

The interaction between the user and the notification is related to whether the user or the application actively initiates the interaction, the time mode in which the user uses the application, the time period in which the user wishes to receive the notification, the importance of the notification content to the user, the personal characteristics of the user (such as concentration of attention, whether it is easy to be disturbed), and contextual factors. The user's interaction with the application can be divided into the following categories according to different initiators: the user initiates interactions, such as taking a taxi, searching, sending messages, etc.; the user actively sets, then the device initiates actively, such as using an alarm clock, a stopwatch; the user actively sets, and the device reminds, then the user decides whether to initiate, such as snapping, fitness, learning, habit formation, etc.; the user does not set, but the device reminds the interactive content, then the user decides whether to initiate, such as an incoming call, a message and real-time news information and other content push; users do not actively set, devices push operational content to attract users, users decide whether to initiate, such as games, videos and other entertainment activities and shopping activities. In addition, the degree of participation of users in different application notifications at different time periods will vary greatly. First of all, for each application, the user will have a relatively regular usage time pattern, and if the user is reminded to use the application at the time he/she is accustomed to logging in to it, there may be a higher response rate to the notification. Secondly, time of users in every day has a division of work, entertainment, rest, etc. Users will be in different tasks or activities in different time periods, and they will have different attention performance and sensitivity to time, which affects the interaction between users and notifications. Among them, the attention situation, the sensitivity to time, the attitude to control, whether it is good at multitasking, sensitivity to privacy etc., are related to personal characteristics, which vary from person to person. At present, when application developers push notifications, there is no clear difference in importance of notifications. But in fact, the importance of different applications and different types of push are significantly different. As a general matter, the message of the task arrangement sent by the tutor is obviously much more important than the gossip news of a certain star that the information application pushes. Last but not the least, the context factor is the most important factor to be considered by the context-aware notification system, including user context, computing context, physical context, social context, etc. User equipment situation, sensor data, notification features, time features, and location features could be acquired and utilized in real application.

4.2   Analyze Aesthetic of Interaction in the Notification System

At present, the context-aware notification system combines explicit and implicit interactions, active and passive interactions, and central and peripheral interactions to provide users with an excellent interactive experience. This has improved operational efficiency and user satisfaction to a certain extent, but at the same time there are still some problems of limited cognitive resources, information overload, interruption, stress, loss of control, privacy and so on.

The interaction modes such as sound, vibration, indicator light and screen pop-up in the notification system are all explicit interactions that the device actively pushes or initiates the requests. From aesthetics of interaction aspect, they not only affect the user's current task, but also may affect the user's cognitive resource allocation, reduce task efficiency, cause the fragmentation of time, and even cause irritability. Interactions initiated by devices such as task reminders, requests, etc., are based on user behavior and context information. However, under the condition of limited cognitive resources, excessive notification messages may result in insufficient cognitive resources, information overload and psychological stress. The modes of displaying icons in the status bar, displaying icons in the history records and other peripheral interactions are used to notify non-important and non-urgent secondary tasks, which are comfortable and effective that can minimize the disruption and consumption of cognitive resources to users. Researchers have found that the distribution of psychological resources is different when users are in different processes of different tasks and interactions. When users engage in complex and difficult task operations, they need to invest more cognitive resources. At this time, the disturbance will cause competition for cognitive resources, which may lead the original task to be interrupted. Task recovery after this kind of interruption may also be more difficult. When engaging in a less difficult task or just completing a task and not starting the next task, the cognitive resources are occupied less, it is possible to process the new task while maintaining the original task state, or to process two items at the same time. In this way, interruptions can be avoided. The context-aware notification system can obtain the context information, analyze the situation, and select the push mode and push timing according to the content importance and context without much cognitive resource consumption and interruptions.

Another study found that mobile phone users receive an average of at least 60 notifications per day, and some even receive 600. If not managed properly, these notifications may disturb users at least 4 times per hour during working hours [5]. Information overload makes users to be immersed in massive amounts of data, which can cause problems such as cognitive overload, excessive psychological stress, and anxiety.

If the context-aware notification system and related middleware obtain context information without explicitly statement about the purpose of obtaining the context information, or the result of the analysis reveals the user's privacy too much, the user may be given a feeling of privacy violation. If you help the user to make judgments and perform tasks too much, it will also make users feel out of control in addition to feeling that privacy is violated. Therefore, clear permission, timely privacy-related feedback, and proper task execution are required to gain users' trust and reduce negative user experience.

5 Discussion and Implication

There are many ways to enhance the interactive aesthetic performance of notification system from the perspective of user-centered and user experience enhancement. For example, the context-aware notification system can perceive the consumption of cognitive resources of users in different contexts, choose the appropriate way (ringing, vibration, visual reminders, etc.) in the appropriate time (non-meeting, leisure, etc.) to attract the attention of users and enhance user perception. Which means, notifying users at the optimal time to obtain the maximum user response rate with minimal interruption and cognitive resource consumption. Urgent and important events can be reminded by the device in an active and explicit manner. Unimportant, non-emergency (contents that are casual and entertaining) can be pushed during the user's rest period or pushed in an implicit way.

The machine learning algorithm can be incorporated into the process of defining the importance of the content of the push content and the search for the appropriate push timing, thus the user's usage patterns are defined through a large number of individual user data.

In the case of having to bother the user, it can be used as a smart assistant to remind and help the user to return to the original task. Such as suspend and maintain the state of the original task and remind user to recover by using timed reminder and forced recovery.

Before using the context data, it is necessary to clearly state the specific data obtained and its usage. After analyzing the context information, the appropriate feedback is also important to eliminate the user's concerns about personal privacy and establish trust in the mobile context-aware system.

In the future, there are varies of topics can be explored, such as the human-computer collaboration model based on mobile context perception, the role orientation of the mobile context-aware system to the user, the relationship between the user's temperament personality and the identity and participation of the context-aware system. As the ultimate goal, smarter and more natural services will be provided to users.

References

1. Temdee, P., Prasad, R.: Context-aware communication and computing: applications for smart environment (2018)
2. Schilit, B., Adams, N., Want, R.: Context-aware computing applications. In: First Workshop on Mobile Computing Systems and Applications, pp. 85–90. IEEE Computer Society (1994)
3. Pielot, M., Rello, L.: The do not disturb challenge: a day without notifications. In: ACM Conference Extended Abstracts on Human Factors in Computing Systems, pp. 1761–1766. ACM (2015)
4. Ho, J., Intille, S.S.: Using context-aware computing to reduce the perceived burden of interruptions from mobile devices. In: SIGCHI Conference on Human Factors in Computing Systems, pp. 909–918. ACM (2005)
5. Pradhan, S., Qiu, L., Parate, A., et al.: Understanding and managing notifications. In: IEEE INFOCOM - IEEE Conference on Computer Communications (2017)
6. Schmidt, A.: Implicit human computer interaction through context. Pers. Technol. 4(2–3), 191–199 (2000)
7. Hausen, D.: Peripheral interaction-exploring the design space (2014)
8. Tractinsky, N.: Aesthetics and apparent usability: empirically assessing cultural and methodological issues. In: Proceedings of the ACM SIGCHI Conference on Human Factors in Computing Systems, pp. 115–122. ACM (1997)
9. Kurosu, M., Kashimura, K.: Apparent usability vs. inherent usability: experimental analysis on the determinants of the apparent usability. In: Conference Companion on Human Factors in Computing Systems, pp. 292–293. ACM (1995)
10. Hassenzahl, M.: Aesthetics in interactive products: correlates and consequences of beauty. In: Product Experience, pp. 287–302 (2008)
11. Djajadiningrat, J.P., Overbeeke, C.J., Wensveen, S.A.G.: Augmenting fun and beauty: a pamphlet. In: Proceedings of DARE 2000 on Designing Augmented Reality Environments, pp. 131–134. ACM (2000)
12. Lenz, E., Diefenbach, S., Hassenzahl, M.: Aesthetics of interaction: a literature synthesis. In: Proceedings of the 8th Nordic Conference on Human-Computer Interaction: Fun, Fast, Foundational, pp. 628–637. ACM (2014)

Research on Kansei Engineering System Establishment for Elderly Product Design

Min Shi[(✉)]

Fuzhou University of International Studies and Trade, Fuzhou, China
1310052572@qq.com

Abstract. The problem of aging has become an important issue in today's society. It is the social responsibility of scholars to study into it. The purpose of this study is to find out elderly's Kansei needs based on the living conditions of different regions in China. Through an investigation of the living habits of the elderly over 80 years old, the requirements of the design of the elderly products are analyzed. According to the analysis of the connotation and extension of the elderly living habits, the preferred Kansei image is sought, and corresponding design elements are extracted. A system that derives the preferred Kansei image with appropriate design elements is established. In this paper, Kansei Engineering research method is used to investigate the visual, auditory, perceptual and behavioral responses of the elderly and then establish a Kansei Engineering Forwarding System with Kansei adjectives database, design element data base and corresponding logical deduction rules. First, we studied the awareness, personality, aesthetics, diversity, happiness and comfort feelings of the elderly. Followed by interviews and questionnaire surveys to acquire elderly's physiological and psychological characteristics, lifestyle and use environment of daily products. Then an experiment was carried out to measure elderly's Kansei preference and to identify the corresponding design elements. Finally, a Kansei Engineering System for new design patterns in line with the elderly's Kansei preference is established. And the product design and development for the elderly can be carried out with the system. According to the research results, the above-mentioned forward Kansei Engineering System that transforms Kansei image into specific design elements to enhance the experience of the products pays more attention to the Kansei preference of elderly users while pursuing product quality. Hopefully, the elderly people can feel the Kansei value of the design and lead a creative life.

Keywords: Aging · Hybrid Kansei engineering · Image · Product design

1 Introduction

1.1 Background and Purpose of the Research

Research of elderly product design has been made in each field. As science and technology progresses, the different interaction modes and information arising from elderly conceptual design are also Kansei elements that must be mastered by designers, which is also a design direction of high-tech industry in recent years. At present deep

© Springer Nature Switzerland AG 2019
M. Kurosu (Ed.): HCII 2019, LNCS 11566, pp. 486–495, 2019.
https://doi.org/10.1007/978-3-030-22646-6_36

researches of social state and environment of ageing have been made in the profession of product design. However, the research and application of image terms of elderly Kansei is not mature and deep enough. This paper aims to find out living states of the elderly which are varying from place to place and transform the Kansei of elderly group into design elements. The research field of "Kansei engineering" focuses on exploring the mutual relations between "people" and "objects", which opens a new way for exploring more Kansei researches from the perspective of engineering. Moreover, for designers whose work is to create "objects", Kansei engineering is a technology to "transform the Kansei or images expected by people into design elements", survey the factors of elderly older than 80 such as living habits and analyze the feelings and demands of elderly as the main appeal. Through analysis and deduction of connotation and extension of living state of the elderly, factors of Kansei elements are created and the Kansei image language is sought. Kansei factors are derived to the system of conceptual characteristics of design.

1.2 Scope and Methods of Research

By means of Kansei Engineering System, this paper integrates perceptual experience of users such as vision, hearing and touch into the product development design, which includes:

1. Assisting to promote the conceptual design capacity of products;
2. Establishing an information system concerning product design.

The research will explore the connection between the Kansei of elderly and product design elements through the sensory systems with frequent interaction with information products such as vision, hearing, smell, touch and taste of elderly and establish the theoretical foundation for applying senses and Kansei engineering in the information products in the future.

2 Kansei Factors of Elderly

In the 1980s, Dr. Herbert A. Simon, a professor with Carnegie Mellon University of the US and a winner of Nobel Economy Prize in 1978, argued that the development of three emerging academic fields, namely "design science", "psychology" and "information science" at that time would bring a chance of another start to the engineering science, and therefore advocated developing "humanity science" [1].

As science and technology progresses, the media for passing information to the elderly keep renewing. Different information creates different modes of interaction for sensory organs of the humankind. Accurate data can be acquired through instruments and equipment, which are shown in Table 1.

Table 1. Physical measurement methods of Kansei engineering

Type of sense	Measurement item	Measurement instrument
Vision	Color	Color photometer
	Light intensity	Luminosity instrument
	Eye movement	Eye tracker
	Direction	Protractor
Hearing	Sound intensity	Sound pressure meter
	Sound frequency	FFT instrument
Skin sensation	Hardness	Body pressure distributor
	Roughness	Roughness instrument
	Temperature	Thermometer/Thermocouple
	Humidity	Humidometer
Touch	Weight	Electronic scale
	Speed	Tachometer
	Direction	Compass
	Strength	Electromyograph

The design direction of high-tech industries in recent years is to integrate accurate data into key industries such as people's livelihood, information, service and communication and stress the feelings, experience and demands of users as the main appeal [2], as shown in Table 2.

Table 2. Survey of physiological characteristics and behavioral response of the elderly

Area/country	Percentage in age structure of the population (%)			Aging index (%)
	0–20	21–65	Above 66	
The world	27	65	8	29.63
Developed countries	17	67	16	94.12
Developing countries	30	64	6	20.00
Japan	13	64	23	176.92
Germany	14	66	20	142.86
France	18	65	17	94.44
The UK	18	66	16	88.89
Canada	17	69	14	82.35
Australia	19	68	13	68.42
The US	20	67	13	65.00
New Zealand	21	66	13	61.90
South Korea	17	73	10	58.82
Singapore	18	73	9	50.00
China	19	73	8	42.11
Malaysia	32	64	4	12.50
Philippines	35	61	4	11.43

3 Analysis of Kansei Image of Elderly

The treatment of Kansei information by the elderly can be discussed under two stages. The first one is the stage of somatic sense, and the second one is consciousness. The treatment of somatic sense and consciousness is mainly differentiated through their time sequence. Usually the former appears after consciousness and is completed in a short time. The cognitive stage occurs through somatic sense. Under the cognitive stage, consciousness integrates all characteristics of somatic sense information to form complete cognitive information before it is applied for designing.

3.1 Analysis of Kansei Image of Somatic Senses of the Elderly

Vision
With the growth of age, our cornea gradually loses gloss and the capability of our eyes to refract lights grows poorer. The function of our iris sphincter muscle declines, which causes our pupils to shrink and the lights that enter our eyes will be reduced. Our crystalline lens will become yellow and turbid. And the visual perception cells of our retina will die and decrease gradually. The declining of a series of our physiological regulation functions will directly affect the changes of our visual acuity, brightness, space, colors and information processing (Fig. 1).

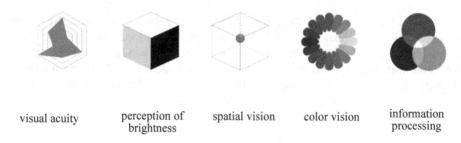

| visual acuity | perception of brightness | spatial vision | color vision | information processing |

Fig. 1. Schematic diagram of visual perception (Color figure online)

Changes of vision acuity: Taking 20 years as the benchmark, to guarantee the same level of vision, the contrast ratio of target and background is 2 at the age of 60, and the rate of declining will grow faster after the age of 60, and the contrast ratio will reach 6 at the age of 80. Changes of perception of brightness: The adaptability to brightness and darkness will decline to different extents. For an adult, for every growth of 13 years in age, the luminosity required will need to double. Changes of spatial vision: Due to the declining of peripheral vision and visual field, the elderly usually cannot see the objects before their eyes. Since their ability to observe the distance and three dimensions of an object has declined, the elderly cannot accurately identify the distance and height of the object. In addition, due to the decline of their visual acuity, the boundary of the object observed by them will become vague, as a result of which their perception of spatial depth declines. Changes of color vision: Since their crystalline lens becomes yellow and turbid, the crystalline lens will absorb blue light selectively. As a result, the elderly's capability to identify blue will decline more significantly than their capability to identify red and green. Changes of visual information processing: The elderly needs a longer time to find out "9" from a matrix of "6". The interval between two flashing points needs to be long enough for them to identify. That is to say, the capability of the elderly to process visual information such as visual search and visual coding has declined.

Complications and other diseases that occur with the growth of age and impacts of environment are shown in Table 3.

Table 3. Blurring degree of vision of the elderly due to illness

Cause	Low eyesight	Blindness
Presbyopia	√	
Senile cataract	√	√
High myopia	√	√
Age-related macular degeneration	√	√
Diabetic retinopathy	√	
Glaucoma	√	
Keratonosus	√	
Eyeball and optic atrophy	√	√

The visual performance of the elderly declines. According to the research made by some scholar, the minimal acceptable visual angle preferred by the elderly is 0.75°, and sighting distance is 43 cm. After conversion, it is equivalent to a height of characters at 5.62 mm, which can also be found in Fig. 2 "Smallest Identifiable Sizes of Characters for Different Age Groups in JIS Specifications as a reference for you, shown as below.

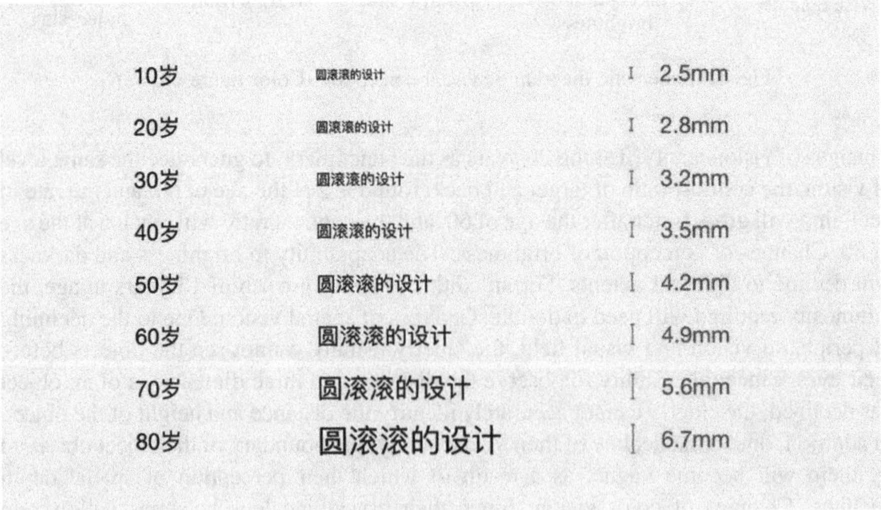

10岁	圆滚滚的设计	I 2.5mm
20岁	圆滚滚的设计	I 2.8mm
30岁	圆滚滚的设计	I 3.2mm
40岁	圆滚滚的设计	I 3.5mm
50岁	圆滚滚的设计	I 4.2mm
60岁	圆滚滚的设计	I 4.9mm
70岁	圆滚滚的设计	I 5.6mm
80岁	圆滚滚的设计	I 6.7mm

Fig. 2. Schematic diagram of smallest identifiable sizes of characters for different age groups

Design strategy under impacts of vision: In lighting design of rooms for elderly, reflected light should be preferred and the switch should come with a dim indicator light and a big size to make it convenient for the elderly to find the switch. Particularly at night when the elderly go to toilet, it is difficult for them to find the position of the switch in darkness. If the light directly goes into their eyes, it will be too dazzling for them to see clearly.

Hearing

What happens most commonly is that the elderly has decreased hearing and cannot hear clearly unless we speak louder. The physiological structure of our hearing organ is composed of auricle, auricular media and auricular internal. The auricle of the elderly is filled with piles of hard cerumen. The hair cells in their cochlea of auricular internal and the cells of their auditory nerve passage have declined and died, and the cells of their cochlea receive an insufficient blood supply. All these causes contribute to the declining hearing of the elderly, which is mainly reflected as follows.

Insensitive response to high-frequency sound waves. The pitch of the sounds must be very high: An adult in 30s can hear the sounds of 4 dB with a frequency of 6,000 Hz. Under the same frequency of sounds, for the elderly at 80 the sound intensity needs to be increased by 40 dB or even higher. The selective attention of hearing of the elderly declines. As we know, in "cocktail party effect", we can neglect other dialogues or noises in the environment when our attention is focused on the speech of someone. As we grow old, our selective attention of hearing will begin to decline.

Design strategy under impacts of hearing: A lot of electronic products come with a voice reminder against any strong and sharp sounds, so as to control the frequencies of sounds within the elderly's range of audibility.

Kansei image term: They cannot hear low pitch sound and dislike high pitch sound, prefer slow speech and quietness.

Touch, Taste and Smell

It is relatively slow for the elderly to identify things by touching, tasting or smelling. Due to the degeneration of cells in the skin, the touch and temperature feel of the elderly will weaken and their sense of pain will become relatively blunt. In general, due to the ageing of their sensory organ system and the declining of various sensory abilities and functions, they become not sensitive to peculiar smells and their sense of touch also becomes weaker. The quantity of sensitive touch points on the skin of the elderly above 60 years declines, their skin begins to wrinkle and become less elastic, senile plaques appear, glands shrink and sweat glands become less. As a result, the minimal sensory stimuli intensity required for the skin to sense touch need to grow gradually at the old ages. Besides, the elderly's senses of temperature and pain will become more blunt, so they are prone to bruises and burns.

In 1954, in a psychology experiment conducted by the laboratory of Canada McGill University, the students were asked to put on a pair of specially-made semi-transparent plastic spectacles (to deprive them of vision), cover their hands and arms with paper-made gloves and sleeves (to deprive them of touch) and lie quietly in a special room filled with monotonous buzz (to deprive them of hearing). Generally the respondents could not bear it for over three days. And after the experiment, they felt restless, their attention became disorderly and their thinking was disturbed. They could not think as normal people did, and their wit also declined to a poor level. The experiment indicates that though senses are a kind of simple and low-level psychological activities, the depriving of senses will surely affect the complex and high-level psychological phenomena such as memory and thinking.

Dimensions of Human Body and Muscular and Skeleton System

The muscular and skeleton systems of the elderly decline, their response becomes slow, their flexibility declines, and the intensity and control ability of their muscles keep declining too. Generally the muscular strength of average people reaches the peak at the ages of 20–30 years and begins to fall later on. The muscular strength of average people at the age of 70 will only be half of that at the age of 30.

For the elderly, the muscular strength of lower limbs is an important stamina factor, which plays a very important role in daily activities (such as walking, going upstairs and downstairs, maintaining balance). According to the researches, the muscles and muscular strength of human body reach the peak at the age of around 20–30. After that, our physical functions will begin to decline slowly. As the number of muscular fiber is reduced and the density of fiber decreases, the skin begins to shrink and the muscular tissue will be changed. As the fat mass of human body grows, the strength, elasticity and tone, moving speed of skin will decline gradually.

Muscular strength refers to the ability of muscular tissue to make a single contraction against a resistant force. Muscular endurance refers to the maximum ability of a muscle group to contract continually. The muscular strength and endurance will decline distinctively due to old age and lack of movement. William (1999) pointed out that the age is a main factor for the reduction of muscles. Muscular strength declines gradually with ageing and lack of exercise, which will lower the mobility of human body, lead to movement disorders and increase the chance for the elderly to be harmed in accidents.

The reduction of muscles is most common in the normal process of ageing, which is not caused by singular factor, but caused by the reciprocal effect of two systems, namely, nerve and muscle, due to the reduction of body movement. As we grow old, the number and size of our muscular cells will fall. The distinctive fall of muscle mass happens at the age of around 50. Due to the reduction of muscle mass, muscular strength becomes poor. A proper amount of movement may improve our conditions due to the reduction of muscle mass caused by ageing and enhance our muscular strength or endurance. Meanwhile, Tominaga Tesuo (2000) measured the changes of muscle mass with ultrasound and discovered that muscle mass was lost naturally by 3–5% in every 10 years after the age of 25. The mass of knee extending muscle, knee bending muscle, dorsum pedis bending muscle, pelma bending muscle, elbow extending muscle and elbow bending muscle at the age of 70 is respectively 60%, 80%, 70%, 67%, 76% and 87% of that at the age of 20, which is because of the reduction of muscular fiber in the motor unit.

Kansei image term: The strength declines when muscle contracts, which affects our mobility.

3.2 Analysis of Cognitive Kansei Image of the Elderly

Cognitive functions refer to our mental abilities to understand and reflect objective things, such as attention, imagination, learning, memory and logical thinking. With the cognitive ageing, the elderly's duration of attention is affected, their ability to receive information declines and their memory grows weaker. The weakening of memory worsens some logical inference ability of the elderly. As a result, their analysis of senses becomes slow, it takes a longer time for them to move and respond and the elderly will be deprived of the ability to perform daily life activities and cannot live independently.

Attention

Our living environment is filled with a lot of stimuli, which will compete for our attention. Attention is an ability to focus on specific stimuli. When we pay attention to specific stimuli, we will gain perception, while the stimuli beyond our attention will be vague and neglected.

In the era of Internet fragmentation, all of us find it difficult to focus our attention. That is because various stimuli come in succession, we have to divert our attention. However, for physiological reasons, the elderly's attention becomes blunt and cannot last long, without the accuracy and speed required for the control of attention in their youth.

Kansei image term: The elderly's attention is also characterized by inertia. It is quite difficult for them to neglect the irrelevant or disturbing information that is retained in their work memory.

Memory

Memory is the foundation for the humankind to learn different behaviors and a mental phenomenon in which information is saved after being received. Our memory is mainly classified as sensory memory, short-term memory and long-term memory. Sensory memory is the retaining of sensory stimuli in a short time. For example, we can observe still images of 24 frames/second in a film as successive images. Short-term memory refers to the memory system which can save a small amount of information within a short time. For example, in the "magical number rule 7 ± 2" often mentioned in the interactive design, error will begin to occur after we memorize 5 9 groups of information. After short-term memory is memorized repeatedly, it will become long-term memory and can be saved permanently.

The memory disorders of the elderly are mainly reflected in short-term memory, retaining of memory and the difficulty to learn new knowledge. Short-term memory will decline with the growth of age, which is not because we cannot pay affective attention to relevant information, but because we cannot effectively neglect the irrelevant information. As a result, the limited capacity of short-term memory system will be overloaded.

After the age of 50, our memory performance will begin to grow weaker and our memory of numbers and memory that do not rely on language will begin to decline. It takes longer time to remember a thing, and the ability to save new memories is poorer than youngsters.

However, the elderly can well remember past things related with their life, or the long-term memory practiced logically. For example, our grandpas and grandmas often tell us the stories that happened when they were young.

Kansei image term: Repeated recital, dictation and use can generate images in our brain.

Thinking

Thinking is a process of analysis, comparison, summary, conclusion and abstraction based on the information acquired by us from senses and perception to form concepts, inferences and judgments, which is the highest form of cognitive activities of the humankind.

The knowledge of the elderly may increase with age. However the agility, smoothness, flexibility, uniqueness and creativity of their thinking will become poorer than that of young age.

Kansei image term: Our perception and memory will decline with the growth of age along with the loss of concept, logical inference and solving ability.

In the era of Internet fragmentation, all of us find it difficult to focus our attention. That is because various stimuli come in succession, we have to divert our attention. However, for physiological reasons, the elderly's attention becomes blunt and cannot last long, without the accuracy and speed required for the control of attention in their youth.

By the above analysis of the Kansei image of the elderly and analysis of factors, the main factors that determine the images of interactive design are found so as to provide the designers with a direction for interactive design in the future. Regression analysis is used to explore the association between somatic feel and perceptual elements and Kansei evaluation and their mutual influence is concluded. The research method of KES (Kansei Engineering System) is shown as below Fig. 3. Designers begin to pay attention to the subtle physiology, psychology and emotions of the elderly. Products that analyze Kansei factors and can reflect the ideas of users will surely emerge. The thought will be established in which the development of new technologies is based on the physiological and psychological factors of the humankind. Therefore, we are convinced that in the 21st century, more attention will be paid to the elderly.

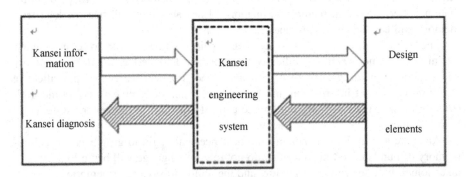

Fig. 3. Schematic diagram of mixed Kansei engineering

4 Conclusion

Through the above analysis and research, the forward Kansei engineering system and reference to Kansei physical data can effectively support the product development of designers when designers consider "producing Kansei products", as shown in Fig. 3.

The macroscopic factors of products include basic background information of target groups for designing such as financial situation, consuming power, behavioral habits, brand awareness of products, development trend of the market, basic development direction. The macroscopic Kansei semantics of products will be analyzed with forward Kansei engineering.

Focusing on the research of the elderly and their consciousness, individuality, aesthetics, diversity, happiness and comfort, the aforementioned forward and backward Kansei engineering systems are integrated into a mixed system that can convert in two ways. According to the research of elderly products, more attention should be paid to the Kansei understanding of products while pursuing product quality. We should create life for the elderly based on Kansei design and create a system to convert Kansei into specific design elements, thereby enhancing the experience of products.

References

1. 『商品開発と感性(感性工学シリーズ)』　長町三生 / 海文堂出版 2005/05 出版　252 p 21cm. ISBN 4303723916
2. 『感性工学のおはなし』長町三生　/ 日本規格協会　1995/07 出版 209 p 19cm. ISBN 4542901866
3. 『感性商品学感性工学の基礎と応用』　長町三生 / 海文堂出版 1993/09 出版　186 p 21cm. ISBN 4303728209
4. 『感性工学(海文堂サイエンス・らいぶらり) 感性をデザインに活かすテクノロジー』長町三生 / 海文堂出版 1989/11 出版 138 p 19cmX14cm. ISBN 4303713201
5. 『语义学概论』　李福印着 北京大学出版社
6. Li, F.: Introduction to Semantics. Peking University Press, Beijing

Narrative, Storytelling, Discourse and Dialogue

A Multimodal Chatbot System for Enhancing Social Skills Training for Security Guards

Stein de Bever[1], Daniel Formolo[1(✉)], Shuai Wang[1], and Tibor Bosse[2]

[1] Department of Computer Science, Vrije Universiteit, Amsterdam, The Netherlands
d.formolo@vu.nl
[2] Behavioural Science Institute, Radboud Universiteit, Nijmegen, The Netherlands

Abstract. Chatbots are typically used in dialogue systems for various purposes such as customer service and information acquisition. This paper explores enhancement of social skills training for security guards with the use of chatbots. More specifically, we designed a chatbot using text and voice as input to study the acceptance and the impact of the system to training security guards in deal with stress situations. The result of a pilot experiment and a survey are presented and discussed. Finally, we discuss possible improvements and future work.

Keywords: Chatbots · Serious games · Training · Role-playing ·
Security employees · Intelligent agents

1 Introduction

Essential skills dealing with inter-personal connections and social interactions can be crucial in the success of many jobs. Good communication and interpersonal skills are therefore essential. However, to improve such skills, one needs to learn from practice rather than books. Typically, companies employ professional actors and deliver role-playing sessions for the training of new recruits, which can be costly, time-consuming and hard to organize. Alternatively, training based on serious games is less costly. Serious games make use of conversational agents, also known as chatbots. Most chatbots uses auditory or textural input/output while some more advanced ones uses both with avatars. These programs are typically used in dialogue systems for various purposes such as customer service and information acquisition. Although it costs a lot to develop such a system, the advantage is that they can be scaled to simultaneously interact with a large group of users, making it viable. In addition, it is local and time independent, which reduces the requirements for interaction, making it more flexible and adaptable than traditional methods. For these reasons, chatbots can potentially be used in a wider variety of instructional situations [5]. In this paper, we study how the use of chatbots for social skills training can make a difference in engagement and knowledge gain of security guards candidates[1].

---

[1] This paper is based on the bachelor thesis of Stein de Bever.

© Springer Nature Switzerland AG 2019
M. Kurosu (Ed.): HCII 2019, LNCS 11566, pp. 499–513, 2019.
https://doi.org/10.1007/978-3-030-22646-6_37

We designed and implemented the chatbots on campus and conducted our experiment and collected the data at a local mid-scale company named Workrate[2] with the aid of their staff. The company has 634 employees and provides security service for ports, air cargo, company offices and their data centres. Many of the employees are university students who work part-time to cover duties such as reception, control rounds, mobile surveillance, etc. A security guard interact with officers, customers and staff during his or her daily duties. Such duties can be demanding on inter-personal interaction, especially in case of criminal cases or potentially harmful occasions. Improper means of interaction may cause harm to staff, victims or even results in life threatening scenarios and cause damage properties and reputation. New recruits are therefore required to pass a practical exam to demonstrate essential skills in the form of three role-playing games before they get on duty. To improve the passing rate and reduce the cost in training, the companies offer trail role-playing training sessions. These sessions with professional actors can be costly, time-consuming, location-dependent, and therefore hard to organize. The company suffers from low passing rate. The interpersonal skills and the result of such training differ significantly from person to person due to the lack of practice. Since such role-play dialogues are hard to practice alone and practical sessions with actors have several drawbacks, it is natural to consider chatbots as an alternative. Despite chatbots are interactive, less costly and location-independent, they have their own drawbacks. They can suffer from imperfection in the interpretation of voice and the lack of emotion. In this paper, we intend to explore the following research question, which infers two sub-questions:

- Can social skills training for security guards be improved by using chatbots?
  - To what extent do people accept chatbots as tools for social skills training?
  - Which means of interaction with chatbots has better training effects (text input or free speech, or combined)?

In the following section, some background information and related literature are presented. Sections 3 and 4 are the design and the implementation of our chatbots respectively. The results are presented in Sect. 5. Finally, in Sect. 6, we discuss the results and outline some future work.

2   Background and Related Work

Chatbots are interactive computer programs that takes auditory or textual inputs and respond with informative answers. Thanks to the advance in Natural Language Processing in recent years, chatbots embrace applications in customer service, information acquisition, education, professional training and so on.

In the study by Bayan et al. the potential use of chatbots in education is addressed [9]. In later research conducted by Hoffmann et al. [5], a virtual assistant support students with the basics of a study area. That gives more time to

---

[2] https://www.workrate.eu/en/.

the teacher focuses on more complex topics of that area. They further compared to traditional e-learning systems and studied features in providing knowledge in this interactive way. Both state that chatbots had positive impact on the results of the student [5,9]. Abbassi et al. [1] studied learning with chatbots vs. conventional search engines for the teaching of Object-oriented Programming. They concluded that the learning outcomes by using chatbots are significantly better when compared with learning through conventional search engines. In addition, chatbots have also been used in medical domains to deal with depression [2] and stress [6]. Some distinct chatbots can make use of emotions to provide psychiatric counseling service in mental healthcare [7]. Closer to our research is the case study by Bosse et al. [4] where they studied how conversational agents can be used for public transport employees in dealing with aggressive customers. The case study showed that the employees managed to enhance their social skills after training with conversational agents. As a result, the training employees manage stress situations more effectively.

In contrast with existing work, we focus on engagement and the comparison of the efficiency of text and auditory input for social skills training in contexts where people confront others and have to make decisions under pressure. We also study how adding chatbots to the classical approach in training would improve the passing rate. The next section describes the design of our chatbots for the training of security guards trainees, which we will refer to as users.

3   Chatbot System Design

In this project, two versions of chatbots have been developed using the Watson Assistant[3]. One using voice and text and another using only text. The voice component approximates users of real scenarios. It also includes time pressure to the user replies to the chatbot. By the other hand, translating voice in text can inject wrong inputs to the chatbot by imprecise algorithms, untypical accents or environmental noise. Those disturbs can affect the user experience. Moreover, because the lack of time pressure in speak and finalize the answer in one shot, dummy users would rather start by texting then using voice at beginning. Therefore both voice and text might be considered to study the efficiency of the chatbot applied to this context. The aim is to assist users to learn how to deal with certain scenarios in security service. In the case of the voice and text approach, the idea is that voice is the main input and the text is an alternative channel to the user.

Despite the voice and text inputs, the core of the chatbot shares the same *dialogue tree*. In a *dialogue tree* an answer has to be given to progress from one node to another. According to the user's input and the conditions of the node, the next node is determined. Figure 1 is an example of a *dialogue tree*.

At each round of the conversation, there are 3 types of response: a correct response, a partially correct response and an incorrect response. An incorrect response will redirects to a node that gives the right answer for that round of

---

[3] Formerly Watson Conversation: https://www.ibm.com/watson/ai-assistant/.

interaction. This prevents the user from restarting the entire use case due to one mistake. In addition, the node redirects back to itself which forces the user to fill in the right answer before continuing. For every partially correct answer, there is a separate branch in the *dialogue tree* which eventually reaches the final node. This branch would lead down to a separate final node. This would be very time consuming as there are partially correct answers at almost every step. For the clarity of the experiment, the complete list of necessary steps at the end of every use case is provided. The users are instructed to check if they take every right step and self-monitor the learning progress.

The system runs on an on-line platform. The interaction with the chatbot is in Dutch. Appendix B contains an sample use case provided by the company. Figure 2 depicts an example of a conversation. To reduce misunderstanding and improve the usability of the system, two instruction web-pages were created with a brief introduction to the experiment. Each version starts with an introduction video per version of the chatbot was embedded to explain the details of the experiment respectively. Further down the web-pages are the links to the chatbot and the corresponding use cases. More details of the web-page and chatbot can be found in Appendix A. The next section provides more details about the implementation and the experimental setup.

4   Research Method

The chatbots have been evaluated in a pilot experiment that consisted of two parts, to which we will refer as separate experiments for practical reasons. In Experiment 1, the objective learning effect of both variants of the chatbot were evaluated. This was done by comparing the skills of a group of users who practiced with the combined (voice and text-based) chatbot with a group of users who used the text-based chatbot (Experiment 1A), as well as with a control group, which are users who did not use any chatbot (Experiment 1B). In Experiment 2, a survey was used to measure the subjective acceptance of people who worked with the chatbot. The design of both experiments is described below. Together with a description is provided of the material that was used for both experiments.

4.1   Material

The use cases selected for our study have been inspired by the material that the users need to study for their final exam. In total, 36 use cases have been provided by the company. These use cases have some similar steps in their structure. At the same time, diverse use cases were chosen that treat different events. For instance, two use cases cover attempted arson, another covers the case with a person trapped in the elevator, while another covers the event of an incorrectly parked car. This was done to show the participants that, across a variety of circumstances, similar steps have to be undertaken to reach the desired result.

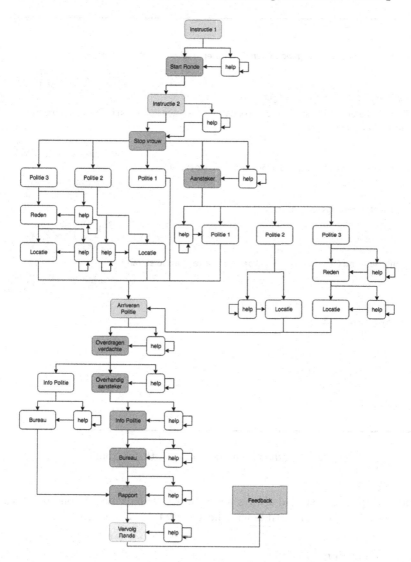

Fig. 1. Dialog tree of use case 1

Nevertheless, the users do not have any guarantee that the same use cases will be used for training as for their final exam.

To pass the practical exam, users have to be familiar with some general protocols that are reflected in many use cases. Some of these protocols can be applied in many different events. For example, some use cases expect the same actions at the beginning with the user saying: 'Security to Central Post, I am starting my round'. Another example is that, when speaking about an unknown

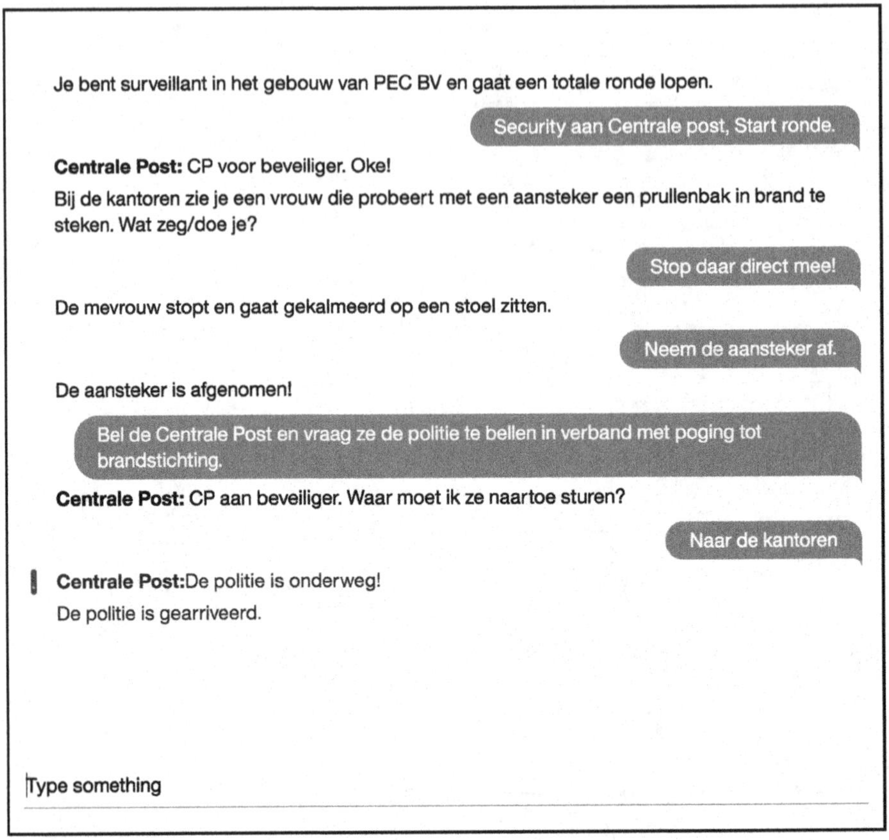

Je bent surveillant in het gebouw van PEC BV en gaat een totale ronde lopen.

> Security aan Centrale post, Start ronde.

Centrale Post: CP voor beveiliger. Oke!

Bij de kantoren zie je een vrouw die probeert met een aansteker een prullenbak in brand te steken. Wat zeg/doe je?

> Stop daar direct mee!

De mevrouw stopt en gaat gekalmeerd op een stoel zitten.

> Neem de aansteker af.

De aansteker is afgenomen!

> Bel de Centrale Post en vraag ze de politie te bellen in verband met poging tot brandstichting.

Centrale Post: CP aan beveiliger. Waar moet ik ze naartoe sturen?

> Naar de kantoren

Centrale Post: De politie is onderweg!
De politie is gearriveerd.

Type something

Fig. 2. Example interaction with the chatbot

person or object, one should always describe the primary and secondary features (e.g., 'the red BMW convertible with license plate AB-CD-12').

4.2 Experiment 1

As mentioned above, Experiment 1 (see Fig. 3) consisted of two sub-experiments, called Experiment 1A and 1B. The aim of Experiment 1A was to compare the differences in the learning effect between the two variants of the chatbot. The aim of Experiment 1B was explore the difference between learning with and without chatbots. In total 10 users participated in the experiment, among which 6 were male and 4 were female. The free-speech version was randomly assigned to 5 participants and the text-based version to the other 5 participants, of which one participant dropped out. First, the participants were provided with the learning material, which they could study by themselves before hand for a week. After that, they attended a lesson day (including a practice exam) given by the company. On that day, they were informed about what to expect during the exam and what are the potential pitfalls. Also some use cases were practiced by role playing with a colleague. After the lesson day, all participants were asked to practice by interacting with (either the combined or the text-based version of) the chatbot every day for 30 min for a period of 5 to 7 days. After that, they took a practical exam with real actors. This practical exam took place at the exam center in Amersfoort. To pass the exam, the users was presented with three use cases in which (s)he was expected to act accordingly to the steps. A third person was assessing and grading the trainee based on a checklist.

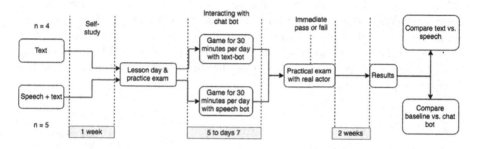

Fig. 3. Design of Experiment 1A

To test the hypothesis that learning with the combined chatbot leads is more effective than learning with the text-based chatbot, the average grades of the two groups were compared. Since the power of the analysis is very low $(n = 9)$, no statistical test could be applied.

As a follow-up (Experiment 1B), we were interested in the question whether learning with (any of the two versions of) our chatbot is equally effective (or perhaps more effective) compared to the traditional form of learning. To this end, the grades of the 9 participants of Experiment 1B were compared to the grades of a baseline group of 29 candidates who took the exam after learning the material from a book instead of an interactive chatbot. Among these 29 candidates, 20 were male and 9 were female. The grades of these candidates were collected in the period between January 1st and May 31st, 2018. To test the hypothesis that the performance of both groups is the same, an unpaired t-test was applied. Hence, the independent variable of this analysis was the applied method of interactive learning and the dependent variable the average grade of the examinees.

4.3   Experiment 2

To obtain more qualitative results about people's opinion on the chatbot as a training intervention, 29 users were asked to fill in a questionnaire about their experience with the chatbot. This group consisted of the 9 participants from Experiment 1A and 20 additional participants who have passed the exam. These 20 employees were asked to interact with the combined version of the chatbot for a week before filling in the questionnaire. Among these 20 employees, 13 were male and 7 were female. The questionnaire contained a number of questions using a 5-point Likert scale as well as some open questions asking for the participants' opinion about their understanding of the use cases and the added value or downside of using chatbots for social skills training. See Appendix C for more details.

Figure 4 summarizes the experiments. In Experiment 1, nine users were divided into two groups: five of them using the combined voice+text chatbot and four of them using the text-based chatbot. After comparing their grades with each other, their grades were also compared with the grades of a baseline group formed by 29 candidates that did not use the chatbot. For Experiment 2, another group of 20 employees that already have took the exam in the past was asked to use the voice+text-based chatbot and fill in a survey. The same survey was filled in by the group of 9 users from the first experiment, and the answers of both groups were analyzed.

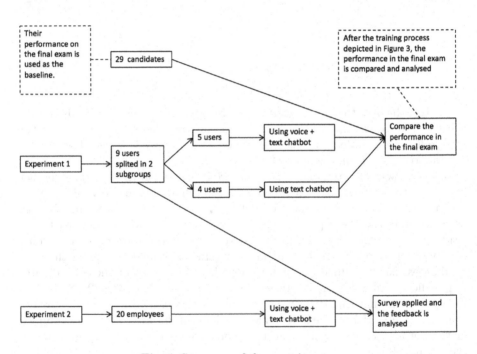

Fig. 4. Summary of the experiments

5   Results

The results of Experiment 1A are shown in Fig. 5. As can be visually observed in the figure, there is not much difference in the grades across the two groups: the users who used the text-based system (mean grade 5.4) performed very similar

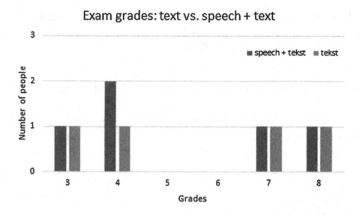

Fig. 5. Experiment 1A: exam grades of users who used the chatbot system.

as the users who used the combined system (mean grade 5.2). Due to the low power of this experiment, no statistical analysis was conducted.

For Experiment 1B, the grades of Experiment 1A were taken together, and were compared to the grades of a group who learned for the exam via traditional means (i.e., from a textbook). The results for this group are shown in Fig. 6. As can be seen, the results are similar to the results of the users who used the chatbot. Both populations have a low frequency in the grades 5 and 6, and a higher frequency in the grades 3, 4, 7 and 8.

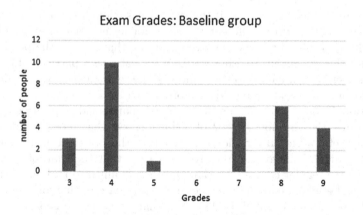

Fig. 6. Experiment 1B: exam grades of users who did not use the chatbot system.

To test if there is indeed no statistical difference in average score between the two populations, a two-sided t-test with unequal variances was applied. The significance level is set to $\alpha = 0.05$ with 14 degrees of freedom. This test pointed out that first group (mean score 5.33) did not obtain a statistically different grade from the second group (mean score 5.96) (p = 0.45).

In addition, the aim of Experiment 2 was to obtain some qualitative results about the users' opinion about the chatbot. The main results (for a selection of relevant questions) are reported in Table 1.

Table 1. Experiment 2: results of the survey for questions 6, 7, 8 and 11.

Question	Totally disagree	Disagree	Neutral	Agree	Totally agree
Q.6. There was enough variation in use cases	0%	5%	10%	80%	5%
Q.7. Training with the chat bot is a useful addition for studying for the practical exam	0%	0%	5%	65%	30%
Q.8. By training with the chat bot I perceived studying for the practical exam as less boring	0%	0%	5%	75%	20%
Q.11. I wouldn't mind to keep training with an extended version of the chatbot in the future	0%	5%	40%	35%	20%

Question 6 aimed to find out if the system has enough variation on the use cases as the system covers different use cases for an effective training process. The results in Table 1 are very positive signalling that 85% of the participants agrees with this statement. In other words, it indicates that participants thought that the selection of use cases covered most of the relevant scenarios. Still, there is room for improvement by including more use cases.

Question 7 aimed to find out if the participants had a positive attitude towards using the chatbot. Row 2 of Table 1 shows that 95% considered the chatbot a useful addition for the preparation of the practical exam. Only 5% remained neutral. This gives a positive indication that the chatbot is a useful addition to the regular course material. Question 8 aimed to find out if the participants of the survey had an increased motivation for studying for the practical exam. The results in Row 3 of Table 1 show that again 95% was positive on the statement: studying for the practical exam is less boring when having a chatbot. Similarly, only 5% remained neutral.

Finally, Question 11 was designed to find out whether it is interesting for the company to continue with the chatbot as an addition to the course material. Row 4 of Table 1 shows that 35% agrees with the statement and 20% totally agrees. When asked about which use cases were more beneficial (Question 4), the answers clearly indicated the most complex use cases, with a long dialogue. They were considered more challenging, realistic and covering several aspects needed in the training. That indicates the advantage of using interactive training that move the users to dynamic interactions. This fact is confirmed by the answers to Question 5 which asked the opposite of Question 4: it inquired about the less useful use cases, i.e. the scenarios that helped people less in the learning process. The answer, again was clear and indicated the shortest and less complex use cases as bringing a small contribution to the training process.

6   Discussion

The primary results of our study indicate that users who prepared for the exam with the chatbot system did not obtain different grades than who used a traditional text book method. This finding can be interpreted both positively and negatively: the bad news is that the chatbot does not lead to better scores, but the good news is that it does not lead to worse scores either. In addition, the results of the survey seemed to indicated that people were positive about the added value of the chatbot system. Therefore, it can still be considered as an interesting alternative to textbooks, which stimulates people to spend more time on learning.

Indeed, other studies have already hinted at the potentially positive impact of using chatbots [1,5,9] or virtual agents [3] on engagement and learning effect. These papers point out similar advantages as were observed in our survey, and during after-session discussions with our participants. Most of the users mentioned as advantages of using a chatbot that it is less repetitive and more engaging than simply reading the use cases. As such, the chatbot system presents an interactive environment which enables users to 'learn by doing'.

Nevertheless, a number of limitations of our study could be mentioned. Firstly, there is no way to assure if the users really practised 30 min per day for a minimum of 5 days. If this is not the case, the results would be biased. Secondly, with a sample size of 9 in the experimental group and 29 in the baseline group the experiment was a bit underpowered for adequate statistical analysis. With a larger sample size and more strict instructions and control the statistical significance would be more meaningful. According to Schreiber et al. each group should have at least 10 participants for the results to draw any conclusions about significance [8]. Finally, a third possible weakness in the experiment was that the document with use cases provided by the company might be outdated. The document was drawn up in 2014 and has not been updated since. Many of the use cases have been replaced because of change in protocols or legislation. This was identified during the training and could affect not only the performance with the chatbot but also the traditional approach, because the same material was given to the participants of the experiment to prepare themselves for the final exam. Moreover, it is important to note that not only the system must behave according to the expectations, but it also has to be attractive and engaging, otherwise the users lose interest. When this happens, a chatbot might lose its advantage over traditional tools. This phenomenon could clearly be observed in the results of the survey. Some users mentioned that simple use cases were not challenging and some others lost interest after practicing the same use case for some time. The time invested in the practice period with the chatbot also contributes to the learning effect. For this particular aspect, more time and more variability of use cases will help to improve the final results.

To conclude, our study provides also some hints that the system is promising to enhance user experience. Although the chatbot did not have a significant impact on the average pass rate, it captivates the user interest to spend more time studying, as show the survey results. Furthermore, it prepares users to deal with the social and time pressures of the final exam. To improve the system more use cases could be included and minor characteristics should be refined in future work. One example is to extend the library to recognise other constructions of sentences that have similar meaning, to ensure that different conversation styles will be considered by the chatbot as a correct answer. Moreover, further research is needed to better understand the differences between text-based and speech approaches. Although the current design does not allow us to draw any conclusions about this, a more sophisticated experiment (e.g., using different performance indicators) may shed more light on this topic.

Acknowledgement. This research was supported by the Brazilian scholarship program Science without Borders - CNPq scholarship reference: 233883/2014-2.

Appendix

A   Online System

The two versions of our system are available online via the following webpages:

- text: http://vesci.labs.vu.nl/steinabacus/
- speech and text: http://vesci.labs.vu.nl/steinvox/

Both webpages contain an introduction with instructional video, followed by links to the ten use cases.

B   Example of a Plain Text Use Case

Case: Arson in the fusebox.
Instruction: You are surveillance at PEC BV. and you are walking a full round.

1. Tell the central post that you are starting your full round.
2. The door of a technical room is open and you hear screaming.
3. When you go and look, you encounter a woman that is trying to light a fire in a dust bin.
3. Tell the woman to stop immediately and arrest her on suspicion of Arson.
4. Confiscate the lighter.

5. Ask the Central post if they can call the police.
6. Hand over the woman to the police that has been arrived.
7. Hand over the lighter as evidence.
8. Ask the names of the agents and to which bureau they are taking the suspect.
9. Speak about 'the suspect' and not 'the woman'.
10. Draw up specific report.
11. Tell the central post that everything has been resolved and that you are continuing with your round.

C   Survey Questions

1. Which version of the chatbot have you been using?
   - Speech + text input
   - text input
2. How long did you practice with the chatbot each day?
   - under 10 min
   - 10 to 20 min
   - 20 to 30 min
   - over 30 min
3. For how many days did you use the chatbot?
   - under 5 days
   - 5 days
   - 6 days
   - 7 days
   - over 7 days
4. Which use case did you find most useful and provided the best training? (multiple answers possible)
   - 1. Arson in the fuse box
   - 2. Broken elevator
   - ...
   - 10. Mover
5. Which use case did you find least useful and provided the least best training? (multiple answers possible)
   - 1. Arson in the fuse box
   - 2. Broken elevator
   - ...
   - 10. Mover
6. There was enough variation in use cases.
   (a) Totally disagree
   (b) Disagree
   (c) Neutral
   (d) Agree
   (e) Totally agree
7. I believe practicing with the chatbot is a useful addition to the regular course material.
   (a) Totally disagree

    (b) Disagree
    (c) Neutral
    (d) Agree
    (e) Totally agree

8. By training with the chatbot I perceived studying for the practical exam as less boring.
    (a) Totally disagree
    (b) Disagree
    (c) Neutral
    (d) Agree
    (e) Totally agree

9. What could have been done better regarding the design of the chatbot?

10. What difficulties did you encounter practicing with the chatbot?

11. In the future I would not mind continuing to train with an extended version of the chatbot.
    (a) Totally disagree
    (b) Disagree
    (c) Neutral
    (d) Agree
    (e) Totally agree

12. What is your name?

References

1. Abbasi, S., Kazi, H.: Measuring effectiveness of learning chatbot systems on student's learning outcome and memory retention. Asian J. Appl. Sci. Eng. 3(2), 251–260 (2014)

2. Bickmore, T.W., Puskar, K., Schlenk, E.A., Pfeifer, L.M., Sereika, S.M.: Maintaining reality: relational agents for antipsychotic medication adherence. Interact. Comput. 22(4), 276–288 (2010)

3. Bosse, T., Gerritsen, C., de Man, J.: Evaluation of a virtual training environment for aggression de-escalation. In: Proceedings of Game-On, pp. 48–58 (2015)

4. Bosse, T., Provoost, S.: Towards aggression de-escalation training with virtual agents: a computational model. In: Zaphiris, P., Ioannou, A. (eds.) LCT 2014. LNCS, vol. 8524, pp. 375–387. Springer, Cham (2014). https://doi.org/10.1007/978-3-319-07485-6_37

5. Hoffmann, R., Kowalski, S., Jain, R., Mumtaz, M.: E-universities services in the new social eco-systems: Security risk analysis: Using conversational agents to help teach information security risk analysis (2011)

6. Medeiros, L., Bosse, T.: Testing the acceptability of social support agents in online communities. In: Nguyen, N.T., Papadopoulos, G.A., Jędrzejowicz, P., Trawiński, B., Vossen, G. (eds.) ICCCI 2017. LNCS (LNAI), vol. 10448, pp. 125–136. Springer, Cham (2017). https://doi.org/10.1007/978-3-319-67074-4_13

7. Oh, K.J., Lee, D., Ko, B., Choi, H.J.: A chatbot for psychiatric counseling in mental healthcare service based on emotional dialogue analysis and sentence generation. In: 2017 18th IEEE International Conference on Mobile Data Management (MDM), pp. 371–375. IEEE (2017)

8. Schreiber, J.B., Nora, A., Stage, F.K., Barlow, E.A., King, J.: Reporting structural equation modeling and confirmatory factor analysis results: a review. J. Educ. Res. **99**(6), 323–338 (2006)
9. Shawar, B.A.A., Atwell, E.: A corpus based approach to generalising a chatbot system. Ph.D. thesis, University of Leeds (School of Computing) (2005)

A Study on Narrative Timing Sequence of Animation in Mobile Interfaces

Yutong Dong[✉], Xia Li, and Zhirou Wang

Beijing Key Laboratory of Network System and Network Culture,
Beijing University of Posts and Telecommunications, Beijing, China
dongyutong624@126.com

Abstract. This paper focuses on the narrative features of interactive animation of mobile phone interface, and discusses the design structure and influencing factors of time sequence dimensions in mobile interactive animation. The narrative feature of interactive animation can improve the user's understanding of information and optimize the logic and information transmission efficiency of animation, which plays an important role in improving user experience. Therefore, this paper analyzes the interactive animation of existing mobile phone systems on the market, and summarizes the narrative features of interactive animation, including the characteristics of "micro-event" narrative, strong functional narrative and abstract graphic metaphor narrative. This paper discusses the design structure and influencing factors of time sequence dimensions in mobile interactive animation. The time sequence structure of three basic interactive animation narratives of "linear structure", "parallel structure" and "link structure" is proposed, which provides a new design thinking angle and reference for interactive animation design.

Keywords: Interactive animation · Mobile interfaces · Narrative · Timing sequence

1 Introduction

With the development of the mobile Internet, the number of intelligent terminals is rapidly increasing, and the user's experience requirements for mobile terminals are also higher [1]. Interactive animation plays an important role in the interactive experience of mobile phones. In 1993, Chang and Ungar [2] as well as Hudson and Stasko [3] proposed applying cartoon animation to interfaces. Later, many scholars have proved through research and practice that interactive animation can improve the interface aesthetics, assist user decision-making and improve the interface user experience [4, 5]. Gonzalez [6] conducted an experiment showing that using animation in a graphical user interface can help improve the user's decision-making process. Research by Kraft and Hurtienne shows that animation can help users build a more accurate mental model of the application structure without increasing the burden on the user [7]. Because of its advantages in user experience, animations are widely used in interface interaction design.

© Springer Nature Switzerland AG 2019
M. Kurosu (Ed.): HCII 2019, LNCS 11566, pp. 514–526, 2019.
https://doi.org/10.1007/978-3-030-22646-6_38

In order to further optimize the experience of interactive animation, some scholars study the design theory of interactive animation from the perspective of usability and cognitive psychology. Some scholars promote research in the direction of emotion and brand. Dong proposed that the dynamic effect should be simple and smooth from the perspective of animated sports language [8]. Tan et al. proposed a design method based on imagery. Based on this design method, the animation will be more cultural and brand-oriented [9]. Liu integrated emotional design into animation design to optimize user experience [10]. From the perspective of ease of use, Xu proposes effective design strategies such as simplicity, metaphor paradigm, memory burden minimization, inheritance, manipulation behavior validity, perception principle, and moderate design [11]. Although scholars have proposed strategies for interactive animation design from many aspects, the "12 basic principles of animation" proposed by Johnston and Thomas [12] is still the basis of the actual design of interactive animation. Therefore, interactive animation has some of the same basic features as traditional animation, and narrative is one of them that cannot be ignored.

Narrative organizes events on a timeline according to a certain level and logical relationship by adding time and space elements, and arranges and controls events on the time axis to form an event collection [13] (see Fig. 1). With the development of narratology and the application of narrative to many fields of research, the medium of narrative has become increasingly rich. The narrative research of language, image, animation, film, space, music and other media has gradually formed a system. There are many kinds of narrative media, but the essence of narrative is storytelling. Events are the core of narrative. As a basic unit in narrative, events have different expressions in different media. In movies, story events are film shots, dances are dance moves, and in motion, elemental movements (see Fig. 2). Animations add time attributes and motion patterns to graphics, which increases the narrative nature of the interaction process [9] and improves the efficiency and logic of information communication. Bruner believes that "we mainly organize our experiences and memories of human events in the form of narratives" [14, 15]. There is also evidence that humans can understand the world more easily through narratives [16]. Therefore, due to the narrative nature, the animation is more in line with the user's cognition than the static information or image, which improves the comprehensibility of the information. Narratives can also create an emotional connection with the audience. Information transfer in a relatively flexible manner, rather than mechanically and bluntly [17]. In summary, due to the narrative characteristics, the animations can improve the user experience in the interactive interface.

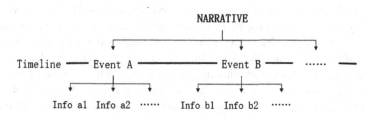

Fig. 1. Narrative

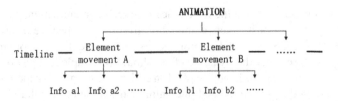

Fig. 2. Animation

Time, distance, path, deformation and shifting are several essential elements in animation design [9]. Time is the basic parameter of animation, and it is also an important parameter that constitutes the characteristics of animation narrative. The time dimension in the study of animation narrative mainly involves three concepts, namely duration, time sequence and time-frequency, that is, the characteristics of an information event can be explained by its position, duration and number of interventions in the narrative sequence [13]. In the current research on the time of animation, most of them study the duration of animation from the perspective of user attention and the appropriateness of animation, while less attention is paid to the study of time sequence. For example, as the time of animation increases, the user's attention and tolerance will plummet [11]. Yang introduces the time and space dimensions into the two-dimensional coordinate system based on the degree of attraction of the user to attention, and analyzes the characteristics in each quadrant [18]. Although Dragicevic starts from the time rhythm and gets the advantage of slowing out the slowing rhythm [19], this conclusion is more suitable for the design of the moving element's time-varying motion curve. However, in more cases, in order to make the interactive animation details richer and more realistic, interactive animation often contains multiple motion elements. The relationship and time sequence between these motion elements can more influence the narrative effect of interactive animation. Interactive animation narrative has similarities with traditional animated narratives and film narratives, but interactive animations have different characteristics from other narrative media. These features make the timing dimension design of interactive animation different from other media, and its timing characteristics are worth studying.

2   Characteristics of Interactive Animation Narrative

The research object selected the mobile phone UI system of the two brands of Xiaomi and VIVO in the Chinese mobile phone market, namely MIUI system and Funtouch system, and selected 40 system animation disassembly analysis. Detailed measurement and charting of the timing, duration, motion profile and motion trajectory of each element in the animation. Obtain the animation time and frequency through the screen recording software, measure the data with AE, and finally draw the data. The chart contains three forms, an animated timing diagram (showing the element motion timing on the time axis (see Fig. 3), a motion graph (representing the motion displacement, rotation, and scaling values over time in a plane rectangular coordinate system (see Fig. 4) and motion trajectory maps (visually depicting motion trajectories in the interface (see Fig. 5). Analyze chart data from the perspective of narrative, focus on the narrative features of interactive interface animation, and the law of timing design in the case of multiple motion elements.

Fig. 3. Timing diagram

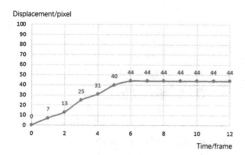

Fig. 4. Motion graph   **Fig. 5.** Motion trajectory maps

2.1 Narrative Through "Micro Events"

The narrative time of traditional animations and movies is as short as a few minutes and as long as a few hours. The interactive animation time should generally not exceed 0.5–1 s [20]. The increase in duration will distract the user. Due to the limited duration of interactive animation, it is difficult to have a complete narrative structure like traditional animation and movies, and to detail the causes, passages, climaxes, and results of events. In more cases, the interactive animation succinctly the information in the interactive interface through "micro events". The "micro event" is the motion of the elements in the interactive animation. The interactive animation narrative conveys the interface information to the user through the "micro event" of the element motion. In the context of limited time, the design of the sequence can bring more layers to the interactive animation design, expand the space for transmitting information, and make it more rhythmic.

2.2 Strong Functionality

Unlike the strong entertainment nature of traditional animations and movies, interactive animation is part of the interface. It is a basic task to satisfy the functional requirements of the user during the interface interaction process. Entertainment is added value. Therefore, the narrative of interactive animation should be based on the clear description of the interactive event as the basic standard. Interactive animation can meet five functional requirements in the interactive interface, namely smooth transition, efficient feedback, enhanced manipulation, help guidance and sublimation experience [18]. Under normal circumstances, interactive animation needs to meet multiple functional requirements in the interface. The deformation design and time dimension design of the elements are affected by these design goals. The design of the animation timing should consider the specific functional requirements and interaction scenarios. Taking the caller animation as an example, the most important function requirement of the caller animation is to guide the user to connect or hang up the phone. The caller animation of the Funtouch system adopts the form of the second change of dot opacity, which shows strong guiding (see Figs. 6 and 7). The MIUI system's caller animation uses three round buttons to jump in order to show the guiding (see Figs. 8 and 9).

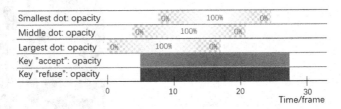

Fig. 6. Timing diagram – Funtouch caller's animation

   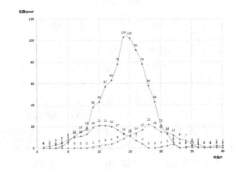

Fig. 7. Timing diagram   **Fig. 8.** Timing diagram – MIUI caller's animation

Fig. 9. Screenshot – MIUI caller's animation

2.3   Interactive Animation Narrative Through Abstract Graphic Metaphor

The elements that move in an animation can be graphics, text, and images, and they can be thought of as characters in the narrative. The position, shape, color, area, opacity, etc. of the element may change with the movement. But just as the character's appearance and character setting at the beginning of the design will affect the development of the story, the movement element also has its relatively fixed nature to form a materialized metaphor, so that the animation conforms to the physical law and is more real and natural. For example, a "small" element should start moving more easily than a "massive" element, and a "smooth surface" element should be easier to start moving and grow faster than a "surface rough" element. The nature of this role metaphor is often determined by the importance and function of the information carried by the element. Not only will it affect the timing sequence of the motion of the elements in the animation, but it will also affect the magnitude, duration, and so on. Take the screen unlock animation in the MIUI system as an example. Through the time sequence difference of the movement of the four regional elements, the four regions of the simulated interface have different degrees of force, which reflects the effect of the paper pressing center drop (see Figs. 10 and 11).

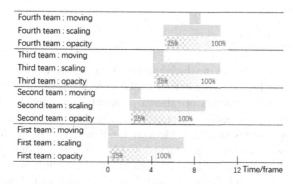

Fig. 10. Timing diagram - screen unlocking animation

Fig. 11. Motion trajectory maps - screen unlocking animation

In summary, the design of the time sequence dimension can help the interactive animation better through the "micro event" narrative, and help improve the narrative effect from the functional and metaphorical narrative. In this paper, from the interactive animation timing research of Xiaomi and VIVO brands, three basic time sequence structures are summarized to expect designers to use the structure and help interactive animation design and improvement.

3   Timing Sequence Structure of Animated Narrative

Timing sequence is the order of events in a narrative and the relationship between the sequence of events in the narrative [13]. The narration of literature and film in order to be more creative will not be carried out in the natural chronological order of the event, so there will be timing arrangements such as flashback and interlude. In order to enable users to understand more clearly the relationship between elements and the hierarchical relationship and interaction logic between interfaces, the animated narrative generally adopts sequential scheduling. Although it is slightly monotonous in timing, it has its own characteristics in the timing combination structure. Based on the syntagmatique theory proposed by Metz in the film narratology [21], this paper selects and enriches the part that fits the animation, and proposes three basic time sequence combination structures of animation.

3.1   Linear Structure

A linear structure is a structure in which another event begins to be described after the event is narrated (see Fig. 12). The events can be movements of different variations of the same element, or movements of different elements (see Figs. 13 and 14: Screen capture animation). The sequential arrangement of events on the time axis forms a linear narrative time series structure. Most of the time series in the linear structure simulates the sequence of real-world events, which will form a visual guide, allowing the user to understand the antecedent consequences of the animation, that is, to better transform the old and new information, and form a real and natural transition experience. At the same time, it can explain the relationship between interface elements and let users understand the interactive logic relationship. Therefore, the interactive animation with linear time sequence structure is more guiding and logical. Because the linear structure has only one element in motion for a period of time, there is only one character in the animated narrative. Although it can quickly focus on the user's attention and convey the information to the user in a simple and intuitive manner, the linear structure can carry a small amount of information per unit time, and the duration is long, which is difficult to avoid. Therefore, it is less used alone in mobile interface animation design.

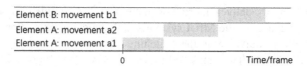

Fig. 12. Linear structure

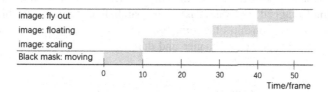

Fig. 13. Timing diagram - screen capture animation

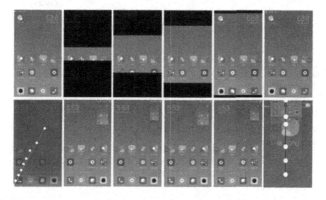

Fig. 14. Motion trajectory maps - screen capture animation

3.2   Parallel Structure

Multiple events are simultaneously described (see Fig. 15). In one case, different variations of a single element move simultaneously. In order to make the animation more delicate, the movement of the element is accompanied by more than one variation, and the combination of displacement, scaling, rotation, opacity, discoloration, and the like is selected according to needs. For example, the animation effect of the image thumbnail enlargement is performed simultaneously with the displacement and the zooming, and the zooming of the pop-up window of the message is accompanied by the change of the opacity. Although combined with a variety of variations, it is often used for widget animations or other simpler feedback. Another situation is the simultaneous movement of multiple elements. Due to the large amount of information carried by the interface, single element motion cannot meet the requirements of interaction and function. A combination of multiple elements is required to form a complete animation to deliver more information or to complete more functional requirements. For example, the MIUI system's dial switching animation (see Figs. 16 and 17) is essentially equivalent to the switching of secondary pages. The elements in the tab bar, background, dial, hands and other interfaces are almost all designed into animations to transform old and new information. The parallel timing structure makes the user aware of the synchronicity of the element motion and the parallel hierarchical relationship between the elements in the time dimension. The overall animation is stronger and not dragged. For this reason, the parallel structure cannot highlight the primary-secondary relationship of information from the time series, and needs other factors such as the magnitude of change and duration.

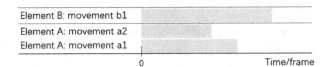

Fig. 15. Parallel structure

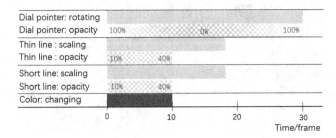

Fig. 16. Timing diagram - dial switching animation

Fig. 17. Motion trajectory maps - dial switching animation

3.3   Link Structure

Another event begins to be described when an event is being narrated (see Fig. 18). Compared with linear structure and parallel structure, the link structure has visual guidance, narrative logic, large amount of information and rich details. At the same time, the link structure improves the problem that the linear structure narrative is not compact and the parallel structure visual focus is dispersed to some extent, so the link structure is used more frequently. The screen unlocking animation of the MIUI system (see Figs. 19 and 20) uses a sequence structure in which each row of numbers is quickly popped up in order to achieve the interactive function requirements and is also very rhythmic. However, the problem with the link structure is that the rhythm of the animated narrative is not easy to grasp, and the timing of the multi-element motion event is not appropriate. It's easier to make the animation messy and not let the user understand the content of the animated narrative.

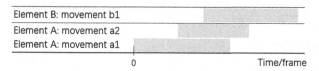

Fig. 18. Link structure

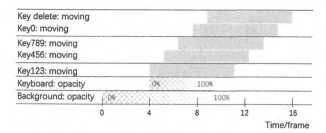

Fig. 19. Timing diagram - digital unlocking animation

Fig. 20. Motion trajectory maps - digital unlocking animation

In the interactive animation narrative, the three basic time series structures are often combined to take advantage of their respective advantages. Regardless of the structure or combination of structures, the purpose is to pass the interface information and interaction logic to the user in a more realistic and natural way through the narrative function. In addition, this paper organizes the timing structure of the MIUI system and the Funtouch system (see Figs. 21 and 22). Through the animation analysis in the MIUI system and the Funtouch system, the Funtouch system animation uses linear time sequence structure more than the MIUI system (see Fig. 21), while the MIUI system uses more parallel and linked time sequence structure (see Fig. 22). Although the details of the 1MIUI system animation are more abundant, the timing structure of the parallel and link makes the animation narrative more compact and rhythmic. Instead of letting the user feel the drag and drop, it highlights the system concept of "fast lightning" and makes the user feel exquisite and fun. The more linear structure in the Funtouch system animation makes the user feel more concise and smooth. The timing sequence and timing structure of the visible animation can help shape the brand features to some extent.

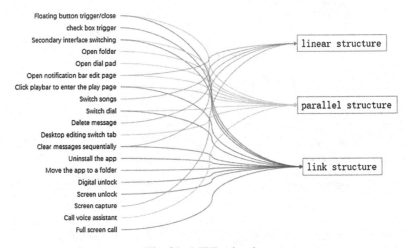

Fig. 21. MIUI animation

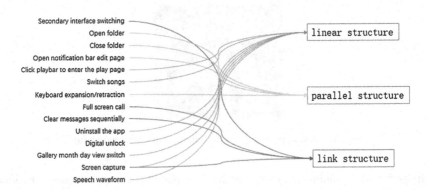

Fig. 22. Funtouch animation

4   Conclusion

Optimizing interactive animation has become an important part of improving the interface experience. Grasping narrative features can better guide the design of interactive animation. Exploring interactive animation design from the perspective of narrative is essentially a visual information design based on time dimension. The time series of design element motion is an important link. The three basic narrative time sequence structures such as linear structure, parallel structure and link structure can provide more reference for interactive animation design. The just-in-time structure not only better communicates the logic between information and information, but also gives users a richer emotional experience and cultural experience.

Acknowledgement. This study is part of the project "Research on Design and Implementation Model of Micro-interaction and Interactive Animation for Improving User Experience" funded by Zhongxing Telecommunication Equipment Corporation.

References

1. Zhang, D., Guo, X., Han, Z.: Security and trusted intelligent mobile terminal. ZTE Technol. J. **21**(05), 39–44 (2015)
2. Chang, B.-W., Ungar, D.: Animation: from cartoons to the user interface. In: Proceedings of the ACM Symposium on User Interface Software and Technology, pp. 45– 55. ACM, New York (1993)
3. Hudson, S.E., Stasko, J.T.: Animation support in a user interface toolkit: flexible, robust, and reusable abstractions. In: Proceedings of the ACM Symposium on User Interface Software and Technology, pp. 57–67. ACM, New York (1993)
4. Bederson, B.B., Boltman, A.: Does animation help users build mental maps of spatial information? In: Proceedings of the IEEE Symposium on Information Visualization (InfoVis 1999), San Francisco, CA, USA, pp. 28–35 (1999)
5. Heer, J., Robertson, G.: Animated transitions in statistical data graphics. IEEE Trans. Vis. Comput. Graph. **13**(6), 1240–1247 (2007)
6. Gonzalez, C.: Does animation in user interfaces improve decision making? In: Tauber, M. J. (ed.) Proceedings of the ACM CHI Conference on Human Factors in Computing Systems, pp. 27– 34. ACM, New York (1996)
7. Kraft, J.F., Hurtienne, J.: Transition animations support orientation in mobile interfaces without increased user effort. In: Proceedings of the 19th International Conference on Human-Computer Interaction with Mobile Devices and Services, Article 17, 6 p. ACM, New York (2017)
8. Dong, T.: Research on the expression forms of animation motion language in UI dynamic design of APP. Appreciation **15**, 182–183 (2017)
9. Tan, H., Liu, J., Tan, Z.: Interaction interface animation design based on imagery. Packag. Eng. **37**(06), 53–56 (2016)
10. Liu, Y.: Emotional design research of interactive interface dynamics. Popular Lit. (04), 97 (2017)
11. Xu, W.: Research on the ease of use of mobile application interface. Ind. Des. (06), 60–61 (2016)

12. Johnston, O., Thomas, F.: The Illusion of Life: Disney Animation. Disney Editions, New York (1981)
13. Liu, J., Zhu, W.: Analysis of the narrative function of dynamic information design. Design (04), 39–42 (2015)
14. Bruner, J.: The narrative construction of reality. Crit. Inq. **18**(1), 1–21 (1991)
15. Bruner, J.: Actual Minds, Possible Worlds. Harvard University Press, Cambridge (2009)
16. Green, M.C., Strange, J.J., Brock, T.C.: Narrative impact: social and cognitive foundations. Philosophy (2003)
17. Sun, Y.: Dynamic image narrative of information visualization. J. Nanjing Univ. Arts (Art and Design) (05), 76–80+190 (2017)
18. Yang, W.: Study on value and dimensions of motion design in user interface. Art Des. (Theory) **2**(05), 47–49 (2016)
19. Dragicevic, P., Bezerianos, A.: Temporal distortion for animated transitions. In: Proceedings of the SIGCHI Conference on Human Factors in Computing Systems (CHI 2011), pp. 2009–2018. ACM, New York (2011)
20. Johnson, J.: Designing with the mind in mind: simple guide to understanding user interface design guidelines, 2nd edn. Elsevier, Morgan Kaufmann is an imprint of Elsevier (2014)
21. Metz, C.: Essais sur la signification au cinema. tome (1968). Klincksieck, Paris (1975)

Experimental Study on Estimation of Opportune Moments for Proactive Voice Information Service Based on Activity Transition for People Living Alone

Mitsuki Komori[1], Yuichiro Fujimoto[1], Jianfeng Xu[2],
Kazuyuki Tasaka[2], Hiromasa Yanagihara[2], and Kinya Fujita[1(✉)]

[1] Graduate School, Tokyo University of Agriculture and Technology,
2-24-16 Nakacho, Koganei, Tokyo 184-8588, Japan
S176615w@st.go.tuat.ac.jp,
{y_fuji,kfujita}@cc.tuat.ac.jp
[2] KDDI Research Inc., 2-1-15 Ohara, Fujimino, Saitama 356-0003, Japan
{ji-xu,ka-tasaka,yanap}@kddi-research.jp

Abstract. Smart speakers that listen to a user's commands and respond vocally are being used in homes across the world. Making smart speakers proactive by delivering information without an explicit command from the user might extend their applications and benefit users. However, such improvements also pose a risk for disturbing users. Therefore, this study aims at developing technology for estimating the opportune moments for information delivery without disturbing the user's daily activity. To analyze the subjective acceptability of users at home, we prototyped an experimental system that detects the activity transitions of participants based on his/her location and body motion using a depth camera and vocally asks his/her acceptability for information delivery at that moment. We conducted an experiment with three participants that lived alone. The results suggested that the acceptability of users relates to the activity patterns both before and after activity transition.

Keywords: Smart speaker · Acceptability · Proactive service · Depth camera · Notification

1 Introduction

Smart speakers that communicate with users in a conversational voice, such as Google Home [1] and Amazon Echo [2], are gaining attention and are being used in to homes around the world. Current smart speakers are manufactured to focus on passive information service. In other words, they wait for the users' vocal request and provide the necessary information. Although they are currently used for passive information delivery, proactive delivery of certain information may benefit users. For instance, a forecast on rainfall just before leaving or a reminder of immediate schedules will be

© Springer Nature Switzerland AG 2019
M. Kurosu (Ed.): HCII 2019, LNCS 11566, pp. 527–539, 2019.
https://doi.org/10.1007/978-3-030-22646-6_39

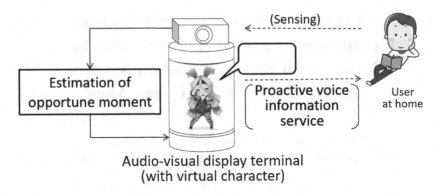

Fig. 1. Concept of proactive voice information service.

appreciated even if they are delivered without an explicit request. As represented by these examples, the proactive service, which satisfies the user's implicit needs, has the potential to make daily-life better.

Another promising scenario of the proactive information service is advertisement delivery. Delivery of an advertisement, which might attract the consumer's interest, may be positively accepted and facilitate a willingness for purchase. However, even if the delivered advertisement is one potentially of interest, a delivery at an inadequate time will be declined by the users and may lead the users to turn off the proactive information delivery function. For avoiding such situations, proactive information delivery needs to be conducted at the right time. Therefore, this study aims to develop a method for estimating the opportune moments for proactive voice information service by sensing the status of the user. Figure 1 represents the concept of this study.

To estimate the chance for information delivery, the acceptability of users for information delivered at unexpected times needs to be investigated first. It has been reported that the cognitive workload of office workers decreases at the breakpoint between tasks [3, 4]. Similarly, the intervals between activities may also be used as information delivery at home. Therefore, we investigated subjectively acceptable moments through a questionnaire targeting housewives, who are one of the conceivable target groups of proactive information delivery at home. We also prototyped an experimental system that estimates the presumable activity boundary based on user motion detected by a depth camera. Then, we conducted a one-week at-home experiment with three participants living alone. The results suggested that the activity pattern before and after activity transitions has some relation with the acceptability of proactive information delivery.

2 Related Work

In conjunction with the worldwide spread of smart speakers, the number of studies on the application of smart speakers is also rapidly increasing [5, 6]. Several studies have tackled the estimation of the opportune moment for information delivery at home. Takemae et al. experimentally investigated the user's preference of each room for notifications [7]. Cumin et al. constructed a simulated house environment and conducted a user study there. They also reported that the location in a room considerably affects acceptability rather than the type of activity [8]. Vastenburg et al. demonstrated that the degree of engagement in the activity, in addition to the urgency of the information, influences the acceptability through at-home experiments [9].

Cognitive workload is known to decrease at the breakpoint between tasks [3, 4]. Tanaka et al. focused on this and proposed an interruptibility estimation algorithm for an office environment [10]. Banerjee et al. also focused on the task breakpoint in a manipulation task. They detected the boundary of motion using a Kinect to estimate the suitable time for voice interruption by a robot [11]. Therefore, this study assumes that users are more acceptable to information delivery at the boundary of activities in a home environment.

3 Questionnaire Survey and Hypothesis

3.1 Questionnaire on Acceptability of Information Delivery at Home

To investigate the variation of subjective notification acceptability at various timings of an activity, we conducted a questionnaire survey with 16 housewives [12]. We requested them to score the acceptability of 61 timings in three levels; acceptable, neither, or not acceptable. We asked them to imagine a proactive smart speaker delivering an advertisement. A few examples of timings are

- Just after cleaning a room.
- While looking at a variety of TV programs after dinner.

Figure 2(a) represents the summaries of answers in the middle, at the break, and the end of an activity. The rate of acceptance in the middle and end of an activity was 7% and 28%, respectively. Although the acceptance rate at the end of an activity is higher, the participants answered more than two-thirds of the cases as not acceptable. Then, we further divided the cases at the end of an activity into two groups based on the existence of a subsequent activity. As a result, the acceptance rate in the cases without subsequent tasks was 49% while only 15% of questions were answered as acceptable for cases with a subsequent to-do task, as shown in Fig. 2(b). These results suggest that the absence of a subsequent to-do task, i.e., the time allowed for rest, is the key to the acceptance of information delivery.

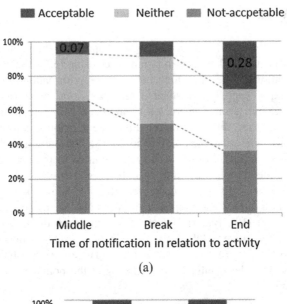

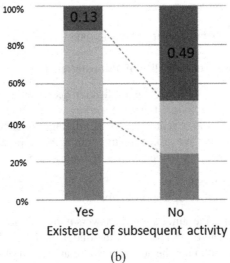

Fig. 2. Results of questionnaire for notification acceptability. (a) Distribution of acceptability scores for various times in relation to the activity being performed. (b) Detailed analysis of the answers for the times at the end of activities. Aggregated for each case with and without subsequent activity.

3.2   Model of Activity Transition and Opportune Moments for Information Delivery

In reference to the results of the questionnaire, this study defines the situation when no to-do task is at hand and the user is thus allowed to rest as a "mental goal" at home; we discuss a model to detect timings for information delivery. Here, we consider a state transition model as shown in Fig. 3.

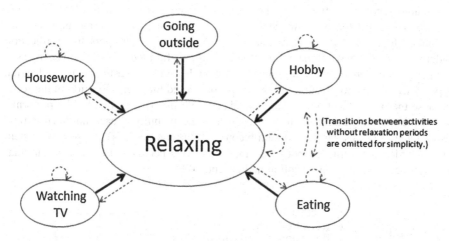

Fig. 3.   Model of activity transition and opportune moments for information delivery. Bold solid arrows indicate better transitions for information delivery

The transitions to "mental goals," i.e., transitions to a relaxation state are represented as the bold solid arrows. This study discusses the feasibility to estimate chances for information delivery by detecting the transition of activities and judging whether the current state is a relaxation state. The transition in activities is expected to be related to the motion of the user. In particular, moving to another location in the room may be a sign of activity transition. For instance, we sometimes move to a desk to use a PC and sometimes move to a table to eat. The motion of arms can reflect activity transition. As for the recognition of the relaxation state, the posture and the location may provide some input. For instance, in a statistical sense, users that are standing or walking are thought to be engaged in an activity or busy, whereas users that are sitting or lying down may be considered to be free or in a relaxed state. Users lying on a bed are also presumed to be more relaxed.

4   Experimental System

4.1   System Overview

We developed an experimental system for collecting users' subjective acceptability scores together with their behavioral data at various timings at their home. Figure 4 illustrates the processing flow of the system. The system consists of a Kinect v2 and a laptop PC (OS: Windows10, CPU: Core i7 - 2.0 GHz, RAM: 8 GB). The system continuously monitors the user's position and motion based on the body tracking function of Kinect for Windows SDK 2.0 [13]. If any specific movements, which are presumed to relate with activity transition, are detected, it triggers the notification judgment process. Next, if the notification condition is fulfilled, the system vocally asks the participant "Do you have a minute?". Although we plan to estimate and reflect the type of activity on notification judgment, we only used the user's location in the room because the user's location is naturally related with the activity that he/she performs. We requested the participants to answer his/her acceptability at each notification time using finger gestures, and the system recorded it through an RGB image. The system also recorded the estimated body part locations twice per second to analyze the relationship between the user's motion and acceptability.

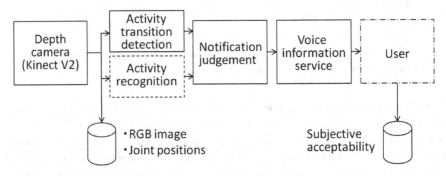

Fig. 4. Processing flow of experimental system.

4.2   Notification Judgement

As discussed later in Sect. 4.3, we focused on the position transfer and reaching action of users as index behaviors for activity transitions, which was verified in our previous study [14]. To avoid excessively frequent notifications, we set minimum blocking periods, which guarantees the participants will not be notified even if the notification condition is satisfied, to 8 min. Contrarily, in the case that no activity transition has been detected for 30 min, the system also provided a notification to the user for a comparison.

4.3 Activity Transition Detection

Most people will have several places in a room where they spend more hours, such as a desk, table, or sofa. We consider a situation when a person has just finished an activity and tries to start another one. If the person does not have a tool required for the activity such as a smartphone, PC, or book at hand, he or she will move to the place where the tool is and may come back to the original place. Alternatively, if the person tries to start an action that needs to be done at a specific place, he or she will also move, for instance, move to the table for lunch. Therefore, we used the position transfer in a room as an index for activity transition. The prototyped system detects the moment when the target user settles in a place after moving from another place farther than 0.6 m. We used the 3D position of the waist provided by Kinect v2 as the position of the user. The system detected the settlement of the user if the total travel distance in 5 s was less than 0.2 m.

When starting a new activity, we often extend our arms for taking something. We also extend our arms at the end of the activity to put the used object on the table or other places. Thus, the system used this reaching action as another indicator of activity transition. In particular, the system detected a sequence of hand motions, where the arm is extended to some extent and then returns close to the body.

5 Experiment for Analyzing the Relationship Between User's Acceptability to Voice Information Delivery and Activity Pattern Before and After Transition

5.1 Overview of Experiment

We conducted an experiment to collect users' acceptability scores at various timings at home using the prototyped experimental system as described in Sect. 4. We recruited three male volunteers who were studying at graduate school for the ease of experiment. Each of them was living alone in an apartment with a single living room. The experiment was conducted after an ethical review by a committee at the university.

Figure 5 illustrates an example of the experimental environment. Kinect v2 was installed at 1.6 m from the floor with 10° of depression angle to capture the entire room. On weekdays, the system recorded the data for 4 to 5 h from the time the user came home until the time the user went to bed. On holidays, it recorded the data for 6 to 7 h from the time the user awoke until the evening. We collected the data of 118 h for 21 days in total (a week for each participant).

During operation, the system intermittently requested vocally the participants to answer their acceptability at the timings as explained in the last section. We instructed the participants to imagine that the notification is the delivery of an advertisement, which might attract the interest of the participant. We requested the participants to score their subjective acceptability in five levels (1: low, 5: high) and indicate the score using finger signs to the camera when the notification is heard.

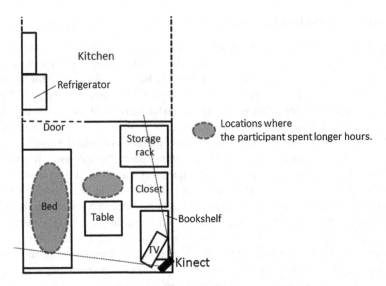

Fig. 5. An example of the experimental environment. Magenta-colored regions indicate the locations where the participant spent longer hours

We also instructed the participants to live as usual except for answering the acceptability as much as possible. In consideration of their privacy, we allowed them to temporally turn off the system when they do not want the data recorded. Furthermore, after the experiment, they checked the recorded RGB images to find and delete the ones that they do not want to share.

5.2   Results

We analyzed 407 responses collected in the experiment and compressed the acceptability scores of 1 and 2 to "Not acceptable," 3 to "Neither," and 4 and 5 to "Acceptable." The numbers of the answers for not acceptable, neither, and acceptable were 164, 39, and 204, respectively. As we expected, the acceptability for voice notifications in real-life situations varied depending on the timing of delivery.

Then, we checked whether the acceptability at the end of the activity was higher than at the middle of the activity, with an expectation that was obtained from the questionnaire survey described in Sect. 3. We categorized the notifications into stationary (non-moving) and non-stationary (moving) groups. The non-stationary group represents the notifications that were delivered within 30 s after the detection of the position transfer of the participant, which implies a transition in activity.

Figure 6 shows the rates of the answers. The rate of acceptance at stationary situations was 49% while the rate at non-stationary scenes was 54%. Contrary to our expectations, their difference was apparently negligible. However, because they should originally have different natures, we further analyzed them.

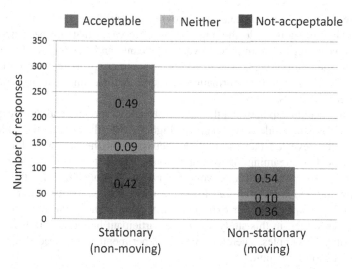

Fig. 6. Distribution of acceptability scores for notifications provided while in stationary (non-moving) and non-stationary (moving) situations.

At first, we focused on the 103 responses answered just after moving, which are summarized in the right bar in Fig. 6. Because our activity in the living room loosely relates with the location, we speculated that the acceptability has some relationship with the settled location after the transfer. Thus, we divided the responses for each location after moving as shown in Fig. 7.

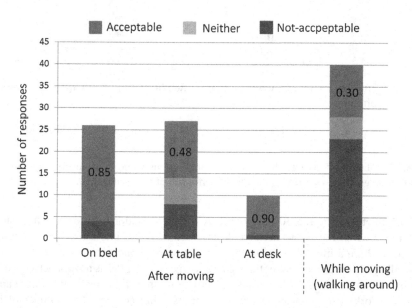

Fig. 7. Distribution of acceptability scores for notifications while in non-stationary (while or after moving) situations. Aggregated for each location being settled after moving.

The average rate of acceptance after moving was 69%, while the rate of moving was 30%. The situation while moving includes the cases that the participants were doing housework (e.g., cleaning with a vacuum cleaner and washing) and cases where they went to the restroom. The lower acceptance rate confirms that the timing while moving is not appropriate for information delivery; and the times staying at a specific location after moving is better.

As for the relationship between the settled place after moving and the acceptability, the rate of acceptance while on the bed was higher (85%) than that at the table (48%). The post-survey revealed that most of the activities on the bed were for fun (e.g., gaming and video streaming on a smartphone), while the measurable portion of activities at the table were for life or work, such as having lunch or using the PC. These activities for life and work appeared to be the major causes for the lower acceptance rate at the table. Contrary to our expectations, the rate of acceptance at the desk was high (90%). However, in this study, only one participant had a desk in his home, and there were only 10 samples. Therefore, further experimentation is needed for obtaining a general result on this point.

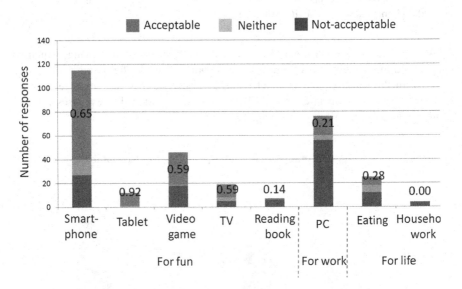

Fig. 8. Distribution of acceptability scores for notifications while in stationary (non-moving) situations. Aggregated for each activity being performed at the notification.

To further analyze the 304 responses answered at stationary (non-moving) situations, as shown in Fig. 8, we divided all observed activities into three types; activities for fun, work, and life. We refer to the use of a smartphone, tablet, video game, TV, and reading a book as a fun activity. We refer to the use of a PC as a work activity since each participant worked on their research activity on their PC. Finally, we refer eating and housework such as cleaning and washing as a life activity. The number of life activities were the smallest among the three types (29). The rate of acceptance while doing housework was 0% (0/4), and the rate while eating was only 22% (7/22). These results confirmed that the notification during a life activity is inappropriate in terms of acceptability. The rate of acceptance while during a work activity (i.e., PC) was also only 16/76 (21%). It suggested that the notification during work activities is inappropriate as well. On the other hand, the rate of acceptance during a fun activity was higher than 60%, and all the activities except reading a book have high acceptability (smartphone: 75/115, tablet: 11/12, video game: 27/46, TV: 11/19, and reading book: 1/7). It suggested that the times while being engaged in a fun activity are the potential opportune moments for proactive vocal information delivery.

6 Discussion

The result suggested that when the user settles at a place after moving from another position is the chance for information delivery. Furthermore, in the cases that users were settled on a bed, which would be one of the typical places where a user relaxes, the voice notifications appeared to be more accepted. The result also suggested that while users are engaging in a fun activity, such as using a smartphone, is a chance for notification. Furthermore, some of the feedback provided through the post-survey suggested that users tend to accept notifications at higher probability during a fun activity after eating, taking a bath, and PC work. These example cases correspond to both the time at the activity transition and the time while relaxing; that is the "mental goal" discussed in Sect. 3.2.

However, even in those situations, 20% to 30% of the notifications were evaluated as not acceptable. In practical use, two or three times of inappropriate notifications out of 10 will be too much and unaffordable. Therefore, a further exploration for more appropriate timing is needed. In this study, we focused only on the activity transitions that can be judged based on externally-observable information (i.e., moving). Meanwhile, smartphones and PCs occupied most activities, at least in this experiment. Such multi-functional devices are used for various activities; and thus, the acceptability of the user might differ from the activities performed on the device. For instance, the post-survey revealed that the notifications while using application software for communication are not acceptable most of the time.

In contrast, acceptability for the notifications while playing a game depends on the concentration on the activity. Therefore, to identify the more appropriate times, we need to explore the effective information related to smartphone use such as application types for more accurate estimation. Furthermore, the use of smartphones as a media for information delivery is another promising option. Smartphones are also useful in detecting user activity. However, they are sometimes stored in a bag or left for charging. Consequently, it appears promising to coordinate smart speakers installed in a room and smartphones carried and occasionally used by a user.

In addition, the development of an algorithm for judging appropriate timings using the explored indices, in conjunction with the user position and body motion used in this study, are also needed. Although this study discussed the acceptability of proactive vocal information delivery at various times in real-life scenarios, the small number of participants limits the discussion on the generality of the observed tendencies. A further experiment with more participants should be conducted to reveal the common rules at the opportune moments for proactive vocal information delivery.

7 Conclusion

In this study, based on the questionnaire survey, we prototyped an experimental system which detects the activity transition of a user and notifies the user vocally for a proactive information service. We also collected the subjective acceptability scores for the notification delivered at various timings in an actual living environment with three participants living alone over 21 days.

The results revealed that the notifications are more accepted when the user is settled on a bed after moving from another place and while the user is using a smartphone after eating, housework, or working on a PC. It suggested the necessity for detecting the user activity and its transition for estimating an opportune moment for information delivery. One promising direction is to utilize the information on smartphone use in combination with the sensor data provided by a smart speaker installed in a room. It is also necessary to conduct experiments with a greater number of participants for the further discussion on general tendency and individual differences.

References

1. Google Home. https://madeby.google.com/intl/en_us/home/. Accessed 1 Dec 2018
2. Amazon Echo. https://www.amazon.com/Amazon-Echo-Bluetooth-Speaker-with-WiFi-Alexa/dp/B00X4WHP5E. Accessed 1 Dec 2018
3. Mark, G.J., Gonzalez, V.M., Harris, J.: No task left behind? Examining the nature of fragmented work. In: Proceedings of the SIGCHI Conference on Human Factors in Computing Systems, pp. 321–330. ACM, New York (2005)
4. Iqbal, S.T., Bailey, B.P.: Investigating the effectiveness of mental workload as a predictor of opportune moments for interruption. In: Proceedings of the SIGCHI Conference on Human Factors in Computing Systems, pp. 1489–1492. ACM, New York (2005)
5. Porcheron, M., Fischer, J.E., Reeves, S., Sharples, S.: Voice interface in everyday life. In: Proceedings of the SIGCHI Conference on Human Factors in Computing Systems, p. 640. ACM, New York (2018)
6. Luria, M., Hoffman, G., Zuckerman, O.: Comparing social robot, screen and voice interfaces for smart-home control. In: Proceedings of the SIGCHI Conference on Human Factors in Computing Systems, pp. 580–592. ACM, New York (2017)
7. Takemae, Y., Chaki, S., Ohno, T., Yoda, I., Ozawa, S.: Analysis of human interruptibility in the home environment. In: Extended Abstracts on Human Factors in Computing Systems, pp. 2681–2686. ACM, New York (2007)
8. Cumin, J., Lefebvre, G., Ramparany, F., Crowley, J.: Inferring availability for communication in smart homes using context. In: IEEE International Conference on Pervasive Computing and Communications (PerCom) Workshops (2018)

9. Vastenburg, M.H., Keyson, D.V., de Ridder, H.: Considerate home notification systems: a field study of acceptability of notifications in the home. Pers. Ubiquit. Comput. **12**(8), 555–566 (2008)
10. Tanaka, T., Fukazawa, S., Takeuchi, K., Nonaka, M., Fujita, K.: Study of uninterruptibility estimation method for office worker during PC work. J. Inf. Process. Soc. Jpn. **53**(1), 126–137 (2012)
11. Banerjee, S., Silva, A., Feigh, K., Chernova, S.: Effects of interruptibility-aware robot behavior. arXiv:1804.06383 (2018)
12. Fujimoto, Y., Komori, M., Xu, J., Tasaka, K., Yanagihara, H., Fujita, K.: Preliminary study on modeling opportune time for proactive auditory information service. In: Proceedings of the 80th National Convention of Information Processing Society of Japan, 5E-03. IPSJ, Tokyo (2018)
13. Shotton, J., et al.: Real-time human pose recognition in parts from single depth images. Commun. ACM **56**(1), 116–124 (2013)
14. Fujimoto, Y., Nagasawa, Y., Xu, J., Tasaka, K., Yanagihara, H., Fujita, K.: Possibility of estimation on information provision based on body movement toward push-type information service. In: Proceedings of Human Interface Symposium, 7D1-5. HIS, Kyoto (2017)

The Tension Experience - Performance in Alternate Realities

Dario Mesquita[1]([⊠]) [iD], Sérgio Nesteriuk[2]([⊠]) [iD],
and João Massarolo[1]([⊠]) [iD]

[1] Federal University of São Carlos, São Paulo, Brazil
dario.mirg@gmail.com, massarolo@terra.com
[2] Anhembi Morumbi University, São Paulo, Brazil
nesteriuk@hotmail.com

Abstract. This paper aims to discuss the notion of performance in the alternate reality game based on an analysis of the *Tension Experience* project, conducted in 2016 under the direction of Darren Lynn Bousman, which features the use of immersive theater strategies in a number of special contexts, and the use of multiple media support to create an emerging fictional universe so that each participant has a unique and personalized experience. *Tension Experience* establishes a form of blind performance in a narrative game with no rules or clear objectives, that seeks to enter the daily life of its participants, providing an experience that acts between the fictional and the non-fictional. In this way, the work updates some traditional strategies of alternating reality games as an immersive entertainment format, with a greater focus on narrative and role-playing aspects at the expense of hidden puzzles and mysteries.

Keywords: Alternate reality game · Performance · Immersive theater

1 Introduction

The alternate reality games – ARGs – appeared in the 2000s aiming to create a ludic experience with immersive qualities. They work as a game without clear rules and specific goals that goes on for an indefinite period of time and that is developed through the coordinated use of multiple medias (internet, TV, mobile, etc.) in association to actions in physical environments, in a way to keep a coherent narrative unit that is also related to the reality of the participants, in a combination of fictional and non-fictional elements.

In this way, it is created a structure that endorses the fictional universe that unfolds through the daily life of the involved ones, as a second layer of reality full of challenges that demand an active participation of the subjects in various performing actions that are ambiguous for happening not according to rules that are duly established, but rules that must be explored to be figured out. Those are characteristics that give to the experience of ARG strong immersive shapes, reconfiguring the classic understanding that one has of games as an experience with specific and limited space, time, and rules. This broad the possibilities of performance by the participants and their social, emotional, and cognitive dimensions, intensifying an immersion process in the experience.

© Springer Nature Switzerland AG 2019
M. Kurosu (Ed.): HCII 2019, LNCS 11566, pp. 540–549, 2019.
https://doi.org/10.1007/978-3-030-22646-6_40

The alternate reality game has qualities that support a whole contemporary artistic trend in which, as Canton [5] points out, "materializes through a constant negotiation between art and life, life and art", which is also visible in the spectrum of mediatic entertainment in the last decades, which Works that increasingly use strategies of mediatic convergence to provide actions where the public participates [10].

For having such characteristics, ARG has been strategically used in entertainment, in many fields (cinema, TV, advertising, etc.) as a way to involve the public directly with elements of mediated fictional universes. For example, *The Tension Experience* project - led by movie director Darren Lynn Bousman and writer Clint Sears - uses strategies of the alternate reality game together with those of the immersive theater in order to create intense emotional experiences for its participants, requiring of them a different mode of performance from what is traditionally practiced in the media and theater. In order to understand this performance dimension in the ARG, this article aims to analyze the elements of the alternate reality game as well as *The Tension Experience* project and its relationship with the immersive theater in order to understand how the performance of participants in this form of playful experience, whose main aesthetic is the lack of well-defined boundaries between fiction and non-fiction.

2   The Origins of Alternate Reality

In 2001, in one of the first trailers [2] and posters (see Fig. 1) of the A.I. Artificial Intelligence (United States, A.I. Artificial Intelligence, 2001), directed by Steven Spielberg, some viewers noticed something unusual in the credits of the work team. Among the listed professionals came the name of Jeanine Salla, credited as a sentient machine therapist - which also appeared on promotional posters. By researching her on the internet, in addition to discovering Jeanine Salla's personal website, the audience was also led to a set of interlinked websites set in the year 2142 that dealt with the technical, social, philosophical, and sentimental problems of artificial intelligence.

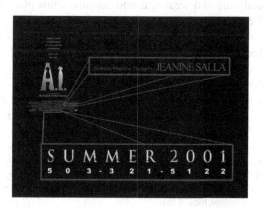

Fig. 1. Poster details of *A.I.- Artificial Intelligence* (2001) which were the rabbit hole to ARG *The Beast*

Slowly, Jeanine Salla proved to be a gateway to an investigative adventure about the death in unusual circumstances of her friend Evan Chan, with internet users as her main allies. To solve this enigma, several puzzles were created, ranging from websites, e-mails, and recorded links to those who were willing to explore this world, in a four-month conspiracy plot, from April to June 2001, involving about of 7,480 members of the main group of participants, known as Cloudmakers [12].

The experience came without any official announcement and happened thanks to the public's curiosity about the clues left in the promotional trailers of the film - although it did not directly involve any character in the film, approaching only their fictional world. What many regarded as a game, due to the puzzle challenges proposed by it[1], it did not have an official name and its existence was not even confirmed by the production crew of the film. Subsequently, what was only referred to as the A.I. marketing campaign or its web game [18], was named The Beast[2] by its makers Sean Stewart (writer), Elan Lee (director and producer), and Pete Fenlon (content manager) under the supervision of Jordan Weisman, who was then the creative director of the Entertainment Division of Microsoft Games Studios - who signed a contract for the development of a franchise of games based on the A.I. movie. The original project of the games was canceled by Microsoft shortly after the results of A.I.'s poor reception in its debut (July 2001) and The Beast was closed as well in the same period instead of keeping going until December, as it was originally planned, when videogames based on the universe of the movie would finally be released [12].

The proposal of The Beast, as Sean Stewart claimed in an interview to McGonigal [12], was to create mediatic evidence of a fictional world as if it actually existed, and then to break it "into thousands of small pieces and buried them in the midst of 70 billion pieces of online content". In this way, the experience would not be constituted as a sensorial simulated reality, but an alternative world that was accessible by objects of everyday communication, which occurred in a persistent and parallel way to the daily life of the participants.

The Beast is considered to be the precursor of the form of ludic experience that has become known as an alternate reality game, defined by Martin [11] as games that take "the substance of daily life and weaves it into narratives that place layers of meaning and interaction in the real world". This additional layer is what Christy Dena [6] points out as the main aesthetic of alternate realities design, which seeks to reduce the evidence that could characterize it as fictional in order to create a truthfulness of the facts so that they can be treated as plausible events.

Since then, other projects of this nature have been created, whether linked to audiovisual works, such as *Lost* (ABC, 2004–2010) and its *Lost Experience* (2006) [20]; to publicity, such as the *Guaraná Antarctica*'s campaign known as *Uncertain*

---

[1] About the challenges, Andre Phillips, one of the participants, stated in an interview: "the puzzles made us read Goedel, Escher, and Bach, translate from German and Japanese, even from an obscure language called Kannada, decipher Morse and Enigma codes, and execute an incredible range of operations in sound and image files" [16].

[2] The name came from an internal joke of the makers because of the number of documents created for the game, which accounted for 666 files, the number of the beast, as revealed by writer Sean Stewart in his blog [19].

Zone (2007) [7] made in partnership with Editora Abril; or used in independent projects such as *Perplex City* (2005–2007) [14], produced by the British game company Mind Candy, which took over as a business model the sale of decks with jigsaw puzzles, which were brought from a reality parallel to ours. Aimed at a specific niche audience that has arose after 2001, the ARGs did not have major changes in their basic formula, always developing through the internet, especially with investigative plots that usually refer to conspiracy theories hidden between websites and discussion forums.

These strategies are also found in *The Tension Experience* project, which began in 2016 in Los Angeles, to create experiences focused especially on actions inspired by immersive theater, in which performances "use expansive installations and environments that have mobile audiences and which invite the audience to participate" [3], removing their status as an observer and becoming co-author of the narrative represented.

In this sense, the first experience was divided into two parts: (1) *Indoctrination*, an ARGs that extended from February to September 2016, involving the articulation between a fictional world and daily world through the internet, in addition to live interactions of characters with some participants (estimated around 40); (2) *Ascension*, a ticketed immersive play inside a warehouse[3]. The experience has as main motto to follow the trajectory of Addison Barrow (Sabrina Kern), a young actress who, when moving to Los Angeles, is seduced by an organization called The *O.O.A. Institute*, a facade for a secret society with touches of religious worship where a series of intrigues of power among the leaders - called Gatekeepers – happens [4].

The Tension Experience is inserted in a context of works focused on the performance of the audience, who stops being only a viewer to become a user in an experience open to modifications that evade a mere mechanical interactivity, having the participation as something substantial for the progress of the experience. But before any specific analysis on the project, it is necessary to delineate some characteristics of the alternate reality games, better defining the way in which the performance of the participants is constituted.

3   Alternate Reality Game and Performance in the Dark

According to McGonigal [12], the main focus in alternate reality games is to create immersive situations for the player without resorting to interactive and sensory strategies that constitute a virtual world apart. In the case of ARGs, the participants' day-to-day communication devices are used to blur the boundaries between gaming and non-gaming (fiction and non-fiction). The motto "this is not a game" (TINAG)[4], was defining in the first alternate reality games, in the sense of defending the quest to hide the projected/artificial nature of the ARG and to place it as an obscure layer of reality that is hidden between encrypted messages. Following this precept defined first

---

[3] The presentations occurred Thursday through Sunday hourly from 6:00 to 11:00 pm, with a audience of 8-12 people each show, totalizing 300 members per week [15].

[4] The words came in a trailer for the A.I. movie, aired on North American television on June 7th, 2001, blinking rapidly in red letters along with credits [11].

by Elan Lee in a conference in 2002 [12], who worked on The Best, the ARGs should follow three principles: 1 - "Tell no one", the game should not be announced, so that it arouses people's greater interest in knowing more about mysteries, providing the feeling of dealing with something unique, so they enjoy sharing it with others; 2 - "Do not build a space for the game", that is to say, do not confine the experience to a single environment; 3 - "Do not build a Game", the instructions and rules should not be clear, nor even have specific objectives, just as the daily routine does not have properly clarified rules.

Faced with these qualities, McGonigal classifies ARGs as ubiquitous games, which create a persistent ludic infrastructure by rethinking the reality and functioning of their technical devices for ludic purposes. This breaks with Huizinga's [9] classic notion of the game as an activity apart from ordinary life, with well-defined space, time, and rules that runs within dedicated places and projects for this, as a magic circle, "that is to say, places that are forbidden, isolated, closed, sacred, within which certain rules are respected. All of them are temporary worlds within the habitual world, dedicated to the practice of a space activity".

The transposition of these boundaries of the game would happen by the activation of affordances of gameplay in the everyday world. As McGonigal [12] explains, affordances refer to the fundamental properties in goals, determining how they can be manipulated and used. They are sensory cues that help users to understand how to interact with the properties of things and cognitively build the environment. The perception of affordance depends on the skill of the user who is taking a particular action that will produce an effect in relation to a specific object. This response may be predicted or directly observed, and is also a culturally recognizable property (such as a door-opening knob) or empirically accessible by exploiting the object's utilities. In this way, the ARGs would be activities that give new meanings and ludic functions to reality, updating the relationship between its participants and the environment, which originates a reactive system that unfolds in fragmented narratives, revealing an universe hidden as yet.

As McGonigal [12] explains, alternate reality games would be game structures that activate certain properties of the world: "[…] transforming everyday objects and places into interactive platforms; game structures also activate players by making them more responsive to potential calls to interaction. This is because the act of exposing previously unperceived affordances creates a more meaningful relationship between the actor and the object or the space in the world."

But, as the author comments, these features arise only by the performance of the subject with the encrypted messages. On the concept of performance, Zumthor [22] says that "performance is recognition" because it "accomplishes, concretizes, makes something go from virtuality to the present". An act that is situated in a cultural and situational context, as an emergency that escapes the common course of things, a "phenomenon that leaves this context at the same time as in that it finds place" [22]. An action that, for the author, modifies the knowledge of the subjects involved and gives new forms to the perception of the environment, leaving the mere mechanical function of communication.

McGonigal understands the performance of ARG participants through the concept of dark play formulated by Shechner [17]. The author uses the concept to refer to ludic activities in which the participants are not sure whether they are playing, because " Unlike carnivals or ritual clowns whose inversions of established order are sanctioned by the authorities, dark play is truly subversive, its agendas always hidden." [16], such as a mouse trapped in a maze or a person captured unnoticed by a game of deception. For him, there is always a danger in these experiences, because of the delicate limit between the security of representations and the risk to the daily life of those involved. The reward for the participants occurs through fraud, disturbance, and excess - that is to say, by strong emotional engagement, which for the McGonigal is transformed into pleasure in discovering the occult and to be surprised to reveal the staging or farce.

This intensity in engagement can be measured by the time that the participants of the ARG The Beast took to solve the puzzles of the first stage of the project. The producers estimated a three-month deadline for everything to be solved, but when the ARG was released, the mysteries of the first stage were solved in about one day only.

However, as pointed out by researchers such as McGonigal [12] and Dena [6], the commitment of participants is not proportional to the number of participants. Few people actually engage in these kinds of experiences, even when they have a broad reach across the internet. The ARGs have come to be known as projects aimed at a specific niche of the audience that is avid to look out for puzzles and that like to solve complex problems and speculate in online groups about possible narrative paths of a still obscure fictional world.

As Mind Candy's co-founder Dan Hon [8] complained during his talk on the Everything *We Know About Transmedia Is Wrong!* panel at the PICNIC 2010 conference, the ARGs failed to become popular for wasting their time on things nobody want to see or do. He mainly criticizes the producers for using cryptography and puzzles without any narrative justification, since "the number of people interested in mathematical cryptography is negligible; instead, let's do things that entertain people" [8].

In this sense, *The Tension Experience* explores other aspects of the format of what is seen in traditional alternate reality games. In this experiment, the focus shifts from exploration of the subject's cognitive performance in solving puzzles and goes to the action of dealing emotionally with a game in the dark, as defined by Shechner [17]. By incorporating precepts of the immersive theater, which is intensified by the strategies of design of alternate realities previously listed, the ARG seeks to break the daily life of its participants, collecting their personal data in the networks, interfering in the day to day actions with live actors and telephone calls, in actions that demand an active performance of the subject in trying to separate the game from non-game.

4   The Tension Experience and the Immersive Theater

Journalist McKendry [13] reports that the first edition of *The Tension Experience* (and its first part named *Indoctrination*) was primary disclosed to a select audience of media professionals and entertainment journalists living in Los Angeles. Invitations were sent via email from an institution called O.O.A., offering lighting to those who were willing to participate in the experience and learn its secrets. Anyone who accepted the invitation could subscribe to the experience through the institution's website [21] or by telephone. Shortly thereafter, an extensive questionnaire was sent regarding personal information, which came with the following warning: " *The Tension Experience* is a paranoia, fear based experiment. We use personal information and data collected to tailor the experience for each participant involved. By using this website you understand that we will go out of our way to create a unique experience based on YOU. At any time you wish to end your experience with us please email TheTensionExperience@gmail.com. Upon your request all information will be deleted from our servers, and your GAME will end." [16].

After the registration, an interview was scheduled in an isolated warehouse in the city and until this meeting, the user would receive anonymous calls, as reported by Adrew Kasch McKendry [13]: "I receive a series of creepy anonymous phone calls. Some laughing. Music playing. I posted an announcement of my wife's pregnancy on Facebook and a minute later, the phone rings and a creepy voice says 'Congratulations!' and hangs up". In the same statement, Adrew describes his face-to-face meeting in which he had to answer another questionnaire and at the end hitchhike to a crying girl, who supposedly had passed the same test and was desperate. As she leaves the car, the girl declares that they have shown her a picture of him.

This was the tone of the participants experiences for seven months, interacting with characters over the internet or in public places, always having the support of platforms such as the forum of the O.O.A. and its social media, such as Facebook and Twitter, which periodically provided clues about the main plot and broadcast it to short videos. In one of these transmissions [1], the spectator was taken into a car with three occupants. In the background, a casual song was playing, until they all get out of the car and take out an injured man who is soon recognized by the users as one of the characters of the main plot. From such events, participants are becoming aware of the intrigues

Fig. 2. Photographic record of the immersive play that closes the events of *The Tension Experience: Ascension.*

behind the O.O.A. and the role of Addison Barrow (Sabrina Kern) in the power struggle among the group's leaders. Having as its peak a collective event, a second part of the experience named *Ascension*, accessible by the purchase of limited tickets, in which a shed with various scenarios for an immersive play - staged periodically between November and December 2016 (see Fig. 2).

As defined by Belo [3], in the immersive theater there are no barriers between the audience and the actors, having the audience the freedom to interact with the cast and the scenario, and "there is a single central narrative, but each member of the audience creates his own narrative, linked to his experience, there being as many narratives as the number of members of the audience the piece has" [3]. According to the author, such an immersive performance format emerges as a counterpoint to the experience of a world so mediated by technology, where people crave for tactile and intimate experiences.

This form of performance art refers to the experiences and ideas that sought to break the fourth wall of the theater from the 1930s onwards in order to create a viewer emancipated by the intensification of the senses and by creation as a form of consciousness - with such dramatic writers as Bertold Brecht in the epic theater, and Antonin Artaud in the theater of cruelty. In the 1970s, in Brazil, Augusto Boel sought to create pieces with active audiences through the idea of the Theater of the Oppressed, in which the public had the concession to interfere in the direction of the narrative for the outcome of the play, with constant improvisation by the actors.

These features are taken by *The Tension Experience: Ascension* and potentialized through the activation of gameplay's affordances that give rise to performances within the design of the game in the dark - not having a clear awareness of where a performance action begins or ends, tracking at all times loopholes that indicate the limits of zones in which fictional events may be occurring.

As stated by the participant Adrew Kasch [13], each of his friends who joined the experiment stated that they witnessed events different from their own, each with its own narrative, according to the individually constructed profile, making it unlikely to predict any future action. Project's director Darren Bousman also explains that the rules themselves should be obscured so as not to break with the subject's cognitive immersion process, providing different layers and views on the same event.

At the end of each piece, for example, characters are killed in sacrificial rituals, and the audience can intervene and change the ending by speaking a specific Latin phrase that was secretly written in notes that participants had access to during the ARG. However, it requires collective consent for such an act, as he reports in one situation: "One person found it and tried to do it, but he was so meek in his approach that he just muttered it. Everybody turned and looked at him, but he didn't say anything else again. If he would have said it again, it all would have happened." [4]. Despite the apparent failure of the subject, it is incorporated and becomes coherent within the narrative spectrum of performance, for from the recognition of performance, possible worlds open up through participation, resulting in paths of frustration for a single individual (as mentioned above), among other tracks in which it is up to each participant to develop their conclusions.

5   Final Considerations

This article sought to discuss the notion of performance in the alternate reality game from a brief analysis of the *The Tension Experience: Ascension*, which incorporates dynamics of the immersive theater in order to create an experience with a more narrative focus instead of exploring the dynamics of puzzles solutions that were so common in early ARGs. In order to do so, it was made a rescue of the trajectory of what was considered the first alternate reality game, The Beast, made in 2001, based especially on the premise "this is not a game" in order not to expose itself as a game and require participants' ability to decipher hidden puzzles in movie trailers, images, and websites.

In this way, it was possible to point out the main characteristics of the ARGs, focusing especially on how the performance is constituted by the activation of gameplay functionalities in the daily environment, mixing the fictional with the non-fiction, and providing an ambiguous quality in its performance - Something that is representative in *The Tension Experience: Ascension*, for developing its narrative lines in a personalized way to each participant, crossing them in a final collective event having as support the immersive theater, which requires the participation of the audience for its progress. Qualities that corroborate to create a linear performance that requires participants to be guided by experience and discern the events involved with the game through the daily experience.

The experience is focused on developing a greater participation in its narrative dimension, the performance of its participants along with actors, and through personal messages through the platforms. There is an escape from the structure of mysteries in puzzles or activities that require many collaborative actions, attending to the details of the daily life of each participant, within an unique business model based on the purchase of tickets, and with a geographical space of action well delineated - which contributes to all sustainable production logistics, one of the major bottlenecks when it comes to the production of alternate reality games.

The possibility of working on *The Tension Experience* universe in a serialized way, with new projects launched annually, allows experimentation still unprecedented in its format, considering that the alternate reality game projects developed over a long period are rare. Thus, *The Tension Experience* would be an object of study to be followed in its next editions in view of the potentialities of innovation that it can provide for the field of immersive experiences, as well as reflections on performance in the dark.

References

1. A gift for her live streaming. https://www.periscope.tv/w/1MnxnXLQLqBGO. Accessed 24 June 2018
2. A.I. Artificial intelligence - official® trailer [HD]. http://www.springer.com/lncs. Accessed 21 Nov 2016
3. Belo, I.C.: Teatro imersivo: públicos e práticas culturais. ISCTE IUL, Lisboa (2016)

4. Bishop, B.: Cults, chaos, and community: how The Tension Experience rewrote the rules of storytelling. In: The Verge, 22 November 2016. https://www.theverge.com/2016/11/22/13716340/the-tension-experience-lust-darren-lynn-bousman-clint-sears-interview. Accessed 23 May 2018

5. Canton, K.: Do moderno ao contemporâneo. Martins Fontes, São Paulo (2009)

6. Dena, C.: Transmedia Practice: Theorising the Practice of Expressing a Fictional World across Distinct Media and Environments. University of Sydney, Sydney (2009)

7. Desvendando o Zona Incerta video. https://youtu.be/lzGm3KfcnDY. Accessed 10 June 2018

8. Gool, D.: Picnic: everything we know about transmedia is wrong. ARGNet, 26 September 2010. https://www.argn.com/2010/09/picnic_everything_we_know_about_transmedia_is_wrong. Accessed 23 June 2018

9. Huizinga, J.: Homo Ludens, 5th edn. Perspectiva, São Paulo (2004)

10. Jenkins, H.: Cultura da Convergência. 1nd edn. Aleph, São Paulo, 2008

11. Martin, A., Thompson, B., Chatfield, T. (eds.): Alternate reality games white paper. In: International Game Developers Association IGDA (2016)

12. McGonigal, J.: This Might Be a Game: Ubiquitous Play and Performance at the Turn of the Twenty-First Century. University of California, Berkeley (2006)

13. McKendry, R.: The wild, frightening events behind The Tension Experience!. In: 13th Floor, 03 Mar 2016. http://www.the13thfloor.tv/2016/03/03/the-wild-and-frightening-events-behind-the-tension-experience/. Accessed 20 June 2018

14. Perplex City Homepage. http://perplexcity.com/. Accessed 10 June 2018

15. Reilly, M.: No wrong choices: performing alternate reality in The Tension Experience. Int. J. Perform. Arts Digit. Media 15(1), 70–83 (2018)

16. Said, M.: Getting to know The Tension Experience before it gets to know you. In: ARG-Net, 07 Jan 2016. https://www.argn.com/2016/07/getting_to_know_the_tension_experience/. Accessed 24 June 2018

17. Shechner, R.: Performance Studies: An Introduction, 3rd edn. Routledge, New York (2013)

18. Sieberg, D.: Reality blurs, hype builds with Web 'A.I.' game. In: CNN, 03 August 2001. https://web.archive.org/web/20010803071643/http://www.cnn.com:80/SPECIALS/2001/coming.attractions/stories/aibuzz.html. Accessed 03 June 2018

19. Stewart, S.: The Beast (a.k.a. The A.I. Web Game). http://www.seanstewart.org/the-beast-2001-a-k-a-the-a-i-web-game/. Accessed 10 June 2018

20. The lost experience - channel 4 and Hi-ReS! reel. https://youtu.be/oXK8Cp9KjXE. Accessed 10 June 2018

21. The Tension Experience homepage. http://thetensionexperience.com/. Accessed 24 June 2018

22. Zumthor, P.: Performance, recepção, leitura. Cosacnaify, São Paulo (2014)

Transfictionality and Transmedia Storytelling: A Conceptual Distinction

Thiago Mittermayer[1(✉)] and Letícia X. L. Capanema[2]

[1] São Paulo Catholic University (PUC-SP), São Paulo, Brazil
thimitter@gmail.com
[2] Mato Grosso Federal University (UFMT), Cuiabá, Brazil
capanema.leticia@gmail.com

Abstract. This paper proposes the distinction between the concepts of transmedia storytelling and transfictionality. Despite the similarities, both concepts comprehend different meanings, which will be discussed in the current context of convergence culture, marked by the enhancement of interactivity, participatory culture, and media convergence. In this way, the fictional and narrative flows across works and media will be problematized based in the research of Jenkins [1], Ryan [2, 3], and Saint-Gelais [4] as theoretical foundation.

Keywords: Transfictionality · Transmedia storytelling · Fiction · Narrative · Media

1 Introduction

Transmedia storytelling and transfictionality are phenomena that have aroused the interest of the Entertainment Industry and of the researchers in Narratology, Communication, Culture, and Technology. In fact, transmedial and transfictional strategies involve multiple intelligences that comprise creative, technological, and market issues. They are also embedded in traditionally established domains of knowledge, such as narrative studies, and emerging ones, such as HCI research (Human-Computer Interaction). Certainly, these concepts are central for understanding current media culture. However, their definitions often get confused when are not properly delimited. The objective of this paper is to discuss and relate these two concepts from a narratological perspective, without losing sight of their media and technological relations. Although they understand different meanings, the transmedia storytelling and the transfictionality present connections that need to be discussed and, mainly, understood in the current context of convergence culture.

From the observation that the current culture enhances flows and relations across media, narratives, and diegetic universes, we seek, in this article, to understand how the processes of transmediality and transfictionality occur. Thus, we will examine these two concepts more closely supported by Jenkins [1], Ryan [2, 3], and Saint-Gelais [4] studies.

Before that, it is necessary, in this introduction, to clarify a few fundamental concepts for understanding transmedia storytelling and transfictionality, such as: *fiction, narrative,* and *media*. In this way, it will be possible to connect these concepts to the *trans* prefix and to explore its meanings in current media. After this stage, we will

© Springer Nature Switzerland AG 2019
M. Kurosu (Ed.): HCII 2019, LNCS 11566, pp. 550–558, 2019.
https://doi.org/10.1007/978-3-030-22646-6_41

explain what is and what is not understood by transmedia storytelling and the main conceptual confusions with other terminologies, such as: adaptation, remediation, multimodal narration, and even transfiction. Following, we will present an investigation into the notion of transfictionality developed by Saint-Gelais, highlighting the potential of any fiction to construct unlimited worlds. Finally, we will analyze the transmedia storytelling and the transfictionality combined, in order to contribute to the studies on the narrative and fictional flows across works and media.

1.1 Fiction

Under a narratological perspective, fiction is understood as the creation of imagined worlds (diegesis), made up of elements such as characters, events, places, objects, etc., generated by its authors and (re)constructed by the public.[1] The (re)construction of a fictional world also presupposes a kind of silent agreement between the public and the work. That means the reader, spectator, user, gamer or interactor of a fiction is inclined to accept the elements presented to him through the tacit pact that Coleridge[2] called "willing suspension of disbelief." It is a voluntary agreement in which public momentarily disables their incredulity to allow themselves to be convinced by the diegetic universe presented to them.

Although it is formed by mental schemes, fiction does not necessarily oppose reality. Inevitably, the two concepts (fiction and reality) are associated. The philosopher Vilém Flusser presents a unique view on the subject, assuming that fiction cannot be understood as simply the opposite of reality. According to him, (2015, p. 64) [5]: "We must bid farewell to that naive separation between true and false, as Wittgenstein has already said. The disapproval of the fictitious cannot be sustained for long. Observing more precisely, the function of discourse is fiction, or, as we say today, alternative realities."

Eco, in his *Six Walks in the Fictional Woods* [6], reminds us that, as fantastic as they may be, fictional worlds are always "parasites of the real world." (1994, p. 125). Even accepting the pact of fiction, we will always compare it with the reality we know. "In fiction, precise references to the actual world are so closely linked that, after spending some time in the world of the novel and mixing fictional elements with references to reality, as one should, the reader no longer knows exactly where he or she stands." An example, according to Eco, is that some people believe in the actual existence of events and fictional characters, for example, Sherlock Holmes. Thus fiction transports us into

---

[1] This conception of fiction follows the perspective of researchers as: Gérard Genette *Figs. 3* (1972), Thomas Pavel *Univers de la fiction* (1988), Lubomír Doležel *Mimesis and possible worlds* (1988), Jean-Marie Schaeffer *Pourquoi la fiction?* (1999).

[2] The critic and writer Samuel Taylor Coleridge used the expression: 'willing suspension of disbelief' for the first time in his book *Biographia Literaria* (1817) to refer to the agreement between the reader and the work of fiction. In this agreement, the reader accepts as true the postulates created by the fictional world, without necessarily invalidating them when compared to the postulates of reality external to the work.

an imagined world, governed by its own rules and principles, which can resemble or distance enormously from what we call reality. In this sense, fiction is a kind of alternative universe shaped by a narrative that relates, in a certain way, to reality.

1.2   Narrative

On the other hand, narrative refers to the discourse that organizes the elements belonging to a universe (fictional or factual), ordering them according to temporal, enunciative, and others criteria. In the article *Transmedial storytelling and transfictionality* [2], Ryan presents a broad definition of narrative. For the author, narrative is, in general, a sequence of events that develop in time. According to Ryan (2013, p. 364), narratives are mental representations of dynamic models of developing situations – Ryan takes as reference the concept of chronotope (indivisibility of space and time) created by Mikhail Bakhtin. A narrative is characterized by the configuration of a discourse that organizes a succession of events and presents itself through some expressive form (oral, written, audiovisual, etc.). Therefore, we can distinguish fiction from narrative since fiction relates to the creation of worlds, and narrative, to the operation of organizing a discourse. Then, every fiction is structured by a narrative, but not every narrative is fictional.

1.3   Media

Since a fictional narrative organizes elements of a diegetic universe, it can be realized through diverse media, using its language properties. Thus, the media chosen to narrate a particular fiction presents specificities that will shape the narrative. For example, television and film use audiovisual language, such as montage, framing, sound uses, among others. Video game, in turn, is supported by interactive and audiovisual elements. Literature, in textual language. Comics books, textual and visual languages. Therefore, media is here understood as a system of communication that brings together techniques, language, and interaction forms. These systems, or media, present sets of features (aesthetic, narrative, technological, and spectatorial) recognized and shared by the public and the creators in the cultural context. Therefore, we consider media as a form of communication, that is a medium that is a producer of meanings. It is this characteristic that allows media (such as book, radio, television, film, and video games) to communicate innumerable narratives, whether fictional or not.

The current media context, named by Jenkins [1] as convergence culture, is characterized by the coexistence of old and new media, technological and symbolic exchanges, and by the mixing of languages and contents. In addition, profound changes in production systems, distribution and reception, merging the roles, previously delimited, of transmitter and receiver. According to Jenkins (2006, p. 104), convergence culture "makes the flow of content across multiple media platforms inevitable."

2 What Is and What Is not Transmedia Storytelling?

Combining prefix *trans* to the concepts of fiction, narrative, and media, we highlight flows, passages, and displacements that can occur across them. In this sense, transmedia storytelling and transfictionality imply the transposition of diegetic, narrative and/or media borders. To start, it can be inferred that these are strategies that act at the extra-compositional level, through the breaking of limits and the establishment of new relations.

It is known that one of the most important scholars of the transmedia storytelling is Jenkins [1]. The researcher investigated transmedia in popular culture, identifying the expansion of a narrative universe across media. A practice enhanced by technological convergence and by the participatory and collaborative culture. Jenkins notes that media react to current convergence culture by expanding their content across platforms. From this synergy among media, forms of interaction and narrative models emerge, resulting in the phenomenon of the transmedia storytelling. Not surprisingly, Jenkins uses the film *Matrix* (Lana Wachowski, Lilly Wachowski, 1999) as a remarkable case to develop his conception of transmedia storytelling. This transmedia project (composed of films, comics books, and video games) presents a fictional narrative of cyberpunk genre, which narrates the adventures of the Neo, a hacker within an informational universe named Matrix, very similar to cyberspace. For Jenkins (2006, p. 95), Matrix "is entertainment for the age of media convergence, integrating multiple texts to create a narrative so large that it cannot be contained within a single medium".

In academic studies, the transmedia occurrence had already been identified and investigated by other researchers who used different terminologies. Kinder [7], for example, introduces the term 'transmedia intertextuality' (1991, p. 1) which refers to the expansion of an entertainment super-system across different media. Another precursor concept of the transmedia storytelling and the convergence culture is the term 'remediation', developed by Bolter and Grusin [8]. Remediation happens when a new medium reshapes elements of previous media. Bolter and Grusin [8] argue that in this process there is not substitution of one media for another, but a reciprocal movement of repair, reform and remodeling. In this sense, transmediation can be understood as a phenomenon contained in a broader process of remediation, in which different media establish many kinds of connections (technology, language, business), as well as narrative integration.

However, Ryan [2] relativizes the concept of transmedia storytelling. According to her (2013, p. 362): "it is tempting to regard transmedial storytelling as something radically new and revolutionary if not as the narrative form of the future". It should be emphasized that narrative expansion in multiple media is not an unprecedented phenomenon. This practice dates back to the earliest days of human culture and can be identified, for example, in Greek mythology, biblical narratives, fairy tales, and popular stories. All of them are founding narratives of social groups that, at certain times and places, have been massively consumed and propagated through multiple expressive forms. Although it is an old process, the transmedia storytelling finds, in the current culture and technology, propitious circumstances for its potential. "Transmedial storytelling is a response to the proliferation of media and delivery systems that the digital revolution of the past fifty years has brought upon us", writes the author (2013, p. 384).

Although it is a concept well studied today, there is much imprecision in defining transmedia, which is confused with several other similar and related terms. In the paper *Transmedia storytelling: industry buzzword or new narrative experience?* Ryan [4] presents four arguments about what should and should not be transmedia storytelling. In the first argument, the author comments that transmedia is not a simple adaptation. Based on Jenkins, Ryan ([4], p. 2) states that what differentiates adaptation from transmedia storytelling "lies in the fact that adaptation tries (with greater or lesser success) to tell the same story in a different medium, while transmedia storytelling tells different stories about a given storyworld." Second argument for Ryan is that transmedia storytelling presents similarities with Saint-Gelais's concept of transfictionality, but they keep different meanings, which will be better distinguished in the final part of this article. Third, Ryan (ibid., p. 3) declares that "our concept of transmedia storytelling should not include the use of various media platforms to advertise a certain narrative product." After all, products generated to promote a certain work do not necessarily add elements to fictional universe. Finally, the fourth argument is: transmedia storytelling should not be confused with the concept of multimodal narration. This is because this last concept is linked to the idea of several types of signs telling a narrative. As for example in the use of images and texts in children's books, or in the union of music and theater in the opera. Ryan explains the difference between transmedia storytelling and multimodal narration in the following passage:

> While in multimodal narration the different semiotic channels are organically connected, so that the story would make no sense, or at least lose a great deal of its appeal, if one types of signs was disabled, in transmedia storytelling the different semiotic or media objects are autonomous entities that can be consumed separately from each other, and there is no need to consume them all: the user can explore the database more or less thoroughly ([3], p. 4).

In order to progress in our discussion, we choose the seminal definition of Jenkins [9]: transmedia storytelling "represents a process where integral elements of a fiction get dispersed systematically across multiple delivery channels for the purpose of creating a unified and coordinated entertainment experience. Ideally, each medium makes it own unique contribution to the unfolding of the story". However, we cannot ignore Ryan's lucid critiques [2]. She points out that the transmedia process can differ in the way it is constituted and can be understood as a narrative form and/or only as a marketing strategy. The author names "snowball" the transmedia storytelling scheme, which begins with a work that has its narrative expanded through a spontaneous production by fans and other authors. Diversely, the type "project transmedia" would be a more recent practice. In this case, a certain fictional universe is conceived from the outset as a transmedia project. This is, as a narrative that will be created from many media, each one contributing with a part of the whole story. In these cases, there is an explicit interest in marketing the same narrative world that is complemented by various media. Finally, we endorse the idea that the transmedia storytelling is characterized by approaching distinct media for the constitution of a narrative whole, each of which contributes, albeit autonomously, with new elements for the construction of a single diegetic world.

3 Why Is the Concept of Transfictionality Fascinating?

One of the most intriguing aspects of fiction is the ability to construct universes that can be exploited in an unlimited way. There are no fixed boundaries for fiction. It can be as vast and detailed as life is. This inexhaustible ability to compose a diegetic universe was named by Doležel [10] of "indeterminate domain of fiction." In other words, it is the infinite potential of set of elements that create a fictional world. Transfictionality acts precisely in this insatiable narrative desire in which the boundaries of a fiction are not capable of containing possible diegetic relations with others.

Transfictionality concept was examined in-depth by the Canadian researcher Saint-Gelais in his book *Figures Transfuges: transfictionalité et ses enjeux* [3]. Although the author has developed his study within the literature, his contributions are equally pertinent for understanding fictional flows and displacements in other expressive forms. In an interview with Vox Poetique magazine [11], Saint-Gelais states:

> There is transfictionality when two or more texts "share" fictitious elements (i.e., making reference jointly), whether these elements are characters, (sequences of) events or fictional worlds; as for the "texts", it can be as well of texts in the strict sense (novels, news, but also essays in certain cases) as of films, comics, TV episodes, etc.[3] [11].

Therefore, according to him, transfiction designates the relations between different fictions, which share elements of the same diegetic world. As we can see, the author applies the word "text" in the broad sense of any form of discourse, be it textual, sound, visual, or audiovisual. Thus, transfictionality encompasses any and all forms of discourse, whether literary or not. In this way, there is transfictionality when a certain "text" shares fictional elements with other "text(s)", whether they belong to the same or different media.

Saint-Gelais develops the transfictionality definition from Doležel reflections (1998) [10] on "postmodern rewriting", that is the literary practice of re-elaborating fictional texts through the development of their diegetic elements in other texts, through transposition, modification or expansion. Doležel, in turn, engender his studies of "postmodern rewriting" based on Gerard Genette's concept of transtextuality [12].

Genette undertook an important theoretical classification, generating very useful concepts for literature studies, but also applicable to other media. Thus, extending dialogism's notions, from Bakhtin, Genette ([12], p. 9) proposes the term *transtextuality*, defining it as "everything that puts a text in relation to other texts, whether this relation is manifest or secret." Genette distinguishes types of relations between texts, of which we highlight hypertextuality: the derivation of one text (hypertext) from another (hypotext). In this category there are strategies such as parody (textual transformation with ludic function) and pastiche (textual imitation with ludic function).

---

[3] Original text: "Il y a transfictionnalité lorsque deux textes ou davantage «partagent» des éléments fictifs (c'est-à-dire, y font conjointement référence), que ces éléments soient des personnages, des (séquences d') événements ou des mondes fictifs; quant aux «textes», il peut s'agir aussi bien de textes au sens strict (romans, nouvelles, mais aussi essais dans certains cas) que de films, bandes dessinées, épisodes télé, etc.".

Doležel [10] expands Genette's reflections on hypertextuality and states: "literary works are linked not only to the level of texture but also, and not less importantly, on the level of fictional worlds." (1998, p. 202) Therefore, the author is more interested in fictional than in narrative relations. As Saint-Gelais [4] reminds us: "transfictionality and hypertextuality do not cover exactly the same domains." (2011, p. 10). If hypertext establishes imitation and transformation (parody, pastiche), transfiction implies a migration of diegetic elements. Thus, transfictionality can also be understood as a particular form of transtextuality, which is established by sharing fictional elements.

Prequels, sequels, adaptations, spin off, crossover, alternative versions, counter-fictions, fanfictions are some recurring forms of transfictionality in popular culture. These are distinct fictional works (sometimes in different media) that create diegetic intersections, sharing fictional elements. Following the strategies already identified by Doležel and discussed by Saint-Gelais, Ryan [3] writes that transfictionality consists of three operations: "expansion (such as prequels and sequels), modification (such as changing the ending of a story and consequently the fate of characters), and the transposition of plot into a new setting, such as Greek myth being transported into the modern world." (2015, p. 3)

Among the transfictional expansive operations, one of the most common is the migration of characters, who transpose the frontiers of the original work to inhabit others. Recognized in the media industry as spin off, this transfictional strategy is characterized by the derivation of a work from diegetic elements belonging to another. As an example of monomedia transfictionality we can quote the relations between television series *Breaking Bad* (AMC, 2008–2013) and *Better Call Saul* (AMC, 2015-). Although they are autonomous and independent, the series keep a diegetic connection since they share characters, places, and events. *Better Call Saul* appropriates the *Breaking Bad* character Saul to create an extension of the original narrative. Although Saul occupies different diegetic status (in *Breaking Bad* he is secondary and in *Better Call Saul* he is the protagonist) it is the same character that has its narrative arc developed and extended in the derived series.

Another example of transfictionality, this time involving two distinct media (TV and Cinema), is the relation between the film *Psyco* (Alfred Hitchcok, 1960) and the television series *Bates Motel* (A&E, 2013–2017). Although they present big differences, both diegetic universes are linked through the characters Norman Bates, Norma Bates (his mother), and Bates Motel (central place in the narrative development of film, and series). Created 53 years later, the television series takes various elements of the film universe to expand its fiction, developing the previous life of Norman Bates (adolescence and early adult life), thus functioning as a prequel of the film. However, the relations between the two fictional works are more complex than they appear. After all, the character of Norman Bates teenager (series) lives in a contemporary time, in which he uses, for example, modern equipment such as cell phones, iPods, and the Internet. The Norman Bates adult (film) lives in the 1950s, immersed in a technological context and in a setting (scenery and costumes) typical of the fifties. The inconsistencies between series and film reveal a certain detachment from their transfictional relations.

According to Saint-Gelais [4], "transfictionality necessarily leads to a crossing and therefore, at the same time, to a rupture and a contact, and the contact comes to suture, but never perfectly, that which has been broken." (2011, pp. 23–24).[4]

According to Boni [13], from a fictional perspective, the *Bates Motel* series represents "a transfictional expansion of a world in the mode of hyperdiegese."[5] In this sense, if we evaluate the whole *Psyco* transfictional universe[6], we can agree with Boni when she says that the film "is the top of the iceberg, while the many sequels and prequels, including the *Bates Motel*, are the hidden portions, yet ready to emerge with each new media incarnation." (2016, p. 11). The transfictionality notion is often associated with the iceberg figure to illustrate the fascinating "indeterminate domain of fiction", allowing us think of the existence of a diegetic hidden part that remains latent. In transfictional logic, a "text" is nothing more than the top of a diegetic iceberg, from which we access only a fraction of a potentially larger universe.

4 Perspectives: Transmedia + Transfictionality

Although they are distinct concepts, transmedia storytelling and transfictionality have gained importance in the current media culture. They can be seen as strategies that act through fictional, narrative and/or media connections and displacements, enhancing the symbolic production of humanity. We have seen that there is transfictionality when two or more "texts" share fictional elements, such as characters, events, objects, places, etc., increasing the original diegetic universe. Although it has been more extensively studied in the literature, transfictionality can be identified in any form of discourse, and may even involve "texts" of different media. In Ryan's words [2], transfictionality "refers to the migration of fictional entities across different texts, but these texts may belong [or not] to the same medium [...]" (2013, p. 365). Transmedia storytelling, in turn, implies the combining of different media for the composition of a narrative whole. Thus, as Ryan points out (ibid., p. 366), "transmedia storytelling can be regarded as a special case of transfictionality – a transfictionality that operates across many different media."

It is difficult to establish a rigid boundary between transfictionality and transmedia storytelling. Discerning these strategies can become a daunting task. We know that

---

[4] Original texte: "La transfictionalité entraine forcement une traversée, et donc à la fois une rupture et un contact, le second venant suturer, mais jamais parfaitement, ce qui la première a separe." ([4], pp. 23–24).

[5] In his *cult culture* studies, Matt Hills adopts the term *hyperdiegesis* to designate "the creation of a vast and detailed narrative space, only a fraction of which is ever directly seen or encountered within the text, but which nevertheless appears to operate according to principles of internal logic and extension". Matt Hills, Fan Cultures, Londres, New York, Routledge, coll. «Sussex studies in culture and communication», 2002, p. 104 [13].

[6] The *Psyco* transfictional universe comprises a wide variety of works, such as the original Hitchcock's film, the sequels *Psyco II* (Richard, Franklin, 1983) and *Psyco III* (Anthony Perkins, 1986), the prequel *Psyco IV* (Mick Garris, 1990), the remake *Psycho* (Gus Van Sant, 1998), the telefilm *Bates Motel* (NBC, 1987), the TV series *Bates Motel* (A&E, 2013–2017), as well as other productions such as books and graphic novels. Available at: https://en.wikipedia.org/wiki/Psyco_(franchise) (Accessed: 28 January 2019).

concepts are created to identify and to investigate complex objects with clarity and discernment. Although different, these concepts are not mutually exclusive. In many cases, they can illuminate distinct faces of the same phenomenon. When we approach narrative relations between distinct works from a fictional perspective, we are in the field of transfictionality. When we observe the same event from the media relation's angle, we are on transmedia domain.

The assembly of fictional works across different media in a single narrative system has been a very recurrent strategy in popular culture. The value of *transmedia transfictionality* is in the possibility of transcending the original fiction limits, expanding its universe, its events and characters by different media and languages. The transmedia transfictionality concerns the heterogeneous construction of a fictional world and, at the same time, the activation of different language and media. The main condition for an object to be classified as transmedia transfictionality is the verification of a qualitative fictional narrative system composed by different media, each one presenting certain parts and ways of telling stories. Extracompositional flows across "texts" and media involve complex issues, such as narratological, communicational, technological and marketing efforts. Undoubtedly, an intricate phenomenon that finds his potential in convergence culture and provokes attention of public and scholars from different fields of knowledge.

References

1. Jenkins, H.: Convergence Culture. New York University Press, New York (2016)
2. Ryan, M.: Transmedial storytelling and transfictionality. Poet. Today **34**(3), 361–388 (2013). https://doi.org/10.1215/03335372-2325250. Accessed 28 Jan 2019
3. Ryan, M.: Transmedia storyworlds: industry buzzword or new narrative experience? Storyworlds: J. Narrat. Stud. **7**(2), 1–19 (2015). https://muse.jhu.edu/article/602197. Accessed 28 Jan 2019
4. Saint-Gelais, R.: Fictions transfuges: la transfictionalité et ses enjeux. Éditions du Seuil, Paris (2011)
5. Flusser, V.: Communicology: Reflections on the Future. Martins Fontes, São Paulo (2015). (in Portuguese)
6. Eco, U.: Six Walks in the Fictional Woods. Harvard University Press, Cambridge (1994)
7. Kinder, M.: Playing with Power in Movies, Television, and Video Games: From Muppet Babies to Teenage Mutant Ninja Turtles. University of California, Berkeley (1991)
8. Bolter, J., Grusin, R.: Remediation: Understanding New Media. MIT Press, Cambridge (1999)
9. Jenkins, H.: Transmedia storytelling 101 (2017). http://henryjenkins.org/blog/2007/03/transmedia_storytelling_101.html. Accessed 20 Dec 2018
10. Doležel, L.: Heterocosmica: Fiction and Possible Worlds. John Hopkins University Press, Baltimore (1998)
11. Saint-Gelais, R.: Fictions transfuges: la transfictionnalité et ses enjeux. Vox Poetica, 20 April 2012. http://www.vox-poetica.org/entretiens/intStGelais.html. Accessed 15 Dec 2018
12. Genette, G.: Palimpsests: Literature in the Second Degree. Viva Voz, Belo Horizonte (2010)
13. Boni, M.: 'Psycho/Bates Motel: hyperdiégèse et réactivation sélective'. Intermédialités, 28–29 (2016). https://doi.org/10.7202/1041077ar. Accessed: 20 Jan 2019

Generating Graphic Representations of Spoken Interactions from Journalistic Data

Dimitrios Mourouzidis[1], Vasilios Floros[1],
and Christina Alexandris[1,2,3(✉)]

[1] National and Kapodistrian University of Athens, Athens, Greece
mourouzidisd@gmail.com, florosbas2002@yahoo.gr,
calexandris@gs.uoa.gr
[2] European Communication Institute (ECI),
Danube University Krems, Krems, Austria
[3] National and Technical University of Athens, Athens, Greece

Abstract. Generated distinct types of graphic patterns depicting the discourse structure of spoken journalistic texts - interviews or discussions, contribute to a user-independent evaluation of spoken Human-Human conversation and interaction. Distinct types of the graphic representation also function as visual representations of Cognitive Bias. The distinct types of generated graphic representations and values allow the identification of additional, "hidden," Illocutionary Acts, beyond the defined framework of the spoken conversation and interaction.

Keywords: Spoken journalistic texts · Spoken interaction · Dialog flow · Graphic representations · Cognitive bias

1 Introduction

Generating distinct types of graphic patterns depicting the discourse structure of spoken journalistic texts targets to contribute to a user-independent evaluation of spoken Human-Human conversation and interaction. The generated types of graphic patterns describing the discourse structure of an interview or discussion function as visual aids for the evaluation of pragmatic features and the detection of Cognitive Bias. Furthermore, the graphic patterns generated may also enable the identification of additional, "hidden," Illocutionary Acts beyond the defined framework of the spoken conversation and interaction. The distinct types of graphic patterns and visual representations contribute to the evaluation of spoken political and journalistic texts such as interviews, live conversations in the Media, as well as discussions in Parliament, focusing in the discourse component of spoken political and journalistic texts.

The graphic patterns and visual representations are based on the output of an interactive annotation tool for spoken journalistic texts presented in previous research [2]. Specifically, in the interactive annotation tool [2], incoming texts to be processed constitute transcribed data from journalistic texts. The annotation tool was designed to operate with most commercial transcription tools, some of which are available online. The development of the tool is based on data and observations provided by professional

© Springer Nature Switzerland AG 2019
M. Kurosu (Ed.): HCII 2019, LNCS 11566, pp. 559–570, 2019.
https://doi.org/10.1007/978-3-030-22646-6_42

journalists (European Communication Institute, Program M.A in Quality Journalism and Digital Technologies, Danube University at Krems, Athena- Research and Innovation Center in Information, Communication and Knowledge Technologies, Athens - Institution of Promotion of Journalism Ath.Vas. Botsi, Athens and the National and Technical University of Athens, Greece). Since processing speed and the option of re-usability in multiple languages of the written and spoken political and journalistic texts constitutes a basic target of the proposed approach, strategies typically employed in the construction of Spoken Dialog Systems, such as keyword processing in the form of topic detection, were adapted in the developed annotation tool. The functions of the designed and constructed interactive annotation tool [2] include providing the User-Journalist with (a) the tracked indications of the topics handled in the interview or discussion and (b) the graphic pattern of the discourse structure of the interview or discussion. Furthermore, these functions facilitate the comparison between discourse structures of conversations and interviews with similar topics or the same participants/ participant.

2   User Interaction and Relation Types

2.1   Interactive Registration of Relation Types

In the above-stated process of interactive annotation [1, 2], the "Identify Topic" command allows the content of answers, responses and reactions to be checked in respect to the question asked or issue addressed. Specifically, topics in respect to the question asked or issue addressed by the interviewer or moderator are defined at a local level with the activation of the "Identify Topic" command. Topics, treated as local variables, are registered and tracked. Assistance in choice of topic is provided to the user with the automatic signalization of nouns. Nouns are signalized by the Stanford POS Tagger in each turn taken by the speakers in the respective segment in the dialog structure [1]. The use of the registered and tracked keywords, treated as local variables, is crucial for the signalization of each topic and the relations between topics, since automatic Rhetorical Structure Theory (RST) analysis procedures [18, 26] usually involves larger (written) texts and may not produce the required results.

Relation types between topics are determined by the user by activating the "Identify Relation" command. We note that in the domain of journalistic texts, the relations between topics cannot be strictly semantic: automatic processes may result to errors. The user chooses among four available relations between the topic of the question or issue addressed with the topic of the respective response or reaction [2]: "Repetition", "Association", "Generalization" or "Topic Switch".

The "Repetition" relation ("REP" tag) involves the repetition of the same word or synonym and corresponds to the generation of the shortest distance between defined topics, referred to as "Distance 1". A characteristic example is "Britain"-"the UK" [1]. The "Association" relation ("ASOC" tag) is often defined by the user's beliefs and world knowledge, for example, in the relation between "propaganda"-"social-media" [1]. The "Association" relation is represented as a longer line to the next word-node, corresponding to "Distance 2". The generation of the longest distance between defined topics,

"Distance 3", corresponds to the "Generalization" relation ("GEN" tag). The "Generalization" relation is also defined by the user's world knowledge, however, in many cases, this relation can be evaluated with a lexicon or Wordnet, as in the example "police"-"security" [1]. The "Topic Switch" relation ("SWITCH" tag) is used when no evident semantic relations are identified between topics and the relation is perceived as a change (or switch) of topic, for example, in the relation between "security" and "entrepreneurship" [1]."Topic Switch" generates a break in the sequence of topics [1, 2].

Observed differences between identified topic relations among some journalists that are non-native speakers of English [1] (especially in respect to "ASOC" and "SWITCH") may in some cases be attributed to lack of world knowledge of the language community concerned [8, 15, 22]. As noted in previous research [1], these observations imply that the international public may often perceive and receive different and/or incomplete information in respect to evaluating conversation and interaction [3, 11, 16, 25].

2.2   Relation Types and Graphic Representation

The graphic pattern of the discourse structure concerning the interview or discussion is based on the representation of the selected local topics constituting the path of the user's choices and interaction. In particular, path generation of the interaction is modeled and implemented based on user interactions registered in spoken dialog systems (in the domains of consumer complaints and mobile phone services call centers) [7, 14]. A visual representation from the user's interaction is generated, tracking the corresponding selected keywords in the dialog flow. In the present application, the same model is applied for tracking topics and generating models in transcribed spoken journalistic texts [1, 2].

With the interactive generation of registered paths, similar to paths with generated sequences of recognized keywords [7, 14] a keyword (topic) may be repeated ("Repetition" relation) or related to a more general concept (or global variable) [10] ("Generalization" relation) or related to keywords (topics) concerning similar functions ("Association" relation). Similarly to the domain of spoken dialog systems, a keyword involving a new command or function is registered as a new topic ("Topic Switch" relation). Subsequently, the "path" of interaction is generated with the sequence of topics chosen by the user and the perceived relations between them. The generated "path" of interaction forms distinctive visual representations according to its content. Furthermore, topics and words generating diverse reactions and choices from different users may result to the generation of different forms of generated graphic representations for the same conversation or interaction.

3   Evaluation and Cognitive Bias

Generated graphic patterns contribute to a user-independent evaluation of spoken Human-Human conversation and interaction [1], similarly to user-independent evaluation of spoken dialog systems [23], where speed and correctness are of crucial importance [10]. In spoken dialog systems, varying degrees of user's familiarity with dialog systems or user-friendly interfaces in spoken interaction result to different perceptions of successful interactions. Thus, occasional errors may be "forgiven" by the user [6, 13]. Specifically, errors in spoken input or a longer duration of interaction due to complications in the dialog may not always correspond to negative evaluation. In a similar manner, varying degrees of familiarity and bias with topics discussed in spoken journalistic texts result to different perceptions of successful conversations or debates and any complications or mistakes can be "forgiven" by the user [1].

The content and form of the generated graphic representations can contribute in depicting the degree in which all topics are addressed as well as what topics are avoided. Topics introduced in the discussion or interview are avoided by speakers either by changing a topic or by persisting to address the same topic. The degree in which all topics are addressed, as well as what topics are avoided, are evident in the form of the generated graphic representation. For example, multiple breaks in the generated graphic representation correspond to multiple instances of topic switch and the ("New Topic" relation. Furthermore, the generated graphic representation may also depict how participants may be lead or even forced into addressing a topic – by association or generalization (the "Association" and the "Generalization" relations respectively) [1].

The content and form of the generated graphic representations (presented in the following section) may be considered as visual representations of Cognitive Bias [1], where the perceived relations-distances between word-topics perceived by the user are related to Lexical Bias [19]. Additionally, the graphic representations allow the determination of the participants in the conversation or interview who were successful in their spoken interaction and the participants who were less successful. This output targets to by-pass Confidence Bias [9] of users-participants and evaluators [1].

4 Form of Generated Graphic Representations

4.1 Present Approach

As described above, the generated graphic representation is based on the relations of the topics to each other, including distances from one word to another. In previous research [1, 2], Distances 1, 2 and 3 were depicted as vertical lines from top to bottom, in the case of the generation of a tree-like structure, or as horizontal lines from left to right, in the case of the generation of a graph. Topic switches were depicted as breaks in the continuous flow of the generated graphic representation, generating a new, disconnected point or node. This approach envisioned a possible further development with graphic forms similar to discourse trees [5, 12], however, it presented difficulties in matching points of the generated structure to the respective segments of the spoken text.

The present approach targets to allow the alignment of the generated graphic representation with the respective segments of the spoken text, facilitating a possible integration in transcription tools.

Similarly to the approaches presented in previous research [1, 2], the length of the lines between points corresponding to topics depends on the type of distance to the next word-node, with the shortest line corresponding to the relation of "Repetition", related to Distance 1 and the longest line corresponding to the relation of "Generalization", Distance 3.

In the present application, Distances 1, 2 and 3 correspond to the respective values "1", "2" and "3" (y = 1, y = 2 and y = 3) depicted in the generated graphic representation. The "Topic Switch" relation is assigned value "−1" (Fig. 1).

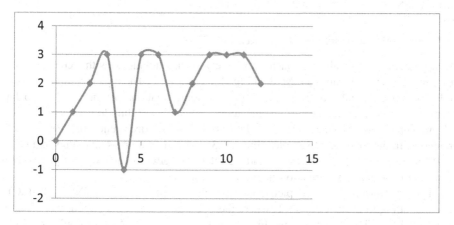

Fig. 1. Distances and values between topics.

The starting point of the graphic representation of the spoken interaction depicted in Fig. 1 is point zero in the time frame (x), where (x, y) = (0, 0). For the 1st second of spoken interaction there is an occurrence of two (2) keywords and one "Repetition" relation between them, represented as value "1" in the y axis (y), where (REP): 1, corresponding to point (1, 1).

From the 1st to the 2nd second (y = 2) of spoken interaction, the 3rd keyword demonstrates an "Association" relation with the previous, 2nd keyword, represented as value "2" in the y axis (y), where (ASOC): 2, corresponding to point (2, 2).

Until the 3rd second of spoken interaction, there is one more 4rth keyword and its relation with the previous, 3rd keyword is an "Generalization" relation, represented as value "3" in the y axis (y), where (GEN): 3, corresponding to point (3, 3).

In the 4rth second of spoken interaction, the 5th keyword demonstrates a "New Topic" relation with the previous, 4rth keyword, represented as value "−1" in the y axis (y), (NEW TOPIC): −1, corresponding to point (4, −1).

Two "Generalization" relations follow in the 5th second and 6th second of spoken interaction, where the relation between the 6th keyword and the previous, 5th keyword and the following 7th keyword is represented as value "3" in the y axis (y), where (GEN): 3, corresponding to points (5, 3) and (6, 3).

In the 7th second of spoken interaction, the 8th keyword there is a "Repetition" relation to the previous, 7th keyword, represented as value "1" in the y axis (y), where (REP): 1, corresponding to point (7, 1). In the 8th second of spoken interaction, the 9th keyword is related to the previous 8th keyword with an "Association" relation, represented as value "2" in the y axis (y), where (ASOC): 2, corresponding to point (8, 2).

A sequence of three "Generalization" relations follow in the 9th to 11th second of spoken interaction, where the relation between the 10th keyword and the previous, 9th keyword and the following 11th and 12th keywords is represented as value "3" in the y axis (y), where (GEN): 3, corresponding to points (9, 3), (10, 3) and (11, 3).

Finally, in the 12th second of spoken interaction, there is one more 13th keyword and its relation with the previous, 12th keyword is an "Association" relation between them (ASSOC): 2, corresponding to point (12, 2).

4.2   Graphic Representation and Relation Type

Dialog segments typically demonstrate a variety of topic relations, with a characteristic example shown in the above-described Fig. 1 and in Fig. 2. The typical variety of topic relations concerns all - or almost all- types of topic relations. Empirical data so far demonstrates a predominance of "Association" relations, a slightly lower occurrence of "New Topic" and "Generalization" relations and a low occurrence of "Repetition" relations. In the following examples (Figs. 2, 3, 4, 5 and 6) we present dialog segments of 12 s (12 s) with 13 word-topics and 12 relations between each word-topic, where x = time in secs and y = relation between two topics.

The example in Fig. 2 depicts two (2) "New Topic" relations (NEW TOPIC), corresponding to Distance y = −1, where there is a switch of topic (where y = −1 and x = {3, 12}). The example in Fig. 2 includes two (2) "Repetition" relations (REP) (where y = 1, και x = {7, 10}), five (5) "Association" relations (ASOC) (where y = 2 and x = {2, 5, 8, 9}) and three (3) "Generalization" relations (GEN), where y = 3 and x = {1, 4, 6}.

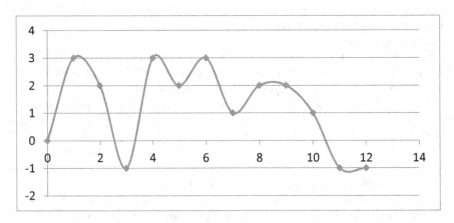

Fig. 2. Typical form of generated graphical representation.

4.3   Graphic Representation of "Repetition" Relations

In contrary to the examples presented in Figs. 1 and 2, a remarkable predominance of specific types of relations results to the generation of characteristic types of graphic representations. As previously described above, the overall shape of the generated graphic representation is dependent on the mostly occurring relation types in the discourse structure of the interview or discussion.

A high frequency of "Repetition" relations is presented in Fig. 3, where seven (7) "Repetition" relations are registered with y = 1 and x = {1, 3, 5, 6, 7, 9, 11, 12}. The same topic is repeated between the points in the above-presented x values.

The graphic representation in Fig. 3 demonstrates a development around the value y = 1 level.

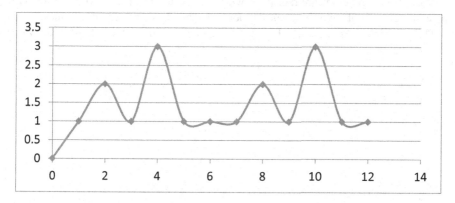

Fig. 3. Generated graphical representation with a "Repetition" relation.

4.4 Graphic Representation of "Association" Relations

The generation of a graphic representation of multiple high peaks is illustrated in the example in Fig. 4, corresponding to transcripts of available online interviews. The characteristic plateau-like shape of the peaks in the generated graphic representation is affected by the relatively high percentage of "Association" relations on the value y = 2 level. The present example (Fig. 4) depicts twelve (12) relations, several of which are "Association" (ASOC) relations, where y = 2 and x = {2, 5, 6, 8, 9, 10}.

The graphic representation in Fig. 4 demonstrates a development around the value y = 2 level.

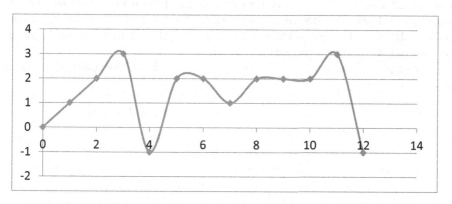

Fig. 4. Generated graphical representation with multiple "Association" relations.

4.5   Graphic Representation of "Topic Switch"

The generation of a graphic representation of many separate sharp peaks is illustrated in the following example in Fig. 5, corresponding to transcripts of available online interviews. In particular, the overall shape of the generated graphic representation is affected by the relatively high percentage of "Topic Switch" relations, creating a characteristic sequence of sharp peaks.

A high frequency of "New Topic" relations is presented in Fig. 4, where eight (8) "New Topic" relations are registered with y = −1, for x = {1, 3, 5, 6, 7, 9, 11, 12}. There is a change of topic between the points in the above-presented x values.

The graphic representation in Fig. 5 demonstrates multiple sharp drops in the value y = −1 level.

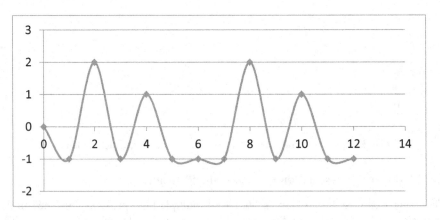

Fig. 5. Generated graphical representation with multiple "Topic Switch" relations.

4.6   Graphic Representation of "Generalization" Relations

The generation of a graphic representation of characteristically high peaks is illustrated in the example in Fig. 6, corresponding to transcripts of available online interviews. The characteristic plateau-like shape of the peaks in the generated graphic representation is affected by the relatively high percentage of "Generalization" relations on value y = 3 level. The present example (Fig. 6) depicts six (6) "Generalization" (GEN) relations, where y = 3 and x = {3, 4, 5, 6, 9, 10, 11} in which the "Generalization" (GEN) relation is repeated six (6) times.

The graphic representation in Fig. 6 demonstrates a development around the value y = 3 level.

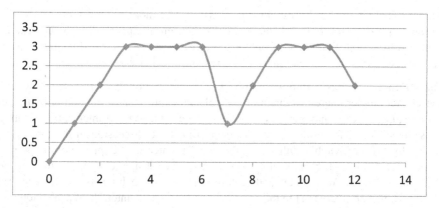

Fig. 6. Generated graphical representation with multiple "Generalization" relations.

5   Detecting Pointers to Speaker Intentions

The above-described graphic representations and values enable the evaluation of the behavior of speakers-participants, depicting Cognitive Bias and may also serve for by-passing Confidence Bias of the user-evaluator of the recorded and transcribed discussion or interview. Furthermore, the above-described graphic representations and values also allow the identification and detection of additional, "hidden" Illocutionary Acts not restricted to "Obtaining Information Asked" or "Providing Information Asked", as defined by the framework of the interview or discussion.

Speech Acts performed by one or multiple speakers-participants usually involve complex Illocutionary Acts beyond the defined framework of the interaction. This feature differentiates Speech Acts in two-party or multiparty discussions or interviews from task-specific dialogs [20] and typical collaborative dialogs [21, 24]. In two-party or multiparty discussions or interviews, the Illocutionary Act [4, 17] performed by the Speakers may not be restricted to "Obtaining Information Asked" or "Providing Information Asked" in the spoken interaction concerned and may involve other or additional intentions regarding the presence of the speakers-participants and their role in the interview or discussion. In particular, the Illocutionary Acts not restricted to "Obtaining Information Asked" or "Providing Information Asked" may be related to one or more categories of Speech Acts defining less explicitly expressed Speaker intentions. Here, we present three frequently detected categories of pointers to "hidden" Speech Acts, namely "Presence", "Express Policy" and "Make Impression". We note that all three Speech Act pointers may be connected to each other and may even occur at the same time. The "Make Impression" Speech Act pointer is distinguished from the other two Speech Act pointer since it is identifiable on the Paralinguistic Level.

The "Presence" Pointer. "Presence" Speech Act pointer is identified by the Speaker's reluctance to answer questions, avoidance of topics, or a polite or symbolic presence in the discussion or interview but not an active participation. Besides the Speaker's silence (Silence/No Answer) as response to questions or statements, a "Presence" pointer is signalized by remaining in the same "safe" topic by repeating the same subject ("Repetition") or by introducing a "safer" and more general topic ("Generalization") or a different topic ("Topic Switch"). "Presence" Speech Act pointers can be identified by a high frequency of one or more of the above-described relations, especially in combination with instances of no response (Silence/No Answer).

The "Express Policy" Pointer. With the "Express Policy" additional "hidden" Speech Act pointer, there is a direct or even blatant expression of opinion or policy. In this case, the Speaker may persist on discussing the same topic of interest by repeating the same subject ("Repetition") or may try to direct the discussion in the topic(s) or interest by "Topic Switch". Unlike the "Presence" pointer, the "Express Policy" pointer is characterized by a higher level of complexity, since it may contain features of the "Presence" Speech Act pointer and features of the "Make Impression" Speech Act pointer. However, in contrast to the case of the "Presence" pointer, the repeated topic(s) or the topics introduced are all - or almost all- semantically or associatively related. Although, as previously described, the "Express Policy" pointer may be related to the "Make Impression" Speech Act pointer, the "Express Policy" Speech Act pointer does not necessarily entail the creation of tension in the discussion or interview.

The "Make Impression" Pointer. With the "Make Impression" Speech Act pointer, the Speaker purposefully creates tension in the interview or discussion. The "Make Impression" pointer is characterized by any of the features of the "Presence" or "Express Policy" Speech Acts pointer. Additionally, the "Make Impression" pointer can also be distinguished from the previous Speech Act pointers in respect to features in the paralinguistic level of one (or all) of the Speakers, including rise of amplitude, prosodic emphasis and other prosodic features, gestures and facial expressions.

6 Conclusions and Further Research

The present application targets to assist evaluation and decision-making process in respect to discussions and interviews in the Media, providing a graphic representation of the discourse structure and aiming to by-pass Cognitive Bias of the user-evaluator. The predominate types of relations, if applicable, are easily identified by the y level value around which the graphic representation is developed.

The time frame generation of the linear structure allows the graphic representation to be presented in conjunction with the parallel depiction of speech signals and transcribed texts, a typical feature of most transcription tools.

Furthermore, the above-described graphic representations and values enable the evaluation of the behavior of speakers-participants, allowing the identification and detection of additional, "hidden" Illocutionary Acts not restricted to "Obtaining Information Asked" or "Providing Information Asked" framework defined by the interview or discussion. In the light of the above, the present application may also be adapted to additional domains, such as education-training and virtual negotiators, since it concerns the evaluation of a user's familiarity, perception and world knowledge. The alignment of the generated graphic representation with the respective segments of the spoken text enable a possible integration of the present application in existing transcription tools.

References

1. Alexandris, C.: Measuring cognitive bias in spoken interaction and conversation: generating visual representations. In: Beyond Machine Intelligence: Understanding Cognitive Bias and Humanity for Well-Being AI Papers from the AAAI Spring Symposium, Stanford University, Technical Report SS-18-03, pp. 204–206. AAAI Press, Palo Alto (2018)
2. Alexandris, C., Nottas, M., Cambourakis, G.: Interactive evaluation of pragmatic features in spoken journalistic texts. In: Kurosu, M. (ed.) HCI 2015. LNCS, vol. 9171, pp. 259–268. Springer, Cham (2015). https://doi.org/10.1007/978-3-319-21006-3_26
3. Alexandris, C.: English, German and the international "semi-professional" translator: a morphological approach to implied connotative features. J. Lang. Transl. **11**(2), 7–46 (2010)
4. Austin, J.L.: How to Do Things with Words (eds. by, J.O. Urmson, M. Sbisà), 2nd edn. University Press, Oxford Paperbacks, Oxford (1962/1976)
5. Carlson, L., Marcu, D., Okurowski, M.E.: Building a discourse-tagged corpus in the framework of rhetorical structure theory. In: Proceedings of the 2nd SIGDIAL Workshop on Discourse and Dialogue, Eurospeech 2001, Denmark, September 2001 (2001)
6. Cohen, P., et al.: Quickset: multimodal interaction for distributed applications. In: Proceedings of the 5th ACM International Multimedia Conference, Seattle, Washington, pp. 31–40. Association for Computing Machinery (ACM) (1997)
7. Floros, V., Mourouzidis, D.: Multiple task management in a dialog system for call centers. Master's thesis, Department of Informatics and Telecommunications, National University of Athens, Greece (2016)
8. Hatim, B.: Communication Across Cultures: Translation Theory and Contrastive Text Linguistics. University of Exeter Press, Exeter (1997)
9. Hilbert, M.: Toward a synthesis of cognitive biases: how noisy information processing can bias human decision making. Psychol. Bull. **138**(2), 211–237 (2012)
10. Lewis, J.R.: Introduction to Practical Speech User Interface Design for Interactive Voice Response Applications. IBM Software Group, USA, Tutorial T09 presented at HCI 2009 San Diego, CA, USA (2009)
11. Ma, J.: A comparative analysis of the ambiguity resolution of two English-Chinese MT approaches: RBMT and SMT. Dalian Univ. Technol. J. **31**(3), 114–119 (2010)
12. Marcu, D.: Discourse trees are good indicators of importance in text. In: Mani, I., Maybury, M. (eds.) Advances in Automatic Text Summarization, pp. 123–136. The MIT Press, Cambridge (1999)
13. Nass, C., Brave, S.: Wired for Speech: How Voice Activates and Advances the Human-Computer Relationship. The MIT Press, Cambridge (2005)
14. Nottas, M., Alexandris, C, Tsopanoglou, A., Bakamidis, S.: A hybrid approach to dialog input in the citzenshield dialog system for consumer complaints. In: Proceedings of HCI 2007, Beijing, People's Republic of China (2007)
15. Paltridge, B.: Discourse Analysis: An Introduction. Bloomsbury Publishing, London (2012)
16. Pan, Y.: Politeness in Chinese Face-to-Face Interaction. Advances in Discourse Processes Series, vol. 67. Ablex Publishing Corporation, Stamford (2000)
17. Searle, J.R.: Speech Acts: An Essay in the Philosophy of Language. Cambridge University Press, Cambridge, MA (1969)
18. Stede, M., Taboada, M., Das, D.: Annotation Guidelines for Rhetorical Structure. Manuscript. University of Potsdam and Simon Fraser University, March 2017 (2017)
19. Trofimova, I.: Observer bias: an interaction of temperament traits with biases in the semantic perception of lexical material. PLoSONE **9**(1), e85677 (2014)

20. Tung, T., Gomez, R., Kawahara, T., Matsuyama, T.: Multi-party human-machine interaction using a smart multimodal digital signage. In: Kurosu, M. (ed.) Human-Computer Interaction. Interaction Modalities and Techniques, Lecture Notes in Computer Science, vol. 8007, pp. 408–415. Springer, Heidelberg (2013). https://doi.org/10.1007/978-3-642-39330-3_43

21. Wang, H., Gailliot, A., Hyden, D., Lietzenmayer, R.: A knowledge elicitation study for collaborative dialogue strategies used to handle uncertainties in speech communication while using GIS. In: Kurosu, M. (ed.) HCI 2013. LNCS, vol. 8007, pp. 135–144. Springer, Heidelberg (2013). https://doi.org/10.1007/978-3-642-39330-3_15

22. Wardhaugh, R.: An Introduction to Sociolinguistics, 2nd edn. Blackwell, Oxford (1992)

23. Williams, J.D., Asadi, K., Zweig, G.: Hybrid Code Networks: practical and efficient end-to-end dialog control with supervised and reinforcement learning. In: Proceedings of the 55th Annual Meeting of the Association for Computational Linguistics, Vancouver, Canada, 30 July–4 August 2017, pp. 665–677. Association for Computational Linguistics (ACL) (2017)

24. Yang, Z., Levow, G.A., Meng, H.: Predicting user satisfaction in spoken dialog system evaluation with collaborative filtering. IEEE J. Sel. Top. Signal Process. **6**(8), 971–981 (2012)

25. Yu, Z., Yu, Z., Aoyama, H., Ozeki, M., Nakamura, Y.: Capture, recognition, and visualization of human semantic interactions in meetings. In: Proceedings of PerCom, Mannheim, Germany (2010)

26. Zeldes, A.: rstWeb - A browser-based annotation interface for rhetorical structure theory and discourse relations. In: Proceedings of NAACL-HLT 2016 System Demonstrations, San Diego, CA, pp. 1–5 (2016). http://aclweb.org/anthology/N/N16/N16-3001.pdf

Author-Driven Approaches to Computational Narrative Design for Games

David John Tree[1](✉) and Alessio Malizia[2](✉)

[1] Games and Visual Effects Research Lab, School of Creative Arts,
University of Hertfordshire, Hatfield, UK
d.tree@herts.ac.uk
[2] School of Creative Arts, University of Hertfordshire, Hatfield, UK
a.malizia@herts.ac.uk

Abstract. Accessible Head Mounted Displays (HMD) have provided mass access to Extended Reality (XR) content as never before. One of the key complaints from HMD owners, however, is the lack of substantial high-quality content (Moore 2017). Coupled with the domain-specific topic of presence, which describes a state beyond the concept of immersion instead with the user feeling part of the virtual world.

Utilizing traditional production techniques cost and the duration of the resultant product are inextricably linked, although some progress reducing manual hours has been made with the introduction of Procedural Content Generation (PCG); the focus of this shift has been on asset creation rather than narratives (Kapadia et al. 2017). While PCG can reduce the cost of production it does not however directly increase the duration of the game. The current solution from developers has been to implement game mechanics to increase the duration of the game, leading to a rise in arcade-style wave shooters (Anon 2018), however, this solution is not applicable to long-form content such as narrative-based Role Playing Games (RPG), story-based first-person action games and interactive narratives.

The intended contribution of this paper is both to describe the challenges to the academic knowledge in procedurally generated content and computational narratives but is also about studying how those approaches can be democratized, enabling wider adoption within the content creation community, with a view to their eventual use within non-entertainment sectors.

Keywords: Interactive narrative · Computational narrative · Agency

1 Introduction

While the introduction of fully automated and mixed-initiative design processes such as Procedural Content Generation (PCG) and Computational Narrative (CN) can reduce the manual hours required to design and produce games, hitherto the impact of these techniques is predominated in the visual and special aspects of video games showing little impact in the players narrative experience. These techniques have demonstrated an ability to improve game duration and reduce overall production cost, however this has been to the detriment of narrative complexity leading to an increase in arcade and

© Springer Nature Switzerland AG 2019
M. Kurosu (Ed.): HCII 2019, LNCS 11566, pp. 571–584, 2019.
https://doi.org/10.1007/978-3-030-22646-6_43

shoot-em-up style video games rather than an elaborated form of content such as Role-Playing Games (RPG), story-based first-person action games and interactive narratives which offer a better or more immersive experience.

Some approaches are available to improve the depth and breadth of games based on mixed-initiative interactive narratives but these have been seldom employed in game engines so far. Such approaches include combining Machine Learning techniques (supervised or unsupervised) with player analytics to model players' behaviour and adapt the storytelling accordingly. Furthermore, Visual Languages can be used to support authors/designers in modelling Non-Player Characters (NPCs) without requiring advanced programming skills.

We believe that by employing such techniques authors, players and producers can benefit in their respective activities, enabling a renewed focus on creativity rather than on technical aspects and requirements. With the end goal of increasing the complexity in the game narrative and therefore the sense of immersion in the game world along with increased productivity. Simultaneously using those approaches pose new research questions and challenges.

For instance, the multimodal possibilities offered by new technologies such as Augmented and Virtual Reality and Conversational Agents are limited if not integrated into the game narrative generating discontinuity in the sense of immersion and cognitive flow (Faiola et al. 2013). A crucial element of games is, for instance, the design of Non-Player Characters (NPCs), However, to improve NPCs behaviour full integration with the game narrative is needed, e.g. by allowing them to use elaborate strategies to achieve the game objectives in a sensible way.

In this paper, we will explore the field of automated and mixed-initiative design of game elements and interactive narratives, describing the state of the art and focusing on two very promising techniques: Procedural Content Generation and Computational Narrative with the aim of informing the community on the research questions and challenges posed by such approaches. We describe also the possibilities offered by such algorithmic approaches that can positively impact player experience, authors ability to focus on narratives and improve publishers/producers benefits in terms of production workflow, cost and duration.

2 Background

2.1 Interactive Narratives

Although Non-linear storytelling is now synonymous with the interactive media, conceptually it has existed for as long as stories have been told. Where in person we might pass some information on to someone else by way of a story, we the storyteller will judge our audience and adapt the story accordingly rather than providing a verbatim account of events.

The introduction of the print media changed this aural tradition to one of accurate, complete reproduction thus changing the passage of information forever. However the yearning for adaptive narratives made its way into printed media, early examples of this non-linear storytelling can be found in the Choose Your Own Adventure (Montgomery et al. 1982) series of books part of a genre of fictional books which enable the reader to select the path and therefore the outcome of the story. This form of interactive fiction is defined as a branching narrative as when plotted the narrative would show a tree-like structure. Fighting fantasy (Jackson and Livingstone 1982) later combined the mechanics of Tabletop Role Playing Games (TRPG) such as the popular dungeons and dragons (Gygax and Arneson 1974) and through this combination, both a feeling of player presence and reader agency was achieved with the added dimension of alea (Caillois and Barash 1961) based gameplay. To achieve this the books included integral character sheets which stored information of previous decisions and the current character status.

Interactive narratives enable the reader limited agency over the narrative by offering the reader a choice at key points throughout the story, thus allowing the reader to select the outcome of the story. Although this agency was initially limited through the printed form it was later explored through hypertexts to enable a more fluid experience as explored by Aarseth (1997).

Due to their printed nature existing artefacts in this field require an entirely manual approach to authoring thus the authoring workload increases exponentially with the number of choices available to the player. Ryan (Ryan 2009) suggests that the holy grail of interactive narratives is the freeform provided by dynamic creation of a narrative within the defined story world. Ryan has long been an investigator within the field of interactive narratives since her acclaimed work "Hamlet on the holodeck" (Murray 1998).

Literature Role Playing Games (LitRPG) is a sub-genre of fiction whereby the protagonist takes part in a Role-Playing Game either digital or tabletop, exploring the character's exploits, with a common trope of highlighting the game mechanics of the world indicating gained experience or achievements mirroring that found within real games. Although not interactive themselves this literary form provides a space for the examination of ethics, methods of interaction and more recently the interaction of human characters with the system. The advantage of this hypothetical exploration is the lack of the implementation stage needed to explore these scenarios in a real game, permitting thinking beyond current systems available and inspiring real-world development.

In the Awaken Online LitRPG series (Bagwell 2016) players partake in a new Virtual Reality Massively Multiplayer Online Role-Playing Game (MMORPG) entitled "Awaken Online" where the Game Manager named Alfred controls not only the ongoing story but the in-game gods and NPC behaviours. The books raise several questions within the VR arena including the ethics of high gore games and the possibility of simulation induced Post Traumatic Stress Disorder as well as the possible therapeutic effects of the simulation environment. More relevant to this paper Bagwell explores the role of an A.I. with unclear directives experimenting to encourage players to engage for longer. Although the anthropomorphized Alfred is portrayed as a sentient intelligence with the Bagwell referencing that the in-game AI had passed the Turing test (Turing 1950) the question of how the success of gameplay and interactive narratives is very relevant and we explore this question in the computational narrative section of this paper.

Continued development of interactive technologies and distribution mediums have led to the inception of Interactive Cinema and TV such as the recent Bandersnatch, a psychological thriller interactive film in the science fiction anthology series Black Mirror made available on streaming by Netflix (Slade 2018). In this interactive film, the audience is forced to make decisions for the protagonist, the designer has encouraged impulse driven response through the application of a time window to provide a choice (ten seconds). The designers provide the viewers with five main endings with slightly different variants within each ending while making use of loops to cull extraneous story elements.

However, the interactive video technologies are still hampered by the pre-generated necessity of the delivery platform, and while some efforts to enable true agency have been made through simultaneous production and viewing (Weber 2016; Montazemi 2017) these only apply to a niche audience and are inaccessible to the general public.

Video games offer a unique environment for the exploration of Artificial Intelligence and more specifically Interactive Narratives as videogame environments are data rich and optimised for the exploitation of interaction (Yannakakis and Togelius 2018). Video games developers can be broadly categorised as either high budget mainstream (AAA) and independently funded studios (Indie) AAA studios have implemented interactive narratives within some titles such as Shadows of Mordor (Productions 2014) which features an adaptive story world with its Nemesis game system, Allowed for the replacement of Non Playing Characters to be replaced through promotion of other NPCs. The developers combined this with the ability of NPC characters who have defeated the player in the past to remember the encounter and to taunt the player on the next instance.

However more ambitious solutions are currently being investigated by Indie studios driven by the need to create efficient methods for producing engaging long-form content. Although in the past this been the downfall of titles which generated large followings within the gaming community such as the now infamous No Man's Sky (Murray et al. 2016) which was initially advertised to create a fully adaptive game space upon release the majority of the procedural content had been removed (Caldwell 2016). This has not dissuaded other Independent studios from pursuing the objective of a fully procedural game space, more recently a crowd-funded title, Pine (Twirlbound 2019), currently under development, proposes to implement a game world that adapts to the player, utilising a combination of generative algorithms.

2.2   Computational Narrative

The convergence of gestural, verbal and interactive media termed multi-modal interaction has become a possibility within recent years due to mass market access to VR motion controls for gestural input (Anon 2012; Robertson 2016a, 2016b) A.I. driven verbal interfaces (Solon 2018) and high-powered home computing, enabling physically accurate rendering of a real-time worlds. With the platforms becoming increasingly stable and defined the prime opportunity for content creation has arrived. As this multi-modal platform matures, we will be investigating combining these systems with computational narratives to enable for the creation of adaptive narrative systems. The following section focuses on current developments in Computational Narratives and later the more specifically on the application of CN within the context of video games.

In their survey, Yannakakis and Togelius (2015) provide a structured approach to the alignment of Artificial Intelligence and Machine Learning Techniques to the applications of these techniques within the video-game domain, demonstrating the reach of the A.I. beyond controlling Non-Playing Characters (NPCs) and identifying gaps in the convergence of these research areas. Although the lack of convergence could be down to inherent incompatibilities of the techniques with the target area, the overall conclusions presented reinforce the need to further investigate linkages between the different areas of AI and ML within the domain of games.

As a subfield of Artificial intelligence, Computational Narrative aims to imbue computational systems with story intelligence, providing those systems with the ability to understand and synthesise information expressed in a narrative form. For the purposes of exploration, this field is often divided into two distinct areas, story analysis and story generation.

Story analysis combines techniques in Natural Language Translation, Sentiment analysis and applies them to a corpus of stories to gain insights into the structures, meaning and emotions expressed with a view to distilling the key structures of stories into an interpretable form.

Vonnegut (2004) posited that all stories have shapes, by plotting the happiness of the protagonist along the Y-axis of Good-fortune and Ill-fortune against an X-axis of beginning to end. This hypothesis has been later ratified by the work of Reagan et al. (2016) developers of the Hedonometer which utilises a big data approach to story analysis applying sentiment analysis to the Project Gutenberg Corpus. Novel to these approaches is the focus on the emotions of the characters rather than to the plot itself, as our focus is on the prescience of the player within the game world and the purpose of the story is to impress emotions, therefore it is vital that we understand the emotional states of both NPCs and possessed characters alike.

In their survey of story generation techniques for authoring computational narratives Kybartas and Bidarra (2017) outline the field of story generation placing papers on a scale comparing input from space automation and plot automation to the generated narrative. They identify that further investigation is warranted into the field of automated space generation which would contravene traditional practice of narrative design where the author designs the world/space before the creation of the story within the world. The authors of this paper also identify that the field of computational narrative needs a standard model of computational narrative that would allow the myriad of bespoke systems to interact to form a succinct narrative, these conclusions are supported by a significant quantity of background research the majority of which is published in subject-specific journals.

Li et al. (2013) pose to address the challenge of story generation within an unknown domain, the paper concludes that, by crowdsourcing the source corpus, their system can generate stories of equal quality to that of untrained humans, this is supported by testing that was run on a sample of 60 participants who were paid to provide feedback on the story generated by the plot graph; the data supports the conclusion that the system has successfully generated a storyline which required a similar level of correction to the human counterpart. It should be noted that the testers were paid, and the experiment was undertaken using Amazon Mechanical Turk which in its nature subsets the population used and may not be representative of culture as a whole.

The conclusions drawn are influential in that they present a working model for resolving the knowledge-intensive training phase of story generation in an affordable and innovative way.

As alluded to earlier, the field of computational narratives is been divided leading to the separate representation of story elements. Valls-Vargas et al. (2017) illuminate this dysfunction between generative and analytical models of computational narrative. Later highlighting the lack of an end to end solution, that would enable the introduction of a partially completed text with the output of a completed narrative with the system having prior knowledge of domain-specific areas. The paper concludes with the presentation of a prototype combined system; combined systems such as this will be vital to the enabling of unsupervised machine learning approaches allowing the system to both generate and evaluate the efficacy of the narratives.

Horswill et al. (2014) provide an overview of papers covered in the 2015 Transactions on Computational Intelligence and AI in games. Concluding that some progress has been made in the field of AI in games and some commercial examples have started to appear. A key challenge in the field is disjoint between the research community and content creators. Highlighting the fear that if the field continues to progress along its current trajectory the AI techniques will continue to be aesthetically unproductive. This argument is supported through the representation methodologies used to analyse the success or failure of the AI systems which are currently predominated by HCI (Human-Computer Interaction) methodologies rather than methodologies utilised by the arts. The conclusions drawn in this paper support the need for a change in the methodology for the analysis and scoring of narrative generation systems to better accommodate aesthetic values.

Riedl (2012) outlines the field of AI in Video Games, specifying four fields of research: Human Level AI, Better Games, Supporting Game Development Practices and New Experiences before identifying the open problems in interactive narrative. A common theme throughout the challenges is the need for further research into the methods and techniques of autonomous drama manager's which take the traditional tabletop games role of dungeon master. Outside the field of AI Riedl highlights the success of applying psychology aware algorithms to guide players through the game world, mitigating players awareness of the game master.

Inspired by Table-top Roleplaying Games (TRPG) Ono and Ogata present a combined system approach to Narrative generation within a game environment through the combination of an Integrated Narrative Generation System (INGS) into the Automated Narrative Generation Game (ANGG). Novelty is found in the use of computer-controlled Game Manager (GM) and Players (PL) in automating both actors within the game, world collaboration is formed where the Game Manager generates the high-level story world and the Players propose enhancements on the low level. In addition to this, the techniques used for the low-level micro level control of the representation are founded on the techniques used in the marketing and film industries making it relevant to this work.

2.3   Agency

Agency is the ability of a player to have an impact on the game world, as highlighted by Harrell and Zhu (2009) often this is misconceived to be the ability of the player to have sole and unencumbered free will. However, Harrell et al. propose that instead agency should be considered in three forms: player agency, system agency, and authorial agency. This theory is supported through the analysis of contemporary media artefact's which align to these concepts and with reference to the mechanics of the real world. While the objective in creating the game world, is not to wholly replicate real-world rules, for the maintenance of the suspension of disbelief a plausible reality is required. Building on this theory of split agency games the memory, reverie machine (Zhu and Harrell 2009), explores this hypothesis through an experimental AI-driven game of agency where the balance of agency is dynamically adapted during gameplay.

Within the context of the game world, system agency can be considered the application of the rules and mechanics of the game, an integral part of the play. The interesting element here is that the application of agency cannot simply be evaluated as a temporal control of an event where a single actor (player, system or author) has control over the current state of the game world. Instead agency should be considered for each element that is controllable, for example in the case of the game cinematic the author has control over the location of a player and the story unfolding around them, however most games will allow the player agency over the player viewport especially in the case of XR content where the restriction of head movement can increase the chances of simulation sickness. (Hettinger and Riccio 1992)

Authorial agency is limited by two factors, that of how the CN system encodes the authors narrative template and how the CN system interprets the author's template to generate the game narrative. However, before these can be investigated, a representational model for computational narratives needs to be agreed. Initial research into this field has revealed that some attempts have been made to move the representational model of computational narratives beyond that of Hierarchical node trees and Directional Acyclic Graph. Such as the model presented by Verbrugge (2003) which combines Petri Nets with bi-directional edge flow to present a hypergraph representation of narrative.

Alternative models for representing these narratives can be seen in the system developed by Poulakos et al. (2016) who have begun to address the democratisation of computational narrative intelligence through the development of a graphical tool integrated into Unity3D games engine. The evidence presented is a small-scale test of computer science students who are inherently and more technically minded, somewhat limiting the validity of the results drawn; nevertheless, the objective of the study was an initial indication of the system and to receive feedback to support additional work. While the conclusions drawn are not in themselves of surprise, indeed implementing a graphical user interface improves accessibility to complex computational systems, the solution itself and the objectives of the paper are aligned with our objectives and one of the possible areas identified for development of a 3D interface for the story world generator is of interest in respect of our identified research question.

3   Research Questions

Through the exploration of existing approaches reported in the literature and adopted by the games industry, we have identified the following open questions relevant to addressing. Furthermore, two methodologies appear to be more adequate to tackle the following research questions to improve the end-users experience: Procedural Content Generation and Computational Narratives. Such approaches present a promising solution but also some quite relevant challenges for the field.

We will focus on three categories of potential end users: authors (e.g. game and narrative designers), players and producers/publishers. Our research questions therefore will be:

1. How can Computational Narratives and Procedural Content Generation assist authors in the design of interactive narratives so that players will have a better experience and producers could benefit by such approaches?
2. How can Computational Narrative and Procedural Content Generation techniques be integrated into existing middle-ware/game engines to enable the democratization of such technology, supporting authors in their narrative design approach and providing a better player experience?
3. How is the feeling of presence impacted by the integration of a computationally generated interactive narrative to improve the quality of player experience, stimulate authors creations and enable game publishers to streamline their production?

4   Challenges

Procedural Content Generation (PCG) is employed in the automatic or semi-automatic design and generation of game elements from level maps to missions and textures. More recently, several approaches and solutions emerged on the market that show promising contributions to the fields of PGC and CN, such as computational creativity, end-user development and interaction design.

Computational Narrative (CN) takes a different but equally promising approach: focusing on story creation through the modelling of existing stories before applying generative algorithms to synthesise new narratives within the same domain. Stories are crucial to provide player's immersion and feeling of suspension of disbelief contributing to the effective and cognitive dimensions of the player's experience.

A combination of these two approaches can be effective in tackling the research question (1): *How can CN and PGC assist authors in the design of interactive narratives so that players will have a better experience and producers could benefit by such approaches?*

PCG can be implemented in form of AI-assisted design tools which assist authors in generating game content: for instance, tools can support the creation of level maps by employing constraints inspired by the quality of player experience. Through the application of supervised machine learning, players can be involved in the co-design of level maps that can be used to train a machine learning algorithm to model constraints based on player's categories as in Bartle's taxonomy of player types (Bartle 1996) and therefore providing an AI-assisted PCG tool. Assuming the authors are non-programmers a visual language can be used to enable an AI-based PCG approach to the design and generation of game levels (Shapiro and Ahrens 2016) Furthermore, producers can benefit by integrating PCG into their production pipeline optimising cost and time to market.

Computational Narrative can provide support to authors in form of tools for generating narratives, such as drama management tools (Mateas and Stern 2003). CN tools need further exploration since few are available and are mainly language-based as in textual adventures where those tools can generate interactive fiction. With the advent of multi-modal interactions more advanced computational narrative tools are needed to take advantage of such technologies and provide more advanced player experiences. Hypermedia visualisation tools in utilising a visual platform will provide great insight in the design of advanced multidimensional narratives (Charles et al. 2011). For instance, first-person narratives might benefit from the so-called believable agent's where NPC (Non-playing Characters) can render more realistic behaviour following the story pattern perhaps modelled on human player data collected while in game. Producers can benefit from CN by integrating a more immersive narrative in their games taking advantage of multi-modal interaction from the very beginning of story authoring in addition to game replay value with new avenues for Downloadable Content (DLC).

While PGC and CN provide a promising approach to the adoption of interactive narratives in games some challenges are still to be addressed to fully employ such approaches:

- How to design Visual Languages or Visual Tools that can help authors design and generate complex and multi-modal interactive narratives.
- How to co-design game elements with players to train AI-assisted tools to support PCG and CN for non-programmers (e.g., authors or designers)
- How to employ Hypermedia visualizations to integrate complex narratives in gameplay.

For such approaches to have an impact in the interactive narrative and game areas PCG and CN should not be restricted to academic research or early adopters, leading to our next research questions (2): *How can Computational Narrative and Procedural Content Generation techniques be integrated into existing middle ware/game engines to enable the democratization of such technology, supporting authors in their narrative design approach and providing a better player experience?*

While PCG has been explored in research, as per evidence from our literature review it has been seldom employed in the mainstream design of games. Content creation software and middleware utilise scripting to automate content generation: e.g. MEL or Python scripting used in Maya to generate content or C# as a scripting language for Unity. Efforts are required from authors to learn to programme, with such environments normally offering APIs (Application Programming Interfaces) but rarely user-friendly visual editors or visual tools. PCG can be used to generate different game elements such as level maps or even quests but such high-level activities will require programming. To allow authors to use PCG in existing game engines means to improve the player experience by allowing authors to focus on the narrative and not on other skills that they might lack. Furthermore, PCG could offer a way of modelling the quality of experience allowing simulation-based testing integrated into game engines, e.g. testing author-driven automatically-generated content by playing the game through a simulated player (an agent). At the same time, such an approach could open game design to authors focused on the narrative more than on the technology to implement it.

Computational Narrative can provide integrated storytelling workflows and patterns for existing game engines allowing the authors to take full advantage of the technical features offered by such middleware. By integrating Computational Narrative in existing game engines NPCs could become more proficient when developed as characters in the narrative using existing storytelling elements, e.g. elements of the Propp's functions (Imabuchi and Ogata 2012) can be modelled in the Computational Narrative aspects of an existing game engine. Taking advantage of the multi-modal interaction features offered by modern game engines agents integrated into a story generated by Computational Narrative could be more realistic and proficient being able to integrate well in the narrative and become more believable improving the player experience.

How to integrate PGC and CN approaches in mainstream game engines to improve the democratization of advanced narratives present some interesting challenges:

- How can game engines provide support to PGC and CN providing authors with user-friendly tools to generate content and design narratives?
- Can we identify open standards to generate game elements and narratives that can be supported by existing game engines?
- Can common narrative elements providing a better player experience be modelled in current game engines in a user-friendly way freeing the authors from technicalities and allowing them to focus on the narrative and player experience?

PGC elements and Computational Narrative must generate believable and immersive content to improve the player's experience and provide game producer with the ability of exploit multi-modal technologies (3): *How is the feeling of presence impacted by the integration of a computationally generated interactive narrative to improve the quality of player experience, stimulate authors creations and enable game publishers in streamlining their production?*

PGC can generate NPCs behaviour and interactions with game levels and actual player. Computational player modelling could learn NPCs behaviour to react consistently to human players. Machine learning algorithms for modelling NPCs could provide a better sense of presence, immersion and multi-modal experience for the players, e.g. the well-known limitation of NPCs in VR environments incapable of looking at player's eyes during dialogues.

Computational Narrative techniques could assist in generating more believable NPCs behaviour when interacting with a player following storytelling patterns. Agents (NPCs) able to plan actions according to a strategy and express behavioural and emotional attitude can offer a better player experience with respect to believability. Looking into integrating results from interactive virtual and conversational agents as well as humans might benefit the feeling of presence and realism of games highly improving the quality of player experience.

How to generate more believable and immersive experiences through PGC and CN approaches provide some interesting challenges:

- Can we employ machine-learning algorithms to model NPCs reactions to actual players' behaviour?
- Can we model players by learning their behaviour from data and patterns accumulated during game plays and inform interactive storytelling and automatically-generated agents to be more believable and thus offer a better player's experience?
- Could we take advantage of existing studies on conversational agents and chatbots to generate more realistic NPCs and improve the player feeling of presence and immersion in games and interactive narratives?

We believe that the challenges identified in this section can be a source of inspiration for future research on author-driven approaches to computational narrative design for games with the aim of improving player experience, authors ability to focus on creativity and publisher's workflow and production management and optimisation.

5   Conclusion

As McGrath (2014) stated referring to C.S. Lewis (Author of the Chronicles of Narnia): "Lewis wanted us to understand that the inner world is shaped by stories." The most relevant gaming and interactive stories experiences are based on complex narratives requiring a huge investment from game producers and publishers. Lately, with the rise of AI-oriented applications, Procedural-Generated Content (PGC) and Computational Narrative (CN) aided stakeholders involved in the creation of interactive experiences. By allowing the author/designer to focus on the narrative and creativity while at the same time increasing productivity, such tools are becoming more and more crucial for interactive, multimodal experiences and game production. Nevertheless, such approaches require integration into existing production pipelines ensuring they improve the player/user experience. Without the utilisation of such techniques, fiscal pressures on game development have led to the dwindling of narrative lead immersive content leading to domination of shoot-em-ups and wave-based arcade shooters.

In this paper, we described some of the existing approaches and the research questions to inform the community of the possibilities and challenges posed by such approaches. Clearly, a multidisciplinary approach is needed to design tools to adequately support both designers and authors in the production of complex narratives within a mixed-initiative approach, disciplines such as artificial intelligence, end-user programming, information visualisation and user experience are just a few examples of the areas that might be involved in tackling such questions and challenges. We believe that PCG and CN can positively impact, not only the production costs and quality of future games and interactive experiences but also the author's abilities to focus more on creativity and less on technical skills while at the same time providing a better player experience.

6   Future Work

We plan to investigate towards a unified dynamic representational system for inter-active narratives within games, using a measure of narratological and ludic success combined with a user interface design measure of success for the author's interaction with this new model. The aim will consists of improving the efficiency of generating immersive narratives that are functionally interactive with a focus on player agency.

Acknowledgements. The Games and Visual Effects Research Lab (G + VERL) is funded by the European Regional Development Fund: Interreg: North Sea Region, Create Converge project.

References

Aarseth, E.J.: Cybertext: Perspectives on Ergodic Literature. Johns Hopkins University Press, Baltimore (1997)

Anon. Leap Motion Unveils World's Most Accurate 3-D Motion Control Technology for Computing—Leap Motion (2012). https://www.leapmotion.com/news/leap-motion-unveils-worlds-most-accurate-3-d-motion-control-technology-for-computing. Accessed 29 May 2018

Anon. Time Carnage - More than Just Another Wave Shooter|VR Game Rankings: Reviews - Previews - Lists, VR Game Rankings (2018). https://www.vrgamerankings.com/single-post/2018/04/18/Time-Carnage—More-than-just-another-wave-shooter. Accessed 31 May 2018

Bagwell, T.: Awaken Online. Book 1 : Catharsis (2016)

Bartle, R.: Hearts, clubs, diamonds, spades: players who suit MUDs. J. MUD Res. 1(1), 19 (1996)

Caillois, R., Barash, M.: Man, Play, and Games. Librairie Gallimard, Paris (1961). https://books.google.co.uk/books/about/Man_Play_and_Games.html?id=bDjOPsjzfC4C&printsec=frontcover&source=kp_read_button&redir_esc=y#v=onepage&q&f=false

Caldwell, B.: The Broken Promise Of No Man's Sky And Why It Matters, Rock paper shotgun (2016). https://www.rockpapershotgun.com/2016/08/17/broken-promises-of-no-mans-sky/

Charles, F., et al.: Timeline-based navigation for interactive narratives. In: Proceedings of the 8th International Conference on Advances in Computer Entertainment Technology, p. 37. ACM (2011)

Faiola, A., et al.: Correlating the effects of flow and telepresence in virtual worlds: enhancing our understanding of user behavior in game-based learning. Comput. Hum. Behav. 29, 1113–1121 (2013). https://doi.org/10.1016/j.chb.2012.10.003

Gygax, G., Arneson, D.: Dungeons and Dragons. TSR, New York (1974)

Harrell, D.F.F., Zhu, J.: Agency play: dimensions of agency for interactive narrative design. In: Proceedings of the AAAI 2009 Spring Symposium on Narrative Intelligence II, aaai.org, pp. 44–52. AAAI Press, Menlo Park (2009). http://www.aaai.org/Papers/Symposia/Spring/2009/SS-09-06/SS09-06-008.pdf

Hettinger, L.J., Riccio, G.E.: Visually induced motion sickness in virtual environments. Presence: Teleoperators Virtual Environ. 1(3), 306–310 (1992). https://doi.org/10.1162/pres.1992.1.3.306

Horswill, I.D., Montfort, N., Young, R.M.: Guest editorial: computational narrative and games. IEEE Trans. Comput. Intell. AI Games 6(2), 93–96 (2014). https://doi.org/10.1109/TCIAIG.2014.2325879

Imabuchi, S., Ogata, T.: A story generation system based on propp theory: as a mechanism in an integrated narrative generation system. In: Isahara, H., Kanzaki, K. (eds.) JapTAL 2012. LNCS (LNAI), vol. 7614, pp. 312–321. Springer, Heidelberg (2012). https://doi.org/10.1007/978-3-642-33983-7_31

Jackson, S., Livingstone, I.: The Warlock of Firetop Mountain (1982). https://www.amazon.co.uk/Warlock-Firetop-Mountain-Fighting-Gamebook/dp/1840463872/ref=oosr. Accessed 25 May 2018

Kapadia, M., et al.: Computational narrative. In: ACM SIGGRAPH 2017 Courses on - SIGGRAPH 2017, pp. 1–118 (2017). https://doi.org/10.1145/3084873.3084931

Kybartas, B., Bidarra, R.: A survey on story generation techniques for authoring computational narratives. IEEE Trans. Comput. Intell. AI Games 9(3), 239–253 (2017). ieeexplore.ieee.org, https://doi.org/10.1109/tciaig.2016.2546063

Li, B., et al.: Story generation with crowdsourced plot graphs. In: Proceedings of the Twenty-Seventh AAAI Conference on Artificial Intelligence, aaai.org, pp. 598–604 (2013)

Ryan, M.-L.: From narrative games to playable stories: toward a poetics of interactive narrative. StoryWorlds J. Narrative Stud. 1(1), 43–59 (2009). https://doi.org/10.1353/stw.0.0003

Mateas, M., Stern, A.: Façade: an experiment in building a fully-realized interactive drama. In: Game Developers Conference, pp. 4–8 (2003)

McGrath, A.: If I Had Lunch with CS Lewis: Exploring the Ideas of CS Lewis on the Meaning of Life. Tyndale House Publishers, Colorado Springs (2014)

Montazemi, P.T.: Device and Method for Playing an Interactive Audiovisual Movie (2017). https://patents.google.com/patent/US20180090177A1/en. Accessed 29 Jan 2019

Montgomery, R.A., Peguy, L., Cannella, M.: The Abominable Snowman. Chooseco, Toronto (1982)

Moore, T.P.: What Steam's Data Reveals About the Health of VR's Ecosystem–VRFocus, VRfocus (2017). https://www.vrfocus.com/2016/07/what-steams-data-reveals-about-the-health-of-vrs-ecosystem/. Accessed 31 May 2018

Murray, J.H.: Hamlet on the Holodeck : The Future of Narrative in Cyberspace. MIT Press, Cambridge (1998). https://mitpress.mit.edu/books/hamlet-holodeck. Accessed 25 May 2018

Murray, S., et al.: 'No Man's Sky'. Hello Games (2016). https://www.nomanssky.com/

Poulakos, S., Kapadia, M., Maiga, Guido M., Zünd, F., Gross, M., Sumner, Robert W.: Evaluating accessible graphical interfaces for building story worlds. In: Nack, F., Gordon, Andrew S. (eds.) ICIDS 2016. LNCS, vol. 10045, pp. 184–196. Springer, Cham (2016). https://doi.org/10.1007/978-3-319-48279-8_17

Productions, M.: Shadows of Mordor. Warner Brothers (2014)

Reagan, A.J., et al.: The emotional arcs of stories are dominated by six basic shapes. EPJ Data Sci. 5(1) (2016). https://doi.org/10.1140/epjds/s13688-016-0093-1

Riedl, M.O.: Interactive narrative: a novel application of artificial intelligence for computer games. In: Proceedings of the 26th AAAI Conference on Artificial Intelligence, pp. 2160–2165 (2012). http://www.aaai.org/ocs/index.php/AAAI/AAAI12/paper/download/5153/5388

Robertson, A.: HTC Vive review|The Verge, The Verge (2016a). https://www.theverge.com/2016/4/5/11358618/htc-vive-vr-review. Accessed 29 May 2018

Robertson, A.: Oculus Touch review: the Oculus Rift is finally complete-The Verge, The Verge (2016b). https://www.theverge.com/2016/12/5/13811232/oculus-touch-rift-vr-motion-controller-review. Accessed 29 May 2018

Shapiro, R.B., Ahrens, M.: Beyond blocks: syntax and semantics. Commun. ACM 59(5), 39–41 (2016)

Slade, D.: Black Mirror: Bandersnatch. Netflix (2018)

Solon, O.: Google's robot assistant now makes eerily lifelike phone calls for you|Technology|The Guardian (2018). https://www.theguardian.com/technology/2018/may/08/google-duplex-assistant-phone-calls-robot-human. Accessed 29 May 2018

Turing, A.: Computing Machinery and Intelligence. Mind **59**(236), 433–460 (1950). https://doi.org/10.1093/mind/LIX.236.433

Twirlbound. 'Pine'. Twirlbound, Breda (2019)

Valls-Vargas, J., Zhu, J., Ontañón, S.: From computational narrative analysis to generation. In: Proceedings of the International Conference on the Foundations of Digital Games - FDG 2017, pp. 1–4 (2017). https://doi.org/10.1145/3102071.3106362

Verbrugge, C.: A structure for modern computer narratives. In: International Conference on Computers and Games, pp. 308–325. Springer (2003). https://doi.org/10.1007/978-3-540-40031-8_21

Vonnegut, K.: Shape of Stories (2004). https://www.youtube.com/watch?v=GOGru_4z1Vc

Weber, T.: Late Shift, Switzerland (2016)

Yannakakis, G.N., Togelius, J.: A panorama of artificial and computational intelligence in games. IEEE Trans. Comput. Intell. AI Games **7**(4), 317–335 (2015). https://doi.org/10.1109/TCIAIG.2014.2339221

Yannakakis, G.N., Togelius, J.: Artificial Intelligence and Games. Springer (2018)

Zhu, J., Harrell, D.F.: Memory, reverie machine: towards a dance of agency in interactive storytelling. In: Proceedings of the International Symposium on Electronic Art (ISEA) Conference, pdfs.semanticscholar.org (2009). https://pdfs.semanticscholar.org/284d/76d352af2528879bb242870360b22b289614.pdf

Author Index

Printed in the United States
By Bookmasters